MICROSOFT® OFFICE

Access 2003

Comprehensive
Concepts and
Techniques

Gary B. Shelly
Thomas J. Cashman
Philip J. Pratt
Mary Z. Last

THOMSON
COURSE TECHNOLOGY

COURSE TECHNOLOGY
25 THOMSON PLACE
BOSTON MA 02210

SHELLY
CASHMAN
SERIES®

Australia • Canada • Denmark • Japan • Mexico • New Zealand • Philippines • Puerto Rico • Singapore
South Africa • Spain • United Kingdom • United States

THOMSON
COURSE TECHNOLOGY

Microsoft Office Access 2003:
Comprehensive Concepts and Techniques, CourseCard Edition

Gary B. Shelly
Thomas J. Cashman
Philip J. Pratt
Mary Z. Last

Managing Editor:
Alexandra Arnold

Senior Acquisitions Editor:
Dana Merk

Product Manager:
Reed Cotter

Editorial Assistant:
Selena Coppock

Print Buyer:
Laura Burns

Series Consulting Editor:
Jim Quasney

Director of Production:
Patty Stephan

Production Editor:
Catherine G. DiMassa

Production Assistant:
Jill Klaffky

Development Editor:
Nancy Lamm

Copy Editors/Proofreaders:
Ginny Harvey
Nancy Lamm
Kim Kosmatka

Interior Designer:
Becky Herrington

Cover Designers:
Ken Russo
Richard Herrera

Illustrators:
Richard Herrera
Andrew Bartel

Compositors:
Jeanne Black
Kellee LaVars

Indexer:
Cristina Haley

Printer:
Banta Menasha

Thomson Course Technology, the Course Technology logo, the Shelly Cashman Series® and **Custom Edition**® are registered trademarks used under license. All other names used herein are for identification purposes only and are trademarks of their respective owners.

Thomson Course Technology reserves the right to revise this publication and make changes from time to time in its content without notice.

ISBN 1-4188-4363-6

MICROSOFT ° OFFICE

Access 2003

Comprehensive Concepts and Techniques

Contents

Project Three

Maintaining a Database Using the Design and Update Features of Access

Integration Feature

Sharing Data among Applications

Project Four

Reports, Forms, and Combo Boxes

Project Five

Enhancing Forms with OLE Fields, Hyperlinks, and Subforms

Project Six

Switchboards, PivotTables, and PivotCharts

Web Feature

Data Access Pages

Project Seven

Advanced Report and Form Techniques

Project Eight

Using Visual Basic for Applications (VBA) and Creating Multi-Page Forms

Project Nine

Administering a Database System

SQL Feature

SQL Feature: Using SQL

Appendix A

Microsoft Access Help System

Appendix B

Speech and Handwriting Recognition

Appendix C

Publishing Office Web Pages to a Web Server

Appendix D

Changing Screen Resolution and Resetting the Access Toolbars and Menus

Appendix E

Microsoft Office Specialist Certification

Appendix F

Database Design

Preface

The Shelly Cashman Series® offers the finest textbooks in computer education. We are proud of the fact that our series of Microsoft Office 4.3, Microsoft Office 95, Microsoft Office 97, Microsoft Office 2000, and Microsoft Office XP textbooks have been the most widely used books in education. With each new edition of our Office books, we have made significant improvements based on the software and comments made by the instructors and students. The *Microsoft Office 2003* books continue with the innovation, quality, and reliability that you have come to expect from the Shelly Cashman Series.

In this *Microsoft Office Access 2003* book, you will find an educationally sound, highly visual, and easy-to-follow pedagogy that combines a vastly improved step-by-step approach with corresponding screens. All projects and exercises in this book are designed to take full advantage of the Access 2003 enhancements. The project material is developed to ensure that students will see the importance of learning Access for future coursework. The popular Other Ways and More About features offer in-depth knowledge of Access 2003, and the new Q&A feature offers students a way to solidify important database concepts. The Learn It Online page presents a wealth of additional exercises to ensure your students have all the reinforcement they need.

Objectives of This Textbook

Microsoft Office Access 2003: Comprehensive Concepts and Techniques, CourseCard Edition is intended for a three-unit course that presents in-depth coverage of Microsoft Office Access 2003. No experience with a computer is assumed, and no mathematics beyond the high school freshman level is required. The objectives of this book are:

- To teach the fundamentals of Access 2003
- To teach students how to design databases
- To acquaint students with the proper procedures to create databases
- To expose students to practical examples of the computer as a useful tool
- To develop an exercise-oriented approach that allows learning by doing
- To introduce students to new input technologies
- To encourage independent study and help those who are working alone
- To assist students preparing to take the Microsoft Office Specialist examination for Microsoft Office Access 2003

Approved by Microsoft as Courseware for Microsoft Office Specialist Certification

Microsoft Office Access 2003: Comprehensive Concepts and Techniques, CourseCard Edition has been approved by Microsoft as courseware for Microsoft Office Specialist certification. After completing the projects and exercises in this book, students will be prepared to take the specialist-level examination for Microsoft Office Access 2003.

By passing the certification exam for a Microsoft software application, students demonstrate their proficiency in that application to employers. This exam is offered at participating centers, corporations, and employment agencies. See Appendix E for additional information about obtaining Microsoft Office Specialist certification and for a table that includes the Microsoft Office Access 2003 skill sets and corresponding page numbers where a skill is discussed in the book, or visit the Web site microsoft.com/officespecialist.

The Shelly Cashman Series Microsoft Office Specialist Center (Figure 1) has links to valuable information on the certification program. The Web page (scsite.com/winoff2003/cert) includes links to general information on certification, choosing an application for certification, preparing for the certification exam, and taking and passing the certification exams.

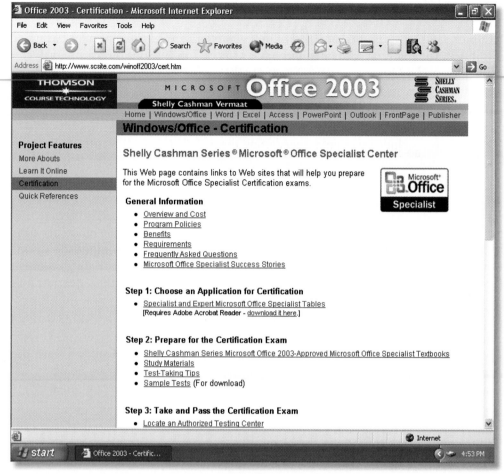

FIGURE 1

The Shelly Cashman Approach

Features of the Shelly Cashman Series *Microsoft Office Access 2003* books include:

- **Project Orientation:** Each project in the book presents a practical problem and complete solution using an easy-to-understand methodology.

- **Step-by-Step, Screen-by-Screen Instructions:** Each of the tasks required to complete a project is identified throughout the project. Full-color screens accompany the steps.

- **Thoroughly Tested Projects:** Unparalleled quality is ensured because every screen in the book is produced by the author only after performing a step, and then each project must pass Thomson Course Technology's award-winning Quality Assurance program.

- **Other Ways Boxes and Quick Reference Summary:** The Other Ways boxes displayed at the end of many of the step-by-step sequences specify the other ways to perform the task completed in the steps. Thus, the steps and the Other Ways box make a comprehensive reference unit.

- **More About and Q&A Features:** These marginal annotations provide background information, tips, and answers to common questions that complement the topics covered, adding depth and perspective to the learning process.

- **Integration of the World Wide Web:** The World Wide Web is integrated into the Access 2003 learning experience by (1) More About annotations that send students to Web sites for up-to-date information and alternative approaches to tasks; (2) a Microsoft Office Specialist Certification Web page so students can prepare for the certification examinations; (3) an Access 2003 Quick Reference Summary Web page that summarizes the ways to complete tasks (mouse, menu, shortcut menu, and keyboard); and (4) the Learn It Online page at the end of each project, which has project reinforcement exercises, learning games, and other types of student activities.

Organization of This Textbook

Microsoft Office Access 2003: Comprehensive Concepts and Techniques, CourseCard Edition provides basic instruction on how to use Access 2003. The material is divided into nine projects, an Integration feature, a Web feature, an SQL feature, six appendices, and a Quick Reference Summary.

Project 1 – Creating and Using a Database   In Project 1, students are introduced to the concept of a database and use Access 2003 to create a database. Topics include creating a database; creating a table; defining the fields in a table; opening a table, adding records to a table, and closing a table; and previewing and printing the contents of a table. Other topics in this project include creating a query using the Simple Query Wizard; using a form to view data; using the Report Wizard to create a report; and using Access Help. Students also learn how to design a database to eliminate redundancy.

Project 2 – Querying a Database Using the Select Query Window   In Project 2, students learn to use queries to obtain information from the data in their databases. Topics include creating queries, running queries, saving queries, and printing the results. Specific query topics include displaying only selected fields; using character data in criteria; specifying parameter queries; using wildcards; using numeric data in criteria; using comparison operators; and creating compound criteria. Other related topics include sorting, joining tables, and restricting records in a join. Students learn to use calculated fields, statistics, and grouping. They also create top-values queries, format fields in queries, and create and use crosstab queries.

Project 3 – Maintaining a Database Using the Design and Update Features of Access   In Project 3, students learn the crucial skills involved in maintaining a database. These topics include using Datasheet view and Form view to add new records, change existing records, delete records, and locate and filter records. Students learn the processes of changing the structure of a table, adding fields, and changing characteristics of existing fields. They change the appearance of a datasheet; create a variety of validation rules and specify referential integrity; perform mass changes and deletions using queries; create single-field and multiple-field indexes; and use subdatasheets to view related data.

Integration Feature – Sharing Data Among Applications   In the Integration feature, students learn how to embed an Excel worksheet in an Access database and how to link a worksheet to a database. Students also learn how to prepare Access data for use in other applications. Topics include embedding worksheets; linking worksheets; using the resulting tables; using the Export command to export database data to an Excel worksheet; using drag-and-drop to export data to a Word document; using the Export command to create a snapshot of a report; and exporting and importing XML data.

Project 4 – Reports, Forms, and Combo Boxes   In Project 4, students learn to create custom reports and forms. Students learn how to change a variety of field properties such as font styles, formats, and colors. Topics include creating queries for reports; using the Report Wizard; modifying a report design; saving a report; sorting and grouping in a report; printing a report; creating a report with groups and subtotals; removing totals from a report; aligning controls; and changing the format of controls. Other topics include creating an initial form using the Form Wizard; modifying a form design; moving fields; and adding calculated fields and combo boxes.

Project 5 – Enhancing Forms with OLE Fields, Hyperlinks, and Subforms   In Project 5, students learn to use date, memo, OLE, and hyperlink fields. Topics include incorporating these fields in the structure of a database; using the Input Mask Wizard; updating the data in these fields and changing table properties; creating a form that uses a subform to incorporate a one-to-many relationship between tables; manipulating subforms on a main form; incorporating date, memo, OLE, and hyperlink fields in forms; and incorporating various visual effects in forms. Students also learn to use the hyperlink fields to access Web pages and to use date and memo fields in a query.

Project 6 – Switchboards, PivotTables, and PivotCharts   In Project 6, students create macros and learn how to create a switchboard system. Students also learn to create and use both PivotTables and PivotCharts. They also learn to create and present information in PivotTable view and PivotChart view. Topics include creating and running macros; creating a switchboard; creating switchboard pages and switchboard items; and using a switchboard.

Web Feature – Data Access Pages   In the Web feature, students learn to create a data access page to enable users to access the data in a database via the Internet. They also learn how to create grouped data access pages, as well as how to create data access pages containing PivotTables and PivotCharts. Topics include creating a data access page using the Page Wizard; previewing a data access page from within Access; and using a data access page. Other topics include creating a grouped data access page in Design View; using a grouped data access page; creating a data access page containing a PivotTable; using a data access page containing a PivotTable; saving a PivotChart as a data access page; and using a data access page containing a PivotChart.

Project 7 – Advanced Report and Form Techniques In Project 7, students learn to use Design view to create complex reports involving data from queries that join multiple tables and also to enhance forms with buttons and combo boxes. Topics include creating a report in Design view; adding fields to a report; including a subreport in a report; adding a date and page number to a report; and creating and printing mailing labels. Topics also include adding command buttons to forms; modifying VBA code associated with a command button; adding a combo box to a form that will be used for searching; modifying the properties of the combo box; as well as using the combo box to search for a record.

Project 8 – Using Visual Basic for Applications (VBA) and Creating Multi-Page Forms In Project 8, students learn to use Visual Basic for Applications (VBA). In addition to learning general VBA concepts, they learn how to create functions in a standard module in VBA; test functions; use functions in queries and forms; associate code with events; create sub procedures in VBA; and create functions to run commands. Additional topics include creating a form using Design view; adding a tab control to a form; adding a subform control to a form; adding charts to a form; and adding an ActiveX control to a form.

Project 9 – Administering a Database System In Project 9, students learn the issues and techniques involved in administering a database management system. Topics include converting a database to other versions of Access; using the Table Analyzer, Performance Analyzer, and Documenter; enabling automatic error checking; creating a custom input mask; using Smart Tags; using SharePoint services; using online collaboration; specifying referential integrity options; setting startup options; setting and removing passwords; specifying the macro security level; encrypting a database; creating and using a replica; synchronizing a Design Master and a replica; splitting a database; creating an MDE file; and specifying user-level security.

SQL Feature – Using SQL In the SQL feature, students learn how to use the SQL language. Topics include entering SQL commands through SQL view; indicating fields to be included; specifying criteria; using compound criteria; using computed fields; sorting; using built-in functions; grouping; and joining tables. Students also see how the SQL commands they enter compare the with SQL commands generated by Access.

Appendices The book includes six appendices. Appendix A presents an introduction to the Microsoft Access Help system. Appendix B describes how to use the Access speech and handwriting recognition capabilities. Appendix C explains how to publish Web pages to a Web server. Appendix D shows how to change the screen resolution and reset the menus and toolbars. Appendix E introduces students to Microsoft Office Specialist certification. Appendix F presents database design techniques, that is, techniques that enable students to design a database to satisfy a set of requirements. The appendix also illustrates the normalization process, which allows students to identify and correct potential problems in database designs.

Quick Reference Summary In Access 2003, you can accomplish a task in a number of ways, such as using the mouse, menu, shortcut menu, and keyboard. The Quick Reference Summary at the back of the book provides a quick reference to each task presented.

Access 2003 CourseCard New! Now includes a free, tear-off Access 2003 CourseCard that provides students with a great way to have Access skills at their fingertips.

End-of-Project Student Activities

A notable strength of the Shelly Cashman Series *Microsoft Office Access 2003* books is the extensive student activities at the end of each project. Well-structured student activities can make the difference between students merely participating in a class and students retaining the information they learn. The activities in the Shelly Cashman Series *Microsoft Office Access 2003* books include the following.

- **What You Should Know** A listing of the tasks completed within a project together with the pages on which the step-by-step, screen-by-screen explanations appear.

- **Learn It Online** Every project features a Learn It Online page that contain 12 exercises. These exercises include True/False, Multiple Choice, Short Answer, Flash Cards, Practice Test, Learning Games, Tips and Tricks, Newsgroup usage, Expanding Your Horizons, Search Sleuth, Office Online Training, and Office Marketplace.

- **Apply Your Knowledge** This exercise usually requires students to open and manipulate a file on the Data Disk that parallels the activities in the project. To obtain a copy of the Data Disk, follow the instructions on the inside back cover of this textbook.

- **In the Lab** Three in-depth assignments per project require students to utilize the project concepts and techniques to solve problems on a computer.

- **Cases and Places** Five unique real-world case-study situations, including one small-group activity.

Instructor Resources CD-ROM

The Shelly Cashman Series is dedicated to providing you with all of the tools you need to make your class a success. Information on all supplementary materials is available through your Course Technology representative or by calling one of the following telephone numbers: Colleges and Universities, 1-800-648-7450; High Schools, 1-800-824-5179; Private Career Colleges, 1-800-347-7707; Canada, 1-800-268-2222; Corporations with IT Training Centers, 1-800-648-7450; and Government Agencies, Health-Care Organizations, and Correctional Facilities, 1-800-477-3692.

The Instructor Resources for this textbook include both teaching and testing aids. The contents of each item on the Instructor Resources CD-ROM (ISBN 0-619-20048-0) are described below.

INSTRUCTOR'S MANUAL The Instructor's Manual is made up of Microsoft Word files, which include detailed lesson plans with page number references, lecture notes, teaching tips, classroom activities, discussion topics, projects to assign, and transparency references. The transparencies are available through the Figure Files described below.

LECTURE SUCCESS SYSTEM The Lecture Success System consists of intermediate files that correspond to certain figures in the book, allowing you to step through the creation of an application in a project during a lecture without entering large amounts of data.

SYLLABUS Sample syllabi, which can be customized easily to a course, are included. The syllabi cover policies, class and lab assignments and exams, and procedural information.

FIGURE FILES Illustrations for every figure in the textbook are available in electronic form. Use this ancillary to present a slide show in lecture or to print transparencies for use in lecture with an overhead projector. If you have a personal computer and LCD device, this ancillary can be an effective tool for presenting lectures.

POWERPOINT PRESENTATIONS PowerPoint Presentations is a multimedia lecture presentation system that provides slides for each project. Presentations are based on project objectives. Use this presentation system to present well-organized lectures that are both interesting and knowledge based. PowerPoint Presentations provides consistent coverage at schools that use multiple lecturers.

SOLUTIONS TO EXERCISES Solutions are included for the end-of-project exercises, as well as the Project Reinforcement exercises.

RUBRICS AND ANNOTATED SOLUTION FILES The grading rubrics provide a customizable framework for assigning point values to the laboratory exercises. Annotated solution files that correspond to the grading rubrics make it easy for you to compare students' results with the correct solutions whether you receive their homework as hard copy or via e-mail.

TEST BANK & TEST ENGINE The ExamView test bank includes 110 questions for every project (25 multiple choice, 50 true/false, and 35 short answer) with page number references and, when appropriate, figure references. A version of the test bank you can print also is included. The test bank comes with a copy of the test engine, ExamView, the ultimate tool for your objective-based testing needs. ExamView is a state-of-the-art test builder that is easy to use. ExamView enables you to create paper-, LAN-, or Web-based tests from test banks designed specifically for your Course Technology textbook. Utilize the ultra-efficient QuickTest Wizard to create tests in less than five minutes by taking advantage of Course Technology's question banks, or customize your own exams from scratch.

LAB TESTS/TEST OUT   The Lab Tests/Test Out exercises parallel the In the Lab assignments and are supplied for the purpose of testing students in the laboratory on the material covered in the project or testing students out of the course.

DATA FILES FOR STUDENTS   All the files that are required by students to complete the exercises are included. You can distribute the files on the Instructor Resources CD-ROM to your students over a network, or you can have them follow the instructions on the inside back cover of this book to obtain a copy of the Data Disk.

ADDITIONAL ACTIVITIES FOR STUDENTS   These additional activities consist of Project Reinforcement Exercises, which are true/false, multiple choice, and short answer questions that help students gain confidence in the material learned.

SAM 2003

SAM 2003 helps you energize your class exams and training assignments by allowing students to learn and test important computer skills in an active, hands-on environment.

SAM 2003 ASSESSMENT   With SAM 2003 Assessment, you create powerful interactive exams on critical applications such as Word, Excel, Access, PowerPoint, Windows, Outlook, and the Internet.

SAM 2003 TRAINING   Invigorate your lesson plan with SAM 2003 Training. Using highly interactive text, graphics, and sound, SAM 2003 Training gives your students the flexibility to learn computer applications by choosing the training method that fits them best. Create customized training units that employ various approaches to teaching computer skills.

SAM 2003 ASSESSMENT AND TRAINING   Designed to be used with the Shelly Cashman Series, SAM 2003 Assessment and Training includes built-in page references so students can create study guides that match the Shelly Cashman Series textbooks you use in class.

Online Content

Course Technology offers textbook-based content for Blackboard, WebCT, and MyCourse 2.1.

BLACKBOARD AND WEBCT   As the leading provider of IT content for the Blackboard and WebCT platforms, Course Technology delivers rich content that enhances your textbook to give your students a unique learning experience.

MYCOURSE 2.1   MyCourse 2.1 is Course Technology's powerful online course management and content delivery system. MyCourse 2.1 allows nontechnical users to create, customize, and deliver Web-based courses; post content and assignments; manage student enrollment; administer exams; track results in the online grade book; and more.

To the Student... Getting the Most Out of Your Book

Welcome to *Microsoft Office Access 2003: Comprehensive Concepts and Techniques, CourseCard Edition*. You can save yourself a lot of time and gain a better understanding of Microsoft Office Access 2003 if you spend a few minutes reviewing the figures and callouts in this section.

1 Project Orientation

Each project presents a practical problem and shows the solution in the first figure of the project. The project orientation lets you see firsthand how problems are solved from start to finish using application software and computers.

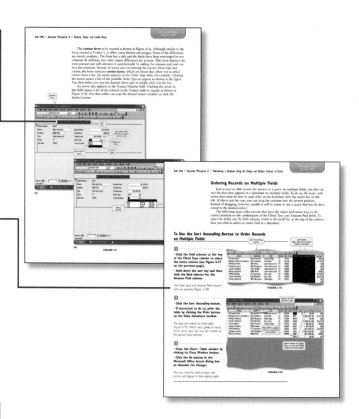

2 Consistent Step-by-Step, Screen-by-Screen Presentation

Project solutions are built using a step-by-step, screen-by-screen approach. This pedagogy allows you to build the solution on a computer as you read through the project. Generally, each step is followed by an italic explanation that indicates the result of the step.

3 More Than Just Step-by-Step

More About and Q&A annotations in the margins of the book and substantive text in the paragraphs provide background information, tips, and answers to common questions that complement the topics covered, adding depth and perspective. When you finish with this book, you will be ready to use Access to solve problems on your own.

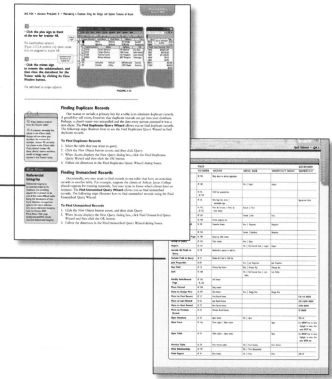

4 Other Ways Boxes and Quick Reference Summary

Other Ways boxes that follow many of the step sequences and a Quick Reference Summary at the back of the book explain the other ways to complete the task presented, such as using the mouse, menu, shortcut menu, and keyboard.

5 Emphasis on Getting Help When You Need It

The first project of each application and Appendix A show you how to use all the elements of the Access Help system. Being able to answer your own questions will increase your productivity and reduce your frustrations by minimizing the time it takes to learn how to complete a task.

6 Review

After you successfully step through a project, a section titled What You Should Know summarizes the project tasks with which you should be familiar. Terms you should know for test purposes are bold in the text.

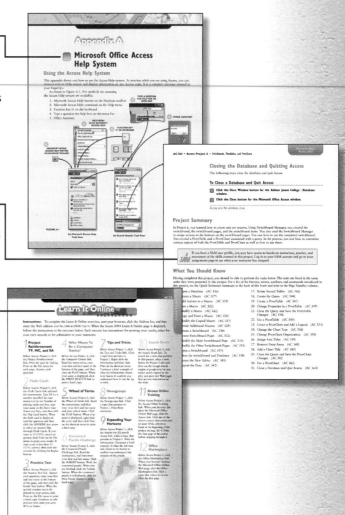

7 Reinforcement and Extension

The Learn It Online page at the end of each project offers reinforcement in the form of review questions, learning games, and practice tests. Also included are Web-based exercises that require you to extend your learning beyond the book.

8 Laboratory Exercises

If you really want to learn how to use the applications, then you must design and implement solutions to problems on your own. Every project concludes with several carefully developed laboratory assignments that increase in complexity.

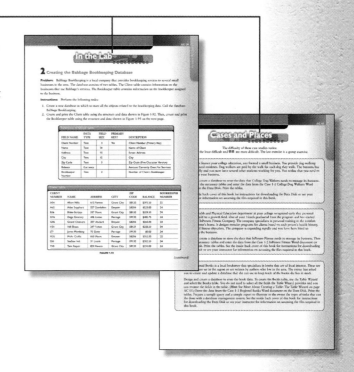

Shelly Cashman Series – Traditionally Bound Textbooks

The Shelly Cashman Series presents the following computer subjects in a variety of traditionally bound textbooks. For more information, see your Course Technology representative or call 1-800-648-7450. For Shelly Cashman Series information, visit Shelly Cashman Online at **scseries.com**

COMPUTERS	
Computers	Discovering Computers 2006: A Gateway to Information, Complete
	Discovering Computers 2006: A Gateway to Information, Introductory
	Discovering Computers 2006: A Gateway to Information, Brief
	Discovering Computers: Fundamentals, Second Edition
	Teachers Discovering Computers: Integrating Technology in the Classroom, Third Edition
	Essential Introduction to Computers, Sixth Edition (40-page)

WINDOWS APPLICATIONS	
Microsoft Office	Microsoft Office 2003: Essential Concepts and Techniques (5 projects)
	Microsoft Office 2003: Brief Concepts and Techniques (9 projects)
	Microsoft Office 2003: Introductory Concepts and Techniques, Second Edition (15 projects)
	Microsoft Office 2003: Advanced Concepts and Techniques (12 projects)
	Microsoft Office 2003: Post Advanced Concepts and Techniques (11 projects)
	Microsoft Office XP: Essential Concepts and Techniques (5 projects)
	Microsoft Office XP: Brief Concepts and Techniques (9 projects)
	Microsoft Office XP: Introductory Concepts and Techniques, Windows XP Edition (15 projects)
	Microsoft Office XP: Introductory Concepts and Techniques, Enhanced Edition (15 projects)
	Microsoft Office XP: Advanced Concepts and Techniques (11 projects)
	Microsoft Office XP: Post Advanced Concepts and Techniques (11 projects)
Integration	Teachers Discovering and Integrating Microsoft Office: Essential Concepts and Techniques, Second Edition
	Integrating Microsoft Office XP Applications and the World Wide Web: Essential Concepts and Techniques
PIM	Microsoft Outlook 2002: Essential Concepts and Techniques • Microsoft Office Outlook 2003: Introductory Concepts and Techniques
Microsoft Works	Microsoft Works 6: Complete Concepts and Techniques[1] • Microsoft Works 2000: Complete Concepts and Techniques[1]
Microsoft Windows	Microsoft Windows XP: Comprehensive Concepts and Techniques[2]
	Microsoft Windows XP: Brief Concepts and Techniques
	Microsoft Windows 2000: Comprehensive Concepts and Techniques[2]
	Microsoft Windows 2000: Brief Concepts and Techniques
	Microsoft Windows 98: Comprehensive Concepts and Techniques[2]
	Microsoft Windows 98: Essential Concepts and Techniques
	Introduction to Microsoft Windows NT Workstation 4
Notebook Organizer	Microsoft Office OneNote 2003: Introductory Concepts and Techniques
Word Processing	Microsoft Office Word 2003: Comprehensive Concepts and Techniques[2] • Microsoft Word 2002: Comprehensive Concepts and Techniques[2]
Spreadsheets	Microsoft Office Excel 2003: Comprehensive Concepts and Techniques[2] • Microsoft Excel 2002: Comprehensive Concepts and Techniques[2]
Database	Microsoft Office Access 2003: Comprehensive Concepts and Techniques[2] • Microsoft Access 2002: Comprehensive Concepts and Techniques[2]
Presentation Graphics	Microsoft Office PowerPoint 2003: Comprehensive Concepts and Techniques[2] • Microsoft PowerPoint 2002: Comprehensive Concepts and Techniques[2]
Desktop Publishing	Microsoft Office Publisher 2003: Comprehensive Concepts and Techniques[2] • Microsoft Publisher 2002: Comprehensive Concepts and Techniques[1]

PROGRAMMING	
Programming	Microsoft Visual Basic .NET: Comprehensive Concepts and Techniques[2] • Microsoft Visual Basic 6: Complete Concepts and Techniques[1] • Java Programming: Comprehensive Concepts and Techniques, Second Edition[2] • Structured COBOL Programming, Second Edition • Understanding and Troubleshooting Your PC • Programming Fundamentals Using Microsoft Visual Basic .NET

INTERNET	
Concepts	Discovering the Internet: Brief Concepts and Techniques • Discovering the Internet: Complete Concepts and Techniques
Browser	Microsoft Internet Explorer 6: Introductory Concepts and Techniques, Windows XP Edition • Microsoft Internet Explorer 5: An Introduction • Netscape Navigator 6: An Introduction
Web Page Creation	Web Design: Introductory Concepts and Techniques • HTML: Comprehensive Concepts and Techniques, Third Edition[2] • Microsoft Office FrontPage 2003: Comprehensive Concepts and Techniques[2] • Microsoft FrontPage 2002: Comprehensive Concepts and Techniques[2] • Microsoft FrontPage 2002: Essential Concepts and Techniques • JavaScript: Complete Concepts and Techniques, Second Edition[1] • Macromedia Dreamweaver MX: Comprehensive Concepts and Techniques[2]

SYSTEMS ANALYSIS	
Systems Analysis	Systems Analysis and Design, Sixth Edition

DATA COMMUNICATIONS	
Data Communications	Business Data Communications: Introductory Concepts and Techniques, Fourth Edition

[1]Also available as an Introductory Edition, which is a shortened version of the complete book, [2]Also available as an Introductory Edition and as a Complete Edition, which are shortened versions of the comprehensive book.

MICROSOFT OFFICE

ACCESS

MICROSOFT
Office Access 2003

Creating and Using a Database

PROJECT

1

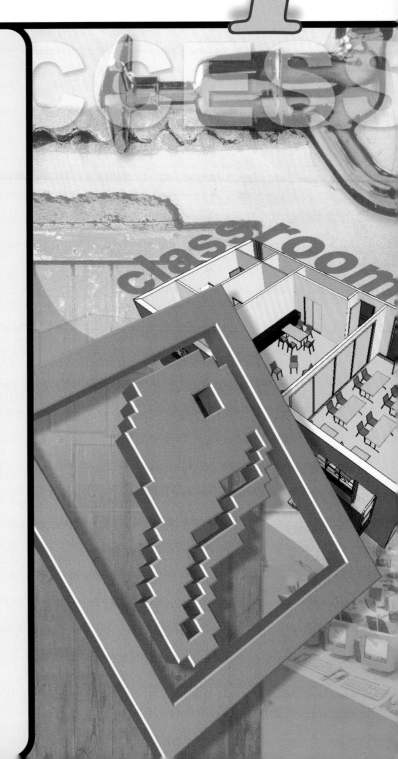

CASE PERSPECTIVE

Ashton James College (AJC) has a solid reputation in the community, delivers quality computer courses, and has a faculty of highly professional, dedicated instructors. Its graduates are among the top achievers in the state. Recently, at the urging of area businesses that depend on the college-educated workforce, AJC has begun to offer corporate computer training through its Continuing Education department. The programs have proved to be very popular, and the client list is growing rapidly.

AJC employs several trainers to teach these corporate courses. It assigns each client to a specific trainer. The trainer contacts the client to determine the particular course the client requires. The trainer then customizes a program for that particular client. The trainer will schedule all the necessary training sessions.

To ensure that operations run smoothly, Ashton James College needs to maintain data on its trainers and their clients. The AJC administration wants to organize the data in a database, managed by a database management system such as Access. In this way, AJC can keep its data current and accurate while program administrators analyze the data for trends and produce a variety of useful reports. Your task is to help the director of continuing education at Ashton James College, Dr. Robert Gernaey, create and use the database.

As you read through this project, you will learn how to use Access to create a database.

MICROSOFT
Office Access 2003

Creating and Using a Database

You will have mastered the material in this project when you can:

- Describe databases and database management systems
- Start Access
- Describe the features of the Access desktop
- Create a database
- Create a table and add records
- Close a table

- Close a database and quit Access
- Open a database
- Print the contents of a table
- Create and use a simple query
- Create and use a simple form
- Create and print a custom report
- Design a database to eliminate redundancy

What Is Microsoft Office Access 2003?

Microsoft Office Access 2003 is a powerful database management system (DBMS) that functions in the Windows environment and allows you to create and process data in a database. Some of the key features are:

- **Data entry and update** Access provides easy mechanisms for adding, changing, and deleting data, including the capability of making mass changes in a single operation.
- **Queries (questions)** Access makes it possible to ask complex questions concerning the data in the database and then receive instant answers.
- **Forms** Access allows the user to produce attractive and useful forms for viewing and updating data.
- **Reports** Access report creation tools make it easy to produce sophisticated reports for presenting data.
- **Web support** Access allows you to save objects, reports, and tables in HTML format so they can be viewed using a browser. You also can import and export documents in XML format. Access's capability of creating data access pages allows real-time access to data in the database via the Internet.

What Is New in Access?

This latest version of Access has many new features to make you more productive. You can view information on dependencies between various database objects. You can enable error checking for many common errors in forms and reports. You can add smart tags to fields in tables, queries, forms, or data access pages. Access now has a command to backup a database. Many wizards provide more options for sorting data. You can export to, import from, or link to a Windows SharePoint Services list. Access now offers enhanced XML support.

Project One — Ashton James College Database

Creating, storing, sorting, and retrieving data are important tasks. In their personal lives, many people keep a variety of records such as names, addresses, and telephone numbers of friends and business associates, records of investments, records of expenses for tax purposes, and so on. For effective use of this data, users must have quick access to it. Businesses also must be able to store and access information quickly and easily.

The term **database** describes a collection of data organized in a manner that allows access, retrieval, and use of that data. A **database management system**, such as Access, is a software tool that allows you to use a computer to create a database; add, change, and delete data in the database; sort the data in the database; retrieve data in the database; and create forms and reports using the data in the database.

In Access, a database consists of a collection of tables. Figure 1-1 shows a sample database for Ashton James College, which consists of two tables. The Client table contains information about the clients to which Ashton James College provides services. The college assigns each client to a specific trainer. The Trainer table contains information about the trainers to whom these clients are assigned.

Client table

fields

CLIENT NUMBER	NAME	ADDRESS	CITY	STATE	ZIP CODE	AMOUNT PAID	CURRENT DUE	TRAINER NUMBER
BS27	Blant and Sons	4806 Park	Lake Hammond	TX	76653	$21,876.00	$892.50	42
CE16	Center Services	725 Mitchell	San Julio	TX	78364	$26,512.00	$2,672.00	48
CP27	Calder Plastics	7300 Cedar	Lake Hammond	TX	76653	$8,725.00	$0.00	48
EU28	Elba's Furniture	1445 Hubert	Tallmadge	TX	77231	$4,256.00	$1,202.00	53
FI28	Farrow-Idsen	829 Wooster	Cedar Ridge	TX	79342	$8,287.50	$925.50	42
FL93	Fairland Lawn	143 Pangborn	Lake Hammond	TX	76653	$21,625.00	$0.00	48
HN83	Hurley National	3827 Burgess	Tallmadge	TX	77231	$0.00	$0.00	48
MC28	Morgan-Alyssa	923 Williams	Crumville	TX	76745	$24,761.00	$1,572.00	42
PS82	PRIM Staffing	72 Crestview	San Julio	TX	78364	$11,682.25	$2,827.50	53
TE26	Telton-Edwards	5672 Anderson	Dunston	TX	77893	$8,521.50	$0.00	48

records

clients of trainer Belinda Perry

Trainer table

TRAINER NUMBER	LAST NAME	FIRST NAME	ADDRESS	CITY	STATE	ZIP CODE	HOURLY RATE	YTD EARNINGS
42	Perry	Belinda	261 Porter	Burdett	TX	76734	$23.00	$27,620.00
48	Stevens	Michael	3135 Gill	Rockwood	TX	78884	$21.00	$23,567.50
53	Gonzalez	Manuel	265 Maxwell	Camino	TX	76574	$24.00	$29,885.00
67	Danville	Marty	1827 Maple	Dunston	TX	77893	$20.00	$0.00

trainer Belinda Perry

FIGURE 1-1

More About

Databases in Access 2003

In some DBMSs, every table, query, form, or report is stored in a separate file. This is not the case in Access 2003, in which a database is stored in a single file on disk. The file contains all the tables, queries, forms, reports, and programs created for this database.

The rows in the tables are called **records**. A record contains information about a given person, product, or event. A row in the Client table, for example, contains information about a specific client.

The columns in the tables are called fields. A **field** contains a specific piece of information within a record. In the Client table, for example, the fourth field, City, contains the city where the client is located.

The first field in the Client table is the Client Number. Ashton James College assigns a number to each client. As is common to the way in which many organizations format client numbers, Ashton James College calls it a *number*, although it actually contains letters. The AJC client numbers consist of two uppercase letters followed by a two-digit number.

These numbers are unique; that is, no two clients are assigned the same number. Such a field can be used as a **unique identifier**. This simply means that a given client number will appear only in a single record in the table. Only one record exists, for example, in which the client number is CP27. A unique identifier also is called a **primary key**. Thus, the Client Number field is the primary key for the Client table.

The next seven fields in the Client table are Name, Address, City, State, Zip Code, Amount Paid, and Current Due. The Amount Paid field contains the amount that the client has paid Ashton James College year-to-date (YTD), but before the current period. The Current Due field contains the amount due to AJC for the current period.

For example, client BS27 is Blant and Sons. The address is 4806 Park in Lake Hammond, Texas. The Zip code is 76653. The client has paid $21,876.00 for training services so far this year. The amount due for the current period is $892.50.

AJC assigns each client a single trainer. The last field in the Client table, Trainer Number, gives the number of the client's trainer.

The first field in the Trainer table, Trainer Number, is the number Ashton James College assigns to the trainer. These numbers are unique, so Trainer Number is the primary key of the Trainer table.

The other fields in the Trainer table are Last Name, First Name, Address, City, State, Zip Code, Hourly Rate, and YTD Earnings. The Hourly Rate field gives the trainer's hourly billing rate, and the YTD Earnings field contains the total amount that AJC has paid the trainer for services so far this year.

For example, Trainer 42 is Belinda Perry. Her address is 261 Porter in Burdett, Texas. The Zip code is 76734. Her hourly billing rate is $23.00, and her YTD earnings are $27,620.00.

The trainer number appears in both the Client table and the Trainer table. It relates clients and trainers. For example, in the Client table, you see that the trainer number for client BS27 is 42. To find the name of this trainer, look for the row in the Trainer table that contains 42 in the Trainer Number field. After you have found it, you know the client is assigned to Belinda Perry. To find all the clients assigned to Belinda Perry, however, you must look through the Client table for all the clients that contain 42 in the Trainer Number field. Her clients are BS27 (Blant and Sons), FI28 (Farrow-Idsen), and MC28 (Morgan-Alyssa).

The last trainer in the Trainer table, Marty Danville, has not been assigned any clients yet; therefore, his trainer number, 67, does not appear on any row in the Client table.

Figure 1-1 on page AC 5 shows the data that must be maintained in the database. The first step is to create the database and the tables it contains. In the process, you must define the fields included in the two tables, as well as the type of data each field will contain. Then, you must add the appropriate records to the tables. Finally, you will print the contents of the tables. After you have completed these tasks, you will create a query, a form, and a report.

Starting Access

If you are stepping through this project on a computer, and you want your screen to agree with the figures in this book, then you should change your computer's resolution to 800 × 600. For more information on how to change the resolution on your computer, see Appendix D. To start Access, Windows must be running. The following steps show how to start Access.

To Start Access

1

• **Click the Start button on the Windows taskbar, point to All Programs on the Start menu and then point to Microsoft Office on the All Programs submenu.**

Windows displays the Start menu, the All Programs submenu, and the Microsoft Office submenu (Figure 1-2).

More About

The Access Help System

Need Help? It is no further than the Type a question for help box on the menu bar in the upper-right corner of the window. Click the box that contains the text, Type a question for help (Figure 1-3 on the next page), type help, and then press the ENTER key. Access responds with a list of topics you can click to learn about obtaining help on any Access-related topic. To find out what is new in Access 2003, type what is new in Access in the Type a question for help box.

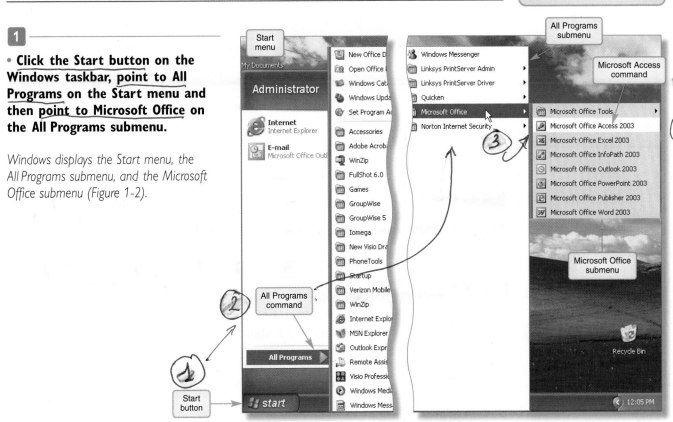

FIGURE 1-2

2

- **Click Microsoft Office Access 2003.**

Access starts. After several seconds, the Access window appears (Figure 1-3).

3

- **If the Access window is not maximized, double-click its title bar to maximize it.**

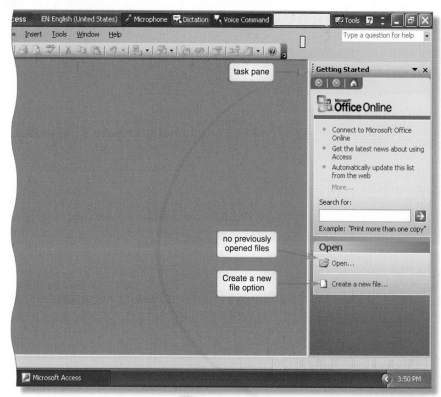

FIGURE 1-3

The screen in Figure 1-3 illustrates how the Access window looks the first time you start Access after installation on most computers. Access displays a task pane on the right side of the screen at startup. A **task pane** is a separate window that enables users to carry out some Access tasks more efficiently. When you start Access, it displays the Getting Started task pane, which is a small window that provides commonly used links and commands that allow you to open files, create new files, or search Office-related topics on the Microsoft Web site. The task pane is used only to create a new database and then it is closed.

If the Office Speech Recognition software is installed and active on your computer, then when you start Access the Language bar is displayed on the screen. The **Language bar** allows you to speak commands and dictate text. It usually is located on the right side of the Windows taskbar next to the notification area and changes to include the speech recognition functions available in Access. In this book, the Language bar is closed. For additional information about the Language bar, see the next page and Appendix B. The following steps show how to close the Language bar if it appears on the screen.

To Close the Language Bar

1

• **Right-click the Language bar to display a list of commands.**

The Language bar shortcut menu appears (Figure 1-4).

2

• **Click Close the Language bar.**
• **Click the OK button.**

The Language bar disappears.

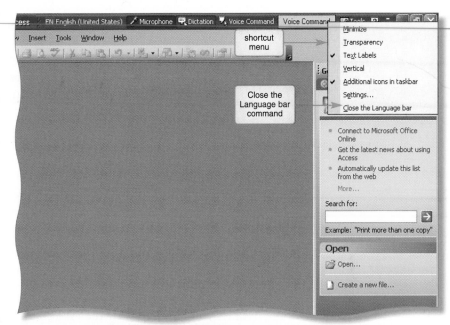

FIGURE 1-4

Speech Recognition

With the **Office Speech Recognition software** installed and a microphone, you can speak the names of toolbar buttons, menus, menu commands, list items, alerts, and dialog box controls, such as OK and Cancel. You also can dictate field entries, such as text and numbers. To indicate whether you want to speak commands or dictate cell entries, you use the Language bar. The Language bar can be in one of three states: (1) **restored**, which means it is displayed somewhere in the Access window (Figure 1-5a); (2) **minimized**, which means it is displayed on the Windows taskbar (Figure 1-5b); or (3) **hidden**, which means you do not see it on the screen. If the Language bar is hidden and you want it to display, then do the following:

1. Right-click an open area on the Windows taskbar at the bottom of the screen.
2. Point to Toolbars and then click Language bar on the Toolbars submenu.

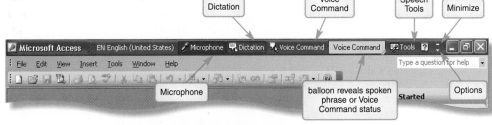

(a) Language Bar in Access Window with Microphone Enabled

(b) Language Bar Minimized on Windows Taskbar

FIGURE 1-5

If the Language bar command is dimmed on the Toolbars submenu or if the Speech command is dimmed on the Tools menu, the Office Speech Recognition software is not installed.

Creating a New Database

In Access, all the tables, reports, form, and queries that you create are stored in a single file called a database. Thus, before creating any of these objects, you first must create the database that will hold them. You can use either the Database Wizard or the Blank database option in the task pane to create a new database. The Database Wizard can guide you by suggesting some commonly used databases. If you choose to create a database using the Database Wizard, you would use the following steps.

To Create a Database Using the Database Wizard

1. Click the New button on the Database toolbar and then click the On my computer link in the New File task pane.
2. When Access displays the Template dialog box, click the Databases tab, and then click the database that is most appropriate for your needs.
3. Follow the instructions in the Database Wizard dialog box to create the database.

Because you already know the tables and fields you want in the Ashton James College database, you would use the Blank database option in the task pane rather than the Database Wizard. The following steps illustrate how to use the Blank database option to create a database on a floppy disk in drive A.

To Create a New Database

1

• **Insert a formatted floppy disk in drive A.**

• **Click the New button on the Database toolbar to display the task pane.**

• **Click the Blank database option in the task pane, and then click the Save in box arrow.**

Access displays the File New Database dialog box and the Save in list appears (Figure 1-6a). Your File name text box may display db1.mdb, rather than db1.

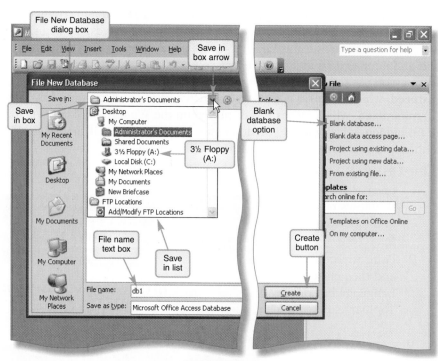

FIGURE 1-6a

2

- **Click 3½ Floppy (A:).**
- **Click the File name text box.**
- **Use the BACKSPACE key or the DELETE key to delete db1 and then type** Ashton James College **as the file name.**

The file name is changed to Ashton James College (Figure 1-6b).

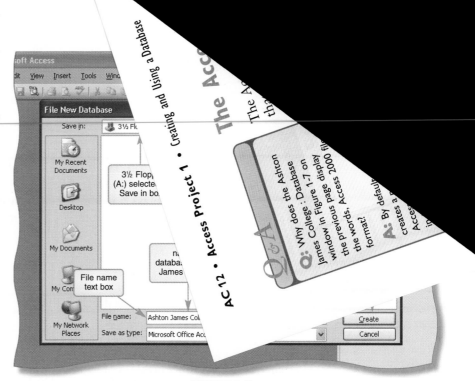

FIGURE 1-6b

3

- **Click the Create button to create the database.**

The Ashton James College database is created. The Ashton James College : Database window appears in the Microsoft Access window (Figure 1-7). The task pane does not appear.

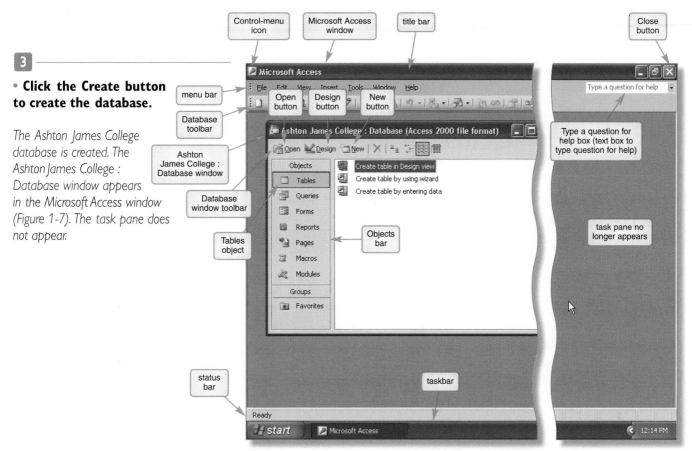

FIGURE 1-7

...ss Window

...ccess window (Figure 1-7 on the previous page) contains a variety of features ...t play important roles when you are working with a database.

Title Bar

The **title bar** is the top bar in the Microsoft Access window. It includes the title of the application, Microsoft Access. The icon on the left is the Control-menu icon. Clicking this icon displays a menu from which you can close the Access window. The button on the right is the Close button. Clicking the Close button closes the Access window.

Menu Bar

The **menu bar** is displayed below the title bar. It is a special toolbar that displays the menu names. Each menu name represents a menu of commands that you can use to retrieve, store, print, and manipulate data. When you point to a menu name on the menu bar, the area of the menu bar is displayed as a selected button. Access shades selected buttons in light orange and surrounds them with a blue outline. To display a menu, such as the Edit menu, click the Edit menu name on the menu bar (Figures 1-8a and 1-8b). A **menu** is a list of commands. If you point to a command on the menu with an arrow to its right, a **submenu** is displayed from which you can choose a command.

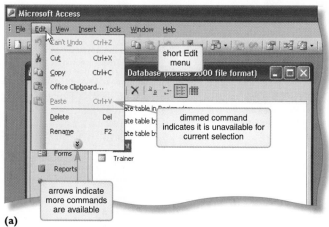

(a)

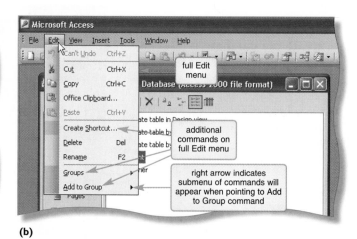

(b)

FIGURE 1-8

When you click a menu name on the menu bar, Access displays a **short menu** listing the most recently used commands (Figure 1-8a). If you wait a few seconds or click the arrows at the bottom of the short menu, the full menu appears. The **full menu** lists all the commands associated with a menu (Figure 1-8b). You also can display a full menu immediately by double-clicking the menu name on the menu bar. In this book, always have Access display the full menu using one of the following techniques.

1. Click the menu name on the menu bar and then wait a few seconds.
2. Click the menu name and then click the arrows at the bottom of the short menu.

3. Click the menu name and then point to the arrows at the bottom of the short menu.
4. Double-click the menu name.

Both short and full menus display some **dimmed commands** that appear gray, or dimmed, instead of black, which indicates they are not available for the current selection. A command with a medium blue shading to the left of it on a full menu is called a **hidden command** because it does not display on a short menu. As you use Access, it automatically personalizes the short menus for you based on how often you use commands. That is, as you use hidden commands, Access *unhides* them and places them on the short menu.

Toolbars

Below the menu bar is a toolbar. A **toolbar** contains buttons that allow you to perform certain tasks more quickly than using the menu bar. Each button contains a picture, or **icon**, depicting its function. When you move the mouse pointer over a button, the name of the button appears below it in a **ScreenTip**. The toolbar shown in Figure 1-7 on page AC 11 is the Database toolbar. The specific toolbar or toolbars that appear will vary, depending on the task on which you are working. Access routinely displays the toolbar or toolbars you will need for the task. If you want to change these or simply to determine what toolbars are available for the given task, consult Appendix D.

Taskbar

The Windows **taskbar** at the bottom of the screen displays the Start button, any active windows, and the current time.

Status Bar

Immediately above the Windows taskbar is the **status bar**. It contains special information that is appropriate for the task on which you are working. Currently, it contains the word, Ready, which means Access is ready to accept commands.

Database Window

The **Database window**, referred to in Figure 1-7 as the Ashton James College : Database window, is a special window that allows you to access easily and rapidly a variety of objects such as tables, queries, forms, and reports. To do so, you will use the various components of the window.

Shortcut Menus

Rather than use toolbars to accomplish a given task, you also can use **shortcut menus**, which are menus that display the actions available for a particular item. To display the shortcut menu for an item, right-click the item; that is, point to the item and then click the right mouse button. Figures 1-9a and 1-9b on the next page illustrate the use of toolbars and shortcut menus to perform the same task, namely to print the contents of the Client table. In the figure, the tables you will create in this project already have been created.

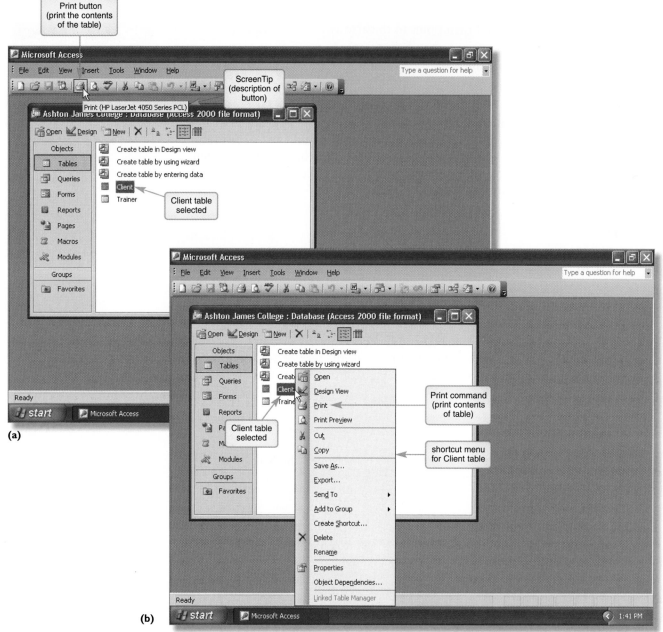

FIGURE 1-9

Before the action illustrated in Figure 1-9a, you would have to select the Client table by clicking it. Then, you would point to the Print button on the toolbar as shown in the figure. When you point to a button on a toolbar, the ScreenTip appears, indicating the purpose of the button, in this case Print. When you click the button, the corresponding action takes place. In this case, Access will print the contents of the Client table.

To use a shortcut menu to perform the same task, you would right-click the Client table, which produces the shortcut menu shown in Figure 1-9b. You then would click the desired command, in this case the Print command, on the shortcut menu. The corresponding action then takes place.

You can use whichever option you prefer. Many professionals who use Access will use a combination. If it is simplest to use the shortcut menu, which often is the case, they will use the shortcut menu. If it is simpler just to click a toolbar button, they will do that. The steps in this text follow this approach; that is, using a combination of both options. The text indicates how to accomplish the task using the other approach, as well. Thus, if the steps use a shortcut menu, the Other Ways box at the end of the steps will indicate how you could accomplish the task using a toolbar button. If the steps use a button, the Other Ways box will indicate how you could accomplish the task with a shortcut menu.

AutoCorrect

Not visible in the Access window, the **AutoCorrect** feature of Access works behind the scenes, correcting common mistakes when you complete a text entry in a cell. AutoCorrect makes three types of corrections for you:

1. Corrects two initial capital letters by changing the second letter to lowercase.
2. Capitalizes the first letter in the names of days.
3. Replaces commonly misspelled words with their correct spelling. For example, it will change the misspelled word *recieve* to *receive* when you complete the entry. AutoCorrect will correct the spelling automatically of more than 400 commonly misspelled words.

Creating a Table

An Access database consists of a collection of tables. After you have created the database, you must create each of the tables within it. In this project, for example, you must create both the Client and Trainer tables shown in Figure 1-1 on page AC 5.

To create a table, you describe the structure of the table to Access by describing the fields within the table. For each field, you indicate the following:

1. **Field name** — Each field in the table must have a unique name. In the Client table (Figure 1-10a and 1-10b on the next page), for example, the field names are Client Number, Name, Address, City, State, Zip Code, Amount Paid, Current Due, and Trainer Number.

Structure of Client table

FIELD NAME	DATA TYPE	FIELD SIZE	PRIMARY KEY?	DESCRIPTION
Client Number	Text	4	Yes	Client Number (Primary Key)
Name	Text	20		Client Name
Address	Text	15		Street Address
City	Text	15		City
State	Text	2		State (Two-Character Abbreviation)
Zip Code	Text	5		Zip Code (Five-Character Version)
Amount Paid	Currency			Amount Paid by Client This Year
Current Due	Currency			Current Due from Client This Period
Trainer Number	Text	2		Number of Client's Trainer

FIGURE 1-10a

Client table

CLIENT NUMBER	NAME	ADDRESS	CITY	STATE	ZIP CODE	AMOUNT PAID	CURRENT DUE	TRAINER NUMBER
BS27	Blant and Sons	4806 Park	Lake Hammond	TX	76653	$21,876.00	$892.50	42
CE16	Center Services	725 Mitchell	San Julio	TX	78364	$26,512.00	$2,672.00	48
CP27	Calder Plastics	7300 Cedar	Lake Hammond	TX	76653	$8,725.00	$0.00	48
EU28	Elba's Furniture	1445 Hubert	Tallmadge	TX	77231	$4,256.00	$1,202.00	53
FI28	Farrow-Idsen	829 Wooster	Cedar Ridge	TX	79342	$8,287.50	$925.50	42
FL93	Fairland Lawn	143 Pangborn	Lake Hammond	TX	76653	$21,625.00	$0.00	48
HN83	Hurley National	3827 Burgess	Tallmadge	TX	77231	$0.00	$0.00	48
MC28	Morgan-Alyssa	923 Williams	Crumville	TX	76745	$24,761.00	$1,572.00	42
PS82	PRIM Staffing	72 Crestview	San Julio	TX	78364	$11,682.25	$2,827.50	53
TE26	Telton-Edwards	5672 Anderson	Dunston	TX	77893	$8,521.50	$0.00	48

FIGURE 1-10b

Q: Do all database management systems use the same data types?

A: No. Different database management systems have different available data types. Even data types that are essentially the same can have different names. The Access 2003 Text data type, for example, is referred to as Character in some systems and Alpha in others.

More About

Primary Keys

In some cases, the primary key consists of a combination of fields rather than a single field. For more information about determining primary keys in such situations, visit the Access 2003 More About Web page (scsite.com/ac2003/more) and click Primary Keys.

2. **Data type** — Data type indicates to Access the type of data the field will contain. Some fields can contain only numbers. Others, such as Amount Paid and Current Due, can contain numbers and dollar signs. Still others, such as Name and Address, can contain letters.

3. **Description** — Access allows you to enter a detailed description of the field.

You also can assign field widths to text fields (fields whose data type is Text). This indicates the maximum number of characters that can be stored in the field. If you do not assign a width to such a field, Access assumes the width is 50.

You also must indicate which field or fields make up the primary key; that is, the unique identifier, for the table. In the Ashton James College database, the Client Number field is the primary key of the Client table and the Trainer Number field is the primary key of the Trainer table.

The rules for field names are:

1. Names can be up to 64 characters in length.

2. Names can contain letters, digits, and spaces, as well as most of the punctuation symbols.

3. Names cannot contain periods, exclamation points (!), accent graves (`), or square brackets ([ ]).

4. The same name cannot be used for two different fields in the same table.

Each field has a **data type**. This indicates the type of data that can be stored in the field. The data types you will use in this project are:

1. **Text** — The field can contain any characters. A maximum number of 255 characters is allowed in a field whose data type is Text.

2. **Number** — The field can contain only numbers. The numbers either can be positive or negative. Fields are assigned this type so they can be used in arithmetic operations. Fields that contain numbers but will not be used for arithmetic operations usually are assigned a data type of Text. The Trainer Number field, for example, is a text field because the trainer numbers will not be involved in any arithmetic.

3. **Currency** — The field can contain only monetary data. The values will appear with currency symbols, such as dollar signs, commas, decimal points, and with two digits following the decimal point. Like numeric fields, you can use currency fields in arithmetic operations. Access assigns a size to currency fields automatically.

Table 1-1 shows the other data types that are available.

Table 1-1 Additional Data Types	
DATA TYPE	DESCRIPTION
Memo	Field can store a variable amount of text or combinations of text and numbers where the total number of characters may exceed 255.
Number	Field can store numeric data that can be used in mathematical calculations.
Date/Time	Field can store dates and times.
AutoNumber	Field can store a unique sequential number that Access assigns to a record. Access will increment the number by 1 as each new record is added.
Yes/No	Field can store only one of two values. The choices are Yes/No, True/False, or On/Off.
OLE Object	Field can store an OLE object, which is an object linked to or embedded in the table.
Hyperlink	Field can store text that can be used as a hyperlink address.
Lookup Wizard	Field can store a value from another table or from a list of values by using a list box or combo box. Choosing this data type starts the Lookup Wizard, which assists in the creation of the field. The field then is a Lookup field. The data type is set based on the values you selected in the wizard. If the values are text for example, the field is assigned the Text data type.

The field names, data types, field widths, primary key information, and descriptions for the Client table are shown in Figure 1-10a on page AC 15.

With the information in Figures 1-10a and 1-10b, you are ready to begin creating the table. The following steps illustrate how to create a table.

To Create a Table

1

• **Click the New button on the Database window toolbar.**

The New Table dialog box appears (Figure 1-11).

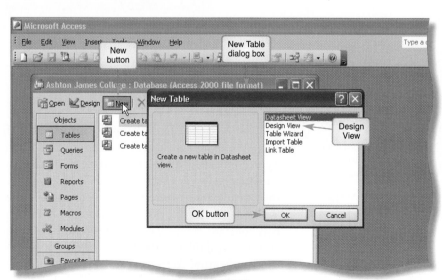

FIGURE 1-11

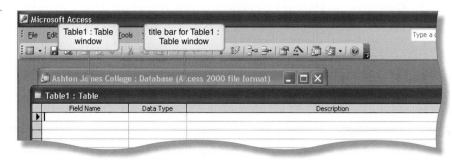

2

• **Click Design View and then click the OK button.**

The Table1 : Table window appears (Figure 1-12).

FIGURE 1-12

3

• **Double-click the title bar of the Table1 : Table window to maximize the window.**

Access displays the maximized Table1 : Table window (Figure 1-13).

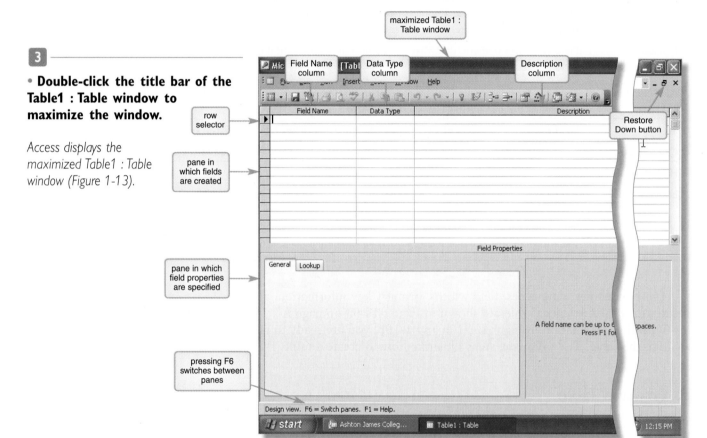

FIGURE 1-13

Defining the Fields

The next step in creating the table is to define the fields by specifying the required details in the Table window, which include entries in the Field Name, Data Type, and Description columns and additional information in the Field Properties pane in the lower portion of the Table window. You press the F6 key to move from the upper **pane** (portion of the screen), the one where you define the fields, to the lower pane, the one where you define field properties. As you define the fields, the **row selector** (Figure 1-13), the small box or bar that, when you click it, selects the entire row, indicates the field you currently are describing. It is positioned on the first field, indicating Access is ready for you to enter the name of the first field in the Field Name column.

The following steps show how to define the fields in the table.

To Define the Fields in a Table

1

• **Type** Client Number **(the name of the first field) in the Field Name column, and then press the TAB key.**

The words, Client Number, appear in the Field Name column and the insertion point advances to the Data Type column, indicating you can enter the data type (Figure 1-14). The word, Text, one of the possible data types, currently appears. The arrow indicates a list of data types is available by clicking the arrow.

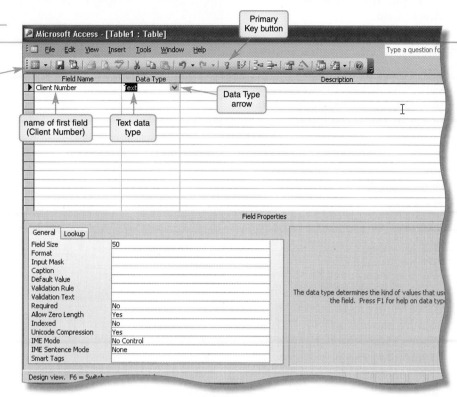

FIGURE 1-14

2

• **Because Text is the correct data type, press the TAB key to move the insertion point to the Description column, type** Client Number (Primary Key) **as the description, and then click the Primary Key button on the Table Design toolbar.**

The Client Number field is the primary key as indicated by the key symbol that appears in the row selector (Figure 1-15). A ScreenTip, which is a description of the button, appears.

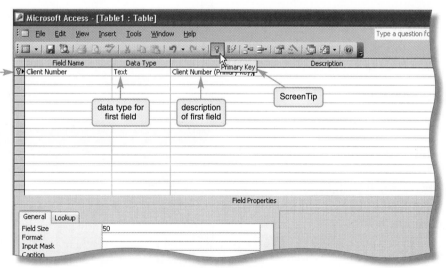

FIGURE 1-15

3

• **Press the F6 key.**

The current entry in the Field Size property box (50) is selected (Figure 1-16).

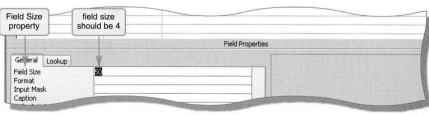

FIGURE 1-16

4

• **Type** 4 **as the size of the Client Number field.**

• **Press the** F6 **key to return to the Description column for the Client Number field, and then press the** TAB **key to move to the Field Name column in the second row.**

The insertion point moves to the second row just below the field name Client Number (Figure 1-17).

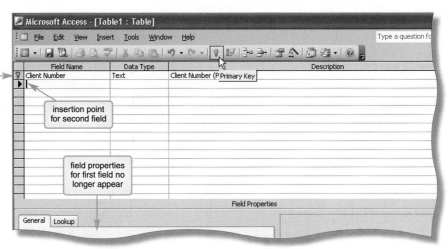

FIGURE 1-17

5

• **Use the techniques illustrated in Steps 1 through 4 to make the entries from the Client table structure shown in Figure 1-10a on page AC 15 up through and including the name of the Amount Paid field.**

• **Click the Data Type box arrow.**

The additional fields are entered (Figure 1-18). A list of available data types appears in the Data Type column for the Amount Paid field.

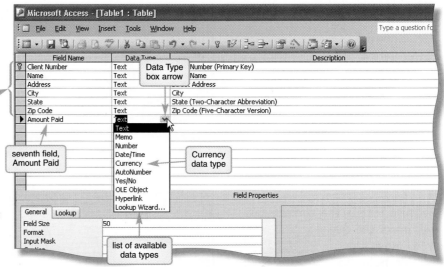

FIGURE 1-18

6

• **Click Currency and then press the** TAB **key.**

• **Make the remaining entries from the Client table structure shown in Figure 1-10a.**

All the fields are entered (Figure 1-19).

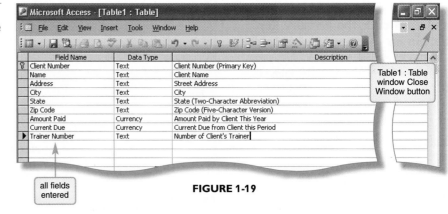

FIGURE 1-19

The description of the table is now complete.

Correcting Errors in the Structure

When creating a table, check the entries carefully to ensure they are correct. If you make a mistake and discover it before you press the TAB key, you can correct the error by repeatedly pressing the BACKSPACE key until the incorrect characters are removed. Then, type the correct characters. If you do not discover a mistake until later, you can click the entry, type the correct value, and then press the ENTER key.

If you accidentally add an extra field to the structure, select the field by clicking the row selector (the leftmost column on the row that contains the field to be deleted). After you have selected the field, press the DELETE key. This will remove the field from the structure.

If you forget a field, select the field that will follow the field you want to add by clicking the row selector, and then press the INSERT key. The remaining fields move down one row, making room for the missing field. Make the entries for the new field in the usual manner.

If you made the wrong field a primary key field, click the correct primary key entry for the field and then click the Primary Key button on the Table Design toolbar.

As an alternative to these steps, you may want to start over. To do so, click the Close Window button for the Table1 : Table window and then click the No button in the Microsoft Office Access dialog box. The initial Microsoft Access window is displayed and you can repeat the process you used earlier.

Closing and Saving a Table

The Client table structure now is complete. The final step is to close and save the table within the database. At this time, you should give the table a name.

Table names are from 1 to 64 characters in length and can contain letters, numbers, and spaces. The two table names in this project are Client and Trainer.

The following steps close and save the table.

To Close and Save a Table

1

• **Click the Close Window button for the Table1 : Table window (see Figure 1-19). (Be sure not to click the Close button on the Microsoft Access title bar, because this would close Microsoft Access.)**

The Microsoft Office Access dialog box appears (Figure 1-20).

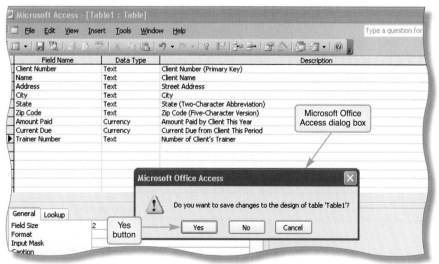

FIGURE 1-20

2

• **Click the Yes button in the Microsoft Office Access dialog box, and then type** Client **as the name of the table.**

The Save As dialog box appears (Figure 1-21). The table name is entered.

3

• **Click the OK button in the Save As dialog box.**

The table is saved. The window containing the table design no longer is displayed.

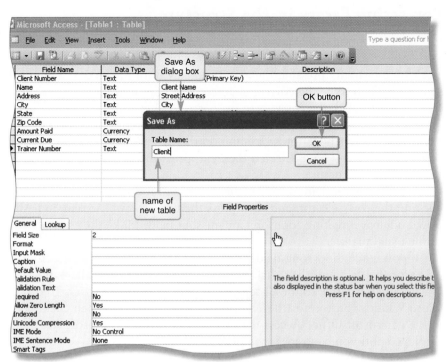

FIGURE 1-21

Adding Records to a Table

Creating a table by building the structure and saving the table is the first step in a two-step process. The second step is to add records to the table. To add records to a table, the table must be open. When making changes to tables, you work in Datasheet view. In **Datasheet view**, the table is represented as a collection of rows and columns called a **datasheet**. It looks very much like the tables shown in Figure 1-1 on page AC 5.

You often add records in phases. You may, for example, not have enough time to add all the records in one session. To illustrate this process, this project begins by adding the first two records in the Client table (Figure 1-22). The remaining records are added later.

CLIENT NUMBER	NAME	ADDRESS	CITY	STATE	ZIP CODE	AMOUNT PAID	CURRENT DUE	TRAINER NUMBER
BS27	Blant and Sons	4806 Park	Lake Hammond	TX	76653	$21,876.00	$892.50	42
CE16	Center Services	725 Mitchell	San Julio	TX	78364	$26,512.00	$2,672.00	48

Client table (first 2 records)

FIGURE 1-22

The following steps illustrate how to open the Client table and then add records.

To Add Records to a Table

1

• **Right-click the Client table in the Ashton James College : Database window.**

The shortcut menu for the Client table appears (Figure 1-23). The Ashton James College : Database window is maximized because the previous window, the Client : Table window, was maximized. (If you wanted to restore the Database window to its original size, you would click the Restore Window button.)

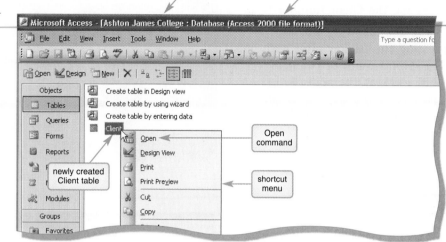

FIGURE 1-23

2

• **Click Open on the shortcut menu.**

*Access displays the Client : Table window (Figure 1-24). The window contains the Datasheet view for the Client table. The **record selector**, the small box or bar that, when clicked, selects the entire record, is positioned on the first record. The status bar at the bottom of the window also indicates that the record selector is positioned on record 1.*

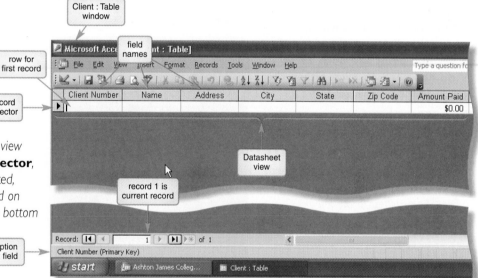

FIGURE 1-24

3

• **Type BS27 as the first client number (see Figure 1-22). Be sure you type the letters in uppercase as shown in the table in Figure 1-22 so they are entered in the database correctly.**

The client number is entered, but the insertion point is still in the Client Number field (Figure 1-25). The pencil icon in the record selector column indicates that the record is being edited but changes to the record are not saved yet. Microsoft Access also creates a row for a new record.

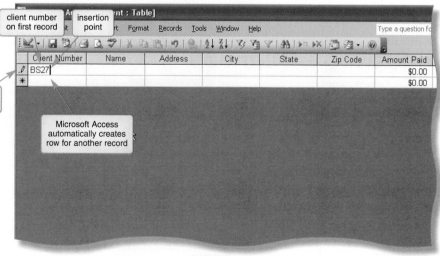

FIGURE 1-25

Microsoft Office
Access 2003

4

• **Press the TAB key to complete the entry for the Client Number field.**

• **Type the following entries, pressing the TAB key after each one:** Blant and Sons **as the name,** 4806 Park **as the address,** Lake Hammond **as the city,** TX **as the state, and** 76653 **as the Zip code.**

The Name, Address, City, State, and Zip Code fields are entered (Figure 1-26).

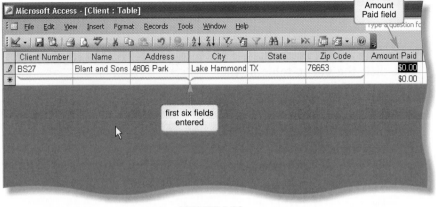

FIGURE 1-26

5

• **Type** 21876 **as the Amount Paid amount and then press the TAB key. (You do not need to type dollar signs or commas. In addition, because the digits to the right of the decimal point are both zeros, you do not need to type either the decimal point or the zeros.)**

• **Type** 892.50 **as the current due amount and then press the TAB key.**

• **Type** 42 **as the trainer number to complete data entry for the record.**

The fields have shifted to the left (Figure 1-27). The Amount Paid and Current Due values appear with dollar signs and decimal points. The insertion point is positioned in the Trainer Number field.

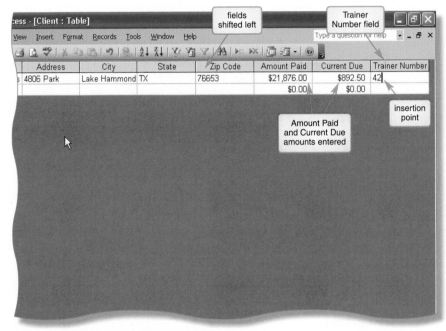

FIGURE 1-27

6

• **Press the TAB key.**

The fields shift back to the right, the record is saved, and the insertion point moves to the client number field on the second row (Figure 1-28).

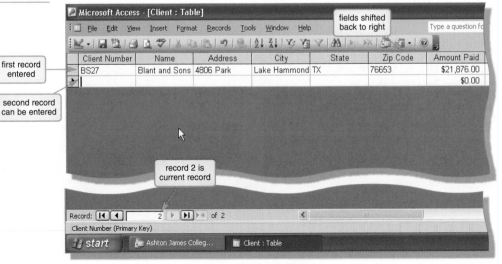

FIGURE 1-28

7

• **Use the techniques shown in Steps 3 through 6 to add the data for the second record shown in Figure 1-22 on page AC 22.**

The second record is added and the insertion point moves to the Client Number field on the third row (Figure 1-29).

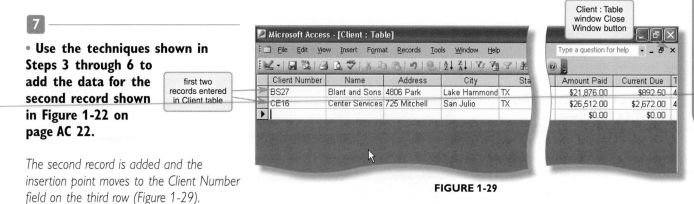

FIGURE 1-29

As soon as you have entered or modified a record and moved to another record, the original record is saved. This is different from other applications. The rows entered in a spreadsheet, for example, are not saved until the entire spreadsheet is saved.

Correcting Errors in the Data

Check your entries carefully to ensure they are correct. If you make a mistake and discover it before you press the TAB key, correct it by pressing the BACKSPACE key until the incorrect characters are removed and then typing the correct characters.

If you discover an incorrect entry later, correct the error by clicking the incorrect entry and then making the appropriate correction. If the record you must correct is not on the screen, use any technique, such as the UP ARROW and DOWN ARROW keys to move to it. If the field you want to correct is not visible on the screen, use the horizontal scroll bar along the bottom of the screen to shift all the fields until the one you want appears. Then make the correction.

If you add an extra record accidentally, select the record by clicking the record selector that immediately precedes the record. Then, press the DELETE key. This will remove the record from the table. If you forget a record, add it using the same procedure as for all the other records. Access will place it in the correct location in the table automatically.

If you cannot determine how to correct the data, you are, in effect, stuck on the record. Access neither allows you to move to any other record until you have made the correction, nor allows you to close the table. If you encounter this situation, simply press the ESC key. Pressing the ESC key will remove from the screen the record you are trying to add. You then can move to any other record, close the table, or take any other action you desire.

More About

Correcting Errors in the Data

You also can undo changes to a field by clicking the Undo typing button on the Table Datasheet toolbar. If you already have moved to another record and want to delete the record you just added, click Edit on the menu bar and then click Undo Saved Record.

Closing a Table and Database and Quitting Access

It is a good idea to close a table as soon as you have finished working with it. It keeps the screen from getting cluttered and prevents you from making accidental changes to the data in the table. If you no longer will work with the database, you should close the database as well. With the creation of the Client table complete, you also can quit Access at this point.

The steps on the next page close the table and the database and then quit Access.

To Close a Table and Database and Quit Access

1

• **Click the Close Window button for the Client : Table window.**

The datasheet for the Client table no longer appears (Figure 1-30).

2

• **Click the Close Window button for the Ashton James College : Database window.**

The Ashton James College : Database window no longer appears.

3

• **Click the Close button for the Microsoft Access window.**

The Microsoft Access window closes and the Windows desktop appears.

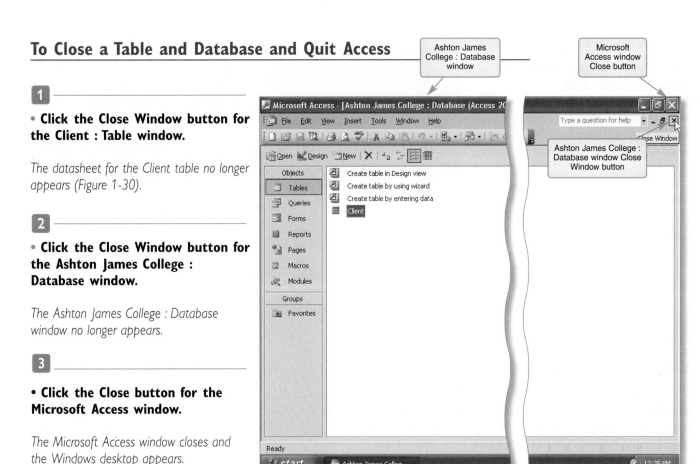

FIGURE 1-30

Opening a Database

To work with any of the tables, reports, or forms in a database, the database must be open. The following steps open the database from within Access.

To Open a Database

1

• **Start Access following the steps on pages AC 7 and AC 8.**

• **If the task pane appears, click its Close button.**

• **Click the Open button on the Database toolbar.**

The Open dialog box appears (Figure 1-31).

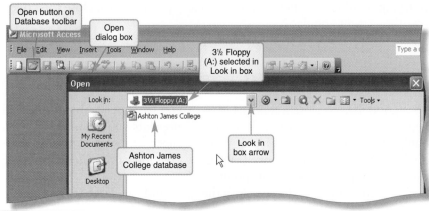

FIGURE 1-31

2

• **Be sure 3½ Floppy (A:) folder appears in the Look in box. If not, click the Look in box arrow and click 3½ Floppy (A:).**

• **Click Ashton James College.**

Access displays the Open dialog box (Figure 1-32). The 3½ Floppy (A:) folder appears in the Look in box and the files on the floppy disk in drive A are displayed. (Your list may be different.)

3

• **Click the Open button in the Open dialog box.**

• **If a Security Warning dialog box appears, click the Open button.**

The database opens and the Ashton James College : Database window appears.

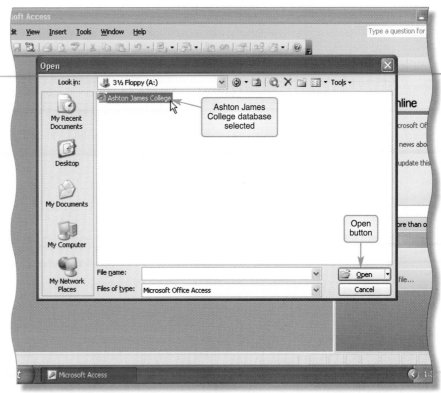

FIGURE 1-32

Adding Additional Records

You can add records to a table that already contains data using a process almost identical to that used to add records to an empty table. The only difference is that you place the insertion point after the last data record before you enter the additional data. To do so, use the **Navigation buttons**, which are buttons used to move within a table, found near the lower-left corner of the screen shown in Figure 1-34 on the next page. The purpose of each of the Navigation buttons is described in Table 1-2.

Table 1-2 Navigation Buttons in Datasheet View	
BUTTON	**PURPOSE**
First Record	Moves to the first record in the table
Previous Record	Moves to the previous record
Next Record	Moves to the next record
Last Record	Moves to the last record in the table
New Record	Moves to the end of the table to a position for entering a new record

The steps on the next page add the remaining records (Figure 1-33 on the next page) to the Client table.

Other Ways

1. On File menu click Open
2. In Getting Started task pane, click name of database
3. Press CTRL + O
4. In Voice Command mode, say "Open"

Q&A

Q: Why click the New Record button? Could you just click the Client Number on the first open record and then add the record?

A: You could click the Client Number on the first open record, provided that record appears on the screen. With only two records in the table, this is not a problem. Once a table contains more records than will fit on the screen, it is easier to click the New Record button.

Client table (last 8 records)

CLIENT NUMBER	NAME	ADDRESS	CITY	STATE	ZIP CODE	AMOUNT PAID	CURRENT DUE	TRAINER NUMBER
CP27	Calder Plastics	7300 Cedar	Lake Hammond	TX	76653	$8,725.00	$0.00	48
EU28	Elba's Furniture	1445 Hubert	Tallmadge	TX	77231	$4,256.00	$1,202.00	53
FI28	Farrow-Idsen	829 Wooster	Cedar Ridge	TX	79342	$8,287.50	$925.50	42
FL93	Fairland Lawn	143 Pangborn	Lake Hammond	TX	76653	$21,625.00	$0.00	48
HN83	Hurley National	3827 Burgess	Tallmadge	TX	77231	$0.00	$0.00	48
MC28	Morgan-Alyssa	923 Williams	Crumville	TX	76745	$24,761.00	$1,572.00	42
PS82	PRIM Staffing	72 Crestview	San Julio	TX	78364	$11,682.25	$2,827.50	53
TE26	Telton-Edwards	5672 Anderson	Dunston	TX	77893	$8,521.50	$0.00	48

FIGURE 1-33

To Add Additional Records to a Table

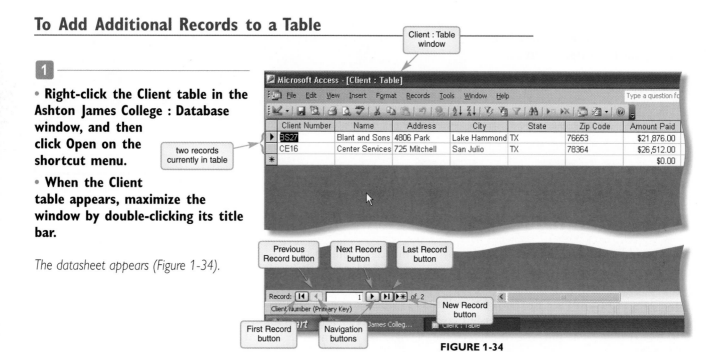

1

• **Right-click the Client table in the Ashton James College : Database window, and then click Open on the shortcut menu.**

• **When the Client table appears, maximize the window by double-clicking its title bar.**

The datasheet appears (Figure 1-34).

FIGURE 1-34

2

• **Click the New Record button.**

Access places the insertion point in position to enter a new record (Figure 1-35).

FIGURE 1-35

3

• **Add the records from Figure 1-33 using the same techniques you used to add the first two records.**

The additional records are added (Figure 1-36).

4

• **Click the Close Window button for the datasheet.**

The window containing the table closes and the Ashton James College : Database window appears.

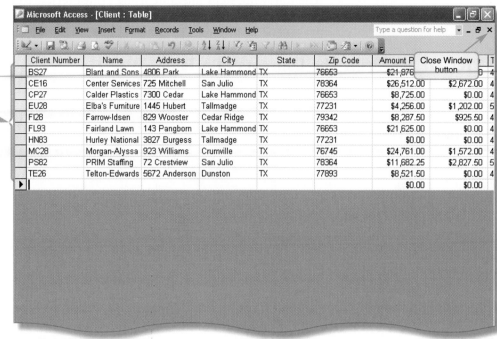

all 10 records entered

Close Window button

Client Number	Name	Address	City	State	Zip Code	Amount P		T
BS27	Blant and Sons	4806 Park	Lake Hammond	TX	76653	$21,876		4
CE16	Center Services	725 Mitchell	San Julio	TX	78364	$26,512.00	$2,672.00	4
CP27	Calder Plastics	7300 Cedar	Lake Hammond	TX	76653	$8,725.00	$0.00	4
EU28	Elba's Furniture	1445 Hubert	Tallmadge	TX	77231	$4,256.00	$1,202.00	5
FI28	Farrow-Idsen	829 Wooster	Cedar Ridge	TX	79342	$8,287.50	$925.50	4
FL93	Fairland Lawn	143 Pangborn	Lake Hammond	TX	76653	$21,625.00	$0.00	4
HN83	Hurley National	3827 Burgess	Tallmadge	TX	77231	$0.00	$0.00	4
MC28	Morgan-Alyssa	923 Williams	Crumville	TX	76745	$24,761.00	$1,572.00	4
PS82	PRIM Staffing	72 Crestview	San Julio	TX	78364	$11,682.25	$2,827.50	5
TE26	Telton-Edwards	5672 Anderson	Dunston	TX	77893	$8,521.50	$0.00	4
						$0.00	$0.00	

FIGURE 1-36

Other Ways

1. Click New Record button on Table Datasheet toolbar
2. On Insert menu click New Record
3. Press CTRL+PLUS SIGN (+)
4. In Voice Command mode, say "Insert, New Record"

Previewing and Printing the Contents of a Table

When working with a database, you often will need to print a copy of the table contents. Figure 1-37 shows a printed copy of the contents of the Client table. (Yours may look slightly different, depending on your printer.) Because the Client table is wider substantially than the screen, it also will be wider than the normal printed page in portrait orientation. **Portrait orientation** means the printout is across the width of the page. **Landscape orientation** means the printout is across the length of the page. Thus, to print the wide database table, use landscape orientation. If you are printing the contents of a table that fit on the screen, you will not need landscape orientation. A convenient way to change to landscape orientation is to preview what the printed copy will look like by using Print Preview. This allows you to determine whether landscape orientation is necessary and, if it is, to change the orientation easily to landscape. In addition, you also can use Print Preview to determine whether any adjustments are necessary to the page margins.

Client   9/15/05

Client Number	Name	Address	City	State	Zip Code	Amount Paid	Current Due	Trainer Number
BS27	Blant and Sons	4806 Park	Lake Hammond	TX	76653	$21,876.00	$892.50	42
CE16	Center Service	725 Mitchell	San Julio	TX	78364	$26,512.00	$2,672.00	48
CP27	Calder Plastics	7300 Cedar	Lake Hammond	TX	76653	$8,725.00	$0.00	48
EU28	Elba's Furniture	1445 Hubert	Tallmadge	TX	77231	$4,256.00	$1,202.00	53
FI28	Farrow-Idsen	829 Wooster	Cedar Ridge	TX	79342	$8,287.50	$925.50	42
FL93	Fairland Lawn	143 Pangborn	Lake Hammond	TX	76653	$21,625.00	$0.00	48
HN83	Hurley National	3827 Burgess	Tallmadge	TX	77231	$0.00	$0.00	48
MC28	Morgan-Alyssa	923 Williams	Crumville	TX	76745	$24,761.00	$1,572.00	42
PS82	PRIM Staffing	72 Crestview	San Julio	TX	78364	$11,682.25	$2,827.50	53
TE26	Telton-Edwards	5672 Anderson	Dunston	TX	77893	$8,521.50	$0.00	48

FIGURE 1-37

The following steps illustrate using Print Preview to preview and then print the Client table.

To Preview and Print the Contents of a Table

1

• **Right-click the Client table.**

The shortcut menu for the Client table appears (Figure 1-38).

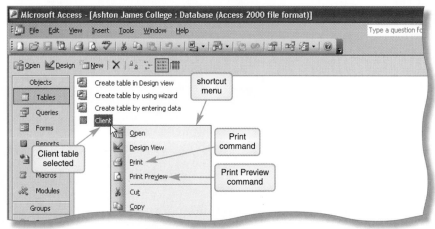

FIGURE 1-38

2

• **Click Print Preview on the shortcut menu.**

• **Point to the approximate position shown in Figure 1-39.**

The preview of the report appears. The mouse pointer shape changes to a magnifying glass, indicating you can magnify a portion of the report.

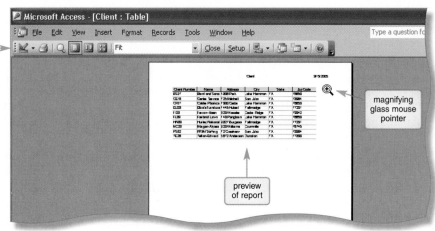

FIGURE 1-39

3

• **Click the magnifying glass mouse pointer in the approximate position shown in Figure 1-39.**

The portion surrounding the mouse pointer is magnified (Figure 1-40). The last field that appears is the Zip Code field. The Amount Paid, Current Due, and Trainer Number fields do not appear. To display the additional fields, you will need to switch to landscape orientation.

r	Name	Address	City	State	Zip Code
	Blant and Sons	4806 Park	Lake Hammon	TX	76653
	Center Service	725 Mitchell	San Julio	TX	78364
	Calder Plastics	7300 Cedar	Lake Hammon	TX	76653
	Elba's Furniture	1445 Hubert	Tallmadge	TX	77231
	Farrow-Idsen	829 Wooster	Cedar Ridge	TX	79342
	Fairland Lawn	143 Pangborn	Lake Hammon	TX	76653
	Hurley National	3827 Burgess	Tallmadge	TX	77231
	Morgan-Alyssa	923 Williams	Crumville	TX	76745
	PRIM Staffing	72 Crestview	San Julio	TX	78364
	Telton-Edward	5672 Anderson	Dunston	TX	77893

FIGURE 1-40

4

• **Click the Setup button on the Print Preview toolbar.**

Access displays the Page Setup dialog box (Figure 1-41).

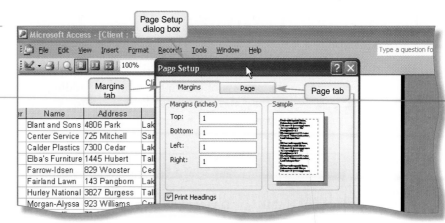

FIGURE 1-41

5

• **Click the Page tab.**

*The Page sheet appears (Figure 1-42). The Portrait option button currently is selected. (**Option button** refers to the round button that indicates choices in a dialog box. When the corresponding option is selected, the button contains within it a solid circle. Clicking an option button selects it, and deselects all others.)*

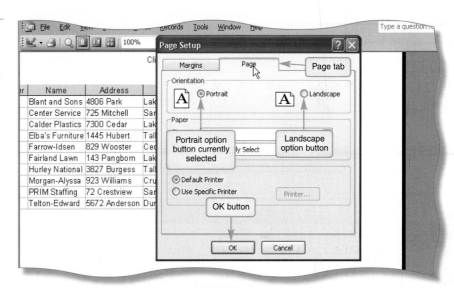

FIGURE 1-42

6

• **Click Landscape, and then click the OK button.**

The orientation is changed to landscape as shown by the report that appears on the screen (Figure 1-43). The last field that is displayed is the Trainer Number field; so all fields currently appear. If they did not, you could decrease the left and right margins; that is, the amount of space left by Access on the left and right edges of the report.

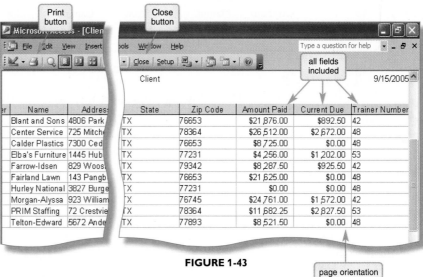

FIGURE 1-43

7

• **Click the Print button to print the report, and then click the Close button on the Print Preview toolbar.**

The report prints. It looks like the report shown in Figure 1-37 on page AC 29. The Print Preview window closes and the Ashton James College : Database window appears.

Creating Additional Tables

A database typically consists of more than one table. The Ashton James College database contains two, the Client table and the Trainer table. You need to repeat the process of creating a table and adding records for each table in the database. In the Ashton James College database, you need to create and add records to the Trainer table. The structure and data for the table are given in Figure 1-44.

Structure of Trainer table

FIELD NAME	DATA TYPE	FIELD SIZE	PRIMARY KEY?	DESCRIPTION
Trainer Number	Text	2	Yes	Trainer Number (Primary Key)
Last Name	Text	10		Last Name of Trainer
First Name	Text	8		First Name of Trainer
Address	Text	15		Street Address
City	Text	15		City
State	Text	2		State (Two-Character Abbreviation)
Zip Code	Text	5		Zip Code (Five-Character Version)
Hourly Rate	Currency			Hourly Rate of Trainer
YTD Earnings	Currency			YTD Earnings of Trainer

Trainer table

TRAINER NUMBER	LAST NAME	FIRST NAME	ADDRESS	CITY	STATE	ZIP CODE	HOURLY RATE	YTD EARNINGS
42	Perry	Belinda	261 Porter	Burdett	TX	76734	$23.00	$27,620.00
48	Stevens	Michael	3135 Gill	Rockwood	TX	78884	$21.00	$23,567.50
53	Gonzalez	Manuel	265 Maxwell	Camino	TX	76574	$24.00	$29,885.00
67	Danville	Marty	1827 Maple	Dunston	TX	77893	$20.00	$0.00

FIGURE 1-44

The following steps show how to create the table.

More About

Printing the Contents of a Table

You can change the margins, paper size, paper source, or the printer that will be used to print the report. To change the margins, select the Margins sheet in the Page Setup dialog box and then enter the appropriate margin size. To change the paper size, paper source, or the printer, select the Page sheet in the Page Setup dialog box, click the appropriate down arrow, and then select the desired option.

To Create an Additional Table

1

- **Make sure the Ashton James College database is open.**

- **Click the New button on the Database window toolbar, click Design View, and then click the OK button.**

- **Enter the data for the fields for the Trainer table from Figure 1-44. Be sure to click the Primary Key button when you enter the Trainer Number field.**

The entries appear (Figure 1-45).

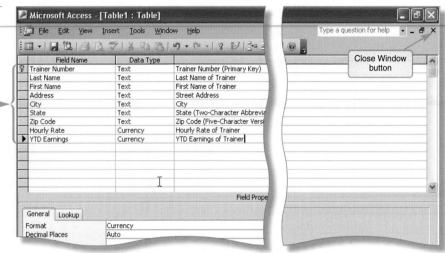

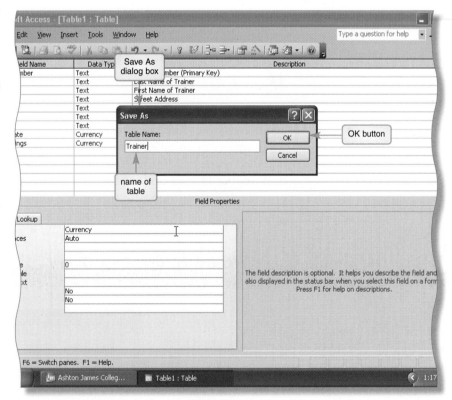

FIGURE 1-45

2

- **Click the Close Window button, click the Yes button in the Microsoft Office Access dialog box when asked if you want to save the changes, and then type** Trainer **as the name of the table.**

The Save As dialog box appears (Figure 1-46). The table name is entered.

3

- **Click the OK button.**

The table is saved in the Ashton James College database. The window containing the table structure no longer appears.

FIGURE 1-46

Adding Records to the Additional Table

Now that you have created the Trainer table, use the steps on the next page to add records to it.

To Add Records to an Additional Table

1

• **Right-click the Trainer table, and then click Open on the shortcut menu. Enter the Trainer data from Figure 1-44 on page AC 32 into the Trainer table.**

The datasheet displays the entered records (Figure 1-47).

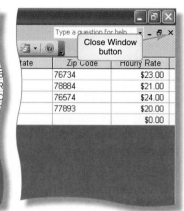

2

• **Click the Close Window button for the Trainer : Table window.**

Access closes the table and removes the datasheet from the screen.

FIGURE 1-47

The records are now in the table.

Using Queries

Queries are simply questions, the answers to which are in the database. Access contains a powerful query feature. Through the use of this feature, you can ask a wide variety of complex questions. For simple requests, however, such as listing the number, name, and trainer number of all clients, you do not need to use the query feature, but instead can use the Simple Query wizard.

The following steps use the Simple Query wizard to create a query to display the number, name, and trainer number of all clients.

To Use the Simple Query Wizard to Create a Query

1

• **With the Tables object selected and the Client table selected, click the New Object button arrow on the Database toolbar.**

A list of objects that can be created is displayed (Figure 1-48).

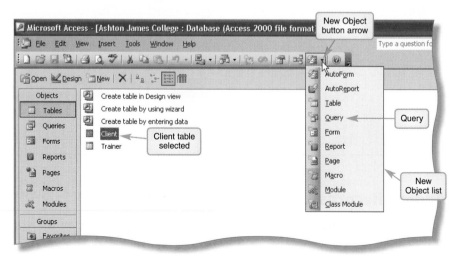

FIGURE 1-48

2

• **Click Query on the New Object list.**

The New Query dialog box appears (Figure 1-49).

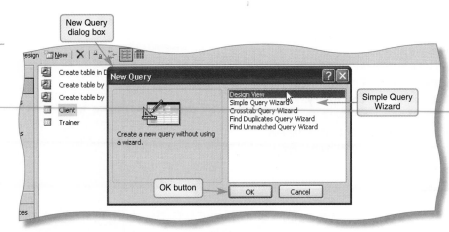

FIGURE 1-49

3

• **Click Simple Query Wizard, and then click the OK button.**

Access displays the Simple Query Wizard dialog box (Figure 1-50). It contains a list of available fields and a list of selected fields. Currently no fields are selected for the query.

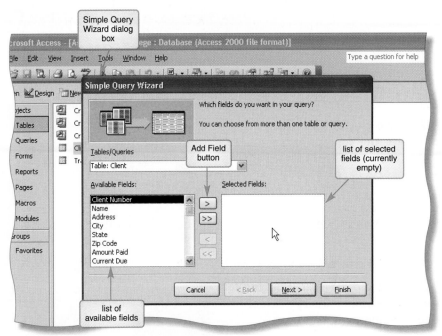

FIGURE 1-50

4

• **Click the Add Field button to add the Client Number field.**

• **Click the Add Field button a second time to add the Name field.**

• **Click the Trainer Number field, and then click the Add Field button to add the Trainer Number field.**

The fields are selected (Figure 1-51).

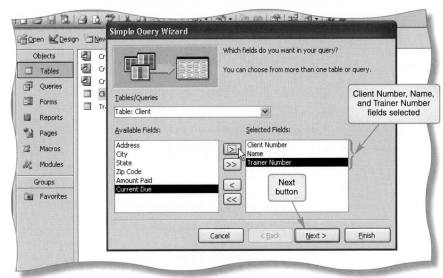

FIGURE 1-51

5

• **Click the Next button, and then type** Client-Trainer Query **as the name for the query.**

The Simple Query Wizard dialog box displays the new query name (Figure 1-52).

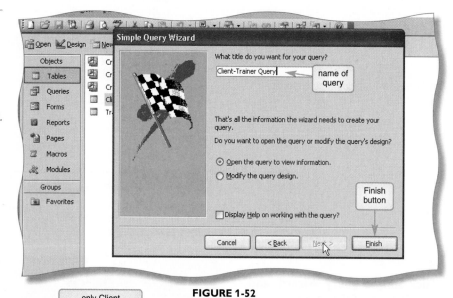

FIGURE 1-52

6

• **Click the Finish button to complete the creation of the query.**

Access displays the query results (Figure 1-53). The results contain all records, but only contain the Client Number, Name, and Trainer Number fields.

7

• **Click the Close Window button for the Client-Trainer Query : Select Query window.**

Access closes the query and the Ashton James College : Database window appears.

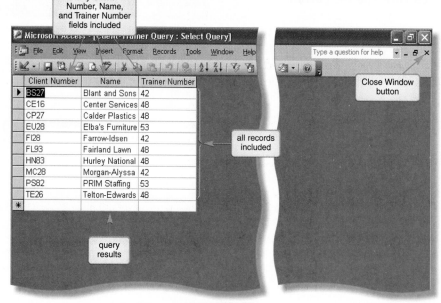

FIGURE 1-53

The query is complete. You can use it at any time you like in the future without needing to repeat the above steps.

Using a Query

After you have created and saved a query, you can use it at any time in the future by opening it. To open a saved query, click the Queries object on the Objects bar, right-click the query, and then click Open on the shortcut menu. To print the results, click the Print button on the toolbar. If you want to change the design of the query, click Design View on the shortcut menu rather than Open. To print the query without first opening it, click Print on the shortcut menu.

You often want to restrict the records that are included. For example, you might only want to include those clients whose trainer number is 42. In such a case, you need to enter the 42 as a **criterion**, which is a condition that the records to be included must satisfy. To do so, you will open the query in Design view, enter the criterion below the appropriate field, and then run the query. The following steps show how to enter a criterion to include only clients of trainer 42 and then run the query.

To Use a Query

1

• **If necessary, click the Queries object. Right-click the Client-Trainer Query.**

The shortcut menu for the Client-Trainer Query is displayed (Figure 1-54).

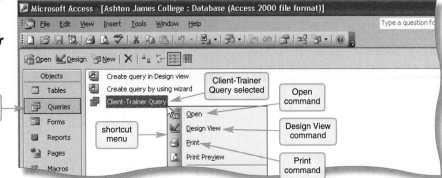

FIGURE 1-54

2

• **Click Design View on the shortcut menu.**

The query appears in Design view (Figure 1-55).

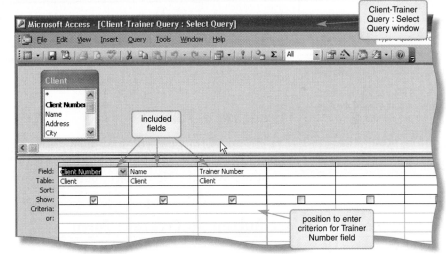

FIGURE 1-55

3

• **Click the Criteria row in the Trainer Number column of the grid, and then type** 42 **as the criterion.**

The criterion is typed (Figure 1-56).

FIGURE 1-56

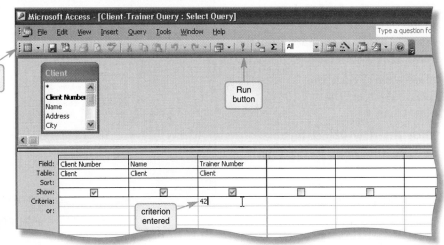

4

• **Click the Run button on the Query Design toolbar.**

Access displays the results (Figure 1-57). Only the clients of trainer 42 are included.

5

• **Close the window containing the query results by clicking its Close Window button.**

• **When asked if you want to save your changes, click the No button.**

The results no longer appear. The changes to the query are not saved.

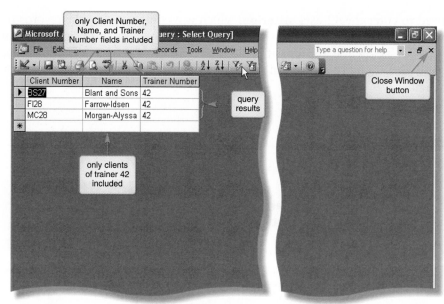

FIGURE 1-57

Other Ways

1. On Query menu click Run
2. In Voice Command mode, say "Run"

Q&A

Q: If you saved the query, what would happen the next time you ran the query?

A: You would see only clients of trainer 42.

Using a Form to View Data

In creating tables, you have used Datasheet view; that is, the data on the screen appeared as a table. You also can use **Form view**, in which you see data contained in a form.

Creating a Form

To use Form view, you first must create a form. The simplest way to create a form is to use the New Object button on the Database toolbar. The following steps illustrate using the New Object button to create a form for the Client table.

To Use the New Object Button to Create a Form

1

• **Make sure the Ashton James College database is open, the Database window appears, and the Client table is selected.**

• **If necessary, click the Tables object on the Objects bar.**

• **Click the New Object button arrow on the Database toolbar.**

A list of objects that can be created appears (Figure 1-58).

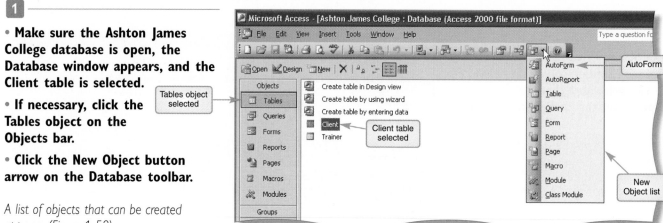

FIGURE 1-58

2

• **Click AutoForm on the New Object list.**

After a brief delay, the form appears (Figure 1-59). If you do not move the mouse pointer after clicking the New Object button, the ScreenTip for the Properties button may appear when the form opens. Access displays the Formatting toolbar when a form is created. (When you close the form, this toolbar no longer appears.)

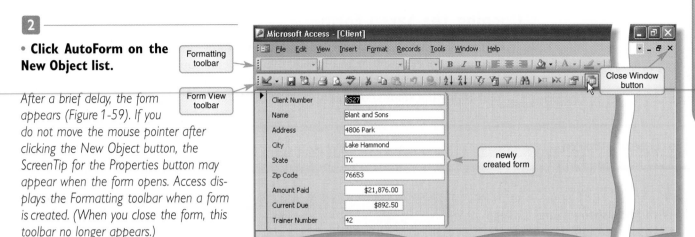

FIGURE 1-59

Other Ways

1. On Insert menu click AutoForm
2. In Voice Command mode, say "New Object, AutoForm"
3. In Voice Command mode, say "Insert, AutoForm"

Closing and Saving the Form

Closing a form is similar to closing a table. The only difference is that you will be asked if you want to save the form unless you previously have saved it. The following steps close the form and save it as Client.

To Close and Save a Form

1

• **Click the Close Window button for the Client window (see Figure 1-59).**

Access displays the Microsoft Office Access dialog box (Figure 1-60).

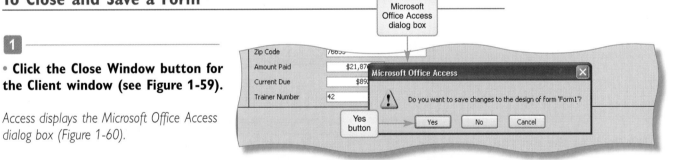

FIGURE 1-60

2

• **Click the Yes button.**

The Save As dialog box appears (Figure 1-61). The name of the table (Client) becomes the name of the form automatically. This name could be changed, if desired.

3

• **Click the OK button.**

The form is saved as part of the database and the form closes. The Ashton James College : Database window is redisplayed.

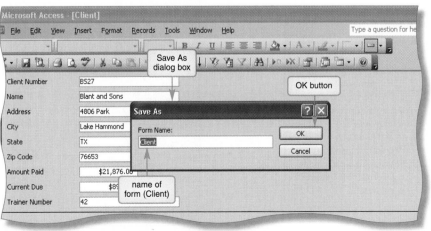

FIGURE 1-61

Opening the Saved Form

After you have saved a form, you can use it at any time in the future by opening it. Opening a form is similar to opening a table. Before opening the form, however, the Forms object, rather than the Tables object, must be selected.

The following steps show how to open the Client form.

To Open a Form

1

• **With the Ashton James College database open and the Database window on the screen, click Forms on the Objects bar, and then right-click the Client form.**

The list of forms appears (Figure 1-62). The shortcut menu for the Client form appears.

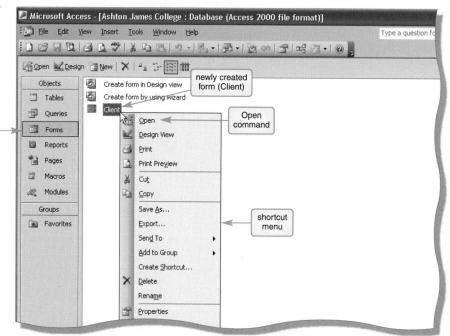

FIGURE 1-62

2

• **Click Open on the shortcut menu.**

The Client form appears (Figure 1-63).

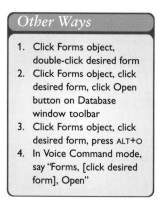

Other Ways

1. Click Forms object, double-click desired form
2. Click Forms object, click desired form, click Open button on Database window toolbar
3. Click Forms object, click desired form, press ALT+O
4. In Voice Command mode, say "Forms, [click desired form], Open"

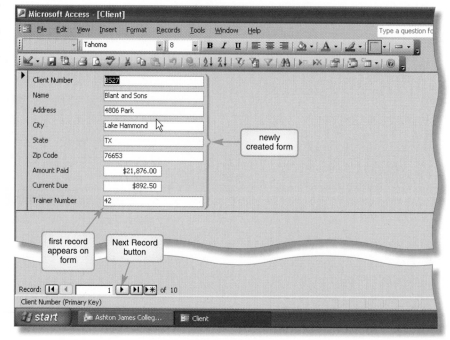

FIGURE 1-63

Using the Form

You can use the form just as you used Datasheet view. You use the Navigation buttons to move between records. You can add new records or change existing ones. To delete the record appearing on the screen, after selecting the record by clicking its record selector, press the DELETE key. Thus, you can perform database operations using either Form view or Datasheet view.

Because you can see only one record at a time in Form view, to see a different record, such as the fifth record, you must use the Navigation buttons to move to it. The following step illustrates moving from record to record in Form view.

To Use a Form

1

• **Click the Next Record button four times.**

Access displays the fifth record on the form (Figure 1-64).

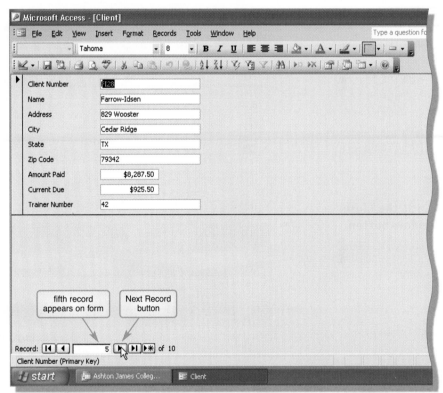

fifth record appears on form

Next Record button

FIGURE 1-64

Switching Between Form View and Datasheet View

In some cases, after you have seen a record in Form view, you will want to switch to Datasheet view to see the collection of records. The steps on the next page show how to switch from Form view to Datasheet view.

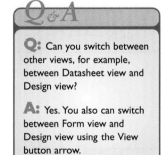

Q: Can you switch between other views, for example, between Datasheet view and Design view?

A: Yes. You also can switch between Form view and Design view using the View button arrow.

To Switch from Form View to Datasheet View

 1

• **Click the View button arrow on the Form View toolbar.**

The list of available views appears (Figure 1-65).

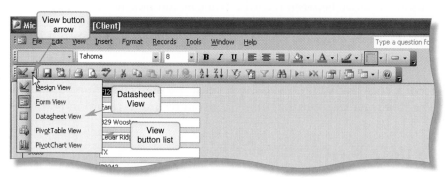

FIGURE 1-65

2

• **Click Datasheet View.**

The table appears in Datasheet view (Figure 1-66). The record selector is positioned on the fifth record.

3

• **Click the Close Window button.**

The Client window closes and the datasheet no longer appears.

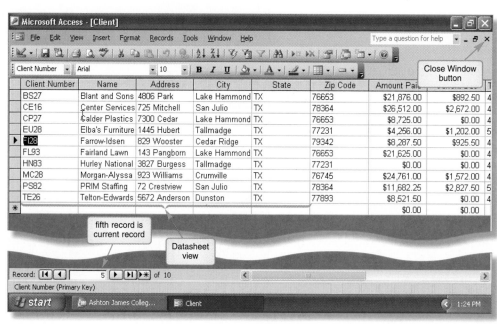

FIGURE 1-66

Other Ways

1. On View menu click Datasheet View
2. In Voice Command mode, say "View, Datasheet View"

Creating a Report

Earlier in this project, you printed a table using the Print button. The report you produced was shown in Figure 1-37 on page AC 29. While this type of report presented the data in an organized manner, the format is very rigid. You cannot select the fields to appear, for example; the report automatically includes all the fields and they appear in precisely the same order as in the table. A way to change the title of the table is not available. Therefore, it will be the same as the name of the table.

In this section, you will create the report shown in Figure 1-67. This report features significant differences from the one in Figure 1-37. The portion at the top of the report in Figure 1-67, called a **page header**, contains a custom title. The contents of this page header appear at the top of each page. The **detail lines**, which are the lines that are printed for each record, contain only those fields you specify and in the order you specify.

Client Amount Report

Client Number	Name	Amount Paid	Current Due
BS27	Blant and Sons	$21,876.00	$892.50
CE16	Center Services	$26,512.00	$2,672.00
CP27	Calder Plastics	$8,725.00	$0.00
EU28	Elba's Furniture	$4,256.00	$1,202.00
FI28	Farrow-Idsen	$8,287.50	$925.50
FL93	Fairland Lawn	$21,625.00	$0.00
HN83	Hurley National	$0.00	$0.00
MC28	Morgan-Alyssa	$24,761.00	$1,572.00
PS82	PRIM Staffing	$11,682.25	$2,827.50
TE26	Telton-Edwards	$8,521.50	$0.00

FIGURE 1-67

The following steps show how to create the report in Figure 1-67.

To Create a Report

1

• **Click Tables on the Objects bar, and then make sure the Client table is selected.**

• **Click the New Object button arrow on the Database toolbar.**

The list of available objects appears (Figure 1-68).

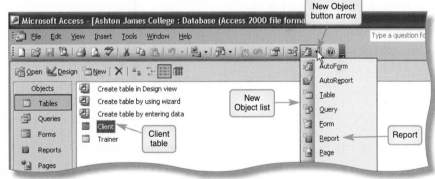

FIGURE 1-68

2

• **Click Report.**

Access displays the New Report dialog box (Figure 1-69).

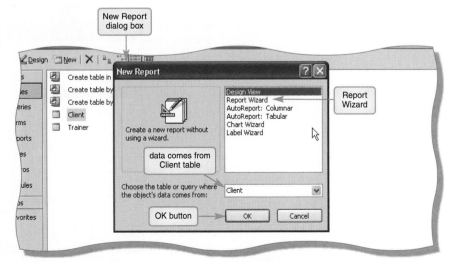

FIGURE 1-69

3

• **Click Report Wizard, and then click the OK button.**

Access displays the Report Wizard dialog box (Figure 1-70). As you click the Next button in this dialog box, a series of options helps you create the report.

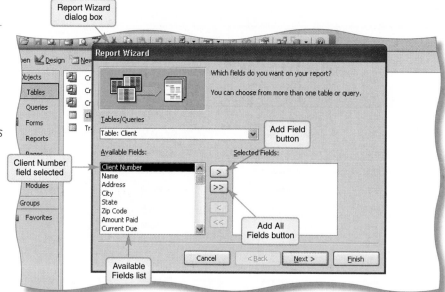

FIGURE 1-70

4

• **Click the Add Field button to add the Client Number field.**

• **Click the Add Field button to add the Name field.**

• **Add the Amount Paid and Current Due fields just as you added the Client Number and Name fields.**

The fields for the report appear in the Selected Fields box (Figure 1-71).

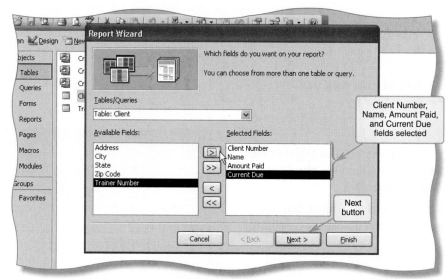

FIGURE 1-71

5

• **Click the Next button.**

The Report Wizard dialog box displays options to specify any grouping that is to take place (Figure 1-72).

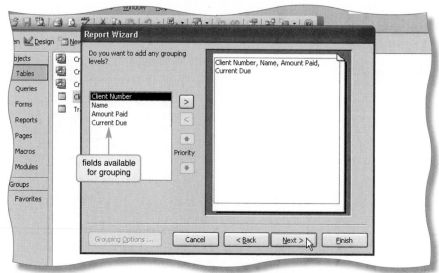

FIGURE 1-72

6

• **Because you will not specify any grouping, click the Next button in the Report Wizard dialog box.**

• **Click the Next button a second time because you will not need to change the sort order for the records.**

The Report Wizard dialog box displays options for changing the layout and orientation of the report (Figure 1-73).

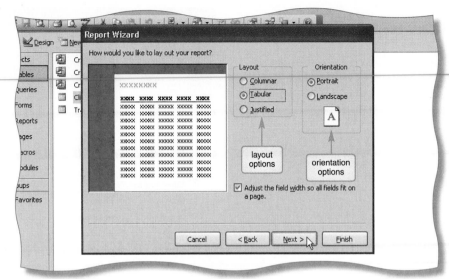

FIGURE 1-73

7

• **Make sure that Tabular is selected as the Layout and Portrait is selected as the Orientation, and then click the Next button.**

The Report Wizard dialog box displays options you can select for the style of the report (Figure 1-74).

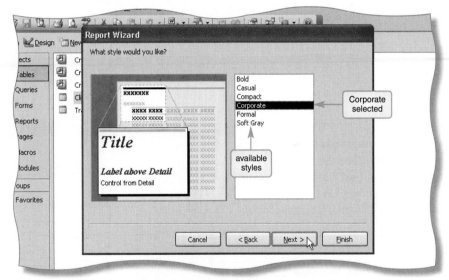

FIGURE 1-74

8

• **Be sure the Corporate style is selected, click the Next button, and then type** Client Amount Report **as the new title.**

The Report Wizard dialog box displays the new title of the report (Figure 1-75).

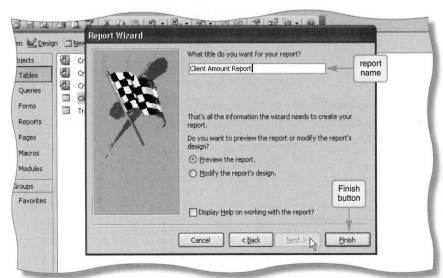

FIGURE 1-75

9

• **Click the Finish button.**

Access displays a preview of the report (Figure 1-76). Your report may look slightly different, depending on your printer.

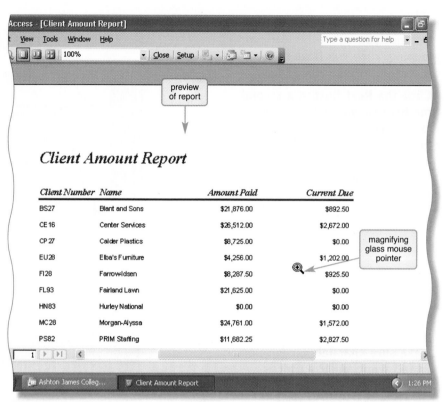

FIGURE 1-76

10

• **Click the magnifying glass mouse pointer anywhere within the report to see the entire report.**

The entire report appears (Figure 1-77).

11

• **Click the Close Window button in the Client Amount Report window.**

The report no longer appears. It has been saved automatically using the name Client Amount Report.

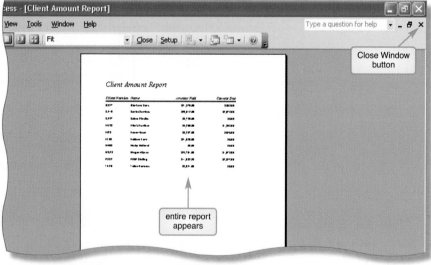

FIGURE 1-77

Other Ways

1. On Objects bar click Reports, double-click Create report by using wizard
2. On Objects bar click Reports, click New on Database window toolbar
3. On Insert menu click Report
4. In Voice Command mode, say "Insert, Report"

Printing the Report

With the report created, you can preview the report to determine if you need to change the orientation or the page margins. You also can print the report. If you want to print specific pages or select other print options, use the Print command on the File menu. The following steps on the next page show how to print a report using the shortcut menu.

To Print a Report

1

- **If necessary, click Reports on the Objects bar in the Database window.**
- **Right-click the Client Amount Report.**

The Client Amount Report is selected and the shortcut menu appears (Figure 1-78).

2

- **Click Print on the shortcut menu.**

The report prints. It should look similar to the one shown in Figure 1-67 on page AC 43.

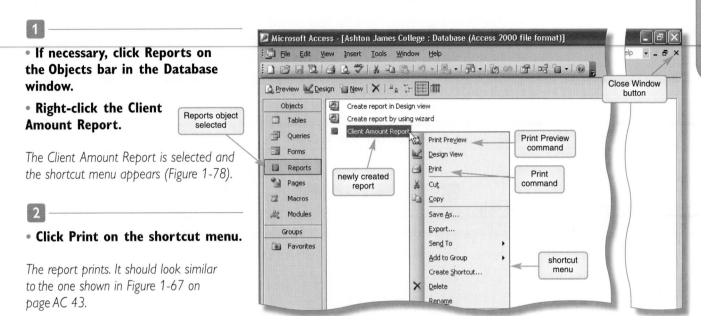

FIGURE 1-78

Closing the Database

After you have finished working with a database, you should close it. The following step closes the database by closing its Database window.

To Close a Database

1 **Click the Close Window button for the Ashton James College : Database window.**

Access Help System

At any time while you are using Access, you can get answers to questions by using the Access Help system. You can activate the Access Help system by using the Type a question for help box on the menu bar, by clicking the Microsoft Access Help button on the toolbar, or by clicking Help on the menu bar (Figure 1-79 on the next page). Used properly, this form of online assistance can increase your productivity and reduce your frustrations by minimizing the time you spend learning how to use Access.

The section on the next page shows how to get answers to your questions using the Type a question for help box. Additional information about using the Access Help system is available in Appendix A.

More About

The Access Help System

The best way to become familiar with the Access Help system is to use it. Appendix A includes detailed information on the Access Help system and exercises that will help you gain confidence in using it.

Obtaining Help Using the Type a Question for Help Box on the Menu Bar

The Type a question for help box on the right side of the menu bar lets you type in free-form questions, such as *how do I save* or *how do I create a Web page* or, you can type in terms, such as *copy*, *save*, or *formatting*. Access responds by displaying a list of topics related to what you entered. The following steps show how to use the Type a question for help box to obtain information on removing a primary key.

To Obtain Help Using the Type a Question for Help Box

1

• **Click the Type a question for help box on the right side of the menu bar.**

• **Type** how do I remove a primary key **in the box (Figure 1-79).**

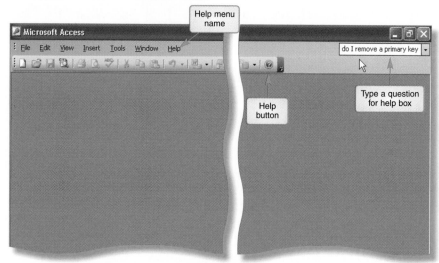

FIGURE 1-79

2

• **Press the ENTER key.**

Access displays the Search Results task pane, which includes a list of topics relating to the question, how do I remove a primary key (Figure 1-80). Your list may be different.

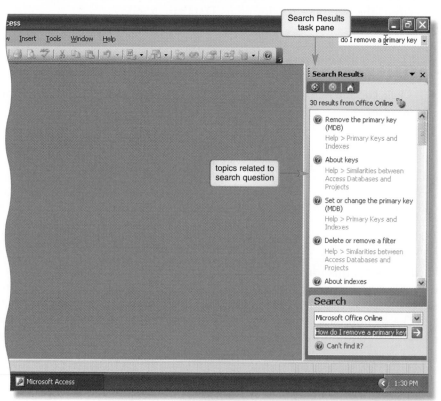

FIGURE 1-80

3

• **Point to the Remove the primary key (MDB) topic.**

The mouse pointer changes to a hand indicating it is pointing to a link (Figure 1-81).

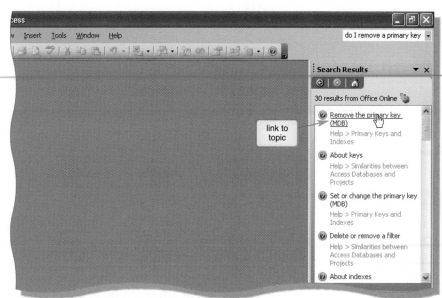

FIGURE 1-81

4

• **Click Remove the primary key (MDB).**

Access displays a Microsoft Office Access Help window that provides Help information about removing the primary key (Figure 1-82). Your window may be in a different position.

5

• **Click the Close button on the Microsoft Office Access Help window title bar.**

The Microsoft Access Help window closes.

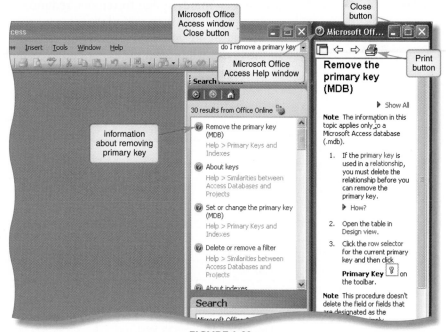

FIGURE 1-82

Use the buttons in the upper-left corner of the Microsoft Office Access Help window (Figure 1-82) to navigate through the Help system, and change the appearance and print the contents of the window.

As you enter questions and terms in the Type a question for help box, Access adds them to its list. Thus, if you click the Type a question for help box arrow, a list of previously asked questions and terms will appear.

Quitting Access

After you close a database, you can open another database, create a new database, or simply quit Access and return to the Windows desktop. The following step quits Access.

To Quit Access

1 **Click the Close button in the Microsoft Access window (see Figure 1-82 on the previous page).**

More About

Database Design: Design Method

A variety of methods have been developed for designing complex databases given a set of input and output requirements. For more information about database design methods, visit the Access 2003 More About Web page (scsite.com/ac2003/more) and click Database Design.

Designing a Database

Database design refers to the arrangement of data into tables and fields. In the example in this project, the design is specified, but in many cases, you will have to determine the design based on what you want the system to accomplish.

With large, complex databases, the database design process can be extensive. Major sections of advanced database textbooks are devoted to this topic. Often, however, you should be able to design a database effectively by keeping one simple principle in mind: design to remove redundancy. **Redundancy** means storing the same fact in more than one place.

To illustrate, you need to maintain the following information shown in Figure 1-83. In the figure, all the data is contained in a single table. Notice that the data for a given trainer (number, name, address, and so on) occurs on more than one record.

CLIENT NUMBER	NAME	ADDRESS	...	CURRENT DUE	TRAINER NUMBER	LAST NAME	FIRST NAME	...
BS27	Blant and Sons	4806 Park	...	$892.50	42	Perry	Belinda	...
CE16	Center Services	725 Mitchell	...	$2,672.00	48	Stevens	Michael	...
CP27	Calder Plastics	7300 Cedar	...	$0.00	48	Stevens	Michael	...
EU28	Elba's Furniture	1445 Hubert	...	$1,202.00	53	Gonzalez	Manuel	...
FI28	Farrow-Idsen	829 Wooster	...	$925.50	42	Perry	Belinda	...
FL93	Fairland Lawn	143 Pangborn	...	$0.00	48	Stevens	Michael	
HN83	Hurley National	3827 Burgess	...	$0.00	48	Stevens	Michael	
MC28	Morgan-Alyssa	923 Williams	...	$1,572.00	42	Perry	Belinda	
PS82	PRIM Staffing	72 Crestview	...	$2,827.50	53	Gonzalez	Manuel	
TE26	Telton-Edwards	5672 Anderson	...	$0.00	48	Stevens	Michael	

Client table — duplicate trainer names

FIGURE 1-83

More About

The Quick Reference

For a table that lists how to complete tasks covered in this book using the mouse, menu, shortcut menu, and keyboard, see the Quick Reference Summary at the back of this book, or visit the Access 2003 Quick Reference Web page (scsite.com/ac2003/qr).

Storing this data on multiple records is an example of redundancy, which causes several problems, including:

1. Redundancy wastes space on the disk. The name of trainer 42 (Belinda Perry), for example, should be stored only once. Storing this fact several times is wasteful.

2. Redundancy makes updating the database more difficult. If, for example, Belinda Perry's name changes, her name would need to be changed in several different places.

3. A possibility of inconsistent data exists. If, for example, you change the name of Belinda Perry on client FI28's record to Belinda Martin, but do not change it on client BS27's record, the data is inconsistent. In both cases, the trainer number is 42, but the names are different.

The solution to the problem is to place the redundant data in a separate table, one in which the data no longer will be redundant. If, for example, you place the data for trainers in a separate table (Figure 1-84), the data for each trainer will appear only once.

More About

Database Design: Normalization

A special technique, called normalization, identifies and eliminates redundancy. For more information about normalization, visit the Access 2003 More About Web page (scsite.com/ac2003/more) and click Normalization.

trainer data is in separate table

Trainer table

TRAINER NUMBER	LAST NAME	FIRST NAME	ADDRESS	CITY	STATE	ZIP CODE	HOURLY RATE	YTD EARNINGS
42	Perry	Belinda	261 Porter	Burdett	TX	76734	$23.00	$27,620.00
48	Stevens	Michael	3135 Gill	Rockwood	TX	78884	$21.00	$23,567.50
53	Gonzalez	Manuel	265 Maxwell	Camino	TX	76574	$24.00	$29,885.00

Client table

CLIENT NUMBER	NAME	ADDRESS	CITY	STATE	ZIP CODE	AMOUNT PAID	CURRENT DUE	TRAINER NUMBER
BS27	Blant and Sons	4806 Park	Lake Hammond	TX	76653	$21,876.00	$892.50	42
CE16	Center Services	725 Mitchell	San Julio	TX	78364	$26,512.00	$2,672.00	48
CP27	Calder Plastics	7300 Cedar	Lake Hammond	TX	76653	$8,725.00	$0.00	48
EU28	Elba's Furniture	1445 Hubert	Tallmadge	TX	77231	$4,256.00	$1,202.00	53
FI28	Farrow-Idsen	829 Wooster	Cedar Ridge	TX	79342	$8,287.50	$925.50	42
FL93	Fairland Lawn	143 Pangborn	Lake Hammond	TX	76653	$21,625.00	$0.00	48
HN83	Hurley National	3827 Burgess	Tallmadge	TX	77231	$0.00	$0.00	48
MC28	Morgan-Alyssa	923 Williams	Crumville	TX	76745	$24,761.00	$1,572.00	42
PS82	PRIM Staffing	72 Crestview	San Julio	TX	78364	$11,682.25	$2,827.50	53
TE26	Telton-Edwards	5672 Anderson	Dunston	TX	77893	$8,521.50	$0.00	48

FIGURE 1-84

Notice that you need to have the trainer number in both tables. Without it, no way exists to tell which trainer is associated with which client. The remaining trainer data, however, was removed from the Client table and placed in the Trainer table. This new arrangement corrects the problems of redundancy in the following ways:

1. Because the data for each trainer is stored only once, space is not wasted.
2. Changing the name of a trainer is easy. You have only to change one row in the Trainer table.
3. Because the data for a trainer is stored only once, inconsistent data cannot occur.

Designing to omit redundancy will help you to produce good and valid database designs.

More About

Microsoft Certification

The Microsoft Office Specialist Certification program provides an opportunity for you to obtain a valuable industry credential — proof that you have the Access 2003 skills required by employers. For more information, see Appendix E, or visit the Access 2003 Certification Web page (scsite.com/ac2003/cert).

Project Summary

In Project 1, you learned about databases and database management systems. You learned how to create a database and how to create the tables within a database. You saw how to define the fields in a table by specifying the characteristics of the fields. You learned how to open a table, how to add records to it, and how to close it. You also printed the contents of a table. You learned how to use the Simple Query wizard to create a query that included columns from a table as well as how to enter a criterion to restrict the rows that were included. You created a form to view data on the screen and also created a custom report. You learned how to use Microsoft Access Help. Finally, you learned how to design a database to eliminate redundancy.

 If you have a SAM user profile, you may have access to hands-on instruction, practice, and assessment of the skills covered in this project. Log in to your SAM account and go to your assignments page to see what your instructor has assigned.

What You Should Know

Having completed this project, you should be able to perform the tasks below. The tasks are listed in the same order they were presented in this project. For a list of the buttons, menus, toolbars, and commands introduced in this project, see the Quick Reference Summary at the back of this book and refer to the Page Number column.

1. Start Access   (AC 7)
2. Close the Language Bar   (AC 9)
3. Create a New Database   (AC 10)
4. Create a Table   (AC 17)
5. Define the Fields in a Table   (AC 19)
6. Close and Save a Table   (AC 21)
7. Add Records to a Table   (AC 23)
8. Close a Table and Database and Quit Access (AC 26)
9. Open a Database   (AC 26)
10. Add Additional Records to a Table   (AC 28)
11. Preview and Print the Contents of a Table (AC 30)
12. Create an Additional Table   (AC 33)
13. Add Records to an Additional Table   (AC 34)
14. Use the Simple Query Wizard to Create a Query (AC 34)
15. Use a Query   (AC 37)
16. Use the New Object Button to Create a Form (AC 38)
17. Close and Save a Form   (AC 39)
18. Open a Form   (AC 40)
19. Use a Form   (AC 41)
20. Switch from Form View to Datasheet View (AC 42)
21. Create a Report   (AC 43)
22. Print a Report   (AC 47)
23. Close a Database   (AC 47)
24. Obtain Help Using the Type a Question for Help Box   (AC 48)
25. Quit Access   (AC 50)

Learn It Online

Instructions: To complete the Learn It Online exercises, start your browser, click the Address bar, and then enter the Web address scsite.com/ac2003/learn. When the Access 2003 Learn It Online page is displayed, follow the instructions in the exercises below. Each exercise has instructions for printing your results, either for your own records or for submission to your instructor.

1 Project Reinforcement TF, MC, and SA

Below Access Project 1, click the Project Reinforcement link. Print the quiz by clicking Print on the File menu for each page. Answer each question.

2 Flash Cards

Below Access Project 1, click the Flash Cards link and read the instructions. Type 20 (or a number specified by your instructor) in the Number of playing cards text box, type your name in the Enter your Name text box, and then click the Flip Card button. When the flash card is displayed, read the question and then click the ANSWER box arrow to select an answer. Flip through Flash Cards. If your score is 15 (75%) correct or greater, click Print on the File menu to print your results. If your score is less than 15 (75%) correct, then redo this exercise by clicking the Replay button.

3 Practice Test

Below Access Project 1, click the Practice Test link. Answer each question, enter your first and last name at the bottom of the page, and then click the Grade Test button. When the graded practice test is displayed on your screen, click Print on the File menu to print a hard copy. Continue to take practice tests until you score 80% or better.

4 Who Wants To Be a Computer Genius?

Below Access Project 1, click the Computer Genius link. Read the instructions, enter your first and last name at the bottom of the page, and then click the PLAY button. When your score is displayed, click the PRINT RESULTS link to print a hard copy.

5 Wheel of Terms

Below Access Project 1, click the Wheel of Terms link. Read the instructions, and then enter your first and last name and your school name. Click the PLAY button. When your score is displayed, right-click the score and then click Print on the shortcut menu to print a hard copy.

6 Crossword Puzzle Challenge

Below Access Project 1, click the Crossword Puzzle Challenge link. Read the instructions, and then enter your first and last name. Click the SUBMIT button. Work the crossword puzzle. When you are finished, click the Submit button. When the crossword puzzle is redisplayed, click the Print Puzzle button to print a hard copy.

7 Tips and Tricks

Below Access Project 1, click the Tips and Tricks link. Click a topic that pertains to Project 1. Right-click the information and then click Print on the shortcut menu. Construct a brief example of what the information relates to in Access to confirm you understand how to use the tip or trick.

8 Newsgroups

Below Access Project 1, click the Newsgroups link. Click a topic that pertains to Project 1. Print three comments.

9 Expanding Your Horizons

Below Access Project 1, click the Expanding Your Horizons link. Click a topic that pertains to Project 1. Print the information. Construct a brief example of what the information relates to in Access to confirm you understand the contents of the article.

10 Search Sleuth

Below Access Project 1, click the Search Sleuth link. To search for a term that pertains to this project, select a term below the Project 1 title and then use the Google search engine at google.com (or any major search engine) to display and print two Web pages that present information on the term.

11 Access Online Training

Below Access Project 1, click the Access Online Training link. When your browser displays the Microsoft Office Online Web page, click the Access link. Click one of the Access courses that covers one or more of the objectives listed at the beginning of the project on page AC 4. Print the first page of the course before stepping through it.

12 Office Marketplace

Below Access Project 1, click the Office Marketplace link. When your browser displays the Microsoft Office Online Web page, click the Office Marketplace link. Click a topic that relates to Access. Print the first page.

Apply Your Knowledge

1 Changing Data, Creating Queries, and Creating Reports

Instructions: Start Access. Open the database Begon Pest Control from the Data Disk. See the inside back cover for instructions for downloading the Data Disk or see your instructor for information about accessing the files required in this book.

Begon Pest Control is a company that performs pest control services for commercial businesses. Begon has a database that keeps track of its technicians and customers. The database has two tables. The Customer table contains data on the customers who use the services of Begon. The Technician table contains data on the individuals employed by Begon. The structure and data are shown for the Customer table in Figure 1-85 and for the Technician table in Figure 1-86.

Structure of Customer table

FIELD NAME	DATA TYPE	FIELD SIZE	PRIMARY KEY?	DESCRIPTION
Customer Number	Text	4	Yes	Customer Number (Primary Key)
Name	Text	20		Customer Name
Address	Text	15		Street Address
City	Text	15		City
State	Text	2		State (Two-Character Abbreviation)
Zip Code	Text	5		Zip Code (Five-Character Version)
Balance	Currency			Amount Owed by Customer
Technician Number	Text	3		Number of Customer's Technician

Customer table

CUSTOMER NUMBER	NAME	ADDRESS	CITY	STATE	ZIP CODE	BALANCE	TECHNICIAN NUMBER
AT23	Atlas Repair	220 Beard	Kady	TN	42514	$335.00	203
AZ01	AZ Auto	412 Beechwood	Conradt	TN	42547	$300.00	210
BL35	Blanton Shoes	443 Chedder	Kady	TN	42514	$290.00	210
CJ45	C Joe Diner	87 Fletcher	Carlton	TN	52764	$0.00	214
CM90	Cramden Co.	234 Fairlawn	Conradt	TN	42546	$355.00	203
HI25	Hill Crafts	245 Beard	Kady	TN	42514	$334.00	210
KL50	Klean n Dri	378 Stout	Carlton	TN	52764	$365.00	210
MC10	Moss Carpet	109 Fletcher	Carlton	TN	52764	$398.00	203
PV83	Prime Video	734 Lanton	Conradt	TN	42547	$0.00	214
SE05	Servete Mfg Co.	879 Redfern	Kady	TN	42515	$343.00	210

FIGURE 1-85

Apply Your Knowledge

Structure of Technician table

FIELD NAME	DATA TYPE	FIELD SIZE	PRIMARY KEY?	DESCRIPTION
Technician Number	Text	3	Yes	Technician Number (Primary Key)
Last Name	Text	10		Last Name of Technician
First Name	Text	8		First Name of Technician
Address	Text	15		Street Address
City	Text	15		City
State	Text	2		State (Two-Character Abbreviation)
Zip Code	Text	5		Zip Code (Five-Character Version)
Hourly Rate	Currency			Hourly Pay Rate

Technician table

TECHNICIAN NUMBER	LAST NAME	FIRST NAME	ADDRESS	CITY	STATE	ZIP CODE	HOURLY RATE
203	Estevez	Miguel	467 Clay	Kady	TN	42517	$11.50
210	Hillsdale	Rachel	78 Parkton	Conradt	TN	42547	$11.75
214	Liu	Chou	897 North	Carlton	TN	52764	$11.65
220	Short	Chris	111 Maple	Conradt	TN	42547	$11.50

FIGURE 1-86

Instructions: Perform the following tasks:

1. Open the Customer table and change the Technician Number for customer KL50 to 214.
2. Print the Customer table.
3. Use the Simple Query Wizard to create a new query to display and print the customer number, name, and technician number for records in the Customer table as shown in Figure 1-87 on the next page.
4. Save the query as Customer-Technician Query and then close the query.
5. Open the Customer-Technician Query in Design View and restrict the query results to only those customers whose technician number is 210.
6. Print the query but do not save the changes.
7. Create the report shown in Figure 1-88 on the next page for the Customer table.
8. Print the report.

(continued)

Apply Your Knowledge

Changing Data, Creating Queries, and Creating Reports *(continued)*

FIGURE 1-87

Customer Amount Report

Customer Number	Name	Balance
AT23	Atlas Repair	$335.00
AZ01	AZ Auto	$300.00
BL35	Blanton Shoes	$290.00
CJ45	C Joe Diner	$0.00
CM90	Cramden Co.	$355.00
HI25	Hill Crafts	$334.00
KL50	Klean n Dri	$365.00
MC10	Moss Carpet	$398.00
PV83	Prime Video	$0.00
SE05	Servete Mfg Co.	$343.00

FIGURE 1-88

In the Lab

1 Creating the Birds2U Database

Problem: Birds2U is a new online retailer. The company specializes in products for bird and nature enthusiasts. The database consists of two tables. The Item table contains information on items available for sale. The Supplier table contains information on the companies that supply the items.

Instructions: Perform the following tasks:

1. Create a new database in which to store all the objects related to the items for sale. Call the database Birds2U.
2. Create the Item table using the structure shown in Figure 1-89. Use the name Item for the table.
3. Add the data shown in Figure 1-89 to the Item table.
4. Print the Item table.

In the Lab

Structure of Item table

FIELD NAME	DATA TYPE	FIELD SIZE	PRIMARY KEY?	DESCRIPTION
Item Code	Text	4	Yes	Item Code (Primary Key)
Description	Text	20		Description of Item
On Hand	Number			Number of Units On Hand
Cost	Currency			Cost of Item
Selling Price	Currency			Selling Price of Item
Supplier Code	Text	2		Code of Item's Supplier

Item table

ITEM CODE	DESCRIPTION	ON HAND	COST	SELLING PRICE	SUPPLIER CODE
BA35	Bat House	14	$43.50	$45.50	21
BB01	Bird Bath	2	$82.10	$86.25	13
BE19	Bee Box	7	$39.80	$42.50	21
BL06	Bluebird House	9	$14.35	$15.99	13
BU24	Butterfly Box	6	$36.10	$37.75	21
GF12	Globe Feeder	12	$14.80	$16.25	05
HF01	Hummingbird Feeder	5	$11.35	$14.25	05
PM05	Purple Martin House	3	$67.10	$69.95	13
SF03	Suet Feeder	7	$8.05	$9.95	05
WF10	Window Feeder	10	$14.25	$15.95	05

FIGURE 1-89

5. Create the Supplier table using the structure shown in Figure 1-90 on the next page. Use the name Supplier for the table.
6. Add the data shown in Figure 1-90 to the Supplier table.
7. Print the Supplier table.
8. Create a form for the Supplier table. Use the name Supplier for the form.
9. Open the form you created and change the address for Supplier Code 17 to 56 Beechwood.
10. Create and print the report shown in Figure 1-91 on the next page for the Item table.

(continued)

Creating the Birds2U Database *(continued)*

Structure of Supplier table

FIELD NAME	DATA TYPE	FIELD SIZE	PRIMARY KEY?	DESCRIPTION
Supplier Code	Text	2	Yes	Supplier Code (Primary Key)
Name	Text	20		Supplier Name
Address	Text	15		Street Address
City	Text	15		City
State	Text	2		State (Two-Character Abbreviation)
Zip Code	Text	5		Zip Code (Five-Character Version)
Telephone Number	Text	12		Telephone Number (999-999-9999 Version)

Supplier table

SUPPLIER CODE	NAME	ADDRESS	CITY	STATE	ZIP CODE	TELEPHONE NUMBER
05	All Birds Supply	234 Southward	Elgin	AZ	85165	602-555-6756
13	Bird Casa Ltd	38 Junction	Grandber	TX	78628	512-555-3402
17	Lawn Fixtures	56 Beecham	Holligan	CA	95418	707-555-4545
21	Natural Woods	67 Main	Ghostman	MI	49301	610-555-3333

FIGURE 1-90

Inventory Report

Item Code	Description	On Hand	Cost
BA35	Bat House	14	$43.50
BB01	Bird Bath	2	$82.10
BE19	Bee Box	7	$39.80
BL06	Bluebird House	9	$14.35
BU24	Butterfly Box	6	$36.10
GF12	Globe Feeder	12	$14.80
HF01	Hummingbird Feeder	5	$11.35
PM05	Purple Martin House	3	$67.10
SF03	Suet Feeder	7	$8.05
WF10	Window Feeder	10	$14.25

FIGURE 1-91

2 Creating the Babbage Bookkeeping Database

Problem: Babbage Bookkeeping is a local company that provides bookkeeping services to several small businesses in the area. The database consists of two tables. The Client table contains information on the businesses that use Babbage's services. The Bookkeeper table contains information on the bookkeeper assigned to the business.

Instructions: Perform the following tasks:

1. Create a new database in which to store all the objects related to the bookkeeping data. Call the database Babbage Bookkeeping.
2. Create and print the Client table using the structure and data shown in Figure 1-92. Then, create and print the Bookkeeper table using the structure and data shown in Figure 1-93 on the next page.

Structure of Client table

FIELD NAME	DATA TYPE	FIELD SIZE	PRIMARY KEY?	DESCRIPTION
Client Number	Text	3	Yes	Client Number (Primary Key)
Name	Text	20		Name of Client
Address	Text	15		Street Address
City	Text	15		City
Zip Code	Text	5		Zip Code (Five-Character Version)
Balance	Currency			Amount Currently Owed for Services
Bookkeeper Number	Text	2		Number of Client's Bookkeeper

Client table

CLIENT NUMBER	NAME	ADDRESS	CITY	ZIP CODE	BALANCE	BOOKKEEPER NUMBER
A54	Afton Mills	612 Revere	Grant City	58120	$315.50	22
A62	Atlas Suppliers	227 Dandelion	Empeer	58216	$525.00	24
B26	Blake-Scripps	557 Maum	Grant City	58120	$229.50	24
D76	Dege Grocery	446 Linton	Portage	59130	$485.75	34
G56	Grand Cleaners	337 Abelard	Empeer	58216	$265.00	22
H21	Hill Shoes	247 Fulton	Grant City	58121	$228.50	24
J77	Jones Plumbing	75 Getty	Portage	59130	$0.00	24
M26	Mohr Crafts	665 Maum	Empeer	58216	$312.50	22
S56	SeeSaw Ind.	31 Liatris	Portage	59130	$362.50	34
T45	Tate Repair	824 Revere	Grant City	58120	$254.00	24

FIGURE 1-92

(continued)

In the Lab

Creating the Babbage Bookkeeping Database *(continued)*

Structure of Bookkeeper table

FIELD NAME	DATA TYPE	FIELD SIZE	PRIMARY KEY?	DESCRIPTION
Bookkeeper Number	Text	2	Yes	Bookkeeper Number (Primary Key)
Last Name	Text	10		Last Name of Bookkeeper
First Name	Text	8		First Name of Bookkeeper
Address	Text	15		Street Address
City	Text	15		City
Zip Code	Text	5		Zip Code (Five-Character Version)
Hourly Rate	Currency			Hourly Rate
YTD Earnings	Currency			Year-to-Date Earnings

Bookkeeper table

BOOKKEEPER NUMBER	LAST NAME	FIRST NAME	ADDRESS	CITY	ZIP CODE	HOURLY RATE	YTD EARNINGS
22	Lewes	Johanna	26 Cotton	Portage	59130	$14.50	$18,245.00
24	Rodriguez	Mario	79 Marsden	Grant City	58120	$13.50	$17,745.50
34	Wong	Choi	263 Topper	Empeer	58216	$14.00	$16,750.25

FIGURE 1-93

3. Change the Bookkeeper Number for client J77 to 34.
4. Use the Simple Query Wizard to create a new query to display and print the Client Number, Name, and Bookkeeper Number for all clients where the bookkeeper number is 24.
5. Create and print the report shown in Figure 1-94 for the Client table.

Balance Due Report

Client Number	*Name*	*Balance*
A54	Afton Mills	$315.50
A62	Atlas Suppliers	$525.00
B26	Blake-Scripps	$229.50
D76	Dege Grocery	$485.75
G56	Grand Cleaners	$265.00
H21	Hill Shoes	$228.50
J77	Jones Plumbing	$0.00
M26	Mohr Crafts	$312.50
S56	SeeSaw Ind.	$362.50
T45	Tate Repair	$254.00

FIGURE 1-94

In the Lab

3 Creating the City Guide Database

Problem: The local chamber of commerce publishes a guide for newcomers. To help finance the guide, the chamber includes advertisements from local businesses. Advertising representatives receive a commission based on the advertising revenues they generate. The database consists of two tables. The Advertiser table contains information on the businesses that advertise in the guide. The Ad Rep table contains information on the advertising representative assigned to the account.

Instructions Part 1: Using the data shown in Figures 1-95 and 1-96 on the next page create the City Guide database, the Advertiser table, and the Ad Rep table. Note that the Ad Rep table uses the number data type. Print the tables. Then, create a form for the Advertiser table.

Structure of Advertiser table

FIELD NAME	DATA TYPE	FIELD SIZE	PRIMARY KEY?	DESCRIPTION
Advertiser Number	Text	4	Yes	Advertiser Number (Primary Key)
Name	Text	20		Name of Advertiser
Address	Text	15		Street Address
Zip Code	Text	5		Zip Code (Five-Character Version)
Telephone Number	Text	8		Telephone Number (999-9999 Version)
Balance	Currency			Amount Currently Owed
Amount Paid	Currency			Amount Paid Year-to-Date
Ad Rep Number	Text	2		Number of Advertising Representative

Data for Advertiser table

ADVERTISER NUMBER	NAME	ADDRESS	ZIP CODE	TELEPHONE NUMBER	BALANCE	AMOUNT PAID	AD REP NUMBER
A228	Adam's Music	47 Berton	19363	555-0909	$90.00	$565.00	26
B103	Barbecue Joint	483 Cantor	19363	555-8990	$185.00	$825.00	29
C048	Chloe's Salon	10 Main	19362	555-2334	$0.00	$375.00	29
C135	Creative Toys	26 Jefferson	19362	555-1357	$130.00	$865.00	32
D217	Dog Groomers	33 Maple	19362	555-2468	$290.00	$515.00	26
G346	Gold's Clothes	196 Lincoln	19364	555-3579	$0.00	$805.00	29
M321	Meat Shoppe	234 Magnolia	19363	555-6802	$215.00	$845.00	29
P124	Palace Theatre	22 Main	19364	555-8024	$65.00	$180.00	26
S111	Suds n Spuds	10 Jefferson	19365	555-5791	$465.00	$530.00	32
W456	Western Wear	345 Oaktree	19363	555-7913	$105.00	$265.00	26

FIGURE 1-95

(continued)

Creating the City Guide Database *(continued)*

Structure for Ad Rep table

FIELD NAME	DATA TYPE	FIELD SIZE	PRIMARY KEY?	DESCRIPTION
Ad Rep Number	Text	2	Yes	Advertising Rep Number (Primary Key)
Last Name	Text	10		Last Name of Advertising Rep
First Name	Text	8		First Name of Advertising Rep
Address	Text	15		Street Address
City	Text	15		City
Zip Code	Text	5		Zip Code (Five-Character Version)
Comm Rate	Number	Double		Commission Rate on Advertising Sales
Commission	Currency			Year-to-Date Total Commissions

Data for Ad Rep table

AD REP NUMBER	LAST NAME	FIRST NAME	ADDRESS	CITY	ZIP CODE	COMM RATE	COMMISSION
26	Febo	Jen	57 Barton	Crescent	19111	0.09	$6,500.00
29	Martinson	Kyle	87 Pearl	Newton	19124	0.08	$6,250.00
32	Rogers	Elena	45 Magret	San Luis	19362	0.09	$7,000.00

FIGURE 1-96

Instructions Part 2: Correct the following error. The ad rep assigned to the Meat Shoppe account should be Elena Rogers. Use the form you created to make the correction, and then print the form showing the corrected record. To print the form, open the form, click File on the menu bar, and then click Print. Click Selected Records(s) as the Print Range. Click the OK button.

Instructions Part 3: Create a query to find which accounts Kyle Martinson represents. Print the results. Prepare an advertiser status report that lists the advertiser's number, name, balance currently owed, and amount paid to date.

Cases and Places

The difficulty of these case studies varies:
■ are the least difficult and ■■ are more difficult. The last exercise is a group exercise.

1 ■ To help finance your college education, you formed a small business. You provide dog-walking services to local residents. Dog walkers are paid by the walk for each dog they walk. The business has grown rapidly and you now have several other students working for you. You realize that you need to computerize your business.

Design and create a database to store the data that College Dog Walkers needs to manage its business. Then create the necessary tables and enter the data from the Case 1-1 College Dog Walkers Word document on the Data Disk. Print the tables. See the inside back cover of this book for instructions for downloading the Data Disk or see your instructor for information on accessing the files required in this book.

2 ■ The Health and Physical Education department at your college recognized early that personal training would be a growth field. One of your friends graduated from the program and has started a company, InPerson Fitness Company. The company specializes in personal training in the comfort of the customer's home. It designs exercise programs for clients based on each person's health history, abilities, and fitness objectives. The company is expanding rapidly and you have been hired to computerize the business.

Design and create a database to store the data that InPerson Fitness needs to manage its business. Then create the necessary tables and enter the data from the Case 1-2 InPerson Fitness Word document on the Data Disk. Print the tables. See the inside back cover of this book for instructions for downloading the Data Disk or see your instructor for information on accessing the files required in this book.

3 ■■ Regional Books is a local bookstore that specializes in books that are of local interest. These are books that are set in the region or are written by authors who live in the area. The owner has asked you to create and update a database that she can use to keep track of the books she has in stock.

Design and create a database to store the book data. To create the Books table, use the Table Wizard and select the Books table. You do not need to select all the fields the Table Wizard provides and you can rename the fields in the table. (*Hint*: See More About Creating a Table: The Table Wizard on page AC 15.) Enter the data from the Case 1-3 Regional Books Word document on the Data Disk. Print the tables. Prepare a sample query and a sample report to illustrate to the owner the types of tasks that can be done with a database management system. See the inside back cover of this book for instructions for downloading the Data Disk or see your instructor for information on accessing the files required in this book.

Cases and Places

4 ■■ The Campus Housing office at the local university provides a listing of available off-campus rentals by private owners. The office would like to make this listing available on the campus Web site. The administrator has asked you to create and update a database that can store information about available off-campus housing. The housing list is in the Case 1-4 Campus Housing Word document on the Data Disk. A listing that has 0 bedrooms is either an efficiency apartment or a room for rent in a home. Distance indicates the rental unit's distance in miles from the university. Parking signifies whether reserved parking is available with the unit.

Design and create a database to meet the needs of the Campus Housing office. Then create the necessary tables, enter the data from the Case 1-4 Campus Housing Word document on the Data Disk. Print the tables. Prepare a sample form, sample query, and sample report to illustrate to the office the types of tasks that can be done with a database management system. See the inside back cover of this book for instructions for downloading the Data Disk or see your instructor for information on accessing the files required in this book.

5 ■■ **Working Together** Conducting a job search requires careful preparation. In addition to preparing a resume and cover letter, you will need to research the companies for which you are interested in working and contact these companies to let them know of your interest and qualifications. Microsoft Access can help you manage the job search process. The Database Wizard includes a Contact Management template that can create a database that will help you keep track of your job contacts.

Have each member of your team explore the features of the Database Wizard and determine individually which fields should be included in a Contact Management database. As a group, review your choices and decide on one common design. Prepare a short paper for your instructor that explains why your team chose those particular fields to include in the database.

After agreeing on the database design, assign one member to create the database using the Database Wizard. Every other team member should research a company and add the data to the database. Print the alphabetical contact listing that the Database Wizard creates. Turn in the short paper and the report to your instructor.

Querying a Database Using the Select Query Window

CASE PERSPECTIVE

Dr. Gernaey and his colleagues are eager for Ashton James College (AJC) to obtain the benefits they anticipated when they set up the database of client and trainer data. One immediate benefit they expect is the capability of easily asking questions such as the following concerning the data in the database and rapidly getting the answers.

1. What are the name, the amount paid, and the current due of client CP27?
2. Which clients' names begin with Fa?
3. Which clients are located in Lake Hammond?
4. Which clients have a current due of $0.00?
5. Which clients have an amount paid that is more than $20,000.00?
6. Which clients of trainer 48 have an amount paid that is more than $20,000.00?
7. In what cities are all the clients located?
8. How many hours has each trainer worked so far this year?
9. What is the client number and name of each client, and what is the number and name of the trainer to whom each client is assigned?

AJC needs to find information about clients located in a specific city, but they want to enter a different city each time they ask the question. A parameter query would enable this. They also have a special way they want to summarize their data and a crosstab query will present the data in the desired form.

Your task is to assist the administration of AJC in obtaining answers to these and other questions using Access query features.

As you read through this project, you will learn how to query a database and use the Select Query window.

Querying a Database Using the Select Query Window

Objectives:

You will have mastered the material in this project when you can:

- Create and run queries
- Print query results
- Include fields in the design grid
- Use text and numeric data in criteria
- Create and use parameter queries
- Save a query and use the saved query
- Use compound criteria in queries
- Sort data in queries
- Join tables in queries
- Perform calculations in queries
- Use grouping in queries
- Create crosstab queries

Introduction

A database management system such as Access offers many useful features, among them the capability of answering questions such as those posed by the administration of Ashton James College (Figure 2-1). The answers to these questions, and many more, are found in the database, and Access can find the answers quickly. When you pose a question to Access, or any other database management system, the question is called a query. A **query** is simply a question represented in a way that Access can understand.

Thus, to find the answer to a question, you first create a corresponding query using the techniques illustrated in this project. After you have created the query, you instruct Access to run the query; that is, to perform the steps necessary to obtain the answer. Access then will display the answer in Datasheet view.

Project Two — Querying the Ashton James College Database

The steps in this project obtain answers to the questions posed by the administration of Ashton James College. These include the questions shown in Figure 2-1, as well as many other questions that may be deemed important.

What are the name, the amount paid, and the current due for client CP27?

Which clients' names begin with Fa?

In what cities are all the clients located?

Which clients are located in Lake Hammond?

Which clients of trainer 48 have an amount paid that is more than $20,000.00?

Client table

CLIENT NUMBER	NAME	ADDRESS	CITY	STATE	ZIP CODE	AMOUNT PAID	CURRENT DUE	TRAINER NUMBER
BS27	Blant and Sons	4806 Park	Lake Hammond	TX	76653	$21,876.00	$892.50	42
CE16	Center Services	725 Mitchell	San Julio	TX	78364	$26,512.00	$2,672.00	48
CP27	Calder Plastics	7300 Cedar	Lake Hammond	TX	76653	$8,725.00	$0.00	48
EU28	Elba's Furniture	1445 Hubert	Tallmadge	TX	77231	$4,256.00	$1,202.00	53
FI28	Farrow-Idsen	829 Wooster	Cedar Ridge	TX	79342	$8,287.50	$925.50	42
FL93	Fairland Lawn	143 Pangborn	Lake Hammond	TX	76653	$21,625.00	$0.00	48
HN83	Hurley National	3827 Burgess	Tallmadge	TX	77231	$0.00	$0.00	48
MC28	Morgan-Alyssa	923 Williams	Crumville	TX	76745	$24,761.00	$1,572.00	42
PS82	PRIM Staffing	72 Crestview	San Julio	TX	78364	$11,682.25	$2,827.50	53
TE26	Telton-Edwards	5672 Anderson	Dunston	TX	77893	$8,521.50	$0.00	48

CLIENT NUMBER	NAME	AMOUNT PAID	CURRENT DUE
FI28	Farrow-Idsen	$8,287.50	$925.50
FL93	Fairland Lawn	$21,625.00	$0.00

CLIENT NUMBER	NAME	ADDRESS
BS27	Blant and Sons	4806 Park
CP27	Calder Plastics	7300 Cedar
FL93	Fairland Lawn	143 Pangborn

CLIENT NUMBER	NAME	AMOUNT PAID	CURRENT DUE
CP27	Calder Plastics	$8,725.00	$0.00

CITY
Cedar Ridge
Crumville
Dunston
Lake Hammond
Tallmadge

CLIENT NUMBER	NAME	AMOUNT PAID	CURRENT DUE	TRAINER NUMBER
CE16	Center Services	$26,512.00	$2,672.00	48
FL93	Fairland Lawn	$21,625.00	$0.00	48

FIGURE 2-1

Microsoft Office
Access 2003

Opening the Database

If you are stepping through this project on a computer, and you want your screen to agree with the figures in this book, then you should change your computer's resolution to 800 × 600. For more information on how to change the resolution on your computer, see Appendix D. Before creating queries, first you must open the database. The following steps summarize the procedure to complete this task, once you have started Access.

To Open a Database

1. **Click the Open button on the Database toolbar.**

2. **If necessary, click the Look in box arrow and then click 3½ Floppy (A:). Click Ashton James College, the database created in Project 1. (If you did not complete the steps in Project 1, see your instructor for a copy of the database.)**

3. **Click the Open button in the Open dialog box. If a Security Warning dialog box appears, click the Open button.**

The database opens and the Ashton James College : Database window appears.

Creating and Running Queries

You create a query by making entries in a special window called a **Select Query window**. Once the database is open, the first step in creating a query is to select the table for which you are creating a query in the Database window. Then, you use the New Object button to design the new query in the Select Query window. It typically is easier to work with the Select Query window if it is maximized. Thus, as a standard practice, maximize the Select Query window as soon as you have created it. In addition, it often is useful to resize both panes within the window. This enables you to resize the field list that appears in the upper pane so more fields appear.

The following steps initiate creating a query.

To Create a Query

1

• **Be sure the Ashton James College database is open, the Tables object is selected, and the Client table is selected.**

• **Click the New Object button arrow on the Database toolbar.**

The list of available objects appears (Figure 2-2).

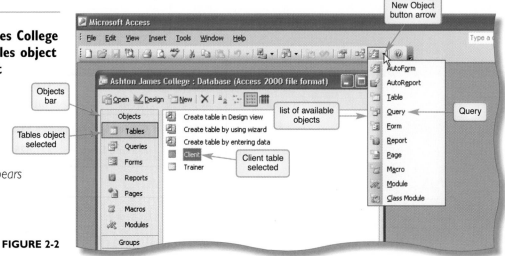

FIGURE 2-2

2

• **Click Query.**

Access displays the New Query dialog box (Figure 2-3).

FIGURE 2-3

3

• **With Design View selected, click the OK button.**

The Query1 : Select Query window appears (Figure 2-4).

FIGURE 2-4

4

• **Maximize the Query1 : Select Query window by double-clicking its title bar, and then drag the line separating the two panes to the approximate position shown in Figure 2-5.**

*The Query1 : Select Query window is maximized. The upper pane contains a field list for the Client table. The lower pane contains the **design grid**, which is the area where you specify fields to be included, sort order, and the criteria the records you are looking for must satisfy. The mouse pointer shape indicates you can drag the line.*

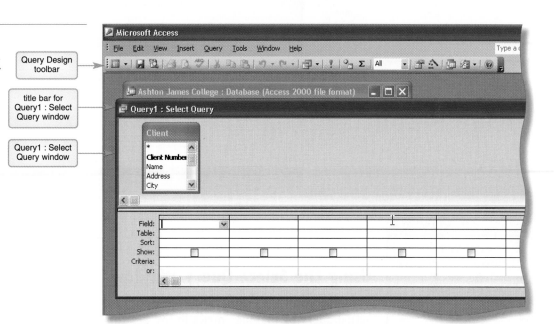

FIGURE 2-5

Microsoft Office
Access 2003

5

• **Drag the lower edge of the field box down far enough so all fields in the Client table are displayed (Figure 2-6).**

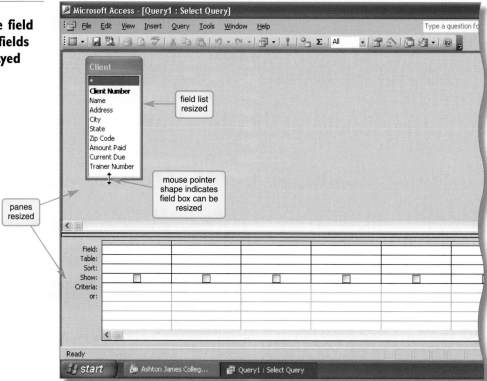

FIGURE 2-6

Using the Select Query Window

Once you have created a new Select Query window, you are ready to create the actual query by making entries in the design grid in the lower pane of the window. You enter the names of the fields you want included in the Field row in the grid. You also can enter criteria, such as the fact that the client number must be a specific number, such as CP27, in the Criteria row of the grid. When you do so, only the record or records that match the criterion will be included in the answer.

Displaying Selected Fields in a Query

Only the fields that appear in the design grid will be included in the results of the query. Thus, to include only certain fields, place only these fields in the grid, and no others. If you place the wrong field in the grid inadvertently, click Edit on the menu bar and then click Delete to remove it. Alternatively, you could click Clear Grid on the Edit menu to clear the entire design grid and then start over.

The following step creates a query to show the client number, name, and trainer number for all clients by including only those fields in the design grid.

To Include Fields in the Design Grid

1

• If necessary, maximize the **Query1 : Select Query** window containing the field list for the **Client** table in the upper pane of the window and an empty design grid in the lower pane.

• Double-click the **Client Number** field in the field list to include it in the query.

• Double-click the **Name** field to include it in the query, and then double-click the **Trainer Number** field to include it as well.

The Client Number, Name, and Trainer Number fields are included in the query (Figure 2-7).

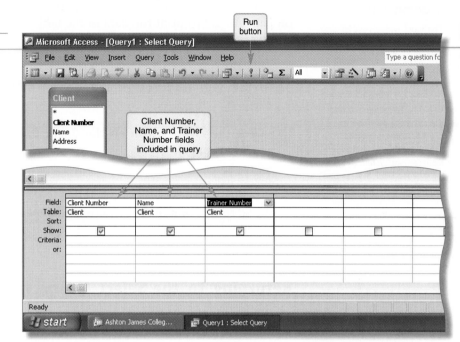

FIGURE 2-7

Running a Query

Once you have created the query, you run the query to produce the results using the Run button on the Query Design toolbar. Access performs the steps necessary to obtain and display the answer. The set of records that makes up the answer will be displayed in Datasheet view. Although it looks like a table that is stored on your disk, it really is not. The records are constructed from data in the existing Client table. If you were to change the data in the Client table and then rerun this same query, the results would reflect the changes. The following step runs the query.

To Run the Query

1

• Click the **Run** button on the **Query Design toolbar** (see Figure 2-7).

The query is executed and the results appear (Figure 2-8).

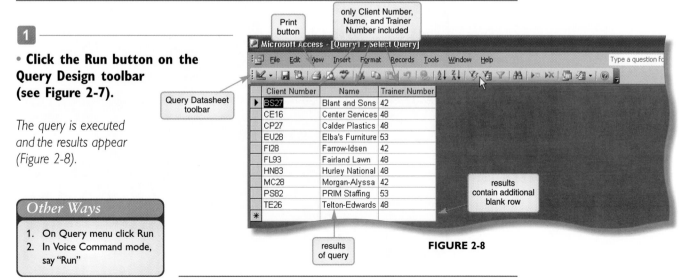

FIGURE 2-8

More About

Queries: SQL

The most widespread of all the query languages is a language called SQL. In SQL, users type commands such as SELECT CURRENT DUE FROM CUSTOMER WHERE CITY = "Tallmadge" to find the current due amounts of all customers located in Tallmadge. Many database management systems, including Access, offer SQL as one option for querying databases. For more information, visit the Access 2003 More About Web page (scsite.com/ac2003/more) and click SQL.

Printing the Results of a Query

To print the results of a query, use the same techniques you learned in Project 1 on page AC 29 to print the data in the table. The following step prints the current query results.

To Print the Results of a Query

1 **Click the Print button on the Query Datasheet toolbar (see Figure 2-8 on the previous page).**

The results print.

If the results of a query require landscape orientation, switch to landscape orientation before you click the Print button as indicated in Project 1 on page AC 31.

Returning to the Select Query Window

You can examine the results of a query on your screen to see the answer to your question. You can scroll through the records, if necessary, just as you scroll through the records of any other table. You also can print a copy of the table. In any case, once you are finished working with the results, you can return to the Select Query window to ask another question. The following steps illustrate how to return to the Select Query window.

To Return to the Select Query Window

1

• **Click the View button arrow on the Query Datasheet toolbar.**

The Query View list appears (Figure 2-9).

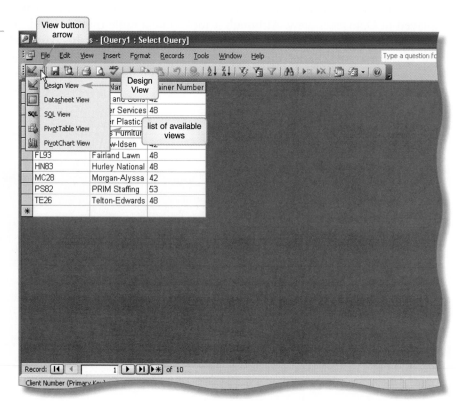

FIGURE 2-9

2

* **Click Design View.**

The Query1 : Select Query window is redisplayed (Figure 2-10).

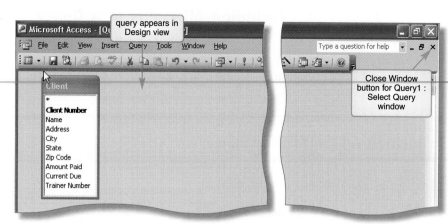

FIGURE 2-10

Other Ways

1. On View menu click Design View
2. In Voice Command mode, say "View, Design View"

Notice that the icon on the View button is the Design View icon. This indicates that the next time you want to display the window in Design view, you need only click the View button.

Closing a Query

To close a query, close the Select Query window. When you do so, Access displays the Microsoft Office Access dialog box asking if you want to save your query for future use. If you think you will need to create the same exact query often, you should save the query. For now, you will not save any queries. You will see how to save them later in the project. The following steps close a query without saving it.

To Close the Query

1

* **Click the Close Window button for the Query1 : Select Query window (see Figure 2-10).**

Access displays the Microsoft Office Access dialog box (Figure 2-11). Clicking the Yes button saves the query and clicking the No button closes the query without saving.

2

* **Click the No button in the Microsoft Office Access dialog box.**

The Query1 : Select Query window closes. The query is not saved.

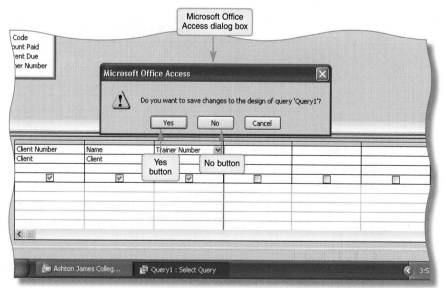

FIGURE 2-11

Other Ways

1. On File menu click Close
2. In Voice Command mode, say "File, Close"

Including All Fields in a Query

If you want to include all fields in a query, you could select each field individually. A simpler way to include all fields is available, however. By selecting the asterisk (*) in the field list, you are indicating that all fields are to be included. The following steps use the asterisk to include all fields.

To Include All Fields in a Query

1

• **Be sure you have a maximized Query1 : Select Query window with resized upper and lower panes, an expanded field list for the Client table in the upper pane, and an empty design grid in the lower pane. (See Steps 1 through 5 on pages AC 68 through AC 70 to create the query and resize the window.)**

• **Double-click the asterisk at the top of the field list.**

The maximized Query1 : Select Query window displays two resized panes. The table name, Client, followed by a period and an asterisk is added to the design grid, indicating all fields are included (Figure 2-12).

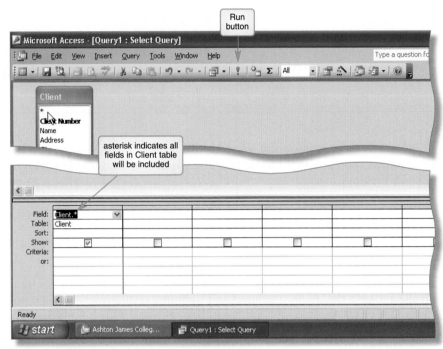

FIGURE 2-12

2

• **Click the Run button.**

The results appear and all fields in the Client table are included (Figure 2-13).

3

• **Click the View button on the Query Datasheet toolbar to return to the Query1 : Select Query window.**

The Query1 : Select Query window replaces the datasheet.

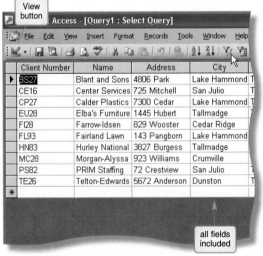

FIGURE 2-13

Other Ways

1. Drag asterisk from field list to design grid
2. Click column in grid, click arrow, click Client.*

Clearing the Design Grid

If you make mistakes as you are creating a query, you can fix each one individually. Alternatively, you simply may want to clear the query; that is, clear out the entries in the design grid and start over. One way to clear out the entries is to close the Select Query window and then start a new query just as you did earlier. A simpler approach, however, is to use the Clear Grid command on the Edit menu. The following steps clear the design grid.

To Clear the Design Grid

 1

• **Click Edit on the menu bar.**

The Edit menu appears (Figure 2-14).

 2

• **Click Clear Grid.**

Access clears the design grid so you can enter your next query.

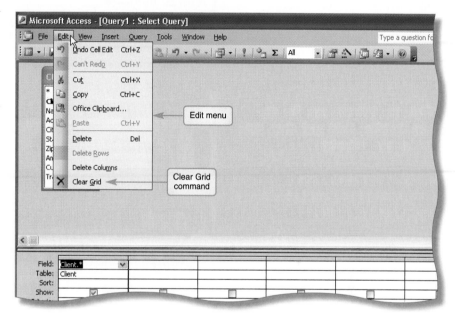

FIGURE 2-14

Entering Criteria

When you use queries, usually you are looking for those records that satisfy some criterion. You might want the name, amount paid, and current due amounts of the client whose number is CP27, for example, or of those clients whose names start with the letters, Fa. To enter criteria, enter them in the Criteria row in the design grid below the field name to which the criterion applies. For example, to indicate that the client number must be CP27, you first must add the Client Number field to the design grid. You then would type CP27 in the Criteria row below the Client Number field.

The next examples illustrate the types of criteria that are available.

Using Text Data in Criteria

To use **text data** (data in a field whose data type is Text) in criteria, simply type the text in the Criteria row below the corresponding field name. The steps on the next page query the Client table and display the client number, name, amount paid, and current due amount of client CP27.

To Use Text Data in a Criterion

1

• **One by one, double-click the Client Number, Name, Amount Paid, and Current Due fields to add them to the query.**

The Client Number, Name, Amount Paid, and Current Due fields are added to the design grid (Figure 2-15).

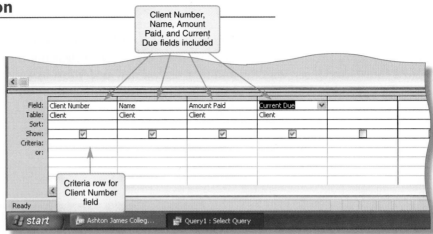

Client Number, Name, Amount Paid, and Current Due fields included

Criteria row for Client Number field

FIGURE 2-15

2

• **Click the Criteria row for the Client Number field and then type** CP27 **as the criterion.**

The criterion is entered (Figure 2-16). When the mouse pointer is in the Criteria box, its shape changes to an I-beam.

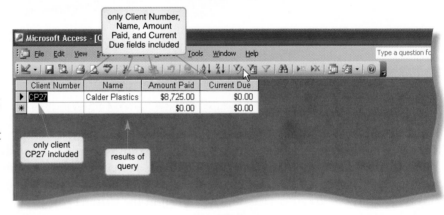

client number must be CP27

FIGURE 2-16

3

• **Click the Run button to run the query.**

The results appear (Figure 2-17). Only client CP27 is included. (The extra blank row contains $0.00 in the Amount Paid and Current Due fields. Unlike text fields, which are left blank, number and currency fields in the extra row contain 0. Because the Amount Paid and Current Due fields are currency fields, the values are displayed as $0.00.)

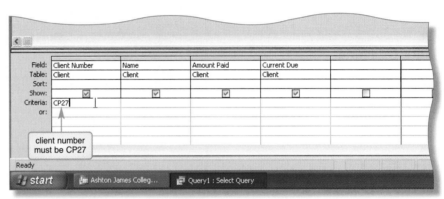

only Client Number, Name, Amount Paid, and Current Due fields included

only client CP27 included

results of query

FIGURE 2-17

Using Wildcards

Two special wildcards are available in Microsoft Access. **Wildcards** are symbols that represent any character or combination of characters. The first of the two wildcards, the **asterisk** (*), represents any collection of characters. Thus Fa* represents the letters, Fa, followed by any collection of characters. The other wildcard symbol is the **question mark** (?), which represents any individual character. Thus t?m represents the letter, T, followed by any single character followed by the letter, m, such as Tim or Tom.

The following steps use a wildcard to find the number, name, and address of those clients whose names begin with Fa. Because you do not know how many characters will follow the Fa, the asterisk is appropriate.

To Use a Wildcard

- **Click the View button on the Query Datasheet toolbar to return to the Query1 : Select Query window.**
- **If necessary, click the Criteria row below the Client Number field.**
- **Use the DELETE or BACKSPACE key as necessary to delete the current entry (CP27).**
- **Click the Criteria row below the Name field.**
- **Type** Fa* **as the criterion.**

The criterion is entered (Figure 2-18).

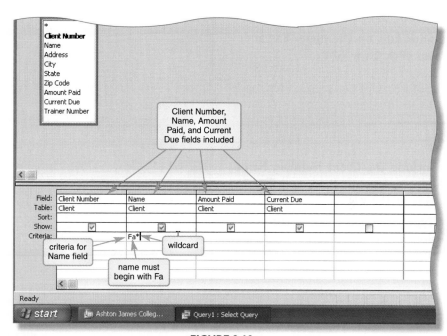

FIGURE 2-18

- **Click the Run button to run the query.**
- **If instructed to do so, print the results by clicking the Print button on the Query Datasheet toolbar.**

The results appear (Figure 2-19). Only the clients whose names start with Fa are included.

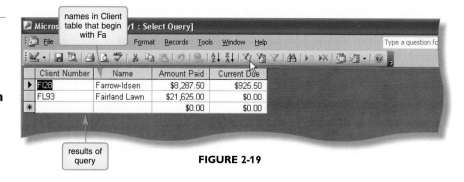

FIGURE 2-19

Criteria for a Field Not in the Result

In some cases, you may have criteria for a particular field that should not appear in the results of the query. For example, you may want to see the client number, name, address, and amount paid for all clients located in Lake Hammond. The criteria involve the City field, which is not one of the fields to be included in the results.

To enter a criterion for the City field, it must be included in the design grid. Normally, this also would mean it would appear in the results. To prevent this from happening, remove the check mark from its Show check box in the Show row of the grid. The steps on the next page illustrate the process by displaying the client number, name, and amount paid for clients located in Lake Hammond.

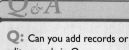

Q&A

Q: Can you add records or edit records in Query Datasheet view?

A: Yes. If the data in the query result is based on one table, you can add and edit records just as you did when the table was displayed in Table Datasheet view.

To Use Criteria for a Field Not Included in the Results

• **Click the View button on the Query Datasheet toolbar to return to the Query1 : Select Query window.**

• **Click Edit on the menu bar and then click Clear Grid.**

Access clears the design grid so you can enter the next query.

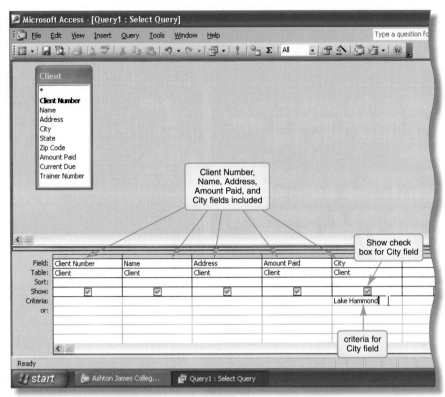

FIGURE 2-20

2

• **Include the Client Number, Name, Address, Amount Paid, and City fields in the query.**

• **Type** Lake Hammond **as the criterion for the City field.**

The fields are included in the grid, and the criterion for the City field is entered (Figure 2-20).

3

• **Click the Show check box to remove the check mark.**

The check mark is removed from the Show check box for the City field (Figure 2-21), indicating it will not show in the result. Because the City field is a text field, Access has added quotation marks before and after Lake Hammond automatically.

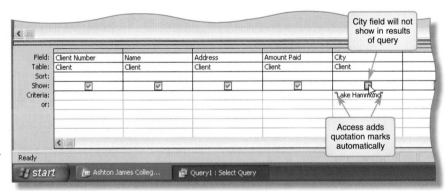

FIGURE 2-21

4

• **Click the Run button to run the query.**

• **If instructed to do so, print the results by clicking the Print button.**

The results appear (Figure 2-22). The City field does not appear. The only clients included are those located in Lake Hammond.

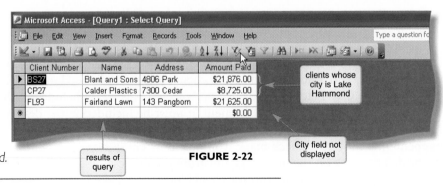

FIGURE 2-22

Creating a Parameter Query

Rather than giving a specific criterion when you first create the query, on occasion, you may want to be able to enter part of the criterion when you run the query and then have the appropriate results appear. For example, to include all the clients located in Tallmadge, you could enter Tallmadge as a criterion in the City field. From that point on, every time you ran the query, only the clients in Tallmadge would appear.

A better way is to allow the user to enter the city at the time the query is run. Thus a user could run the query, enter Tallmadge as the city and then see all the clients in Tallmadge. Later, the user could run the same query, but enter Lake Hammond as the city, and then see all the clients in Lake Hammond. To do this, you create a **parameter query**, which is a query that prompts for input whenever it is run. You enter a parameter, rather than a specific value as the criterion. You create one by enclosing a value in a criterion in square brackets. It is important that the value in the brackets does not match the name of any field. If you enter a field name in square brackets, Access assumes you want that particular field and will not prompt the user for input. For example, you could place [Enter City] as the criterion in the City field.

The following steps create a parameter query that will prompt the user to enter a city, and then display the client number, name, address, and amount paid for all clients located in that city.

To Create and Run a Parameter Query

1

• **Click the View button on the Query Datasheet toolbar to return to the Query1 : Select Query window.**

• **Erase the current criterion in the City column, and then type [Enter City] as the new criterion.**

The criterion is entered (Figure 2-23).

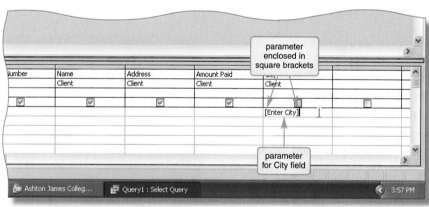

FIGURE 2-23

2

• **Click the Run button to run the query.**

Access displays the Enter Parameter Value dialog box (Figure 2-24). The value (Enter City) previously entered in brackets appears in the dialog box.

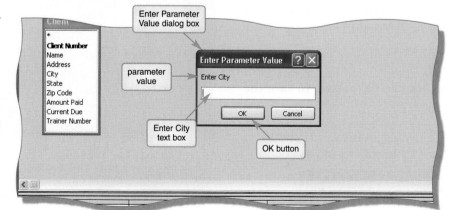

FIGURE 2-24

3

• **Type** Tallmadge **in the Enter City text box and then click the OK button.**

The results appear (Figure 2-25). Only clients whose city is Tallmadge are included. The city name is not displayed in the results.

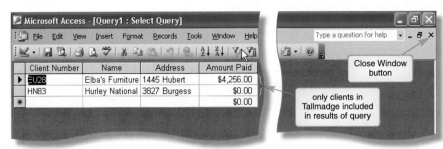

FIGURE 2-25

Each time you run this query, you will be asked to enter a city. Only clients in the city you enter will be included in the results.

Saving a Query

In many cases, you will construct a query you will want to use again. By saving the query, you will eliminate the need to repeat all your entries. The following steps illustrate the process by saving the query you just have created and assigning it the name Client-City Query. You can save with either the query design or the query results appearing on the screen.

To Save a Query

1

• **Click the Close Window button for the Query1 : Select Query window containing the query results.**

• **Click the Yes button in the Microsoft Office Access dialog box when asked if you want to save the changes to the design of the query.**

• **Type** Client-City Query **in the Query Name text box.**

The Save As dialog box appears with the query name you typed (Figure 2-26).

2

• **Click the OK button to save the query.**

Access saves the query and closes the Query1 : Select Query window.

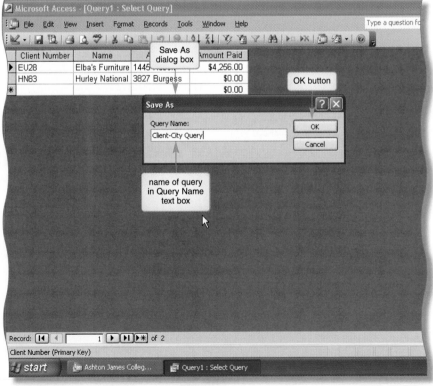

FIGURE 2-26

1. On File menu click Save
2. Press CTRL+S

Using a Saved Query

Once you have saved a query, you can use and manipulate it at any time in the future by opening it. When you right-click the query in the Database window, Access displays a shortcut menu containing commands that allow you to open, print, and change the design of the query. You also can print the results by clicking the Print button on the toolbar. If you want to print the query results without first opening the query, you would click Print on the shortcut menu.

The query is run against the current database. Thus, if changes have been made to the data since the last time you ran it, the results of the query may be different. The following steps use the query named Client-City Query.

More About

Saved Queries

Forms and reports can be based on either tables or saved queries. To create a report or form based on a query, click the Query tab, select the query, click the New Object button arrow, and then click the appropriate command (Report or Form). From that point on, the process is the same as for a table.

To Use a Saved Query

1

• **Click Queries on the Objects bar, and then right-click Client-City Query.**

The shortcut menu for Client-City Query appears (Figure 2-27).

2

• **Click Open on the shortcut menu, type** Tallmadge **in the Enter City text box, and then click the OK button.**

The results appear. They look like the results shown in Figure 2-25.

3

• **Click the Close Window button for the Client-City Query : Select Query window containing the query results.**

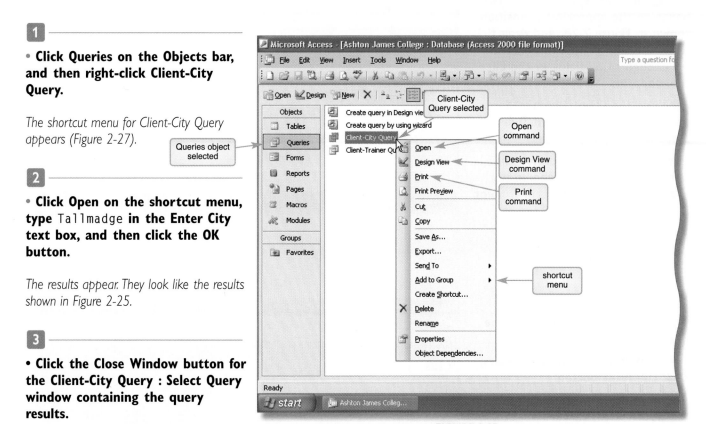

FIGURE 2-27

You can use the query at any time by following the above steps. Each time you do so, you will be prompted to enter a city. Only the clients in that city will be displayed in the results.

Using Numeric Data in Criteria

To enter a number in a criterion, type the number without any dollar signs or commas. The steps on the next page display all clients whose current due amount is $0.00.

Microsoft Office
Access 2003

To Use a Number in a Criterion

1

• **Click the Tables object on the Objects bar and ensure the Client table is selected.**

• **Click the New Object button arrow on the Database toolbar, click Query, and then click the OK button in the New Query dialog box.**

• **Drag the line separating the two panes to the approximate position shown in Figure 2-28, and drag the lower edge of the field box down far enough so all fields in the Client table appear.**

• **Include the Client Number, Name, Amount Paid, and Current Due fields in the query.**

• **Type 0 as the criterion for the Current Due field. You should not enter a dollar sign or decimal point in the criterion.**

The fields are selected and the criterion is entered (Figure 2-28).

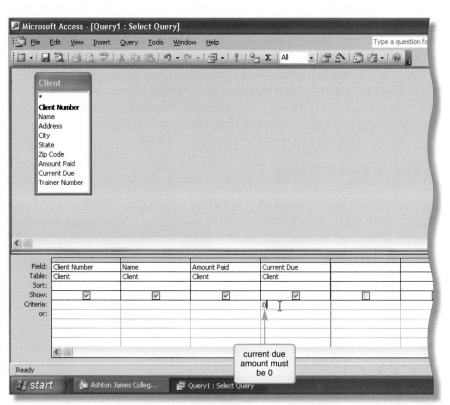

FIGURE 2-28

2

• **Click the Run button to run the query.**

• **If instructed to print the results, click the Print button.**

The results appear (Figure 2-29). Only those clients that have a current due amount of $0.00 are included.

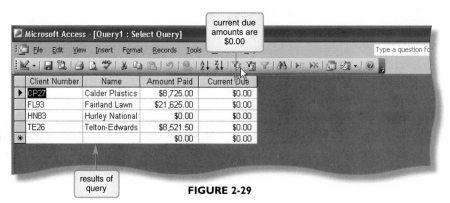

FIGURE 2-29

Using Comparison Operators

Unless you specify otherwise, Access assumes that the criteria you enter involve equality (exact matches). In the last query, for example, you were requesting those clients whose current due amount is equal to 0 (zero). If you want something other than an exact match, you must enter the appropriate **comparison operator**. The comparison operators are > (greater than), < (less than), >= (greater than or equal to), <= (less than or equal to), and NOT (not equal to).

The following steps use the > operator to find all clients whose amount paid is more than $20,000.00.

To Use a Comparison Operator in a Criterion

1

• **Click the View button on the Query Datasheet toolbar to return to the Query1 : Select Query window.**

• **Erase the 0 in the Current Due column.**

• **Type >20000 as the criterion for the Amount Paid field. Remember that you should not enter a dollar sign, a comma, or decimal point in the criterion.**

The fields are selected and the criterion is entered (Figure 2-30).

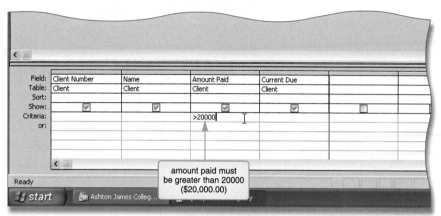

FIGURE 2-30

2

• **Click the Run button to run the query.**

• **If instructed to print the results, click the Print button.**

The results appear (Figure 2-31). Only those clients who have an amount paid greater than $20,000.00 are included.

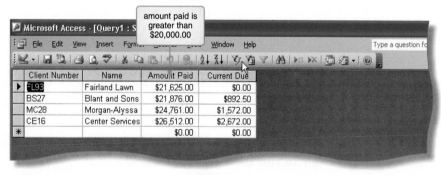

FIGURE 2-31

Using Compound Criteria

Often you will have more than one criterion that the data for which you are searching must satisfy. This type of criterion is called a **compound criterion**. Two types of compound criteria exist.

In an **AND criterion**, each individual criterion must be true in order for the compound criterion to be true. For example, an AND criterion would allow you to find those clients that have an amount paid greater than $20,000.00 and whose trainer is trainer 48.

Conversely, an **OR criterion** is true provided either individual criterion is true. An OR criterion would allow you to find those clients that have an amount paid greater than $20,000.00 or whose trainer is trainer 48. In this case, any client whose amount paid is greater than $20,000.00 would be included in the answer whether or not the client's trainer is trainer 48. Likewise, any client whose trainer is trainer 48 would be included whether or not the client had an amount paid greater than $20,000.00.

Using AND Criteria

To combine criteria with AND, place the criteria on the same line. The following steps use an AND criterion to find those clients whose amount paid is greater than $20,000.00 and whose trainer is trainer 48.

To Use a Compound Criterion Involving AND

1

• **Click the View button on the Query Datasheet toolbar to return to the Query1 : Select Query window.**

• **Include the Trainer Number field in the query.**

• **Type** 48 **as the criterion for the Trainer Number field.**

Criteria have been entered for the Amount Paid and Trainer Number fields (Figure 2-32).

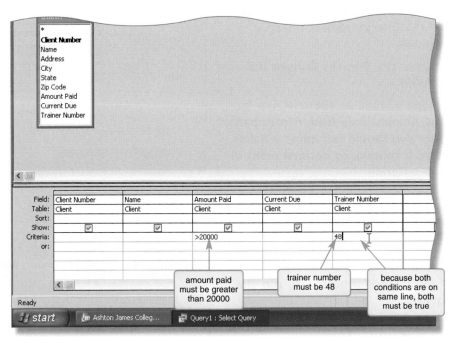

FIGURE 2-32

2

• **Click the Run button to run the query.**

• **If instructed to print the results, click the Print button.**

The results appear (Figure 2-33). Only the clients whose amount paid is greater than $20,000.00 and whose trainer number is 48 are included.

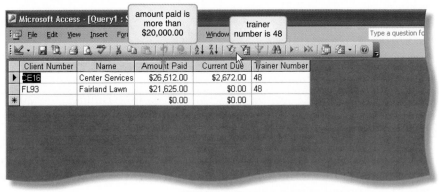

FIGURE 2-33

Using OR Criteria

To combine criteria with OR, the criteria must go on separate lines in the Criteria area of the grid. The following steps use an OR criterion to find those clients whose amount paid is greater than $20,000.00 or whose trainer is trainer 48 (or both).

To Use a Compound Criterion Involving OR

1

• **Click the View button on the Query Datasheet toolbar to return to the Query1 : Select Query window.**

2

• **If necessary, click the Criteria entry for the Trainer Number field and then use the BACKSPACE key or the DELETE key to erase the entry ("48").**

• **Click the or row (below the Criteria row) for the Trainer Number field and then type 48 as the entry.**

The criteria are entered for the Amount Paid and Trainer Number fields on different lines (Figure 2-34).

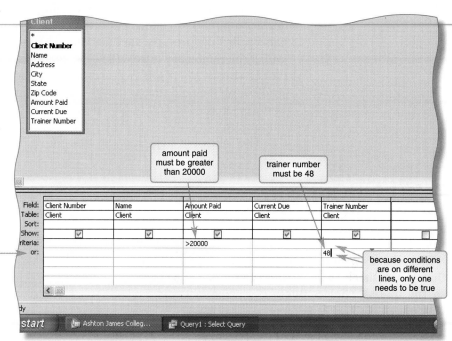

FIGURE 2-34

3

• **Click the Run button to run the query.**

• **If instructed to print the results, click the Print button.**

The results appear (Figure 2-35). Only those clients whose amount paid is greater than $20,000.00 or whose trainer number is 48 are included.

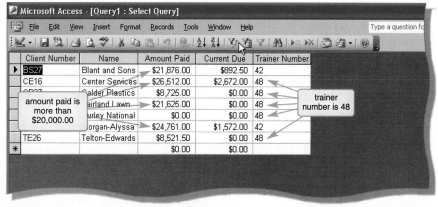

FIGURE 2-35

Sorting Data in a Query

In some queries, the order in which the records appear really does not matter. All you need be concerned about are the records that appear in the results. It does not matter which one is first or which one is last.

In other queries, however, the order can be very important. You may want to see the cities in which clients are located and would like them arranged alphabetically. Perhaps you want to see the clients listed by trainer number. Further, within all the clients of any given trainer, you might want them to be listed by amount paid.

To order the records in the answer to a query in a particular way, you **sort** the records. The field or fields on which the records are sorted is called the **sort key**. If you are sorting on more than one field (such as sorting by amount paid within trainer number), the more important field (Trainer Number) is called the **major key** (also called the **primary sort key**) and the less important field (Amount Paid) is called the **minor key** (also called the **secondary sort key**).

To sort in Microsoft Access, specify the sort order in the Sort row of the design grid below the field that is the sort key. If you specify more than one sort key, the sort key on the left will be the major sort key and the one on the right will be the minor key.

The following steps sort the cities in the Client table.

To Sort Data in a Query

1

• **Click the View button on the Query Datasheet toolbar to return to the Query1 : Select Query window.**

• **Click Edit on the menu bar and then click Clear Grid.**

2

• **Include the City field in the design grid.**

• **Click the Sort row below the City field, and then click the Sort row arrow that appears.**

The City field is included (Figure 2-36). A list of available sort orders appears.

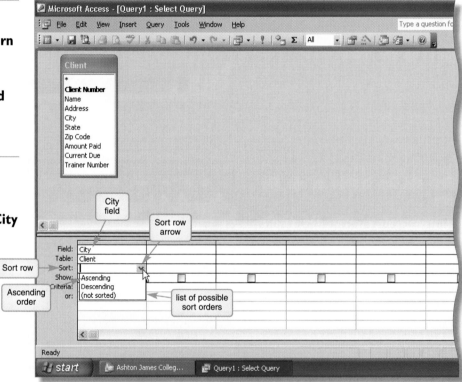

FIGURE 2-36

3

• **Click Ascending.**

Ascending is selected as the order (Figure 2-37).

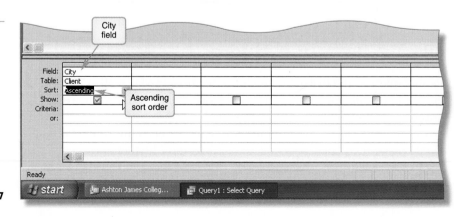

FIGURE 2-37

4

- **Click the Run button to run the query.**
- **If instructed to print the results, click the Print button.**

*The results contain the cities from the Client table (Figure 2-38). The cities appear in alphabetical order. Duplicates, also called **identical rows**, are included.*

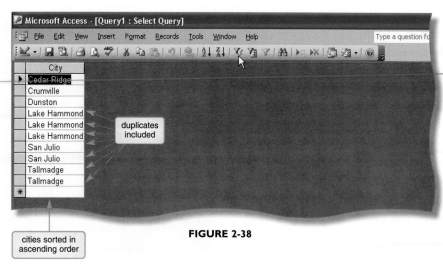

FIGURE 2-38

Omitting Duplicates

When you sort data, duplicates normally are included. In Figure 2-38, for example, San Julio appeared twice, Lake Hammond appeared three times, and Tallmadge appeared twice. To sort to eliminate duplicates, use the Properties button on the Query Design toolbar or the Properties command on the shortcut menu to display the item's property sheet. A **property sheet** is a window containing the various properties of the object. To omit duplicates, you will use the property sheet to change the Unique Values property.

The following steps produce a sorted list of the cities in the Client table in which each city is listed only once.

To Omit Duplicates

1

- **Click the View button on the Query Datasheet toolbar to return to the Query1 : Select Query window.**
- **Click the second field in the design grid (the empty field following City). You must click the second field or you will not get the correct results and will have to repeat this step.**
- **Click the Properties button on the Query Design toolbar.**

Access displays the Query Properties sheet (Figure 2-39). (If your sheet looks different, you clicked the wrong place and will have to repeat the step.)

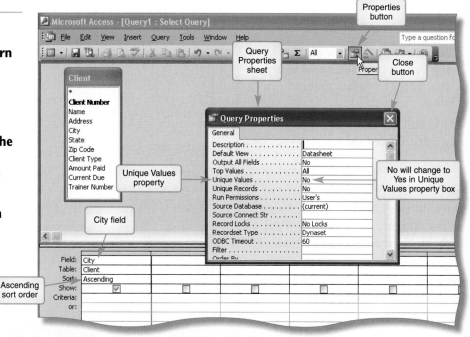

FIGURE 2-39

2

• Click the **Unique Values** property box, and then click the arrow that appears to produce a list of available choices for Unique Values.

• Click **Yes** and then close the Query Properties sheet by clicking its Close button.

• Click the **Run** button to run the query.

• If instructed to print the results, click the Print button.

The results appear (Figure 2-40). The cities are sorted alphabetically. Each city is included only once.

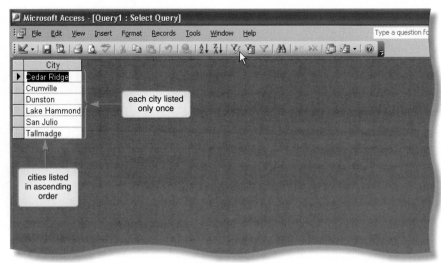

FIGURE 2-40

Sorting on Multiple Keys

The next example lists the number, name, trainer number, and amount paid for all clients. The data is to be sorted by amount paid (low to high) within trainer number, which means that the Trainer Number field is the major key and the Amount Paid field is the minor key.

The following steps accomplish this sorting by specifying the Trainer Number and Amount Paid fields as sort keys.

To Sort on Multiple Keys

1

• Click the **View** button on the Query Datasheet toolbar to return to the Query1 : Select Query window.

• Click **Edit** on the menu bar and then click **Clear Grid**.

2

• Include the Client Number, Name, Trainer Number, and Amount Paid fields in the query in this order.

• Select **Ascending** as the sort order for both the Trainer Number field and the Amount Paid field (Figure 2-41).

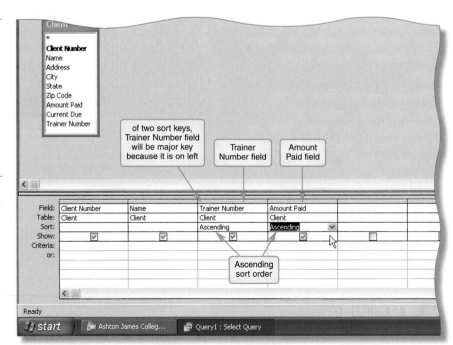

FIGURE 2-41

3

• **Click the Run button to run the query.**

• **If instructed to print the results, click the Print button.**

The results appear (Figure 2-42). The clients are sorted by trainer number. Within the collection of clients having the same trainer, the clients are sorted by amount paid.

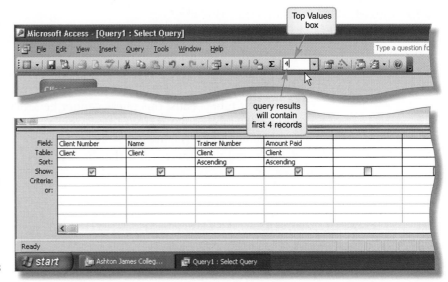

within trainer numbers, clients sorted by amount paid

overall order is by trainer number

FIGURE 2-42

It is important to remember that the major sort key must appear to the left of the minor sort key in the design grid. If you attempted to sort by amount paid within trainer number, but placed the Amount Paid field to the left of the Trainer Number field, your results would be incorrect.

Creating a Top-Values Query

Rather than show all the results of a query, you may want to show only a specified number of records or a percentage of records. Creating a **top-values query** allows you to quantify the results. When you sort records, you can limit results to those records having the highest (descending sort) or lowest (ascending sort) values. To do so, first create a query that sorts the data in the desired order. Next, use the Top Values box on the Query Design toolbar to change the number of records to be included from All to the desired number. The following steps show the first four records that were included in the results of the previous query.

To Create a Top-Values Query

1

• **Click the View button on the Query Datasheet toolbar to return to the Query1 : Select Query window.**

• **Click the Top Values box on the Query Design toolbar, and then type 4 as the new value.**

The value in the Top Values box is changed from All to 4 (Figure 2-43).

Top Values box

query results will contain first 4 records

FIGURE 2-43

> ### More About
>
> ### Joining Tables
>
> One of the key features that distinguishes database management systems from file systems is the capability of joining tables, that is, of creating queries that draw data from two or more tables. Several types of joins are available. Both an inner join type and an outer join type are illustrated in this project. An inner join is the default join in Access. Access will select all records from two tables that have the same value in the fields that are joined. Outer joins are used to show all the records in one table as well as the common records, that is, the records that share the same value in the join field.

2

• **Click the Run button to run the query.**

• **If instructed to print the results, click the Print button.**

The results appear (Figure 2-44). Only the first four records are included.

3

• **Close the query by clicking the Close Window button for the Query1 : Select Query window.**

• **When asked if you want to save your changes, click the No button.**

The Query1 : Select Query window closes. The query is not saved.

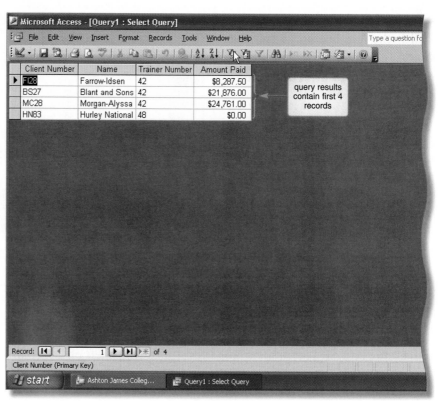

FIGURE 2-44

Other Ways

1. Click Properties button on Query Design toolbar
2. On View menu click Properties
3. Right-click any open area in upper pane, click Properties on shortcut menu
4. In Voice Command mode, say "Properties"

When you run a top-values query, it is important to change the value in the Top Values box back to All. If you do not change the Top Values value back to all, the previous value will remain in force. Consequently, you may very well not get all the records you should in the next query.

A good practice whenever you use a top-values query is to close the query as soon as you are done. That way, you will begin your next query from scratch, which guarantees that the value is set back to All.

Joining Tables

The Ashton James College database needs to satisfy a query that requires values from the Client table and the Trainer table. Specifically, the query needs to list the number and name of each client along with the number and name of the client's trainer. The client's name is in the Client table, whereas the trainer's name is in the Trainer table. Thus, this query cannot be satisfied using a single table. You need to **join** the tables; that is, to find records in the two tables that have identical values in matching fields (Figure 2-45). In this example, you need to find records in the Client table and the Trainer table that have the same value in the Trainer Number fields.

Give me the number and name of each client along with the number and name of each client's trainer.

Client table

CLIENT NUMBER	NAME	...	TRAINER NUMBER
BS27	Blant and Sons	...	42
CE16	Center Services	...	48
CP27	Calder Plastics	...	48
EU28	Elba's Furniture	...	53
FI28	Farrow-Idsen	...	42
FL93	Fairland Lawn	...	48
HN83	Hurley National	...	48
MC28	Morgan-Alyssa	...	42
PS82	PRIM Staffing	...	53
TE26	Telton-Edwards	...	48

Trainer table

TRAINER NUMBER	LAST NAME	FIRST NAME	...
42	Perry	Belinda	...
48	Stevens	Michael	...
53	Gonzalez	Manuel	...
67	Danville	Marty	...

Trainer table

CLIENT NUMBER	NAME	...	TRAINER NUMBER	LAST NAME	FIRST NAME	...
BS27	Blant and Sons	...	42	Perry	Belinda	...
CE16	Center Services	...	48	Stevens	Michael	...
CP27	Calder Plastics	...	48	Stevens	Michael	...
EU28	Elba's Furniture	...	53	Gonzalez	Manuel	...
FI28	Farrow-Idsen	...	42	Perry	Belinda	...
FL93	Fairland Lawn	...	48	Stevens	Michael	...
HN83	Hurley National	...	48	Stevens	Michael	...
MC28	Morgan-Alyssa	...	42	Perry	Belinda	...
PS82	PRIM Staffing	...	53	Gonzalez	Manuel	...
TE26	Telton-Edwards	...	48	Stevens	Michael	...

FIGURE 2-45

To join tables in Access, first you bring field lists for both tables to the upper pane of the Select Query window. Access will draw a line, called a **join line**, between matching fields in the two tables indicating that the tables are related. You then can select fields from either table. Access will join the tables automatically.

The first step is to select the Trainer table in the Database window and create a new query. Then, add the Client table to the query. A join line will appear connecting the Trainer Number fields in the two field lists. This join line indicates how the tables are related; that is, linked through these matching fields. (If you fail to give the matching fields the same name, Access will not insert the line. You can insert it manually, however, by clicking one of the two matching fields and dragging the mouse pointer to the other matching field.)

The steps on the next page create a new query, add the Client table and then select the appropriate fields.

Q&A

Q: Assuming you want the Trainer Number field to be the major key and the Amount Paid field to be the minor key as in the previous steps, how could you display the Amount Paid field before the Trainer Number field?

A: Include the Trainer Number field, the Amount Paid field, and then the Trainer Number field a second time. Select Ascending as the sort order for the first Trainer Number field and for the Amount Paid field. Remove the check mark from the Show check box for the first Trainer Number field. Thus, the first Trainer Number field will be part of the sort key, but will not appear in the results. The second Trainer Number field will appear in the results after the Amount Paid field.

To Join Tables

1

• **With the Tables object selected and the Trainer table selected, click the New Object button arrow on the Database toolbar.**

• **Click Query, and then click the OK button.**

• **Drag the line separating the two panes to the approximate position shown in Figure 2-46, and then drag the lower edge of the field list box down far enough so all fields in the Trainer table appear.**

• **Click the Show Table button on the Query Design toolbar.**

Access displays the Show Table dialog box (Figure 2-46).

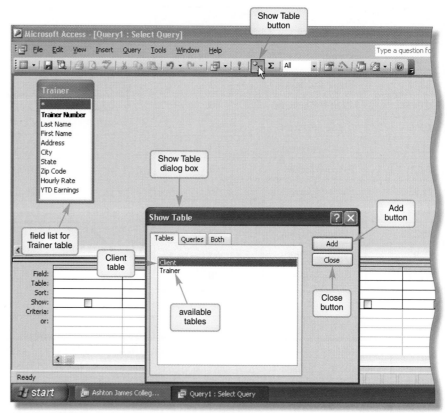

FIGURE 2-46

2

• **Be sure the Client table is selected, and then click the Add button.**

• **Close the Show Table dialog box by clicking the Close button.**

• **Expand the size of the field list so all the fields in the Client table appear.**

The field lists for both tables appear (Figure 2-47). A join line connects the two field lists.

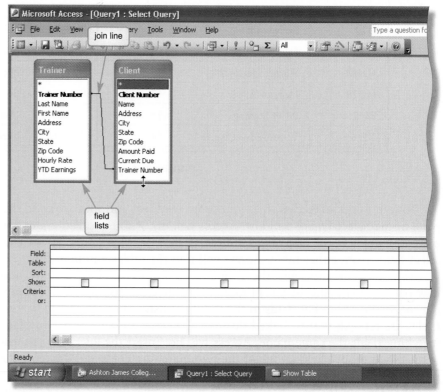

FIGURE 2-47

3

• **Include the Trainer Number, Last Name, and First Name fields from the Trainer table as well as the Client Number and Name fields from the Client table.**

• **Select Ascending as the sort order for both the Trainer Number field and the Client Number field.**

The fields from both tables are selected (Figure 2-48).

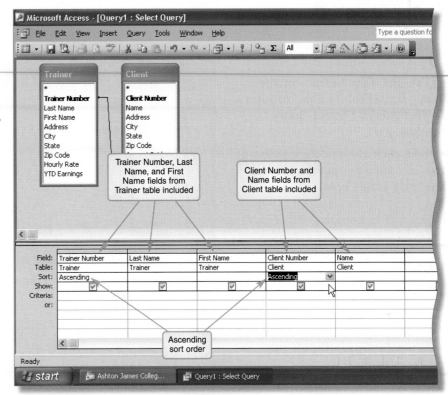

FIGURE 2-48

4

• **Click the Run button to run the query.**

• **If instructed to print the results, click the Print button.**

The results appear (Figure 2-49). They contain data from both the Trainer and Client tables. The records are sorted by trainer number and within trainer number by client number.

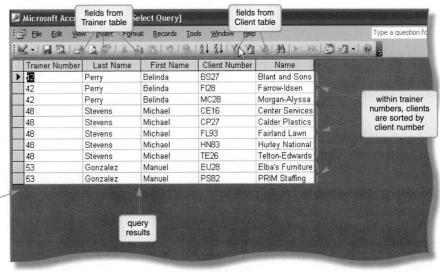

FIGURE 2-49

Changing Join Properties

Normally records that do not match will not appear in the results of a join query. A trainer such as Marty Danville, for whom no clients currently exist, for example, would not appear. To cause such a record to be displayed, you need to change the **join properties**, which are the properties that indicate which records appear in a join, of the query as the steps on the next page illustrate.

Other Ways

1. On Query menu click Show Table
2. Right-click any open area in upper pane, click Show Table on shortcut menu
3. In Voice Command mode, say "Show Table"

To Change Join Properties

1

• **Click the View button on the Query Datasheet toolbar to return to the Query1 : Select Query window.**

• **Right-click the middle portion of the join line (the portion of the line that is not bold).**

The shortcut menu appears (Figure 2-50). (If Join Properties does not appear on your shortcut menu, you did not point to the appropriate portion of the join line. You will need to right-click again.)

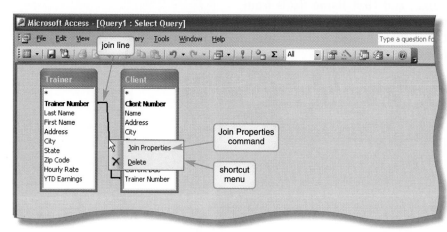

FIGURE 2-50

2

• **Click Join Properties on the shortcut menu.**

Access displays the Join Properties dialog box (Figure 2-51).

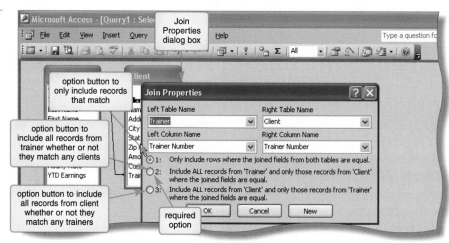

FIGURE 2-51

3

• **Click option button 2 to include all records from the Trainer table regardless of whether or not they match any clients.**

• **Click the OK button.**

• **Run the query by clicking the Run button.**

• **If instructed to print the results, click the Print button.**

The results appear (Figure 2-52).

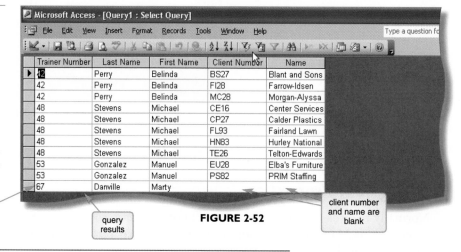

FIGURE 2-52

With the change to the join properties, trainer 67 is included, even though the trainer does not have any clients.

Restricting Records in a Join

Sometimes you will want to join tables, but you will not want to include all possible records. In such cases, you will relate the tables and include fields just as you did before. You also will include criteria. For example, to include the same fields as in the previous query, but only those clients whose amount paid is more than $20,000.00, you will make the same entries as before, but also include >20000 as a criterion for the Amount Paid field.

The following steps modify the query from the previous example to restrict the records that will be included in the join.

To Restrict the Records in a Join

1

• **Click the View button on the Query Datasheet toolbar to return to the Query1 : Select Query window.**

• **Add the Amount Paid field to the query.**

• **Type >20000 as the criterion for the Amount Paid field and then click the Show check box for the Amount Paid field to remove the check mark.**

The Amount Paid field appears in the design grid (Figure 2-53). A criterion is entered for the Amount Paid field, and the Show check box is empty, indicating that the field will not appear in the results of the query.

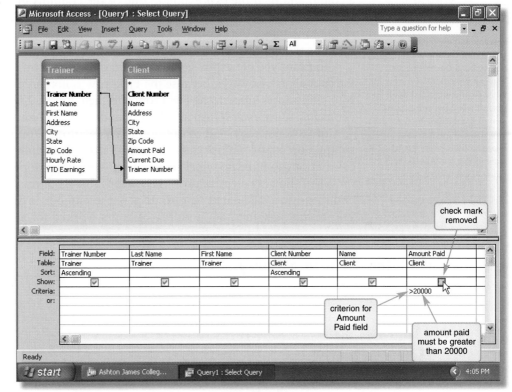

FIGURE 2-53

2

• **Click the Run button to run the query.**

• **If instructed to print the results, click the Print button.**

The results appear (Figure 2-54). Only those clients with an amount paid greater than $20,000.00 are displayed in the result. The Amount Paid field does not appear.

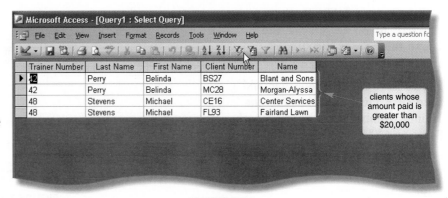

FIGURE 2-54

Calculations

Many types of calculations are available for use in queries. For example, you can add the values in two fields together, or you can calculate the sum or average of the values in one field.

Using Calculated Fields

More About

The Expression Builder

Access includes a tool to help you create complex expressions. If you click Build on the shortcut menu (see Figure 2-55), Access displays the Expression Builder dialog box. The dialog box includes an expression box, operator buttons, and expression elements. You use the expression box to build the expression. You can type parts of the expression directly and paste operator buttons and expression elements into the box. You also can use functions in expressions. For more information, visit the Access 2003 More About Web page (scsite.com/ac2003/more) and click Expression Builder and Functions.

Suppose that Ashton James College wants to know the number of hours worked by each trainer. This poses a problem because the Trainer table does not include a field for hours worked. You can calculate it, however, because the number of hours worked is equal to the YTD earnings divided by the hourly rate. A field that can be computed from other fields is called a **calculated field**.

To include calculated fields in queries, you enter a name for the calculated field, a colon, and then the expression in one of the columns in the Field row. Any fields included in the expression must be enclosed in square brackets ([ ]). For the number of hours worked, for example, you will type Hours Worked:[YTD Earnings]/[Hourly Rate] as the expression.

You can type the expression directly into the Field row. You will not be able to see the entire entry, however, because the Field row is not large enough. The preferred way is to select the column in the Field row and then use the Zoom command on its shortcut menu. When Access displays the Zoom dialog box, you can enter the expression.

You are not restricted to division in calculations. You can use addition (+), subtraction (-), or multiplication (*). You also can include parentheses in your calculations to indicate which calculations should be done first.

The following steps remove the Client table from the query (it is not needed), and then use a calculated field to display the number, last name, hourly rate, year-to-date earnings, and number of hours worked for all trainers.

To Use a Calculated Field in a Query

1

• **Click the View button on the Query Datasheet toolbar to return to the Query1 : Select Query window.**

• **Right-click any field in the Client table field list.**

• **Click Remove Table on the shortcut menu to remove the Client table from the Query1 : Select Query window.**

• **Click Edit on the menu bar and then click Clear Grid. Include the Trainer Number, Last Name, Hourly Rate, and YTD Earnings.**

• **Right-click the Field row in the first open column in the design grid.**

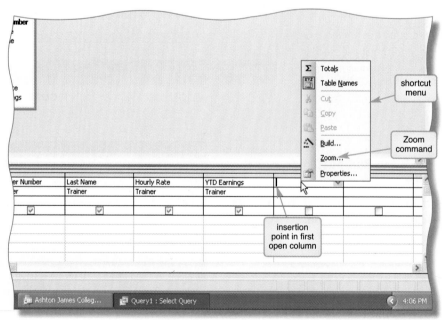

FIGURE 2-55

The shortcut menu appears (Figure 2-55).

2

- **Click Zoom on the shortcut menu.**
- **Type** Hours Worked:[YTD Earnings]/[Hourly Rate] **in the Zoom dialog box that appears.**

Access displays the Zoom dialog box (Figure 2-56). The expression you typed appears within the dialog box.

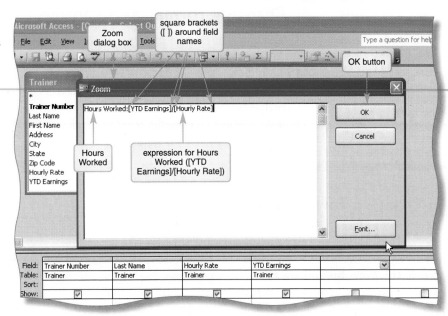

FIGURE 2-56

3

- **Click the OK button.**

A portion of the expression you entered appears in the fifth field in the design grid (Figure 2-57).

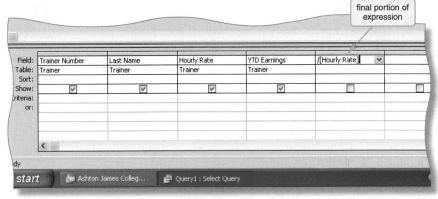

FIGURE 2-57

4

- **Click the Run button to run the query.**
- **If instructed to print the results, click the Print button.**

The results appear (Figure 2-58). Microsoft Access has calculated and displayed the number of hours worked for each trainer.

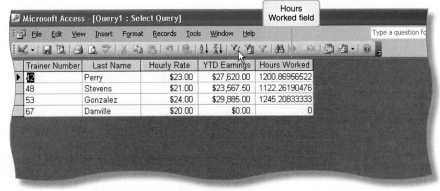

FIGURE 2-58

Other Ways

1. Press SHIFT+F2

Instead of clicking Zoom on the shortcut menu, you can click Build. Access displays the Expression Builder dialog box that provides assistance in creating the expression. If you know the expression you will need, however, usually it is easier to enter it using the Zoom command.

More About

Calculated Fields

Because it is easy to compute values in a query, it is not necessary to store calculated fields, also called computed fields, in a database. It is not necessary, for example, to store the total amount (the amount paid amount plus the current due amount), because it can be calculated whenever it is required.

Changing Format and Caption

You can change the way items appear in the results of a query by changing their format. You also can change the heading at the top of a column in the results by changing the caption. Just as when you omitted duplicates, you will make this change by using the field's property sheet. In the property sheet, you can change the desired property, such as the format, the number of decimal places, or the caption. The following steps change the format of Hours Worked to Fixed and the number of decimal places to 1, thus guaranteeing that the number on each row will contain exactly one decimal place. They also change the caption of the Hourly Rate field to Rate.

To Change a Format and a Caption

1

• **Click the View button on the Query Datasheet toolbar to return to the Query1 : Select Query window.**

• **If necessary, click the Hours Worked field in the design grid, and then click the Properties button on the Query Design toolbar.**

• **Click the Format box, click the Format box arrow, and then click Fixed.**

• **Click the Decimal Places box, and then type 1 as the number of decimal places.**

Access displays the Field Properties sheet (Figure 2-59). The format is changed to Fixed and the number of decimal places is set to 1.

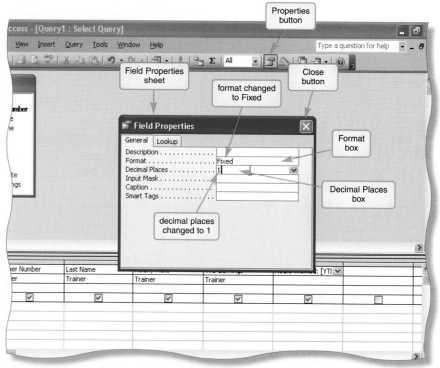

FIGURE 2-59

2

• **Close the Field Properties sheet by clicking its Close button.**

• **Click the Hourly Rate field in the design grid, and then click the Properties button on the Query Design toolbar.**

• **Click the Caption box, and then type Rate as the caption.**

Access displays the Field Properties sheet (Figure 2-60). The caption is changed to Rate.

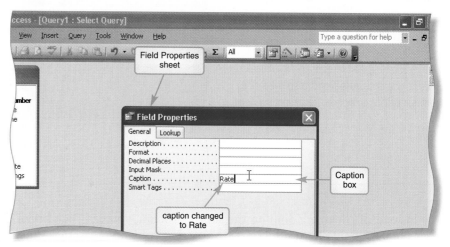

FIGURE 2-60

3

• **Click the Run button to run the query.**

• **If instructed to print the results, click the Print button.**

The results appear (Figure 2-61). The Hourly Rate caption is changed to Rate. The numbers in the Hours Worked column all contain exactly one decimal place.

4

• **Click the Close Window button for the Query1 : Select Query window.**

• **When asked if you want to save your changes, click the No button.**

The Query1 : Select Query window closes. The query is not saved.

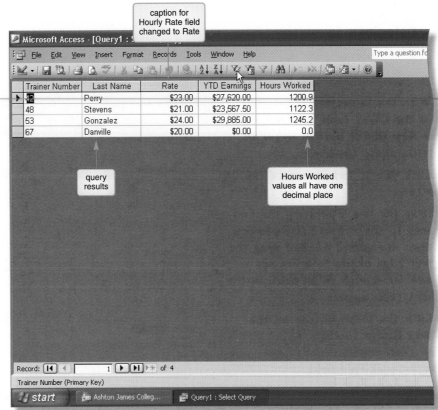

caption for Hourly Rate field changed to Rate

query results

Hours Worked values all have one decimal place

Trainer Number	Last Name	Rate	YTD Earnings	Hours Worked
42	Perry	$23.00	$27,620.00	1200.9
48	Stevens	$21.00	$23,567.50	1122.3
53	Gonzalez	$24.00	$29,885.00	1245.2
67	Danville	$20.00	$0.00	0.0

Record: [◄] [◄] [1] [►] [►►] [►*] of 4

Trainer Number (Primary Key)

FIGURE 2-61

If you had saved the query, the changes you made to the properties would be saved along with the query.

Calculating Statistics

Microsoft Access supports the built-in statistics: COUNT, SUM, AVG (average), MAX (largest value), MIN (smallest value), STDEV (standard deviation), VAR (variance), FIRST, and LAST. These statistics are called aggregate functions. An **aggregate function** is a function that performs some mathematical function against a group of records. To use any of these aggregate functions in a query, you include it in the Total row in the design grid. The Total row routinely does not appear in the grid. To include it, click the Totals button on the Query Design toolbar.

The steps on the next page create a new query for the Client table and then calculate the average amount paid for all clients.

Other Ways

1. On View menu click Properties
2. Right-click field in design grid, click Properties on shortcut menu
3. In Voice Command mode, say "Properties"

More About

Calculating Statistics

Virtually all database management systems support the basic set of statistical calculations: sum, average, count, maximum, and minimum as part of their query feature. Some systems, including Access, add several more, such as standard deviation, variance, first, and last.

To Calculate Statistics

1

- **With the Tables object selected and the Client table selected, click the New Object button arrow on the Database toolbar.**

- **Click Query, and then click the OK button.**

- **Drag the line separating the two panes to the approximate position shown in Figure 2-62, and drag the lower edge of the field list box down far enough so all fields in the Client table appear.**

- **Click the Totals button on the Query Design toolbar, and then double-click the Amount Paid field.**

The Total row now is included in the design grid (Figure 2-62). The Amount Paid field is included, and the entry in the Total row is Group By.

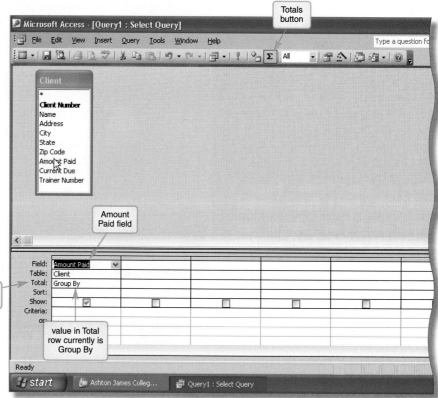

FIGURE 2-62

2

- **Click the Total row in the Amount Paid column, and then click the Total row arrow that appears.**

The list of available options appears (Figure 2-63).

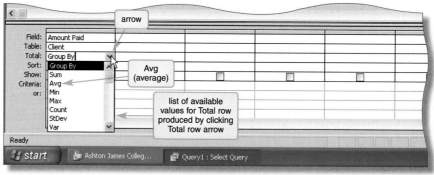

FIGURE 2-63

3

- **Click Avg.**

Avg is selected (Figure 2-64).

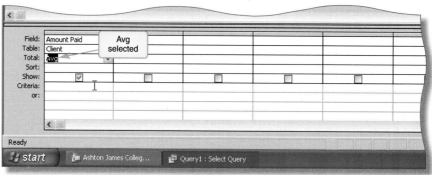

FIGURE 2-64

4

- **Click the Run button to run the query.**
- **If instructed to print the results, click the Print button.**

The result appears (Figure 2-65), showing the average amount paid for all clients.

average amount paid by all clients

FIGURE 2-65

Other Ways

1. On View menu click Totals
2. Right-click any open area in upper pane, click Totals on shortcut menu
3. In Voice Command mode, say "Totals"

Using Criteria in Calculating Statistics

Sometimes calculating statistics for all the records in the table is appropriate. In other cases, however, you will need to calculate the statistics for only those records that satisfy certain criteria. To enter a criterion in a field, first you select Where as the entry in the Total row for the field and then enter the criterion in the Criteria row. The following steps use this technique to calculate the average amount paid for clients of trainer 48.

To Use Criteria in Calculating Statistics

1

- **Click the View button on the Query Datasheet toolbar to return to the Query1 : Select Query window.**

2

- **Include the Trainer Number field in the design grid.**
- **Produce the list of available options for the Total row entry just as you did when you selected Avg for the Amount Paid field.**
- **Use the vertical scroll bar to move through the options until the Where option appears.**

The list of available options appears (Figure 2-66). The Group By entry in the Trainer Number field may not be highlighted on your screen depending on where you clicked in the Total row.

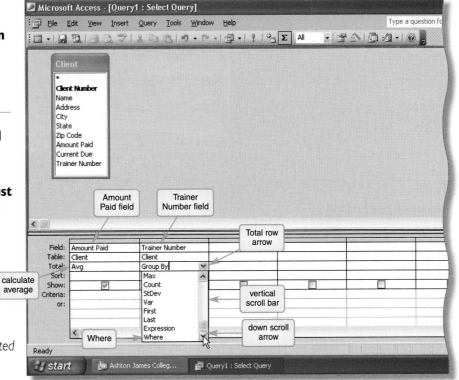

Amount Paid field

Trainer Number field

Total row arrow

calculate average

vertical scroll bar

down scroll arrow

Where

FIGURE 2-66

3

- **Click Where.**
- **Type** 42 **as the criterion for the Trainer Number field.**

Where is selected as the entry in the Total row for the Trainer Number field and 42 is entered in the Criteria row (Figure 2-67).

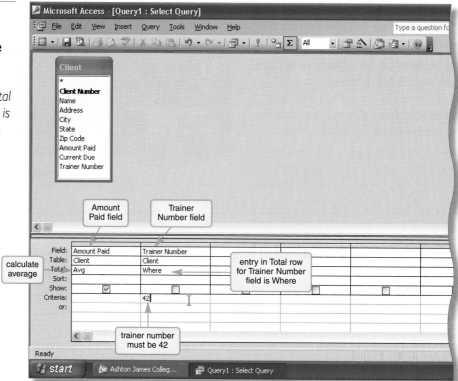

FIGURE 2-67

4

- **Click the Run button to run the query.**
- **If instructed to print the results, click the Print button.**

The results appear (Figure 2-68), giving the average amount paid for clients of trainer 42.

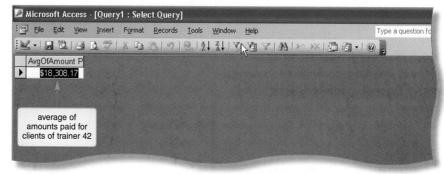

FIGURE 2-68

Grouping

Another way statistics often are used is in combination with grouping; that is, statistics are calculated for groups of records. You may, for example, need to calculate the average amount paid for the clients of each trainer. You will want the average for the clients of trainer 42, the average for clients of trainer 48, and so on.

Grouping means creating groups of records that share some common characteristic. In grouping by Trainer Number, for example, the clients of trainer 42 would form one group, the clients of trainer 48 would be a second, and the clients of trainer 53 form a third group. The calculations then are made for each group. To indicate grouping in Access, select Group By as the entry in the Total row for the field to be used for grouping.

The following steps calculate the average amount paid for clients of each trainer.

To Use Grouping

1

• **Click the View button on the Query Datasheet toolbar to return to the Query1 : Select Query window.**

• **Click Edit on the menu bar and then click Clear Grid.**

• **Include the Trainer Number field.**

• **Include the Amount Paid field, and then click Avg as the calculation in the Total row.**

The Trainer Number and Amount Paid fields are included (Figure 2-69). Group By currently is the entry in the Total row for the Trainer Number field, which is correct; thus, it was not changed.

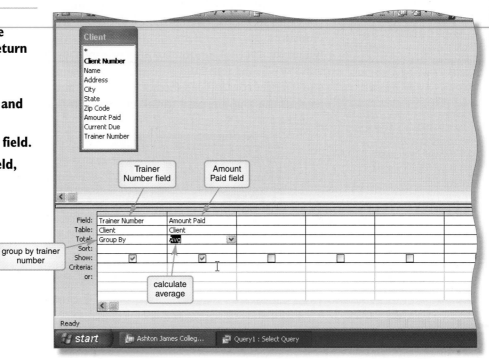

FIGURE 2-69

2

• **Click the Run button to run the query.**

• **If instructed to print the results, click the Print button.**

The results appear (Figure 2-70), showing each trainer's number along with the average amount paid for the clients of that trainer. Because the results are grouped by trainer number, a single row exists for each trainer summarizing all the clients of that trainer.

3

• **Close the query by clicking the Close Window button for the Query1 : Select Query window.**

• **When asked if you want to save your changes, click the No button.**

The Query1 : Select Query window closes. The query is not saved.

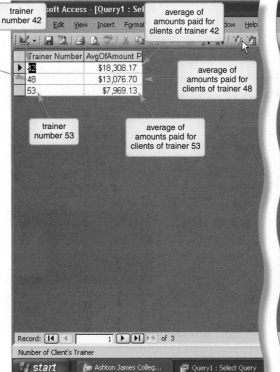

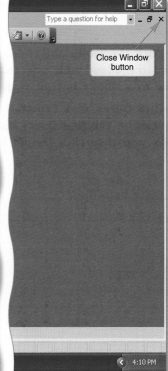

FIGURE 2-70

Microsoft Office
Access 2003

Crosstab Queries

Crosstab queries are useful for summarizing data. A **crosstab query** calculates a statistic (for example, sum, average, or count) for data that is grouped by two different types of information. One of the types will appear down the side of the resulting datasheet, and the other will appear across the top. Figure 2-71 shows a crosstab in which the total of amount paid is grouped by both city and trainer number with cities down the left-hand side and trainer numbers across the top. For example, the entry in the row labeled Cedar Ridge and in the column labeled 42 represents the total of the amount paid for all clients of trainer 42 who live in Cedar Ridge.

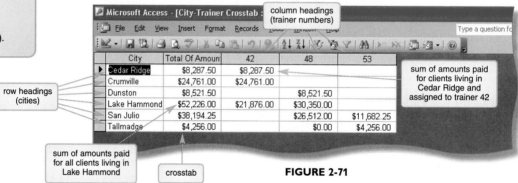

FIGURE 2-71

The following steps use the Crosstab Query wizard to create a crosstab query.

To Create a Crosstab Query

1

• **With the Tables object selected and the Client table selected, click the New Object button arrow.**

• **Click Query, click Crosstab Query Wizard in the New Query dialog box, and then click the OK button.**

Access displays the Crosstab Query Wizard dialog box (Figure 2-72).

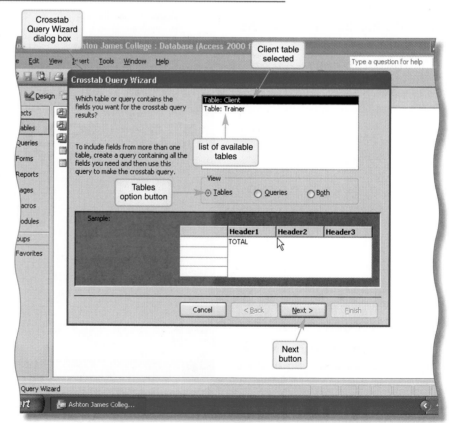

FIGURE 2-72

2

• **With the Tables option button selected and the Client table selected, click the Next button.**

• **Click the City field, and then click the Add Field button.**

The Crosstab Query Wizard dialog box displays options for selecting field values as row headings (Figure 2-73). The City field is selected as the field whose values will provide the row headings.

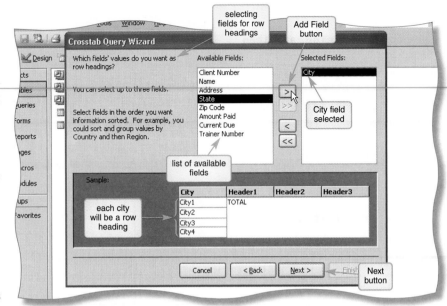

FIGURE 2-73

3

• **Click the Next button, and then click the Trainer Number field.**

The Crosstab Query Wizard dialog box displays options for selecting field values as column headings (Figure 2-74). The Trainer Number field is selected as the field whose values will provide the column headings.

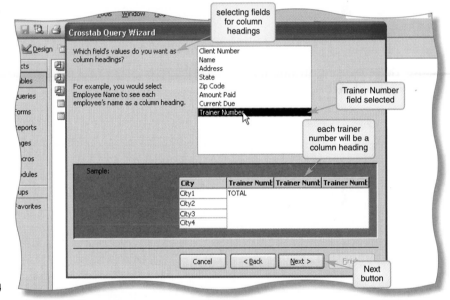

FIGURE 2-74

4

• **Click the Next button, click the Amount Paid field, and then click Sum.**

The Crosstab Query Wizard dialog box displays options for selecting fields for calculations for column and row intersections (Figure 2-75). The Amount Paid field is selected as the field whose value will be calculated for each row and column intersection. Because Sum is the selected function, the calculation will be the total amount paid.

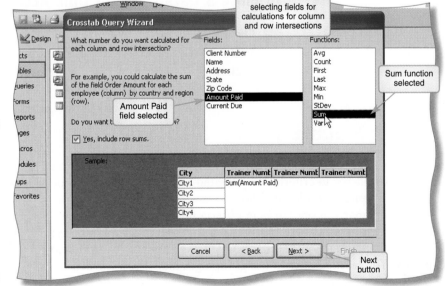

FIGURE 2-75

5

• **Click the Next button, and then type** `City-Trainer Crosstab` **as the name of the query.**

The Crosstab Query Wizard dialog box displays options for naming and viewing the query and modifying the design (Figure 2-76). The name is entered.

6

• **Click the Finish button.**

• **If instructed to print the results, click the Print button.**

The results now can appear. They look like the results shown in Figure 2-71 on page AC 104.

7

• **Close the query by clicking its Close Window button.**

The query no longer appears.

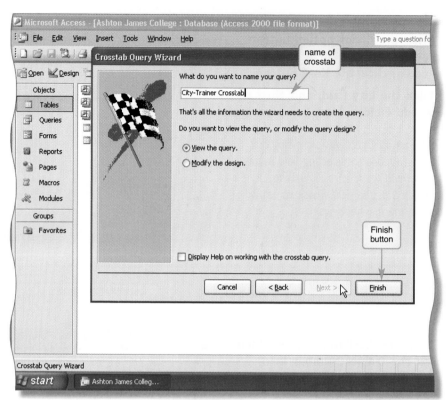

FIGURE 2-76

The query containing the crosstab now can be run just like any other query.

Closing a Database and Quitting Access

The following steps close the database and quit Access.

To Close a Database and Quit Access

1 **Click the Close Window button for the Ashton James College : Database window.**

2 **Click the Close button for the Microsoft Access window.**

Project Summary

In Project 2, you created and ran a variety of queries. You saw how to select fields in a query. You used text data and wildcards in criteria. You created a parameter query, which allowed users to enter a criterion when they run the query. You learned how to save a query for future use and how to use a query you have saved. You also used comparison operators in criteria involving numeric data. You combined criteria with both AND and OR. You saw how to sort the results of a query, how to join tables, how to restrict the records in a join, and how to change join properties. You created computed fields and calculated statistics. You changed formats and captions. You learned how to use grouping. Finally, you learned how to create a crosstab query.

If you have a SAM user profile, you may have access to hands-on instruction, practice, and assessment of the skills covered in this project. Log in to your SAM account and go to your assignments page to see what your instructor has assigned.

What You Should Know

Having completed this project, you should be able to perform the tasks below. The tasks are listed in the same order they were presented in this project. For a list of the buttons, menus, toolbars, and commands introduced in this project, see the Quick Reference Summary at the back of this book and refer to the Page Number column.

1. Open a Database (AC 68)
2. Create a Query (AC 68)
3. Include Fields in the Design Grid (AC 71)
4. Run the Query (AC 71)
5. Print the Results of a Query (AC 72)
6. Return to the Select Query Window (AC 72)
7. Close the Query (AC 73)
8. Include All Fields in a Query (AC 74)
9. Clear the Design Grid (AC 75)
10. Use Text Data in a Criterion (AC 76)
11. Use a Wildcard (AC 77)
12. Use Criteria for a Field Not Included in the Results (AC 78)
13. Create and Run a Parameter Query (AC 79)
14. Save a Query (AC 80)
15. Use a Saved Query (AC 81)
16. Use a Number in a Criterion (AC 82)
17. Use a Comparison Operator in a Criterion (AC 83)
18. Use a Compound Criterion Involving AND (AC 84)
19. Use a Compound Criterion Involving OR (AC 85)
20. Sort Data in a Query (AC 86)
21. Omit Duplicates (AC 87)
22. Sort on Multiple Keys (AC 88)
23. Create a Top-Values Query (AC 89)
24. Join Tables (AC 92)
25. Change Join Properties (AC 94)
26. Restrict the Records in a Join (AC 95)
27. Use a Calculated Field in a Query (AC 96)
28. Change a Format and a Caption (AC 98)
29. Calculate Statistics (AC 100)
30. Use Criteria in Calculating Statistics (AC 101)
31. Use Grouping (AC 103)
32. Create a Crosstab Query (AC 104)
33. Close a Database and Quit Access (AC 106)

Learn It Online

Instructions: To complete the Learn It Online exercises, start your browser, click the Address bar, and then enter the Web address scsite.com/ac2003/learn. When the Access 2003 Learn It Online page is displayed, follow the instructions in the exercises below. Each exercise has instructions for printing your results, either for your own records or for submission to your instructor.

1 Project Reinforcement TF, MC, and SA

Below Access Project 2, click the Project Reinforcement link. Print the quiz by clicking Print on the File menu for each page. Answer each question.

Flash Cards

Below Access Project 2, click the Flash Cards link and read the instructions. Type 20 (or a number specified by your instructor) in the Number of playing cards text box, type your name in the Enter your Name text box, and then click the Flip Card button. When the flash card is displayed, read the question and then click the ANSWER box arrow to select an answer. Flip through Flash Cards. If your score is 15 (75%) correct or greater, click Print on the File menu to print your results. If your score is less than 15 (75%) correct, then redo this exercise by clicking the Replay button.

3 Practice Test

Below Access Project 2, click the Practice Test link. Answer each question, enter your first and last name at the bottom of the page, and then click the Grade Test button. When the graded practice test is displayed on your screen, click Print on the File menu to print a hard copy. Continue to take practice tests until you score 80% or better.

4 Who Wants To Be a Computer Genius?

Below Access Project 2, click the Computer Genius link. Read the instructions, enter your first and last name at the bottom of the page, and then click the PLAY button. When your score is displayed, click the PRINT RESULTS link to print a hard copy.

5 Wheel of Terms

Below Access Project 2, click the Wheel of Terms link. Read the instructions, and then enter your first and last name and your school name. Click the PLAY button. When your score is displayed, right-click the score and then click Print on the shortcut menu to print a hard copy.

6 Crossword Puzzle Challenge

Below Access Project 2, click the Crossword Puzzle Challenge link. Read the instructions, and then enter your first and last name. Click the SUBMIT button. Work the crossword puzzle. When you are finished, click the Submit button. When the crossword puzzle is redisplayed, click the Print Puzzle button to print a hard copy.

7 Tips and Tricks

Below Access Project 2, click the Tips and Tricks link. Click a topic that pertains to Project 2. Right-click the information and then click Print on the shortcut menu. Construct a brief example of what the information relates to in Access to confirm you understand how to use the tip or trick.

8 Newsgroups

Below Access Project 2, click the Newsgroups link. Click a topic that pertains to Project 2. Print three comments.

9 Expanding Your Horizons

Below Access Project 2, click the Expanding Your Horizons link. Click a topic that pertains to Project 2. Print the information. Construct a brief example of what the information relates to in Access to confirm you understand the contents of the article.

10 Search Sleuth

Below Access Project 2, click the Search Sleuth link. To search for a term that pertains to this project, select a term below the Project 2 title and then use the Google search engine at google.com (or any major search engine) to display and print two Web pages that present information on the term.

11 Access Online Training

Below Access Project 2, click the Access Online Training link. When your browser displays the Microsoft Office Online Web page, click the Access link. Click one of the Access courses that covers one or more of the objectives listed at the beginning of the project on page AC 66. Print the first page of the course before stepping through it.

12 Office Marketplace

Below Access Project 2, click the Office Marketplace link. When your browser displays the Microsoft Office Online Web page, click the Office Marketplace link. Click a topic that relates to Access. Print the first page.

Apply Your Knowledge

1 Querying the Begon Pest Control Database

Instructions: Start Access. Open the Begon Pest Control database that you modified in Apply Your Knowledge 1 in Project 1 on page AC 54. (If you did not complete this exercise, see your instructor for a copy of the modified database.) Perform the following tasks:

1. Create a query for the Customer table and add the Name and Address fields to the design grid.
2. Find only those records where the client has an address on Fletcher. Run the query and change the address for the client on 109 Fletcher to 190 Fletcher. Print the results. Return to Design view and clear the grid.
3. Add the Customer Number, Name, City, and Balance fields to the design grid. Sort the records in ascending order by City and descending by Balance. Run the query and print the results. Return to Design view.
4. Modify the query to allow the user to enter a different city each time the query is run. Run the query to find all customers who live in Kady. Print the query results. Save the query as Customer-City Query.
5. Open the Customer-City Query in Design view. Run the query to find all customers who live in Carlton but restrict retrieval to the top two records. Print the results. Close the query without saving it.
6. Create a new query for the Technician table and then join the Technician and Customer tables. Add the Technician Number, First Name and Last Name fields from the Technician table and the Customer Number, and Name fields from the Customer table. Sort the records in ascending order by Technician Number and Customer Number. All technicians should appear in the result even if they currently have no customers. Run the query and print the results.
7. Restrict the records retrieved in task 6 above to only those customers who have a balance greater than $350.00. Run the query and print the results. Close the query without saving it.
8. Create and print the crosstab shown in Figure 2-77. The crosstab groups total of customers' balances by city and technician number.

City	Total Of Balance	203	210	214
Carlton	$763.00	$398.00		$365.00
Conradt	$655.00	$355.00	$300.00	$0.00
Kady	$1,302.00	$335.00	$967.00	

FIGURE 2-77

In The Lab

1 Querying the Birds2U Database

Problem: The management of Birds2U has determined a number of questions it wants the database management system to answer. You must obtain the answers to the questions posed by management.

Instructions: Use the database created in the In the Lab 1 of Project 1 on page AC 57 for this assignment or see your instructor for information on accessing the files required for this book. Perform the following tasks:

1. Open the Birds2U database and create a new query to display and print the Item Code, Description, On Hand, and Selling Price for all records in the Item table.
2. Display and print the Item Code, Description, Cost, and Supplier Code fields for all products where the Supplier Code is 13.

(continued)

In the Lab

1 Querying the Birds2U Database *(continued)*

3. Display and print the Item Code and Description fields for all items where the description includes the letters "bird."

4. Display and print the Item Code and Description fields for all items with a cost less than $15.00.

5. Display and print the Item Code and Description fields for all products that have a selling price greater than $50.00.

6. Display and print all fields for those items with a selling price greater than $30.00 and where the number on hand is at least 5.

7. Display and print all fields for those items that have a supplier code of 13 or a selling price less than $16.00.

8. Include the Item Code, Description, On Hand, and Selling Price in the design grid. Change the caption for the On Hand column to In Stock and sort the records in descending order by selling price. Run the query and print the results. Run the query again but this time limit retrieval to the top 3 records.

9. Join the Supplier table and the Item table. Display the Supplier Code and Name from the Supplier table and the Item Code, Description, On Hand, and Cost from the Item table. Sort the records in ascending order by Supplier Code and by Item Code. All suppliers should display in the result even if they currently supply no items. Run the query and print the results. Save the query as Suppliers and Items.

10. Restrict the records retrieved in task 9 above to only those products where number on hand is less than 5. Run the query and print the results. Close the query and do not save the changes.

11. Create a new query for the Item table and include the Item Code and Description fields in the design grid. Calculate the on-hand value (on hand * cost) for all records in the table. Run the query and print the results.

12. Display and print the average selling price of all items.

13. Display and print the average selling price of items grouped by supplier code.

2 Querying the Babbage Bookkeeping Database

Problem: Babbage Bookkeeping has determined a number of questions it wants the database management system to answer. You must obtain the answers to the questions posed by the bookkeeping service.

Instructions: Use the database created in the In the Lab 2 of Project 1 on page AC 59 for this assignment or see your instructor for information on accessing the files required for this book. Perform the following tasks:

1. Open the Babbage Bookkeeping database and create a new query for the Client table.

2. Display and print the Name and Balance fields for all clients where the bookkeeper number is 24.

3. Display and print the Client Number, Name, and Balance fields for all clients located in Empeer with a balance greater than $300.00.

4. Display and print the Client Number, Name, and Address fields for all clients with an address on Maum.

5. Display and print the cities in ascending order. Each city should appear only once.

6. Create a query that will allow the user to enter the city to search when the query is run. The query results should display the Client Number, Name, and Bookkeeper Number. Test the query by searching for those records where the client is located in Portage. Save the query as Client-City Query.

7. Include the Client Number, Name, and Balance fields in the design grid. Sort the records in descending order by the Balance field. Display and print the top half of the records.

In the Lab

8. Display and print the Client Number, Name, and Balance fields for all clients where the bookkeeper number is 24 or 34 and the balance is greater than $300.00. (*Hint:* Use Microsoft Access Help to solve this problem.)

9. Display and print the First Name, Last Name, and Hourly Rate fields from the Bookkeeper table and the Client Number, Name, and Balance fields from the Client table. Sort the records in ascending order by bookkeeper's last name and client's name.

10. Create a new query for the Bookkeeper table and include the Bookkeeper Number, First Name, Last Name, and Hourly Rate in the design grid. Calculate the number of hours each bookkeeper has worked (YTD Earnings/Hourly Rate). Display hours worked as an integer (0 decimal places). Run the query and print the results.

11. Display and print the following statistics: the total balance for all clients; the total balance for clients of bookkeeper 22; and the total balance for each bookkeeper.

12. Create the crosstab shown in Figure 2-78. The crosstab groups total of clients' balances by city and bookkeeper number. Save the crosstab as City-Bookkeeper Crosstab. Print the crosstab.

City	Total Of Balance	22	24	34
Empeer	$1,102.50	$577.50	$525.00	
Grant City	$1,027.50	$315.50	$712.00	
Portage	$848.25			$848.25

FIGURE 2-78

3 Querying the City Guide Database

Problem: The chamber of commerce has determined a number of questions it wants the database management system to answer. You must obtain the answers to the questions posed by the chamber.

Instructions: Use the database created in the In the Lab 3 of Project 1 on page AC 61 for this exercise or see your instructor for information on accessing the files required for this book. Print the answers to each question.

Instructions Part 1: Create a new query for the Advertiser table and include the Advertiser Number, Name, Balance, and Amount Paid fields in the design grid. Answer the following questions: (1) Which advertisers' names begin with C? (2) Which advertisers are located on Main? (3) Which advertisers have a current balance of $0.00? (4) Which advertisers have a balance greater than $150.00 and have an amount paid greater than $800.00? (5) Which five advertisers have the highest balances? (6) For each advertiser, what is the total of the current balance and the amount paid?

Instructions Part 2: Join the Ad Rep table and the Advertiser table. Include the Ad Rep Number, First Name, and Last Name from the Ad Rep table and the Advertiser Number, Name, and Balance from the Advertiser table in the design grid. Sort the records in ascending order by Ad Rep Number and Advertiser Number. Perform the following: (1) Calculate the pending commission (comm rate * balance) for each ad rep. The pending commission should display as currency. (2) Restrict retrieval to only those records where the pending commission is greater than $20.00.

Instructions Part 3: Calculate the following statistics: (1) What is the average balance for advertisers assigned to ad rep 26? (2) What is the total amount paid of all advertisers? (3) What is the total balance for each ad rep?

Cases and Places

The difficulty of these case studies varies:
■ are the least difficult and ■■ are more difficult. The last exercise is a group exercise.

1 ■ Use the College Dog Walkers database you created in Cases and Places 1 in Project 1 on page AC 63 for this assignment or see your instructor for information on accessing the files required for this book. Perform the following: (a) Display and print the number and name of all customers who live on Easton. (b) Display and print the number, name, telephone number, and balance for all customers who have a balance of at least $40.00. (c) Display and print the number, name, balance, walker first name, and walker last name for all customers. Sort the records in ascending order by walker last name. (d) Display and print the average balance of all customers. (e) Display and print the average balance of customers grouped by walker. (f) Display and print the total balance of all customers.

2 ■ Use the InPerson Fitness Company database you created in Cases and Places 2 in Project 1 on page AC 63 for this assignment or see your instructor for information on accessing the files required for this book. Perform the following: (a) Display and print the number, client name, and balance for all clients of a particular trainer. The owner should be able to enter a different trainer number each time the query is run. (b) Display and print the number, client name, and total of balance due and amount paid. (c) Display and print the number, client name, and balance of all clients whose amount paid is greater than $400.00. (d) Display and print the trainer number, trainer name, client number, client name, client address, and client telephone number for all clients. Sort the data ascending by trainer number and client number. (e) Display and print the total amount paid and total balance grouped by trainer.

3 ■■ Use the Regional Books database you created in Cases and Places 3 in Project 1 on page AC 63 for this assignment or see your instructor for information on accessing the files required for this book. Perform the following: (a) List the book code, title, and on-hand value (units on hand * price) of all books. (b) List the book code, title, and price of all paperback books. (c) List the book code, title, price, and publisher name for all books where there are less than 3 books on hand. (d) Display and print the book code, title, and author for all books. (e) Find the lowest priced book and the highest priced book.

4 ■■ Use the Campus Housing database you created in Cases and Places 4 in Project 1 on page AC 64 for this assignment or see your instructor for information on accessing the files required for this book. Display and print the following: (a) List all rental units that are located two miles or less from campus. (b) List all rental units that have parking and allow pets. (c) List all three-bedroom apartments that rent for less than $1,000.00 a month. (d) Find the average rent for two-bedroom apartments. (e) List the owners of all units that are efficiencies or rooms for rent. (f) List the different lease terms in ascending order. Each lease term should display only once.

5 ■■ **Working Together** Create an additional query for each of the four databases described in the Cases and Places. Each team must create a parameter query, a top values query, a crosstab query, and an aggregate query. Select the database to use to create each specific query type. Use all four databases, that is, one database per specific query type. Run each of the queries and print the results. Write a one-page paper that lists the queries the team created and explains why the team chose those queries.

Maintaining a Database Using the Design and Update Features of Access

PROJECT

3

Client data

CASE PERSPECTIVE

Dr. Gernaey and his colleagues at Ashton James College have received many benefits from the database they created and loaded, including the ability to ask questions concerning the data in the database. They now face the task of keeping the database up-to-date. As they take on new clients and trainers, they will need to add new records and make changes to existing records.

Access offers many features for maintaining a database that they want to utilize. For example, they must change the structure of the database to categorize the clients by type. They will do this by adding a Client Type field to the Client table. They discovered the Name field was too short to contain the name of one of the clients, so they will enlarge the size of the field. Along with these changes, they want to change the appearance of a datasheet when displaying data.

They would like the ability to make mass updates, that is, to update many records in a single operation. They want rules that make sure users can enter only valid data into the database, and they want to ensure that it is not possible for the database to contain a client who is not associated with a specific trainer. Finally, they want to improve the efficiency of certain types of processing, specifically sorting and retrieving data. Your task is to help the administration accomplish these goals.

As you read through this project, you will learn how to use the Access design and update features to maintain a database.

Maintaining a Database Using the Design and Update Features of Access

Objectives

You will have mastered the material in this project when you can:

- Add, change, and delete records
- Search for records
- Filter records
- Update a table design
- Format a datasheet
- Use queries to update records
- Specify validation rules, default values, and formats
- Create and use a Lookup field
- Specify referential integrity
- Use a subdatasheet
- Sort records
- Create indexes

Introduction

Once a database has been created and loaded with data, it must be maintained. **Maintaining the database** means modifying the data to keep it up-to-date, such as adding new records, changing the data for existing records, and deleting records. Updating can include mass updates or mass deletions; that is, updates to, or deletions of, many records at the same time.

In addition to adding, changing, and deleting records, maintenance of a database can involve the need to **restructure the database** periodically; that is, to change the database structure. This can include adding new fields to a table, changing the characteristics of existing fields, and removing existing fields. It also can involve the creation of indexes, which are similar to indexes found in the back of books. Indexes are used to improve the efficiency of certain operations.

Figure 3-1 summarizes some of the various types of activities involved in maintaining a database.

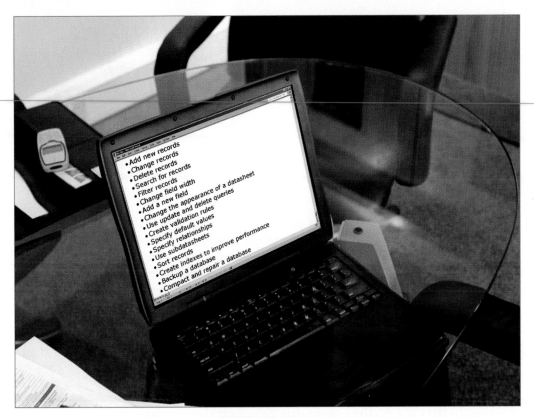

FIGURE 3-1

Project Three — Maintaining the Ashton James College Database

The steps in this project show how to make changes to the data in the Ashton James College database. They also illustrate how to search for records as well as filter records. The steps restructure the database, that is, make changes that meet the needs of the user, in this case, Ashton James College. This includes adding an additional field as well as increasing the width of one of the existing fields. Other changes modify the structure of the database in a way that prevents users from entering invalid data. Steps are presented to create indexes that reduce the time it takes for some operations, for example, those involving sorting the data.

Opening the Database

If you are stepping through this project on a computer and you want your screen to match the figures in this book, then you should change your computer's resolution to 800 × 600. For more information on how to change the resolution on your computer, see Appendix D. Before carrying out the steps in this project, first you must open the database. The steps on the next page start Access and open the database. The steps assume that the Ashton James College database is located on a disk in drive A. If your database is located anywhere else, you will need to adjust the appropriate steps.

More About

The Access Help System

Need Help? It is no further than the Type a question for help box on the menu bar in the upper-right corner of the window. Click the box that contains the text, Type a question for help (Figure 3-3), type help, and then press the ENTER key. Access responds with a list of topics you can click to learn about obtaining help on any Access-related topic. To find out what is new in Access 2003, type what is new in Access in the Type a question for help box.

To Open a Database

1 Click the Start button on the Windows taskbar, point to All Programs on the Start menu, point to Microsoft Office on the All Programs submenu, and then click Microsoft Office Access 2003 on the Microsoft Office submenu.

2 If the Access window is not maximized, double-click its title bar to maximize it.

3 If the Language bar appears, right-click it and then click Close the Language bar on the shortcut menu.

4 Click the Open button on the Database toolbar.

5 If necessary, click the Look in box arrow and then click 3½ Floppy (A:). Click Ashton James College, the database modified in Project 2. (If you did not complete the steps in Project 2, see your instructor for a copy of the database.)

6 Click the Open button in the Open dialog box. If the Security Warning dialog box appears, click the Open button.

The database opens and the Ashton James College : Database window appears.

Updating Records

Keeping the data in a database up-to-date requires updating records in three ways: adding new records, changing the data in existing records, and deleting existing records.

Adding Records

In Project 1, you added records to a database using Datasheet view; that is, as you were adding records, the records were appearing on the screen in the form of a datasheet, or table. When you need to add additional records, you can use the same techniques.

In Project 1, you used a form to view records. This is called Form view. You also can use **Form view** to update the data in a table. To add new records, change existing records, or delete records, you will use the same techniques you used in Datasheet view. The following steps add a record to the Client table with a form, for example. These steps use the Client form created in Project 1.

To Use a Form to Add Records

1

• **With the Ashton James College database open, click Forms on the Objects bar, and then right-click the Client form.**

The list of forms appears (Figure 3-2). The shortcut menu for the Client form also appears.

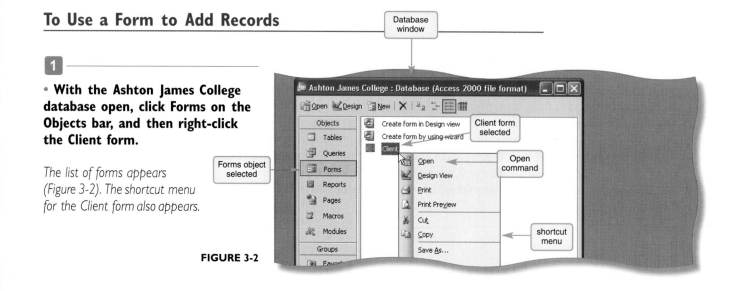

FIGURE 3-2

2

- **Click Open on the shortcut menu.**

The form for the Client table appears (Figure 3-3). Your toolbars may be arranged differently.

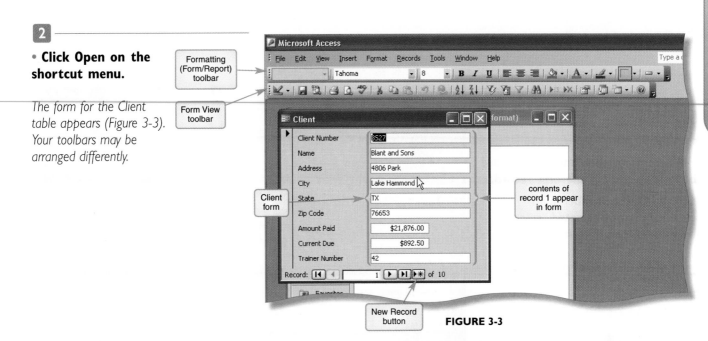

FIGURE 3-3

3

- **Click the New Record button on the Navigation bar, and then type the data for the new record as shown in Figure 3-4. Press the TAB key after typing the data in each field, except after typing the data for the final field (Trainer Number).**

The record appears.

4

- **Press the TAB key.**

The record now is added to the Client table and the contents of the form are erased.

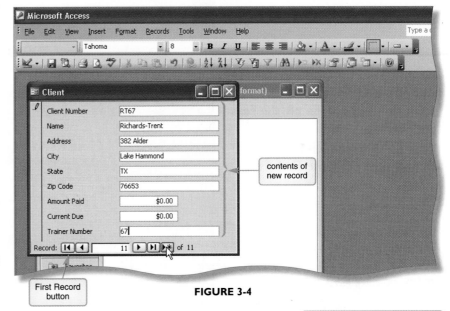

FIGURE 3-4

Searching for a Record

In the database environment, **searching** means looking for records that satisfy some criteria. Looking for the client whose number is FL93 is an example of searching. The queries in Project 2 also were examples of searching. Access had to locate those records that satisfied the criteria.

A need for searching also exists when using Form view or Datasheet view. To update client FL93, for example, first you need to find the client.

You need a way to be able to go directly to a record just by giving the value in some field. This is the function of the Find button. Before clicking the Find button, select the field for the search.

The steps on the next page show how to search for the client whose number is FL93.

Other Ways

1. Click New Record button on Form View toolbar
2. On Insert menu click New Record
3. In Voice Command mode, say "Insert, New Record"

To Search for a Record

1

- **Make sure the Client table is open and the form for the Client table is displayed.**
- **If necessary, click the First Record button to display the first record.**
- **If the Client Number field currently is not selected, select it by clicking the field name.**

The first record appears on the form (Figure 3-5).

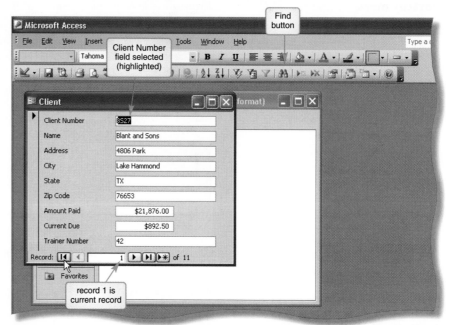

FIGURE 3-5

2

- **Click the Find button on the Form View toolbar.**
- **Type FL93 in the Find What text box and then click the Find Next button.**

Access displays the Find and Replace dialog box, locates the record for client FL93, and displays it in the Client form (Figure 3-6). The Find What text box contains the entry, FL93.

3

- **Click the Cancel button in the Find and Replace dialog box.**

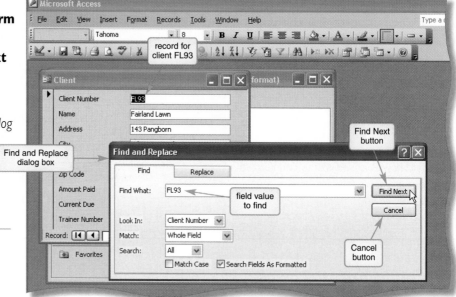

FIGURE 3-6

Other Ways

1. On Edit menu click Find
2. Press CTRL+F
3. In Voice Command mode, say "Find"

In some cases, after locating a record that satisfies a criterion, you might need to find the next record that satisfies the same criterion. For example, if you just found the first client whose trainer number is 42, you then may want to find the second such client, then the third, and so on. To do so, repeat the same process. You will not need to retype the value each time, however.

Changing the Contents of a Record

After locating the record to be changed, select the field to be changed by clicking the field. You also can press the TAB key repeatedly. Then make the appropriate changes. (Clicking the field automatically produces an insertion point. If you use the TAB key, you will need to press F2 to produce an insertion point.)

Normally, Access is in **Insert mode**, so the characters typed will be inserted at the appropriate position. To change to **Overtype mode**, press the INSERT key. The letters, OVR, will appear near the bottom right edge of the status bar. To return to Insert mode, press the INSERT key. In Insert mode, if the data in the field completely fills the field, no additional characters can be inserted. In this case, you would need to increase the size of the field before inserting the characters. You will see how to do this later in the project.

The following steps use Form view to change the name of client FL93 to Fairland Lawns by inserting the letter s after Lawn. Sufficient room exists in the field to make this change.

Q&A

Q: Why can you not use the Next Record button to find client FL93?

A: In a small table, repeatedly clicking the Next Record button until client FL93 is on the screen may not be particularly difficult. In a large table with many records, however, this would be extremely cumbersome.

To Update the Contents of a Field

1

• **Click in the Name field text box for client FL93 after the word Lawn, and then type s (the letter s) to change the name.**

The name is changed. The mouse pointer shape is an I-beam (Figure 3-7).

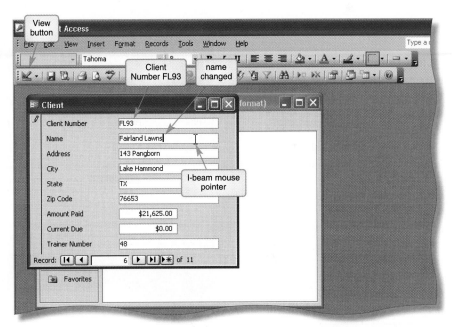

FIGURE 3-7

Once you move to another record or close this table, the change to the name will become permanent.

Switching Between Views

Sometimes, after working in Form view where you can see all fields, but only one record, it is helpful to see several records at a time. To do so, switch to Datasheet view. The steps on the next page switch from Form view to Datasheet view.

More About

The View Button

You can use the View button to switch easily between viewing the form, called Form view, and viewing the design of the form, called Design view. To switch to Datasheet view, you *must* click the down arrow, and then click Datasheet view in the list that appears.

To Switch from Form View to Datasheet View

1

• **Click the View button arrow on the Form View toolbar (see Figure 3-7 on the previous page).**

The View button list appears (Figure 3-8).

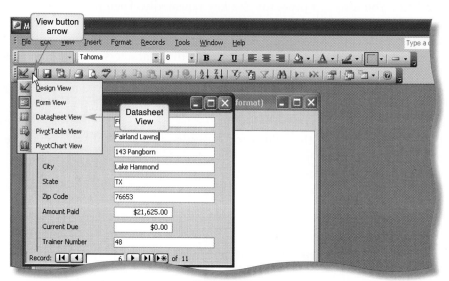

FIGURE 3-8

2

• **Click Datasheet View, and then maximize the window containing the datasheet by double-clicking its title bar.**

The datasheet appears (Figure 3-9). The position in the table is maintained. The current record selector points to client FL93, the client that appeared on the screen in Form view. The Name field, the field in which the insertion point appears, is selected. The new record for client RT67 is currently the last record in the table. When you close the table and open it later, client RT67 will be in its appropriate location.

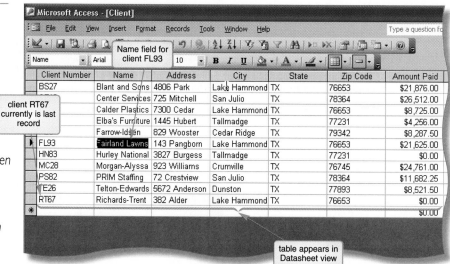

FIGURE 3-9

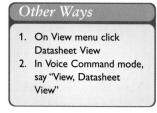

Other Ways

1. On View menu click Datasheet View
2. In Voice Command mode, say "View, Datasheet View"

If you want to return to Form view, use the same process. The only difference is that you click Form View rather than Datasheet View.

Filtering Records

You can use the Find button in either Datasheet view or Form view to locate a record quickly that satisfies some criterion (for example, the client number is FL93). All records appear, however, not just the record or records that satisfy the criterion. To have only the record or records that satisfy the criterion appear, use a **filter**. Three types of filters are available: Filter By Selection, Filter By Form, and Advanced Filter/Sort. You can use a filter in either Datasheet view or Form view.

Using Filter By Selection

The simplest type of filter is called **Filter By Selection**. To use Filter By Selection, you first must give Access an example of the data you want by selecting the data within the table. The following steps use Filter By Selection in Datasheet view to display only the records for clients in San Julio.

To Use Filter By Selection

1

• **Click the City field on the second record.**

The insertion point appears in the City field on the second record (Figure 3-10). The city on this record is San Julio.

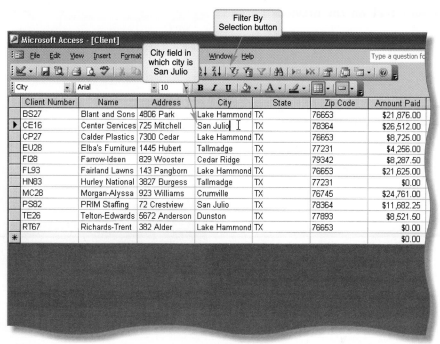

FIGURE 3-10

2

• **Click the Filter By Selection button on the Table Datasheet toolbar (see Figure 3-10).**

• **If instructed to do so, print the results by clicking the Print button on the Table Datasheet toolbar.**

Only the clients located in San Julio appear (Figure 3-11).

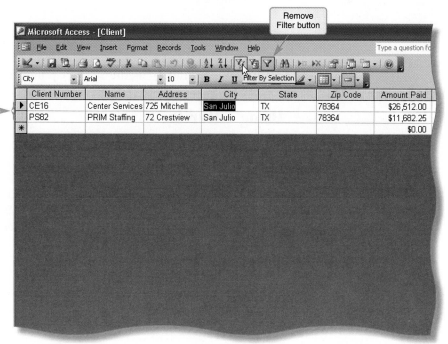

FIGURE 3-11

To redisplay all the records, remove the filter as shown in the following step.

To Remove a Filter

1

• **Click the Remove Filter button on the Table Datasheet toolbar (see Figure 3-11 on the previous page).**

All records appear (Figure 3-12).

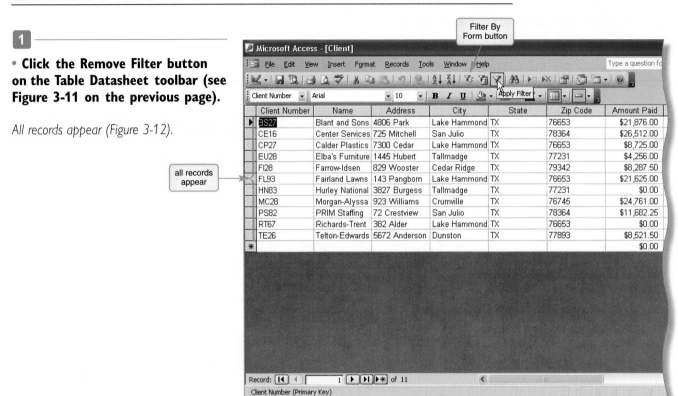

FIGURE 3-12

Other Ways

1. On Records menu point to Filter, click Filter By Selection on Filter submenu
2. In Voice Command mode, say "Filter By Selection"

After you remove the filter, the button changes from the Remove Filter button to the Apply Filter button as the ScreenTip indicates.

Using Filter By Form

Filter By Selection is a quick and easy way to filter by the value in a single field. For more complex criteria, however, it is not appropriate. For example, you could not use Filter By Selection to restrict the records to those for which the city is Lake Hammond and the trainer number is 42. For this type of query, in which you want to specify multiple criteria, you can use **Filter By Form**. The following steps illustrate using this filtering method in Datasheet view.

To Use Filter By Form

1

• **Click the Filter By Form button on the Table Datasheet toolbar (see Figure 3-12).**

• **Click the City field (San Julio may appear in the field), click the arrow that appears, and then click Lake Hammond.**

• **Click the right scroll arrow so the Trainer Number field is on the screen, click the Trainer Number field, click the down arrow that appears, and then click 42.**

The form for filtering appears (Figure 3-13). Lake Hammond is selected as the city, and 42 is selected as the trainer number.

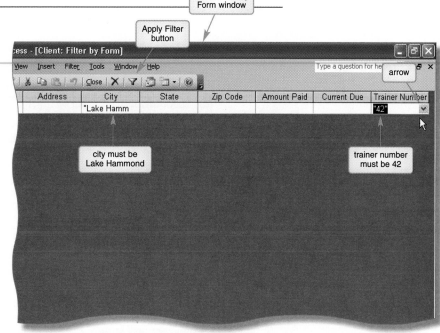

FIGURE 3-13

2

• **Click the Apply Filter button on the Filter/Sort toolbar.**

• **If instructed to do so, print the results by clicking the Print button on the Table Datasheet toolbar.**

The only record included is the record on which the city is Lake Hammond and the trainer number is 42 (Figure 3-14).

FIGURE 3-14

3

• **Click the Remove Filter button on the Table Datasheet toolbar.**

All records are shown.

Other Ways

1. On Records menu point to Filter, click Filter By Form on Filter submenu
2. In Voice Command mode, say "Filter By Form"

Using Advanced Filter/Sort

In some cases, your criteria may be too complex even for Filter By Form. For example, you might want to include any client for which the city is Lake Hammond and the trainer is number 42. You also may want to include any client of trainer 48, no matter where the client is located. Further, you might want to have the results sorted by name. To filter records using complex criteria, you need to use **Advanced Filter/Sort** as illustrated in the steps on the next page.

To Use Advanced Filter/Sort

1

• **Click Records on the menu bar, and then point to Filter.**

The Filter submenu appears (Figure 3-15).

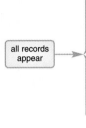

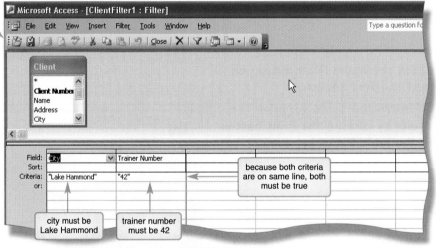

FIGURE 3-15

2

• **Click Advanced Filter/Sort.**

Access displays the ClientFilter1 : Filter window (Figure 3-16). The screen looks just like the screens you used to create queries. The city and trainer number criteria from the previous filter appear. If you were creating a different filter, you could delete these.

FIGURE 3-16

3

• **Type** 48 **as the criterion in the second Criteria row (the or row) of the Trainer Number column, double-click the Name field to add the field to the filter, click the Sort row for the Name column, click the arrow that appears, and then click Ascending.**

The additional criteria for the Trainer Number field are entered (Figure 3-17). The data will be sorted on Name in ascending order.

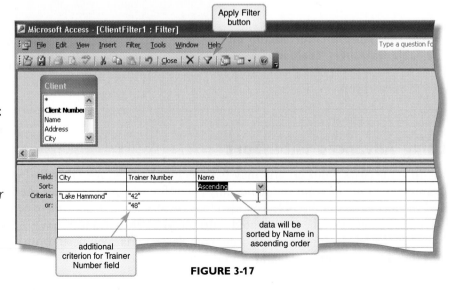

FIGURE 3-17

4

- **Click the Apply Filter button on the Filter/Sort toolbar.**

- **If instructed to do so, print the results by clicking the Print button on the Table Datasheet toolbar.**

The filtered data appears (Figure 3-18). Only the clients who satisfy the criteria in the filter are included. The clients are ordered by name.

5

- **Click the Remove Filter button on the Table Datasheet toolbar.**

All records are shown.

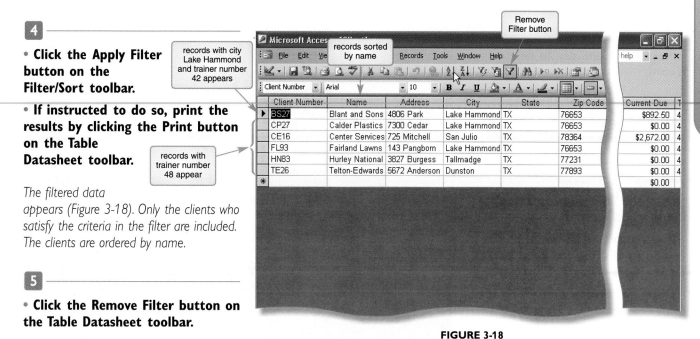

FIGURE 3-18

Deleting Records

When records no longer are needed, **delete the records** (remove them) from the table. For example, suppose client EU28 no longer is served by Ashton James College and its final payment is made. The record for that client should be deleted. The following steps delete client EU28.

To Delete a Record

1

- **With the datasheet for the Client table on the screen, click the record selector of the record in which the client number is EU28.**

The record is selected (Figure 3-19).

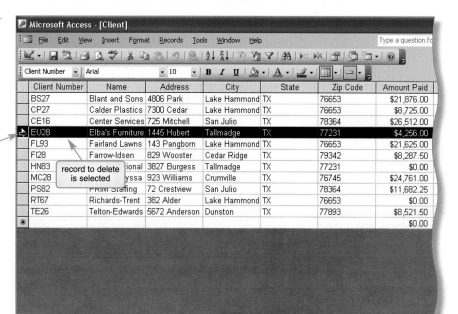

FIGURE 3-19

- **Press the DELETE key to delete the record.**

Access displays the Microsoft Office Access dialog box (Figure 3-20). The message indicates that one record will be deleted.

- **Click the Yes button to complete the deletion.**
- **If instructed to do so, print the results by clicking the Print button on the Table Datasheet toolbar.**
- **Close the window containing the table by clicking its Close Window button.**

The record is deleted and the table no longer appears.

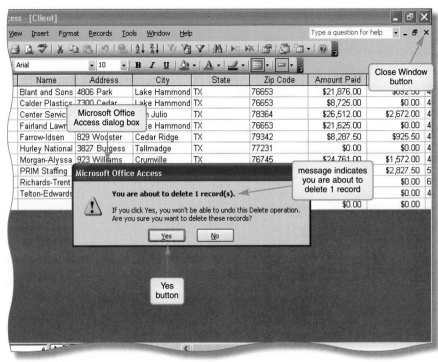

FIGURE 3-20

Other Ways

1. Click Delete Record button on Table Datasheet toolbar
2. On Edit menu click Delete
3. In Voice Command mode, say "Delete"

You can delete records using a form just as you delete records using a datasheet. To do so, first navigate to the record to be deleted. For example, you can use the Navigation buttons or you can locate the desired record using the Find button. The following steps illustrate how to delete a record in Form view after you have located the record to be deleted.

To Delete a Record in Form View

1. Click the Record Selector (the triangle in front of the record) to select the entire record.
2. Press the DELETE key.
3. When Access displays the dialog box asking if you want to delete the record, click the Yes button.

More About

Changing the Structure

A major advantage of using a full-featured database management system is the ease with which you can change the structure of the tables that make up the database. In a non-database environment, changes to the structure can be very cumbersome, requiring difficult and time-consuming changes to many programs.

Changing the Structure

When you initially create a database, you define its **structure**; that is, you indicate the names, types, and sizes of all the fields. In many cases, the structure you first define will not continue to be appropriate as you use the database.

Characteristics of a given field may need to change. For example, a client name might be stored incorrectly in the database. In this example, the name Morgan-Alyssa actually should be Morgan-Alyssa Academy. The Name field is not large enough, however, to hold the correct name. To accommodate this change, you need to restructure the database by increasing the width of the Name field.

It may be that a field currently in the table no longer is necessary. If no one ever uses a particular field, it is not needed in the table. Because it is occupying space and serving no useful purpose, it should be removed from the table. You also would need to delete the field from any forms, reports, or queries that include it.

To make any of these changes, you first must open the table in Design view.

Changing the Size of a Field

The following steps change the size of the Name field from 20 to 25 to accommodate the change of name from Morgan-Alyssa to Morgan-Alyssa Academy.

To Change the Size of a Field

1

• **In the Database window, click Tables on the Objects bar, and then right-click Client.**

The shortcut menu for the Client table appears (Figure 3-21).

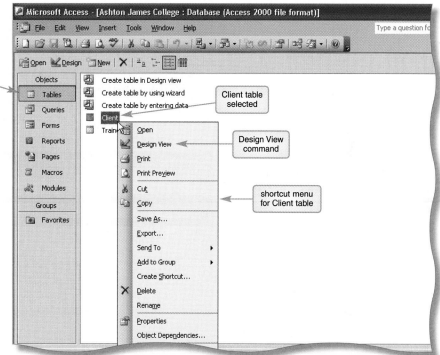

FIGURE 3-21

2

• **Click Design View on the shortcut menu.**

Access displays the Client : Table window (Figure 3-22).

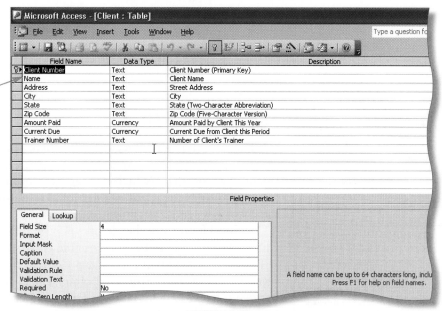

FIGURE 3-22

3

• **Click the row selector for the Name field.**

The Name field is selected (Figure 3-23).

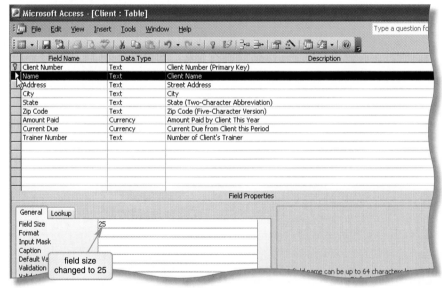

FIGURE 3-23

4

• **Press F6 to select the field size, type 25 as the new size, and then press F6 again.**

The field size is changed (Figure 3-24).

FIGURE 3-24

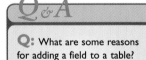

Q: What are some reasons for adding a field to a table?

A: Tables frequently need to be expanded to include additional fields for a variety of reasons. Users' needs can change. The field may have been omitted by mistake when the table first was created. Government regulations may change in such a way that an organization needs to maintain additional information.

Adding a New Field

The next step is to categorize the clients of the Ashton James College database. To do so, you must add an additional field, Client Type. The possible values for Client Type are EDU (which indicates the client is an educational institution), MAN (which indicates the client is a manufacturing organization), or SER (which indicates the client is a service organization).

To be able to store the client type, the following steps add a new field, called Client Type, to the table. The possible entries in this field are EDU, MAN, and SER. The new field will follow Zip Code in the list of fields; that is, it will be the seventh field in the restructured table. The current seventh field (Amount Paid) will become the eighth field, Current Due will become the ninth field, and so on. The following steps add the field.

To Add a Field to a Table

1

• **Click the row selector for the Amount Paid field, and then press the INSERT key to insert a blank row.**

A blank row appears in the position for the new field (Figure 3-25).

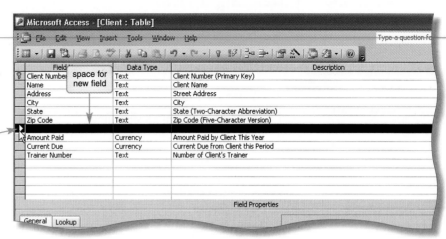

FIGURE 3-25

2

• **Click the Field Name column for the new field.**

• **Type** Client Type **as the field name and then press the TAB key. Select the Text data type by pressing the TAB key.**

• **Type** Client Type (EDU - Education, MAN - Manufacturing, SER - Service) **as the description.**

• **Press F6 to move to the Field Size text box, type** 3 **(the size of the Client Type field), and then press F6 again.**

The entries for the new field are complete (Figure 3-26).

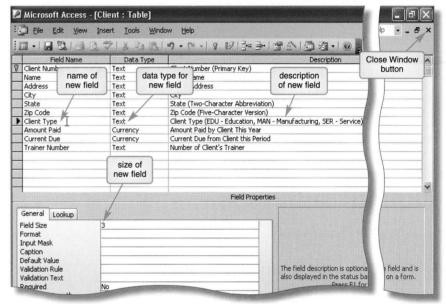

FIGURE 3-26

3

• **Close the Client : Table window by clicking its Close Window button.**

The Microsoft Office Access dialog box is displayed (Figure 3-27).

4

Click the Yes button to save the changes.

The changes are saved.

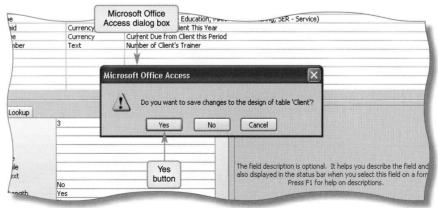

FIGURE 3-27

The Client Type field now is included in the table and available for use.

Other Ways

1. Click Insert Rows button on Table Design toolbar
2. On Insert menu click Rows
3. In Voice Command mode, say "Insert Rows"

Deleting a Field

If a field in one of your tables no longer is needed; for example, it serves no useful purpose or it may have been included by mistake, you should delete the field. The following steps illustrate how to delete a field.

To Delete a Field

1. Open the table in Design view.
2. Click the row selector for the field to be deleted.
3. Press the DELETE key.
4. When Access displays the dialog box requesting confirmation that you want to delete the field, click the Yes button.

When you save your changes to the table structure, the field will be removed from the table.

More About

Moving a Field in a Table Structure

If you add a field to a table and later realize the field is in the wrong location, you can move the field. To do so, click the row selector for the field twice, and then drag the field to the new location.

Updating the Restructured Database

Changes to the structure are available immediately. The Name field is longer, although it does not appear that way on the screen, and the new Client Type field is included.

To make a change to a single field, such as changing the name from Morgan-Alyssa to Morgan-Alyssa Academy, click the field to be changed, and then make the necessary correction. If the record to be changed is not on the screen, use the Navigation buttons (Next Record, Previous Record) to move to it. If the field to be corrected simply is not visible on the screen, use the horizontal scroll bar along the bottom of the screen to shift all the fields until the correct one appears. Then make the change.

The following step changes the name of Morgan-Alyssa to Morgan-Alyssa Academy.

More About

Changing Data Types

It is possible to change the data type for a field that already contains data. Before you change a data type, however, you should consider what effect the change will have on other database objects, such as forms, queries, and reports. For example, you could convert a Text field to a Memo field or to a Hyperlink field. You also could convert a Number field to a Currency field or vice versa.

To Update the Contents of a Field

1

• **Be sure the Client table is selected in the Database window, and then click the Open button on the Database window toolbar.**

• **Click to the right of the final a in Morgan-Alyssa (client MC28), press the SPACEBAR, and then type** Academy **to change the name.**

The name is changed from Morgan-Alyssa to Morgan-Alyssa Academy (Figure 3-28). Only the final portion of the name currently appears.

FIGURE 3-28

Changing the Appearance of a Datasheet

You can change the appearance of a datasheet in a variety of ways. You can resize columns and rows. You can change the font, the font size, the font style, and the color. You also can change the color of the gridlines in the datasheet as well as the cell effects.

Resizing Columns

The Access default column sizes do not always allow all the data in the field to appear. You can correct this problem by **resizing** the column (changing its size) in the datasheet. In some instances, you actually may want to reduce the size of a column. The State field, for example, is short enough that it does not require all the space on the screen that is allotted to it.

Both types of changes are made the same way. Position the mouse pointer on the right boundary of the column's **field selector** (the line in the column heading immediately to the right of the name of the column to be resized). The mouse pointer will change to a two-headed arrow with a vertical bar. You then can drag the line to resize the column. In addition, you can double-click in the line, in which case Access will determine the **best fit** for the column.

The following steps illustrate the process for resizing the Name column to the size that best fits the data.

To Resize a Column

1

• **Point to the right boundary of the field selector for the Name field.**

The mouse pointer shape changes to a bar with a double-arrow, indicating that the column can be resized (Figure 3-29).

FIGURE 3-29

2

• **Double-click the right boundary of the field selector for the Name field.**

The Name column has been resized (Figure 3-30).

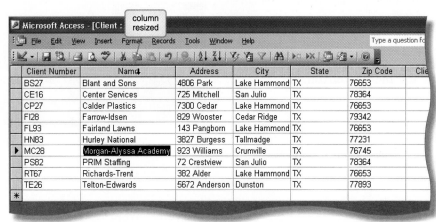

FIGURE 3-30

3

• **Use the same technique to resize the Client Number, Address, City, State, Zip Code, Client Type, and Amount Paid columns to best fit the data.**

The columns have been resized (Figure 3-31).

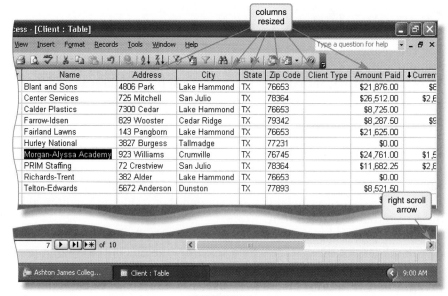

FIGURE 3-31

4

• **If necessary, click the right scroll arrow to display the Current Due and Trainer Number columns, and then resize the columns to best fit the data.**

All the columns have been resized (Figure 3-32).

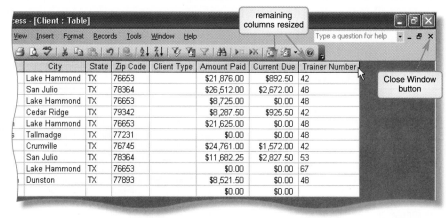

FIGURE 3-32

5

• **Close the Client : Table window by clicking its Close Window button.**

The Microsoft Office Access dialog box is displayed (Figure 3-33). Changing a column width changes the layout, or design, of a table.

6

• **Click the Yes button.**

The next time the datasheet is displayed, the columns will have the new widths.

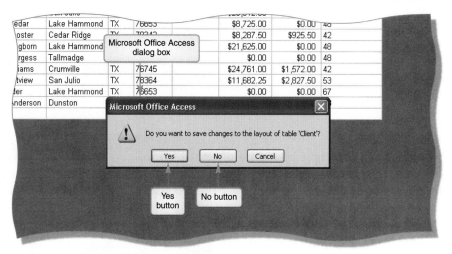

FIGURE 3-33

The change to the layout is saved.

Formatting a Datasheet

In addition to changing the column size, you can format a datasheet in other ways. You can change various aspects of the font, including the font itself, the font style, the size, and the color. You can change the cell effects to make the cells appear raised or sunken, and you can change the gridline color.

The changes to the datasheet will be reflected not only on the screen, but also when you print or preview the datasheet.

In this section, the following steps illustrate how to change the font in the datasheet and the format of the datasheet grid. You then will preview what the datasheet would look like when it is printed. At this point, you can print the datasheet if you so desire. Finally, you will close the datasheet without saving the changes. That way, the next time you view the datasheet, it will appear in its original format.

These steps show how to open the Trainer table in Datasheet view and then change the font.

To Change the Font in a Datasheet

1

• **With the Tables object selected and the Trainer table selected, click the Open button on the Database Window toolbar.**

• **Click Format on the menu bar.**

Access displays the Trainer table in Datasheet view (Figure 3-34). The Format menu appears.

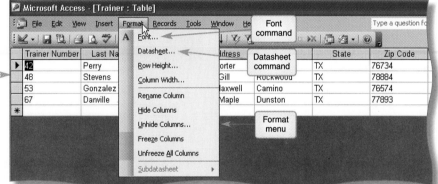

FIGURE 3-34

2

• **Click Font, click Arial Rounded MT Bold in the Font list, and then click 9 in the Size list. (If you do not have Arial Rounded MT Bold available, click another similar font.)**

Access displays the Font dialog box (Figure 3-35). Arial Rounded MT Bold is selected as the font style and 9 is selected as the font size.

3

• **Click the OK button.**

The font is changed.

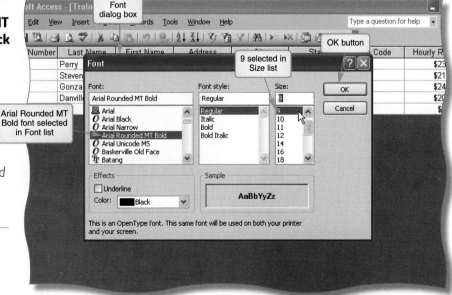

FIGURE 3-35

The following steps change the format of the grid.

To Change the Format of the Datasheet Grid

1

• **Click Format on the menu bar, and then click Datasheet.**

Access displays the Datasheet Formatting dialog box (Figure 3-36).

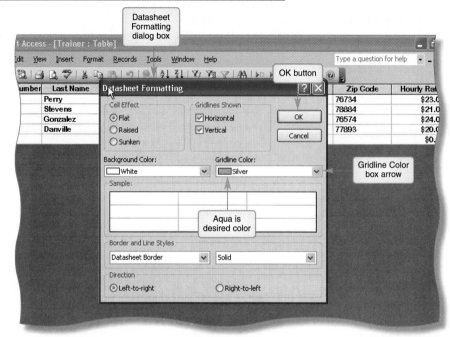

FIGURE 3-36

2

• **Click the Gridline Color box arrow, click Aqua, and then click the OK button.**

• **Resize the columns to best fit the data.**

The gridline color is changed to aqua and the columns have been resized (Figure 3-37).

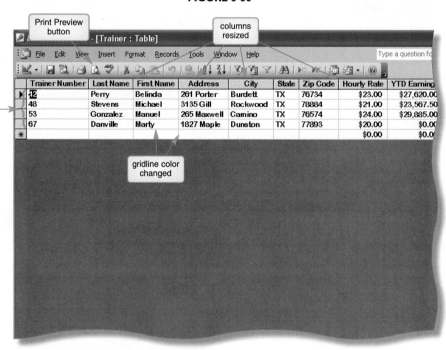

FIGURE 3-37

Other Ways

1. Right-click any open area outside datasheet, click Font on shortcut menu
2. In Voice Command mode, say "Format, Font"

The following steps use Print Preview to preview the changes to the datasheet.

To Use Print Preview

1

• **Click the Print Preview button on the Table Datasheet toolbar.**

• **If instructed to do so, print the results by clicking the Print button on the Print Preview toolbar.**

Access displays the preview window (Figure 3-38). The changes in the datasheet format are reflected in the preview.

2

• **Click the Close button on the Print Preview toolbar.**

The preview no longer appears.

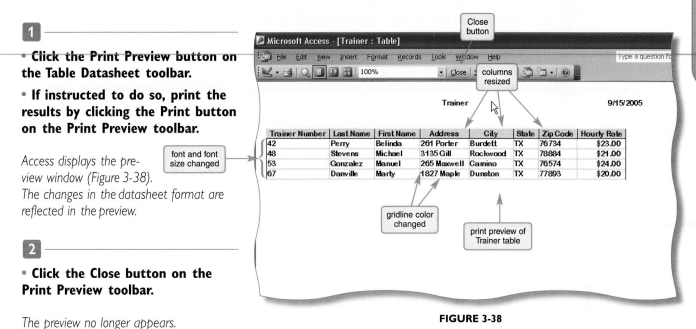

FIGURE 3-38

To print the datasheet, click the Print button on either the Table Datasheet toolbar or the Print Preview toolbar. The changes to the format are reflected in the printout.

The following steps show how to close the datasheet without saving the changes to the format.

To Close the Datasheet Without Saving the Format Changes

1 **Click the Close Window button for the Trainer : Table window.**

2 **Click the No button in the Microsoft Office Access dialog box when asked if you want to save your changes.**

Because the changes are not saved, the next time you open the Trainer table it will appear in the original format (see Figure 3-34 on page AC 133). If you had saved the changes, the changes would be reflected in its appearance.

Mass Changes

In some cases, rather than making individual changes, you will want to make mass changes. That is, you will want to add, change, or delete many records in a single operation. You can do this with queries. An update query allows you to make the same change to all records satisfying some criterion. If you omit the criterion, you will make the same changes to all records in the table. A delete query allows you to delete all the records satisfying some criterion. You can add the results of a query to an existing table by using an append query. You also can add the results to a new table by using a make-table query.

Q: Can you format query results?

A: Yes. You can format the results of a query in Query Datasheet view just as you can in Table Datasheet view. You can resize columns, change various aspects of the font, change cell effects, and change gridline colors.

More About

Action Queries

An action query is a query that makes changes to many records in just one operation. The four types of action queries are: delete, update, append, and make-table.

More About

Resizing Columns

After you have changed the size of a field, the forms you have created will not reflect your changes. If you used the AutoForm command, you can change the field sizes simply by recreating the form. To do so, right-click the form, click Delete on the shortcut menu, and then create the form as you did in Project 1.

Using an Update Query

The Client Type field is blank on every record. One approach to entering the information for the field would be to step through the entire table, assigning each record its appropriate value. If most of the clients have the same type, a simpler approach is available.

In the Ashton James College database, for example, most clients are type SER. Initially, you can set all the values to SER. To accomplish this quickly and easily, you can use an **update query**, which is a query that makes the same change to all the records satisfying a criterion. Later, you can change the type for educational institutions and manufacturing organizations.

The process for creating an update query begins the same as the process for creating the queries in Project 2. You select the table for the query and then use the Query Type button to change to an update query. In the design grid, an extra row, Update To, appears. Use this additional row to indicate the way the data will be updated. If a criterion is entered, then only those records that satisfy the criterion will be updated.

The following steps change the value in the Client Type field to SER for all the records. Because all records are to be updated, criteria are not required.

To Use an Update Query to Update All Records

1

• **With the Client table selected, click the New Object button arrow on the Database toolbar and then click Query. With Design View selected in the New Query dialog box, click the OK button.**

• **Be sure the Query1 : Select Query window is maximized.**

• **Resize the upper and lower panes of the window as well as the Client field list so all fields in the Client table field list appear (see Figure 2-6 on page AC 70 in Project 2).**

Click the Query Type button arrow on the Query Design toolbar.

The list of available query types appears (Figure 3-39).

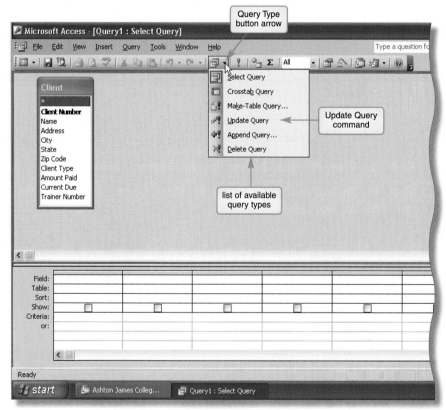

FIGURE 3-39

2

• **Click Update Query, double-click the Client Type field to select the field, click the Update To row in the first column of the design grid, and then type** SER **as the new value.**

The Client Type field is selected (Figure 3-40). In an update query, the Update To row appears in the design grid. The value to which the field is to be changed is entered as SER. Because no criteria are entered, the Client Type value on every row will be changed to SER.

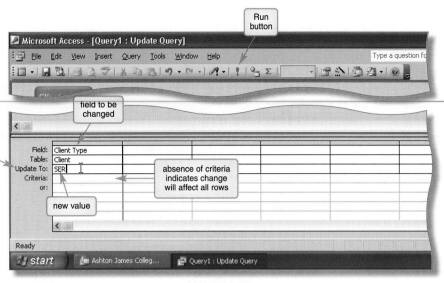

FIGURE 3-40

3

• **Click the Run button on the Query Design toolbar.**

The Microsoft Office Access dialog box is displayed (Figure 3-41). The message indicates that 10 rows (records) will be updated by the query.

4

• **Click the Yes button.**

The changes are made.

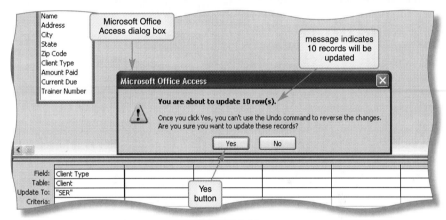

FIGURE 3-41

Other Ways

1. On Query menu click Update Query
2. Right-click any open area in upper pane, point to Query Type on shortcut menu, click Update Query on Query Type submenu
3. In Voice Command mode, say "Query, Update Query"

Using a Delete Query

In some cases, you may need to delete several records at a time. If, for example, all clients in a particular Zip code are to be serviced by another firm, the clients with this Zip code can be deleted from the Ashton James College database. Instead of deleting these clients individually, which could be very time-consuming in a large database, you can delete them in one operation by using a **delete query**, which is a query that will delete all the records satisfying the criteria entered in the query.

You can preview the data to be deleted in a delete query before actually performing the deletion. To do so, click the View button arrow on the Query Design toolbar and then click Datasheet View after you create the query, but before you run it. The records to be deleted then would appear in Datasheet view. To delete the records, click the View button arrow on the Query Datasheet toolbar and then click Design View to return to Design view. Click the Run button on the Query Design toolbar, and then click the Yes button in the Microsoft Office Access dialog box when asked if you want to delete the records.

The steps on the next page use a delete query to delete any client whose Zip code is 77893 without first previewing the data to be deleted. (Only one such client currently exists in the database.)

Q: Why should you preview the data before running a delete query?

A: If you inadvertently enter the wrong criterion and do not realize it before you click the Yes button, you will delete the incorrect set of records. Worse yet, you might not even realize that you have done so.

To Use a Delete Query to Delete a Group of Records

1

- **Click Edit on the menu bar and then click Clear Grid to clear the grid.**
- **Click the Query Type button arrow on the Query Design toolbar.**

The list of available query types appears (Figure 3-42).

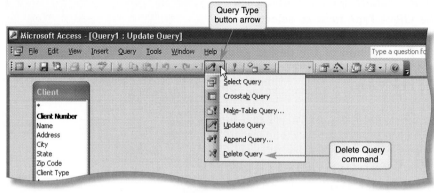

FIGURE 3-42

2

- **Click Delete Query, double-click the Zip Code field to select the field, and then click the Criteria row.**
- **Type** 77893 **as the criterion.**

The criterion is entered in the Zip Code column (Figure 3-43). In a delete query, the Delete row appears in the design grid.

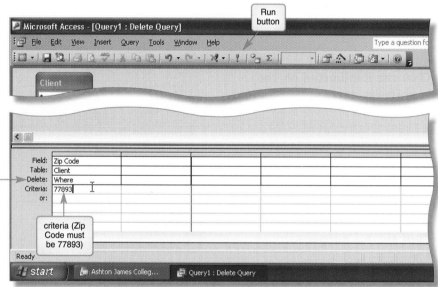

FIGURE 3-43

3

- **Click the Run button on the Query Design toolbar to run the query.**

The Microsoft Office Access dialog box is displayed (Figure 3-44). The message indicates the query will delete 1 row (record).

4

- **Click the Yes button.**
- **Close the Query window. Do not save the query.**

The client with Zip code 77893 has been removed from the table.

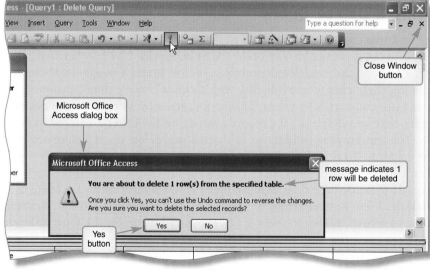

FIGURE 3-44

Using Append and Make-Table Queries

An **append query** adds a group of records from one table to the end of another table. For example, suppose that Ashton James College acquires some new clients and a database containing a table with those clients. To avoid entering all this information manually, you can append it to the Client table in the Ashton James College database using the append query. The following steps illustrate how to create an append query.

Other Ways

1. On Query menu click Delete Query
2. Right-click any open area in upper pane, point to Query Type on shortcut menu, click Delete Query on Query Type submenu
3. In Voice Command mode, say "Query, Delete Query"

To Create an Append Query

1. Create a select query for the table containing the records to append.
2. In the design grid, indicate the fields to include, and then enter any necessary criteria.
3. Run the query to be sure you have specified the correct data, and then return to the design grid.
4. Click the Query Type button arrow on the Query Design toolbar, and then click Append Query.
5. When Access displays the Append Query dialog box, specify the name of the table to receive the new records and its location. Run the query by clicking the OK button.
6. When Access indicates the number of records to be appended, click the OK button.

The records then are added to the indicated table.

In some cases, you might want to add the records to a new table, that is, a table that has not yet been created. If so, use a **make-table query** to add the records to a new table. Access will create this table as part of the process and add the records to it.

Validation Rules

You now have created, loaded, queried, and updated a database. Nothing you have done so far, however, makes sure that users enter only valid data. To ensure the entry of valid data, you create **validation rules**; that is, rules that a user must follow when entering the data. As you will see, Access will prevent users from entering data that does not follow the rules. The steps also specify **validation text**, which is the message that will appear if a user violates the validation rule.

Validation rules can indicate a **required field**, a field in which the user actually must enter data. For example, by making the Name field a required field, a user actually must enter a name (that is, the field cannot be blank). Validation rules can make sure a user's entry lies within a certain **range of values**; for example that the values in the Amount Paid field are between $0.00 and $90,000.00. They can specify a **default value**; that is, a value that Access will display on the screen in a particular field before the user begins adding a record. To make data entry of client numbers more convenient, you also can have lowercase letters appear automatically as uppercase letters. Finally, validation rules can specify a collection of acceptable values; for example, that the only legitimate entries for the Client Type field are EDU, MAN, and SER.

Specifying a Required Field

To specify that a field is to be required, change the value for the Required property from No to Yes. The steps on the next page specify that the Name field is to be a required field.

To Specify a Required Field

1

• **With the Database window open, the Tables object selected, and the Client table selected, click the Design button on the Database Window toolbar.**

Name field selected

• **Select the Name field by clicking its row selector.**

Access displays the Client : Table window (Figure 3-45). The Name field is selected.

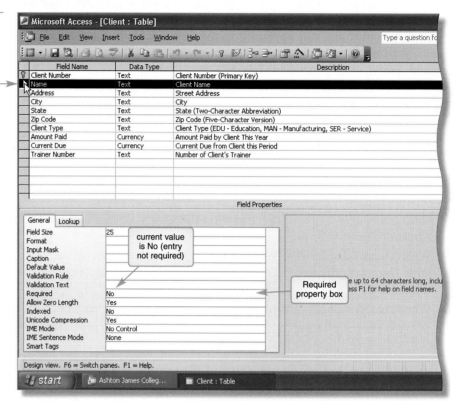

FIGURE 3-45

2

• **Click the Required property box in the Field Properties pane, and then click the down arrow that appears.**

• **Click Yes in the list.**

The value in the Required property box changes to Yes (Figure 3-46). It now is required that the user enter data into the Name field when adding a record.

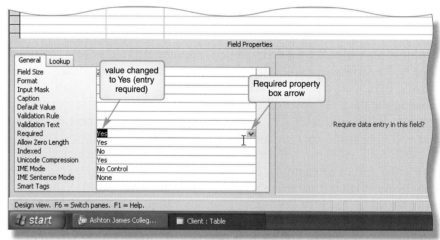

FIGURE 3-46

Specifying a Range

The following step specifies that entries in the Amount Paid field must be between $0.00 and $90,000.00. To indicate this range, the criterion specifies that the amount paid amount must be both >= 0 (greater than or equal to 0) and <= 90000 (less than or equal to 90000).

To Specify a Range

1

• **Select the Amount Paid field by clicking its row selector. Click the Validation Rule property box to produce an insertion point, and then type** >=0 and <=90000 **as the rule.**

• **Click the Validation Text property box to produce an insertion point, and then type** Must be between $0.00 and $90,000.00 **as the text.**

The validation rule and text are entered (Figure 3-47). In the Validation Rule property box, Access automatically changed the lowercase letter, a, to uppercase in the word, and. In the Validation Text property box, you should type all the text, including the dollar signs, decimal points, and comma.

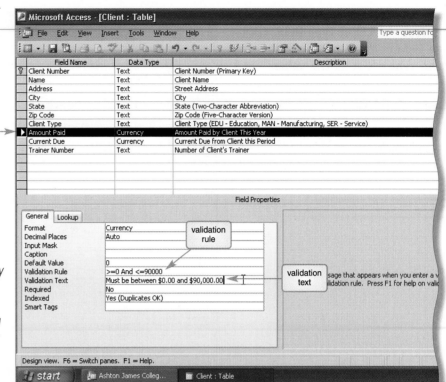

FIGURE 3-47

Users now will be prohibited from entering an amount paid amount that either is less than $0.00 or greater than $90,000.00 when they add records or change the value in the Amount Paid field.

Specifying a Default Value

To specify a default value, enter the value in the Default Value property box. The step on the next page specifies SER as the default value for the Client Type field. This simply means that if users do not enter a client type, the type will be SER.

To Specify a Default Value

1

• **Select the Client Type field. Click the Default Value property box, and then type =SER as the value.**

The Client Type field is selected. The default value is entered in the Default Value property box (Figure 3-48).

Client Type field selected

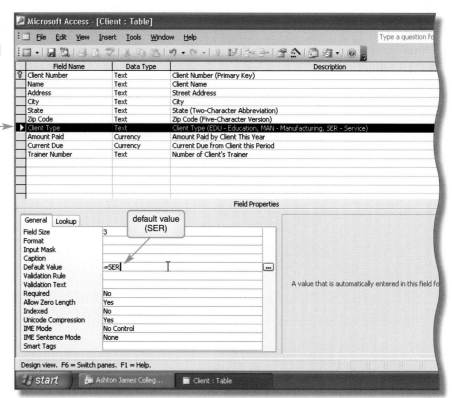

default value (SER)

FIGURE 3-48

From this point on, if users do not make an entry in the Client Type field when adding records, Access will set the value equal to SER.

Specifying a Collection of Legal Values

The only **legal values** for the Client Type field are EDU, MAN, and SER. An appropriate validation rule for this field can direct Access to reject any entry other than these three possibilities. The following step specifies the legal values for the Client Type field.

To Specify a Collection of Legal Values

1

• **Make sure the Client Type field is selected.**

• **Click the Validation Rule property box and then type** =EDU or =MAN or =SER **as the validation rule.**

• **Click the Validation Text property box and then type** Must be EDU, MAN, or SER **as the validation text.**

The Client Type field is selected. The validation rule and text have been entered (Figure 3-49). In the Validation Rule property box, Access automatically inserted quotation marks around the EDU, MAN, and SER values and changed the lowercase letter, o, to uppercase in the word, or.

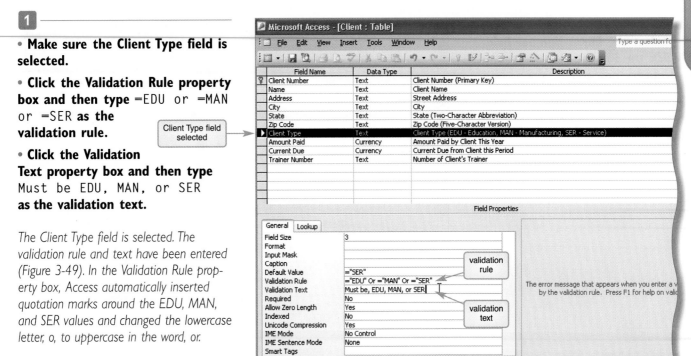

FIGURE 3-49

Users now will be allowed to enter only EDU, MAN, or SER in the Client Type field when they add records or make changes to this field.

Using a Format

To affect the way data appears in a field, you can use a **format**. To use a format with a Text field, you enter a special symbol, called a **format symbol**, in the field's Format property box. The Format property uses different settings for different data types. The following step specifies a format for the Client Number field in the Client table and illustrates the way you enter a format. The format symbol used in the example is >, which causes Access to display lowercase letters automatically as uppercase letters. The format symbol < causes Access to display uppercase letters automatically as lowercase letters.

More About

Relationships and Lookup Wizard Fields

You cannot change the data type for a field that participates in a relationship between two tables. For example, you cannot change the data type for the Trainer Number field in the Client table to Lookup Wizard because a one-to-many relation exists between the Trainer table and the Client table. If you want to change the data type for the Trainer Number field, first you must delete the relationship in the Relationships window, change the data type to Lookup Wizard, and then re-create the relationship.

To Specify a Format

1

• **Select the Client Number field. Click the Format property box and then type > (Figure 3-50).**

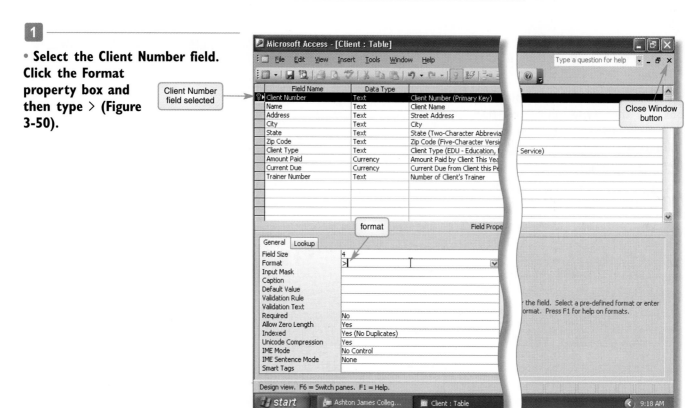

FIGURE 3-50

From this point on, any lowercase letters will appear automatically as uppercase when users add records or change the value in the Client Number field.

Saving Rules, Values, and Formats

The following steps save the validation rules, default values, and formats.

To Save the Validation Rules, Default Values, and Formats

1

• **Click the Close Window button for the Client : Table window to close the window (see Figure 3-50).**

The Microsoft Office Access dialog box is displayed, asking if you want to save your changes (Figure 3-51).

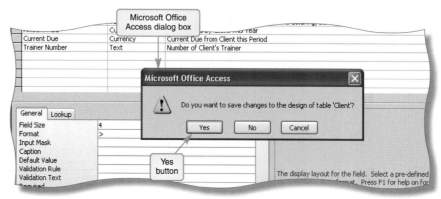

FIGURE 3-51

2

• **Click the Yes button to save the changes.**

The Microsoft Office Access dialog box is displayed (Figure 3-52). This message asks if you want the new rules applied to current records. If this were a database used to run a business or to solve some other critical need, you would click Yes. You would want to be sure that the data already in the database does not violate the rules.

3

• **Click the No button.**

The changes are saved. Existing data is not tested.

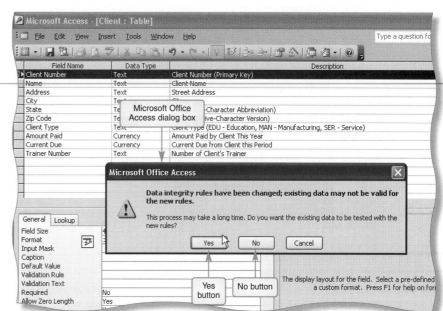

FIGURE 3-52

Updating a Table that Contains Validation Rules

When updating a table that contains validation rules, Access provides assistance in making sure the data entered is valid. It helps in making sure that data is formatted correctly. Access also will not accept invalid data. Entering a number that is out of the required range, for example, or entering a value that is not one of the possible choices, will produce an error message in the form of a dialog box. The database will not be updated until the error is corrected.

If the client number entered contains lowercase letters, such as st21 (Figure 3-53), Access will display the data automatically as ST21 (Figure 3-54).

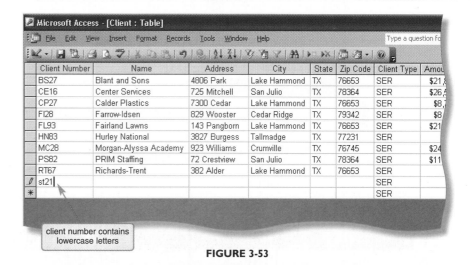

FIGURE 3-53

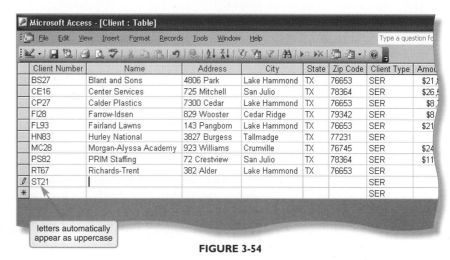

FIGURE 3-54

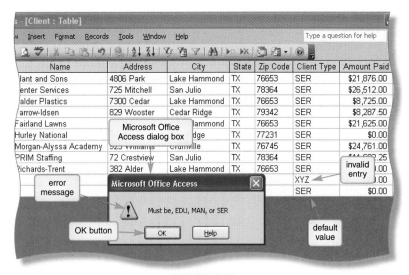

FIGURE 3-55

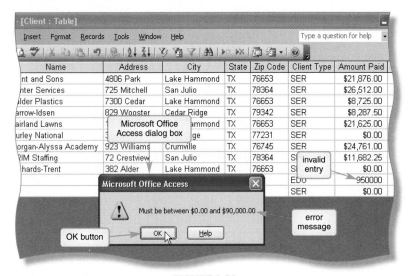

FIGURE 3-56

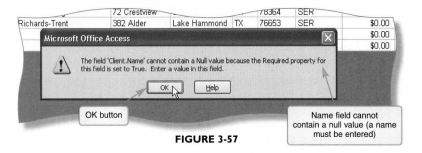

FIGURE 3-57

If the client type is not valid, such as XYZ, Access will display the text message you specified (Figure 3-55) and not allow the data to enter the database.

If the amount paid value is not valid, such as 950000, which is too large, Access also displays the appropriate message (Figure 3-56) and refuses to accept the data.

If a required field contains no data, Access indicates this by displaying an error message as soon as you attempt to leave the record (Figure 3-57). The field must contain a valid entry before Access will move to a different record.

When entering data into a field with a validation rule, you may find that Access displays the error message and you are unable to make the necessary correction. It may be that you cannot remember the validation rule you created or it was created incorrectly. In such a case, you neither can leave the field nor close the table because you have entered data into a field that violates the validation rule.

If this happens, first try again to type an acceptable entry. If this does not work, repeatedly press the BACKSPACE key to erase the contents of the field and then try to leave the field. If you are unsuccessful using this procedure, press the ESC key until the record is removed from the screen. The record will not be added to the database.

Should the need arise to take this drastic action, you probably have a faulty validation rule. Use the techniques of the previous sections to correct the existing validation rules for the field.

Creating a Lookup Field

Currently, the data type for the Client Type field is text. Users must enter a type. The validation rules ensure that they can enter only a valid type, but they do not assist the users in making the entry. To assist them in the data-entry process, you can change the Client Type field to a lookup field. A **Lookup field** allows the user to select from a list of values.

To change a field to a lookup field that selects from a list of values, use the Lookup Wizard data type as shown in the following steps.

To Create a Lookup Field

1

- **If necessary, click the Tables object. Click Client and then click the Design button on the Database Window toolbar.**
- **Click the Data Type column for the Client Type field, and then click the arrow.**

The list of available data types appears (Figure 3-58).

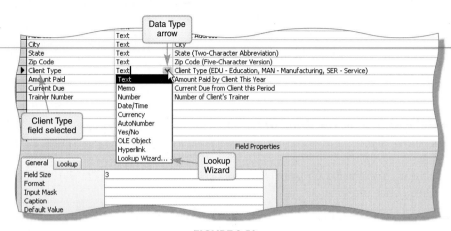

FIGURE 3-58

2

- **Click Lookup Wizard, and then click the "I will type in the values that I want" option button.**

Access displays the Lookup Wizard dialog box with options for creating a lookup column (Figure 3-59).

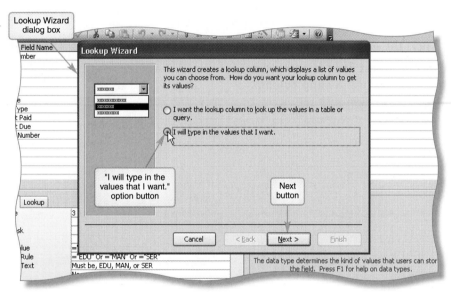

FIGURE 3-59

3

- **Click the Next button.**

The Lookup Wizard dialog box displays options for the number of columns and their values (Figure 3-60). In this screen, you enter the list of values.

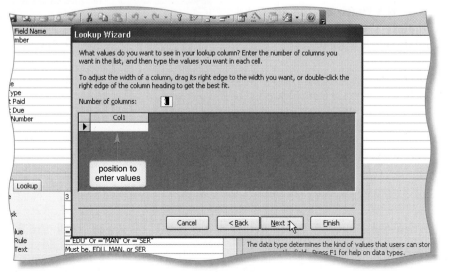

FIGURE 3-60

4

• **Click the first row of the table (below Col1), and then type** EDU **as the value in the first row.**

• **Press the DOWN ARROW key, and then type** MAN **as the value in the second row.**

• **Press the DOWN ARROW key, and then type** SER **as the value in the third row.**

The list of values for the lookup column is entered (Figure 3-61).

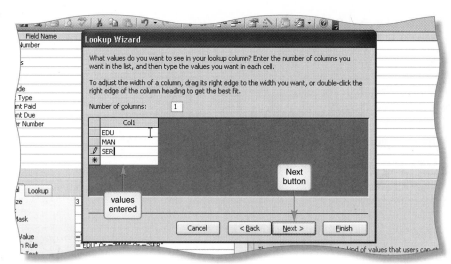

FIGURE 3-61

5

• **Click the Next button.**

• **Ensure Client Type is entered as the label for the lookup column.**

• **The label is entered (Figure 3-62).**

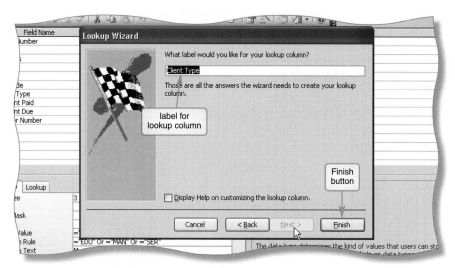

FIGURE 3-62

6

• **Click the Finish button to complete the definition of the Lookup Wizard field.**

Client Type is now a Lookup Wizard field, but the data type still is Text because the values entered in the wizard were entered as text (Figure 3-63).

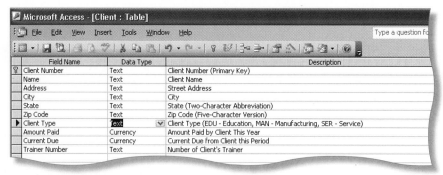

FIGURE 3-63

7

• **Click the Close Window button on the Client : Table window title bar to close the window.**

• **When the Microsoft Office Access dialog box is displayed, click the Yes button to save your changes.**

The Client Type field is now a lookup field and the changes are saved.

Using a Lookup Field

Earlier, you changed all the entries in the Client Type field to SER. Thus, you have created a rule that will ensure that only legitimate values (EDU, MAN, or SER) can be entered in the field. You also made Client Type a Lookup field. You can make changes to a Lookup field by clicking the field to be changed, clicking the arrow that appears in the field, and then selecting the desired value from the list.

The following steps change the Client Type value on the second and sixth records to MAN and on the seventh and ninth records to SER.

More About

Lookup Fields

You also can create a lookup field that looks up the values in a table or query. To do so, click the "I want the lookup column to look up values in a table or query." option button (Figure 3-59 on AC 147) in the Lookup Wizard dialog box.

To Use a Lookup Field

1

- **Make sure the Client table is displayed in Datasheet view.**
- **Click to the right of the SER entry in the Client Type field on the second record.**

An insertion point and down arrow appear in the Client Type field on the second record (Figure 3-64).

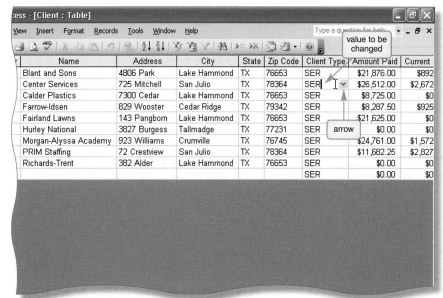

FIGURE 3-64

2

- **Click the down arrow.**

The list of values for the Client Type field appears (Figure 3-65).

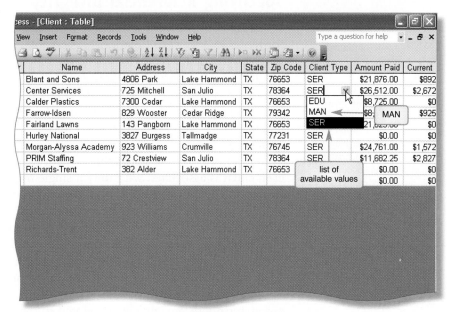

FIGURE 3-65

- Click MAN to change the value.
- In a similar fashion, change the SER on the sixth record to MAN, on the seventh record to EDU, and on the ninth record to EDU (Figure 3-66).
- If instructed to do so, print the results by clicking the Print button on the Table Datasheet.

4

- Close the Client : Table window by clicking its Close Window button.

The Client Type field changes now are complete.

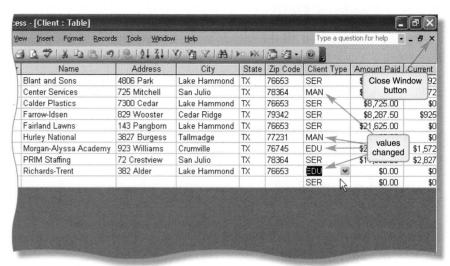

FIGURE 3-66

Referential Integrity

The property that ensures that the value in a foreign key must match that of another table's primary key is called **referential integrity**. A **foreign key** is a field in one table whose values are required to match the *primary key* of another table. In the Client table, the Trainer Number field is a foreign key that must match the primary key of the Trainer table; that is, the trainer number for any client must be a trainer currently in the Trainer table. A client whose trainer number is 92, for example, should not be stored because no such trainer exists.

Specifying Referential Integrity

In Access, to specify referential integrity, you must define a relationship between the tables by using the Relationships command. Access then prohibits any updates to the database that would violate the referential integrity.

The type of relationship between two tables specified by the Relationships command is referred to as a **one-to-many relationship**. This means that *one* record in the first table is related to (matches) *many* records in the second table, but each record in the second table is related to only *one* record in the first. In the Ashton James College database, for example, a one-to-many relationship exists between the Trainer table and the Client table. *One* trainer is associated with *many* clients, but each client is associated with only a single trainer. In general, the table containing the foreign key will be the *many* part of the relationship.

When specifying referential integrity, two ways exist to handle deletions. In the relationship between clients and trainers, for example, deletion of a trainer for whom clients exist, such as trainer number 42, would violate referential integrity. Any clients for trainer number 42 no longer would relate to any trainer in the database. The normal way to avoid this problem is to prohibit such a deletion. The other option is to **cascade the delete**, that is, have Access allow the deletion but then automatically delete any clients related to the deleted trainer.

Two ways also exist to handle the update of the primary key of the Trainer table. In the relationship between trainers and clients, for example, changing the trainer number for trainer 42 to 62 in the Trainer table would cause a problem. Clients are in the Client table on which the trainer number is 42. These clients no longer would relate to any trainer. Again, the normal way of avoiding the problem is to prohibit this type of update. The other option is to **cascade the update**; that is, have Access allow the update but then automatically make the corresponding change for any client whose trainer number was 42. It now will be 62.

The following steps use the Relationships command to specify referential integrity by specifying a relationship between the Trainer and Client tables. The steps also ensure that update will cascade, but that delete will not.

More About

Relationships: Printing Relationships

You can obtain a printed copy of your relationships after you have created them. To do so, first click the Relationships button to display the relationships. Next click File on the menu bar and then click Print Relationships. When Access displays the Print Preview window, click the Print button on the Print Preview toolbar

To Specify Referential Integrity

1

• **With the Database window displaying, click the Relationships button on the Database toolbar.**

Access displays the Show Table dialog box (Figure 3-67).

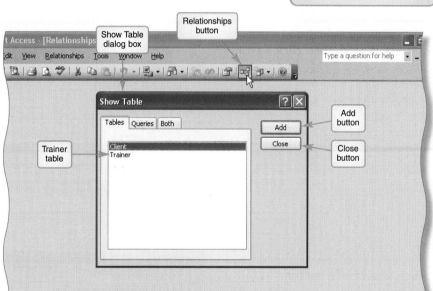

FIGURE 3-67

2

• **Click the Trainer table and then click the Add button. Click the Client table, click the Add button again, and then click the Close button in the Show Table dialog box.**

• **Resize the field lists that appear so all fields are visible.**

Field lists for the Trainer and Client tables appear (Figure 3-68). The lists have been resized so all fields are visible.

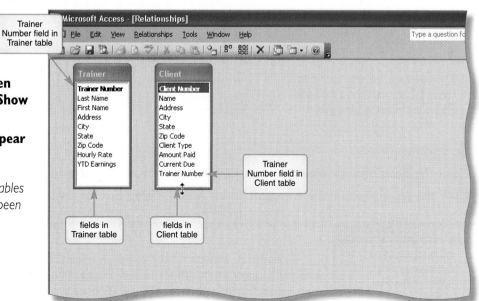

FIGURE 3-68

3

• **Drag the Trainer Number field in the Trainer table field list to the Trainer Number field in the Client table field list.**

Access displays the Edit Relationships dialog box (Figure 3-69). The correct fields (the Trainer Number fields) have been identified as the matching fields.

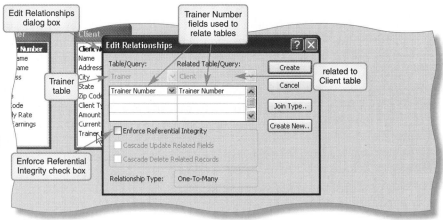

FIGURE 3-69

4

• **Click Enforce Referential Integrity to select it, and then click Cascade Update Related Fields to select it.**

The Enforce Referential Integrity and Cascade Update Related Fields check boxes are selected (Figure 3-70).

FIGURE 3-70

5

• **Click the Create button.**

*Access creates the relationship and displays it visually with the **relationship line** joining the two Trainer Number fields (Figure 3-71). The number 1 at the top of the relationship line close to the Trainer Number field in the Trainer table indicates that the Trainer table is the one part of the relationship. The infinity symbol at the other end of the relationship line indicates that the Client table is the many part of the relationship.*

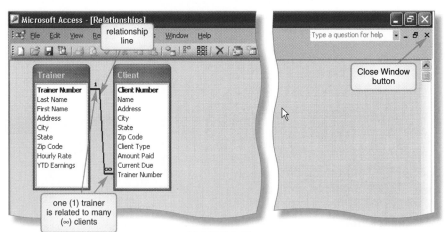

FIGURE 3-71

6

• **Close the Relationships window by clicking its Close Window button.**
• **Click the Yes button in the Microsoft Office Access dialog box to save the relationship you created.**

Other Ways

1. On Tools menu click Relationships
2. Right-click Database window, click Relationships on shortcut menu

Referential integrity now exists between the Trainer and Client tables. Access now will reject any number in the Trainer Number field in the Client table that does not match a trainer number in the Trainer table. Attempting to add a client whose

Trainer Number field does not match would result in the error message shown in Figure 3-72.

A deletion of a trainer for whom related clients exist also would be rejected. Attempting to delete trainer 53 from the Trainer table, for example, would result in the message shown in Figure 3-73.

Access would, however, allow the change of a trainer number in the Trainer table. Then it automatically makes the corresponding change to the trainer number for all the trainer's clients. For example, if you changed the trainer number of trainer 42 to 62, the same 62 would appear in the trainer number field for clients.

Using Subdatasheets

Now that the Trainer table is related to the Client table, it is possible to view the clients of a given trainer when you are viewing the datasheet for the Trainer table. The clients for the trainer will appear below the trainer in a **subdatasheet**. The fact that such a subdatasheet is available is indicated by a plus sign that appears in front of the rows in the Trainer table. The following steps display the subdatasheet for trainer 48.

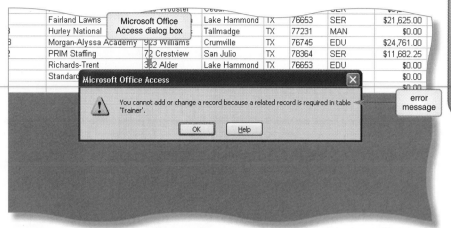

FIGURE 3-72

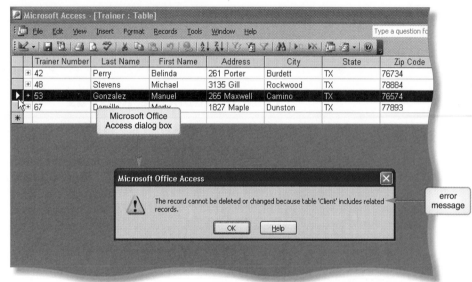

FIGURE 3-73

To Use a Subdatasheet

1

• **With the Database window on the screen, the Tables object selected, and the Trainer table selected, click the Open button on the Database Window toolbar.**

The datasheet for the Trainer table appears (Figure 3-74).

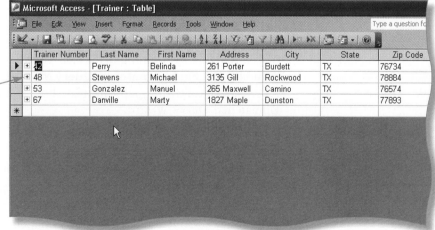

FIGURE 3-74

2

• **Click the plus sign in front of the row for trainer 48.**

The subdatasheet appears (Figure 3-75). It contains only those clients that are assigned to trainer 48.

3

• **Click the minus sign to remove the subdatasheet, and then close the datasheet for the Trainer table by clicking its Close Window button.**

The datasheet no longer appears.

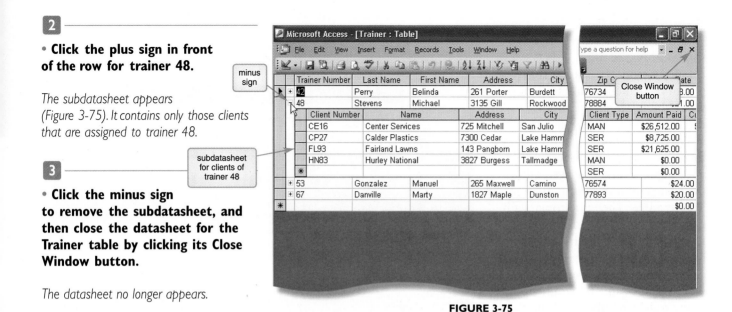

FIGURE 3-75

Finding Duplicate Records

One reason to include a primary key for a table is to eliminate duplicate records. A possibility still exists, however, that duplicate records can get into your database. Perhaps, a client's name was misspelled and the data entry person assumed it was a new client. The **Find Duplicates Query Wizard** allows you to find duplicate records. The following steps illustrate how to use the Find Duplicates Query Wizard to find duplicate records.

To Find Duplicate Records

1. Select the table that you want to query.
2. Click the New Object button arrow, and then click Query.
3. When Access displays the New Query dialog box, click the Find Duplicates Query Wizard and then click the OK button.
4. Follow the directions in the Find Duplicates Query Wizard dialog boxes.

Finding Unmatched Records

Occasionally, you may want to find records in one table that have no matching records in another table. For example, suppose the clients of Ashton James College placed requests for training materials. You may want to know which clients have no requests. The **Find Unmatched Query Wizard** allows you to find unmatched records. The following steps illustrate how to find unmatched records using the Find Unmatched Query Wizard.

To Find Unmatched Records

1. Click the New Object button arrow, and then click Query.
2. When Access displays the New Query dialog box, click Find Unmatched Query Wizard and then click the OK button.
3. Follow the directions in the Find Unmatched Query Wizard dialog boxes.

Ordering Records

Normally, Access sequences the records in the Client table by client number whenever listing them because the Client Number field is the primary key. You can change this order, if desired.

Using the Sort Ascending Button to Order Records

To change the order in which records appear, use the Sort Ascending or Sort Descending buttons. Either button reorders the records based on the field in which the insertion point is located.

The following steps order the records by city using the Sort Ascending button.

To Use the Sort Ascending Button to Order Records

1

• **With the Database window on the screen, the Tables object selected, and the Client table selected, click the Open button on the Database Window toolbar.**

• **Click the City field on the first record (any other record would do as well).**

An insertion point appears in the City field (Figure 3-76).

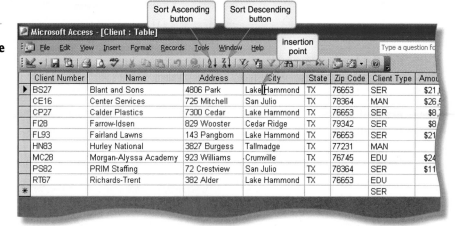

FIGURE 3-76

2

• **Click the Sort Ascending button on the Table Datasheet toolbar.**

• **If instructed to do so, print the table by clicking the Print button on the Table Datasheet toolbar.**

The rows now are ordered by city (Figure 3-77).

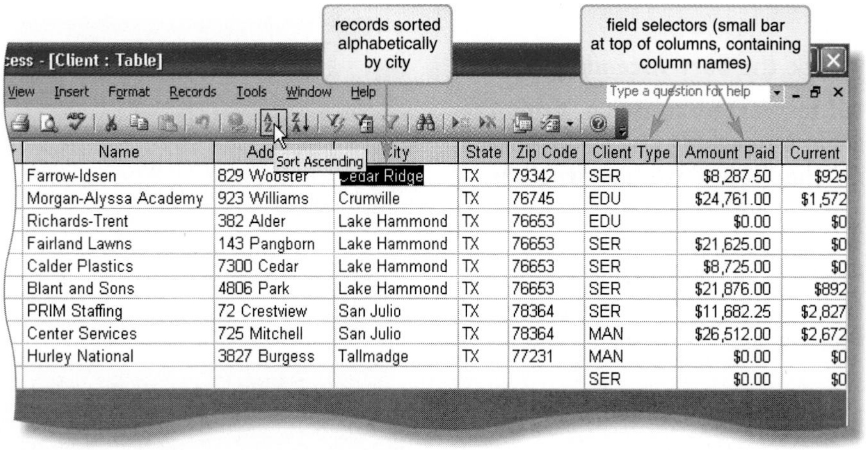

FIGURE 3-77

If you wanted to sort the data in reverse order, you would use the Sort Descending button instead of the Sort Ascending button.

Other Ways

1. On Records menu point to Sort, click Sort Ascending on Sort submenu
2. In Voice Command mode, say "Sort Ascending"

Ordering Records on Multiple Fields

Just as you are able to sort the answer to a query on multiple fields, you also can sort the data that appears in a datasheet on multiple fields. To do so, the major and minor keys must be next to each other in the datasheet with the major key on the left. (If this is not the case, you can drag the columns into the correct position. Instead of dragging, however, usually it will be easier to use a query that has the data sorted in the desired order.)

The following steps order records that have the major and minor keys in the correct position on the combination of the Client Type and Amount Paid fields. To select the fields, use the field selector, which is the small bar at the top of the column that you click to select an entire field in a datasheet.

To Use the Sort Ascending Button to Order Records on Multiple Fields

1

• **Click the field selector at the top of the Client Type column to select the entire column (see Figure 3-77 on the previous page).**

• **Hold down the SHIFT key and then click the field selector for the Amount Paid column.**

The Client Type and Amount Paid columns both are selected (Figure 3-78).

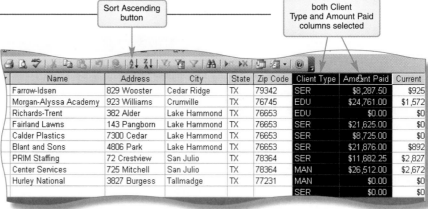

FIGURE 3-78

2

• **Click the Sort Ascending button.**

• **If instructed to do so, print the table by clicking the Print button on the Table Datasheet toolbar.**

The rows are ordered by client type (Figure 3-79). Within each group of clients of the same type, the rows are ordered by the amount paid amount.

3

• **Close the Client : Table window by clicking its Close Window button.**

• **Click the No button in the Microsoft Office Access dialog box to abandon the changes.**

The next time the table is open, the records will appear in their original order.

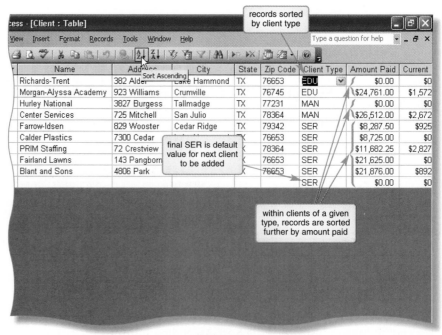

FIGURE 3-79

Creating and Using Indexes

You already are familiar with the concept of an index. The index in the back of a book contains important words or phrases together with a list of pages on which the given words or phrases can be found. An **index** for a table is similar. Figure 3-80, for example, shows the Client table along with an index built on client names. In this case, the items of interest are names instead of keywords or phrases as is the case in the back of this book. The field or fields on which the index is built is called the **index key**. Thus, in Figure 3-80, the Name field is the index key. (The structure of an index actually is a little more complicated than the one shown in the figure and is beyond the scope of this book. The concept is the same, however, and the structure shown in the figure illustrates the important concepts.)

Index on Name

NAME	RECORD NUMBER
Blant and Sons	1
Calder Plastics	3
Center Services	2
Fairland Lawns	5
Farrow-Idsen	4
Hurley National	6
Morgan-Alyssa Academy	7
PRIM Staffing	8
Richards-Trent	9

Client Table

RECORD NUMBER	CLIENT NUMBER	NAME	ADDRESS	CITY	STATE	ZIP CODE	...
1	BS27	Blant and Sons	4806 Park	Lake Hammond	TX	76653	...
2	CE16	Center Services	725 Mitchell	San Julio	TX	78364	...
3	CP27	Calder Plastics	7300 Cedar	Lake Hammond	TX	76653	...
4	FI28	Farrow-Idsen	829 Wooster	Cedar Ridge	TX	79342	...
5	FL93	Fairland Lawns	143 Pangborn	Lake Hammond	TX	76653	...
6	HN83	Hurley National	3827 Burgess	Tallmadge	TX	77231	...
7	MC28	Morgan-Alyssa Academy	923 Williams	Crumville	TX	76745	...
8	PS82	PRIM Staffing	72 Crestview	San Julio	TX	78364	...
9	RT67	Richards-Trent	382 Alder	Lake Hammond	TX	76653	...

FIGURE 3-80

Each name occurs in the index along with the number of the record on which the corresponding client is located. Further, the names appear in the index in alphabetical order. If Access were to use this index to find the record on which the name is Farrow-Idsen, for example, it could scan the names in the index rapidly to find Farrow-Idsen. Once it did, it would determine the corresponding record number (4) and then go immediately to record 4 in the Client table, thus finding this client more quickly than if it had to look through the entire Client table one record at a time. Indexes make the process of retrieving records very fast and efficient. (With relatively small tables, the increased efficiency associated with indexes will not be as apparent as in larger tables. In practice, it is common to encounter tables with thousands, tens of thousands, or even hundreds of thousands of records. In such cases, the increase in efficiency is dramatic. In fact, without indexes, many operations in such databases simply would not be practical. They would take too long to complete.)

Because no two clients happen to have the same name, the Record Number column contains only single values. This may not always be the case. Consider the index on the Zip Code field shown in Figure 3-81 on the next page. In this index, the Record Number column contains several values, namely all the records on which the corresponding Zip code appears. The first row, for example, indicates that Zip code 76653 is found on records 1, 3, 5, and 9; the fourth row indicates that Zip code 78364 is found on records 2 and 8. If Access were to use this index to find all clients in Zip code 78364, it could scan the Zip codes in the index rapidly to find

More About

Indexes

The most common structure for high-performance indexes is called a B-tree. It is a highly efficient structure that supports very rapid access to records in the database as well as a rapid alternative to sorting records. Virtually all systems use some version of the B-tree structure. For more information about B-tree indexes, visit the Access 2003 More About Web page (scsite.com/ac2003/more) and click B-tree.

78364. Once it did, it would determine the corresponding record numbers (2 and 8) and then go immediately to these records. It would not have to examine any other records in the Client table.

Index on Zip Code			Client Table							
ZIP CODE	RECORD NUMBER		RECORD NUMBER	CLIENT NUMBER	NAME	ADDRESS	CITY	STATE	ZIP CODE	...
76653	1, 3, 5, 9		1	BS27	Blant and Sons	4806 Park	Lake Hammond	TX	76653	...
76745	7		2	CE16	Center Services	725 Mitchell	San Julio	TX	78364	...
77231	6		3	CP27	Calder Plastics	7300 Cedar	Lake Hammond	TX	76653	...
78364	2, 8		4	FI28	Farrow-Idsen	829 Wooster	Cedar Ridge	TX	79342	...
79342	4		5	FL93	Fairland Lawns	143 Pangborn	Lake Hammond	TX	76653	...
			6	HN83	Hurley National	3827 Burgess	Tallmadge	TX	77231	...
			7	MC28	Morgan-Alyssa Academy	923 Williams	Crumville	TX	76745	...
			8	PS82	PRIM Staffing	72 Crestview	San Julio	TX	78364	...
			9	RT67	Richards-Trent	382 Alder	Lake Hammond	TX	76653	...

FIGURE 3-81

Another benefit of indexes is that they provide an efficient way to order records. That is, if the records are to appear in a certain order, Access can use an index instead of physically having to rearrange the records in the database. Physically rearranging the records in a different order can be a very time-consuming process.

To use the index to order records, use record numbers in the index; that is, simply follow down the Record Number column, listing the corresponding clients. In this index, you would first list the client on record 1 (Blant and Sons), then the client on record 3 (Calder Plastics), then the client on record 2 (Center Services), and so on. The clients would be listed alphabetically by name without actually sorting the table.

To gain the benefits from an index, you first must create one. Access automatically creates an index on the primary key as well as some other special fields. If, as is the case with both the Client and Trainer tables, a table contains a field called Zip Code, for example, Access will create an index for it automatically. You must create any other indexes you feel you need, indicating the field or fields on which the index is to be built.

Although the index key usually will be a single field, it can be a combination of fields. For example, you might want to sort records by amount paid within client type. In other words, the records are ordered by a combination of fields: Client Type and Amount Paid. An index can be used for this purpose by using a combination of fields for the index key. In this case, you must assign a name to the index. It is a good idea to assign a name that represents the combination of fields. For example, an index whose key is the combination of the Client Type and Amount Paid fields might be called TypePaid.

How Does Access Use an Index?

Access creates an index whenever you request that it do so. It takes care of all the work in setting up and maintaining the index. In addition, Access will use the index automatically.

If you request that data be sorted in a particular order and Access determines that an index is available that it can use to make the process efficient, it will do so. If no index is available, it still will sort the data in the order you requested; it will just take longer.

Similarly, if you request that Access locate a particular record that has a certain value in a particular field, Access will use an index if an appropriate one exists. If not, it will have to examine each record until it finds the one you want.

In both cases, the added efficiency provided by an index will not be apparent readily in tables that have only a few records. As you add more records to your tables, however, the difference can be dramatic. Even with only 50 to 100 records, you will notice a difference. You can imagine how dramatic the difference would be in a table with 50,000 records.

When Should You Create an Index?

An index improves efficiency for sorting and finding records. On the other hand, indexes occupy space on your disk. They also require Access to do extra work. Access must keep all the indexes that have been created up-to-date. Thus, both advantages and disadvantages exist to using indexes. Consequently, the decision as to which indexes to create is an important one. The following guidelines should help you in this process.

Create an index on a field (or combination of fields) if one or more of the following conditions are present:

1. The field is the primary key of the table (Access will create this index automatically).
2. The field is the foreign key in a relationship you have created.
3. You frequently will need your data to be sorted on the field.
4. You frequently will need to locate a record based on a value in this field.

Because Access handles 1 automatically, you need only to concern yourself about 2, 3, and 4. If you think you will need to see client data arranged in order of amount paid amounts, for example, you should create an index on the Amount Paid field. If you think you will need to see the data arranged by amount paid within trainer number, you should create an index on the combination of the Trainer Number field and the Amount Paid field. Similarly, if you think you will need to find a client given the client's name, you should create an index on the Name field.

Creating Single-Field Indexes

A **single-field index** is an index whose key is a single field. In this case, the index key is to be the Name field. In creating an index, you need to indicate whether to allow duplicates in the index key; that is, two records that have the same value. For example, in the index for the Name field, if duplicates are not allowed, Access would not allow the addition of a client whose name is the same as the name of a client already in the database. In the index for the Name field, duplicates will be allowed. The steps on the next page create a single-field index.

More About

Changing Table Properties

You can change the properties of a table by opening the table in Design view and then clicking the Properties button on the Table Design toolbar. Access will display the property sheet for the table. To display the records in a table in an order other than primary key order (the default sort order), use the Order By property. For example, to display the Client table automatically in Name order, click the Order By property box, type Client.Name in the property box, close the property sheet, and save the change to the table design. When you open the Client table in Datasheet view, the records will be sorted in Name order.

To Create a Single-Field Index

1

• **With the Database window on the screen, the Tables object selected, and the Client table selected, click the Design button on the Database Window toolbar.**

• **Be sure the Client : Table window is maximized.**

• **Click the row selector to select the Name field.**

• **Click the Indexed property box in the Field Properties pane.**

• **Click the down arrow that appears.**

The Indexed list appears (Figure 3-82). The items in the list are No (no index), Yes (Duplicates OK) (create an index and allow duplicates), and Yes (No Duplicates) (create an index but reject (do not allow) duplicates).

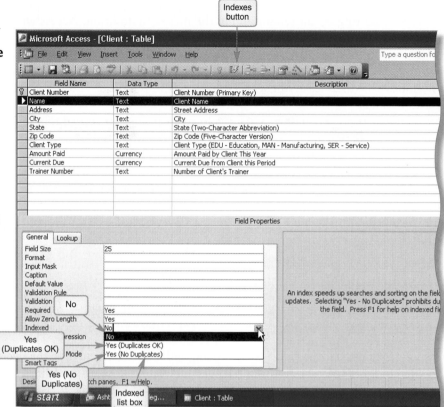

FIGURE 3-82

2

• **Click the Yes (Duplicates OK) item in the list.**

The index on the Name field now will be created and is ready for use as soon as you save your work.

Creating Multiple-Field Indexes

Creating **multiple-field indexes**, that is, indexes whose key is a combination of fields, involves a different process from creating single-field indexes. To create multiple-field indexes, you will use the Indexes button, enter a name for the index, and then enter the combination of fields that make up the index key. The following steps create a multiple-field index with the name TypePaid. The key will be the combination of the Client Type field and the Amount Paid field.

To Create a Multiple-Field Index

1

- **Click the Indexes button on the Table Design toolbar (see Figure 3-82).**

- **Click the blank row (the row following Name) in the Index Name column in the Indexes: Client dialog box.**

- **Type** TypePaid **as the index name, and then press the TAB key.**

Access displays the Indexes: Client dialog box. It shows the indexes that already have been created and allows you to create additional indexes (Figure 3-83). The index name has been entered as TypePaid. An insertion point appears in the Field Name column. The index on the Client Number field is the primary index and was created automatically by Access. The index on the Name field is the one just created. Access created other indexes (for example, the Zip Code and Amount Paid fields) automatically. In this dialog box, you can create additional indexes.

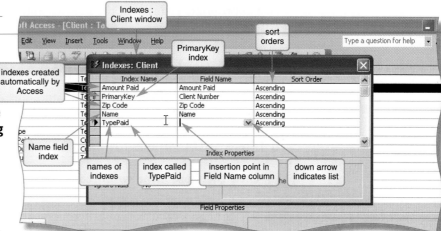

FIGURE 3-83

2

- **Click the down arrow in the Field Name column to produce a list of fields in the Client table. Select Client Type.**

- **Press the TAB key three times to move to the Field Name column on the following row.**

- **Select the Amount Paid field in the same manner as the Client Type field.**

Client Type and Amount Paid are selected as the two fields for the TypePaid index (Figure 3-84). The absence of an index name on the row containing the Amount Paid field indicates that it is part of the previous index, TypePaid.

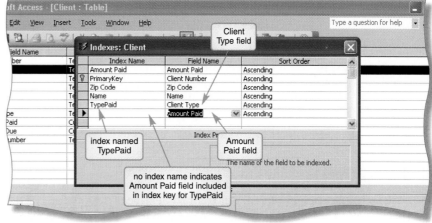

FIGURE 3-84

3

- **Close the Indexes: Client dialog box by clicking its Close button, and then close the Client : Table window by clicking its Close Window button.**

- **Click the Yes button in the Microsoft Office Access dialog box to save your changes.**

The indexes are created and Access displays the Database window.

Other Ways

1. On View menu click Indexes
2. In Voice Command mode, say "Indexes"

The indexes are created. Access will use them automatically whenever possible to improve efficiency of ordering or finding records. Access also will maintain them automatically. That is, whenever the data in the Client table is changed, Access will make appropriate changes in the indexes automatically.

Closing the Database and Quitting Access

The following steps close the database and quit Access.

To Close a Database and Quit Access

1 **Click the Close Window button for the Ashton James College : Database window.**

2 **Click the Close button for the Microsoft Access window.**

The database and Access close.

Special Database Operations

The special operations involved in maintaining a database are backup, recovery, compacting a database, and repairing a database.

Backup and Recovery

It is possible to damage or destroy a database. Users can enter data that is incorrect; programs that are updating the database can end abnormally during an update; a hardware problem can occur; and so on. After any such event has occurred, the database may contain invalid data. It even may be totally destroyed.

Obviously, you cannot allow a situation in which data has been damaged or destroyed to go uncorrected. You must somehow return the database to a correct state. This process is called **recovery**; that is, you say that you **recover** the database.

The simplest approach to recovery involves periodically making a copy of the database (called a **backup copy** or a **save copy**). This is referred to as **backing up** the database. If a problem occurs, you correct the problem by copying this backup copy over the actual database, often referred to as the **live database**.

To backup the database that is currently open, you use the Back Up Database command on the File menu. In the process, Access suggests a name that is a combination of the database name and the current date. For example, if you back up the Ashton James College database on April 20, 2005, Access will suggest the name Ashton James College_2005-04-20. You can change this name if you desire, although it is a good idea to use this name. By doing so, it will be easy to distinguish between all the backup copies you have made to determine which is the most recent. In addition, if you discover that a critical problem occurred on April 18, 2005, you may want to go back to the most recent backup before April 18. If, for example, the database was not backed up on April 17 but was backed up on April 16, you would use Ashton James College_2005-04-16.

The following steps back up a database to a file on a hard disk or high-capacity removable disk. You should check with your instructor before completing these steps.

To Backup a Database

1. Open the database to be backed up.
2. Click File on the menu bar, and then click Back Up Database.
3. Selected the desired location in the Save in box. If you do not want the name Access has suggested, enter the desired name in the File name text box.
4. Click the Save button.

Access creates a backup copy with the desired name in the desired location. Should you ever need to recover the database using this backup copy, you can simply copy it over the live version.

Compacting and Repairing a Database

As you add more data to a database, it naturally grows larger. Pictures will increase the size significantly. When you delete objects (for example, records, tables, forms, or pictures), the space previously occupied by the object does not become available for additional objects. Instead, the additional objects are given new space, that is, space that was not already allocated. If you decide to change a picture, for example, the new picture will not occupy the same space as the previous picture, but instead it will be given space of its own.

To remove this wasted space from the database, you must **compact** the database. Compacting the database makes an additional copy of the database, one that contains the same data, but does not contain the wasted space that the original does. The original database will still exist in its unaltered form.

A typical three-step process for compacting a database is as follows:

1. Compact the original database (for example, Ashton James College) and give the compacted database a different name (for example, Ashton James College Compacted).
2. Assuming that the compacting operation completed successfully, delete the original database (Ashton James College).
3. Also assuming that the compacting operation completed successfully, rename the compacted database (Ashton James College Compacted) with the name of the original database (Ashton James College).

Of course, if a problem occurs in the compacting operation, you should continue to use the original database; that is, do not complete Steps 2 and 3.

The operation can be carried out on a floppy disk, provided sufficient space is available. If the database to be compacted occupies more than half the floppy disk, however, Access may not have enough room to create the compacted database. In such a case, you should first copy the database to a hard disk or network drive. (You can use whatever Windows technique you prefer for copying files to do so.) You then can complete the process on the hard disk or network drive.

In addition to compacting the database, the same operation is used to **repair** the database in case of problems. If Microsoft Access reports a problem with the database or if some aspect of the database seems to be behaving in an unpredictable fashion, you should run the Compact and Repair operation to attempt to correct the problem. If Access is unable to repair the database, you will need to revert to your most recent backup copy.

More About

Compacting and Repairing a Database

You can require Access to compact a database automatically whenever the database is closed. To do so, click Tools on the menu bar and then click Options. When Access displays the Options dialog box, click the General tab. Click the Compact on Close check box.

More About

Backup and Recovery

Before making changes to the database, such as the changes made in this project, it is a good idea to make a copy of the database. Then, if a problem occurs that damages either the data in the database or the structure of the database, you can recover the database by copying the backup copy over it.

Q: Is it possible to compact an open database?

A: Yes, to do so, click Tools on the menu bar, point to Database Utilities, and then click Compact and Repair Database on the Database Utilities submenu.

The following steps compact a database and repair any problems after you have copied the database to a hard disk. If you have not copied the database to a hard disk, check with your instructor before completing these steps.

To Compact and Repair a Database

1. Be sure the database is closed. Click Tools on the menu bar, point to Database Utilities, and then click Compact and Repair Database on the Database Utilities submenu.
2. In the Database to Compact From dialog box, select the database to be compacted and then click the Compact button.
3. In the Compact Database Into dialog box, enter a new name for the compacted database and then click the Save button in the Database to Compact From dialog box.
4. Assuming the operation is completed successfully, delete the original database and rename the compacted database as the original name.

The database now is the compacted form of the original.

Project Summary

In Project 3, you learned how to maintain a database. You saw how to use Form view to add records to a table. You learned how to locate and filter records. You saw how to change the contents of records in a table and how to delete records from a table. You restructured a table, both by changing field characteristics and by adding a new field. You saw how to make a variety of changes to the appearance of a datasheet. You learned how to make changes to groups of records and delete a group of records. You created a variety of validation rules that specified a required field, a range, a default value, legal values, and a format. You examined the issues involved in updating a table with validation rules. You also saw how to specify referential integrity. You learned how to view related data by using subdatasheets. You learned how to order records. You saw how to improve performance by creating single-field and multiple-field indexes.

If you have a SAM user profile, you may have access to hands-on instruction, practice, and assessment of the skills covered in this project. Log in to your SAM account and go to your assignments page to see what your instructor has assigned.

What You Should Know

Having completed this project, you should be able to perform the tasks below. The tasks are listed in the same order they were presented in this project. For a list of the buttons, menus, toolbars, and commands introduced in this project, see the Quick Reference Summary at the back of this book and refer to the Page Number column.

1. Open a Database   (AC 115)
2. Use a Form to Add Records   (AC 116)
3. Search for a Record   (AC 118)
4. Update the Contents of a Field   (AC 119)
5. Switch from Form View to Datasheet View (AC 120)
6. Use Filter By Selection   (AC 121)
7. Remove a Filter   (AC 122)
8. Use Filter By Form   (AC 123)
9. Use Advanced Filter/Sort   (AC 124)
10. Delete a Record   (AC 125)
11. Delete a Record in Form View   (AC 126)
12. Change the Size of a Field   (AC 127)
13. Add a Field to a Table   (AC 129)
14. Delete a Field   (AC 130)
15. Update the Contents of a Field   (AC 130)
16. Resize a Column   (AC 131)
17. Change the Font in a Datasheet   (AC 133)
18. Change the Format of the Datasheet Grid (AC 134)
19. Use Print Preview   (AC 135)
20. Close the Datasheet Without Saving the Format Changes   (AC 135)
21. Use an Update Query to Update All Records (AC 136)
22. Use a Delete Query to Delete a Group of Records (AC 138)
23. Create an Append Query   (AC 139)
24. Specify a Required Field   (AC 140)
25. Specify a Range   (AC 141)
26. Specify a Default Value   (AC 142)
27. Specify a Collection of Legal Values   (AC 143)
28. Specify a Format   (AC 144)
29. Save the Validation Rules, Default Values, and Formats   (AC 144)
30. Create a Lookup Field   (AC 147)
31. Use a Lookup Field   (AC 149)
32. Specify Referential Integrity   (AC 151)
33. Use a Subdatasheet   (AC 153)
34. Find Duplicate Records   (AC 154)
35. Find Unmatched Records   (AC 154)
36. Use the Sort Ascending Button to Order Records (AC 155)
37. Use the Sort Ascending Button to Order Records on Multiple Fields   (AC 156)
38. Create a Single-Field Index   (AC 160)
39. Create a Multiple-Field Index   (AC 161)
40. Close a Database and Quit Access   (AC 162)
41. Backup a Database   (AC 163)
42. Compact and Repair a Database   (AC 164)

Learn It Online

Instructions: To complete the Learn It Online exercises, start your browser, click the Address bar, and then enter the Web address scsite.com/ac2003/learn. When the Access 2003 Learn It Online page is displayed, follow the instructions in the exercises below. Each exercise has instructions for printing your results, either for your own records or for submission to your instructor.

1 Project Reinforcement TF, MC, and SA

Below Access Project 3, click the Project Reinforcement link. Print the quiz by clicking Print on the File menu for each page. Answer each question.

Flash Cards

Below Access Project 3, click the Flash Cards link and read the instructions. Type 20 (or a number specified by your instructor) in the Number of playing cards text box, type your name in the Enter your Name text box, and then click the Flip Card button. When the flash card is displayed, read the question and then click the ANSWER box arrow to select an answer. Flip through Flash Cards. If your score is 15 (75%) correct or greater, click Print on the File menu to print your results. If your score is less than 15 (75%) correct, then redo this exercise by clicking the Replay button.

3 Practice Test

Below Access Project 3, click the Practice Test link. Answer each question, enter your first and last name at the bottom of the page, and then click the Grade Test button. When the graded practice test is displayed on your screen, click Print on the File menu to print a hard copy. Continue to take practice tests until you score 80% or better.

4 Who Wants To Be a Computer Genius?

Below Access Project 3, click the Computer Genius link. Read the instructions, enter your first and last name at the bottom of the page, and then click the PLAY button. When your score is displayed, click the PRINT RESULTS link to print a hard copy.

5 Wheel of Terms

Below Access Project 3, click the Wheel of Terms link. Read the instructions, and then enter your first and last name and your school name. Click the PLAY button. When your score is displayed, right-click the score and then click Print on the shortcut menu to print a hard copy.

6 Crossword Puzzle Challenge

Below Access Project 3, click the Crossword Puzzle Challenge link. Read the instructions, and then enter your first and last name. Click the SUBMIT button. Work the crossword puzzle. When you are finished, click the Submit button. When the crossword puzzle is redisplayed, click the Print Puzzle button to print a hard copy.

7 Tips and Tricks

Below Access Project 3, click the Tips and Tricks link. Click a topic that pertains to Project 3. Right-click the information and then click Print on the shortcut menu. Construct a brief example of what the information relates to in Access to confirm you understand how to use the tip or trick.

8 Newsgroups

Below Access Project 3, click the Newsgroups link. Click a topic that pertains to Project 3. Print three comments.

9 Expanding Your Horizons

Below Access Project 3, click the Expanding Your Horizons link. Click a topic that pertains to Project 3. Print the information. Construct a brief example of what the information relates to in Access to confirm you understand the contents of the article.

10 Search Sleuth

Below Access Project 3, click the Search Sleuth link. To search for a term that pertains to this project, select a term below the Project 3 title and then use the Google search engine at google.com (or any major search engine) to display and print two Web pages that present information on the term.

11 Access Online Training

Below Access Project 3, click the Access Online Training link. When your browser displays the Microsoft Office Online Web page, click the Access link. Click one of the Access courses that covers one or more of the objectives listed at the beginning of the project on page AC 114. Print the first page of the course before stepping through it.

12 Office Marketplace

Below Access Project 3, click the Office Marketplace link. When your browser displays the Microsoft Office Online Web page, click the Office Marketplace link. Click a topic that relates to Access. Print the first page.

Apply Your Knowledge

1 Maintaining the Begon Pest Control Database

Instructions: Start Access. Open the Begon Pest Control database that you modified in Apply Your Knowledge 1 in Project 2 on page AC 109. (If you did not complete this exercise, see your instructor for a copy of the modified database.) Perform the following tasks:

1. Open the Customer table in Design view as shown in Figure 3-85.

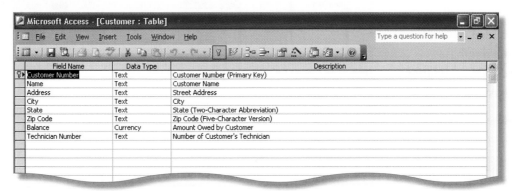

FIGURE 3-85

2. Increase the size of the Name field to 25.
3. Format the Customer Number and State fields so any lowercase letters appear in uppercase.
4. Make the Name field a required field.
5. Specify that balance amounts must be less than or equal to $2,000.00. Include validation text.
6. Create an index that allows duplicates for the Name field.
7. Save the changes to the structure.
8. Open the Customer table in Datasheet view.
9. Change the name of customer SE05 to Servete Manufacturing and the address of customer MC10 to 109 Fletcher.
10. Resize the Name column so the complete name for customer SE05 appears. Resize the remaining columns to the best fit.
11. Close the table and click the Yes button to save the changes to the layout of the table.
12. Print the table. If necessary, change the margins so the table prints on one page in landscape orientation.
13. Open the Customer table and use Filter By Selection to find the record for client CM90. Delete the record.
14. Remove the filter and then print the table.
15. Sort the data in descending order by balance.
16. Print the table in landscape orientation. Close the table. If you are asked to save changes to the design of the table, click the No button.
17. Establish referential integrity between the Technician table (the one table) and the Customer table (the many table). Cascade the update but do not cascade the delete. Print the Relationships window by making sure the Relationships window is open, clicking File on the menu bar, and then clicking Print Relationships. When Access displays the Print Preview window, click the Print button on the Print Preview toolbar. Do not save the report.
18. Backup the database.

1 Maintaining the Birds2U Database

Problem: The management of Birds2U recently acquired some items from a store that is going out of business. You now need to append these new items to the current item table. Because the business has expanded, you also need to change the database structure and add some validation rules to the database.

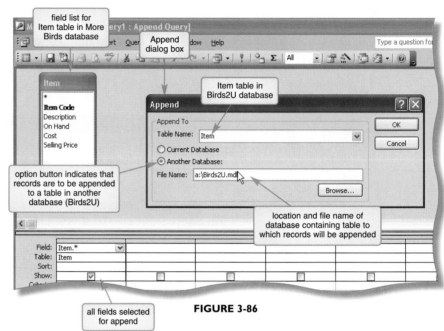

FIGURE 3-86

Instructions: Use both the Birds2U database created in the In the Lab 1 of Project 1 on page AC 56 and the More Birds database for this assignment. Perform the following tasks:

1. Open the More Birds database from the Data Disk.
2. Create a new query for the Item table and double-click the asterisk in the field list to add all fields to the query.
3. Change the query type to an Append Query. When Access displays the Append dialog box, make the entries shown in Figure 3-86 and then click the OK button. If your Birds2U database is not located on the floppy disk in drive A, you will need to enter the appropriate information in the File name text box.
4. Click the Run button on the Query Design toolbar to run the append query. Click the Yes button in the Microsoft Office Access dialog box that displays the message that you are about to append 4 rows.
5. Close the append query without saving it, and then close the More Birds database. Open the Birds2U database, and then open the Item table in Datasheet view. The table should contain 14 records.
6. The items added from the More Birds database do not have a supplier assigned to them. Assign items BS10, FS11, and LM05 to supplier 17. Assign item BO22 to supplier 21.
7. Resize the columns to best fit the data and print the Item table. Save the changes to the layout.
8. Using a query, delete all records in the Item table where the description starts with the letter S. (*Hint:* Use Help to solve this problem.) Close the query without saving it. Print the Item table.
9. Open the Supplier table in Design view and add a new field to the end of the table. Name the field, Fax Number. This new field has the same data type and length as Telephone Number. Enter the same comment as Telephone Number but replace Telephone with Fax. Save the change to the table design.
10. Add the following data to the Fax Number field.
11. Resize all columns in the Supplier table to the best fit.
12. Print the table on one page in landscape orientation. Save the change to the layout.
13. Specify referential integrity between the Supplier table (the one table) and the Item table (the many table). Cascade the update but not the delete. Print the Relationships window.
14. Compact the database.

05	602-555-6574
13	512-555-8967
17	707-555-9991
21	610-555-3344

In the Lab

2 Maintaining the Babbage Bookkeeping Database

Problem: Babbage Bookkeeping is expanding rapidly and needs to make some database changes to handle the expansion. The company needs to know more about its clients, such as the type of business and it needs to ensure that data that is entered in the database is valid. It also needs to add some new clients to the database.

Instructions: Use the Babbage Bookkeeping database created in the In the Lab 2 of Project 1 on page AC 59 or see your instructor for information about accessing the files required for this book. Perform the following tasks:

1. Open the Babbage Bookkeeping database and then open the Client table in Design view.
2. Add the field, Client Type, to the Client table. The field should appear after the Zip Code field. Define the field as text with a width of 3. This field will contain data on the type of client. The client types are MAN (Manufacturing), RET (Retail), and SER (Service). Save these changes to the structure.
3. Using a query, change all the entries in the Client Type column to RET. This will be the type of most clients. Do not save the query.
4. Open the Client table and resize all columns to best fit the data. Print the table in landscape orientation. Save the changes to the layout of the table.
5. Create the following validation rules for the Client table and save the changes to the table. List the steps involved on your own paper.
   a. Increase the size of the Name field to 25 and make the Name field a required field.
   b. Specify the legal values MAN, RET, and SER for the Client Type field. Include validation text.
   c. Assign a default value of RET to the Client Type field.
   d. Ensure that any letters entered in the Client Number field appear as uppercase.
   e. Specify that balance must be less than or equal to $1,500.00. Include validation text.
   f. Make the Client Type field a Lookup field.
6. Make the following changes to the Client table. You can use either the Find button or Filter By Selection to locate the records to change:
   a. Change the client type for clients G56, J77, and T45 to SER.
   b. Change the client type for clients B26 and S56 to MAN.
   c. Change the name of client S56 to SeeSaw Industries.
7. Add the following clients to the Client table:

| C21 | Crompton Meat Market | 72 Main | Empeer | 58216 | RET | $0.00 | 24 |
| L50 | Lou's Salon | 124 Fulton | Grant City | 58121 | SER | $125.00 | 34 |

8. Resize the Name column to best fit the new data, and save the changes to the layout of the table.
9. Open the Client table and use Filter By Form to find all records where the client has a balance of $0.00 and has the Client Type of SER. Delete these records.
10. Remove the filter, change the font to Courier New and the font size to 9. Change the gridline color to blue. Print the table in landscape orientation. Close the Client table and do not save any changes.
11. Specify referential integrity between the Bookkeeper table (the one table) and the Client table (the many table). Cascade the update but not the delete. Print the Relationships window. Do not save the report.
12. Compact the database and then backup the database.

3 Maintaining the City Guide Database

Problem: The chamber of commerce has determined that some changes must be made to the database structure. Another field must be added. Because several individuals update the data, the chamber also would like to add some validation rules to the database. Finally, some additions and deletions are required to the database.

Instructions: Use the database created in the In the Lab 3 of Project 1 on page AC 61 for this exercise or see your instructor for information about accessing the files required for this book.

Instructions Part 1: Several changes must be made to the database structure. For example, the chamber would like to categorize the businesses that advertise in the guide. It has determined that the businesses should be categorized as Retail, Dining, or Service establishments and suggest you use the advertiser types RET, DIN, and SER, respectively. Further, the chamber has identified advertisers A228, C135, G346, M321, and W456 as retail businesses. Advertisers C048, D217, P124, and S111 are service establishments and advertiser B103 is a restaurant. The chamber wants to ensure that only those types are entered and it wants to provide some type of lookup to help the individuals that do the data entry. It also wants to ensure that an entry always appears in the Name field and that any letters entered in the Advertiser Number field appear in uppercase. Because it often sorts the data by advertiser name, it wants to make the sorting process more efficient. Make the changes to the database structure and then print the Advertiser table. Place the Advertiser Type field after the Telephone Number field. To ensure that the table prints on one page, adjust the column widths to best fit the data and print the table in landscape orientation.

Instructions Part 2: The chamber has acquired three new advertisers. These advertisers are:

A245	AAA Diner	23 Berton	19363	555-0998	DIN	$50.00	$0.00	26
F410	Fran's Nails	145 Lincoln	19362	555-4218	SER	$75.00	$0.00	32
M111	Main Street Grille	20 Main	19364	555-4455	DIN	$0.00	$0.00	29

Also, the owner of Chloe's Salon has sold the business and the new owner now wants to advertise under the name, Clara for Hair. Another advertiser, Gold's Clothes, has gone out of business. Use the Advertiser form you created in Project 1 to make these changes. To show the chamber that you have made the appropriate changes, adjust column widths, and print the Advertiser table. Be sure the table prints on one page.

Instructions Part 3: Because the ad reps work on commission, the chamber wants to make sure that advertisers are not assigned to an ad rep that is not in the database. It also wants the ability to change an ad rep number in the Ad Rep table and have the change applied to the Advertiser table. Create the appropriate relationship that would satisfy the chamber's needs and print the relationship. Then, change the ad rep number for ad rep 26 to 21. Print the Advertiser table. Be sure the table prints on one page.

Cases and Places

The difficulty of these case studies varies:
■ are the least difficult and ■■ are more difficult. The last exercise is a group exercise.

1 ■ Use the College Dog Walkers database you created in Case Study 1 of Project 1 on page AC 63 for this assignment or see your instructor for information about accessing the files required for this book. Perform each of the following tasks and then print the results:

(a) Melissa Menteer recently married. Her new name is Melissa MacFarlandson.

(b) Frank Bishop adopted a stray dog and now has two dogs that are walked. Frank's per walk amount has been increased to $12.00. Frank's new balance is $30.00.

(c) The minimum per walk amount is now $8.00. The new minimum per walk amount should be the default for all new customers. No per walk amount should be less than $8.00 or more than $24.00.

(d) Specify referential integrity. Cascade the update but not the delete.

(e) Compact and then backup the database.

2 ■ Use the InPerson Fitness Company database you created in Case Study 2 of Project 1 on page AC 63 for this assignment or see your instructor for information about accessing the files required for this book. Perform each of these tasks and then print the results:

(a) Create an index on the Amount Paid and Balance fields in the Client table. Sort the records in the table in descending order by amount paid and balance.

(b) Add a Telephone Number field to the Trainer table. The field should appear after the First Name field. The field should have the same length and the same comment as the Telephone Number field in the Client table. The telephone number for trainer 203 is 555-0101. For trainer 205 and 207, the telephone numbers are 555-1243 and 555-2662, respectively.

(c) Resize the columns in both tables to best fit the data.

(d) Change the cell effect for the Trainer table to Sunken and change the gridline color to red.

(e) Specify referential integrity. Cascade the update but not the delete.

(f) Compact and then backup the database.

3 ■■ Use the Regional Books database you created in Case Study 3 of Project 1 on page AC 63 for this assignment or see your instructor for information about accessing the files required for this book:

(a) The bookstore has added a used book section. Add a field to the database to indicate whether a book is used or new. All books currently in the database are new books.

(b) All books must have a title and the units on hand should never be less than 0.

(c) The default sort order for the Books table should be by title rather than book code (*Hint*: See More About Changing Table Properties on page AC 159 to solve this problem.)

(d) The title for the book 5890 actually is Great Regional Recipes and Food.

(e) Add the used book, County Politics to the database and use 9867 as the book code. County Politics was written by Estelle Dearling and published by VanNestor. The book is a hardback and sells for $7.95. There is only one copy of the book.

(f) The owner sold the last copy of Quirky Architecture, and the book is now out of print.

(g) Determine whether any records are in one table that do not have related records in another table.

(h) Analyze the database and determine if you have a one-to-many relationship between any tables. If so, specify referential integrity between the tables. Cascade the update but not the delete.

Cases and Places

4 ◼◼ Use the Campus Housing database you created in Case Study 4 of Project 1 on page AC 64 for this assignment or see your instructor for information about accessing the files required for this book:

(a) Determine which units are located less than 2 miles from campus and have parking or which units allow pets. Sort the records by distance.

(b) All units must have at least one bathroom.

(c) The only valid lease terms are 3, 6, 9, and 12 months. Most units have a lease term of 9 months.

(d) Many users sort the data in ascending order by bedroom and bathroom. The users are complaining about the length of time it takes to sort the records.

(e) The unit that is located .25 miles from campus no longer is for rent.

(f) Alan Kindall has increased the rent on all his units by $25.00.

(g) Determine whether your database contains any duplicate records.

(h) Analyze the database and determine if you have a one-to-many relationship between any tables. If so, specify referential integrity. Cascade the update but not the delete.

5 ◼◼ **Working Together** With a make-table query, a user can create a new table from one or more tables in the database. The table can be stored in the same database or a new database. As a team, use the Access Help system to learn more about make-table queries. Then, choose one of the Cases and Places databases and create a make-table query. The query must use two tables to create one new table and must store the table in a new database that your team must create. For example, for the Birds2U database, the owner could create a table named Supplier Call List that would include the item code, description, and cost of each item as well as the supplier name and telephone number. Write a one-page paper that (1) explains the purpose for which the new table is intended and (2) suggests at least two additional uses for make-table queries.

Open the Contact Management database that you created in Project 1. As a team, review the data types for each of the fields that are in the database. Do any of these data types need to be changed? For example, is there a Text field that is storing notes about the company? Change the data types as necessary and write a one-page paper that explains your reasons for changing (or not changing) the data types in the Contact Management database.

Make a copy of the College Dog Walkers database and name it University Dog Walkers. Research the purpose of the Find Unmatched Query Wizard and the Find Duplicates Query Wizard. Create queries using each of these wizards. Did the queries perform as expected? Open each query in Design view and modify it, for example, add another field to the query. What happened to the query results? Write a one-page paper that explains the purpose of each query wizard and describes your experiences with creating and modifying the queries.

MICROSOFT
Office Access 2003

Sharing Data among Applications

CASE PERSPECTIVE

Harton-Janes Clinic specializes in physical therapy. Employees have been using Microsoft Excel to automate a variety of tasks for several years. When deciding to maintain patient data, the administrators decided to maintain the data as an Excel worksheet. Employees recently completed Microsoft Office training at Ashton James College (AJC) and now have decided they need to maintain the data in an Access database. They need an easy way to copy the data to Access.

AJC has determined that it needs to export (copy) some of the data in its database to other formats. Some users need the data in Excel, others want it placed in a Microsoft Word document, and still others want the ability to send a report via e-mail.

AJC would like to export the Client and Trainer tables in such a way that they can be imported easily to a database of a related organization, AJ Consulting, which handles various accounting functions for AJC. The users have learned that the easiest way to do this is to use XML (Extensible Markup Language).

As you read through this Integration Feature, you will learn how to use Access to convert data in the manner desired by Harton-Janes Clinic and Ashton James College.

O b j e c t i v e s

You will have mastered the material in this Integration Feature when you can:

- Import or link an Excel worksheet
- Export data to Excel and Word
- Create report snapshots
- Export and import XML data

Introduction

It is not uncommon for people to use an application for some specific purpose, only to find later that another application may be better suited. For example, an organization such as Harton-Janes Clinic initially might keep data in an Excel worksheet, only to discover later that the data would be better maintained in an Access database. The following are some common reasons for using a database instead of a worksheet:

1. The worksheet contains a great deal of redundant data. As discussed in Project 1 on pages AC 50 and AC 51, databases can be designed to eliminate redundant data.

2. The worksheet would need to be larger than Excel can handle. Excel has a limit of 16,384 rows. In Access, no such limit exists.

3. The data to be maintained consists of multiple interrelated items. For example, the Ashton James College database maintains data on two items, clients and trainers, and these items are interrelated. A client has a single trainer and each trainer is responsible for several clients. The Ashton James College database is a very simple one. Databases easily can contain thirty or more interrelated items.

4. You want to use the extremely powerful query and report capabilities of Microsoft Access.

Regardless of the reasons for making the change from a worksheet to a database, it is important to be able to make the change easily. In the not-too-distant past, converting data from one tool to another often could be a very difficult, time-consuming task. Fortunately, an easy way of converting data from Excel to Access is available.

Figures 1a and 1b illustrate the conversion process. The type of worksheet that can be converted is one in which the data is stored as a **list**, that is, a labeled series of rows in which each row contains the same type of data. For example, in the worksheet in Figure 1a, the first row contains the labels, which are entries indicating the type of data found in the column. The entry in the first column, for example, is Patient Number, indicating that all the other values in the column are patient numbers. The entry in the second column is Last Name, indicating that all the other values in the column are last names. Other than the first row, which contains the labels, all the rows contain precisely the same type of data shown in the Access database in Figure 1b: a patient number in the first column, a last name in the second column, a first name in the third column, and so on.

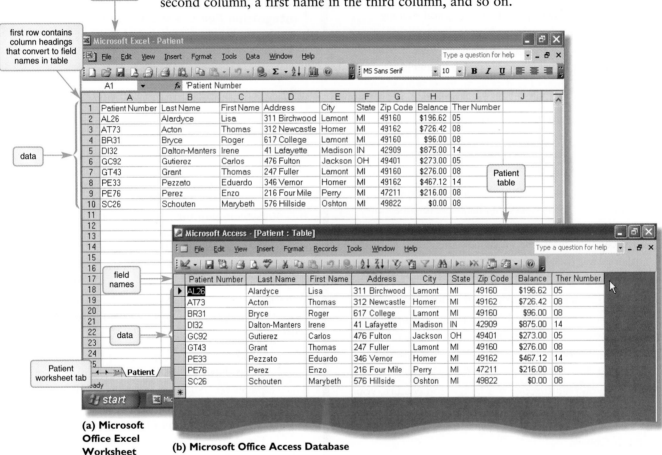

(a) Microsoft Office Excel Worksheet

(b) Microsoft Office Access Database

FIGURE 1

As the figures illustrate, the worksheet, shown in Figure 1a, is copied to a database table, shown in Figure 1b. The columns in the worksheet become the fields. The column headings in the first row of the worksheet become the field names. The rows of the worksheet, other than the first row, which contains the labels, become the records in the table. In the process, each field will be assigned the data type that seems the most reasonable, given the data currently in the worksheet.

Conversely, you can copy data from an Access database so that another application (for example, Excel) can use the data. Several different ways exist to export data. The two most common are to use the Export command on the File menu, which you will use to export a query to an Excel worksheet (Figure 2a), and to use drag-and-drop, which you will use to export a query to a Word document (Figure 2b).

At times you may want to send a report to a user via e-mail. It would be prohibitive to send the whole database to the other user, just so the user could print or view the report. In addition, doing so would require the other user to have Microsoft Access installed. A better way is to create a snapshot of the report. A **snapshot** is a special file that contains the report exactly as it appears when printed (Figure 2c). The other user then can use the Snapshot Viewer, which is a Microsoft Office tool, to view or print the report.

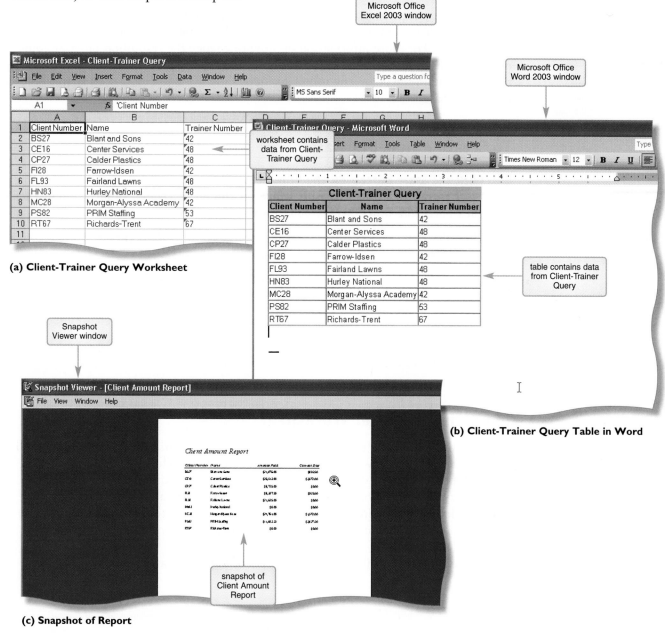

(a) Client-Trainer Query Worksheet

(b) Client-Trainer Query Table in Word

(c) Snapshot of Report

FIGURE 2

You also can export and import data using XML, which is a format for exchanging data between dissimilar applications. The XML format allows you to export and import both data and structure of multiple related tables in a single operation.

More About

Importing Data: Databases

You can use the Import command to import objects, such as tables, queries, reports, and forms from other databases. When you select a database in the Import dialog box, Access displays the Import Objects dialog box. You then can select the type of object to import. Click the Options button in the Import Objects dialog box to display a list of options. For example, you can import only the structure of a table or you can import both the structure and the data.

Convert Data from Other Applications to Access

The process of converting data to an Access database, referred to as **importing**, uses an Import wizard. Specifically, if the data is copied from an Excel worksheet, the process will use the **Import Spreadsheet Wizard**. The wizard takes you through some basic steps, asking a few simple questions. After you have answered the questions, the wizard will perform the conversion, creating an appropriate table in the database and filling it with the data from the worksheet.

Creating an Access Database

If you are stepping through this project on a computer and you want your screen to match the figures in this book, then you should change your computer's resolution to 800 × 600. For more information on how to change the resolution on your computer, see Appendix D. Before converting the data, you need to create the database that will contain the data. The following steps show how to create the Harton-Janes Clinic database.

To Create a New Database

1 Click the Start button on the Windows taskbar, click All Programs on the Start menu, point to Microsoft Office on the All Programs submenu, and then click Microsoft Office Access 2003 on the Microsoft Office submenu.

2 Click the New button on the Database toolbar, and then click Blank database in the New area of the New File task pane.

3 Click the Save in box arrow in the File New Database dialog box and then click 3½ Floppy (A:).

4 Erase the current entry in the File name text box, type Harton-Janes Clinic as the file name, and then click the Create button.

Access creates the database. It is open and ready for use.

Importing an Excel Worksheet

To convert the data, use the Import Spreadsheet Wizard. In the process, you will indicate that the first row contains the column headings. These column headings then will become the field names in the Access table. In addition, you will indicate the primary key for the table. As part of the process, you can, if you desire, choose not to include all the fields from the worksheet in the resulting table. You should be aware that some of the steps might take a significant amount of time for Access to execute.

The following steps illustrate the process of importing an Excel worksheet.

To Import an Excel Worksheet

1

- **With the Harton-Janes Clinic database open, right-click in the open area of the Database window.**

The shortcut menu appears (Figure 3).

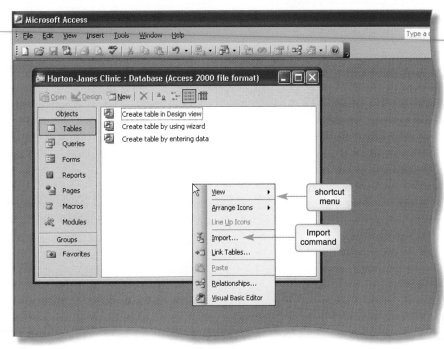

FIGURE 3

2

- **Click Import.**
- **When Access displays the Import dialog box, click the Files of type box arrow and then click Microsoft Excel.**
- **If necessary, select 3½ Floppy (A:) in the Look in list.**
- **Make sure the Patient workbook is selected, and then click the Import button.**
- **When Access displays the Import Spreadsheet Wizard dialog box, if necessary, click Show Worksheets and then click the Next button.**
- **Be sure the Patient worksheet is selected, and then click the Next button.**

Access displays the Import Spreadsheet Wizard dialog box requesting you to indicate whether the first row contains column headings (Figure 4).

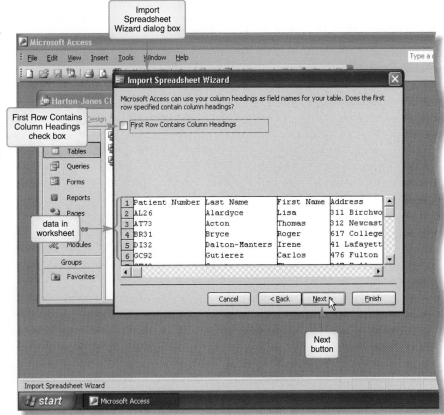

FIGURE 4

3

• **If necessary, click First Row Contains Column Headings to select it.**

• **Click the Next button.**

The Import Spreadsheet Wizard dialog box displays options for storing data in a new table or in an existing table (Figure 5).

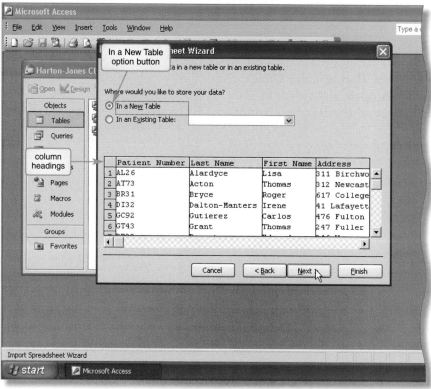

FIGURE 5

4

• **If necessary, click In a New Table to select it and then click the Next button.**

• **Because the Field Options need not be specified, click the Next button.**

The Import Spreadsheet Wizard dialog box displays options for defining a primary key for the new Access table (Figure 6). Options allow Access to add a special field to serve as the primary key, allow the user to choose an existing field to serve as the primary key, or allow the user to indicate no primary key. Most of the time, one of the existing fields will serve as the primary key. In this worksheet, for example, the Patient Number serves as the primary key.

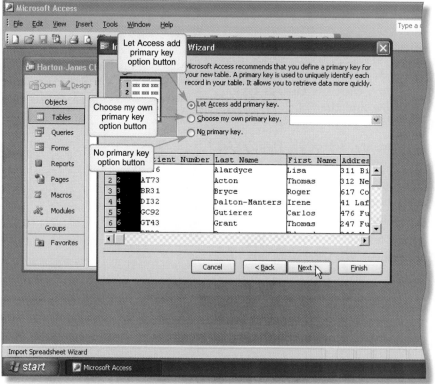

FIGURE 6

5

• **Click Choose my own primary key.**

• **Because the Patient Number field, which is the correct field, is already selected as the primary key, click the Next button. (If some other field were to be the primary key, you could click the down arrow and select the other field from the list of available fields.)**

• **Be sure Patient appears in the Import to Table text box.**

• **Click the Finish button.**

The worksheet is converted into an Access table named Patient. When the process is completed, Access displays the Import Spreadsheet Wizard dialog box (Figure 7).

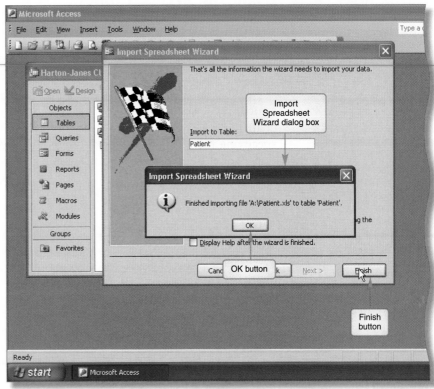

FIGURE 7

6

• **Click the OK button.**

Access has created the table (Figure 8). The table name appears in the Database window.

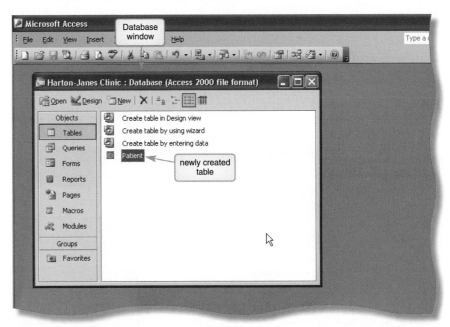

FIGURE 8

> ### Other Ways
>
> 1. On File menu click Get External Data, click Import
> 2. In Voice Command mode, say "File, Get External Data, Import"

More About

The Access Help System

Need Help? It is no further than the Type a question for help box on the menu bar in the upper-right corner of the window. Click the box that contains the text, Type a question for help (Figure 1b on page AC 174), type `help`, and then press the ENTER key. Access responds with a list of topics you can click to learn about obtaining help on any Access-related topic. To find out what is new in Access 2003, type `what is new in Access` in the Type a question for help box.

Using the Access Table

After the Access version of the table has been created, you can treat it as you would any other table. You can open the table in Datasheet view (Figure 1b on page AC 174). You can make changes to the data. You can create queries that use the data in the table.

By clicking Design View on the table's shortcut menu, you can view the table's structure and make any necessary changes to the structure. The changes may include changing field sizes and types (for those that may not be correct), creating indexes, specifying the primary key, or adding additional fields. If you have imported multiple tables that are to be related, you will need to relate the tables. To accomplish any of these tasks, use the same steps you used in Project 3. In the Patient table shown in Figure 1b, for example, the columns have been resized to best fit the data.

Linking versus Importing

When an external table or worksheet is imported, or converted, into an Access database, a copy of the data is placed as a table in the database. The original data still exists, just as it did before, but no further connection exists between it and the data in the database. Changes to the original data do not affect the data in the database. Likewise, changes in the database do not affect the original data.

It also is possible to **link** data stored in a variety of formats to Access databases by selecting Link instead of Import on the shortcut menu. (The available formats include several other database management systems as well as a variety of nondatabase formats, including Excel worksheets.) With linking, the connection is maintained.

When an Excel worksheet is linked, for example, the worksheet is not stored in the database. Instead Access simply establishes a connection to the worksheet so you can view or edit the data in either Access or Excel. Any change made in either one will be immediately visible in the other. For example, if you would change an address in Access and then view the worksheet in Excel, you would see the new address. If you add a new row in Excel and then view the table in Access, the row would appear as a new record.

To identify that a table is linked to other data, Access places an arrow in front of the table (Figure 9). In addition, the Excel icon in front of the name identifies the fact that the data is linked to an Excel worksheet.

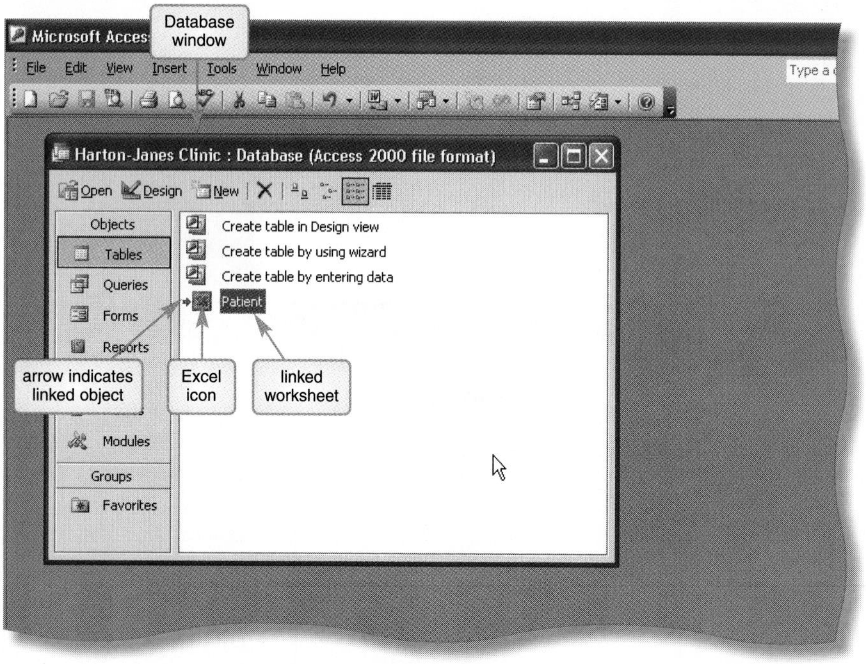

FIGURE 9

After you link tables between a worksheet and a database or between two databases, you can modify many of the linked table's features. For example, you can rename the linked table, set view properties, and set links between tables in queries. If you move, rename, or modify linked tables, you can use the **Linked Table Manager** to update the links. To do so, use the Tools menu, click Database Utilities, and then click Linked Table Manager. The Linked Table Manager dialog box that appears includes instructions on how to update the links.

Closing the Database

The following step shows how to close the database by closing its Database window.

To Close a Database

1 Click the Close button for the Harton-Janes Clinic : Database window.

Copy Data from Access to Other Applications

Exporting is the process of copying database objects to another database, to a worksheet, or to some other format so another application (for example, Excel) can use the data. Several ways exist for exporting data. The two most common are to use the Export command, which you will use to export a query to Excel, and to use drag-and-drop, which you will use to export a query to a Word document. You also will use the Export command to export a report as a snapshot.

Opening the Database

Before exporting the Ashton James College data, you first must open the database. The following steps show how to open a database.

To Open a Database

1 Click the Open button on the Database toolbar.

2 If necessary, click the Look in box arrow and then click 3½ Floppy (A:). Click Ashton James College, the database modified in Project 3. (If you did not complete the steps in Project 3, see your instructor for a copy of the database.)

3 Click the Open button in the Open dialog box. If a Security Warning dialog box appears, click the Open button.

Access opens the Ashton James College database in the Database window.

Using the Export Command to Export Data to Excel

One way to export data to Excel, as well as to a variety of other formats, is to select the database object to be exported and then select the Export command on the shortcut menu. After you have selected the command, indicate the file type (for example, Microsoft Excel 97-2003) and then click the Save button. For some of the formats, including Excel, you can select Save formatted, in which case the export process will attempt to preserve as much of the Access formatting of the data as possible. You also can select Autostart in which case, the application receiving the data will start automatically once the data is exported. The resulting data then will appear in the application.

The steps on the next page show how to use the Export command to export the Client-Trainer Query to Excel.

Q: How could you export records from a table?

A: The process of exporting records from a table is identical to that of exporting records from a query. Simply select the Tables object and then the table containing the records to be exported before selecting the Export command. All records and fields from the table then will be exported.

To Use the Export Command to Export Data to Excel

• **Click Queries on the Objects bar, and then right-click Client-Trainer Query.**

The shortcut menu appears (Figure 10).

2

• **Click Export.**

• **If necessary, click the Save in box arrow and then click 3½ Floppy (A:).**

• **Click the Save as type box arrow, and then click Microsoft Excel 97-2003 in the Save as type list.**

• **Be sure the file name is Client-Trainer Query, and then click the Export button.**

The worksheet is created.

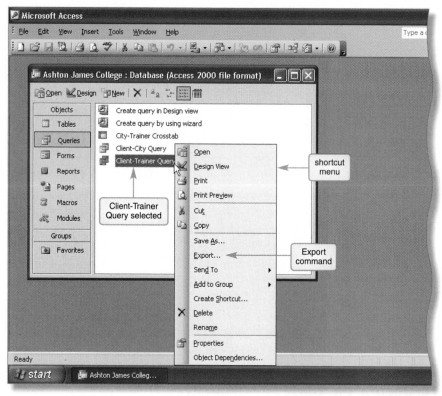

FIGURE 10

To view the worksheet, you could open it in Excel. You then could make any changes to it. For example, you could resize the columns to best fit the data by double-clicking the right edge of the column heading. Figure 2a on page AC 175 shows the worksheet displayed in Excel with the columns resized.

Using Drag-and-Drop to Export Data to Word

When using the Export command, Microsoft Word is not one of the available file types. You would need to select one of the file types that can be imported into Word, export from Access to the selected file type, and then import the file that is created into Word. A simpler way to export to Word is to use the drag-and-drop method. In this method, both Access and Word must be open simultaneously. You then drag the object to be imported from Access to the Word document. The following steps show how to export the Client-Trainer Query to Word using the drag-and-drop method.

Q: Can you use drag-and-drop to export data to Excel?

A: Yes. You can use drag-and-drop to export data to Excel just as you can to export data to Word. Be sure that Excel is running instead of Word. Drag the table or query from the Database window in Access to the Excel worksheet. The records will be converted to rows in the worksheet and the fields will be converted to columns.

To Use Drag-and-Drop to Export Data to Word

- **Click the Start button on the Windows taskbar, point to All Programs on the Start menu, point to Microsoft Office on the All Programs submenu, and then click Microsoft Office Word 2003 on the Microsoft Office submenu.**

- **Close the Getting Started task pane.**

- **Click the Microsoft Access button on the taskbar to return to Microsoft Access.**

- **Click the Restore Down button or resize the Access window so the Access window does not occupy the full screen.**

- **Be sure the Queries object is selected.**

- **Drag the Client-Trainer Query icon to the upper-left corner of the Word document. Do not release the mouse button.**

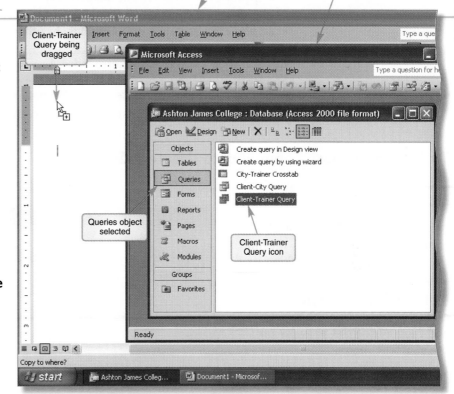

FIGURE 11

Microsoft Office Word is displayed in a maximized window (Figure 11). Microsoft Office Access is displayed in a resized, smaller window. The Queries object is selected and the Client-Trainer Query is selected. The mouse pointer indicates that the Client-Trainer Query is being dragged to Word.

- **Release the mouse button and then click the Save button on the Standard toolbar in Microsoft Word.**

- **Type** Client-Trainer Query **in the File name text box, and then click the Save button in the Save As dialog box.**

- **Click in the Word window to deselect the table.**

The data from the query is inserted in the Word document. The title of the query appears in bold at the top of the document. The data is inserted as a Word table. The document is saved. It looks like the one shown in Figure 2b on page AC 175.

- **Quit Word by clicking its Close button.**

- **Maximize the Microsoft Office Access window by double-clicking its title bar.**

Microsoft Word no longer appears. The file is saved and available for use.

Using the Export Command to Create a Snapshot

If you want to send a report to someone via e-mail, the simplest way is to create a snapshot of the report. The **snapshot** is stored in a separate file with an extension of snp. This file contains all the details of the report, including fonts, effects (for example, bold or italic), and graphics. In other words, the contents of the snapshot file look precisely like the report. The snapshot file can be viewed by anyone having the Snapshot Viewer; Microsoft Office Access 2003 is *not* required. You can use the **Snapshot Viewer** to e-mail the snapshot; the recipient can use the Snapshot Viewer to view or print the snapshot.

The following steps illustrate how to create a snapshot.

To Use the Export Command to Create a Snapshot

• **If the Microsoft Access Database window is not maximized, maximize the window by double-clicking its title bar.**

• **Click the Reports object, right-click the Client Amount Report, and then click Print Preview on the shortcut menu.**

• **Right-click the preview of the report.**

Access displays the Client Amount Report window with a preview of the report (Figure 12). The shortcut menu appears.

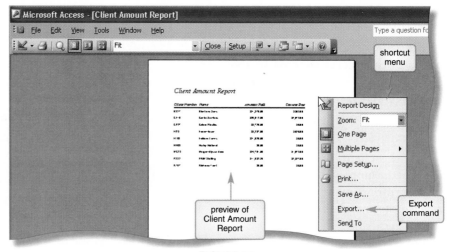

FIGURE 12

• **Click Export.**

• **If necessary, click the Save in box arrow and then click 3½ Floppy (A:).**

• **Click the Save as type box arrow, select Snapshot Format, be sure the Autostart check box is checked, and then click the Export button.**

• **If a Microsoft Office Access dialog box is displayed asking if you want to install Snapshot Viewer, click the No button and see your instructor.**

The snapshot of the report is created. It looks similar to the one in Figure 2c on page AC 175.

3

• **Click the Close button for the Snapshot Viewer - [Client Amount Report] window.**

• **Click the Close button on the Print Preview toolbar.**

The Snapshot Viewer and Print Preview windows close. Access displays the Database window.

You can e-mail the snapshot to other users. The other users can use the Snapshot Viewer to view the report online or to print the report.

XML

Just as Hypertext Markup Language (HTML) is the standard language for creating and displaying Web pages, **Extensible Markup Language** (**XML**) is the standard language for describing and delivering data on the Web. XML is a data interchange format that allows you to exchange data between dissimilar systems or applications. With XML, you can describe both the data and the structure (**schema**) of the data. You can export tables, queries, forms, or reports.

When exporting XML data, you can choose to export multiple related tables in a single operation to a single XML file. If you later import this XML data to another database, you will import all the tables in a single operation. Thus, the new database would contain each of the tables. All the fields would have all the correct data types and sizes. The primary keys would be correct, and the tables would be related exactly as they were in the original database.

Exporting XML Data

To export XML data, you use the same Export command you used to export to other formats. You then select XML as the Save as type. You indicate whether to just save the data or to save both the data and the schema (that is, the structure). If you have made changes to the appearance of the data, such as changing the font, and want these changes saved as well, you save what is termed the **presentation**. The data is saved in a file with the XML extension, the schema is saved in a file with the XSD extension, and the presentation is saved in a file with the XSL extension. The default choice, which usually is appropriate, is to save both the data and schema, but not the presentation. If multiple tables are related, such as the Client and Trainer tables in the Ashton James College data, you can export both tables to a single file.

The following steps export both the Client and Trainer tables to a single XML file called Client. The steps save the data and the schema, but do not save the presentation.

More About

The Quick Reference

For a table that lists how to complete tasks covered in this book using the mouse, menu, shortcut menu, and keyboard, see the Quick Reference Summary at the back of this book, or visit the Access 2003 Quick Reference Web page (scsite.com/ac2003/qr).

Q & A

Q: What are some advantages of report snapshots?

A: When you use Access to create a report snapshot, you can distribute reports electronically to users both inside and outside your organization. You do not need to photocopy or mail printed reports. Instead, users can view the reports online and print only the reports they need.

To Export XML Data

1

- **Click the Tables object, and then right-click Client.**

The shortcut menu for the Client table appears (Figure 13).

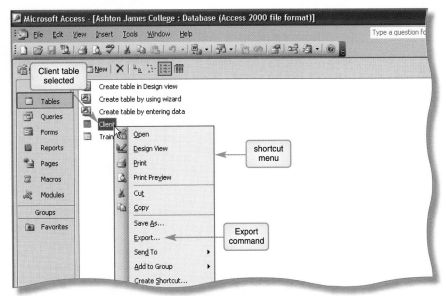

FIGURE 13

2

• **Click Export on the shortcut menu.**

• **Click the Save as type box arrow, scroll down, and then click XML in the list.**

• **If necessary, select 3½ Floppy (A:) in the Save in list.**

Access displays the Export Table 'Client' As dialog box (Figure 14). The file name is Client and the Save as type is XML.

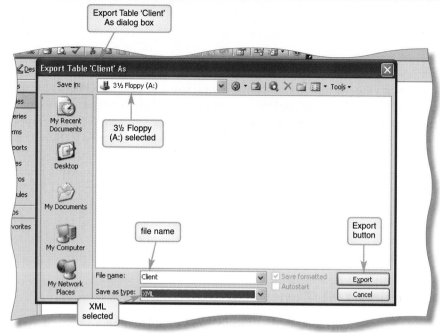

FIGURE 14

3

• **Click the Export button.**

Access displays the Export XML dialog box (Figure 15). The current selections call for the data and schema to be exported. The presentation will not be exported.

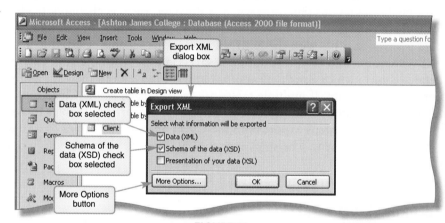

FIGURE 15

4

• **Click the More Options button.**

Access displays the Export XML dialog box (Figure 16). The Data tab is selected.

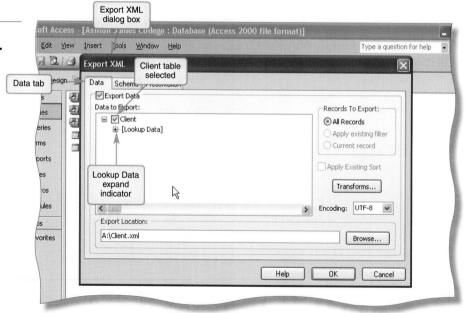

FIGURE 16

5

• **Click the expand indicator (the plus sign) to the left of [Lookup Data], and then click the Trainer check box to select the Trainer table.**

Both the Client table and the Trainer table are selected (Figure 17). The export location is A:\Client.xml.

6

• **Click the OK button.**

• **Click the Close button for the Microsoft Access [Ashton James College : Database (Access 2000 file format)] window.**

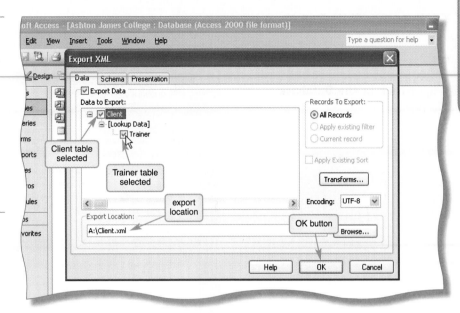

FIGURE 17

The data and structure for both the Client table and the Trainer table are exported to the file named Client. The file also contains the relationship between the two tables. The Ashton James College database is closed.

Creating an Access Database

Before importing the data, you need to create the database that will contain the data. The following steps create the AJ Consulting database.

To Create a New Database

1 Click the New button on the Database toolbar, and then click Blank database in the New area of the New File task pane.

2 If necessary, click the Save in box arrow in the File New Database dialog box and then click 3½ Floppy (A:).

3 Type AJ Consulting in the File name text box and then click the Create button.

Access creates the database. It is open and ready for use.

Importing XML Data

To import XML data, use the Import command and select XML as the type. You then select the XML file that contains the data to be imported. The steps on the next page import the Client and Trainer tables stored in the XML file called Client.

To Import XML Data

1

• **Right-click in the Database window.**

The shortcut menu for the Database window appears (Figure 18).

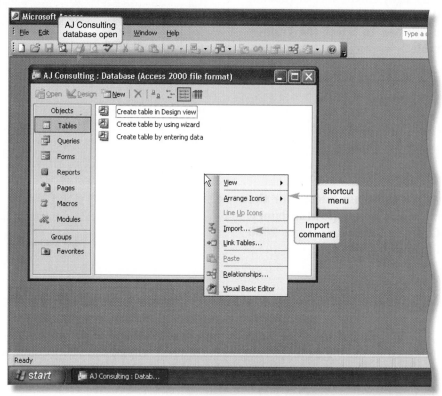

FIGURE 18

2

• **Click Import on the shortcut menu.**

• **Click the Files of type box arrow, scroll down, and then click XML in the list.**

• **If necessary, select 3½ Floppy (A:) in the Look in list.**

• **Click the Client file. (Do not click the xsd version. If you do, you will import both tables, but none of the data. That is, the tables will be empty.)**

Access displays the Import dialog box (Figure 19). The Client file is selected. XML is the file type.

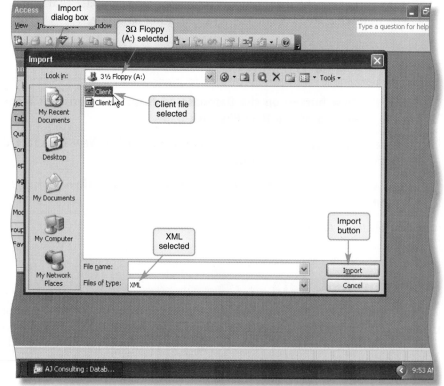

FIGURE 19

• **Click the Import button.**

Access displays the Import XML dialog box (Figure 20). Both the Client and Trainer tables will be imported. Clicking the expand indicator to the left of either table will display a list of fields in the table.

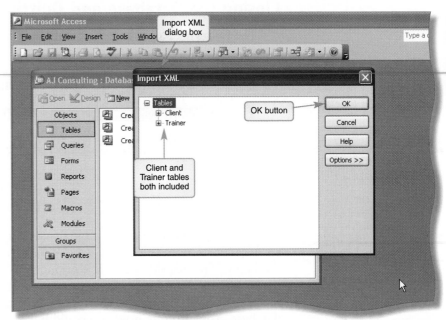

FIGURE 20

• **Click the OK button.**

The data is imported and the Microsoft Office Access dialog box is displayed (Figure 21).

• **Click the OK button.**

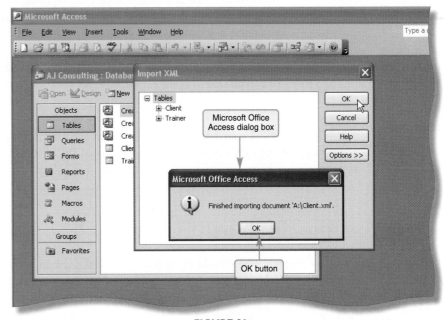

FIGURE 21

Both tables have been imported as part of this single Import operation. In addition to having the same data, the fields in both tables have precisely the same data types and sizes as in the original database. Also, the same fields have been designated primary keys.

Closing the Database and Quitting Access

The following steps close the database and quit Access.

To Close a Database and Quit Access

1 Click the Close Window button for the AJ Consulting : Database window.

2 Click the Close button for the Microsoft Access window.

Integration Feature Summary

The Integration Feature covered the process of integrating an Excel worksheet into an Access database. To convert a worksheet to an Access table, you learned to use the Import Spreadsheet Wizard. Working with the wizard, you identified the first row of the worksheet as the row containing the column headings and you indicated the primary key. The wizard then created the table for you and placed it in a new database. You also saw how you could link data instead of importing it.

You learned to use the Export command and used it to export data to an Excel worksheet. You also learned to use the drag-and-drop feature and used it to export data to a Word document. The project illustrated how to use the Export command to create a snapshot of a report. You learned how to export XML data. You exported both structure and data for multiple related tables in a single operation. Finally, you learned how to import the XML data to a separate database and discovered that a single import operation imported both tables and their structures.

 If you have a SAM user profile, you may have access to hands-on instruction, practice, and assessment of the skills covered in this project. Log in to your SAM account and go to your assignments page to see what your instructor has assigned.

What You Should Know

Having completed this project, you should be able to perform the tasks below. The tasks are listed in the same order they were presented in this project. For a list of the buttons, menus, toolbars, and commands introduced in this project, see the Quick Reference Summary at the back of this book and refer to the Page Number column.

1. Create a New Database   (AC 176)
2. Import an Excel Worksheet   (AC 177)
3. Close a Database   (AC 181)
4. Open a Database   (AC 181)
5. Use the Export Command to Export Data to Excel   (AC 182)
6. Use Drag-and-Drop to Export Data to Word (AC 183)
7. Use the Export Command to Create a Snapshot (AC 184)
8. Export XML Data   (AC 185)
9. Create a New Database   (AC 187)
10. Import XML Data   (AC 188)
11. Close a Database and Quit Access   (AC 190)

In the Lab

1 Importing Data to an Access Database

Problem: CAC Logo Company has been using Excel for a number of tasks. The company sells logo-imprinted novelty items and clothing to organizations. CAC uses several worksheets to keep track of inventory, and customers. CAC realizes that the customer data would be better handled if maintained in an Access database. The company wants to maintain the items inventory in Excel worksheets but also would like to be able to use the query and report features of Access.

Instructions: For this assignment, you will need two files: Customer.xls and Logo Items.xls. These files are on the Data Disk. See the inside back cover of this book for instructions for downloading the Data Disk or see your instructor for information about accessing the files required for this book. Perform the following tasks:

1. Start Access and create a new database in which to store all the objects for CAC Logo Company. Call the database CAC Logo Company.
2. Import the Customer worksheet shown in Figure 22 into Access. The worksheet is in the Customer workbook on the Data Disk.
3. Use Customer as the name of the Access table and Customer Number as the primary key.
4. Open the Customer table in Datasheet view and resize the columns to best fit the data. Print the table.
5. Link the Logo Items worksheet shown in Figure 23 to the database. The worksheet is in the Logo Items workbook on the Data Disk.
6. Open the linked Logo Items table in Datasheet view and resize the columns to best fit the data. Print the table.
7. Rename the linked Logo Items table as Items. Then, use the Linked Table Manager to update the link between the Excel worksheet and the Access table. (If the Linked Table Manager wizard is not installed on your computer, see your instructor before continuing.)

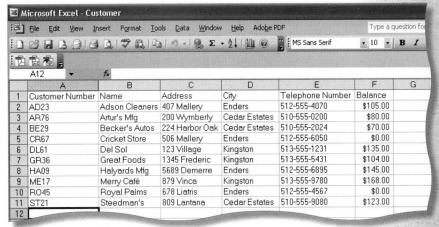

FIGURE 22

FIGURE 23

(continued)

In the Lab

Importing Data to an Access Database *(continued)*

8. Print the Items table.
9. Link the Trainer table in the AJ Consulting database to the CAC Logo database. Trainers of AJ Consulting may become potential sales reps for CAC Logo.
10. Rename the Trainer table as Potential Sales Reps. Then, use the Linked Table Manager to update the link between the two tables.
11. Print the Potential Sales Rep table.

2 Exporting Data to Other Applications

Problem: Begon Pest Control wants to be able to export some of the data in the Access database to other applications. The company wants to export the City-Technician Crosstab query for further processing in Excel. It also wants to use the Customer-Technician query in a Word document as well as e-mail the Customer Amount Report to the company's accounting firm. The company has decided to branch out and offer pest control services that will focus on outside pest control, that is, pest control for lawns and gardens. It wants to export the Customer and Technician tables as a single XML file and then import it to a new database.

Instructions: Start Access. Open the Begon Pest Control database that you modified in Apply Your Knowledge 1 in Project 3 on page AC 167. (If you did not complete this exercise, see your instructor for a copy of the modified database.) Perform the following tasks:

1. Export the City-Technician Crosstab query to Excel as shown in Figure 24.
2. Resize the columns to best fit the data as shown in Figure 24.
3. Print the Excel worksheet.
4. Use drag-and-drop to place the Customer-Technician query in a Word document.
5. Print the Word document.
6. Preview the Customer Amount Report and then export the report as a snapshot.
7. Open the report in the Snapshot Viewer and print it. (If a Microsoft Office Access dialog box is displayed asking if you want to install Snapshot Viewer, click the No button and see your instructor.)
8. Export both the Customer and Technician tables in XML format. Be sure that both tables are exported to the same file.
9. Create a new database called Begon Garden Services.
10. Import the Customer file containing both the Customer and Technician tables to the Begon Garden Services database.
11. Change the name of customer CJ45 to C Joseph Diner.
12. Change the first name of technician 220 to Christy.
13. Print the Customer and Technician tables.

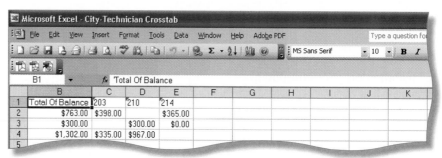

FIGURE 24

MICROSOFT
Office Access 2003

Reports, Forms, and Combo Boxes

PROJECT

4

CASE PERSPECTIVE

Dr. Gernaey and his colleagues at Ashton James College have realized several benefits from using the database of clients and trainers. AJC hopes to realize additional benefits using two custom reports that meet their specific needs. The first report is organized by client type and includes subtotals of both the amount paid and current due amounts for the clients of that type. In addition, it includes grand totals of both of these amounts. The second report groups the clients by trainer number. Similarly to the first report, the second report includes subtotals of the amount paid and current due amounts after each group, and displays grand totals at the end.

AJC also wants to improve the data entry process by using a custom form. The form will have a title with the fields arranged in two columns. It will include the total amount, which will be calculated automatically by adding the amount paid and current due amounts. To assist users in entering the correct client type, users should be able to select from a list of possible client types. To assist users in entering the correct trainer number, users should be able to select from a list of existing trainers. Your task is to help the administration in accomplishing these goals.

As you read through this project, you will learn how to use the Access Report and Form Wizards as well as the various design windows to create custom reports and forms.

MICROSOFT
Office Access 2003

Reports, Forms, and Combo Boxes

OBJECTIVES

You will have mastered the material in this project when you can:

- Create a report using the Report Wizard
- Use sorting and grouping in a report
- Move controls
- Change properties
- Add totals and subtotals to a report
- Align and format controls
- Remove controls
- Change labels and column headings

- Use multiple tables in a report
- Remove unwanted controls
- Understand report design considerations
- Use the Form Wizard to create a form
- Add a calculated field, combo box, and title to a form
- Understand form design considerations

Introduction

This project creates two reports and a form. The first report is shown in Figure 4-1. This report includes the client type, number, name, address, city, amount paid, and current due for each client. It is similar to the one produced by clicking the Print button on the toolbar. It has some significant differences, however.

Not all fields are included. The Client table includes a State field, a Zip Code field, and a Trainer Number field, none of which are included in this report. It also contains an additional feature — grouping. **Grouping** means creating separate collections of records sharing some common characteristic. In the report shown in Figure 4-1, for example, the records have been grouped by client type. There are three separate groups: one for client type EDU, one for client type MAN, and one for client type SER. The appropriate client type appears before each group, and the total of the amount paid and current due amounts for the clients in the group (called a **subtotal**) appears after the group. At the end of the report is a grand total of the amount paid and current due amounts for all groups. Finally, the words, Subtotal and Grand Total, are a different color.

The second report is shown in Figure 4-2. Like the report in Figure 4-1, the data is grouped, although this time it is grouped by trainer number. This report, however, encompasses data from both the Trainer table and the Client table. Not only does the trainer number appear before each group, but the first name and last name of the trainer appear as well. In addition, the column headings have been split over two lines.

Client Account Summary

Client Type	Number	Name	Address	City	Amount Paid	Current Due
EDU						
	MC28	Morgan-Alyssa Academy	923 Williams	Crumville	$24,761.00	$1,572.00
	RT67	Richards-Trent	382 Alder	Lake Hammond	$0.00	$0.00
				Subtotal:	$24,761.00	$1,572.00
MAN						
	CE16	Center Services	725 Mitchell	San Julio	$26,512.00	$2,672.00
	HN83	Hurley National	3827 Burgess	Tallmadge	$0.00	$0.00
				Subtotal:	$26,512.00	$2,672.00
SER						
	BS27	Blant and Sons	4806 Park	Lake Hammond	$21,876.00	$892.50
	CP27	Calder Plastics	7300 Cedar	Lake Hammond	$8,725.00	$0.00
	FL93	Fairland Lawns	143 Pangborn	Lake Hammond	$21,625.00	$0.00
	FI28	Farrow-Idsen	829 Wooster	Cedar Ridge	$8,287.50	$925.50
	PS82	PRIM Staffing	72 Crestview	San Julio	$11,682.25	$2,827.50
				Subtotal:	$72,195.75	$4,645.50
				Grand Total:	$123,468.75	$8,889.50

FIGURE 4-1

Trainer/Client Report

Trainer Number	First Name	Last Name	Client Number	Name	Amount Paid	Current Due
42	Belinda	Perry				
			BS27	Blant and Sons	$21,876.00	$892.50
			FI28	Farrow-Idsen	$8,287.50	$925.50
			MC28	Morgan-Alyssa Academy	$24,761.00	$1,572.00
					$54,924.50	$3,390.00
48	Michael	Stevens				
			CE16	Center Services	$26,512.00	$2,672.00
			CP27	Calder Plastics	$8,725.00	$0.00
			FL93	Fairland Lawns	$21,625.00	$0.00
			HN83	Hurley National	$0.00	$0.00
					$56,862.00	$2,672.00
53	Manuel	Gonzalez				
			PS82	PRIM Staffing	$11,682.25	$2,827.50
					$11,682.25	$2,827.50
67	Marty	Danville				
			RT67	Richards-Trent	$0.00	$0.00
					$0.00	$0.00
					$123,468.75	$8,889.50

FIGURE 4-2

The **custom form** to be created is shown in Figure 4-3a. Although similar to the form created in Project 1, it offers some distinct advantages. Some of the differences are merely aesthetic. The form has a title and the fields have been rearranged in two columns. In addition, two other major differences are present. This form displays the total amount and will calculate it automatically by adding the amount paid and current due amounts. Second, to assist users in entering the correct client type and trainer, the form contains **combo boxes**, which are boxes that allow you to select entries from a list. An arrow appears in the Client Type field, for example. Clicking the arrow causes a list of the possible client types to appear as shown in the figure. You then either can type the desired client type or simply click it in the list.

An arrow also appears in the Trainer Number field. Clicking the arrow in this field causes a list of the trainers in the Trainer table to appear as shown in Figure 4-3b. You then either can type the desired trainer number or click the desired trainer.

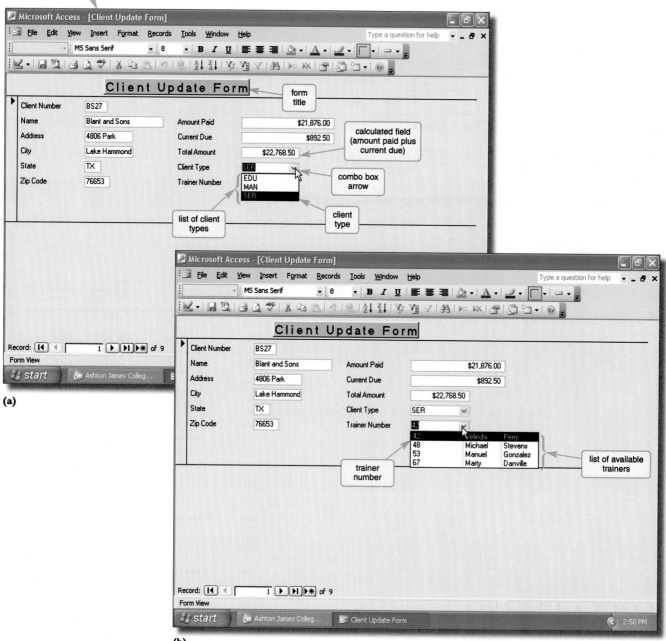

(a)

(b)

FIGURE 4-3

Project Four — Reports, Forms, and Combo Boxes

The steps in this project show how to create reports for the Ashton James College database. The steps also illustrate how to create a custom data-entry form for the database.

Note: When you create forms and reports, you can increase the size of a database substantially. A database containing pictures, for example, can get very large, too large for a diskette. Because these projects illustrate adding pictures to tables as well as to forms and reports, the Ashton James College database is located on disk C. The steps in these projects assume the database is located in a folder called Data on disk C and the pictures (bmp files) are located in a folder called Pictures on disk C. You will use these pictures in Project 5. You are encouraged to copy both your databases and your pictures to disk C, to a network disk, or to a Zip disk. If you cannot do so, you will be instructed which steps to skip in these projects.

Opening the Database

Before you can create the reports and the form, you must open the database. If you are stepping through this project on a computer and you want your screen to match the figures in this book, then you should change your computer's resolution to 800 x 600. For more information on how to change the resolution on your computer, see Appendix D. The following steps, which start Access and open the database, assume that the database is located in a folder called Data on disk C. If your database is located anywhere else, you will need to make the appropriate adjustments in the steps.

To Open a Database

1. Click the Start button on the Windows taskbar, point to All Programs on the Start menu, point to Microsoft Office on the All Programs submenu, and then click Office Access 2003 on the Microsoft Office submenu.

2. If the Access window is not maximized, double-click its title bar to maximize it.

3. If the Language bar appears, right-click it and then click Close the Language bar on the shortcut menu.

4. Click Open on the Database toolbar, and then click Local Disk (C:) in the Look in box. Double-click the Data folder, and then make sure the Ashton James College database is selected.

5. Click the Open button in the Open dialog box. If a Security Warning dialog box appears, click the Open button.

The database opens and the Ashton James College : Database window appears.

More About

The Access Help System

Need Help? It is no further than the Type a question for help box on the menu bar in the upper-right corner of the window. Click the box that contains the text, Type a question for help (Figure 4-3), type help, and then press the ENTER key. Access responds with a list of topics you can click to learn about obtaining help on any Access-related topic. To find out what is new in Access 2003, type what is new in Access in the Type a question for help box.

More About

Creating a Report

There are two alternatives to using the Report Wizard to create reports. You can use AutoReport to create a very simple report that includes all fields and records in the table or query. Design view also allows you to create a report from scratch.

Report Creation

The simplest way to create a report design is to use the Report Wizard. For some reports, the Report Wizard can produce exactly the desired report. For others, however, you first must use the Report Wizard to produce a report that is as close as possible to the desired report. Then, use the Report window to modify the report and transform it into the correct report. In either case, once the report is created and saved, you can print it at anytime. Access will use the current data in the database for the report, formatting and arranging it in exactly the way you specified when the report was created.

Creating a Report

Next, you will create a report using the Report Wizard. Access leads you through a series of choices and questions and then creates the report automatically. The following steps illustrate how to create a report.

To Create a Report Using the Report Wizard

1

• **If necessary, in the Database window, click Tables on the Objects bar and then click Client.**

• **Click the New Object button arrow on the Database toolbar.**

The list of available objects appears (Figure 4-4).

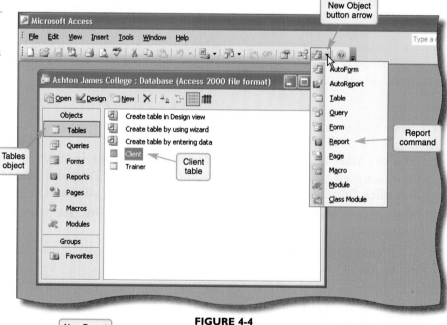

FIGURE 4-4

2

• **Click Report.**

Access displays the New Report dialog box. The Client table is selected (Figure 4-5).

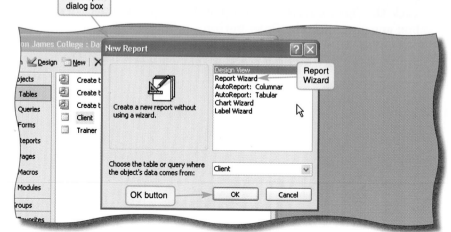

FIGURE 4-5

3

• **Click Report Wizard and then click the OK button.**

The Report Wizard dialog box appears, requesting the fields for the report (Figure 4-6). To add the selected field to the list of fields on the report, use the Add Field button. To add all fields, use the Add All Fields button.

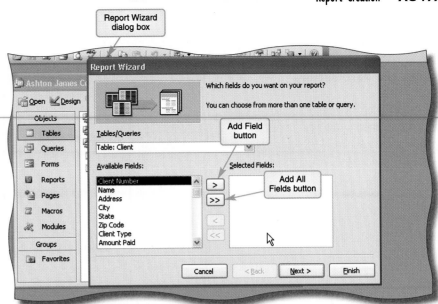

FIGURE 4-6

4

• **Click the Client Type field and then click the Add Field button.**

The Client Type field is selected (Figure 4-7).

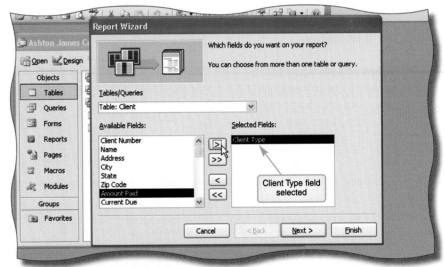

FIGURE 4-7

5

• **Using the same technique, select the Client Number, Name, Address, City, Amount Paid, and Current Due fields.**

The fields are selected (Figure 4-8).

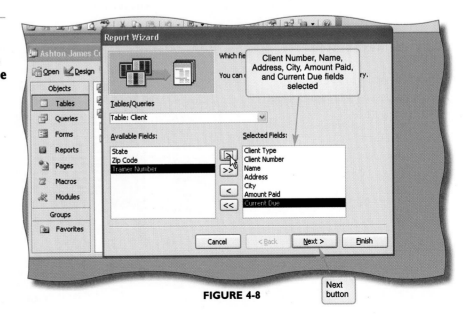

FIGURE 4-8

6

• **Click the Next button.**

The next Report Wizard dialog box appears, requesting the field or fields for grouping levels (Figure 4-9). You do not need to specify grouping at this time.

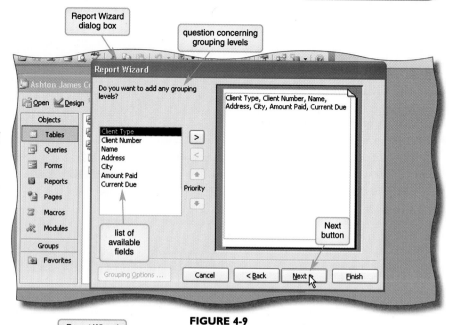

FIGURE 4-9

7

• **Click the Next button.**

The next Report Wizard dialog box appears, requesting the sort order for the report (Figure 4-10). You do not need to specify a sort order at this time.

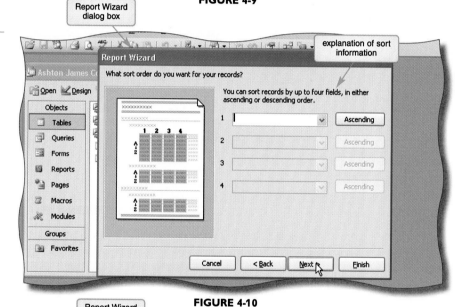

FIGURE 4-10

8

• **Click the Next button.**

The next Report Wizard dialog box appears, requesting your report layout preference (Figure 4-11).

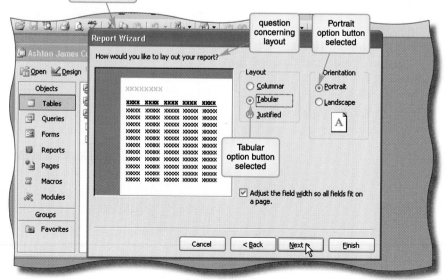

FIGURE 4-11

9

• **Be sure the options selected in the Report Wizard dialog box on your screen match those shown in Figure 4-11, and then click the Next button.**

• **If Corporate is not already selected, click Corporate to select it.**

The next Report Wizard dialog box appears, requesting a style for the report (Figure 4-12). The Corporate style is selected.

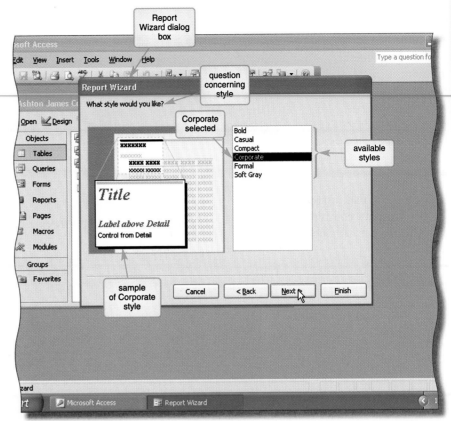

FIGURE 4-12

10

• **Click the Next button and then type** Client Account Summary **as the report title.**

The next Report Wizard dialog box appears, requesting a title for the report (Figure 4-13). Client Account Summary is entered as the title.

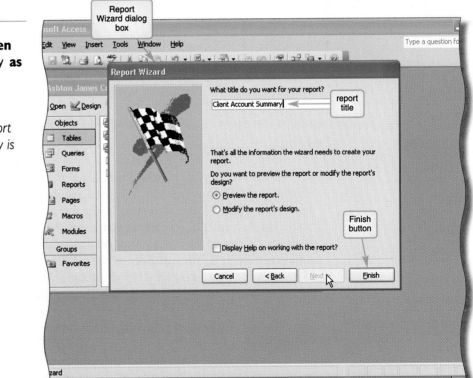

FIGURE 4-13

11

• **Click the Finish button.**

The report design is complete and appears in Print Preview (Figure 4-14).

12

• **Click the Close button in the window containing the report to close the report.**

The report no longer appears.

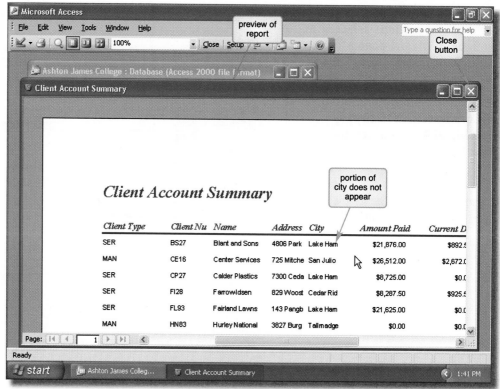

FIGURE 4-14

Other Ways

1. Click Reports on Objects bar, click New button, click Report Wizard to create report
2. Click Reports on Objects bar, double-click Create report by using wizard
3. On Insert menu click Report, click Report Wizard to create report
4. In Voice Command mode, say "Insert, Report"

More About

Adding Fields

If you forget a field when you create a report initially, or if you later decide to add a field to a report, you can use the field list (Figure 4-15). If the field list does not appear, click the Field List button. Then, drag the field from the field list to its proper location in the Report Design window.

Because of the insufficient amount of space allowed in the report shown in Figure 4-14, some of the data does not appear completely. In the City field, for example, Lake Hammond appears as Lake Ham. You will need to correct this problem.

Using Design View

Within the Report window, the different possible views are Design view, Print Preview, and Layout Preview. Use Design view to modify the design (layout) of the report. Use Print Preview to see the report with actual data as it will appear on every page. Use Layout Preview to view the report's layout, which includes just a sample of the data. When you are designing reports, the two most useful views are Design view and Print Preview. You can move from Design view to Print Preview by using the Print Preview button on the Report Design toolbar. To return to Design view after previewing a report, click the button labeled Close on the Print Preview toolbar.

Within Print Preview, you can switch between viewing an entire page and viewing a portion of a page. To do so, click somewhere within the report. When pointing within the report, the mouse pointer will change shape to a magnifying glass.

In Design view, you can modify the design of the report. A toolbox is available in Design view that allows you to create special objects for the report. The toolbox also can obscure a portion of the report, however. You can use the Toolbox button on the Report Design toolbar to remove it and then return it to the screen when needed. Because you use the toolbox frequently when modifying report and form designs, it is desirable to leave it on the screen, however. You can move the toolbox to different positions on the screen using a process referred to as **docking**. The bottom of the screen usually is a good position for it.

The following steps illustrate how to open the report in Design view, remove a field list that is not needed, and dock the toolbox.

To Move to Design View and Dock the Toolbox

1

• **Click the Reports object in the Database window, right-click Client Account Summary, and then click Design View on the shortcut menu.**

• **If necessary, maximize the window.**

The report appears in Design view (Figure 4-15). A field list may appear. The toolbox also may appear.

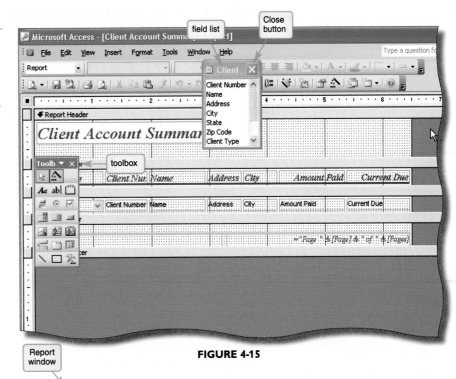

FIGURE 4-15

2

• **If a field list appears, click its Close button to remove the field list from the screen.**

• **If necessary, click the Toolbox button on the Report Design toolbar to display the toolbox.**

• **If the toolbox is not docked at the bottom of the screen, dock it there by dragging its title bar to the bottom of the screen.**

The field list no longer appears, the toolbox is docked at the bottom of the screen, and the window is maximized (Figure 4-16).

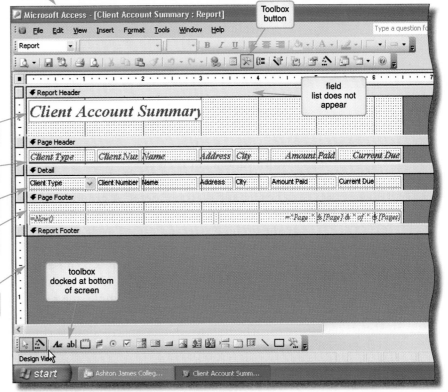

FIGURE 4-16

More About

AutoFormat

When you use the Report Wizard to create a report, you select a style (format) for the report. You can change the style of a report in Design view. To do so, use the AutoFormat command on the Format menu.

More About

Using Queries for Reports

The records in the report will appear in the specified order if you have sorted the data in the query. You also can enter criteria in the query, in which case only records that satisfy the criteria will be included in the report. Reports based on queries open faster than those based on tables.

More About

Grouping in a Report

To force each group to begin on a new page of the report, change the value of the ForceNewPage property for the Group Header section from None to Before Section. The ForceNewPage property does not apply to Page Header or Page Footer sections.

Report Sections

Each portion of the report is described in what is termed a **section**. The sections are labeled on the screen (see Figure 4-16 on the previous page). Notice the following sections: Report Header section, Page Header section, Detail section, Page Footer section, and Report Footer section.

The contents of the **Report Header section** print once at the beginning of the report. The contents of the **Report Footer section** print once at the end of the report. The contents of the **Page Header section** print once at the top of each page, and the contents of the **Page Footer section** print once at the bottom of each page. The contents of the **Detail section** print once for each record in the table.

The various rectangles appearing in Figure 4-16 (Client Account Summary, Client Type, Name, and so on) are called **controls**. All the information on a report or form is contained in the controls. The control containing Client Account Summary displays the report title; that is, it displays the words, Client Account Summary. The control in the Page Header section containing Name displays the word, Name.

The controls in the Detail section display the contents of the corresponding fields. The control containing Name, for example, will display the client's name. The controls in the Page Header section serve as captions for the data. The Client Type control in this section, for example, will display the words, Client Type, immediately above the column of client types, thus making it clear to anyone reading the report that the items in the column are, in fact, client types.

To move, resize, delete, or modify a control, click it. Small squares called sizing handles appear around the border of the control. To move a control, point to the border of the control away from any sizing handle. The mouse pointer shape will change to a hand. You then can drag the control to move it. To resize a control, point to one of the sizing handles. The mouse pointer shape will change to a double-pointing arrow. You then can drag the handle to resize the control. To delete the control, press the DELETE key. Clicking a second time produces an insertion point in the control in order to modify its contents.

Sorting and Grouping

Grouping arranges the records in your report into separate collections of records that share a common characteristic. In the report shown in Figure 4-1 on page AC 195, for example, the records are grouped by client type. Three separate groups are formed, one for each type.

In grouping, reports often include two additional types of sections: a group header and a group footer. A **group header** is printed before the records in a particular group are printed, and a **group footer** is printed after the group. In Figure 4-1, the group header indicates the client type. The group footer includes the total of the amount paid and current due amounts for the clients of that client type. Such a total is called a subtotal, because it is a subset of the overall total.

Within the records in a group, you can choose to further sort the records. In the report in Figure 4-1, for example, the records in each group are sorted by name. You specify both sorting and grouping in the Sorting and Grouping dialog box.

The following steps specify both sorting and grouping for the report.

To Use Sorting and Grouping

1

• **Click the Sorting and Grouping button on the Report Design toolbar.**

The Sorting and Grouping dialog box appears (Figure 4-17).

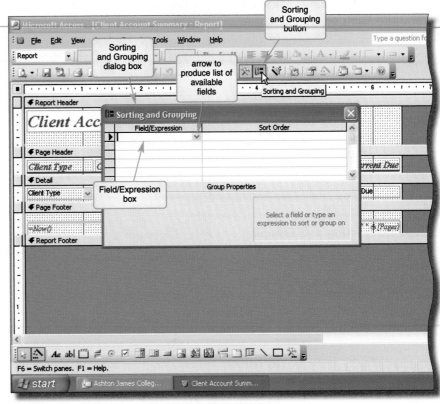

FIGURE 4-17

2

• **Click the down arrow in the Field/Expression box, and then click the Client Type field in the list.**

• **Click the Group Header property box, click the Group Header box arrow, and then click Yes.**

• **Click the Group Footer property box, click the Group Footer box arrow, and then click Yes.**

• **Click the Keep Together property box, click the Keep Together box arrow, and then click With First Detail.**

The Client Type field is selected (Figure 4-18). Because the Group Header and Group Footer properties are changed from No to Yes, the Client Type Header and Client Type Footer sections now are included.

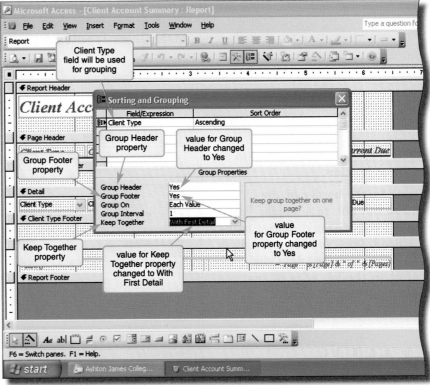

FIGURE 4-18

• **Click the second row in the Field/Expression column, click the arrow, and then select the Name field.**

The Name field is selected (Figure 4-19). This ensures that within all the clients with the same client type, the records will be sorted by Name. No header or footer will be included, because both the Group Header and Group Footer properties still are set to No.

4

• **Close the Sorting and Grouping dialog box by clicking its Close button.**

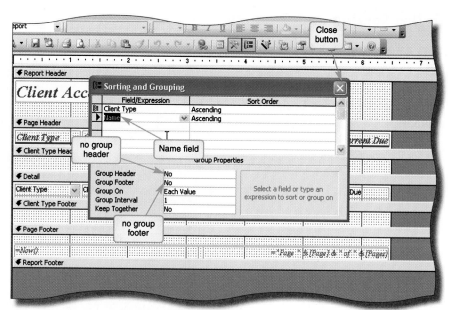

FIGURE 4-19

The records in the report now will be grouped by client type. There will be both a header and a footer for client type. Within each group, the records will be sorted by name.

Moving a Control

To move a control, select it, and then point to the border of the control but away from any sizing handle. The mouse pointer then will be a hand. Drag the control to move it. The following step shows how to move the Client Type control from the Detail section to the Client Type Header section.

To Move a Control

1

• **Click the Client Type control in the Detail section.**

• **Point to the border of the control, but not to a handle. The mouse pointer should change shape to a hand. Once you are pointing in the correct position, drag the control to the left edge of the Client Type Header section.**

The control is moved from the Detail section to the Client Type Header section (Figure 4-20).

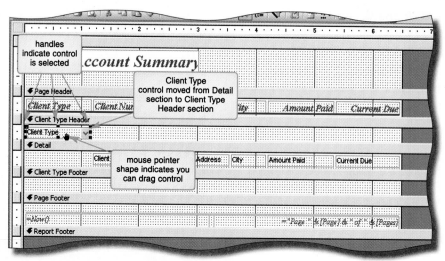

FIGURE 4-20

Changing Properties

Some of the changes you may make will involve using the property sheet for the control to be changed. The **property sheet** for each control is a list of properties that can be modified. By using the property sheet, you can change one or more of the control's properties.

The problem of the missing data in the report shown in Figure 4-14 on page AC 202 can be corrected in several ways.

1. Move the controls to allow more space in between. Then, drag the appropriate handles on the controls that need to be expanded to enlarge them.
2. Use the Font Size property to select a smaller font size. This will allow more data to print in the same space.
3. Use the Can Grow property. By changing the value of this property from No to Yes, the data can be spread over two lines, thus allowing all the data to print. The city of Lake Hammond, for example, will have Lake on one line and Hammond on the next line. Access will split data at natural break points, such as commas, spaces, and hyphens.

The first approach will work, but it can be cumbersome. The second approach also works but makes the report more difficult to read. The third approach, changing the Can Grow property, is the simplest method to use and generally produces a very readable report. The following steps show how to change the Can Grow property for the Detail section.

To Change the Can Grow Property

1

- **Right-click below the section selector for the Detail section.**

The shortcut menu appears (Figure 4-21). (If your shortcut menu looks different, you right-clicked the wrong place and will have to repeat the step.) All the controls in the Detail section are selected.

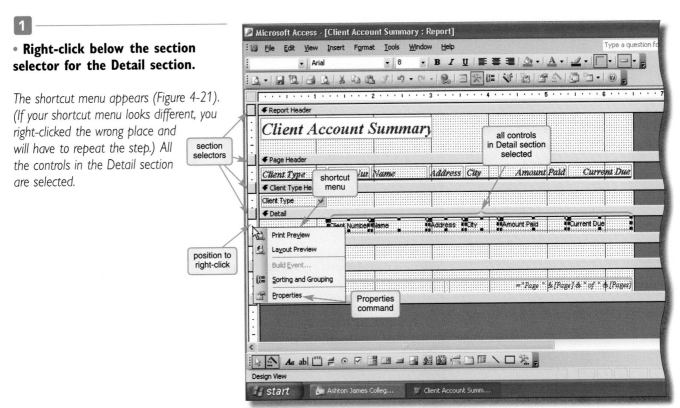

FIGURE 4-21

2

• **Click Properties and then, if necessary, click the All tab to ensure that all available properties appear.**

• **Click the Can Grow property, click the Can Grow property box arrow, and then click Yes in the list that appears.**

The Multiple selection property sheet appears (Figure 4-22). All the properties appear in the All sheet. The value for the Can Grow property has been changed to Yes for all fields in the Detail section.

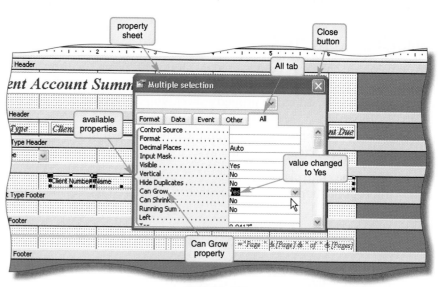

FIGURE 4-22

3

• **Close the property sheet by clicking its Close button.**

The property sheet no longer appears (Figure 4-23).

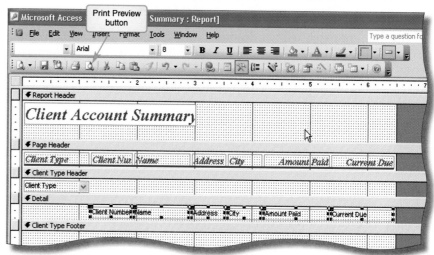

FIGURE 4-23

4

• **Click the Print Preview button.**

A portion of the report appears (Figure 4-24). The addresses and cities now appear completely by extending to a second line. (If your computer shows an entire page, click the portion of the report containing the mouse pointer in the figure.)

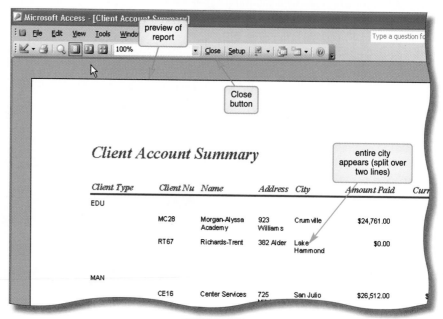

FIGURE 4-24

Adding Totals and Subtotals

To add totals or other statistics to a footer, add a **text box**. A text box is a control that displays data. In the text box, enter an expression that performs the appropriate calculation. You can use any of the aggregate functions: COUNT, SUM, AVG (average), MAX (largest value), MIN (smallest value), STDEV (standard deviation), VAR (variance), FIRST, and LAST. To use a function, type an equal (=) sign, followed by the function name. You then include a set of parentheses containing the item for which you want to perform the calculation. If the item name contains spaces, such as Amount Paid, you must enclose it in square brackets. For example, to calculate the sum of the amount paid values, the expression would be =SUM([Amount Paid]).

Access will perform the calculation for the appropriate collection of records. If you enter this expression in the Client Type Footer section, Access only will calculate the total for clients with the given client type; that is, it will calculate the appropriate subtotal. If you enter the expression in the Report Footer section, Access will calculate the total for all clients.

The following steps illustrate how to add the total of amount paid and current due to both the Client Type Footer section and the Report Footer section. The steps also label the totals in the Client Type Footer section as subtotals and the totals in the Report Footer section as grand totals.

To Add Totals and Subtotals

1

• **Click the Close button on the toolbar to return to Design view.**

• **Click the Text Box tool in the toolbox, and then point to the position shown in Figure 4-25.**

The mouse pointer shape indicates you are placing a text box.

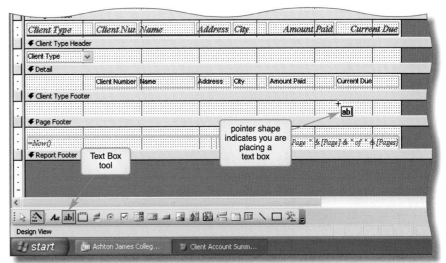

FIGURE 4-25

2

• **Click the position shown in Figure 4-25.**

Access adds a control to the Client Type Footer section (Figure 4-26). The label for the control is Text19: (yours might be different).

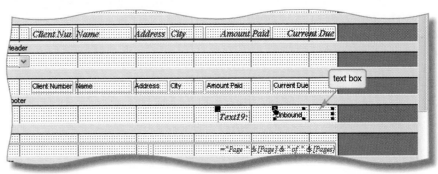

FIGURE 4-26

3

• **Type** =Sum([Current Due]) **in the control, and then press the ENTER KEY.**

The expression is entered in the text box (Figure 4-27). The label still reads Text19. Your number might be different.

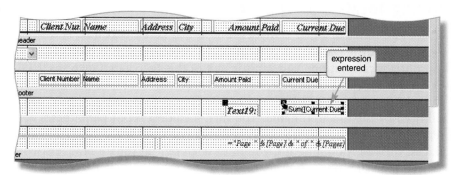

FIGURE 4-27

4

• **Click the label to select it, and then press the DELETE key to delete the label.**

The label is removed from the design (Figure 4-28).

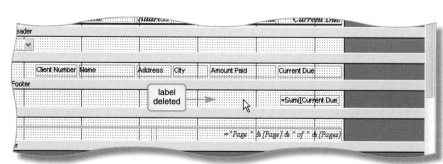

FIGURE 4-28

5

• **Use the Text Box tool to add a second control in the position shown in Figure 4-29.**

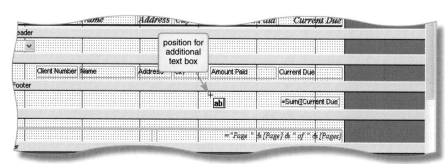

FIGURE 4-29

6

• **Type** =Sum([Amount Paid]) **in the control, and then press the ENTER KEY.**

• **Click the label to select it.**

• **Click the label a second time to produce an insertion point.**

• **Use the DELETE or BACKSPACE key to delete the Text19 (your number might be different).**

• **Type** Subtotal **as the label.**

The expression is entered in the text box (Figure 4-30). The label has been changed to Subtotal:.

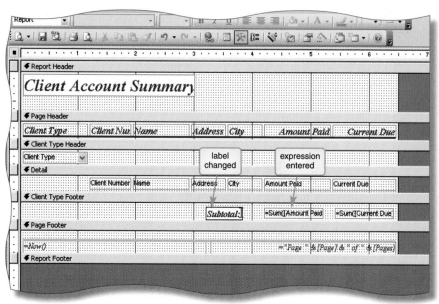

FIGURE 4-30

7

• **Click outside the label to deselect the label.**

• **Click the label a second time to select it.**

• **Move the label to the position shown in Figure 4-31 by dragging the Move handle in the upper-left corner.**

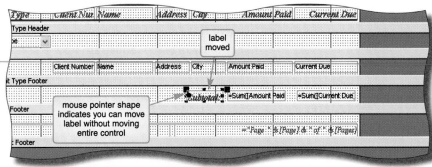

FIGURE 4-31

8

• **Use the techniques in Steps 1 through 7 above to add the controls in the Report Footer section shown in Figure 4-32. The only difference is that the label reads Grand Total: rather than Subtotal:. The expressions in both labels are the same as the expressions you entered earlier. That is, the expression for the control in the Current Due column is =Sum([Current Due]), and the expression in the Amount Paid column is =Sum([Amount Paid]).**

The controls are added to the Report Footer section. When you place the text box controls in the Report Footer section, Access automatically will enlarge the size of the section to accommodate the controls.

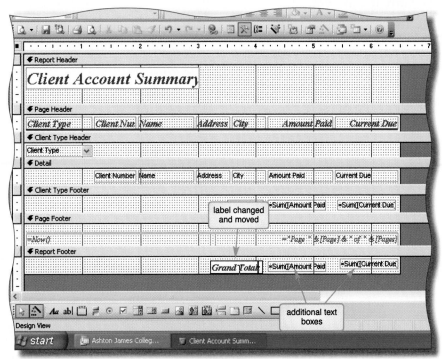

FIGURE 4-32

The report now contains totals and subtotals.

Aligning Controls

There are cases where several controls should be aligned in some fashion. For example, the controls may be aligned so their right edges are even with each other. In another case, controls may be aligned so their top edges are even. To ensure that a collection of controls is aligned properly with each other, select all of the affected controls, and then use the Align command on the Format menu.

There are two ways to select multiple controls. One way is to use a ruler. If you click a position on the horizontal ruler, you will select all the controls for which a portion of the control is under that position on the ruler. Similarly, if you click a position on the vertical ruler, you will select all the controls for which a portion of the control is to the right of that position on the ruler.

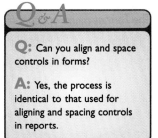

Q&A

Q: Can you align and space controls in forms?

A: Yes, the process is identical to that used for aligning and spacing controls in reports.

The second way to select multiple controls is to select the first control by clicking it. Then, select all the other controls by holding down the SHIFT key while clicking the control.

The following steps illustrate how to select multiple controls and then align them appropriately.

To Align Controls

1

- **Click the horizontal ruler above the Current Due controls.**

The Current Due controls in the Page Header, Detail, Client Type Footer, and Report Footer sections are selected (Figure 4-33). The control that includes the page number also is selected.

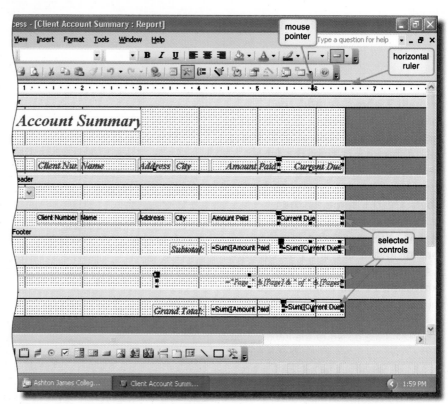

FIGURE 4-33

2

- **Click Format on the menu bar and then point to Align.**

The Format menu appears (Figure 4-34). The Align submenu also appears.

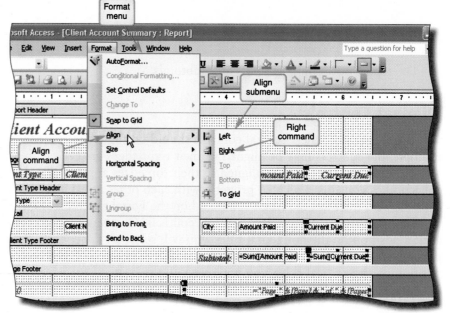

FIGURE 4-34

3

- **Click Right on the Align submenu.**
- **Click the Amount Paid control in the Page Header section to select it.**
- **Press and hold down the SHIFT key and then click the Amount Paid controls in the Detail, Client Type Footer, and Report Footer sections to select them.**
- **Click Format on the menu bar and then point to Align.**

The Current Due controls and the Page Number control are right-aligned (Figure 4-35). The Amount Paid controls are selected. The Format menu and Align submenu appear.

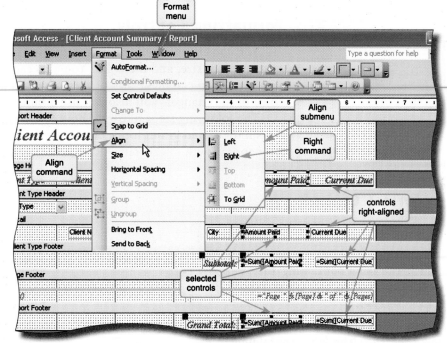

FIGURE 4-35

4

- **Click Right on the Align submenu.**
- **Click the left ruler below the section selector for the Client Type Footer section.**
- **Click Format on the menu bar and then point to Align.**

All the controls in the Client Type Footer section are selected (Figure 4-36). The Format menu and Align submenu appear.

5

- **Click Top on the Align submenu.**
- **Use the same technique to top-align the controls in the Report Footer section.**

All the controls in the Client Type Footer and Report Footer sections are top-aligned.

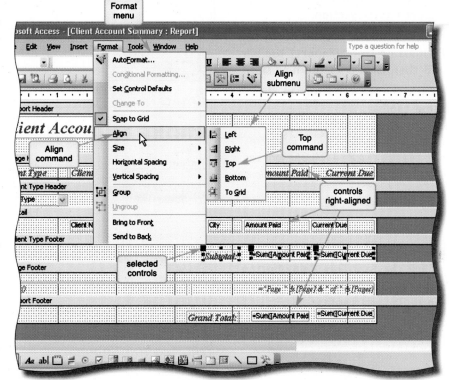

FIGURE 4-36

The controls are all aligned properly. You can use this technique to align any collection of controls.

Formatting Controls

You can change the format of controls in a variety of ways. You can change the font, the font size, and the color. You also can change the way data in the control is displayed. You can make any of these changes using the control's property sheet. For some of the changes, you also can use a button on the Formatting toolbar.

The following steps illustrate how to change the font and color of the labels for the subtotals and grand totals, and remove italics as well as to change the controls so they appear with the currency format (dollars and cents).

To Format Controls

1

• **Click the label containing the word, Subtotal, in the Client Type Footer section.**

• **Press and hold down the SHIFT key and then click the label containing the words, Grand Total, in the Report Footer section.**

• **Click the Font Size arrow on the Formatting (Form/Report) toolbar and then click 8 as the new size.**

• **Click the Italic button on the same toolbar.**

The Subtotal and Grand Total labels are both selected (Figure 4-37). The font size is changed to 8, and the labels are no longer in italics.

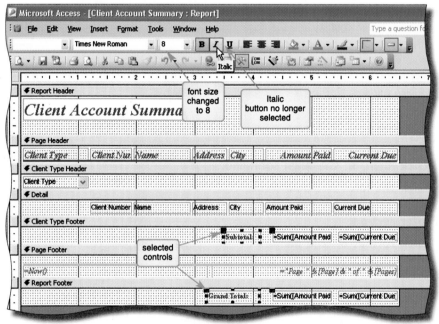

FIGURE 4-37

2

• **Click the Font/Fore Color button arrow on the Formatting (Form/Report) toolbar.**

The color palette appears (Figure 4-38).

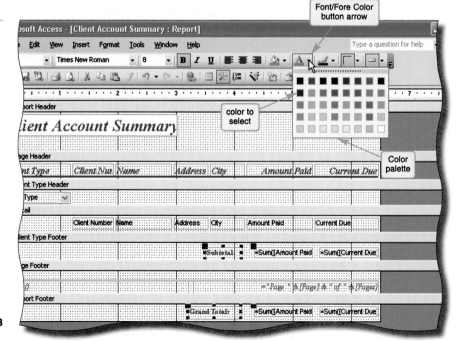

FIGURE 4-38

3

• **Click the color in the second row and first column.**

• **Click the control for the sum of Amount Paid in the Client Type Footer section.**

• **Press and hold down the SHIFT key and click the control for the sum of Amount Paid in the Report Footer section, the control for the sum of Current Due in the Client Type Footer section, and the control for the sum of Current Due in the Report Footer section.**

• **Right-click any of the selected controls.**

The controls are selected and the shortcut menu for the selected controls appears (Figure 4-39).

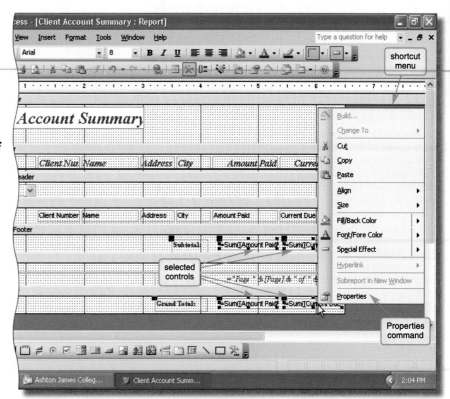

FIGURE 4-39

4

• **Click Properties on the shortcut menu.**

• **Click the Format tab to display only the Format properties, click the Format property box, click the Format property box arrow, and then select Currency.**

The Multiple selection property sheet appears and the Currency format is selected (Figure 4-40).

5

• **Close the property sheet by clicking its Close button.**

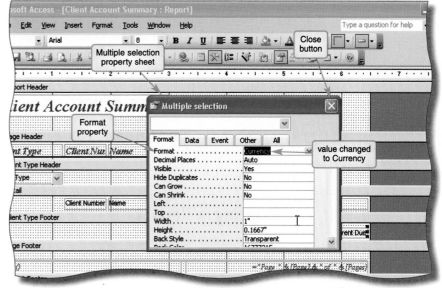

FIGURE 4-40

The format changes now are complete. The steps illustrated using one of the tabs, in this case the Format tab, in the property sheet. You also can use the All tab to display all the properties and then scroll down to find the one you want. If you know the type of property you are looking for and then click the tab for that type of property, you will have a shorter list to scroll through. By clicking the Format tab, for example, only properties that relate to formatting will appear.

Changing Labels

In some cases, the contents of a label may not display completely. For example, the label for Client Number in the Page Header section displays only Client Nu. There are several ways to fix this problem. You can enlarge the size of a label to display the entire contents, you can distribute the text over two lines, or you can delete some of the text that appears in the label. You will see how to distribute text over two lines when the report shown in Figure 4-2 on page AC 195 is created later in this project.

The following step shows how to change a label by deleting text that appears in the label.

To Change a Label

1 Point immediately before the C in Client Nu label in the Page Header section.

2 Click the label to select it.

3 Click it a second time to produce an insertion point before the C, repeatedly press the delete key to delete the word, Client, and the space that immediately follows.

The label is changed to Number.

The changes to the report now are complete and it should look like the report shown in Figure 4-1 on page AC 195.

Closing and Saving a Report

To close a report, close the window using the window's Close Window button in the upper-right corner of the window. Then, indicate whether or not you want to save your changes. The following step shows how to close and save the report.

To Close and Save a Report

1 Close the Report window and then click the Yes button to save the report.

The report no longer appears. The changes are saved.

Printing a Report

To print a report, right-click the report in the Database window, and then click Print on the shortcut menu. The following steps illustrate how to print the Client Account Summary.

To Print a Report

1 If necessary, click the Reports object in the Database window and then right-click Client Account Summary.

2 Click Print on the shortcut menu.

The report prints. It should look like the report shown in Figure 4-1 on page AC 195.

Using Multiple Tables in a Report

You are not restricted to a single table when you create a report. You can use multiple related tables. The report in Figure 4-2 on page AC 195, for example, incorporates data from both the Trainer and Client tables.

Creating a Report Involving Multiple Tables

As you did when you created the first report, you will use the Report Wizard to create the second report. This time, however, you will select fields from two tables. To do so, you will select the first table (for example, Trainer) and then select the fields from this table you would like to include. Next, you will select the second table (for example, Client) and then select the fields from the second table. You will use the wizard to group, sort, and include totals and subtotals. The following steps show how to create a report that incorporates data from both the Trainer and Client tables.

To Create a Report that Involves Multiple Tables

1

• **In the Database window, click the Tables object and then click Trainer.**

• **Click the New Object button arrow on the Database toolbar.**

The list of available objects appears (Figure 4-41).

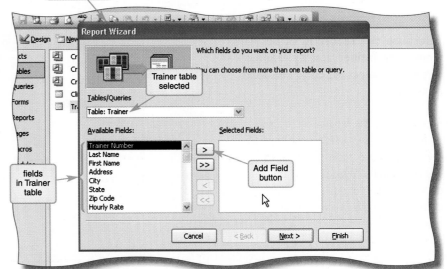

FIGURE 4-41

2

• **Click Report, click Report Wizard, and then click the OK button.**

The Report Wizard dialog box appears, requesting the fields for the report (Figure 4-42). Fields from the Trainer table appear. The Trainer Number field is selected.

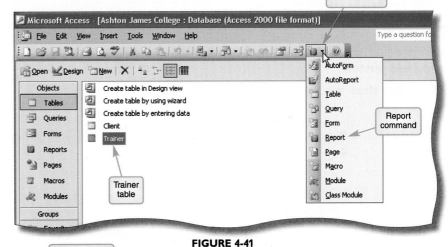

FIGURE 4-42

3

• **Click the Add Field button to add the Trainer Number field.**

• **Add the First Name field by clicking it and then clicking the Add Field button.**

• **Add the Last Name field in the same manner.**

• **Click the Tables/Queries arrow, and then click Table: Client in the Tables/Queries list box.**

The Trainer Number, First Name, and Last Name fields are selected (Figure 4-43). The fields from the Client table appear in the Available Fields box.

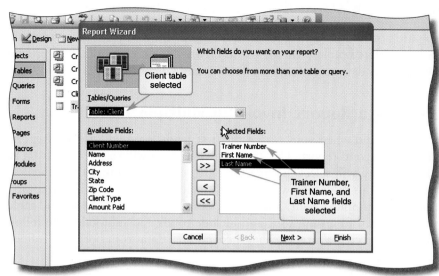

FIGURE 4-43

4

• **Add the Client Number, Name, Amount Paid, and Current Due fields by clicking the field and then clicking the Add Field button.**

• **Click the Next button.**

The next Report Wizard dialog box appears (Figure 4-44). Because the Trainer and Client tables are related, the wizard is asking you to indicate how the data is to be viewed; that is, the way the report is to be organized. The report may be organized by Trainer or by Client.

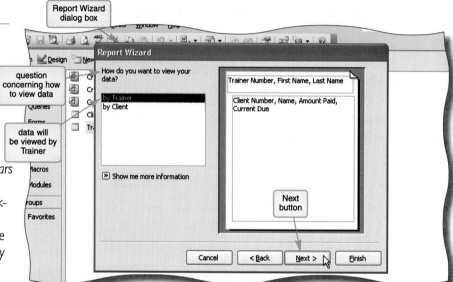

FIGURE 4-44

5

• **Because the report is to be viewed by Trainer and by Trainer already is selected, click the Next button.**

Access groups the report automatically by Trainer Number, which is the primary key of the Trainer table (Figure 4-45). The next Report Wizard dialog box appears, asking for additional grouping levels other than the Trainer Number.

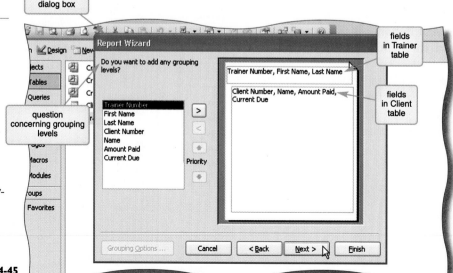

FIGURE 4-45

6

• **Because no additional grouping levels are required, click the Next button.**

• **Click the box arrow in the text box labeled 1 and then click the Client Number field in the list.**

The next Report Wizard dialog box appears, requesting the sort order for detail records in the report; that is, the way in which records will be sorted within each of the groups (Figure 4-46). The Client Number field is selected for the sort order, indicating that within the group of clients of any trainer, the clients will be sorted by client number.

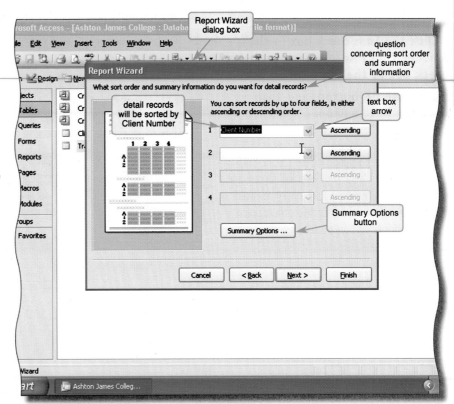

FIGURE 4-46

7

• **Click the Summary Options button.**

The Summary Options dialog box appears (Figure 4-47). This dialog box allows you to indicate any statistics you want calculated in the report by clicking the appropriate check box. You can also indicate whether to show both the detail records and the summary data in the report or to show the summary data only by clicking the appropriate option button.

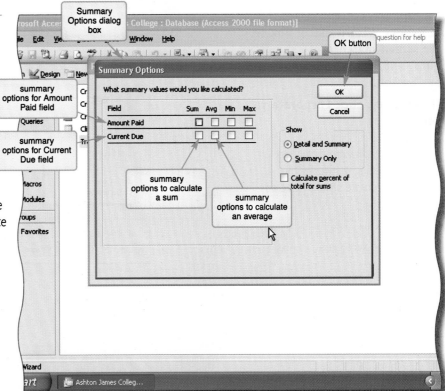

FIGURE 4-47

8

• **Click the Sum check box in the Amount Paid row and the Sum check box in the Current Due row.**

• **Click the OK button, and then click the Next button.**

The next Report Wizard dialog box appears, requesting your report layout preference (Figure 4-48). The Stepped layout, which is the correct one, already is selected. To see the effect of any of the others, click the appropriate option button.

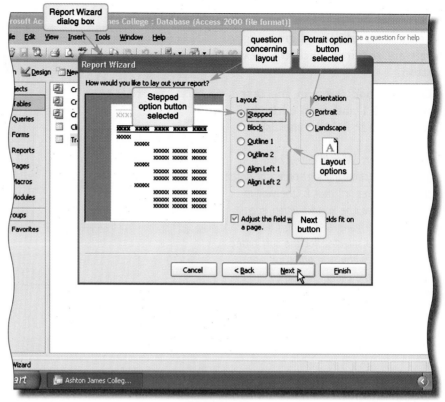

FIGURE 4-48

9

• **Be sure the options selected in the Report Wizard dialog box on your screen match those shown in Figure 4-48, and then click the Next button.**

• **If necessary, click Corporate to select it.**

The next Report Wizard dialog box appears, requesting a style for the report. The Corporate style is selected (Figure 4-49).

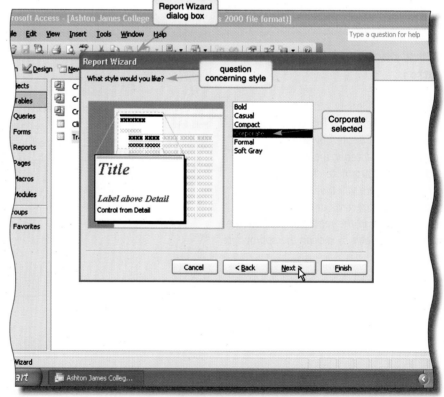

FIGURE 4-49

• **Click the Next button, and then type** Trainer/Client Report **as the report title.**

The next Report Wizard dialog box appears, requesting a title for the report (Figure 4-50). Trainer/Client Report is typed as the title.

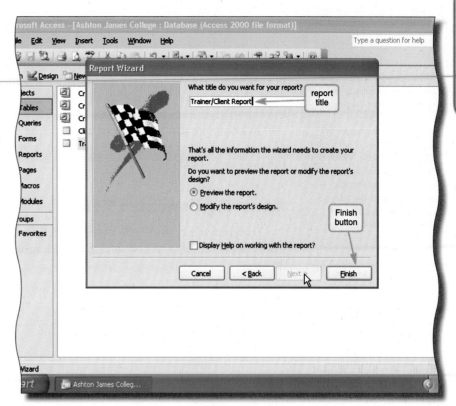

FIGURE 4-50

• **Click the Finish button.**

The report design is complete and appears in the Print Preview window (Figure 4-51).

• **Close the report by clicking the Close Window button for the window containing the report.**

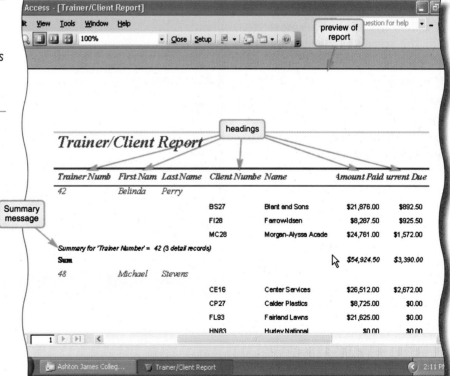

FIGURE 4-51

You will find differences between the report shown in Figure 4-51 on the previous page and the one illustrated in Figure 4-2 on page AC 195. The column headings in Figure 4-51 are on a single line, whereas they extend over two lines in the report in Figure 4-2. In addition, the report in Figure 4-2 does not contain the message that begins, Summary for Trainer Number. Other messages found on the report in Figure 4-51 also are not on the report in Figure 4-2, but they are included in a portion of the report that does not appear.

To complete the report design, you must change the column headings and remove these extra messages. In addition, you will change the Can Grow property for the Name field.

Removing Unwanted Controls

To remove a control you do not need, first click the control to select it. Then, press the DELETE key to remove the unwanted control as the following steps illustrate.

To Remove Unwanted Controls

1

• **Be sure the Reports object is selected in the Database window, right-click Trainer/Client Report, and then click Design View on the shortcut menu.**

• **If a field list appears, remove it from the screen by clicking its Close button.**

• **If necessary, maximize the window.**

• **Click the control at the top of the Trainer Number Footer section.**

The report appears in Design view (Figure 4-52). The control is selected.

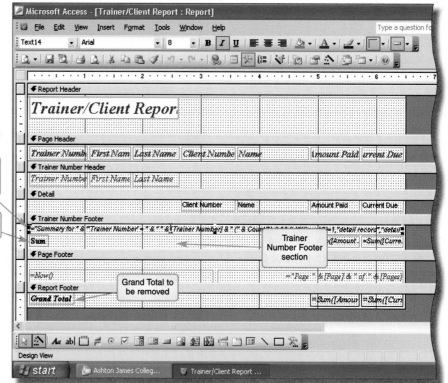

FIGURE 4-52

2

- **Press the DELETE key to delete it.**
- **Click the control that reads Sum, then press the delete key to delete the control.**
- **Click the control that reads Grand Total, then press the delete key to delete the control.**

The controls have been removed (Figure 4-54).

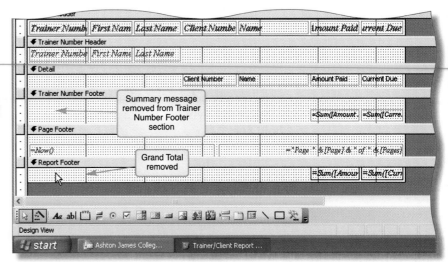

FIGURE 4-53

Changing a Property

Just as in the previous report, there is missing data in the Detail section of the report. The following steps select all the controls in the Detail section and change the Can Grow property for the controls.

To Change a Property

1

- **Right-click below the section selector for the Detail section.**
- **Click Properties and then, if necessary, click the Format tab.**
- **Click the Can Grow property, click the Can Grow property box arrow, and then click Yes in the list that appears.**

The Multiple selection property sheet appears (Figure 4-54). The value for the Can Grow property has been changed to Yes for all fields in the Detail section.

2

- **Close the property sheet by clicking its Close button.**

The property sheet no longer appears.

More About

Enlarging Controls

If you want to make a slight adjustment to a control, it often is easier to hold down the SHIFT key and use the appropriate arrow key.

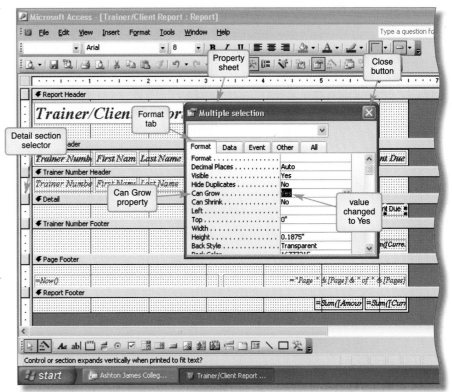

FIGURE 4-54

Enlarging the Page Header Section

The current Page Header section is not large enough to encompass the desired column headings because several of them extend over two lines. Thus, before changing the column headings, you must enlarge the Page Header. To do so, drag the bottom border of the Page Header section down. A bold line in the Page Header section immediately below the column headings also must be dragged down.

The following steps illustrate enlarging the Page Header section and moving the bold line.

To Enlarge the Page Header Section

1

• **Point to the bottom border of the Page Header section. The mouse pointer shape changes to a two-headed vertical arrow with a crossbar.**

• **Drag the mouse pointer down to enlarge the size of the Page Header section.**

The section is enlarged (Figure 4-55).

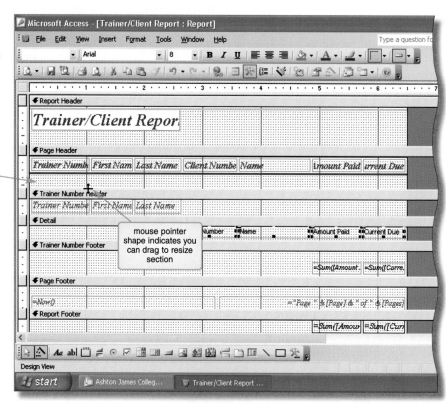

Page Header section expanded

mouse pointer shape indicates you can drag to resize section

FIGURE 4-55

2

• **Click the bold line underneath the column headings in the Page Header section, and then drag the bold line down to the bottom of the Page Header section. The mouse pointer is displayed as a hand when you drag the line.**

The bold line is moved (Figure 4-56).

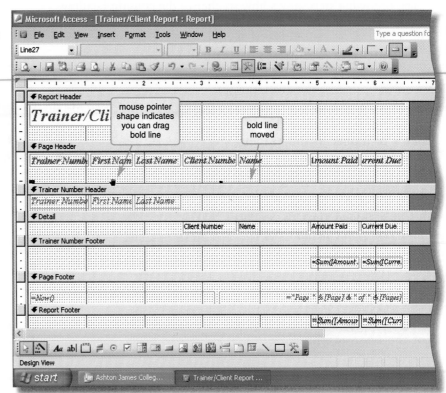

FIGURE 4-56

The page heading now is enlarged appropriately so the column headings can be changed.

Changing Column Headings

To change a column heading, point to the position where you would like to display an insertion point. Click once to select the heading. Handles will appear around the border of the heading after clicking. Then, click a second time to display the insertion point. Then, you can make the desired changes. To delete a character, press the DELETE key to delete the character following the insertion point, or press the BACKSPACE key to delete the character preceding the insertion point. To insert a new character, simply type the character. To move the portion following the insertion point to a second line, press SHIFT+ENTER.

If you click the second time too rapidly, Access will assume you have double-clicked the heading. Double-clicking a control is another way to produce the control's property sheet. If this happens, simply close the property sheet and begin the process again.

More About

Report Design

Proper report design is critical because users judge the value of information based on the way it is presented. Many organizations have formal rules governing the design of printed documents. For more information on report design, visit the Microsoft Access 2003 More About Web page (scsite.com/ac2003/more) and click Report Design.

The following step shows how to change the column headings.

To Change the Column Headings

1

• **Point immediately after the second r in Trainer in the heading for the first field.**

• **Click the column heading for the first field to select it.**

• **Click it a second time to produce an insertion point behind the r, press the DELETE key to delete the space between Trainer and Number, and then press SHIFT+ENTER to extend the headings over two lines.**

• **Using the same technique, change all of the two word headings.**

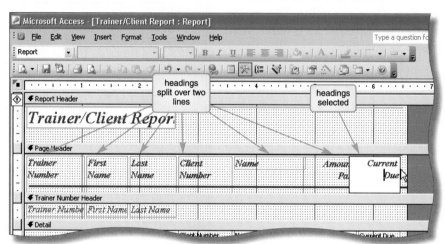

FIGURE 4-57

The headings are split over two lines (Figure 4-57).

Previewing a Report

To see what the report looks like with actual data, preview the report by clicking the Print Preview button on the Report Design toolbar as illustrated in the following step.

To Preview a Report

1 **Click the Print Preview button on the Report Design toolbar. If the entire width of the report does not appear, click anywhere within the report.**

A preview of the report appears. The extra messages have been removed. The column headings have been changed and now extend over two lines. The name for Morgan-Alyssa Academy extends over two lines.

Closing and Saving a Report

To close a report, close the window containing the report. Then, indicate whether you want to save your changes. The following step shows how to close and save the report.

To Close and Save a Report

1 **Click the Close Window button for the window containing the report to close the window. Click the Yes button to save the design of the report.**

Access displays the Database window. The changes are saved.

Printing a Report

To print the report, right-click the report name in the Database window, and then click Print on the shortcut menu as the following step illustrates.

To Print a Report

1 **Be sure the Reports object is selected in the Database window. Right-click Trainer/Client Report and then click Print on the shortcut menu.**

The report prints. It should look like the report shown in Figure 4-2 on page AC 195.

Report Design Considerations

When designing and creating reports, keep in mind the following guidelines.

1. The purpose of any report is to provide specific information. Ask yourself if the report conveys this information effectively. Are the meanings of the rows and columns in the report clear? Are the column captions easily understood? Are all abbreviations used in the report clear to those looking at the report?
2. Be sure to allow sufficient white space between groups. If you feel the amount is insufficient, add more space by enlarging the group footer.
3. You can use different fonts and sizes by changing the appropriate properties. It is important not to overuse them, however. Consistently using several different fonts and sizes often gives a cluttered and amateurish look to the report.
4. Be consistent when creating reports. Once you have decided on a general style, stick with it.

Creating and Using Custom Forms

Thus far, you have used a form to add new records to a table and change existing records. When you did, you created a basic form using the AutoForm command. Although the form did provide some assistance in the task, the form was not particularly pleasing. The standard form stacked fields on top of each other at the left side of the screen. This section covers custom forms that you can use in place of the basic form created by the AutoForm command. To create such a form, first use the Form Wizard to create a basic form. Then, modify the design of this form, transforming it into the one you want.

Beginning the Form Creation

To create a form, select a table for the form and then use the New Object button. Next, use the Form Wizard to create the form. The Form Wizard will lead you through a series of choices and questions. Access then will create the form automatically.

The steps on the next page show how to create an initial form. This form later will be modified to produce the form shown in Figure 4-3 on page AC 196.

More About

Modifying Form Properties

You can modify many of the properties associated with a form. To modify a form property, right-click the form selector (the box in the upper-left corner of the form) and click Properties. For example, to change the default view to continuous form, right-click the form selector, click Properties, click the Default View property, and then click Continuous Form. Other property changes, such as changing the caption for a form are done similarly. For example, you could change the caption for the form from Client Update Form to AJC Client Update Form by clicking the Caption property and entering the new caption name.

More About

Creating Forms

There are two alternatives to using the Form Wizard to create forms. You can use AutoForm to create a very simple form that includes all fields in the table or query. You also can use Design view to create a form totally from scratch.

To Begin Creating a Form

1

• **Make sure the Tables object is selected and then click Client.**

• **Click the New Object button arrow, click Form, and then click Form Wizard. Click the OK button.**

The Form Wizard dialog box appears (Figure 4-58). The Client Number field is selected.

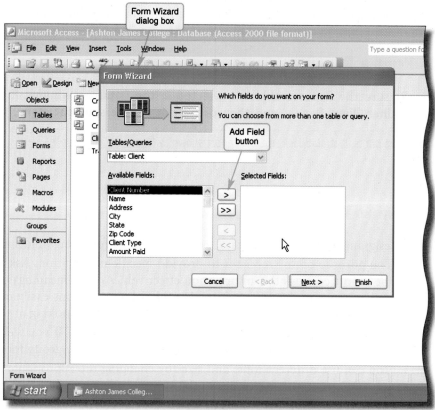

FIGURE 4-58

2

• **Use the Add Field button to add all the fields except the Client Type and Trainer Number fields.**

• **Click the Next button.**

• **When asked for a layout, be sure Columnar is selected, and then click the Next button again.**

The Form Wizard dialog box appears, requesting a form style (Figure 4-59).

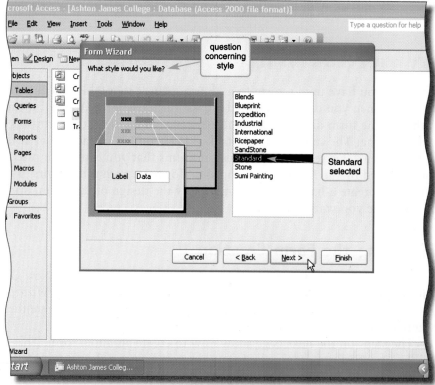

FIGURE 4-59

3

• **Be sure Standard is selected, click the Next button, and then type** Client Update Form **as the title for the form.**

• **Click the Finish button to complete and display the form.**

Access displays the Client Update Form in Form view (Figure 4-60).

4

• **Click the Close Window button for the Client Update Form window to close the form.**

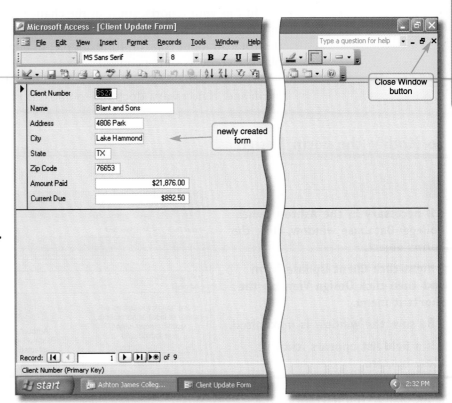

FIGURE 4-60

Modifying the Form Design

To modify the design of an existing form, open the form in Design view. The modifications can include moving fields, adding new fields, and changing field characteristics. In addition, you can add special features, such as combo boxes and titles and change the colors used.

Just as with reports, the various items on a form are called controls. The three types are bound controls, unbound controls, and calculated controls. **Bound controls** are used to display data that comes from the database, such as the client number and name. Bound controls have attached labels that typically display the name of the field that furnishes the data for the control. The **attached label** for the Client Number field, for example, is the portion of the screen immediately to the left of the field. It contains the words, Client Number.

Unbound controls are not associated with data from the database and are used to display such things as the form's title. Finally, **calculated controls** are used to display data that is calculated from other data in the database, such as the Total Amount, which is calculated by adding the amount paid and current due amounts.

To move, resize, delete, or modify a control, click it. Clicking a second time produces an insertion point in the control to let you modify its contents. When a control is selected, handles appear around the border of the control and, if appropriate, around the attached label. If you point to the border of the control, but away from any handle, the pointer shape will change to a hand. You then can drag the control to move it. If an attached label appears, it will move along with the control. If you wish to move the control or the attached label separately, drag the large handle in the upper-left corner of the control or label. To resize the control, drag one of the sizing handles; and to delete it, press the DELETE key.

Other Ways

1. Click Forms on Objects bar, click New button, click Form Wizard
2. Click Forms on Objects bar, double-click Create form by using wizard
3. On Insert menu click Form, click Form Wizard
4. In Voice Command mode, say "Forms, New," click Form Wizard

Just as with reports, some of the changes you wish to make to a control will involve using the property sheet for the control. You will use the property sheet of the Total Amount control, for example, to change the format that Access uses to display the contents of the control.

The following steps illustrate how to modify the design of the Client Update Form and, if necessary, dock the toolbox at the bottom of the screen.

To Modify the Form Design

1

• **If necessary in the Ashton James College: Database window, click the Forms object.**

• **Right-click Client Update Form and then click Design View on the shortcut menu.**

• **Be sure the window is maximized.**

• **If a field list appears, click its Close button.**

• **Be sure the toolbox appears and is docked at the bottom of the screen.**

• **Click the control for the Amount Paid field, and then move the mouse pointer until the shape changes to a hand. (You will need to point to the border of the control but away from any handle.)**

Move handles appear, indicating the field is selected (Figure 4-61). The shape of the mouse pointer changes to a hand.

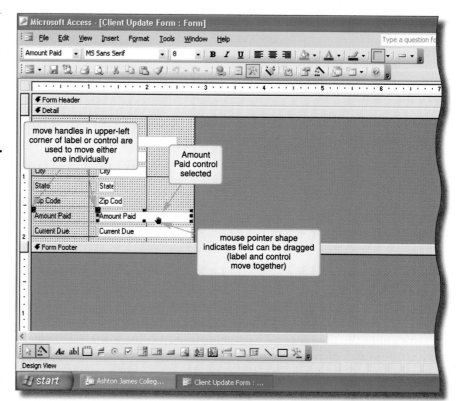

FIGURE 4-61

2

• **Drag the Amount Paid field to the approximate position shown in Figure 4-62.**

The form expands automatically in size to accommodate the new position for the field.

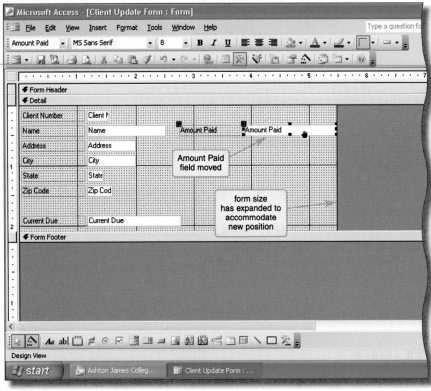

FIGURE 4-62

3

• **Use the same steps to move the Current Due field to the position shown in Figure 4-63.**

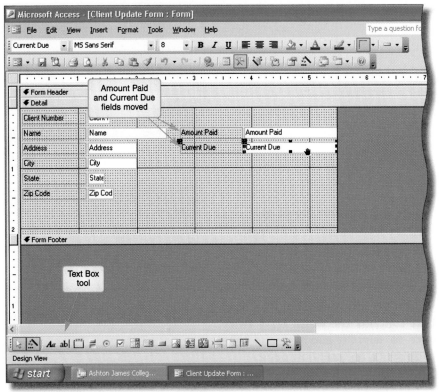

FIGURE 4-63

Adding a Calculated Field

To add a calculated field, use the Text Box tool in the toolbox. Place the text box on the form, and then indicate the contents of the field.

The following steps illustrate how to add the Total Amount field to the form. The total amount is calculated by adding the contents of the Amount Paid field and the contents of the Current Due field.

To Add a Calculated Field

1

• **Click the Text Box tool in the toolbox, and then move the mouse pointer, which has changed shape to a small plus symbol accompanied by a text box, to the position shown in Figure 4-64.**

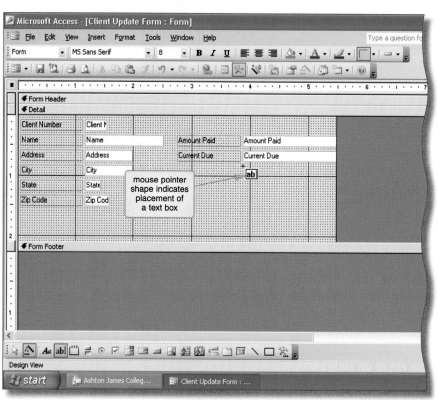

FIGURE 4-64

2

• **Click the position shown in Figure 4-64 to place a text box.**

• **Click inside the text box and type** =[Amount Paid]+[Current Due] **as the expression in the text box.**

• **Click the attached label (the box that contains the word, Text) twice, once to select it and a second time to produce an insertion point.**

• **Use the DELETE key or the BACKSPACE key to delete the current entry.**

• **Type** Total Amount **as the new entry.**

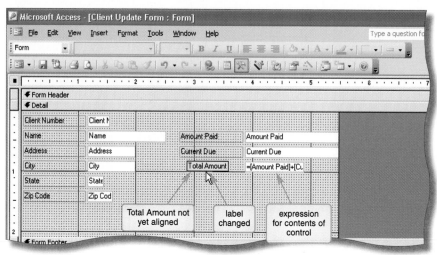

FIGURE 4-65

The expression for the field has been entered and the label has been changed to Total Amount (Figure 4-65).

3

- **Click outside the Total Amount control to deselect it, and then click the control to select it once more. Handles will appear around the control.**

- **Move the label portion so its left edge lines up with the labels for the Amount Paid and Current Due fields by dragging the move handle in its upper-left corner.**

The label is moved (Figure 4-66). The mouse pointer has assumed the pointing finger shape.

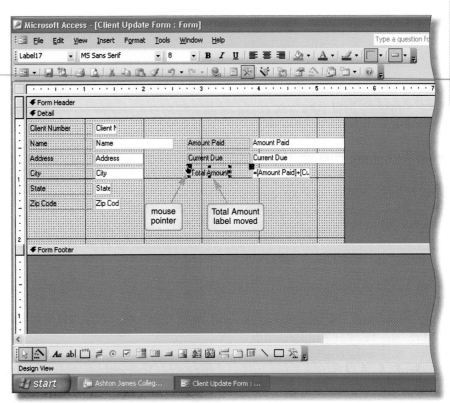

FIGURE 4-66

The control is added to the form. The expression and label are correct and the control is in the correct position.

Changing the Format of a Field

Access automatically formats fields from the database appropriately because it knows their data types. Usually, you will find the formats assigned by Access to be acceptable. For calculated fields, such as Total Amount, however, Access just assigns a general format. The value will not display automatically with two decimal places and a dollar sign.

To change to a special format, such as Currency, which displays the number with a dollar sign and two decimal places, requires using the field's property sheet to change the Format property. The steps on the next page change the format for the Total Amount field to Currency.

To Change the Format of a Field

1

• **Right-click the control for the Total Amount field (the box containing the expression) to produce its shortcut menu, and then click Properties on the shortcut menu.**

• **If necessary, click the All tab so all the properties appear, and then click the Format property.**

Access displays the property sheet for the field (Figure 4-67).

2

• **Click the Format property box arrow to produce a list of available formats.**

• **Scroll down so Currency appears and then click Currency.**

• **Close the property sheet by clicking its Close button.**

The property sheet no longer appears.

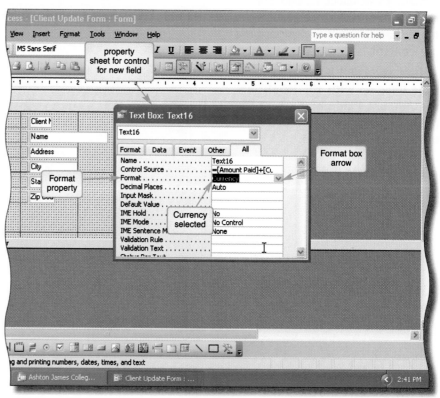

FIGURE 4-67

The values in the Total Amount field will appear in Currency format, which includes a dollar sign and two decimal places.

Combo Boxes

When entering a value for the client type, there are only three legitimate values: EDU, MAN, and SER. When entering a trainer number, the value must match the number of a trainer currently in the Trainer table. To assist the users in entering this data, the form will contain combo boxes. With a combo box, the user can type the data, if that is convenient. Alternatively, the user can click the combo box arrow to display a list of possible values and then select an item from the list.

To place a combo box in the form, use the Combo Box tool in the toolbox. If the Control Wizards tool in the toolbox is selected, you can use a wizard to guide you through the process of creating the combo box. The following steps show how to place a combo box that selects values from a list for the Client Type field on the form.

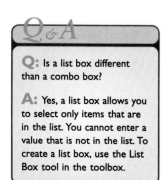

Q: Is a list box different than a combo box?

A: Yes, a list box allows you to select only items that are in the list. You cannot enter a value that is not in the list. To create a list box, use the List Box tool in the toolbox.

To Place a Combo Box that Selects Values from a List

1

• **If necessary, click the Control Wizards tool in the toolbox to select it.**

• **Click the Combo Box tool in the toolbox, and then move the mouse pointer, whose shape has changed to a small plus symbol accompanied by a combo box, to the position shown in Figure 4-68.**

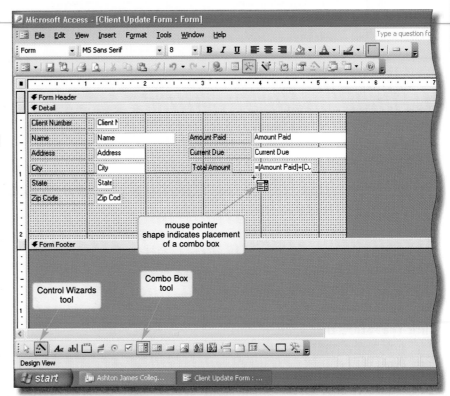

FIGURE 4-68

2

• **Click the position shown in Figure 4-68 to place a combo box.**

• **If necessary, click the "I will type in the values that I want." option button to select it.**

The Combo Box Wizard dialog box appears, requesting that you indicate how the combo box is to receive values for the list (Figure 4-69). The "I will type in the values that I want." option button is selected.

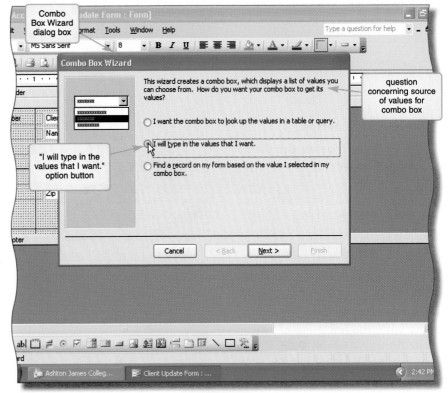

FIGURE 4-69

3

• **Click the Next button in the Combo Box Wizard dialog box, click the first row of the table (under Col1), and then type** EDU **as the entry.**

• **Press the DOWN ARROW key and then type** MAN **as the entry.**

• **Press the DOWN ARROW key again and then type** SER **as the entry.**

The list of values for the combo box is entered (Figure 4-70).

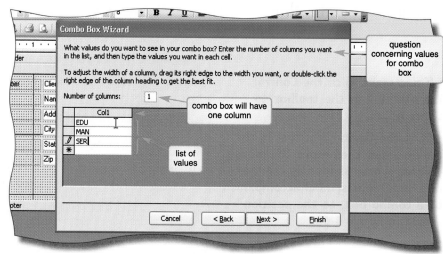

FIGURE 4-70

4

• **Click the Next button.**

• **Click the "Store that value in this field:" option button.**

• **Click the "Store that value in this field:" box arrow and then click Client Type.**

The "Store that value in this field:" option button is selected, and the Client Type field is selected (Figure 4-71).

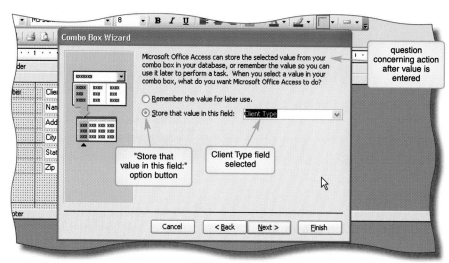

FIGURE 4-71

5

• **Click the Next button.**

• **Type** Client Type **as the label for the combo box.**

The label is entered (Figure 4-72).

6

• **Click the Finish button.**

• **Click the label for the combo box, and then drag its move handle to move the label so its left edge aligns with the left edge of the labels for the Amount Paid, Current Due, and Total Amount fields.**

The combo box is placed on the form.

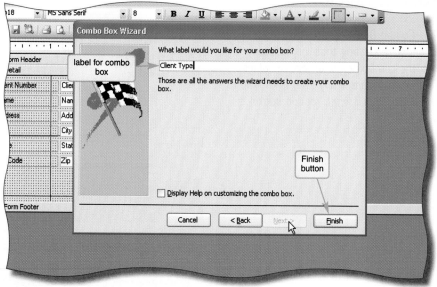

FIGURE 4-72

The steps for placing a combo box to select values from a table are similar to those for placing a combo box to select values from a list. The only difference is the source of the data. The following steps show how to place a combo box that selects values from a related table for the Trainer Number field on the form.

To Place a Combo Box that Selects Values from a Related Table

1

• **With the Control Wizards tool in the toolbox selected, click the Combo Box tool in the toolbox, and then move the mouse pointer, whose shape has changed to a small plus symbol accompanied by a combo box, to the position shown in Figure 4-73.**

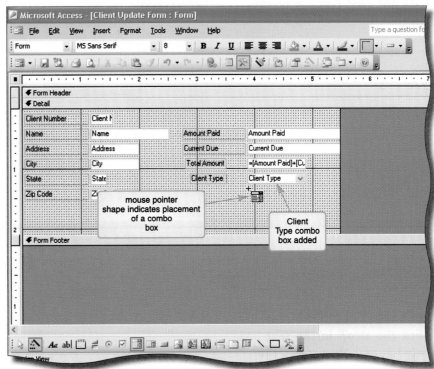

FIGURE 4-73

2

• **Click the position shown in Figure 4-73 to place a combo box.**

• **In the Combo Box Wizard dialog box, click the "I want the combo box to look up the values in a table or query." option button if it is not already selected.**

• **Click the Next button and then click Table: Trainer.**

The Trainer table is selected as the table to provide values for the combo box (Figure 4-74).

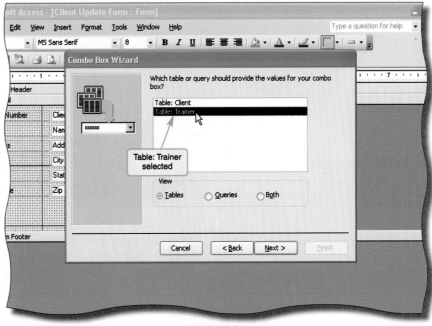

FIGURE 4-74

3

• **Click the Next button.**

• **Click the Add Field button to add the Trainer Number as a field in the combo box.**

• **Click the First Name field and then click the Add Field button.**

• **Click the Last Name field and then click the Add Field button.**

The Trainer Number, First Name, and Last Name fields are selected for the combo box (Figure 4-75).

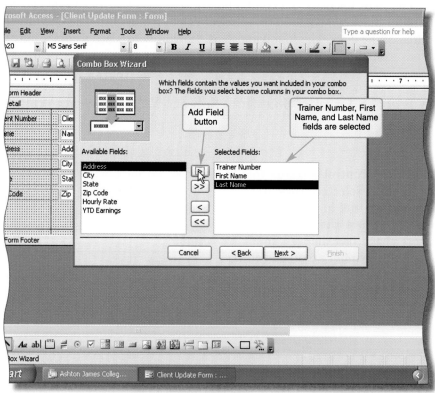

FIGURE 4-75

4

• **Click the Next button.**

• **Click the arrow in the text box labeled 1, and then select the Trainer Number field.**

The rows within the combo box will be sorted by trainer number (Figure 4-76).

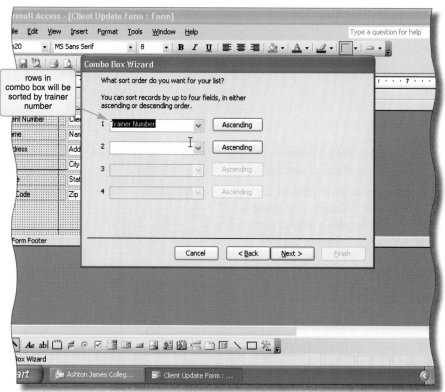

FIGURE 4-76

5

• **Click the Next button.**

The next Combo Box Wizard dialog box appears (Figure 4-77). You can use this dialog box to change the sizes of the fields. You also can use it to indicate whether the key field, in this case the Trainer Number field, should be hidden.

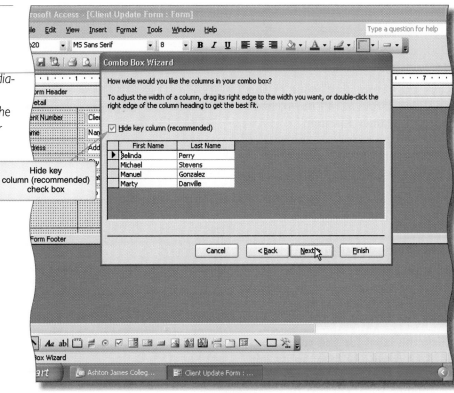

FIGURE 4-77

6

• **Click the "Hide key column (recommended)" check box to remove the check mark to ensure the Trainer Number field appears along with the First Name and Last Name fields.**

• **Resize each column to best fit the data by double-clicking the right-hand border of the column heading.**

• **Click the Next button.**

The Combo Box Wizard dialog box appears, asking you to choose a field that uniquely identifies a row in the combo box (Figure 4-78). The Trainer Number field, which is the correct field, is already selected.

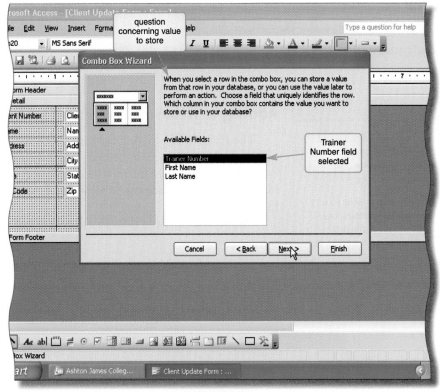

FIGURE 4-78

7

- **Click the Next button.**
- **Click the "Store that value in this field:" option button.**
- **Click the "Store that value in this field:" box arrow, scroll down, and then click Trainer Number.**

The Trainer Number field is selected as the field in which to store the value (Figure 4-79).

8

- **Click the Next button.**
- **Be sure** Trainer Number **is entered as the label for the combo box, and then click the Finish button.**
- **Click the label for the combo box, and then move the label so its left edge aligns with the left edge of the Amount Paid, Current Due, Total Amount, and Client Type fields.**

The combo box is placed on the form.

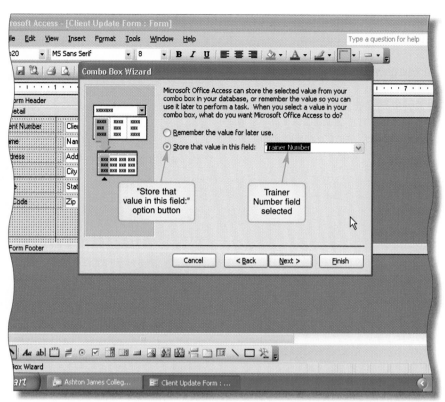

FIGURE 4-79

Adding a Title

The form in Figure 4-3 on page AC 196 contains a title, Client Update Form, that appears in a large, light blue label at the top of the form. To add a title, first expand the Form Header section to allow room for the title. Next, use the Label tool in the toolbox to place the label in the Form Header section. Finally, type the title in the label.

The following steps illustrate how to add a title to the form.

Access Project 4

To Add a Title

1

• **Point to the bottom border of the Form Header section. The mouse pointer changes shape to a two-headed vertical arrow with a crossbar.**

• **Drag the bottom border of the Form Header section to resize the Form Header section to the approximate size shown in Figure 4-80.**

• **Click the Label tool in the toolbox and then move the mouse pointer, whose shape has changed to a small plus symbol accompanied by a label, to the approximate position shown in the figure.**

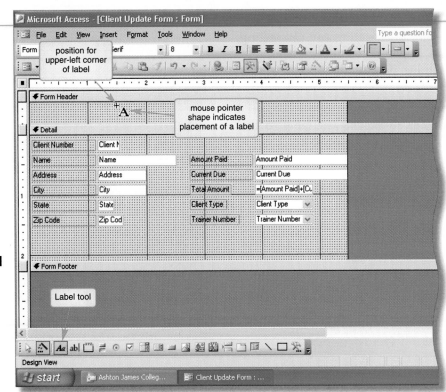

FIGURE 4-80

2

• **Click the mouse pointer in the position in the figure, and then type** Client Update Form **as the contents of the label.**

The label has been placed (Figure 4-81).

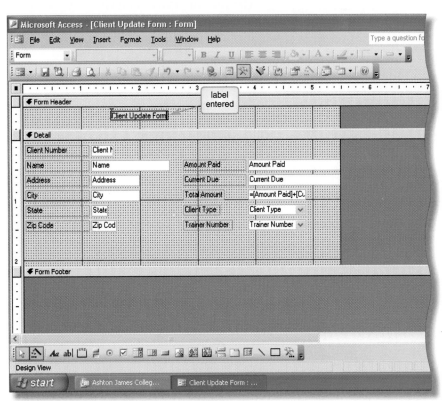

FIGURE 4-81

3

- Click outside the label to deselect it.

- Click the label to select it once again. (Deselecting and reselecting are required to produce the handles around the border of the control.)

- Drag the handle in the lower-right corner to expand the label to the size shown in Figure 4-82.

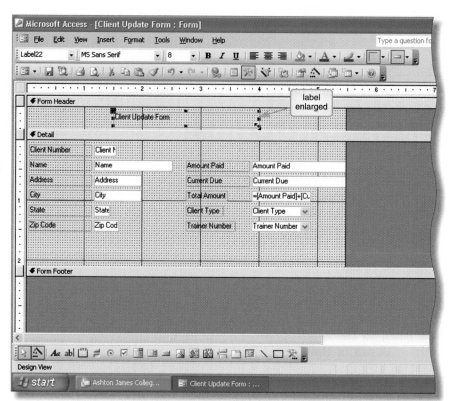

FIGURE 4-82

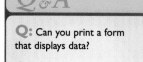
The title currently is much too small for the rectangle, but you can correct that by changing the font size. Changing the font size is just one of the enhancements you can make to the title.

Enhancing a Title

The form now contains a title. You can enhance the appearance of the title by changing various properties of the label containing the title. The following steps change the color of the label, make the label appear to be raised from the screen, change the font size of the title, and change the alignment of the title within the label.

To Enhance a Title

1

• **Right-click the label containing the title.**

The shortcut menu for the label is displayed (Figure 4-83).

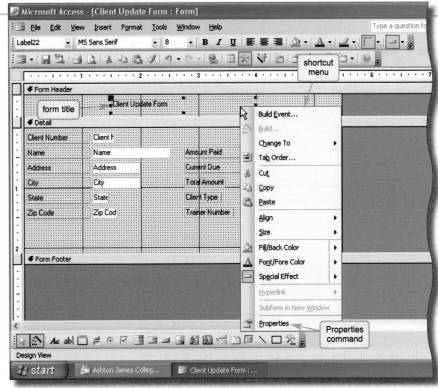

FIGURE 4-83

2

• **Click Properties.**

• **If necessary, click the All tab in the property sheet.**

• **Click the down scroll arrow to display the Back Color property and then click Back Color.**

Access displays the property sheet for the label (Figure 4-84). The insertion point is displayed in the Back Color property and the Build button appears.

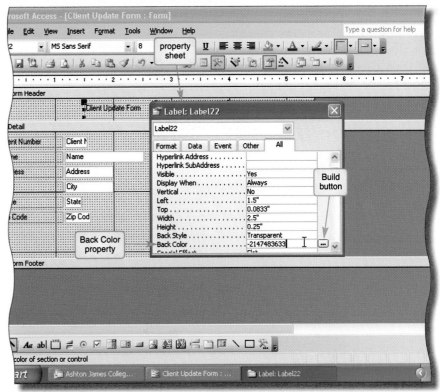

FIGURE 4-84

3

• **Click the Build button.**

The Color palette appears (Figure 4-85).

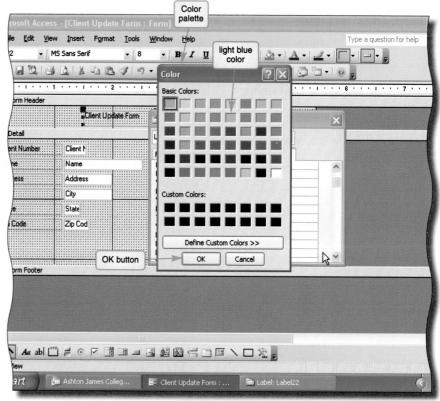

FIGURE 4-85

4

• **Click the color light blue in the second row and fifth column, and then click the OK button.**

• **Scroll down the property sheet, click the Special Effect property, and then click the Special Effect property box arrow.**

The list of available values for the Special Effect property is displayed (Figure 4-86).

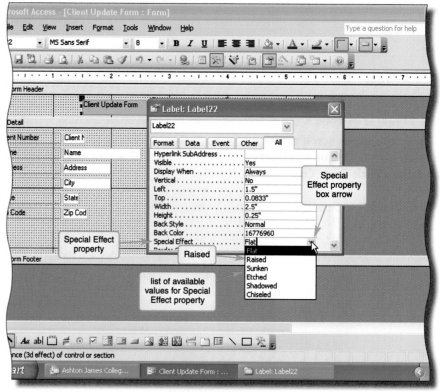

FIGURE 4-86

5

- **Click Raised.**
- **Scroll down the property sheet and then click the Font Size property.**
- **Click the Font Size property box arrow.**
- **Click 14 in the list of font sizes.**
- **Scroll down and then click the Text Align property.**
- **Click the Text Align property box arrow.**

The list of available values for the Text Align property appears (Figure 4-87).

6

- **Click Distribute.**
- **Close the property sheet by clicking its Close button.**
- **If necessary, use the sizing handles to resize the label so the entire title is displayed.**
- **Click outside the label to deselect it.**

The enhancements to the title now are complete.

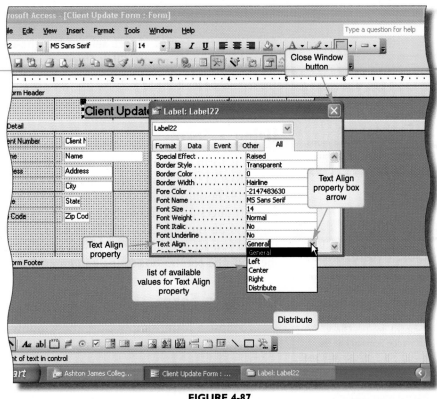

FIGURE 4-87

Saving and Closing a Form

To close a form, close the window using the window's Close Window button. Then, indicate whether you want to save your changes. The following step shows how to close and save the form.

To Close and Save a Form

1 **Click the window's Close Window button to close the window, and then click the Yes button to save the design of the form.**

Access displays the Database window. The changes are saved.

Opening a Form

To open a form, use the Open command on the shortcut menu. The form will appear and can be used to examine and update data. The step on the next page illustrates how to open the Client Update Form.

More About

Microsoft Certification

The Microsoft Office Specialist Certification program provides an opportunity for you to obtain a valuable industry credential - proof that you have the Access 2003 skills required by employers. For more information, see Appendix E, or visit the Microsoft Access 2003 Certification Web page (scsite.com/ac2003/cert).

Other Ways

1. On File menu click Close
2. In Voice Command mode, say "File, Close"

To Open a Form

1 **With the Forms object selected, right-click the Client Update Form to display the shortcut menu. Click Open on the shortcut menu.**

The form appears. It should look like the form shown in Figure 4-3 on page AC 196.

Using a Form

This form contains combo boxes. To use a combo box, click the arrow. Clicking the arrow in the Client Type combo box produces a list of client types (see Figure 4-3a on page AC 196). Clicking the arrow in the Trainer Number combo box produces a list of numbers and the names of available trainers as shown in Figure 4-3b on page AC 196. In either case, you can type the appropriate value from the list you see on the screen or you simply can click the value in the list. With either method, the combo box helps you enter the correct value.

Closing a Form

To close a form, simply close the window containing the form. The following step shows how to close the form.

To Close a Form

1 **Click the Close Window button for the Form window.**

Form Design Considerations

As you design and create custom forms, keep in mind the following guidelines.

1. Remember that someone using your form may be looking at the form for several hours at a time. Forms that are cluttered or contain too many different effects (colors, fonts, frame styles, and so on) can become very hard on the eyes.
2. Place the fields in logical groupings. Fields that relate to each other should be close to one another on the form.
3. If the data that a user will enter comes from a paper form, make the screen form resemble the paper form as closely as possible.

Closing the Database and Quitting Access

The following steps close the database and quit Access.

To Close a Database and Quit Access

1 **Click the Close Window button for the Ashton James College : Database window.**

2 **Click the Close button for the Microsoft Access window.**

Access and the database close.

Project Summary

In Project 4, you used wizards to create two reports and a form, which you then modified in Design view. To create the reports, you learned the purpose of the various sections and how to modify their contents. You used sorting and grouping in a report and saw how to add totals and subtotals. Then, you created and used a custom form. Steps and techniques were presented showing you how to move controls, create new controls, add combo boxes, and add a title. You changed the characteristics of various objects in the form. You also learned general principles to help you design effective reports and forms.

 If you have a SAM user profile, you may have access to hands-on instruction, practice, and assessment of the skills covered in this project. Log in to your SAM account and go to your assignments page to see what your instructor has assigned.

What You Should Know

Having completed this project, you should be able to perform the tasks below. The tasks are listed in the same order they were presented in this project. For a list of the buttons, menus, toolbars, and commands introduced in this project, see the Quick Reference Summary at the back of this book and refer to the Page Number column.

1. Open a Database   (AC 197)
2. Create a Report Using the Report Wizard   (AC 198)
3. Move to Design View and Dock the Toolbox   (AC 203)
4. Use Sorting and Grouping   (AC 205)
5. Move a Control   (AC 206)
6. Change the Can Grow Property   (AC 207)
7. Add Totals and Subtotals   (AC 209)
8. Align Controls   (AC 212)
9. Format Controls   (AC 214)
10. Change a Label   (AC 216)
11. Close and Save a Report   (AC 216, AC 226)
12. Print a Report   (AC 216)
13. Create a Report that Involves Multiple Tables   (AC 217)
14. Remove Unwanted Controls   (AC 222)
15. Change a Property   (AC 223)
16. Enlarge the Page Header Section   (AC 224)
17. Change the Column Headings   (AC 226)
18. Preview a Report   (AC 226)
19. Close and Save a Report   (AC 226)
20. Print a Report   (AC 227)
21. Begin Creating a Form   (AC 228)
22. Modify the Form Design   (AC 230)
23. Add a Calculated Field   (AC 232)
24. Change the Format of a Field   (AC 234)
25. Place a Combo Box that Selects Values from a List   (AC 235)
26. Place a Combo Box that Selects Values from a Related Table   (AC 237)
27. Add a Title   (AC 241)
28. Enhance a Title   (AC 243)
29. Close and Save a Form   (AC 245)
30. Open a Form   (AC 246)
31. Close a Form   (AC 246)
32. Close a Database and Quit Access   (AC 246)

Learn It Online

Instructions: To complete the Learn It Online exercises, start your browser, click the Address bar, and then enter the Web address scsite.com/ac2003/learn. When the Access 2003 Learn It Online page is displayed, follow the instructions in the exercises below. Each exercise has instructions for printing your results, either for your own records or for submission to your instructor.

1 Project Reinforcement TF, MC, and SA

Below Access Project 4, click the Project Reinforcement link. Print the quiz by clicking Print on the File menu for each page. Answer each question.

Flash Cards

Below Access Project 4, click the Flash Cards link and read the instructions. Type 20 (or a number specified by your instructor) in the Number of playing cards text box, type your name in the Enter your Name text box, and then click the Flip Card button. When the flash card is displayed, read the question and then click the ANSWER box arrow to select an answer. Flip through Flash Cards. If your score is 15 (75%) correct or greater, click Print on the File menu to print your results. If your score is less than 15 (75%) correct, then redo this exercise by clicking the Replay button.

3 Practice Test

Below Access Project 4, click the Practice Test link. Answer each question, enter your first and last name at the bottom of the page, and then click the Grade Test button. When the graded practice test is displayed on your screen, click Print on the File menu to print a hard copy. Continue to take practice tests until you score 80% or better.

4 Who Wants To Be a Computer Genius?

Below Access Project 4, click the Computer Genius link. Read the instructions, enter your first and last name at the bottom of the page, and then click the PLAY button. When your score is displayed, click the PRINT RESULTS link to print a hard copy.

5 Wheel of Terms

Below Access Project 4, click the Wheel of Terms link. Read the instructions, and then enter your first and last name and your school name. Click the PLAY button. When your score is displayed, right-click the score and then click Print on the shortcut menu to print a hard copy.

6 Crossword Puzzle Challenge

Below Access Project 4, click the Crossword Puzzle Challenge link. Read the instructions, and then enter your first and last name. Click the SUBMIT button. Work the crossword puzzle. When you are finished, click the Submit button. When the crossword puzzle is redisplayed, click the Print Puzzle button to print a hard copy.

7 Tips and Tricks

Below Access Project 4, click the Tips and Tricks link. Click a topic that pertains to Project 4. Right-click the information and then click Print on the shortcut menu. Construct a brief example of what the information relates to in Access to confirm you understand how to use the tip or trick.

8 Newsgroups

Below Access Project 4, click the Newsgroups link. Click a topic that pertains to Project 4. Print three comments.

9 Expanding Your Horizons

Below Access Project 4, click the Expanding Your Horizons link. Click a topic that pertains to Project 4. Print the information. Construct a brief example of what the information relates to in Access to confirm you understand the contents of the article.

10 Search Sleuth

Below Access Project 4, click the Search Sleuth link. To search for a term that pertains to this project, select a term below the Project 4 title and then use the Google search engine at google.com (or any major search engine) to display and print two Web pages that present information on the term.

11 Access Online Training

Below Access Project 4, click the Access Online Training link. When your browser displays the Microsoft Office Online Web page, click the Access link. Click one of the Access courses that covers one or more of the objectives listed at the beginning of the project on page AC 194 . Print the first page of the course before stepping through it.

12 Office Marketplace

Below Access Project 4, click the Office Marketplace link. When your browser displays the Microsoft Office Online Web page, click the Office Marketplace link. Click a topic that relates to Access. Print the first page.

Apply Your Knowledge

1 Presenting Data in the Begon Pest Control Database

Instructions: Start Access. If you are using the Microsoft Office Access 2003 Complete or the Microsoft Office Access 2003 Comprehensive text, open the Begon Pest Control database that you used in Project 3. Otherwise, see the inside back cover for instructions for downloading the Data Disk or see your instructor for information about accessing the files required for this book. Perform the following tasks:

1. Create the report shown in Figure 4-88.
2. Print the report.
3. Using the Form Wizard, create a form for the Customer table. Include all fields except Technician Number on the form. Use Customer Update Form as the title for the form.

4. Modify the form in the Design window to create the form shown in Figure 4-89. The form includes a combo box for the Technician Number field.
5. Print the form. To print the form, open the form, click File on the menu bar, and then click Print. Click Selected Record(s) as the Print Range. Click the OK button.

Technician/Customer Report

Technician Number	First Name	Last Name	Customer Number	Name	Balance
203	Miguel	Estevez			
			AT23	Atlas Repair	$335.00
			MC10	Moss Carpet	$398.00
					$733.00
210	Rachel	Hillsdale			
			AZ01	AZ Auto	$300.00
			BL35	Blanton Shoes	$290.00
			HI25	Hill Crafts	$334.00
			SE05	Servete Manufacturing	$343.00
					$1,267.00
214	Chou	Liu			
			CJ45	C Joe Diner	$0.00
			KL50	Klean n Dri	$365.00
			PV83	Prime Video	$0.00
					$365.00
					$2,365.00

FIGURE 4-88

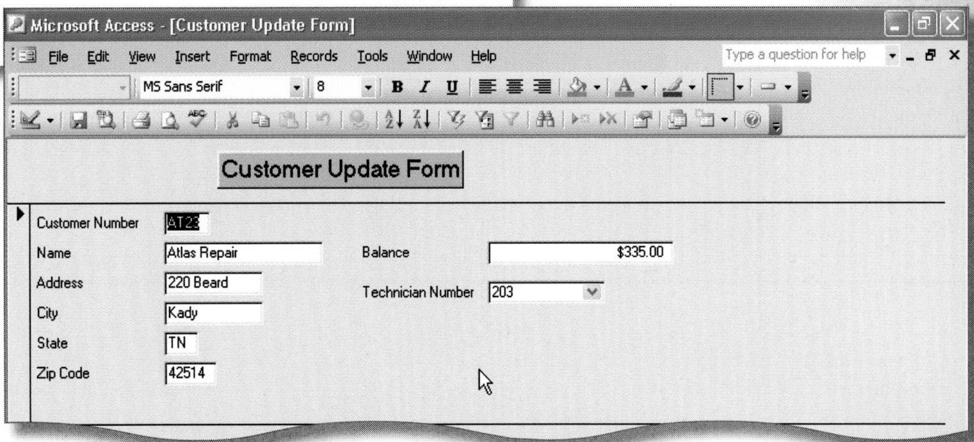

FIGURE 4-89

1 Presenting Data in the Birds2U Database

Problem: The management of Birds2U already has realized the benefits from the database of products and suppliers that you created. The management now would like to prepare reports and forms from the database.

Instructions: If you are using the Microsoft Office Access 2003 Complete or the Microsoft Office Access 2003 Comprehensive text, open the Birds2U database that you used in Project 3. Otherwise, see the inside back cover for instructions for downloading the Data Disk or see your instructor for information about accessing the files required for this book. Perform the following tasks:

1. Create the On Hand Value Report shown in Figure 4-90 for the Item table. The report is sorted by Description. On Hand Value is the result of multiplying On Hand by Cost.

On Hand Value Report

Item Code	Description	On Hand	Cost	On Hand Value
BO22	Barn Owl House	2	$97.50	$195.00
BA35	Bat House	14	$43.50	$609.00
BE19	Bee Box	7	$39.80	$278.60
BB01	Bird Bath	2	$82.10	$164.20
BL06	Bluebird House	9	$14.35	$129.15
BS10	Bunny Sprinkler	4	$41.95	$167.80
BU24	Butterfly Box	6	$36.10	$216.60
FS11	Froggie Sprinkler	5	$41.95	$209.75
GF12	Globe Feeder	12	$14.80	$177.60
HF01	Hummingbird Feeder	5	$11.35	$56.75
LM05	Leaf Mister	3	$29.95	$89.85
PM05	Purple Martin House	3	$67.10	$201.30
WF10	Window Feeder	10	$14.25	$142.50

FIGURE 4-90

In the Lab

2. Print the report.
3. Create the Supplier/Item report shown in Figure 4-91. Profit is the difference between Selling Price and Cost.
4. Print the report.
5. Create the form shown in Figure 4-92. On Hand Value is a calculated control and is the result of multiplying On Hand by Cost. Include a combo box for Supplier Code.
6. Print the form. To print the form, open the form, click File on the menu bar, and then click Print. Click Selected Record(s) as the Print Range. Click the OK button.

Supplier/Item Report

Supplier Code	Name	Item Code	Description	Selling Price	Cost	Profit
05	All Birds Supply					
		GF12	Globe Feeder	$16.25	$14.80	$1.45
		HF01	Hummingbird Feeder	$14.25	$11.35	$2.90
		WF10	Window Feeder	$15.95	$14.25	$1.70
13	Bird Casa Ltd					
		BB01	Bird Bath	$86.25	$82.10	$4.15
		BL06	Bluebird House	$15.99	$14.35	$1.64
		PM05	Purple Martin House	$69.95	$67.10	$2.85
17	Lawn Fixtures					
		BS10	Bunny Sprinkler	$50.00	$41.95	$8.05
		FS11	Froggie Sprinkler	$50.00	$41.95	$8.05
		LM05	Leaf Mister	$34.75	$29.95	$4.80
21	Natural Woods					
		BA35	Bat House	$45.50	$43.50	$2.00
		BE19	Bee Box	$42.50	$39.80	$2.70
		BO22	Barn Owl House	$107.75	$97.50	$10.25
		BU24	Butterfly Box	$37.75	$36.10	$1.65

FIGURE 4-91

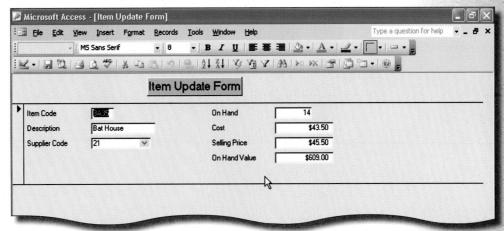

FIGURE 4-92

2 Presenting Data in the Babbage Bookkeeping Database

Problem: Babbage Bookkeeping already has realized several benefits from the database you created. The company now would like to prepare reports and forms from the database.

Instructions: If you are using the Microsoft Office Access 2003 Complete or the Microsoft Office Access 2003 Comprehensive text, open the Babbage Bookkeeping database that you used in Project 3. Otherwise, see the inside back cover for instructions for downloading the Data Disk or see your instructor for information about accessing the files required for this book. Perform the following tasks:

1. Create the Client Income Report shown in Figure 4-93 for the Client table. Group the report by Client Type and sort the records within Client Type by Name.

Client Income Report

Client Type	Client Number	Name	Address	City	Balance
MAN					
	B26	Blake-Scripps	557 Maum	Grant City	$229.50
	S56	SeeSaw Industries	31 Liatris	Portage	$362.50
				Subtotal:	$592.00
RET					
	A54	Afton Mills	612 Revere	Grant City	$315.50
	A62	Atlas Suppliers	227 Dandelion	Empeer	$525.00
	C21	Crompton Meat Market	72 Main	Empeer	$0.00
	D76	Dege Grocery	446 Linton	Portage	$485.75
	H21	Hill Shoes	247 Fulton	Grant City	$228.50
	M26	Mohr Crafts	665 Maum	Empeer	$312.50
				Subtotal:	$1,867.25
SER					
	G56	Grand Cleaners	337 Abelard	Empeer	$265.00
	L50	Lou's Salon	124 Fulton	Grant City	$125.00
	T45	Tate Repair	824 Revere	Grant City	$254.00
				Subtotal:	$644.00
				Grand Total:	$3,103.25

FIGURE 4-93

In the Lab

2. Print the report.
3. Create the Bookkeeper/Client report shown in Figure 4-94. Preview the report to check page margins and orientation. Adjust as necessary.
4. Print the report.
5. Create the form shown in Figure 4-95. Client Type and Bookkeeper Number are combo boxes.
6. Print the form. To print the form, open the form, click File on the menu bar, and then click Print. Click Selected Record(s) as the Print Range. Click the OK button.

Bookkeeper/Client Report

Bookkeeper Number	First Name	Last Name	Client Number	Name	Balance
22	Johanna	Lewes			
			A54	Afton Mills	$315.50
			G56	Grand Cleaners	$265.00
			M26	Mohr Crafts	$312.50
				Average Balance	$297.67
24	Mario	Rodriguez			
			A62	Atlas Suppliers	$525.00
			B26	Blake-Scripps	$229.50
			C21	Crompton Meat Market	$0.00
			H21	Hill Shoes	$228.50
			T45	Tate Repair	$254.00
				Average Balance	$247.40
34	Choi	Wong			
			D76	Dege Grocery	$485.75
			L50	Lou's Salon	$125.00
			S56	SeeSaw Industries	$362.50
				Average Balance	$324.42

FIGURE 4-94

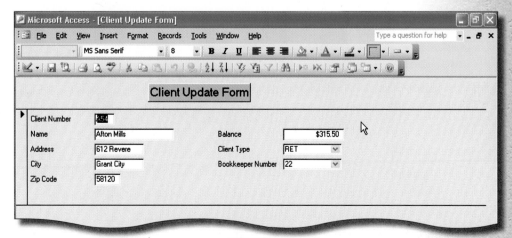

FIGURE 4-95

In the Lab

3 Presenting Data in the City Guide Database

Problem: The chamber of commerce already has realized several benefits from the database you created. The company now would like to prepare reports and forms from the database.

Instructions: If you are using the Microsoft Office Access 2003 Complete or the Microsoft Office Access 2003 Comprehensive text, open the City Guide database that you used in Project 3. Otherwise, see the inside back cover for instructions for downloading the Data Disk or see your instructor for information about accessing the files required for this book. Perform the following tasks:

Instructions Part 1: Create two reports for the chamber of commerce. The first report should be similar to the Client Account Summary report shown in Figure 4-1 on page AC 195. Group the report by Advertiser Type, sort the records within Advertiser Type by Name. The report also should include the address, amount paid, and balance fields. Provide subtotals and a grand total for the Balance and Amount Paid fields. Be sure to align controls appropriately. The second report should be similar to the Trainer/Client Report shown in Figure 4-2 on page AC 195 with the records grouped by Ad Rep Number.

Instructions Part 2: Create a form for the chamber of commerce that is similar to the form shown in Figures 4-3a and 4-3b on page AC 196. Total Amount is the sum of Balance and Amount Paid. Advertiser Type and Ad Rep Number should be combo boxes. Check the alignment and spacing of all controls. Adjust as necessary. Change the Default view for the form to Continuous Forms and the caption for the form to City Guide Advertiser Update Form. Sort the data by Name and print the form.

Cases and Places

The difficulty of these case studies varies:
■ are the least difficult and ■■ are more difficult. The last exercise is a group exercise.

1 ■ If you are using the Microsoft Office Access 2003 Complete or the Microsoft Office Access 2003 Comprehensive text, use the College Dog Walkers database that you used in Project 3. Otherwise, see the inside back cover for instructions for downloading the Data Disk or see your instructor for information about accessing the files required for this book. Use this database and create a form for the Customer table that is similar to that shown in Figure 4-89 on page AC 249.

2 ■ If you are using the Microsoft Office Access 2003 Complete or the Microsoft Office Access 2003 Comprehensive text, use the InPerson Fitness Company database that you used in Project 3. Otherwise, see the inside back cover for instructions for downloading the Data Disk or see your instructor for information about accessing the files required for this book. The InPerson Fitness Company needs a custom report and a custom form. Create a report for the company that is similar to the Trainer/Client Report shown in Figure 4-2 on page AC 195. Create a form for the company that is similar to the form shown in Figures 4-3a and 4-3b on page AC 196. Total Amount is the sum of Balance and Amount Paid.

3 ■■ If you are using the Microsoft Office Access 2003 Complete or the Microsoft Office Access 2003 Comprehensive text, use the Regional Books database that you used in Project 3. Otherwise, see the inside back cover for instructions for downloading the Data Disk or see your instructor for information about accessing the files required for this book. The bookstore owner would like a report that lists books by book type (used or new) with the average price for each type as well as the overall average price for all books. Create a report similar to that shown in Figure 4-1 on page AC 195 that groups books by book type. Within each book type, the records should be sorted by title. The report also should include the book code, units on hand, and price. Create a form similar to that shown in Figure 4-92 on page AC 251. Use a calculated control called Inventory Value that is the result of multiplying units on hand by price. Book type and Publisher code should be combo boxes.

4 ■■ If you are using the Microsoft Office Access 2003 Complete or the Microsoft Office Access 2003 Comprehensive text, use the Campus Housing database that you used in Project 3. Otherwise, see the inside back cover for instructions for downloading the Data Disk or see your instructor for information about accessing the files required for this book. The campus housing office would like an easy way to enter new rentals into the database. Create a custom form for the campus housing office that meets their needs. The form should include combo boxes for bedrooms, bathrooms, lease term, and owner code. Create a report for the campus housing office that lists all rentals grouped by owner. Do not include any subtotals or totals in the report.

Cases and Places

5 ▪▪ **Working Together** The Report and Form Wizards offer several different styles. Each member of the team should pick a different style and create the report shown in Figure 4-2 on page AC 195 and the form shown in Figure 4-3 on page AC 196 using the chosen styles. Compare the styles and as a team vote on which one you prefer. The project gave some general guidelines for designing reports and forms. Use the Internet to find more information about form design guidelines; for example, there are certain fonts that you should not use for a title and certain colors that are harder for individuals to see. Then, as a group, create a form that illustrates poor design features. Include a short write-up that explains what design principles were violated. Be sure to cite your references. Turn in each of the reports and forms that your team created using different styles. Also, turn in the poorly-designed form and the write-up.

Copy the Ashton James College database and rename the database as Team Name_AJC. For example, if your team is Team 1, then name the database Team 1_AJC. View the Trainer/Client Report in Layout view. Print the report. Change the page orientation for the report to landscape and adjust the page margins so that report is centered (approximately) on the page. Print the report in landscape orientation. Hide the report footer for the report and print the report. Unhide the report footer and hide the page header. Print the report. As a team discuss the changes that you made. Include a short write-up that summarizes the team's comments on the changes to the report. Turn in each of the modified reports and the short write-up.

Enhancing Forms with OLE Fields, Hyperlinks, and Subforms

PROJECT

5

CASE PERSPECTIVE

Ashton James College uses its database to keep records about clients and trainers. After several months, however, the administration has found that it needs to maintain additional data on its trainers. AJC needs to store the start date of each trainer in the database. The administration wants the database to contain a comment about each trainer as well as the trainer's picture. Additionally, each trainer now has a page on the Web, and the administration requires easy access to this page from the database. The administration wants to add the Phone Number field to the Trainer table. They also want to type only the digits in the telephone number and then have Access format the number appropriately. If the user enters 5125554625, for example, Access will format the number as (512) 555-4625.

After the proposed fields have been added to the database, they want a form created that incorporates some of the new fields with some of the existing fields. The administration wants the form to include the client number, name, amount paid, and current due amount for the clients of each trainer. Then, they would like to see multiple clients on the screen at the same time. The database should provide the capability of scrolling through all the clients of a trainer and of accessing the trainer's Web page directly from the form. The administration requires queries that use the Start Date and Comment fields.

As you read through this project, you will learn how to make the changes required by Ashton James College.

MICROSOFT
Office Access 2003

Enhancing Forms with OLE Fields, Hyperlinks, and Subforms

Objectives

You will have mastered the material in this project when you can:

- Use date, memo, OLE, and hyperlink fields
- Use the Input Mask wizard
- Update fields and enter data
- Change row and column size
- Create a form with a subform using the Form wizard
- Modify a subform design
- Modify a form design
- Move and resize fields and labels

- Change label alignment and size
- Change the size mode of a picture
- Change special effects and colors of labels
- Add a form title and fine-tune the form
- Change tab stops and tab order
- Use the form to view data and Web pages
- Use Date and Memo fields in a query
- View object dependencies

Introduction

This project creates the form shown in Figure 5-1. The form incorporates the following new features:

- New fields appear on the form. These include the date the trainer started working at the college and the trainer's telephone number.
- The Comment field allows the administration to store notes concerning the trainer. The Comment entry can be as long as the administration desires.
- The Picture field holds a photograph of the trainer.
- The Web Page field enables the user to access the Trainer's Web page directly from the database.
- The form shows data concerning the trainer, and information about the trainer's clients. The clients are displayed in a table on the form.

Trainer Master Form

FIGURE 5-1

Project Five — Enhancing the Ashton James College Forms

The steps in this project create the form required by the administration of Ashton James College. Before creating the form, the structure of the Trainer table must be changed to include the four new fields: Start Date, Comment, Picture, and Web Page. Each of these new fields uses a data type not encountered previously. The Phone Number field must be added and steps taken to ensure that the telephone numbers are entered in an appropriate format. The appropriate data must be entered in these new fields. The manner in which this is achieved depends on the data type. After entering data in the fields, the form including the table of client data is created. Finally, queries are created to obtain the answer to two important questions that reference the new fields.

Opening the Database

If you are stepping through this project on a computer and you want your screen to match the figures in this book, then you should change your computer's resolution to 800 x 600. For more information on how to change the resolution on your computer, see Appendix D. Before modifying the Trainer table and creating the form, you must open the database. The steps on the next page illustrate how to start Access and open the database. These steps assume that the database is located in a folder called Data on disk C. (See the note in Project 4 on page AC 197.) If your database is located anywhere else, you will need to adjust the appropriate steps.

To Open a Database

1 Click the Start button on the Windows taskbar, point to All Programs on the Start menu, point to Microsoft Office on the All Programs submenu, and then click Microsoft Office Access 2003 on the Microsoft Office submenu.

2 If the Access window is not maximized, double-click its title bar to maximize it.

3 If the Language bar appears, right-click it and then click Close the Language bar on the shortcut menu.

4 Click the Open button on the Database toolbar, and then click Local Disk (C:) in the Look in box. Double-click the Data folder and then make sure the database called Ashton James College is selected.

5 Click the Open button. If a Security Warning dialog box appears, click the Open button.

The database opens and the Ashton James College : Database window appears.

More About

OLE Data Type

A field with a data type of OLE can store data such as Word documents, Excel worksheets, pictures, sounds, and other types of binary data created in other programs. For more information, visit the Access 2003 More About Web page (scsite.com/ac2003/more), and then click OLE Fields.

Q: Why use Date as a data type for date fields? Why not simply use Text?

A: If you use Date, the computer will ensure that only legitimate dates are entered in the field. In addition, you can use date arithmetic. For example, you could subtract one date from another to find how many days there are between the two dates. You also can use dates in criteria.

Special Fields

The fields to be added require data types not previously encountered. The Phone Number field uses an input mask. The new data types are:

1. **Date (D)** — The field contains only valid dates.
2. **Memo (M)** — The field contains text that is variable in length. The length of the text stored in memo fields virtually is unlimited.
3. **OLE (O)** — The field contains objects created by other applications that support **OLE (Object Linking and Embedding)** as a server. Object Linking and Embedding is a feature of Microsoft Windows that creates a special relationship between Microsoft Access and the application that created the object. When you edit the object, Microsoft Access returns automatically to the application that created the object.
4. **Hyperlink (H)** — The field contains links to other Office documents or to Web pages. If the link is to a Web page, the field will contain the address of the Web page.

Adding Fields to a Table

You add the new fields to the Trainer table by modifying the design of the table and inserting the fields at the appropriate position in the table structure. The following steps illustrate how to add the Start Date, Comment, Picture, and Web Page fields to the Trainer table.

To Add Fields to a Table

1

- **If necessary, click Tables on the Objects bar.**
- **Right-click Trainer.**

The shortcut menu for the Trainer table appears (Figure 5-2).

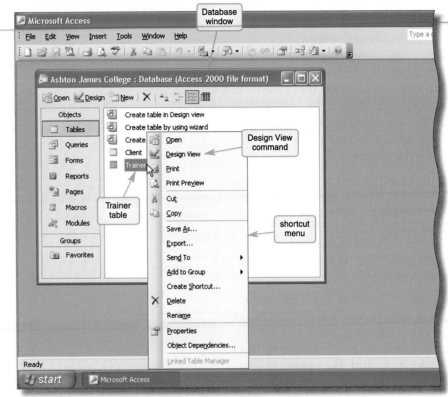

FIGURE 5-2

2

- **Click Design View on the shortcut menu, and then maximize the Microsoft Access – [Trainer : Table] window by double-clicking its title bar.**

The Microsoft Access – [Trainer : Table] window appears (Figure 5-3).

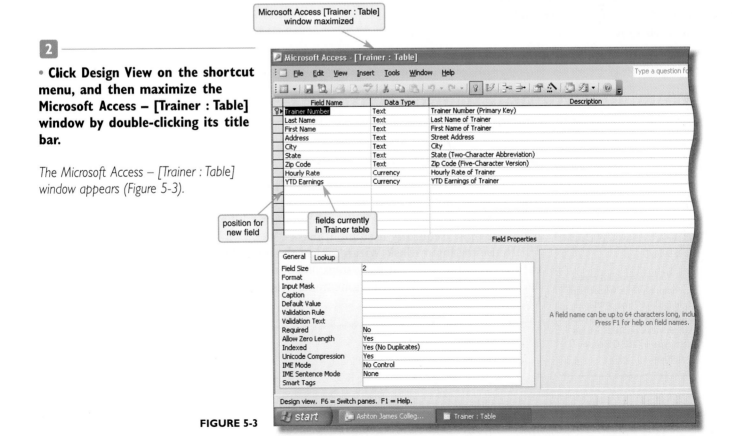

FIGURE 5-3

3

• **Click the position for the new field (Figure 5-3 on the previous page).**

• **Type** Start Date **as the field name, press the TAB key, select Date/Time as the data type, press the TAB key, type** Start Date **as the description, and then press the TAB key to move to the next field.**

• **Type** Comment **as the field name, press the TAB key, select Memo as the data type, press the TAB key, type** Comment Concerning Trainer **as the description, and then press the TAB key to move to the next field.**

• **Type** Picture **as the field name, press the TAB key, select OLE Object as the data type, press the TAB key, type** Picture of Trainer **as the description, and then press the TAB key to move to the next field.**

• **Type** Web Page **as the field name, press the TAB key, select Hyperlink as the data type, press the TAB key, and then type** Address of Trainer's Web Page **as the description.**

The new fields are entered (Figure 5-4).

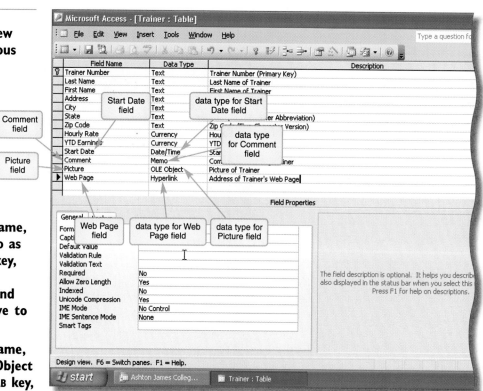

FIGURE 5-4

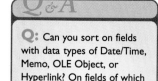

Using the Input Mask Wizard

An **input mask** specifies how the data is to be entered and how it will appear. You can enter an input mask directly or you can use the Input Mask Wizard. The wizard assists you in the creation of the input mask by allowing you to select from a list of the most frequently used input masks.

To use the Input Mask Wizard, select the Input Mask property and then select the Build button. The following steps illustrate how to add the Phone Number field and then specify how the telephone number is to appear by using the Input Mask Wizard.

To Use the Input Mask Wizard

1

• **Click the row selector for the Hourly Rate field, and then press the INSERT key to insert a blank row.**

• **Click the Field Name column for the new field.**

• **Type** Phone Number **as the field name and then press the TAB key.**

• **Select the Text data type by pressing the TAB key.**

• **Type** Phone Number **as the description.**

• **Click the Input Mask property box.**

The data is entered for the field and the Build button appears (Figure 5-5).

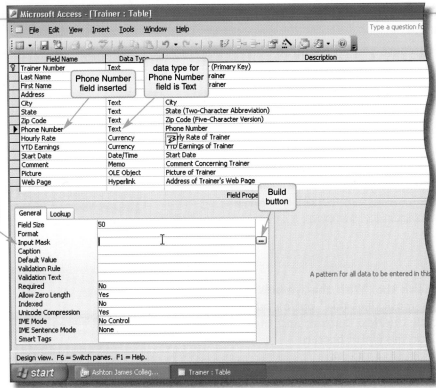

FIGURE 5-5

2

• **Click the Build button.**

• **If a dialog box appears asking you to save the table, click the Yes button. (If a dialog box displays a message that the Input Mask Wizard is not installed, check with your instructor before proceeding with the following steps.)**

• **Ensure that Phone Number is selected.**

The Input Mask Wizard dialog box displays several common input masks (Figure 5-6). Your list may be different. The Phone Number input mask is highlighted.

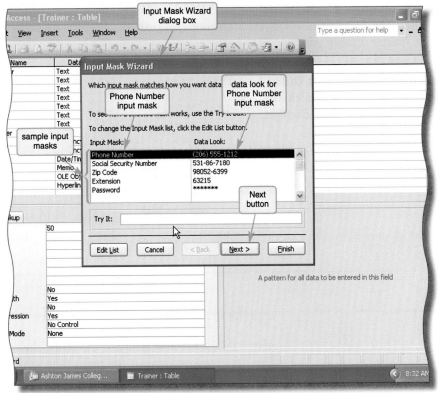

FIGURE 5-6

3

• **Click the Next button.**

• **You then are given the opportunity to change the input mask.**

• **Because you do not need to change the mask, click the Next button a second time.**

The Input Mask Wizard dialog box displays options for storing the data (Figure 5-7). Options allow Access to store the symbols in the mask (the parentheses and the hyphen) in the database or not. Your dialog box may display different numbers in the examples.

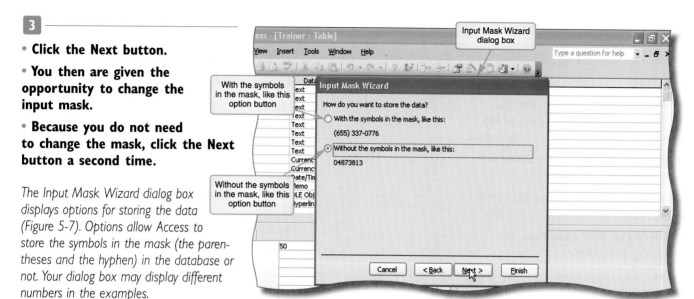

FIGURE 5-7

4

• **Click the "With the symbols in the mask, like this" option button, click the Next button, and then click the Finish button.**

The Input Mask property box displays the input mask (Figure 5-8).

5

• **Click the Close Window button on the Trainer : Table window title bar to close the window.**

• **When the Microsoft Office Access dialog box appears, click the Yes button to save your changes.**

Access saves the changes to the table design.

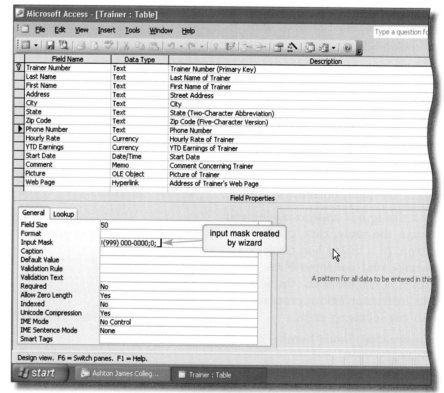

FIGURE 5-8

Updating the New Fields

After adding the new fields to the table, the next task is to enter data into the fields. The data type determines the manner in which this is accomplished. The following sections cover the methods for updating fields with an input mask, date fields, memo fields, OLE fields, and Hyperlink fields.

Entering Data Using an Input Mask

When entering data in a field that has an input mask, Access will insert the appropriate special characters in the proper positions. This means Access will insert the parentheses around the area code, the space following the second parenthesis, and the hyphen in the Phone Number field automatically. The following steps show how to use the input mask to add the telephone numbers.

To Enter Data Using an Input Mask

1

- **If necessary, click the Tables object on the Objects bar, right-click Trainer, and then click Open on the shortcut menu.**
- **Make sure the window is maximized.**
- **Tab to the Phone Number field on the first record.**

Access displays the table in Datasheet view (Figure 5-9). The insertion point is in the Phone Number field on the first record. The parentheses and hyphen do not appear yet. If you click the field, the parentheses and hyphen may appear.

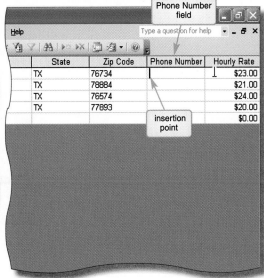

FIGURE 5-9

2

- **Type 5125552512 as the telephone number.**

Access inserts the data in its proper location and displays the telephone number with the appropriate symbols (Figure 5-10). The symbols appear as soon as you begin typing the number.

FIGURE 5-10

3

- **Use the same technique to enter the remaining telephone numbers as shown in Figure 5-11.**

The telephone numbers are entered.

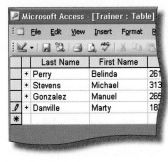
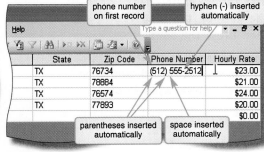

FIGURE 5-11

Entering Data in Date Fields

To enter data in date fields, simply type the dates and include slashes (/). The following steps show how to add the Start Dates for the trainers using Datasheet view.

To Enter Data in Date Fields

1

• **Repeatedly click the right scroll arrow until the new fields appear.**

The fields have shifted to the left (Figure 5-12).

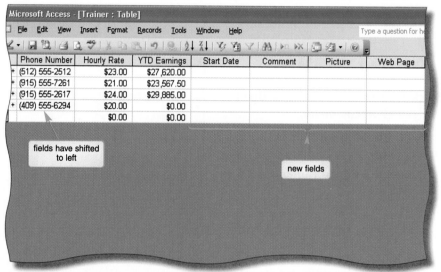

FIGURE 5-12

2

• **Click the Start Date field on the first record, type** 10/12/2003 **as the date on the first record, and then press the DOWN ARROW key.**

• **Type** 5/5/2003 **as the start date on the second record, and then press the DOWN ARROW key.**

• **Type** 2/5/2002 **as the start date on the third record, and then press the DOWN ARROW key.**

• **Type** 8/12/2005 **as the start date on the fourth record.**

The dates are entered (Figure 5-13).

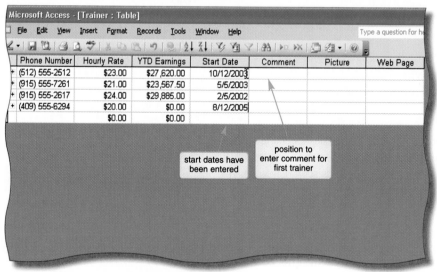

FIGURE 5-13

Entering Data in Memo Fields

To update a memo field, simply type the data in the field. With the current row and column spacing on the screen, only a small portion of the memo will appear. To correct this problem, you will change the spacing later to allow more room for the memo. The following steps show how to enter each trainer's comment.

To Enter Data in Memo Fields

• **If necessary, click the right scroll arrow so the Comment field appears.**

• **Click the Comment field on the first record, and then type** Has done corporate training for 11 years. Has taught introductory computing courses at local colleges for 5 years. **as the entry.**

The last portion of the comment appears (Figure 5-14).

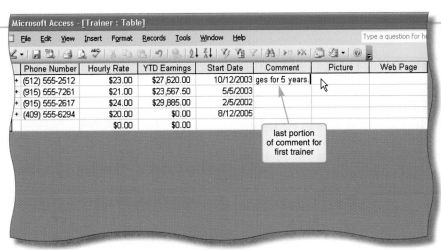

FIGURE 5-14

• **Click the Comment field on the second record, and then type** In previous position, was head of training at Information Technology department for large company. Specialist in database design and development. **as the entry.**

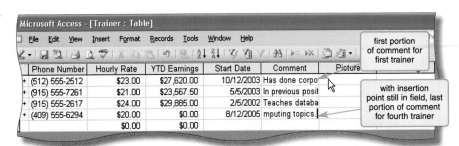

FIGURE 5-15

• **Click the Comment field on the third record, and then type** Teaches database courses at local college and gives database seminars to area industries. **as the entry.**

4

• **Click the Comment field on the fourth record, and then type** New trainer. Was active in tutoring other students in computing topics. **as the entry.**

All the comments are entered (Figure 5-15). The first portion of the comments for the first three trainers appears. Because the insertion point still is in the field for the fourth trainer, only the last portion of the comment appears.

Changing the Row and Column Size

Only a small portion of the comments appears in the datasheet. To allow more of the information to appear, you can expand the size of the rows and the columns. You can change the size of a column by using the field selector. The **field selector** is the bar containing the field name. To change the size of a row, you use a record's **record selector**, which is the small box at the beginning of each record.

Other Ways

1. In Dictation mode, say "[specific text for each comment]"

The following steps describe how to resize the column containing the Comment field and the rows of the table so a larger portion of the Comment field text will appear.

To Change the Row and Column Size

1

• **Drag the line between the column headings for the Comment and Picture columns to the right to resize the Comment column to the approximate size shown in Figure 5-16.**

The mouse pointer changes to a two-headed arrow with a horizontal bar, indicating you can drag the line to resize the column.

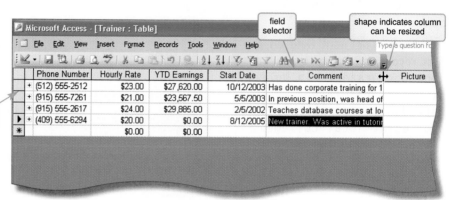

FIGURE 5-16

2

• **Drag the lower edge of the record selector to approximately the position shown in Figure 5-17.**

All the rows are resized at the same time. The comments now appear in their entirety. The last row has a different appearance from the other three because it still is selected.

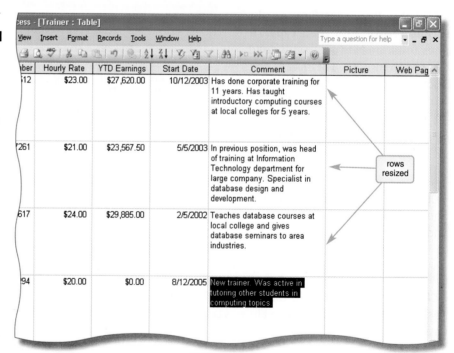

FIGURE 5-17

Other Ways

1. Right-click record selector, click Row Height to change row spacing
2. Right-click field selector, click Column Width to change column size
3. In Voice Command mode, say "Format, Row Height" to change row spacing
4. In Voice Command mode, say "Format, Column Width" to change column size

Entering Data in OLE Fields

To insert data into an OLE field, you use the Insert Object command on the OLE field's shortcut menu. The Insert Object command presents a list of the various types of objects that can be inserted. Access then opens the corresponding application to create the object, for example, Microsoft Drawing. If the object already is created and stored in a file, as is the case in this project, you simply insert it directly from the file.

The following steps illustrate how to insert pictures into the Picture field. The steps assume that the pictures are located in a folder called Pictures on disk C. If your pictures are located elsewhere, you will need to make the appropriate changes.

Note: Because this project illustrates adding pictures to a table, the Ashton James College database is located in a folder called Data on disk C. If your database is on a floppy disk (drive A), copy your database to disk C or to a network disk, or skip the steps in this section so your database will not become too large for your disk.

To Enter Data in OLE Fields

1

• **Ensure the Picture field appears on your screen, and then right-click the Picture field on the first record.**

The shortcut menu for the Picture field appears (Figure 5-18).

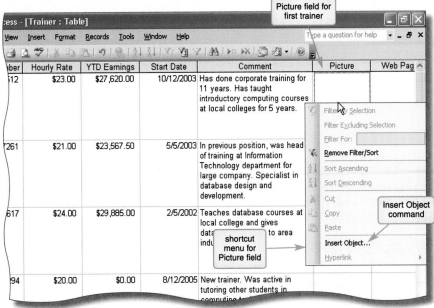

FIGURE 5-18

2

• **Click Insert Object.**

The Microsoft Office Access dialog box displays the Object Type list (Figure 5-19). Your list may be different.

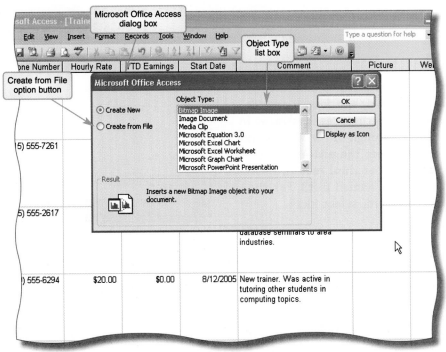

FIGURE 5-19

3

• **Click the Create from File option button, and then click the Browse button.**

• **Navigate to the Pictures folder in the Look in box. (If your pictures are located elsewhere, navigate to the folder where they are located instead of the Pictures folder.)**

The Browse dialog box appears (Figure 5-20). If you do not have the pictures, you will need to locate the folder in which yours are stored.

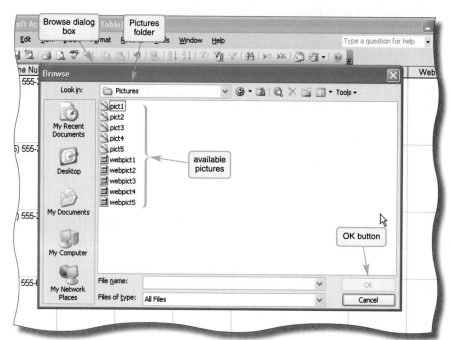

FIGURE 5-20

4

• **Click pict1 and then click the OK button.**

The Browse dialog box closes and the Microsoft Office Access dialog box appears (Figure 5-21). The File text box displays the name of the selected picture.

5

• **Click the OK button.**

6

• **Insert the pictures into the second, third, and fourth records using the techniques illustrated in Steps 1 through 5. For the second record, select the picture named pict2. For the third record, select the picture named pict3. For the fourth record, select pict4.**

The pictures are inserted.

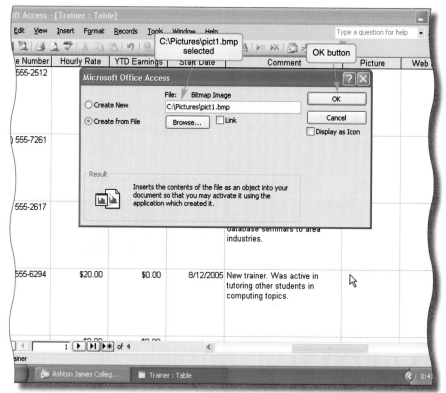

FIGURE 5-21

The entries in the Picture field all should be Bitmap images (BMP). If you see the word Package instead of Bitmap image, there is a problem either with the graphics filters that are installed or with the file associations for BMP files. In that case, you can use a slightly different technique to add the pictures. After right-clicking the Picture field, and clicking Insert Object, *do not* click the Create from File button. Instead, select the Paintbrush Picture object type from the list, select the Paste From command on the Edit menu of the Paintbrush window, select the desired BMP file, and then select the Exit command from the File menu to return to the datasheet. The entry in the Picture field then will be Bitmap image as it should.

Entering Data in Hyperlink Fields

To insert data into a Hyperlink field, you will use the Hyperlink command on the Hyperlink field's shortcut menu. You then edit the hyperlink. You can enter the Web page address for the appropriate Web page or specify a file that contains the document to which you want to link.

The following steps show how to insert the addresses of the trainers' Web pages.

To Enter Data in Hyperlink Fields

1

• **Be sure the Web Page field appears, right-click the Web Page field on the first record, and then point to Hyperlink on the shortcut menu.**

The shortcut menu for the Web Page field is displayed (Figure 5-22). The Hyperlink submenu also appears.

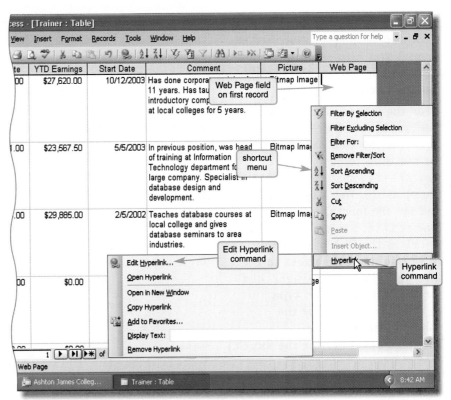

FIGURE 5-22

2

• **Click Edit Hyperlink.**

• **Type** www.scsite.com/
ac2003/trainer1.html **in the
Address text box. (If you do not
have access to the Internet, type**
a:\trainer1.html **in the
Address text box instead of
www.scsite.com/ac2003/
trainer1.html as the Web
page address.)**

*The Insert Hyperlink dialog box displays the
contents of the current folder in the list box.
Your current folder list will be different or a
browsed pages list may appear instead of
the current folder (Figure 5-23).*

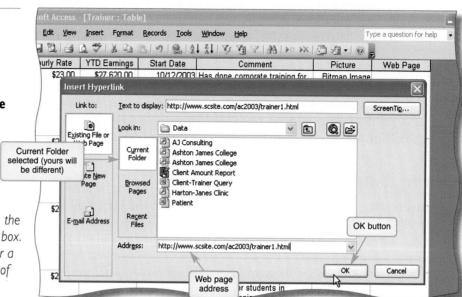

FIGURE 5-23

3

• **Click the OK button.**

• **Use the techniques described in
Steps 1 and 2 to enter Web page
data for the second, third, and
fourth trainers.**

• **For the second trainer, type**
www.scsite.com/ac2003/trainer2
.html **as the Web page address;
for the third, type**
www.scsite.com/ac2003/trainer3
.html **as the Web page address;
and for the fourth, type**
www.scsite.com/ac2003/trainer4
.html **as the Web page address.
(If you do not have access to the
Internet, type** a:\trainer2.html
for the second trainer, type
a:\trainer3.html **for the
third trainer, and type**
a:\trainer4.html **for the fourth.)**

*The Web page data is entered
(Figure 5-24).*

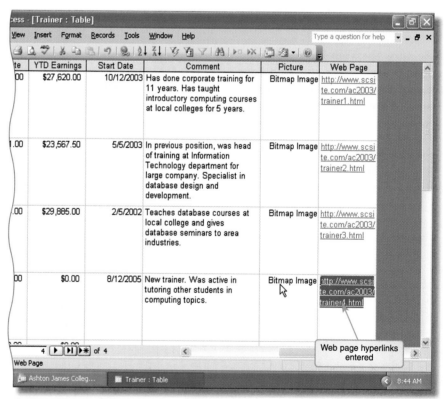

FIGURE 5-24

Other Ways
1. On Insert menu click Hyperlink
2. In Voice Command mode, say "Insert, Hyperlink"

Saving the Table Properties

The row and column spacing are table properties. When changing any table properties, the changes apply only as long as the table is active *unless they are saved*. If they are saved, they will apply every time the table is opened. To save them, simply close the table. If any properties have changed, you will be asked if you want to save the changes. By answering Yes, you can save the changes.

The following steps illustrate how to close the table and save the properties that have been changed.

To Close the Table and Save the Properties

1

• **Close the table by clicking its Close Window button.**

The Microsoft Office Access dialog box appears (Figure 5-25).

2

• **Click the Yes button to save the table properties.**

The properties are saved.

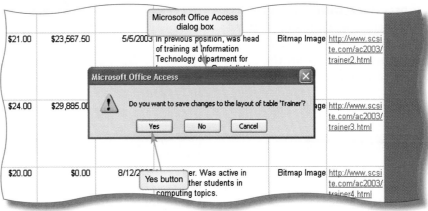

FIGURE 5-25

Although the pictures do not appear on the screen, you can view them at anytime. To view the picture of a particular trainer, right-click the Picture field for the trainer. Click Bitmap Image Object on the shortcut menu, and then click Open. The picture will appear. Once you have finished viewing the picture, close the window containing the picture by clicking its Close button. You also can view the Web page for a trainer, by clicking the trainer's Web Page field.

Advanced Form Techniques

The form in this project includes data from both the Trainer and Client tables. The form will display data concerning one trainer. It also will display data concerning the many clients to which the trainer is assigned. Formally, the relationship between trainers and clients is called a **one-to-many relationship** (*one* trainer services *many* clients).

To include the data for the many clients of a trainer on the form, the client data must appear in a **subform**, which is a form that is contained within another form. The form in which the subform is contained is called the main form. Thus, the **main form** will contain trainer data, and the subform will contain client data.

Creating a Form with a Subform

No special action is required to create a form with a subform if you use the Form Wizard. You must, however, have created previously a one-to-many relationship between the two tables. The Form Wizard will create both the form and subform automatically once you have selected the tables and indicated the general organization of your data. The following steps show how to use the wizard to create the form and subform.

To Create a Form with a Subform Using the Form Wizard

1

• **If necessary, with the Tables object selected, click the Trainer table, and then click the New Object button arrow on the Database toolbar.**

The list of available objects is displayed (Figure 5-26).

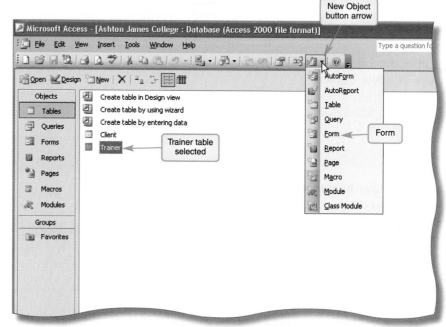

FIGURE 5-26

2

• **Click Form.**

Access displays the New Form dialog box (Figure 5-27).

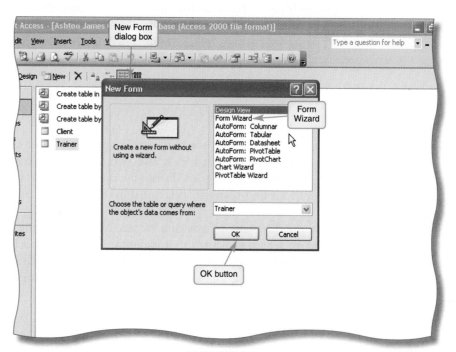

FIGURE 5-27

3

• **Click Form Wizard and then click the OK button.**

• **With the Trainer Number field selected in the Available Fields box, click the Add Field button.**

• **Select the First Name, Last Name, Phone Number, Hourly Rate, YTD Earnings, Start Date, Web Page, Comment, and Picture fields by clicking the field and then clicking the Add Field button.**

• **Click the Table/Queries box arrow.**

The fields from the Trainer table are selected for the form (Figure 5-28). The list of available tables and queries appears.

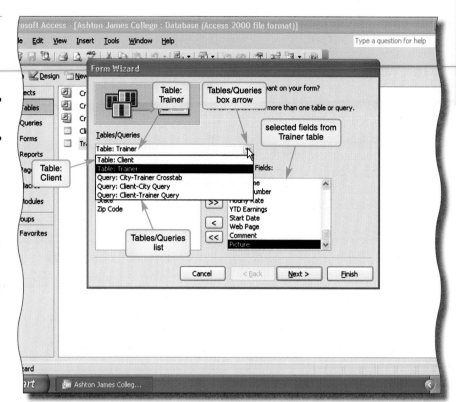

FIGURE 5-28

4

• **Click Table: Client and then select the Client Number, Name, Amount Paid, and Current Due fields.**

The fields are selected (Figure 5-29).

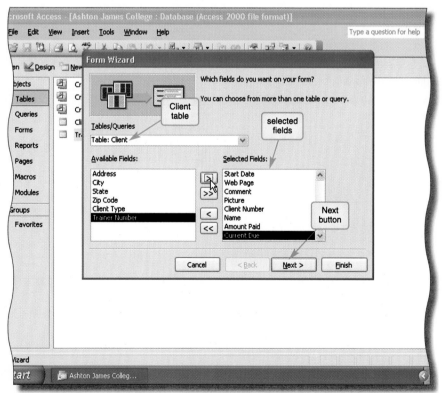

FIGURE 5-29

5

• **Click the Next button.**

The Form Wizard dialog box appears, requesting how you want to view the data: by Trainer or by Client (Figure 5-30). The highlighted selection, by Trainer, is correct. The box on the right indicates visually that the main organization is by Trainer, with the Trainer fields listed at the top. Contained within the form is a subform that contains client data.

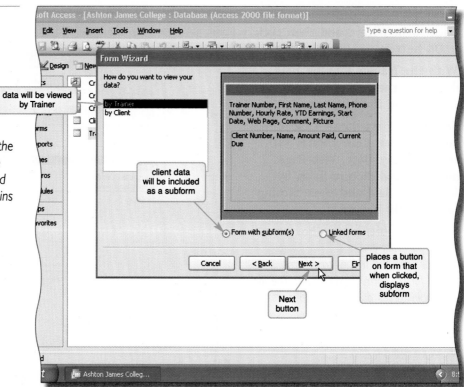

FIGURE 5-30

6

• **Click the Next button.**

Access displays the Form Wizard dialog box requesting the layout for the subform (Figure 5-31). This subform is to appear in Datasheet view.

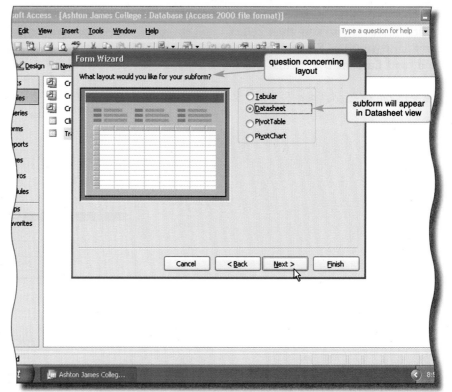

FIGURE 5-31

7

• **Be sure Datasheet is selected and then click the Next button.**

• **Ensure Standard style is selected.**

The Form Wizard dialog box requests a style for the report, and Standard is selected (Figure 5-32).

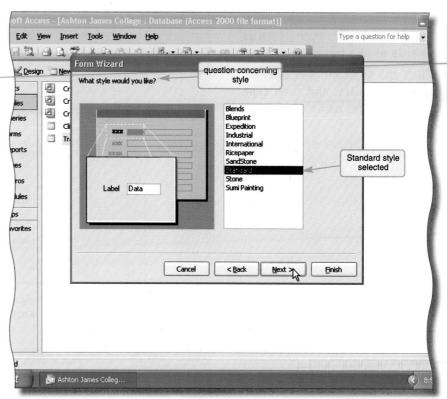

FIGURE 5-32

8

• **Click the Next button.**

The Form Wizard dialog box allows you to change the titles of the form and subform (Figure 5-33).

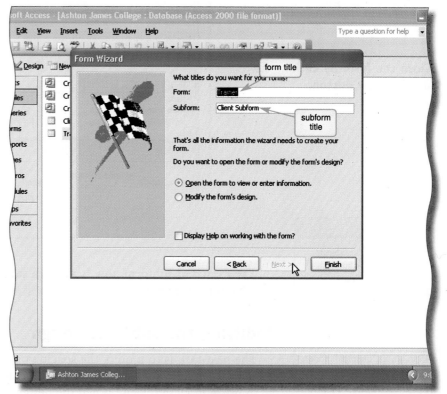

FIGURE 5-33

9

• **Type** Trainer Master Form **as the title of the form.**

• **Click the Subform text box, erase the current entry, and then type** Clients **as the name of the subform.**

The titles are changed (Figure 5-34).

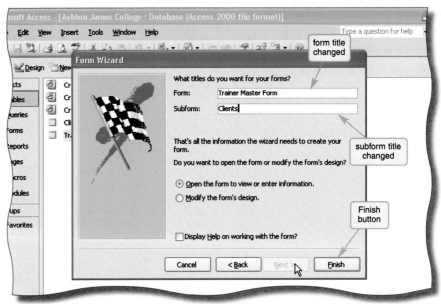

FIGURE 5-34

10

• **Click the Finish button.**

Access displays the form (Figure 5-35). Your form layout may differ slightly. You will modify the layout in the following sections.

11

• **Close the form by clicking its Close Window button.**

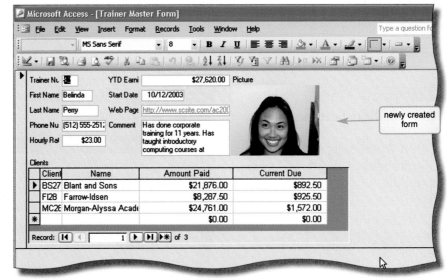

FIGURE 5-35

The form and subform now have been saved as part of the database and are available for future use.

Modifying the Subform Design

The next task is to modify the spacing of the columns in the subform. The columns are much wider than needed. You can correct these problems by opening the subform in Design view. When the design of the subform appears, you then can convert it to Datasheet view. At this point, you can resize each column.

The following steps illustrate how to modify the subform design to improve the column spacing.

To Modify the Subform Design

1

• **With the Forms object selected, right-click Clients.**

The shortcut menu for the subform appears (Figure 5-36).

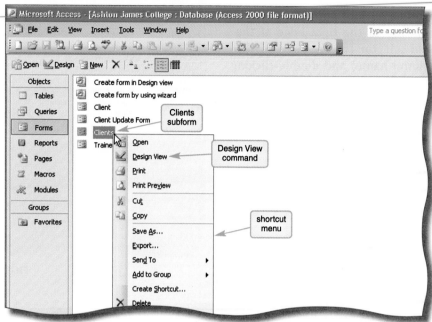

FIGURE 5-36

2

• **Click Design View on the shortcut menu.**

Access displays the form design for the subform (Figure 5-37).

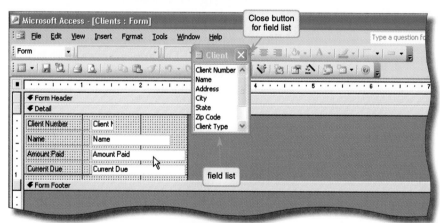

FIGURE 5-37

3

• **If the field list appears, click its Close button.**

• **Click the View button arrow on the Form Design toolbar.**

The View list appears (Figure 5-38).

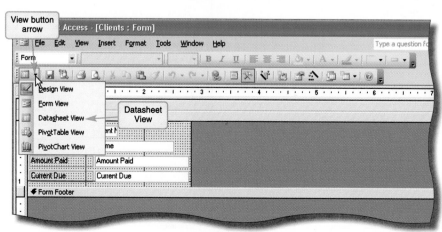

FIGURE 5-38

- **Click Datasheet View to display the subform in Datasheet view.**

- **Resize each of the columns by pointing to the right edge of the field selector (to the right of the column name) and double-clicking.**

Access displays the subform in Datasheet view (Figure 5-39). The columns have been resized. You also can resize each column by dragging the right edge of the field selector.

5

- **Close the subform by clicking its Close Window button.**

The changes are made and saved.

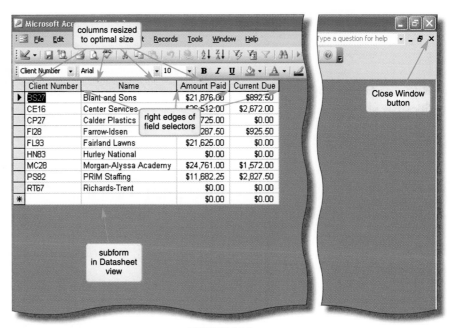

FIGURE 5-39

Modifying the Form Design

The next step is to make several changes to the form. Various objects need to be moved or resized. The properties of the picture need to be adjusted so the entire picture appears. The appearance of the labels needs to be changed and a title needs to be added to the form.

The following steps show how to begin the modification of the form design.

To Modify the Form Design

1

- **Right-click Trainer Master Form.**

The shortcut menu for the form appears (Figure 5-40).

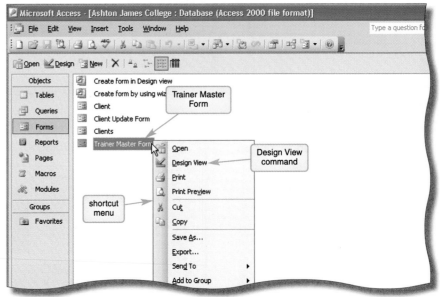

FIGURE 5-40

2

- **Click Design View on the shortcut menu.**
- **Be sure the window is maximized.**
- **If the toolbox does not appear, click the Toolbox button on the toolbar.**
- **Make sure the toolbox is docked at the bottom of the screen. If it is not, drag its title bar to the bottom of the screen to dock it there.**

The form appears in Design view (Figure 5-41). The toolbox is docked at the bottom of the screen.

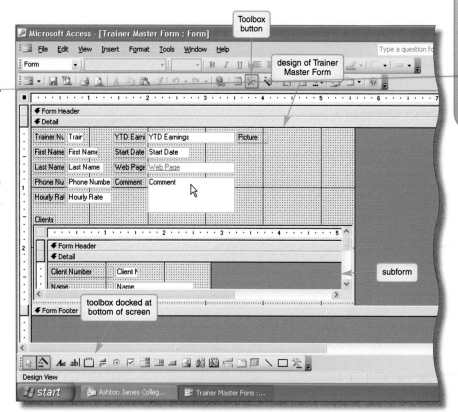

FIGURE 5-41

Your form layout may differ slightly. In the following sections, you will modify the form to match that shown in Figure 5-3 on page AC 261.

Moving and Resizing Fields

Fields on this form can be moved or resized just as they were in the form created in the previous project. First, select the field. To move it, move the mouse pointer to the boundary of the field so it becomes a hand, and then drag the field. To resize a field, drag the appropriate sizing handle. The steps on the next page show how to move certain fields on the form and resize the fields appropriately.

More About

Subforms

When you create forms with subforms, the tables for the main form and the subform must be related. The relationship must have been set previously in the Relationships window. To see if your tables are related, click the Relationships button. Relationships between tables display as lines connecting the tables.

To Move and Resize Fields

1

• **Click the Picture control and then move the mouse pointer until the shape changes to a hand.**

The Picture control is selected and sizing handles appear (Figure 5-42).

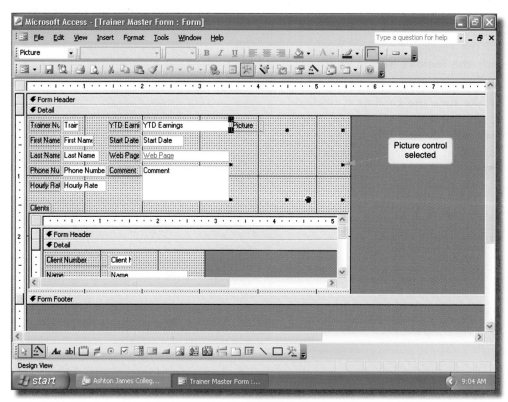

FIGURE 5-42

2

• **Drag the Picture control to approximately the position shown in Figure 5-43.**

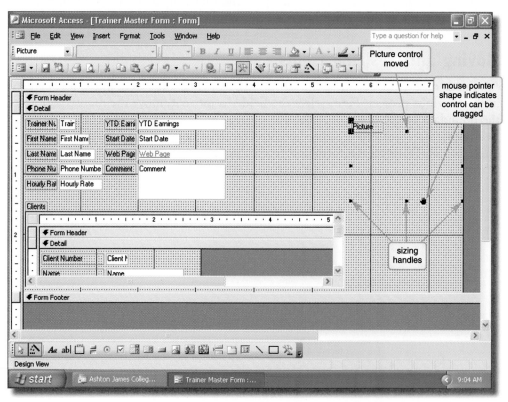

FIGURE 5-43

3

• **Drag the lower sizing handle to approximately the position shown in Figure 5-44.**

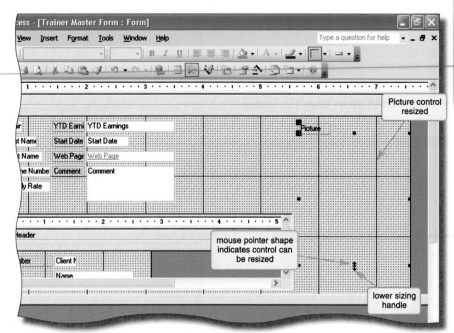

FIGURE 5-44

4

• **Move and resize the Comment control to the approximate position and size shown in Figure 5-45.**

The Comment and Picture controls now are the correct size and in the correct position.

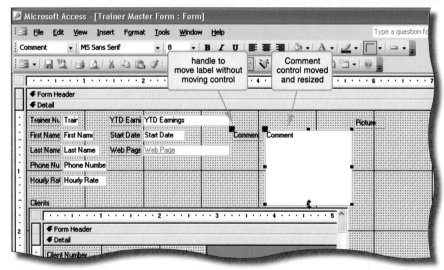

FIGURE 5-45

Moving Labels

To move a label independently from the field with which the label is associated, point to the large, move handle in the upper-left corner of the label. The shape of the mouse pointer changes to a hand with a pointing finger. By dragging this move handle, you will move the label without moving the associated field. The step on the next page illustrates how to move the label of the Comment field without moving the field itself.

To Move a Label

1

• **Be sure the Comment field is selected, and then drag the move handle for its label to the position shown in Figure 5-46.**

The label is moved. The shape of the mouse pointer is a hand with a pointing finger.

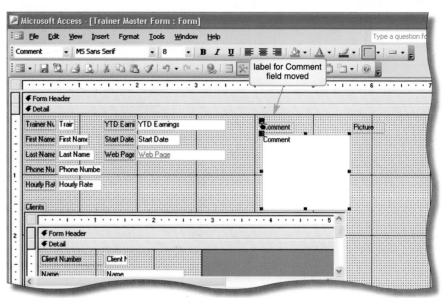

FIGURE 5-46

Moving Remaining Fields

The remaining fields on this form also need to be moved into appropriate positions. The following steps show how to move these fields on the form.

To Move Fields

1

• **Click the Web Page field, move the mouse pointer until the shape changes to a hand, and then drag the field to the position shown in Figure 5-47.**

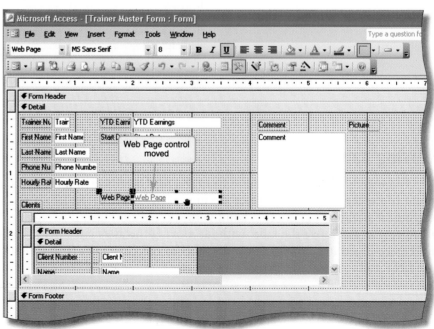

FIGURE 5-47

To Change Special Effects and Colors of Labels

1

• **Click the Trainer Number label to select it.**

• **Select each of the remaining labels by holding down the SHIFT key while clicking the label. Be sure to include the Clients label for the subform.**

• **Right-click one of the selected labels.**

All labels are selected (Figure 5-54). The shortcut menu appears.

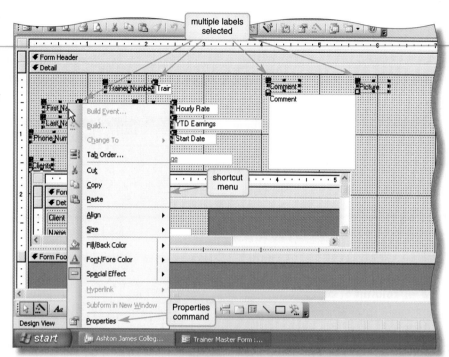

FIGURE 5-54

2

• **Click Properties on the shortcut menu.**

• **Click the Special Effect property, and then click the Special Effect property box arrow.**

The Multiple selection property sheet displays the list of options for the Special Effect property (Figure 5-55). The Flat Special Effect property is highlighted.

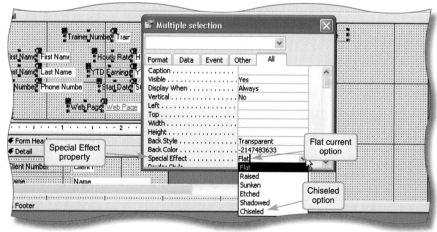

FIGURE 5-55

3

• **Click Chiseled.**

• **If necessary, click the down scroll arrow until the Fore Color property appears, and then click the Fore Color property.**

The Fore Color property is selected (Figure 5-56).

FIGURE 5-56

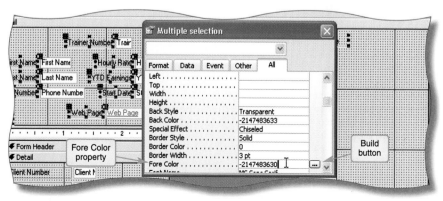

4

• **Click the Build button.**

The Color dialog box appears (Figure 5-57).

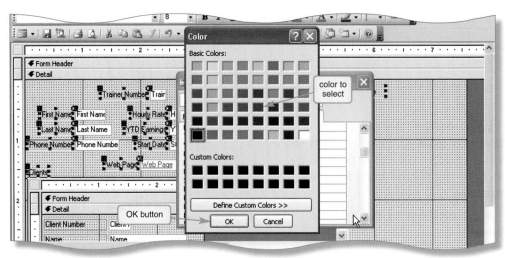

FIGURE 5-57

5

• **Click the color blue in row 4, column 5, and then click the OK button.**
• **Close the Multiple selection property sheet by clicking its Close button.**

The changes to the labels are complete.

6

• **Click the View button to view the form.**

The form appears (Figure 5-58).

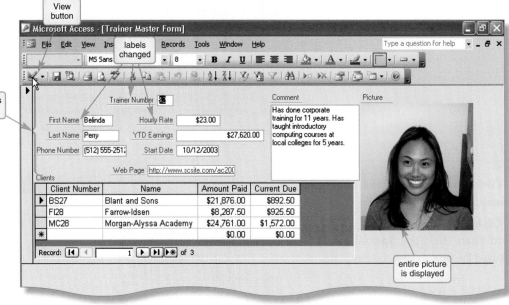

FIGURE 5-58

The fields have been moved, and the appearance of the labels has been changed. The form displays the picture correctly.

Adding a Form Title

The form in Figure 5-1 on page AC 259 includes a title. To add a title to a form, add the title as a label in the Form Header section. To accomplish this task, first you will need to expand the size of the form header to accommodate the title. Then, you can use the Label tool in the toolbox to place the label. After placing the label, you can enter the title in the label. Finally, you can change various properties to improve the title's appearance.

More About

Form Headers

You might wish to add more than just a title to a form header. For example, you might wish to add a picture such as a company logo. To do so, click the Image tool in the toolbox, click the position where you want to place the picture, and then select the picture to insert.

The following steps show how to place a title on the form.

To Add a Form Title

1

• **Click the View button to return to Design view.**

• **Resize the Form Header section by dragging down the line separating the Form Header section from the Detail section to the approximate position shown in Figure 5-59.**

The shape of the mouse pointer changes to a two-headed vertical arrow with a horizontal crossbar, indicating you can drag the line to resize the Form Header section.

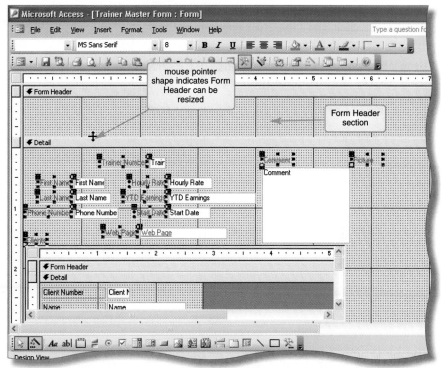

FIGURE 5-59

2

• **Click the Label tool in the toolbox, and then position the mouse pointer as shown in Figure 5-60. The shape of the mouse pointer has changed, indicating you are placing a label.**

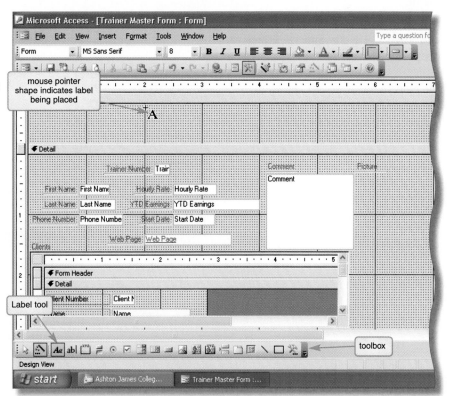

FIGURE 5-60

3

• **Click the position shown in Figure 5-60 on the previous page, and then type** Trainer Master Form **as the title.**

• **Click outside the label to deselect it, and then click the label to select it a second time.**

• **Drag the handle in the lower-right corner to the approximate position shown in Figure 5-61.**

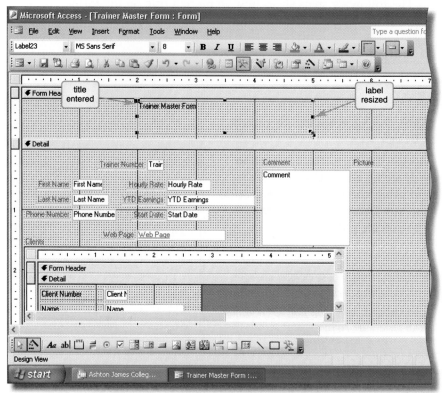

FIGURE 5-61

4

• **Right-click the label and then click Properties on the shortcut menu.**

• **Click the Special Effect property, and then click the Special Effect property box arrow.**

The property sheet displays the list of options for the Special Effect property (Figure 5-62). The Flat Special Effect property is highlighted.

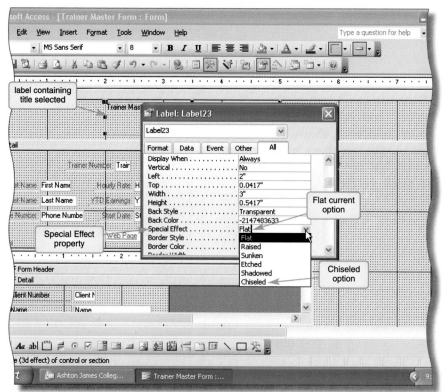

FIGURE 5-62

5

- **Click Chiseled.**
- **Click the down scroll arrow to display the Font Size property.**
- **Click the Font Size property, click the Font Size property box arrow, and then click 12.**
- **If necessary, click the down scroll arrow to display the Font Weight property.**
- **Click the Font Weight property, click the Font Weight property box arrow, and then click Bold.**
- **Close the property sheet by clicking its Close button.**
- **Resize the label to fit the title, and then move the label so it is centered over the form.**

The form header is complete (Figure 5-63).

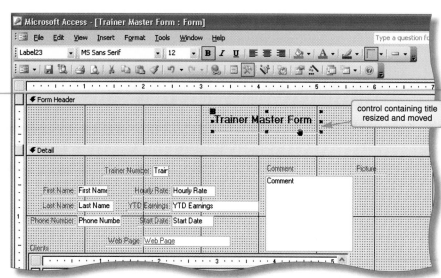

FIGURE 5-63

Fine-Tuning the Form

Once the form is complete, you should fine-tune it; that is, you should make any minor adjustments necessary to make the form look better. If you look at the form in Figure 5-58 on page AC 290, for example, you see that you need to expand the width of the Phone Number control so the entire telephone number appears. You might want to expand the Web Page control so the text box displays more of the Web page address. The following steps show how to fine-tune the form by increasing the size of these two controls.

To Fine-Tune the Form

1 Click the Phone Number control, and then drag the right sizing handle to the right to expand the control.

2 Click the View button to display the form, examine the Phone Number control to see if it is the size you want, and then click the View button to return to the form design.

3 If the Phone Number control is not the desired size, repeat Steps 1 and 2 until it is.

4 Using the techniques shown in Steps 1 through 3, resize the Web Page control to the size you want.

The fine-tuning process now is complete.

Changing Tab Stops

If users repeatedly press the TAB key to move through the controls on the form, they should bypass the Picture control, because they typically would not change the picture. In order to force this to happen, change the Tab Stop property for the control as illustrated in the steps on the next page.

To Change a Tab Stop

1

• **Right-click the Picture control.**

The shortcut menu for the Picture control appears (Figure 5-64).

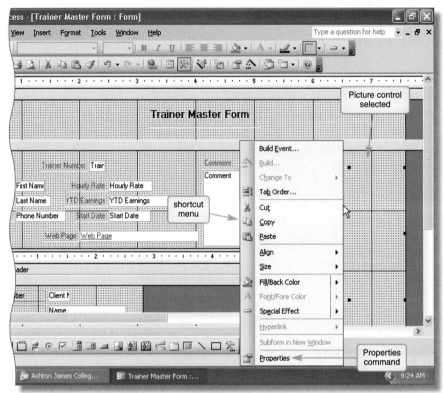

FIGURE 5-64

2

• **Click Properties on the shortcut menu. Make sure the All tab is selected, click the down scroll arrow until the Tab Stop property appears, click the Tab Stop property, click the Tab Stop property box arrow, and then click No.**

The value for the Tab Stop property is changed to No (Figure 5-65).

3

• **Close the property sheet.**
• **With this change, tabbing through the controls on the form will bypass the picture.**

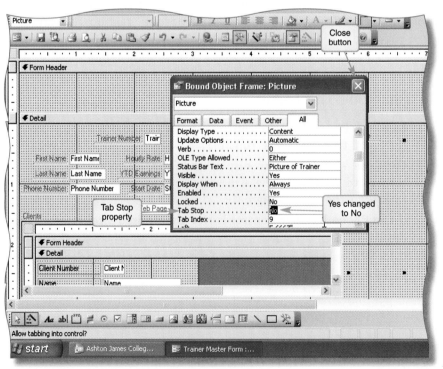

FIGURE 5-65

Changing the Tab Order

Users can repeatedly press the TAB key to move through the fields on a form. Access determines the order in which the fields are encountered in this process. In the default order for this form, the Comment field would come after the Web Page field. With the way the fields are positioned on the form, it would be better for the Comment field to come first. To change the tab order, that is, the order in which fields are encountered when tabbing through a form, use the Tab Order command on the View menu. When the Tab Order dialog box appears, you can change the tab order.

The following steps show how to change the tab order so the Comment field comes before the Web Page field.

More About

Microsoft Certification

The Microsoft Office Specialist Certification program provides an opportunity for you to obtain a valuable industry credential — proof that you have the Access 2003 skills required by employers. For more information, see Appendix E, or visit the Access 2003 Certification Web page (scsite.com/ac2003/cert).

To Change the Tab Order

1

• **Click View on the menu bar.**

The View menu appears (Figure 5-66).

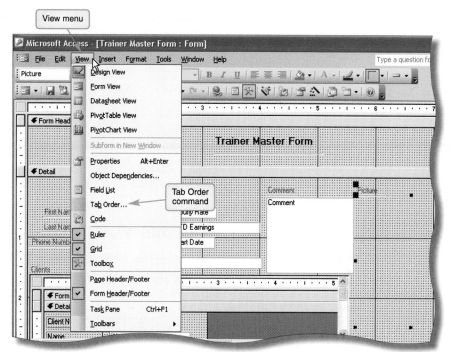

FIGURE 5-66

2

• **Click Tab Order on the View menu, and then click the Comment row to select it.**

The Comment field is selected (Figure 5-67).

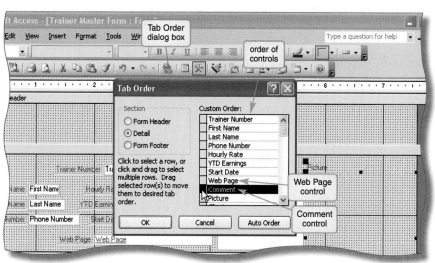

FIGURE 5-67

• **Drag the Comment field above the Web Page field.**

The order is changed (Figure 5-68).

• **Click OK.**

• **Close the window containing the form.**

• **When asked if you want to save the changes to the design of the form, click Yes.**

The tab order now is changed. The form is closed and all the changes have been saved.

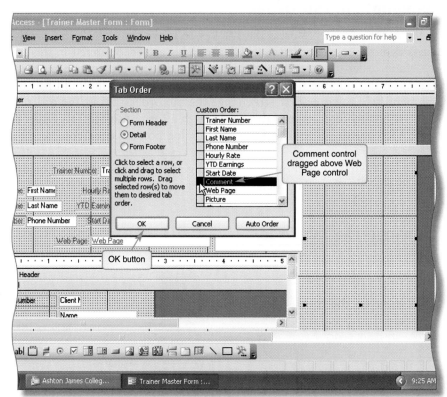

FIGURE 5-68

Viewing Data and Web Pages Using the Form

To use a form to view data, right-click the form in the Database window, and then click Open on the shortcut menu that appears. You then can use the navigation buttons to move among trainers or to move among the clients of the trainer currently shown on the screen. By clicking the trainer's Web Page field, you can display the trainer's Web page. As soon as you close the window containing the Web page, Access returns to the form.

The following steps illustrate how to display data using the form.

To Use the Form to View Data and Web Pages

1

• **If necessary, click Forms on the Objects bar.**

• **Right-click Trainer Master Form and then click Open on the shortcut menu.**

• **Be sure the window containing the form is maximized.**

The form displays the data from the first record (Figure 5-69).

FIGURE 5-69

2

• **Click the Next Record button to move to the second trainer.**

The data from the second record appears (Figure 5-70). If more clients were included than would fit in the subform at a single time, Access would automatically add a vertical scroll bar to the Clients subform. You either can use a scroll bar or the navigation buttons to move among clients.

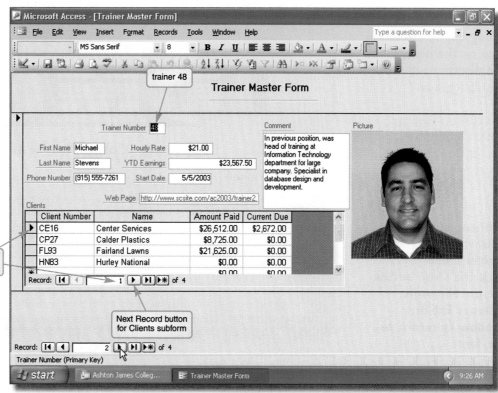

FIGURE 5-70

3

• **Click the subform's Next Record button twice.**

The data from the third client of trainer 48 is selected (Figure 5-71).

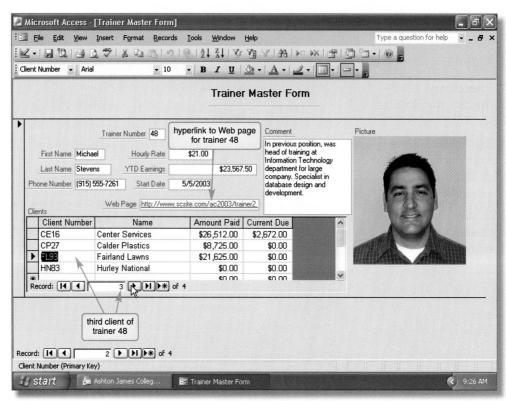

FIGURE 5-71

4

• **Click the Web Page control.**

• **If Access displays a dialog box in either this step or the next, follow the directions given in the dialog box.**

The trainer's Web page appears in the Microsoft Internet Explorer window (Figure 5-72).

5

• **When you have finished viewing the trainer's Web page, click the Close button for the Microsoft Internet Explorer window to return to the form.**

• **Click the Close Window button to close the form.**

The form no longer appears.

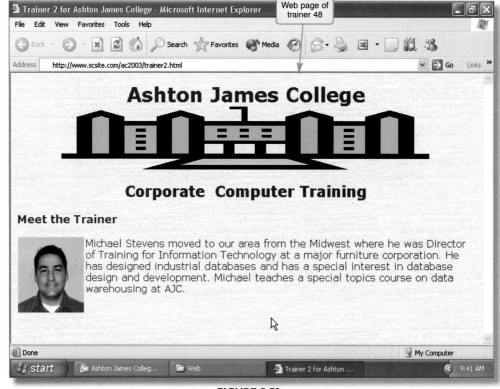

FIGURE 5-72

The previous steps illustrated the way you work with a main form and subform, as well as how to use a hyperlink (the Web Page control in this form). Clicking the navigation buttons for the main form moves to a different trainer. Clicking the navigation buttons for the subform moves to a different client of the trainer whose photograph appears in the main form. Clicking a hyperlink moves to the corresponding document or Web page. The following are other actions you can take within the form:

1. To move from the last field in the main form to the first field in the subform, press the TAB key. To move back to the last field in the main form, press CTRL+SHIFT+TAB.
2. To move from the last field in the subform to the first field in the next record's main form, press CTRL+TAB.
3. To switch from the main form to the subform using the mouse, click anywhere in the subform. To switch back to the main form, click any control in the main form. Clicking the background of the main form will not cause the switch to occur.

Viewing Object Dependencies

In Access, you can view information on dependencies between database objects. Viewing a list of objects that use a specific object helps in the maintenance of a database and avoids errors when changes are made to the objects involved in the dependency. For example, the Trainer Master Form depends on data from the Client table and the Trainer table. The form also depends on the Clients subform. The Object Dependencies command allows you to see the dependencies for any given object or to see what objects depend on the object. The following steps illustrate how to view object dependencies for the Trainer Master Form.

To View Object Dependencies

1 If necessary, click Forms on the Objects bar and then click the Trainer Master Form.

2 Click View on the menu bar and then click Object Dependencies.

3 When the Microsoft Access dialog box appears stating that Access must update dependency information, click OK.

4 Click the "Objects that I depend on" option button.

Access displays the Object Dependencies task pane and lists all the objects on which the Trainer Master Form depends.

Using Date and Memo Fields in a Query

To use date fields in queries, you simply type the dates including the slashes. To search for records with a specific date, you must type the date. You also can use comparison operators. To find all the trainers whose start date is prior to January 1, 2003, for example, you type <1/1/2003 as the criterion.

You also can use memo fields in queries. Typically, you will want to find all the records on which the memo field contains a specific word or phrase. To do so, you use wildcards. For example, to find all the trainers who have the word, database, somewhere in the Comment field, you type *database* as the criterion.

The steps on the next page illustrate how to create and run queries that use date and memo fields.

More About

Quick Reference

For a table that lists how to complete tasks covered in this book using the mouse, menu, shortcut menu, and keyboard, see the Quick Reference Summary at the back of this book, or visit the Access 2003 Quick Reference Web page (scsite.com/ac2003/qr).

More About

Date Fields in Queries: Using Date()

To test for the current date in a query, type Date() in the Criteria row of the appropriate column. Typing <Date() in the Criteria row for Start Date, for example, finds those trainers who started anytime before the date on which you run the query.

More About

Date Fields in Queries: Using Expressions

Expressions have a special meaning in date fields in queries. Numbers that appear in expressions represent numbers of days. The expression <Date()+30 for Start Date finds trainers who started anytime up to 30 days before the day on which you run the query.

To Use Date and Memo Fields in a Query

1

• **In the Database window, click Tables on the Objects bar, and then, if necessary, select the Trainer table.**

• **Click the New Object button arrow on the Database toolbar.**

• **Click Query.**

• **Be sure Design View is highlighted, and then click the OK button.**

• **Be sure the Microsoft Access [Query1 : Select Query] window is maximized.**

• **Resize the upper and lower panes and the Trainer field list so all fields in the Trainer table appear.**

• **Double-click the Trainer Number, First Name, Last Name, Start Date, and Comment fields to include them in the query.**

• **Click the Criteria row under the Comment field and then type** *database* **as the criterion.**

The criterion is entered (Figure 5-73).

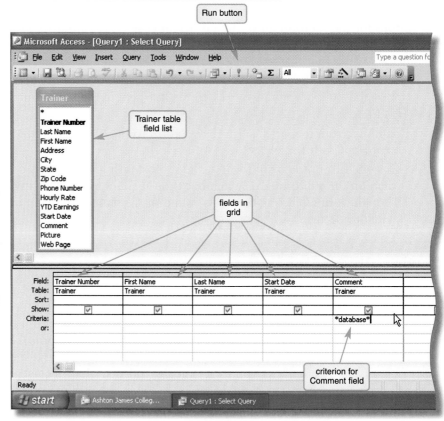

FIGURE 5-73

2

• **Click the Run button on the Query Design toolbar to run the query.**

The results appear in Datasheet view (Figure 5-74). Two records are included. Both records have the word, database, contained within the comment.

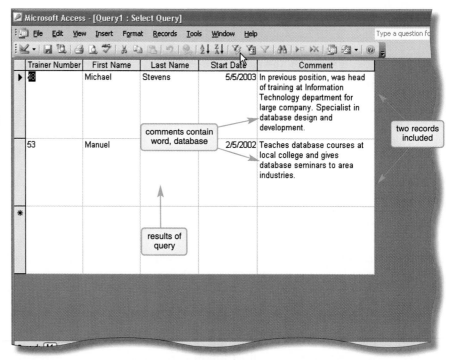

FIGURE 5-74

3

• **Click the View button to return to the Select Query window.**

• **Click the Criteria row under the Start Date field, and then type** <1/1/2003 **as the criterion.**

*The criterion for the Start Date field is entered (Figure 5-75). Access automatically adds the LIKE operator and quotation marks to criteria that use the * wildcard.*

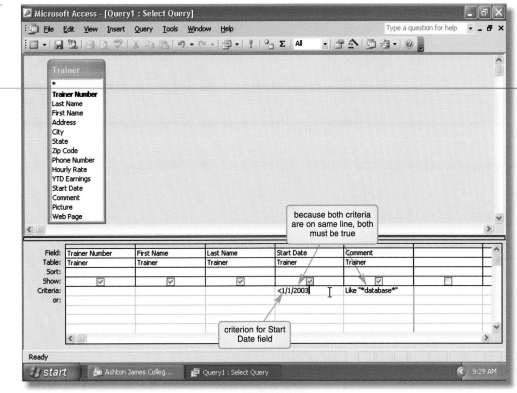

FIGURE 5-75

4

• **Click the Run button to run the query.**

The result contains only a single row, because only one trainer was hired before January 1, 2003 and has a comment entry that contains the word, database (Figure 5-76).

5

• **Close the Select Query window by clicking its Close Window button.**

• **When asked if you want to save the query, click the No button.**

The results of the query are removed from the screen and the Database window again appears.

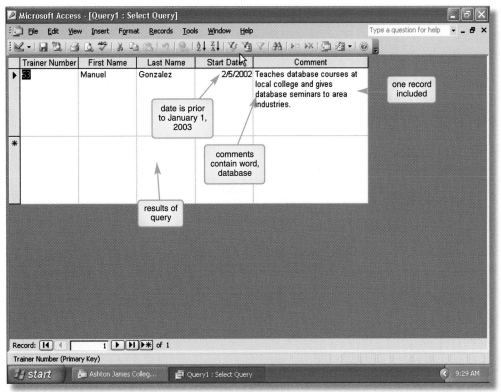

FIGURE 5-76

Closing the Database and Quitting Access

The following steps close the database and quit Access.

To Close a Database and Quit Access

1 **Click the Close Window button for the Ashton James College : Database window.**

2 **Click the Close button for the Microsoft Access window.**

Project Summary

Project 5 introduced you to some additional data types. To maintain the additional data, you learned how to create and work with date, memo, OLE, and Hyperlink fields. You created and used an input mask. You also learned how to use the new data types in a form. You then learned how to build a form on a one-to-many relationship in which you had several records from one of the tables appearing on the screen at the same time in order to create the required form. You learned how to use the form to view trainer and client data as well as to view the trainer's Web page. You saw how to use date and memo fields in queries.

 If you have a SAM user profile, you may have access to hands-on instruction, practice, and assessment of the skills covered in this project. Log in to your SAM account and go to your assignments page to see what your instructor has assigned.

What You Should Know

Having completed this project, you should be able to perform the tasks below. The tasks are listed in the same order they were presented in this project. For a list of the buttons, menus, toolbars, and commands introduced in this project, see the Quick Reference Summary at the back of this book and refer to the Page Number column.

1. Open a Database   (AC 260)
2. Add Fields to a Table   (AC 261)
3. Use the Input Mask Wizard   (AC 263)
4. Enter Data Using an Input Mask   (AC 265)
5. Enter Data in Date Fields   (AC 266)
6. Enter Data in Memo Fields   (AC 267)
7. Change the Row and Column Size   (AC 268)
8. Enter Data in OLE Fields   (AC 269)
9. Enter Data in Hyperlink Fields   (AC 271)
10. Close the Table and Save the Properties (AC 273)
11. Create a Form with a Subform Using the Form Wizard   (AC 274)
12. Modify the Subform Design   (AC 279)
13. Modify the Form Design   (AC 280)
14. Move and Resize Fields   (AC 282)
15. Move a Label   (AC 284)
16. Move Fields   (AC 284)
17. Change Label Alignment   (AC 285)
18. Resize a Label   (AC 287)
19. Change the Size Mode   (AC 288)
20. Change Special Effects and Colors of Labels (AC 289)
21. Add a Form Title   (AC 291)
22. Fine-Tune the Form   (AC 293)
23. Change a Tab Stop   (AC 294)
24. Change the Tab Order   (AC 295)
25. Use the Form to View Data and Web Pages (AC 297)
26. View Object Dependencies   (AC 299)
27. Use Date and Memo Fields in a Query   (AC 300)
28. Close a Database and Quit Access   (AC 302)

Learn It Online

Instructions: To complete the Learn It Online exercises, start your browser, click the Address bar, and then enter the Web address scsite.com/ac2003/learn. When the Access 2003 Learn It Online page is displayed, follow the instructions in the exercises below. Each exercise has instructions for printing your results, either for your own records or for submission to your instructor.

1 Project Reinforcement TF, MC, and SA

Below Access Project 5, click the Project Reinforcement link. Print the quiz by clicking Print on the File menu for each page. Answer each question.

2 Flash Cards

Below Access Project 5, click the Flash Cards link and read the instructions. Type 20 (or a number specified by your instructor) in the Number of playing cards text box, type your name in the Enter your Name text box, and then click the Flip Card button. When the flash card is displayed, read the question and then click the ANSWER box arrow to select an answer. Flip through Flash Cards. If your score is 15 (75%) correct or greater, click Print on the File menu to print your results. If your score is less than 15 (75%) correct, then redo this exercise by clicking the Replay button.

3 Practice Test

Below Access Project 5, click the Practice Test link. Answer each question, enter your first and last name at the bottom of the page, and then click the Grade Test button. When the graded practice test is displayed on your screen, click Print on the File menu to print a hard copy. Continue to take practice tests until you score 80% or better.

4 Who Wants To Be a Computer Genius?

Below Access Project 5, click the Computer Genius link. Read the instructions, enter your first and last name at the bottom of the page, and then click the PLAY button. When your score is displayed, click the PRINT RESULTS link to print a hard copy.

5 Wheel of Terms

Below Access Project 5, click the Wheel of Terms link. Read the instructions, and then enter your first and last name and your school name. Click the PLAY button. When your score is displayed, right-click the score and then click Print on the shortcut menu to print a hard copy.

6 Crossword Puzzle Challenge

Below Access Project 5, click the Crossword Puzzle Challenge link. Read the instructions, and then enter your first and last name. Click the SUBMIT button. Work the crossword puzzle. When you are finished, click the Submit button. When the crossword puzzle is redisplayed, click the Print Puzzle button to print a hard copy.

7 Tips and Tricks

Below Access Project 5, click the Tips and Tricks link. Click a topic that pertains to Project 5. Right-click the information and then click Print on the shortcut menu. Construct a brief example of what the information relates to in Access to confirm you understand how to use the tip or trick.

8 Newsgroups

Below Access Project 5, click the Newsgroups link. Click a topic that pertains to Project 5. Print three comments.

9 Expanding Your Horizons

Below Access Project 5, click the Expanding Your Horizons link. Click a topic that pertains to Project 5. Print the information. Construct a brief example of what the information relates to in Access to confirm you understand the contents of the article.

10 Search Sleuth

Below Access Project 5, click the Search Sleuth link. To search for a term that pertains to this project, select a term below the Project 5 title and then use the Google search engine at google.com (or any major search engine) to display and print two Web pages that present information on the term.

11 Access Online Training

Below Access Project 5, click the Access Online Training link. When your browser displays the Microsoft Office Online Web page, click the Access link. Click one of the Access courses that covers one or more of the objectives listed at the beginning of the project on page AC 258. Print the first page of the course before stepping through it.

12 Office Marketplace

Below Access Project 5, click the Office Marketplace link. When your browser displays the Microsoft Office Online Web page, click the Office Marketplace link. Click a topic that relates to Access. Print the first page.

Apply Your Knowledge

1 Enhancing the Begon Pest Control Database

Instructions: Start Access. If you are using the Microsoft Office Access 2003 Complete or the Microsoft Office Access 2003 Comprehensive text, open the Begon Pest Control database that you used in Project 4. Otherwise, see your instructor for information on accessing the files required for this book. Perform the following tasks:

1. Add the fields, Phone Number, Start Date, and Picture to the Technician table structure as shown in Figure 5-77. Create an input mask for the Phone Number field. Use the same input mask type that you used for the Trainer table in this project.

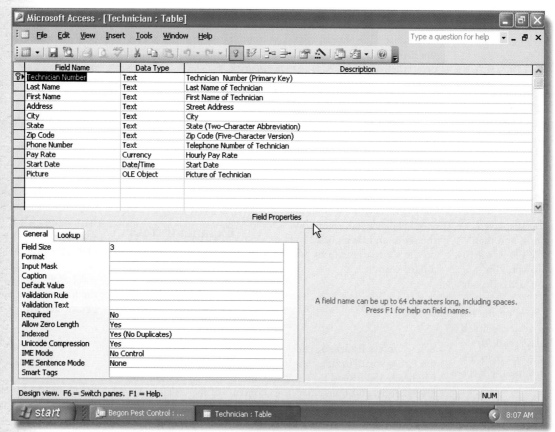

FIGURE 5-77

2. Save the changes to the structure.
3. Add the data shown in Figure 5-78 to the Technician table. Adjust the column width to best fit the size of the data.
4. Print and then close the table. Save the changes to the layout of the table.

Data for Technician Table			
TECHNICIAN NUMBER	PHONE NUMBER	START DATE	PICTURE
203	901-555-6667	11/12/2003	pict2
210	865-555-2112	12/02/2004	pict1
214	901-555-3223	10/16/2004	pict4
220	865-555-5445	01/06/2005	pict5

FIGURE 5-78

Apply Your Knowledge

5. Query the Technician table to find all technicians who started after January 1, 2005. Display the Technician Number, First Name, Last Name, and Pay Rate. Print the results. Do not save the query.

6. Use the Form Wizard to create a form with a subform for the Technician table. Include the Technician Number, First Name, Last Name, Phone Number, Pay Rate, Start Date, and Picture fields from the Technician table. Include the Customer Number, Name, and Balance fields from the Customer table. Users should not be able to tab through the Picture control.

7. Modify the form design to create the form shown in Figure 5-79.

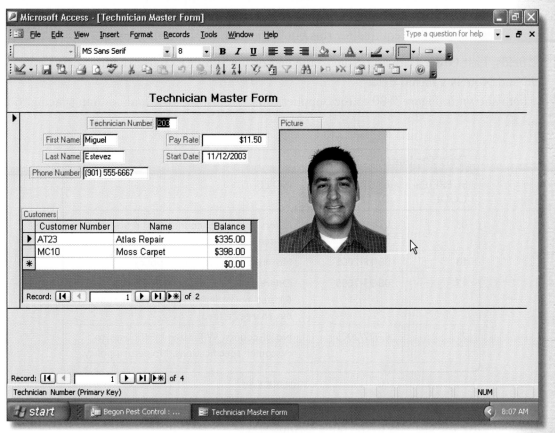

FIGURE 5-79

8. Print the form. To print the form, open the form, click File on the menu bar, click Print, and then click Selected Record(s) as the Print Range. Click the OK button.

1 Enhancing the Birds2U Database

Problem: The management of Birds2U has found that the Birds2U database needs to maintain additional data on suppliers. Management needs to know the last date an order was placed with a supplier and would like to store some notes about each supplier's policies. Birds2U requires a form that displays information about the supplier as well as the items that are purchased from the supplier.

Instructions: If you are using the Microsoft Office Access 2003 Complete or the Microsoft Office Access 2003 Comprehensive text, open the Birds2U database that you used in Project 4. Otherwise, see your instructor for information on accessing the files required for this book. Perform the following tasks:

1. Add the fields, Last Order Date and Note to the end of the Supplier table structure. Last Order Date is a date field and Note is a memo field.
2. Add the data shown in Figure 5-80 to the Supplier table. Adjust the row and column spacing to best fit the data.

Data for Supplier Table		
SUPPLIER CODE	LAST ORDER DATE	NOTE
05	07/10/2005	Offers volume discount when more than 12 items are ordered. Has a return policy.
13	08/18/2005	No discounts. No return policy.
17	08/25/2005	Offers volume discount when more than 6 items are ordered. Has a return policy but charges a fee.
21	07/27/2005	No discounts. Will make birdhouses to customer specifications. No return policy.

FIGURE 5-80

3. Print the table. Save the changes to the table layout.
4. Create the form shown in Figure 5-81 for the Supplier table. Use Supplier Master Form as the name of the form and Items as the name of the subform.

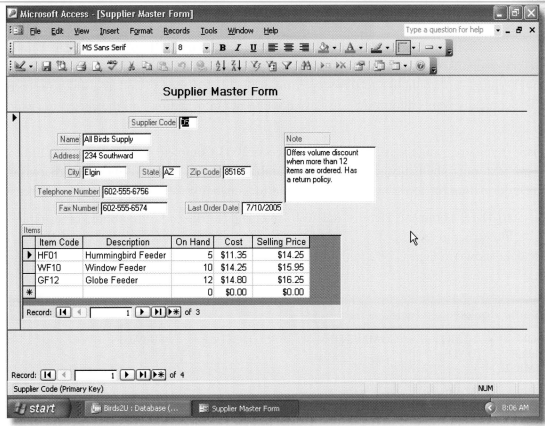

FIGURE 5-81

5. Print the form. To print the form, open the form, click File on the menu bar, click Print, and then click Selected Record(s) as the Print Range. Click the OK button.
6. Query the Supplier table to find all suppliers that accept returns. Include the Supplier Code and Name in the query. Print the results. Do not save the query.

2 Enhancing the Babbage Bookkeeping Database

Problem: Babbage Bookkeeping needs to maintain additional data on the bookkeepers. The company needs to maintain the date a bookkeeper started as well as some notes concerning the bookkeeper's training and abilities. Babbage Bookkeeping also would like to store a picture of the bookkeeper as well as a link to each bookkeeper's Web page. The company wants a form that displays bookkeeper information and the clients for which they are responsible.

Instructions: If you are using the Microsoft Office Access 2003 Complete or the Microsoft Office Access 2003 Comprehensive text, open the Babbage Bookkeeping database that you used in Project 4. Otherwise, see your instructor for information on accessing the files required for this book. Perform the following tasks:

1. Add the Start Date, Comment, Picture, and Web Page fields to the end of the Bookkeeper table. Save the changes to the structure.
2. Add the data shown in Figure 5-82 to the Bookkeeper table. Adjust the row and column spacing to best fit the data.

Data for Bookkeeper Table				
BOOK KEEPER NUMBER	**START DATE**	**COMMENT**	**PICTURE**	**WEB PAGE**
22	06/10/2003	Has a BA in Accounting. Working toward CPA.	pict5	www.scsite.com/ac2003/trainer5.html
24	01/15/2004	Has an AA in Accounting.	pict3	www.scsite.com/ac2003/trainer3.html
34	09/09/2003	Has an AA in Records Management. Working toward BA.	pict1	www.scsite.com/ac2003/trainer1.html

FIGURE 5-82

3. Print the table. Save the changes to the layout of the table.
4. Create the form shown in Figure 5-83 for the Bookkeeper table. Use Bookkeeper Master Form as the name of the form and Accounts as the name of the subform. Change the tab order so users tab to the Web Page field before the Comment field. Users should not be able to tab through the Picture control.

In the Lab

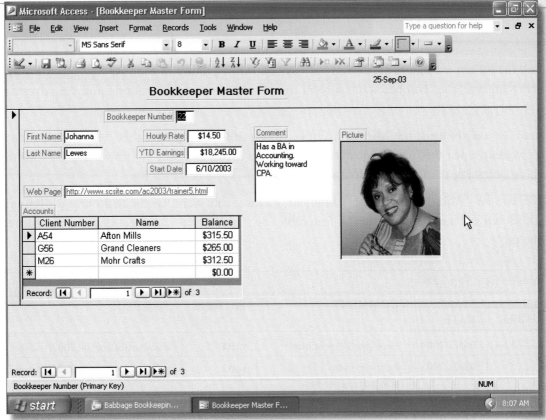

FIGURE 5-83

5. Add the current date to the form. *Hint:* Use Microsoft Office Access Help to solve this problem.
6. Print the form. To print the form, open the form, click File on the menu bar, and then click Print. Click Selected Record(s) as the Print Range. Click the OK button.
7. Query the Bookkeeper table to find all bookkeepers that have an AA degree and started during 2003. Include the Bookkeeper Number, First Name, Last Name, Hourly Rate, and YTD Earnings in the query. Print the query results. Do not save the query.

3 Enhancing the City Guide Database

Problem: The chamber of commerce needs to maintain additional data on the ad reps. The chamber needs to store the date the ad rep started, comments about each ad rep, a picture of each ad rep, and the Web page address of each ad rep. The chamber wants a form that displays ad rep information and the advertisers they represent.

Instructions: If you are using the Microsoft Office Access 2003 Complete or the Microsoft Office Access 2003 Comprehensive text, open the City Guide database that you used in Project 4. Otherwise, see your instructor for information on accessing the files required for this book.

Part 1 Instructions: Add the Start Date, Comment, Picture, and Web Page fields to the Ad Rep table and then add the data shown in Figure 5-84 to the Ad Rep table. Be sure that the datasheet displays the entire comment and print the table.

Data for Ad Rep Table				
AD REP NUMBER	START DATE	COMMENT	PICTURE	WEB PAGE
21	06/12/2004	Excellent copy editor	pict1	www.scsite.com/ac2003/trainer1.html
29	02/06/2005	Records radio advertisements for chamber	pict2	www.scsite.com/ac2003/trainer2.html
32	09/21/2004	Also works as a freelance journalist	pict5	www.scsite.com/ac2003/trainer5.html

FIGURE 5-84

Part 2 Instructions: Create a form for the Ad Rep table that is similar in design to the form shown in Figure 5-1 on page AC 259. Include all fields from the Ad Rep table except the Address, State, and Zip Code fields. Include the Advertiser Number, Name, Balance, and Amount Paid fields from the Advertiser table. Print the form for ad rep 29.

Part 3 Instructions: Find all ad reps that also work as freelance journalists. Include the Ad Rep Number, First Name, and Last Name in the query result. Find all ad reps that started after 2004. Include the Ad Rep Number, First Name, Last Name, Comm Rate, and Commission in the query result.

Cases and Places

The difficulty of these case studies varies:
■ are the least difficult and ■■ are more difficult. The last exercise is a group exercise.

1 ■ Use the College Dog Walkers database that you used in Project 4 for this assignment or see your instructor for information on accessing the files required for this book. Add a Picture field and a Web Page field to the Walker table and add pictures and hyperlinks for all dog walkers. Update the two fields by using appropriate pictures and hyperlinks from the Data Disk. Create a form for the Walker table that is similar in design to the form shown in Figure 5-1 on page AC 259. Include all fields from the Walker table. Include the Customer Number, First Name, Last Name, Per Walk Amount, and Balance fields from the Customer table.

2 ■ Use the InPerson Fitness Company database that you used in Project 4 for this assignment or see your instructor for information on accessing the files required for this book. Add a Start Date, Comment, Picture, and Web Page field to the Trainer table. Add the data shown in Figure 5-85 to the Trainer table. Create a form for the Trainer table that is similar in design to the form shown in Figure 5-1 on page AC 259. Include all fields from the Trainer table. Include the Client Number, First Name, Last Name, Amount Paid, and Balance fields from the Client table. Query the Trainer table to find all trainers that have a degree in recreation management.

Data for Trainer Table				
TRAINER NUMBER	START DATE	COMMENT	PICTURE	WEB PAGE
203	2/5/2005	Working toward a degree in physical therapy. Member of volunteer fire department.	pict1	www.scsite.com/ac2003/trainer1.html
205	3/14/2004	Has a degree in Recreation Management. Runs marathons.	pict3	www.scsite.com/ac2003/trainer3.html
207	6/2/2005	Coaches high school tennis.	pict4	www.scsite.com/ac2003/trainer4.html

FIGURE 5-85

Cases and Places

3 ■■ Use the Regional Books database that you used in Project 4 for this assignment or see your instructor for information on accessing the files required for this book. Regional Books needs to store additional information on publishers. Add the fields and data shown in Figure 5-86 to the Publisher table. Query the database to find all publishers that will fill single orders. Create a Publisher Master Form for the Publisher table. Include all fields in the Book table except the Book Type and Publisher Code. Be sure to include a form header with a title and change the special effects and colors of the labels.

Data for Publisher Table		
PUBLISHER CODE	**ORDER DATE**	**NOTE**
BB	7/21/2005	Will fill single orders and special requests.
PB	7/30/2005	Will fill single orders on an emergency basis only. Ships twice a week.
SI	7/15/2005	Has minimum order requirement of 20 books. Ships weekly.
VN	8/25/2005	Will fill single orders and special requests. Ships daily.

FIGURE 5-86

4 ■■ Use the Campus Housing database that you used in Project 4 for this assignment or see your instructor for information on accessing the files required for this book. Add a Phone Number, Picture, and Web Page field to the Owner table. The Phone Number field should use the same input mask as that shown in the project. Create your own data for the Phone Number field. Update the Picture and Web Page fields by using appropriate pictures and hyperlinks from the Data Disk. Create a form that contains a subform for the Owner table. The subform should display all the fields from the Rental table except Owner Code. Be sure to include a form header with a title and the current date. Change the special effects and colors of the labels.

5 ■■ **Working Together** Copy the Regional Books database and rename the database to your team name. For example, if your team is Team 1, then name the database Team 1 Books. As a team, enhance this Books database by adding a summary description for each book. Make up your own summaries. Add a field to the Publisher table that will store the publisher's Web page. Make up your own Web pages for the publisher or use existing Web pages. For example, use the Course Technology Web page for one of the publisher's Web pages. Modify the Publisher Master Form to include the Web Page field. Determine the object dependencies for all forms and queries in the database. Write a short report that explains what you found and why it is useful information.

Switchboards, PivotTables, and PivotCharts

CASE PERSPECTIVE

The tables, forms, and reports created for Ashton James College are a real benefit for the administration. Although, it is not difficult to use a form or a table, or to print or preview a report, users do have to remember some specific steps. To view client data using a form, for example, they need to first select the Forms object and then open the desired form. To view the same client data in Datasheet view, they need to remember to select the Tables object, after which they must open the correct table. If they want a window maximized, they must take the correct action to maximize it. AJC has heard about switchboard systems that enable users to click a button or two to open any form or table, preview any report, or print any report. The administration would like such a switchboard system because they believe this will improve the user-friendliness of the system, thereby improving employee satisfaction.

The administration also wants to summarize their data in additional ways. While they use the crosstab queries created previously, they want the ability to make changes to the way the data is summarized and presented on the screen. Presenting the query results as PivotTables addresses these needs. Presenting the results as PivotCharts gives the same flexibility in a graphical format. Your task is to help the administration accomplish these goals.

As you read through this project, you will learn how to create the switchboard, a PivotTable, and a PivotChart for Ashton James College.

Switchboards, PivotTables, and PivotCharts

OBJECTIVES

You will have mastered the material in this project when you can:

- Create, add actions to, run, copy, and modify macros
- Create a switchboard and switchboard pages
- Modify switchboard pages
- Use a switchboard
- Import data and create a query
- Create a PivotTable
- Change properties in a PivotTable

- Use a PivotTable
- Create a PivotChart and add a legend
- Change the chart type and organization of a PivotChart
- Remove drop areas in a PivotChart
- Assign axis titles and a chart title in a PivotChart
- Use a PivotChart

Introduction

Previous projects illustrated how to create tables, forms, and reports. Each time a user needs to utilize any of these, however, the user needs to follow a correct series of steps. To open the Client Update Form in a maximized window, for example, requires that a user click Forms on the Objects bar in the Database window, and then right-click the correct form. Next, the user must click Open on the shortcut menu, and then finally double-click the title bar for the window containing the form to maximize the window.

All these steps are unnecessary if the database includes a switchboard system, such as the one shown in Figure 6-1a. A **switchboard** is a form that includes buttons to perform a variety of actions. In this system, the user just clicks a button — View Form, View Table, View Report, Print Report, or Exit Application — to indicate the action to be taken. Other than Exit Application, clicking a button leads to another switchboard. For example, when a user clicks the View Form button, Access displays the View Form switchboard as shown in Figure 6-1b. On this form, the user clicks the button that identifies the form he or she wants to view. Similarly, when the user clicks the View Table button, Access displays a switchboard on which the user clicks a button to indicate the table he or she wants to view. Thus, viewing any form, table, or report, or printing any report requires clicking only two buttons.

The steps in this project show how to create the switchboard system represented in Figures 6-1a and 6-1b. Before doing so, **macros**, which are collections of actions designed to carry out specific tasks, such as opening a form and maximizing the

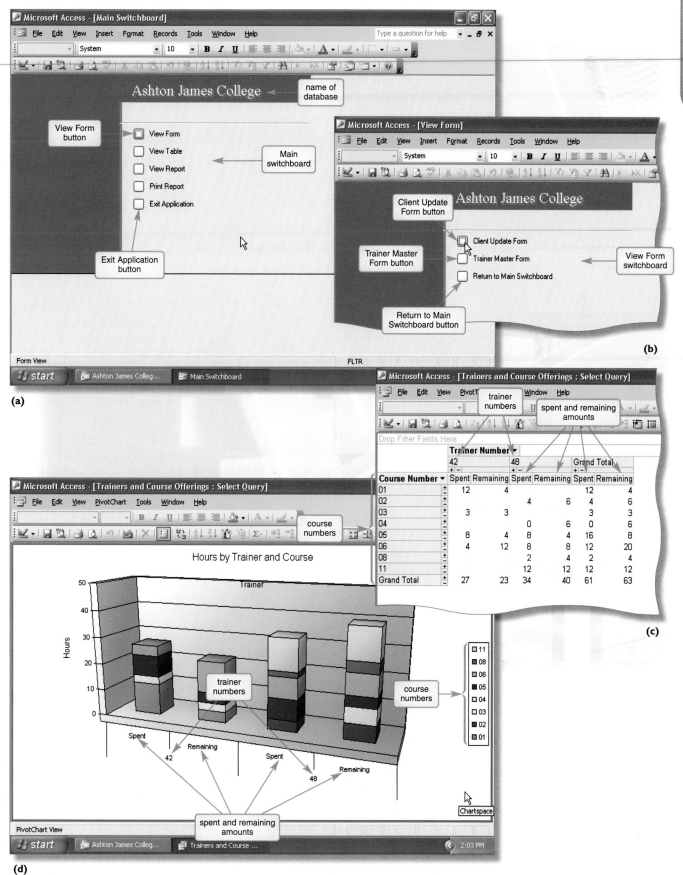

FIGURE 6-1

window containing the form, must be created. Macros are run directly from the Database window. When a macro is run, Access will execute the various steps, called **actions**, in the macro. The switchboard system also uses macros. Clicking certain buttons in the switchboard system will cause the appropriate macros to be run.

Project 2 illustrated the steps for creating a crosstab query, which is a query that calculates a statistic (for example, sum, average, or count) for data that is grouped by two different types of information. A PivotTable is similar (Figure 6-1c on the previous page). Unlike a crosstab, however, a PivotTable is dynamic. In a PivotTable, different levels of detail are shown easily and changes to the organization or layout of the table can be accomplished by dragging items. Checking or unchecking values in drop-down lists can filter data. A PivotChart (Figure 6-1d) presents similar data graphically. Both a PivotTable and a PivotChart representation of a query are created in this project.

Project Six — Switchboards, PivotTables, and PivotCharts

The steps in this project show how to create and test macros and how to use these macros in the switchboard system that Ashton James College requires. With the switchboard system, users can access any form, table, or report simply by clicking the appropriate buttons. The steps add two additional tables to the database. The steps also create a query incorporating this new data, and then use the data in this query to create both a PivotTable and a PivotChart.

Opening the Database

If you are stepping through this project on a computer and you want your screen to match the figures in this book, then you should change your computer's resolution to 800 x 600. For more information on how to change the resolution on your computer, see Appendix D. Before carrying out the steps in this project, first you must open the database. The following steps, which open the database, assume that the database is located in a folder called Data on disk C. (See the note in Project 4 on page AC 197.) If your database is located anywhere else, you will need to make the appropriate adjustments in the steps.

To Open a Database

1 Click the Start button on the Windows taskbar, point to All Programs on the Start menu, point to Microsoft Office on the All Programs submenu, and then click Microsoft Office Access 2003 on the Microsoft Office submenu.

2 If the Access window is not maximized, double-click its title bar to maximize it.

3 If the Language bar appears, right-click it and then click Close the Language bar on the shortcut menu.

4 Click Open on the Database toolbar, and then click Local Disk (C:) in the Look in box. Double-click the Data folder, and then make sure the database called Ashton James College is selected.

5 Click the Open button. If a Security Warning dialog box appears, click the Open button.

The database opens and the Ashton James College : Database window appears.

Creating and Using Macros

A macro consists of a series of actions that Access performs when the macro is run; therefore, you will need to specify the actions when you create the macro. The actions are entered in a special window called a Macro window. Once a macro is created, you can run it from the Database window by right-clicking the macro and then clicking Run on the shortcut menu. Macros also can be associated with items on switchboards. When you click the corresponding button on the switchboard, Access will run the macro. Whether a macro is run from the Database window or from a switchboard, the effect is the same: Access will execute the actions in the macro in the order in which they are entered.

In this project, you will learn how to create macros to open forms and maximize the windows; open tables in Datasheet view; open reports in preview windows; and print reports. As you enter actions, you will select them from a list box. The names of the actions are self-explanatory. The action to open a form, for example, is OpenForm. Thus, it is not necessary to memorize the specific actions that are available.

The following steps demonstrate how to create a macro.

To Create a Macro

1

- **Click the Macros object.**

The list of previously created macros appears (Figure 6-2). Currently, no macros exist.

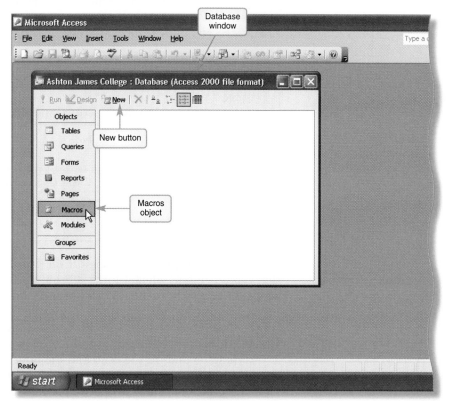

FIGURE 6-2

2

* **Click the New button.**

* **If necessary, maximize the window by double-clicking its title bar.**

The Microsoft Access – [Macro1: Macro] window appears (Figure 6-3).

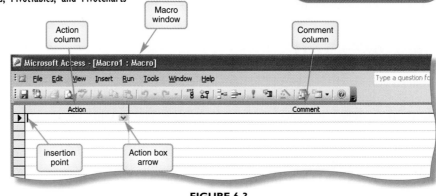

FIGURE 6-3

The Macro Window

The first column in the Macro window is the Action column. You enter the actions you want the macro to perform in this column (Figure 6-3). To enter an action, click the arrow in the Action column and then select the action from the list that appears. Many actions require additional information, called the **arguments** of the action. If you select such an action, the arguments will appear in the lower portion of the Macro window and you can make any necessary changes to them.

The second column in the Macro window is the Comment column. In this column, you enter **comments**, which are brief descriptions of the corresponding action's purpose. The actions, the arguments requiring changes, and the comments for the first macro you will create are shown in Table 6-1.

Table 6-1	Specifications for First Macro		
ACTION	**ARGUMENT TO CHANGE**	**NEW VALUE FOR ARGUMENT**	**COMMENT**
Echo	Echo On	No	Turn echo off to avoid screen flicker
Hourglass			Turn on hourglass
OpenForm	Form Name	Client Update Form	Open Client Update Form
Hourglass	Hourglass On	No	Turn off hourglass
Echo			Turn echo on

The macro begins by turning off the echo. This will eliminate the screen flicker that can be present when a form is being opened. The second action changes the shape of the mouse pointer to an hourglass to indicate that some process is taking place. The third action opens the form called Client Update Form. The fourth action turns off the hourglass, and the fifth action turns the echo back on so the Client Update Form will appear.

Turning on and off the echo and the hourglass are not absolutely necessary. On computers with faster processors, you may not notice a difference between running a macro that includes these actions and one that does not. For computers with slower processors, however, these actions can make a noticeable difference, so they are included here.

Adding Actions to a Macro

To continue creating this macro, enter the actions. For each action, enter the action and comment in the appropriate text boxes, and then make the necessary changes to any arguments. The following steps show how to add the actions to, and save, the macro.

To Add Actions to a Macro

1

• **Click the box arrow in the first row of the Action column to display a list of available actions.**

• **Scroll down until Echo appears.**

The list of available actions appears (Figure 6-4).

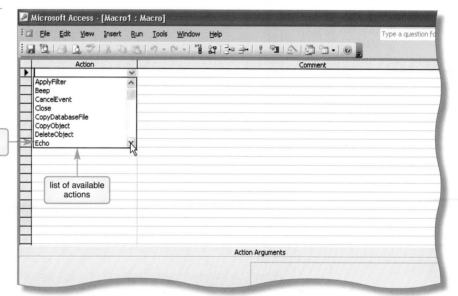

FIGURE 6-4

2

• **Click Echo.**

• **Press the F6 key to move to the Action Arguments for the Echo action.**

• **Click the Echo On box arrow.**

The arguments for the Echo action appear (Figure 6-5). The list of values for the Echo On argument appears.

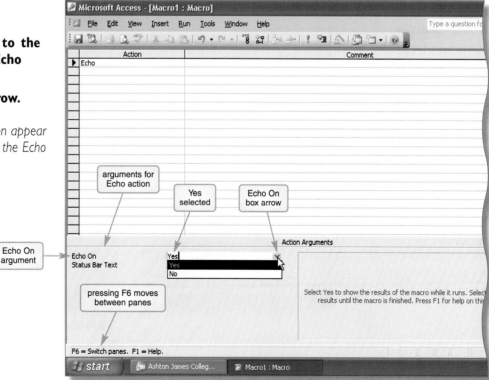

FIGURE 6-5

3

• **Click No.**

• **Press the F6 key to move back to Echo in the Action column, and then press the TAB key.**

• **Type** Turn echo off to avoid screen flicker **in the Comment column, and then press the TAB key.**

The first action and comment are entered (Figure 6-6). The insertion point has moved to the second row.

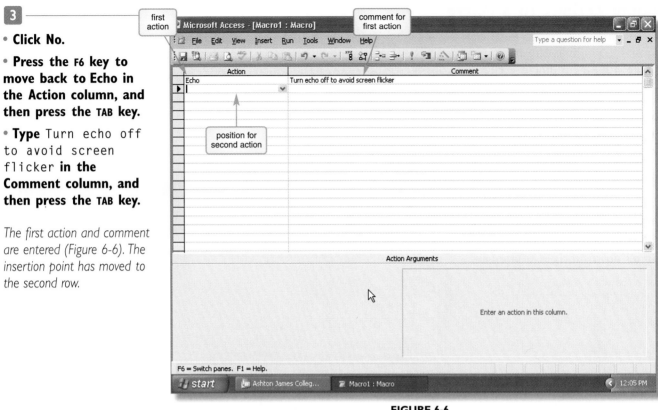

FIGURE 6-6

4

• **Select Hourglass as the action in the second row.**

• **Press the TAB key and then type** Turn on hourglass **as the comment in the second row.**

• **Press the TAB key and then select OpenForm as the third action.**

• **Press the F6 key to move to the Action Arguments, and then click the Form Name box arrow.**

A list of available forms appears (Figure 6-7).

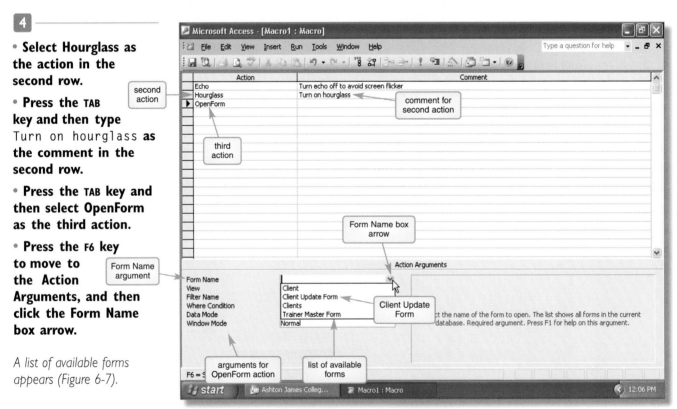

FIGURE 6-7

- **Click Client Update Form, press the F6 key, press the TAB key, and then type** Open Client Update Form **as the comment.**
- **Select Hourglass as the fourth action.**
- **Change the Hourglass On argument to No, and then type** Turn off hourglass **as the comment.**
- **Select Echo as the fifth action, and then type** Turn echo on **as the comment.**

The actions and comments are entered (Figure 6-8).

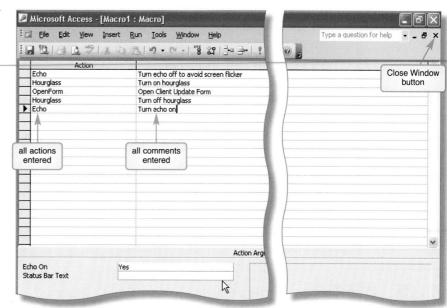

FIGURE 6-8

- **Click the Close Window button to close the macro, click the Yes button to save the macro, type** Open Client Update Form **as the name of the macro.**

The Save As dialog box appears (Figure 6-9).

7

- **Click the OK button.**

The actions and comments have been added to the macro, and the macro is saved.

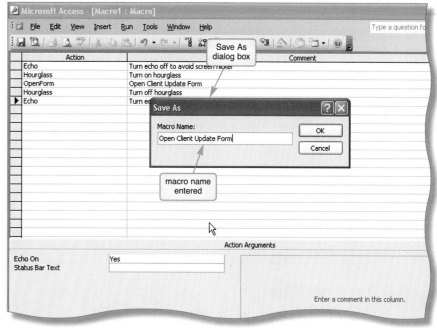

FIGURE 6-9

Running a Macro

To run a macro, select the Macros object in the Database window, right-click the macro, and then select Run on the shortcut menu. The actions in the macro will execute. The steps on the next page illustrate how to run the macro that was just created.

To Run a Macro

1 **Right-click the Open Client Update Form macro and then click Run on the shortcut menu.**

2 **Click the Close Window button on the Client Update Form window title bar.**

The macro runs and displays the Client Update Form. The window containing the form is maximized because the previous windows were maximized. The form no longer appears.

If previous windows had not been maximized, the window containing the form also would not be maximized. In order to ensure that the window containing the form is maximized automatically, you can include the Maximize action in your macro.

Modifying a Macro

To modify a macro, select the macro in the Database window, select Design View on the shortcut menu, and then make the necessary changes. To insert a new action, click the position for the action, or press the INSERT key to insert a new blank row if the new action is to be placed between two actions. Enter the new action, change the values for any necessary arguments, and then enter a comment.

When modifying a macro, two additional columns may appear: the Macro Name column and the Condition column. It is possible to group multiple macros into a single macro group. When doing so, the Macro Name column is used to identify the particular macro within the group. It also is possible to have an action be contingent on a certain condition being true. If so, the condition is entered in the Condition column. Because the macros you are creating are not combined into a macro group and the actions are not dependent on any conditions, you will not need these columns. You can remove these unneeded columns from the screen by clicking the appropriate toolbar buttons.

The following steps show how to modify the macro just created, adding a new step to maximize the form automatically. The steps remove both the Macro Name and the Condition column from the screen.

To Modify a Macro

1

• **Right-click the Open Client Update Form macro.**

The shortcut menu appears (Figure 6-10).

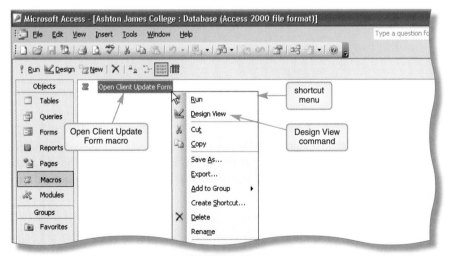

FIGURE 6-10

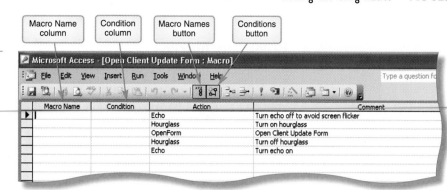

FIGURE 6-11

2

• **Click Design View.**

The macro appears in Design view (Figure 6-11). The Macro Name and Condition columns may be included.

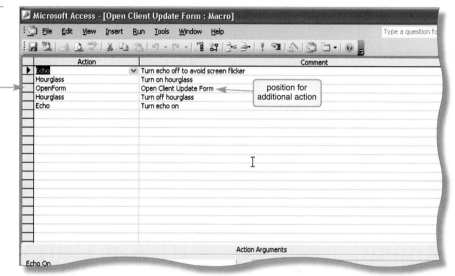

FIGURE 6-12

3

• **If the Macro Name column appears, click the Macro Names button on the Macro Design toolbar to remove the Macro Name column.**

• **If the Condition column appears, click the Conditions button on the Macro Design toolbar to remove the Condition column.**

The Microsoft Access - [Open Client Update Form : Macro] window appears (Figure 6-12). The Macro Name and Condition columns do not appear.

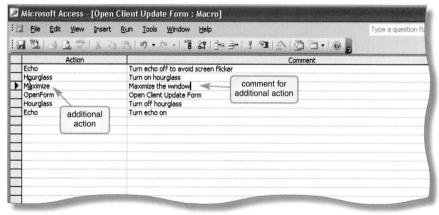

FIGURE 6-13

4

• **Click the row selector on the row containing the OpenForm action to select the row, and then press the INSERT key to insert a new row.**

• **Click the Action column arrow on the new row, select Maximize as the action, and then type** `Maximize the window` **as the comment.**

The new action is entered (Figure 6-13).

5

• **Click the Close Window button, and then click the Yes button to save the changes.**

The macro has been changed and saved.

The next time the macro is run, the form not only will be opened, but the window containing the form also will be maximized automatically.

Other Ways

1. Click Macros on Objects bar, click Macro name, click Design on Macro Design toolbar
2. In Voice Command mode, say "Macros, [click macro name], Design"

More About

Errors in Macros

The order of the actions in a macro may be incorrect. You can move an action by clicking the row selector to the left of the action name to highlight the row. Then click the highlighted row again and drag it to the correct location.

Errors in Macros

Macros can contain errors. For example, if you type the name of the form in the Form Name argument of the OpenForm action instead of selecting it from the list, you may type it incorrectly. Access then will not be able to execute the desired action. In that case, a Microsoft Access dialog box will appear, indicating the error and solution as shown in Figure 6-14.

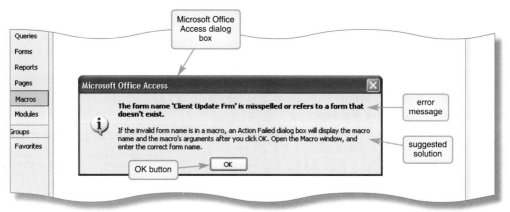

FIGURE 6-14

More About

Finding Problems in Macros

You can single step (run a macro one action at a time) through a macro to observe the results of each action and identify any action that causes an error or produces unexpected results. To single step through a macro, open the macro in Design view, click the Single Step button, and then click the Run button on the Macro Design toolbar. When the Macro Single Step dialog box appears, click the Step button to run the macro one action at a time.

If such a dialog box appears, click the OK button. The Action Failed dialog box then appears (Figure 6-15). The dialog box indicates the macro that was being run, the action that Access was attempting to execute, and the arguments for the action. This information tells you which action needs to be corrected. To make the correction, click the Halt button, and then modify the design of the macro.

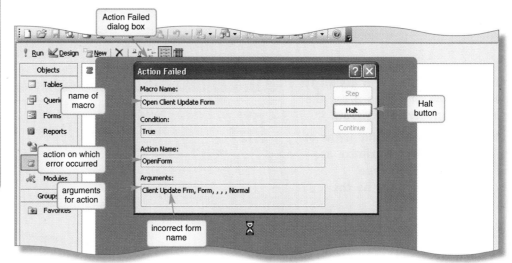

FIGURE 6-15

Additional Macros

The additional macros to be created are shown in Table 6-2. The first column gives the name of the macro, and the second column indicates the actions for the macro. The third column contains the values of those arguments that may need to be changed, and the fourth column contains the comments. (Any arguments not listed can be left as they are.)

Table 6-2 Specifications for Additional Macros

MACRO NAME	ACTION	ARGUMENT(S)	COMMENT
Open Trainer Master Form	Echo	Echo On: No	Turn echo off to avoid screen flicker
	Hourglass	Hourglass On: Yes	Turn on hourglass
	Maximize		Maximize the window
	OpenForm	Form Name: Trainer Master Form	Open Trainer Master Form
	Hourglass	Hourglass On: No	Turn off hourglass
	Echo	Echo On: Yes	Turn echo on
Open Client Table	OpenTable	Table Name: Client	Open Client Table
		View: Datasheet	
	Maximize		Maximize the window
Open Trainer Table	OpenTable	Table Name: Trainer	Open Trainer Table
		View: Datasheet	
	Maximize		Maximize the window
Preview Client Amount Report	OpenReport	Report Name: Client Amount Report	Preview Client Amount Report
		View: Print Preview	
	Maximize		Maximize the window
Print Client Amount Report	OpenReport	Report Name: Client Amount Report	Print Client Amount Report
		View: Print	
Preview Client Account Summary	OpenReport	Report Name: Client Account Summary	Preview Client Account Summary
		View: Print Preview	
	Maximize		Maximize the window
Print Client Account Summary	OpenReport	Report Name: Client Account Summary	Print Client Account Summary
		View: Print	
Preview Trainer/Client Report	OpenReport	Report Name: Trainer/Client Report	Preview Trainer/Client Report
		View: Print Preview	
	Maximize		Maximize the window
Print Trainer/Client Report	OpenReport	Report Name: Trainer/Client Report	Print Trainer/Client Report
		View: Print	

Copying a Macro

When you want to create a new macro, you often find there is an existing macro that is very similar to the one you wish to create. If this is the case, it often is simpler to use a copy of the existing macro and modify it instead of creating a new macro from scratch. The Open Trainer Master Form macro, for example, is very similar to the existing Open Client Update Form macro. Thus, you can make a copy of the Open Client Update Form macro, call it Open Trainer Master Form, and then modify it to the new requirements by changing only the portion that differs from the original macro.

Q&A

Q: One way to construct a new macro from an existing macro is to use Copy and Paste. Are there any other ways?

A: Yes, open the existing macro. Click File on the menu bar, click Save As on the File menu, and then type the name of the new macro. Make the appropriate changes to the new macro.

To make a copy of a macro, you use the clipboard. First, copy the existing macro to the clipboard and then paste the contents of the clipboard. At that point, assign the new name to the macro.

These same techniques will work for other objects as well. If you want to create a new report that is similar to an existing report, for example, use the clipboard to make a copy of the original report, paste the contents, rename it, and then modify the copied report in whatever way you wish.

The following steps illustrate how to use the clipboard to copy and paste the Open Client Update Form macro.

To Copy and Paste a Macro

1

• **Ensure the Macros object is selected, and right-click the Open Client Update Form macro.**

The shortcut menu for the Open Client Update Form macro appears (Figure 6-16).

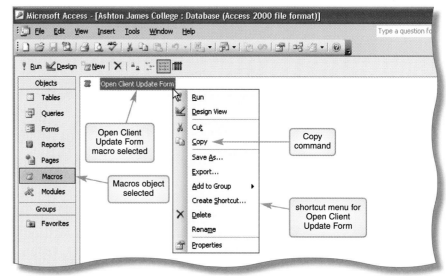

FIGURE 6-16

2

• **Click Copy to copy the macro to the clipboard.**

• **Right-click any open area of the Database window.**

The shortcut menu appears (Figure 6-17).

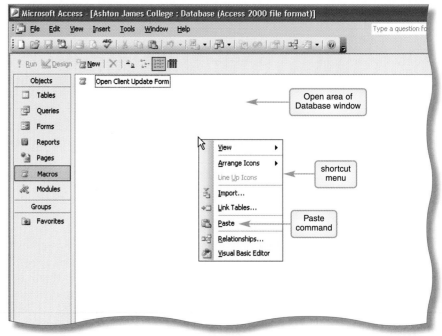

FIGURE 6-17

3

● **Click Paste, type** Open Trainer
Master Form **in the Macro Name
text box in the Paste As dialog box.**

*The Paste As dialog box appears, and the
new macro name is entered in the text box
(Figure 6-18).*

4

● **Click the OK button.**

The new macro is copied and saved.

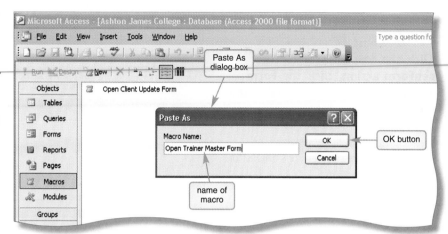

FIGURE 6-18

Modifying the Copied Macro

Once you have copied the macro, you can modify the copy to make any needed
changes. The following steps show how to modify the macro just copied by changing
the Form Name argument for the OpenForm action to Trainer Master Form.

To Modify the Copied Macro

1

● **Right-click the Open Trainer
Master Form macro.**

*The shortcut menu for the macro appears
(Figure 6-19).*

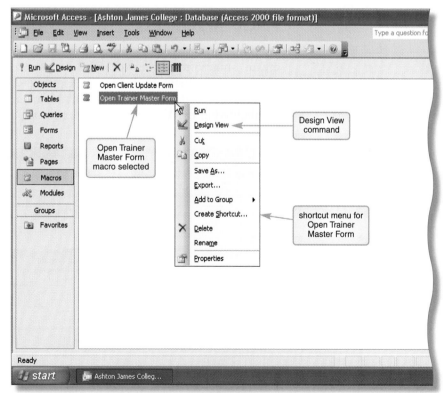

FIGURE 6-19

- **Click Design View.**

- **Click the row selector for the OpenForm action, click the Form Name argument, and then click the Form Name box arrow.**

The macro appears in Design view. The OpenForm action is selected, and the list of available forms appears (Figure 6-20).

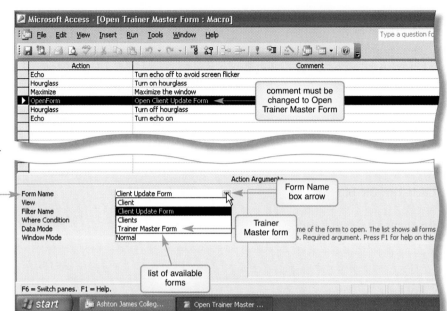

3

- **Click Trainer Master Form to change the Form Name argument.**

- **Click the Comment text box for the OpenForm action, delete the comment, and then type** Open Trainer Master Form **as the new comment.**

- **Click the Close Window button for the Open Trainer Master Form : Macro window, and then click the Yes button to save the changes.**

The changes to the macro have been saved.

FIGURE 6-20

Macro Arguments

Some macros require a change to more than one argument. For example, to create a macro to preview or print a report requires a change to both the Report Name and the View arguments. In Figure 6-21, the OpenReport action displays Client Amount Report in the Report Name argument text box and Print Preview is highlighted in the View argument text box.

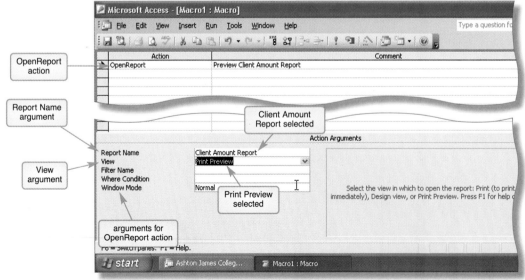

FIGURE 6-21

Creating Additional Macros

You can create additional macros using the same steps you used to create the first macro. You copy an existing macro and then modify the copied macro as needed. The following step shows how to create the additional macros illustrated in Table 6-2 on page AC 325.

To Create Additional Macros

1 **Using the same techniques used to create the Open Client Update Form macro (page AC 319), create each of the macros described in Table 6-2.**

The Open Client Table, Open Trainer Table, Preview Client Amount Report, Print Client Amount Report, Preview Client Account Summary, Print Client Account Summary, Preview Trainer/Client Report, and Print Trainer/Client Report macros are created.

Running the Macros

To run any of the other macros just as you ran the first macro, select the appropriate macro in the Database window and then select Run on the shortcut menu. The appropriate actions then are carried out. Running the Preview Client Amount Report macro, for example, displays the Client Amount Report in a maximized preview window.

Opening Databases Containing Macros

When a database contains macros, there is a chance a computer virus can attach to a macro. To protect against these types of macro viruses, Microsoft Access has a macro level security feature. Various levels of macro security are available, for example: high, medium, and low. If the macro level security is medium or higher, Access displays a Security Warning dialog box when a user attempts to open a database containing macros. If the database comes from a trusted source and you are sure that it does not contain any macro viruses, click Open in the Security Warning dialog box to open the database.

Creating and Using a Switchboard

A switchboard (see Figures 6-1a and 6-1b on page AC 315) is a special type of form. It contains buttons you can click to perform a variety of actions. Buttons on the Main switchboard can lead to other switchboards. Clicking the View Form button, for example, causes Access to display the View Form switchboard. Buttons also can be used to open forms or tables. Clicking the Client Update Form button on the View Form switchboard opens the Client Update Form. Still other buttons cause reports to appear in a preview window or print reports.

Creating a Switchboard

To create a switchboard, you use the Database Utilities command on the Tools menu and then select Switchboard Manager, which is an Access tool that allows you to create, edit, and delete switchboard forms for an application. If you have not previously created a switchboard, you will be asked if you wish to create one. The steps on the next page illustrate how to create a switchboard for the Ashton James College database.

More About

Running a Macro

You can run a macro from any window within Access. To do so, click Macro on the Tools menu, click Run Macro, and then select the macro from the Macro Name list.

More About

Application Systems

An application system is simply an easy-to-use collection of forms, reports, and queries designed to satisfy the needs of some specific user or group of users, such as the users at Ashton James College. A switchboard system is one type of application system that has found widespread acceptance in the Windows environment. For more information about application systems, visit the Access 2003 More About Web page (scsite.com/ac2003/more) and click Application Systems.

To Create a Switchboard

1

• **With the Database window appearing, click Tools on the menu bar, and point to Database Utilities on the Tools menu.**

The Tools menu appears (Figure 6-22). The Database Utilities submenu also appears.

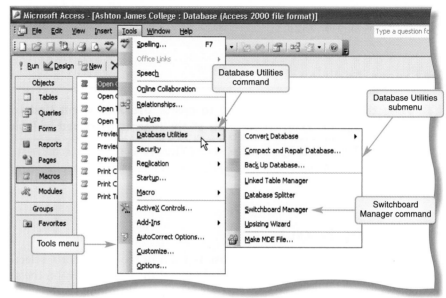

FIGURE 6-22

2

• **Click Switchboard Manager.**

The Switchboard Manager dialog box displays a message indicating that no switchboard currently exists for this database and asks whether to create one (Figure 6-23).

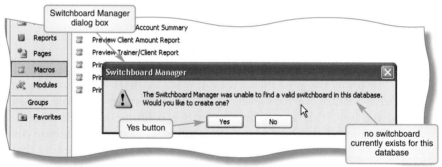

FIGURE 6-23

3

• **Click the Yes button to create a new switchboard.**

The Switchboard Manager dialog box appears and indicates there is only the Main Switchboard (Default) at this time (Figure 6-24).

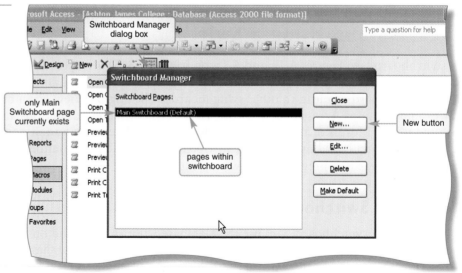

FIGURE 6-24

Creating Switchboard Pages

The next step in creating the switchboard system is to create the individual switchboards within the system. These individual switchboards are called the **switchboard pages**. The switchboard pages to be created are listed in the first column of Table 6-3. You do not have to create the Main Switchboard page because Access has created it automatically (Figure 6-24). To create each of the other pages, use the New button in the Switchboard Manager dialog box, and then enter the name of the page.

Table 6-3	Specifications for Switchboard Pages and Items		
SWITCHBOARD PAGE	**SWITCHBOARD ITEM**	**COMMAND**	**ARGUMENT**
Main Switchboard	View Form	Go to Switchboard	Switchboard: View Form
	View Table	Go to Switchboard	Switchboard: View Table
	View Report	Go to Switchboard	Switchboard: View Report
	Print Report	Go to Switchboard	Switchboard: Print Report
	Exit Application	Exit Application	None
View Form	Client Update Form	Run Macro	Macro: Open Client Update Form
	Trainer Master Form	Run Macro	Macro: Open Trainer Master Form
	Return to Main Switchboard	Go to Switchboard	Switchboard: Main Switchboard
View Table	Client Table	Run Macro	Macro: Open Client Table
	Trainer Table	Run Macro	Macro: Open Trainer Table
	Return to Main Switchboard	Go to Switchboard	Switchboard: Main Switchboard
View Report	View Client Amount Report	Run Macro	Macro: Preview Client Amount Report
	View Client Account Summary	Run Macro	Macro: Preview Client Account Summary
	View Trainer/Client Report	Run Macro	Macro: Preview Trainer/Client Report
	Return to Main Switchboard	Go to Switchboard	Switchboard: Main Switchboard
Print Report	Print Client Amount Report	Run Macro	Macro: Print Client Amount Report
	Print Client Account Summary	Run Macro	Macro: Print Client Account Summary
	Print Trainer/Client Report	Run Macro	Macro: Print Trainer/Client Report
	Return to Main Switchboard	Go to Switchboard	Switchboard: Main Switchboard

The steps on the next page show how to create the switchboard pages.

To Create Switchboard Pages

1

• **Click the New button in the Switchboard Manager dialog box.**

• **Type** View Form **as the name of the new switchboard page.**

The Create New dialog box appears (Figure 6-25). The name of the new page is entered in the Switchboard Page Name text box.

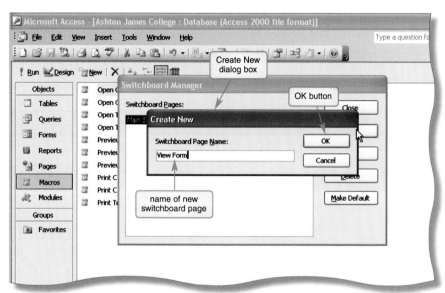

FIGURE 6-25

2

• **Click the OK button to create the View Form switchboard page.**

• **Use the same technique to create the View Table, View Report, and Print Report switchboard pages.**

The Switchboard Manager dialog box displays the newly created switchboard pages in alphabetical order (Figure 6-26).

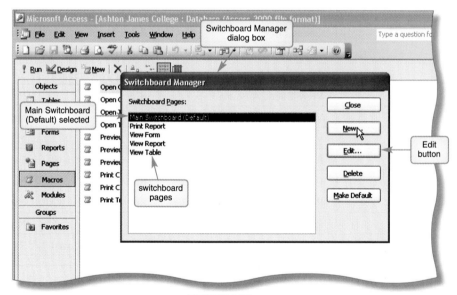

FIGURE 6-26

The switchboard pages now exist. Currently, there are no actions associated with the pages.

Modifying Switchboard Pages

You can modify a switchboard page by using the following procedure. Select the page in the Switchboard Manager dialog box, click the Edit button, and then add new items to the page, move existing items to a different position in the list of items, or delete items. For each item, you can indicate the command to be executed when the item is selected.

The following steps illustrate how to modify the Main Switchboard page.

To Modify the Main Switchboard Page

1

• **With the Main Switchboard (Default) page selected, click the Edit button.**

The Edit Switchboard Page dialog box appears (Figure 6-27).

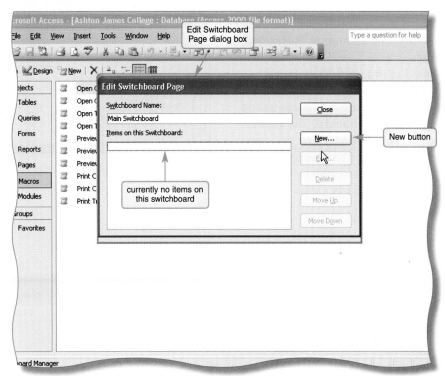

FIGURE 6-27

2

• **Click the New button, type** View Form **as the text, and then click the Switchboard box arrow.**

The Edit Switchboard Item dialog box appears (Figure 6-28). The text is entered, the command is Go to Switchboard, and the list of available switchboards appears.

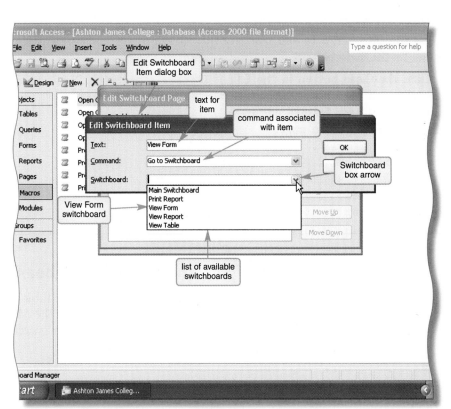

FIGURE 6-28

3

• **Click View Form and then click the OK button to add the item to the switchboard.**

4

• **Using the technique illustrated in Steps 2 and 3, add the View Table, View Report, and Print Report items to the Main Switchboard page. In each case, the command is Go to Switchboard. The names of the switchboards are the same as the name of the items. For example, the switchboard for the View Table item is called View Table.**

5

• **Click the New button, type** Exit Application **as the text, and click the Command box arrow.**

The Edit Switchboard Item dialog box appears (Figure 6-29). The text is entered and the list of available commands appears.

6

• **Click Exit Application and then click the OK button to add the item to the switchboard.**

• **Click the Close button in the Edit Switchboard Page dialog box to indicate you have finished editing the Main Switchboard page.**

The Main Switchboard page now is complete. The Edit Switchboard Page dialog box closes, and the Switchboard Manager dialog box appears.

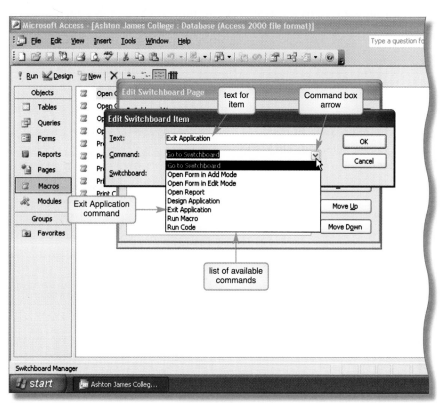

FIGURE 6-29

Modifying the Other Switchboard Pages

The other switchboard pages from Table 6-3 on page AC 331 are modified in exactly the same manner you modified the Main Switchboard page. The following steps illustrate how to modify the other switchboard pages.

To Modify the Other Switchboard Pages

1

• **Click the View Form switchboard page.**

The View Form page is selected (Figure 6-30).

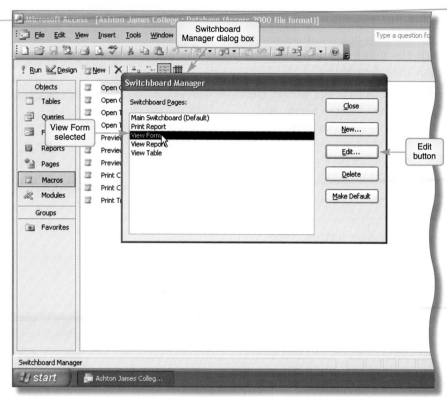

FIGURE 6-30

2

• **Click the Edit button, click the New button to add a new item, type** Client Update Form **as the text, click the Command box arrow, and then click Run Macro.**

• **Click the Macro box arrow.**

The Edit Switchboard Item dialog box appears (Figure 6-31). The text is entered and the command selected. The list of available macros appears.

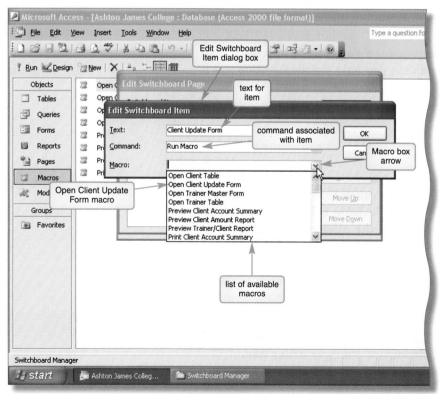

FIGURE 6-31

3

• **Click Open Client Update Form, and then click the OK button.**

• **Click the New button, type** Trainer Master Form **as the text, click the Command box arrow, and then click Run Macro.**

• **Click the Macro box arrow, click Open Trainer Master Form, and then click the OK button.**

The Client Update Form and Trainer Master Form items are added to the switchboard.

4

• **Click the New button, type** Return to Main Switchboard **as the text, and click the Switchboard box arrow.**

The text is entered and the list of available switchboards appears (Figure 6-32).

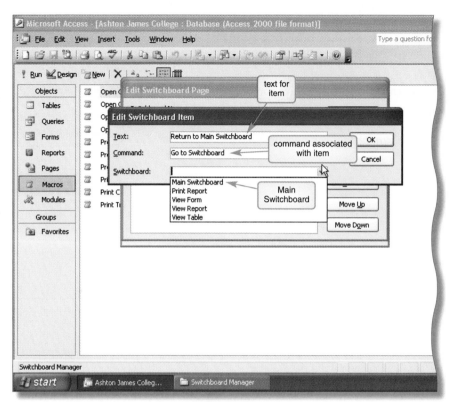

FIGURE 6-32

5

• **Click Main Switchboard in the list of available switchboards, and then click the OK button.**

• **Click the Close button in the Edit Switchboard Page dialog box to indicate you have finished editing the View Form switchboard.**

The View Form switchboard is complete.

6

• **Use the techniques illustrated in Steps 1 through 5 to add the items indicated in Table 6-3 on page AC 331 to the other switchboards.**

The Switchboard Manager dialog box appears (Figure 6-33).

7

• **Click the Close button in the Switchboard Manager dialog box.**

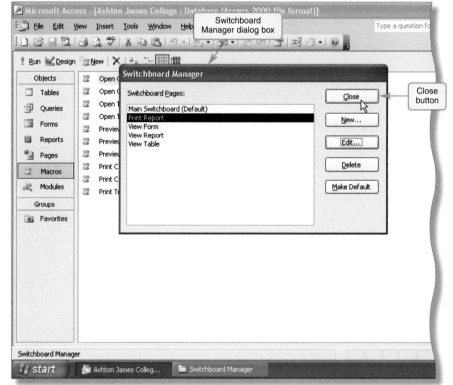

FIGURE 6-33

The switchboard is complete and ready for use. Access has created a form called Switchboard that you will run to use the switchboard. It also has created a table called Switchboard Items. *Do not modify this table.* Switchboard Manager uses this table to keep track of the various switchboard pages and items.

Opening a Switchboard

To use the switchboard, select the Forms object, select the switchboard, and then click Open on the shortcut menu. The Main Switchboard then will appear. To take any action, click the appropriate buttons. When you have finished, click the Exit Application button. The switchboard will be removed from the screen, and the database will be closed. The following steps illustrate opening a switchboard system for use.

To Open a Switchboard

1

• **Click the Forms object and then right-click Switchboard.**

The shortcut menu for the Switchboard appears (Figure 6-34).

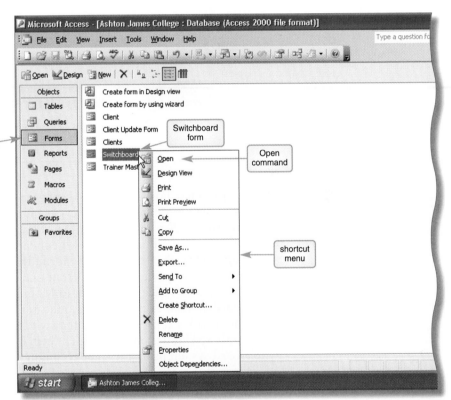

FIGURE 6-34

2

• **Click Open.**

The Main Switchboard appears (Figure 6-35).

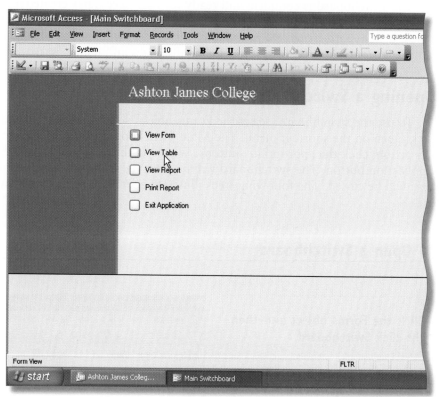

FIGURE 6-35

More About

Displaying Switchboards

It is possible to have the switchboard display automatically when the database is opened. To do so, point to Database Utilities on the Tools menu and then click Switchboard Manager. In the Switchboard Manager dialog box, select the switchboard you want to use as the default switchboard and then click Make Default.

Click the View Form button to display the View Form switchboard page. Click the View Table button to display the View Table switchboard page. Click the View Report button to display the View Report switchboard page. Click the Print Report button to display the Print Report switchboard page. On each of the other switchboard pages, click the button for the form, table, or report you wish to view, or the report you wish to print. To return from one of the other switchboard pages to the Main Switchboard, click the Return to Main Switchboard button. To leave the switchboard system, click the Exit Application button.

If you discover a problem with the switchboard, click Tools on the menu bar, click Database Utilities, and then click Switchboard Manager. You can modify the switchboard system using the same techniques you used to create it.

Closing the Switchboard and Database

To close the switchboard and the database, click the Exit Application button. The following step shows how to close the switchboard.

To Close the Switchboard and Database

1 **Click the Exit Application button.**

The switchboard is removed from the screen. The database closes.

Additional Tables

Before examining PivotTables and PivotCharts, you need to create the two additional tables. The first table, Course, is shown in Figures 6-36a and 6-36b. This table contains the specific courses that the trainers at Ashton James College offer to their customers. Each course has a number and a description. The table also includes the total hours for which the course usually is offered and the increments, that is, the standard time blocks in which the course usually is offered. The first row, for example, indicates that course 01 is called Integrating MS Office Programs. It typically is offered in 4 hour increments for a total of 16 hours.

Q: Can I delete a switchboard?

A: Yes. To delete a switchboard, point to Database Utilities on the Tools menu and then click Switchboard Manager. In the Switchboard Manager dialog box, select the switchboard you want to delete and then click Delete.

Structure of Course Table

FIELD NAME	DATA TYPE	FIELD SIZE	PRIMARY KEY?	DESCRIPTION
Course Number	Text	2	Yes	Course Number (Primary Key)
Course Description	Text	50		Description of Course
Hours	Number			Hours for Typical Offering
Increments	Number			Number of Hours in Typical Session

(a)

Course Table

COURSE NUMBER	COURSE DESCRIPTION	HOURS	INCREMENTS
01	Integrating MS Office Programs	16	4
02	Long Documents with Word	8	4
03	Creating Forms with Word	6	6
04	Newsletters and Graphics with Word	6	6
05	Creating Custom Access Reports	12	4
06	Introduction to Computers	16	4
07	Preventing Pain and Injury at Your Computer	4	2
08	Importing, Exporting, and Linking Data	6	3
09	Presentation Authoring Using PowerPoint	16	4
10	Access Database Projects (ADP)	12	4
11	Excel Programming	24	4

(b)

FIGURE 6-36

The second table, Course Offerings, is shown in Figures 6-37a and 6-37b on the next page. Figure 6-37a, the structure, indicates that the table contains a client number, a course number, the total number of hours for which the course is scheduled, and the number of hours already spent in the course.

Structure of Course Offerings Table

FIELD NAME	DATA TYPE	FIELD SIZE	PRIMARY KEY?	DESCRIPTION
Client Number	Text	4	Yes	Client Number (Portion of Primary Key)
Course Number	Text	2	Yes	Course Number (Portion of Primary Key)
Total Hours	Number	-		Estimate of Total Number of Hours
Hours Spent	Number	-		Hours Already Spent

(a)

Course Offerings Table

CLIENT NUMBER	COURSE NUMBER	TOTAL HOURS	HOURS SPENT
BS27	06	16	4
BS27	03	6	3
CP27	04	6	0
CP27	02	10	4
FI28	01	16	12
FI28	05	12	8
FL93	06	16	8
HN83	05	12	8
HN83	08	6	2
HN83	11	24	12

(b)

FIGURE 6-37

Figure 6-37b gives the data. For example, the first record shows that client number BS27 currently has scheduled course 06 (Introduction to Computers). The course is scheduled for 16 hours, of which they have already spent 4 hours in class.

If you examine the data in Figure 6-37b, you see that the Client Number field cannot be the primary key. The first two records, for example, both have a client number of BS27. The Course Number field also cannot be the primary key. The first and seventh records, for example, both have course number 06. Rather, the primary key is the combination of both of these fields.

Creating the New Tables

The steps to create the new tables are similar to those you have used in creating other tables. The only difference is the way you specify a primary key consisting of more than one field. First, you select both fields that make up the primary key by clicking the row selector for the first field, and then holding down the SHIFT key while clicking the row selector for the second field. Once the fields are selected, you can use the Primary Key button to indicate that the primary key consists of both fields.

The following steps show how to create the tables.

Q: What kind of relationship exists between the Client table and the Course table?

A: If the primary key of the Course Offerings table contains the primary keys for both the Client table and Course table, there is a many-to-many relationship between clients and courses. A client can take many courses and a course can be offered to many clients.

To Create the New Tables

• **Click Open on
the Database
toolbar, and
then click Local
Disk (C:) in the
Look in box.
Click the Data folder,
and then make sure the
database called Ashton
James College is selected.**

• **Click the Open button.**

• **If the Security Warning dialog box
appears, click the Open button.**

• **Click the Tables object.**

• **Click the New button on the
Database window toolbar, click
Design View, and then click the OK
button.**

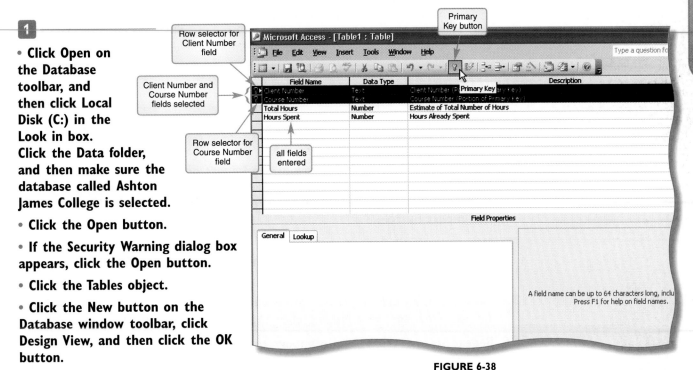

FIGURE 6-38

• **Maximize the window.**

• **Enter the information for the fields in the Course table as indicated in
Figure 6-36a on page AC 339.**

• **Close the window containing the table by clicking its Close Window button.**

• **Click the Yes button to save the changes.**

• **Type** Course **as the name of the table, and then click the OK button.**

• **Click the New button on the Database window toolbar, click Design View, and
then click the OK button.**

• **Enter the information for the fields in the Course Offerings table as indicated
in Figure 6-37a.**

• **Click the row selector for the Client Number field.**

• **Hold down the SHIFT key and then click the row selector for the Course Number
field so both fields are selected.**

• **Click the Primary Key button on the toolbar.**

The primary key consists of both the Client Number and Course Number fields (Figure 6-38).

2

• **Close the window by clicking its Close Window button.**

• **Click the Yes button to save the table.**

• **Type** Course Offerings **as the name of the table, and then click the OK
button to save the table.**

The tables now are created.

Importing the Data

Now that the tables have been created, you need to add data to them. You either could enter the data, or if the data is already in electronic form, you could import the data. The data for the Course and Course Offerings tables are on your Data Disk as text files. The following steps show how to import the data.

To Import the Data

1 With the Ashton James College database open, click File on the menu bar, point to Get External Data, and then click Import.

2 Click the Files of type box arrow in the Import dialog box and then click Text Files. Select the location of the files to be imported (for example, the folder called Data on disk C). Make sure the Course text file is selected. Click the Import button.

3 Make sure the Delimited option button is selected and click the Next button. Click First Row Contains Field Names check box and then click the Next button again.

4 Click the In an Existing Table option button and select the Course table from the list. Click the Next button, click the Finish button, and then click OK.

5 Repeat Steps 1 through 4 to import the Course Offerings text file.

The data for the Course and Course Offerings tables are imported.

More About

Editing Relationships

You can modify existing relationships between tables to change the relationships options such as cascading the update and cascading the delete. To do so, close any open tables in the database and then click the Relationships button on the toolbar. When the Relationships window appears, double-click the relationship line for the relationship you want to edit and then set relationship options.

Relating Several Tables

Now that the tables have been created they need to be related to the existing tables. The Client and Course Offerings tables are related through the Client Number fields in both. The Course and Course Offerings tables are related through the Course Number fields in both. The following steps illustrate the process of relating the tables.

To Relate Several Tables

1 Close any open datasheet on the screen by clicking its Close button. Click the Relationships button on the toolbar. Right-click in the Relationships window and then click Show Table on the shortcut menu. Click the Course Offerings table, click the Add button, click the Course table, click the Add button again, and then click the Close button.

2 Drag the Client Number field from the Client table to the Course Offerings table. Click the Enforce Referential Integrity check box in the Edit Relationships dialog box and then click the Create button.

3 Drag the Course Number field from the Course table to the Course Offerings table. Click Enforce Referential Integrity check box and then click the Create button.

4 Drag the Course and Course Offerings tables to the positions shown in Figure 6-39. Click the Close Window button and then click the Yes button to save the changes.

The relationships are created.

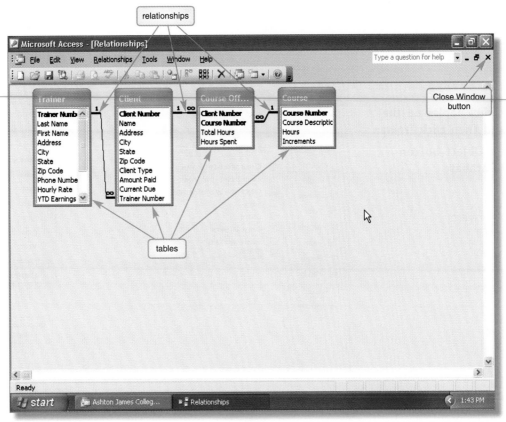

FIGURE 6-39

PivotTables and PivotCharts

There are two alternatives to viewing data in Datasheet view or Form view.
PivotTable view presents data as a **PivotTable**, that is, an interactive table that
summarizes or analyzes data. In a PivotTable, you can show different levels of
detail easily as well as change the organization or layout of the table by dragging
items. You also can filter data by checking or unchecking values in drop-down lists.
PivotChart view presents data as a **PivotChart**, that is, a graphical representation
of the data. In a PivotChart, just as in a PivotTable, you can show different levels of
detail or change the layout by dragging items. You also can filter data by checking or
unchecking values in drop-down lists. You can change the type of chart that appears
as well as customize the chart by adding axis titles, a chart title, and a legend. In this
section, you will create a PivotTable and a PivotChart. Both the PivotTable and the
PivotChart are based on a query.

Creating a Query

Because the PivotTable and PivotChart you will create will be based on a query,
you first must create the query. The steps on the next page show how to create the
necessary query.

To Create the Query

1

- **If necessary, click Tables on the Objects bar, and then click Trainer.**
- **Click the New Object button arrow on the Database toolbar.**

The list of available objects appears (Figure 6-40).

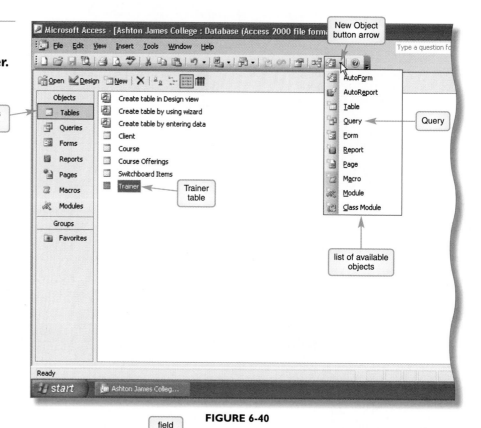

FIGURE 6-40

2

- **Click Query.**
- **Be sure Design View is selected, and then click the OK button.**
- **Be sure the Query1 : Select Query window is maximized.**
- **Resize the upper and lower panes and the Trainer field list so all the fields in the Trainer table appear.**
- **Right-click any open area in the upper pane, click Show Table on the shortcut menu, click the Client table, click the Add button, click the Course Offerings table, click the Add button, and then click the Close button in the Show Table dialog box.**
- **Resize the Client and Course Offering field lists so all the fields appear.**

The Trainer, Client, and Course Offering tables are included (Figure 6-41).

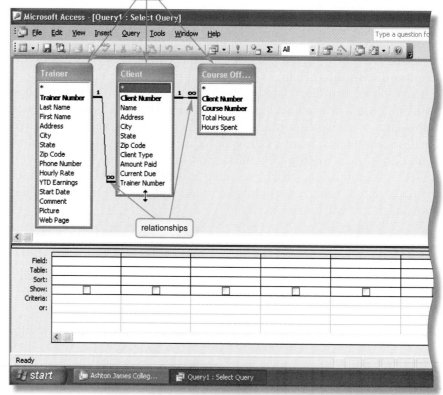

FIGURE 6-41

3

• **Double-click the Trainer Number field from the Trainer table and the Client Number field from the Client table.**

• **Double-click the Course Number and Hours Spent fields from the Course Offerings table.**

• **Right-click the Field row in the first open column.**

The fields are selected. The shortcut menu appears (Figure 6-42).

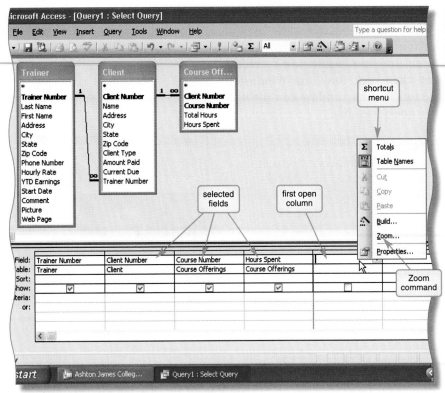

FIGURE 6-42

4

• **Click Zoom on the shortcut menu, type** Hours Remaining:[Total Hours]-[Hours Spent] **in the Zoom dialog box.**

The expression for Hours Remaining is entered (Figure 6-43).

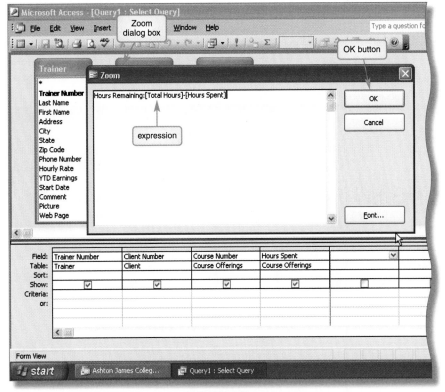

FIGURE 6-43

5

• **Click the OK button, click the Run button on the Query Design toolbar to ensure your results are correct, and then click the Close Window button for the window containing the query results.**

The query results appear (Figure 6-44). (If your results do not look like the ones shown in the figure, return to the query design and make any necessary changes, before attempting to close and save the query.)

6

• **Click the Yes button, type** Trainers and Course Offerings **as the name of the query, and then click the OK button.**

The query is saved and available for use.

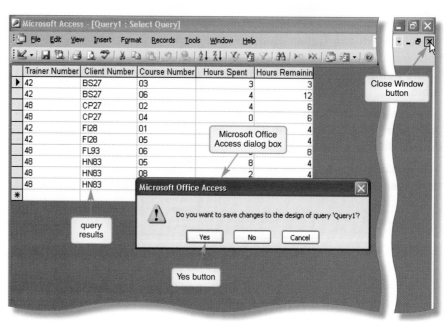

FIGURE 6-44

PivotTables

Figure 6-45 shows a sample PivotTable. The rows in the table represent the courses. The columns represent the trainer numbers. Each column is subdivided into the total of the hours spent and the total of the hours remaining for course offerings for those clients assigned to the trainer. The last column shows the grand total for the items in each row. The last row shows the grand total for items in each column.

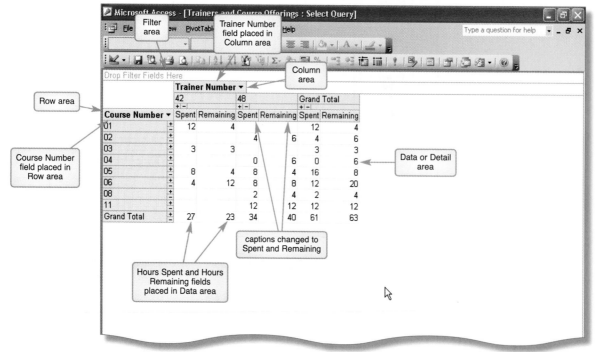

FIGURE 6-45

To create the PivotTable, you place fields in predefined areas of the table called **drop areas**. In the PivotTable in Figure 6-45, the Course Number field has been placed in the Row area, for example. The drop areas are listed and described in Table 6-4.

Table 6-4	PivotTable Drop Areas
AREA	**PURPOSE**
Row	Data from fields in this area will appear as rows in the table.
Column	Data from fields in this area will appear as columns in the table.
Filter	Data from fields in this area will not appear in the table but can be used to restrict the data that appears.
Detail	Data from fields in this area will appear in the detail portion (the body) of the table.
Data	Summary data (for example, a sum) from fields in this area will appear in the detail portion (the body) of the table. Individual values will not appear.

The following steps show how to create a PivotTable using the PivotTable view of the Trainers and Course Offerings query and how to place fields in appropriate drop areas.

To Create a PivotTable

1

• **Click Queries on the Objects bar, right-click the Trainers and Course Offerings query, and then click Open on the shortcut menu. If necessary, maximize the window.**

• **Click the View button arrow.**

The query appears in Datasheet view (Figure 6-46). The list of available views appears.

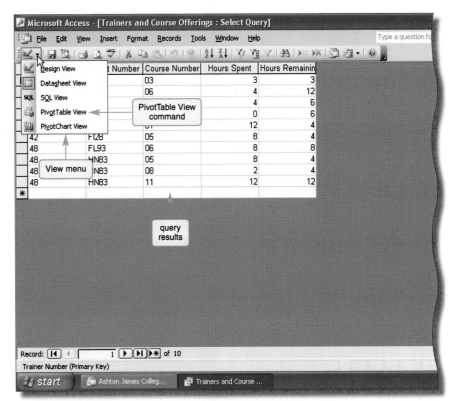

FIGURE 6-46

2

- **Click PivotTable View.**

- **If the PivotTable Field List does not appear, click the Field List button on the PivotTable toolbar to display the field list.**

- **Click Course Number in the field list, and then ensure Row Area appears next to the Add to button.**

The PivotTable appears (Figure 6-47). Course Number is selected in the field list and Row Area is selected.

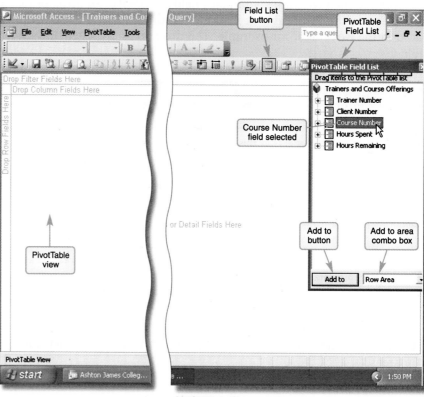

FIGURE 6-47

3

- **Click the Add to button to add the Course Number field to the Row area.**

- **Click the Trainer Number field and then click the arrow to display the list of available areas.**

The list of available areas appears (Figure 6-48). The Trainer Number field is selected.

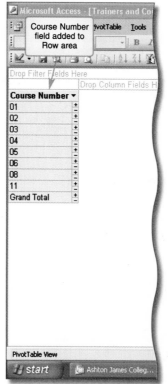
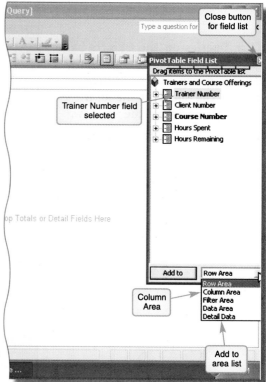

FIGURE 6-48

4

• **Click Column Area and then click the Add to button to add the Trainer Number field to the Column area.**

• **Click Hours Spent, click the arrow to display the list of available areas, click Data Area, and then click the Add to button to add the Hours Spent field to the Data area.**

• **Use the same technique to add the Hours Remaining field to the Data area. Close the PivotTable Field List by clicking its Close button.**

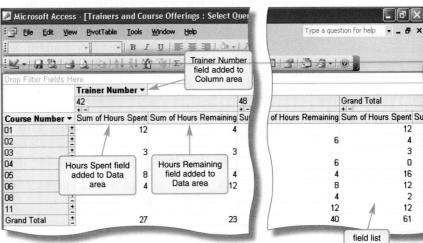

FIGURE 6-49

The fields have been added to appropriate areas of the PivotTable (Figure 6-49).

Changing Properties in a PivotTable

You can use the property sheet for the objects in a PivotTable to change characteristics of the objects. The following steps show how to use the appropriate property sheet to change the caption for Sum of Hours Spent to Spent and for Sum of Hours Remaining to Remaining in order to reduce the size of the columns in the PivotTable.

To Change Properties in a PivotTable

1

• **Right-click the Sum of Hours Spent box, and then click Properties on the shortcut menu.**

• **Click the Captions tab in the property sheet.**

The property sheet and the Caption property appear (Figure 6-50).

2

• **Delete the current entry in the Caption property box, type** Spent **as the new value for the Caption property, and then close the property sheet.**

• **Use the same technique to change the caption for the Sum of Hours Remaining box to Remaining.**

The captions are changed.

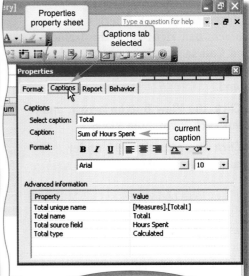

FIGURE 6-50

Saving the PivotTable Changes

To save the changes to the PivotTable view of the query, you save the query. You can do so, by closing the window containing the PivotTable and then clicking the Yes button when asked if you want to save your changes. The following steps close the query and then save the changes.

To Close the Query and Save the PivotTable Changes

1 Click the Close Window button for the window containing the PivotTable.

2 Click the Yes button in the Microsoft Office Access dialog box.

The changes to the layout of the query are saved. In particular, the changes to the PivotTable view of the query are saved.

Using a PivotTable

To use a PivotTable, you must open it. If the PivotTable is associated with a query, this would involve opening the query and then switching to PivotTable view. You then can click appropriate plus (+) or minus (-) signs to hide or show data. You also can click appropriate arrows and then check or uncheck the various items that appear to restrict the data that appears. You can drag items from one location to another to change the layout of the PivotTable. The following steps illustrate how to use the PivotTable view of the Trainers and Course Offerings query.

To Use a PivotTable

1

• **If necessary, click Queries on the Objects bar, right-click the Trainers and Course Offerings query, and then click Open on the shortcut menu.**

• **Click the View button arrow, and then click PivotTable View.**

• **Click the plus sign (+) under trainer number 42.**

The PivotTable appears (Figure 6-51). Data for trainer number 42 is hidden, that is, it does not appear. The column heading for trainer number 42 is changed to No Details. The captions for the other columns are changed to Spent and Remaining. By clicking the appropriate plus sign, you also can hide the data for course numbers or the Grand Total data.

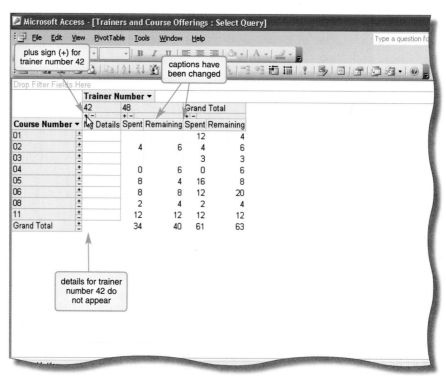

FIGURE 6-51

2

• **Click the minus sign (-) under trainer number 42 to again display data for trainer number 42.**

• **Click the Trainer Number arrow.**

The list of available trainer numbers appears (Figure 6-52). Removing a check mark on a trainer number causes that trainer to be hidden, that is, the trainer number will not appear.

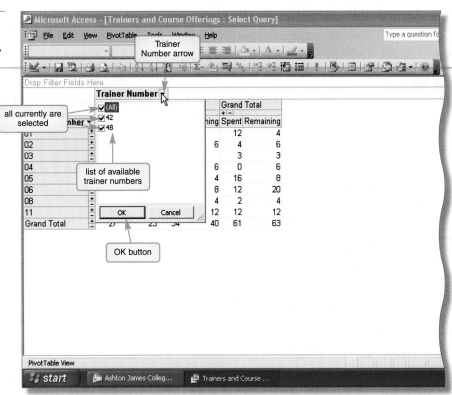

FIGURE 6-52

3

• **Click the Check box for trainer number 42 to remove the check mark, and then click the OK button.**

Trainer number 42 does not appear (Figure 6-53).

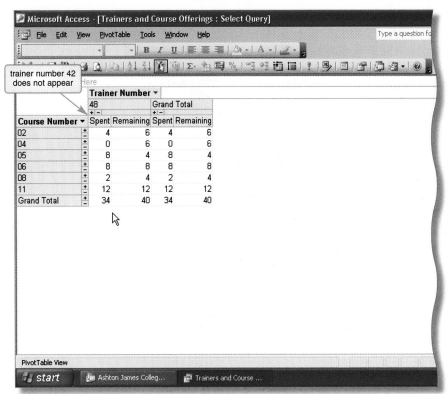

FIGURE 6-53

4

• **Click the Trainer Number arrow, click the All check box to display all trainer numbers, and then click the OK button.**

All trainer numbers appear (Figure 6-54).

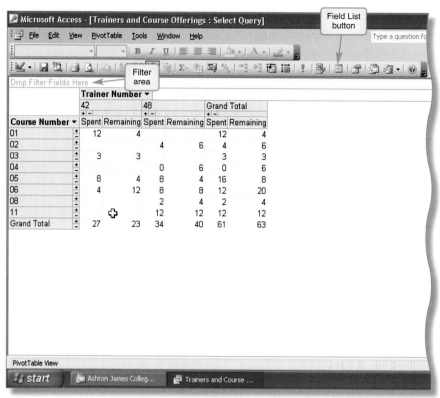

FIGURE 6-54

5

• **Click the Field List button to display the PivotTable Field List. Click Client Number, click the arrow to display a list of available areas, click Filter Area, and then click the Add to button to add the Client Number field to the Filter area.**

• **Click the Client Number arrow.**

The Client Number field is added to the Filter area (Figure 6-55). The list of client numbers used in the query appears.

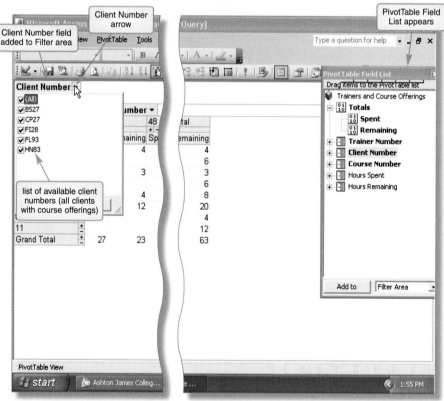

FIGURE 6-55

6

• **Click the check boxes in front of clients BS27 and CP27 to remove the check marks, and then click the OK button.**

The data appearing in the PivotTable is changed (Figure 6-56). The amounts for clients BS27 or CP27 do not appear.

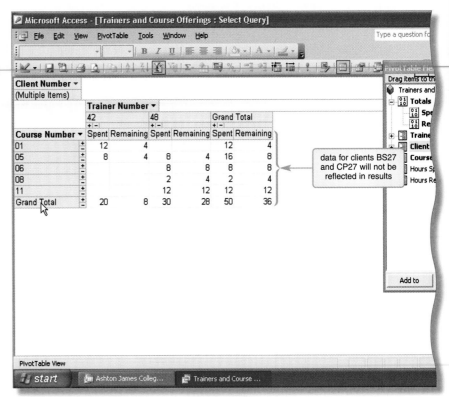

data for clients BS27 and CP27 will not be reflected in results

FIGURE 6-56

7

• **Click the Client Number arrow, click the All check box, and then click the OK button to display data for all clients.**

• **Drag the Trainer Number field from the Column area to the Row area, and then drag Course Number field from the Row area to the Column area.**

The rows and columns in the PivotTable are reversed (Figure 6-57).

8

• **Click the Close Window button for the window containing the PivotTable.**

• **Click the No button when asked if you want to save your changes.**

The PivotTable is closed. The changes are not saved. The next time you open the PivotTable, the changes you just made will not be reflected.

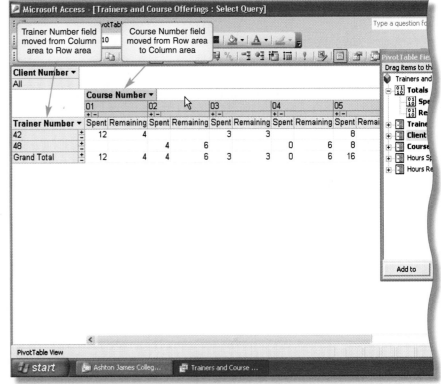

Trainer Number field moved from Column area to Row area

Course Number field moved from Row area to Column area

FIGURE 6-57

PivotCharts

You can create a PivotChart from scratch by placing fields in appropriate drop areas just as you did when you created a PivotTable. The drop areas are shown in Figure 6-58. Their purpose is described in Table 6-5.

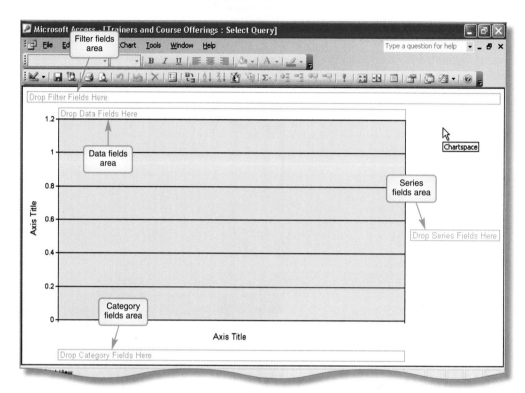

FIGURE 6-58

Table 6-5 PivotChart Drop Areas	
AREA	**PURPOSE**
Series	Data from fields in this area will appear as data series, which are represented by colored data markers such as bars. Related markers constitute a series and are assigned a specific color. The names and colors appear in the chart legend.
Category	Data from fields in this area will appear as categories, that is, related groups of data. Category labels appear across the x-axis (horizontal) of the chart provided the graph type selected has such an axis.
Filter	Data from fields in this area will not appear in the chart but can be used to restrict the data that appears.
Data	Data from fields in this area will be summarized within the chart.

If you are using the PivotChart view of a table or query and already have modified the PivotTable view, much of this work already is done. The same information is used wherever possible. You can, of course, modify any aspect of this information. You can remove fields from drop areas by clicking the field name and then pressing the DELETE key. You can add fields to drop areas just as you did with the PivotTable. You also can make other changes, including adding a legend, changing the chart type, changing captions, and adding titles.

The following steps show how to create a PivotChart using PivotChart view of the Trainers and Course Offerings query and then add a legend.

To Create a PivotChart and Add a Legend

1

• **If necessary, click Queries on the Objects bar, right-click the Trainers and Course Offerings query, and then click Open on the shortcut menu.**

• **Click the View button arrow, and then click PivotChart View.**

• **If the Chart Field List appears, close the field list by clicking its Close button.**

The PivotChart appears (Figure 6-59). It represents the same data specified in the PivotTable.

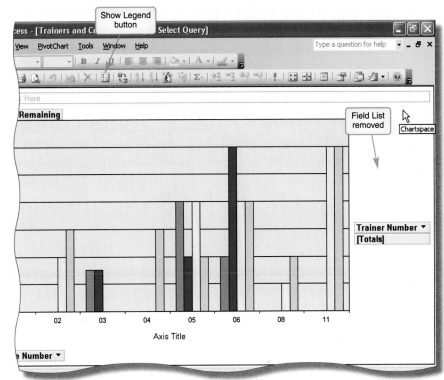

FIGURE 6-59

2

• **Click the Show Legend button.**

A legend appears (Figure 6-60).

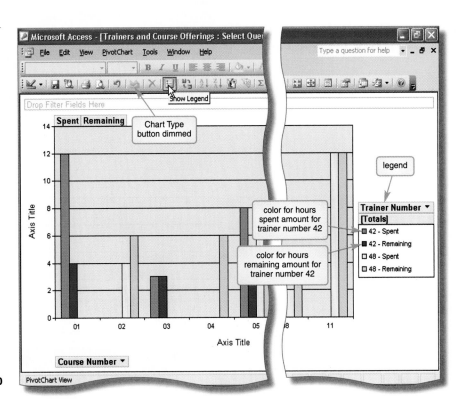

FIGURE 6-60

Changing the Chart Type

Several types of charts are available. To change the chart type, use the Chart Type button, and then select the desired chart type. The following steps illustrate how to change the chart type to 3D Stacked Column.

To Change the Chart Type

1

• **If the Chart Type button is dimmed, click the Chartspace (that is, the white space in the chart).**

The Chart Type button is available (Figure 6-61).

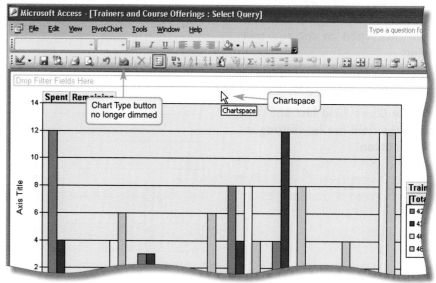

FIGURE 6-61

2

• **Click the Chart Type button on the PivotChart toolbar, and then, if necessary, click the Type tab.**

The list of graph types appears (Figure 6-62). (Your graph types may be arranged differently). The Type tab is selected.

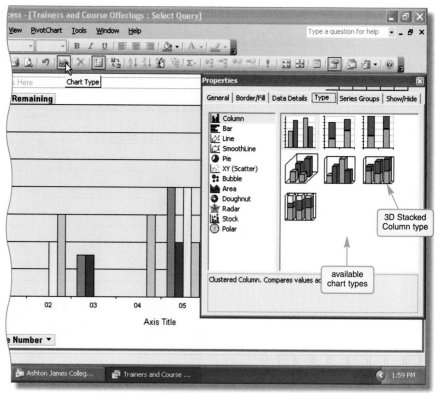

FIGURE 6-62

3

• **Click the 3D Stacked Column type, and then close the Properties window.**

The chart type is changed to 3D Stacked Column (Figure 6-63).

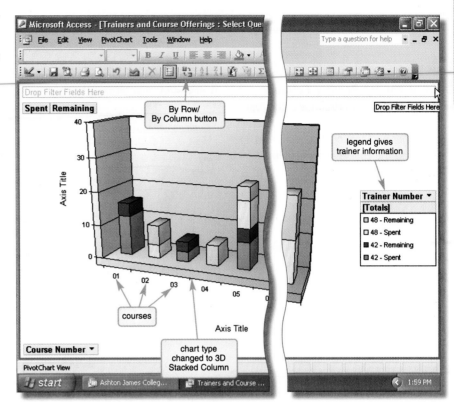

FIGURE 6-63

Changing PivotChart Organization

The chart in Figure 6-63 has the Course numbers along the horizontal axis and trainer numbers in the legend. The heights of the bars represent the total number of hours for each course. Within a bar, the colors represent the trainer and whether the amount represents hours remaining or hours spent (see legend). To change the orientation, you can click the By Row/By Column button. The step on the next page shows how to change the orientation so the trainer numbers appear along the horizontal axis and the courses appear in the legend.

To Change PivotChart Organization

1

• **Click the By Row/By Column button on the PivotChart toolbar.**

The trainer numbers now appear along the x-axis and the courses appear in the legend (Figure 6-64).

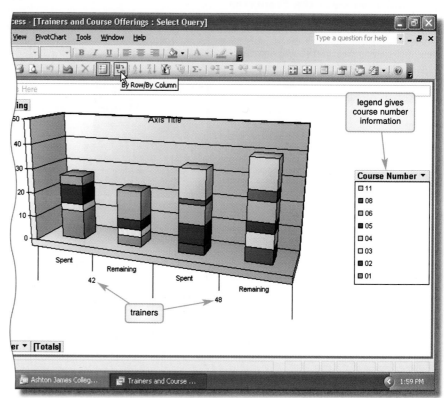

FIGURE 6-64

Assigning Axis Titles

You can assign titles to an axis by right-clicking the Axis Title box for the axis you want to change, selecting Properties on the shortcut menu, and then changing the Caption property to the title you want to assign. The following steps illustrate how to change the two axis titles to Hours and Trainer.

To Assign Axis Titles

1

- **Right-click the axis title to the left of the chart, and then click Properties on the shortcut menu.**
- **Click the Format tab in the Properties window, and then click the Caption box.**
- **Use the BACKSPACE or DELETE key to delete the old caption.**
- **Type** Hours **as the new caption.**

The Properties property sheet appears (Figure 6-65). Your font properties may be different. The caption is changed to Hours.

2

- **Close the property sheet to complete the change of the axis title.**
- **Use the same technique to change the other axis title to Trainer.**

The axis titles are changed.

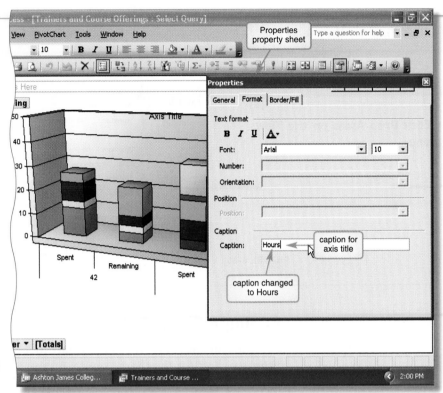

FIGURE 6-65

Removing Drop Areas

You can remove the drop areas from the PivotChart to give the chart a cleaner look. To do so, use the Drop Areas command on the View menu. If you later need to use the drop areas to perform some task, you can return them to the screen by using the Drop Areas command on the View menu a second time. The steps on the next page show how to remove the drop areas.

To Remove Drop Areas

1

• **Click View on the menu bar.**

The View menu appears (Figure 6-66).

2

• **Click Drop Areas on the View menu.**

The drop areas no longer appear.

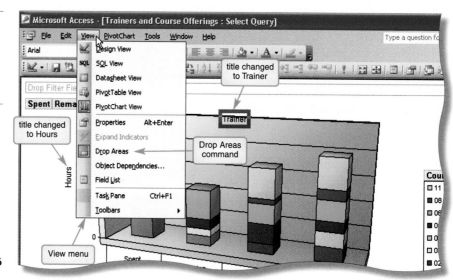

FIGURE 6-66

Adding a Chart Title

You can add a title to a PivotChart by clicking the Add Title button in the property sheet for the chart. You then can change the Caption property for the newly added title to assign the title of your choice. The following steps illustrate how to add a title to the PivotChart and then change the title's Caption property to Hours by Trainer and Course.

To Add a Chart Title

1

• **Right-click anywhere in the Chartspace (the white space) of the PivotChart, click Properties on the shortcut menu, and then, if necessary, click the General tab.**

• **Click the Add Title button.**

The property sheet appears (Figure 6-67). The General tab is selected. The chart now includes a title.

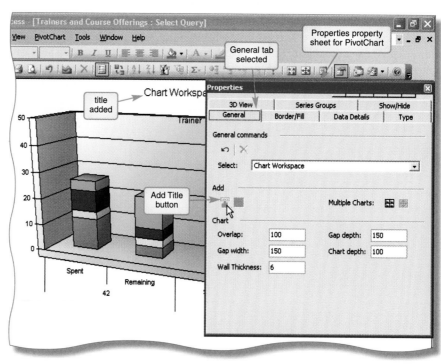

FIGURE 6-67

2

- **Close the Properties property sheet, right-click the newly added title, and then click Properties on the shortcut menu.**

- **When the Properties property sheet appears, click the Format tab.**

- **Click the Caption box, and then use the BACK-SPACE or DELETE key to erase the old caption.**

- **Type** Hours by Trainer and Course **as the new caption.**

The property sheet appears (Figure 6-68). The caption is changed.

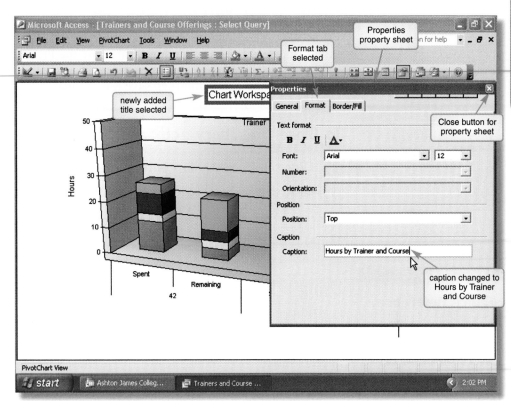

FIGURE 6-68

3

- **Close the property sheet by clicking its Close button.**

The chart has the desired title (Figure 6-69).

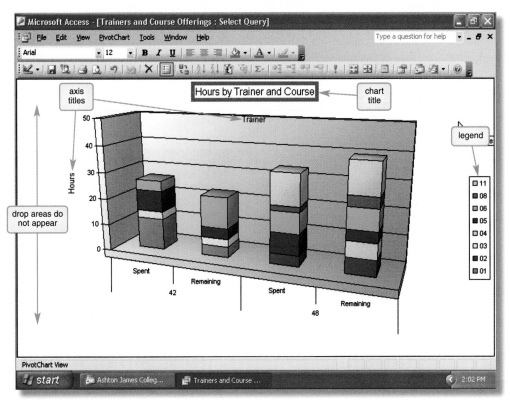

FIGURE 6-69

Saving the PivotChart Changes

To save the changes to the PivotChart view of the query, you save the query. You can do so, by closing the window containing the PivotChart and then clicking the Yes button when asked if you want to save your changes. The following steps show how to close the query and then save the changes.

To Close the Query and Save the PivotChart Changes

1 **Click the Close Window button for the window containing the PivotChart.**

2 **Click the Yes button in the Microsoft Office Access dialog box.**

The changes to the layout of the query are saved. In particular, the changes to the PivotChart view of the query are saved.

Using a PivotChart

To use a PivotChart, you first must open it. If the PivotChart is associated with a query, this would involve opening the query and then switching to PivotChart view. You then can check or uncheck the various items that appear to restrict the data that appears. In order to do so, the drop areas must appear. If they do not, use the Drop Areas command on the View menu to display them. You then can click the arrows. You also can drag fields to the drop areas.

You can make the same types of changes you made when you first created the PivotChart. You can change the chart type. You can change the orientation by clicking the By Row/By Column button. You can add or remove a legend. You can change titles. The following steps show how to use the PivotChart view of the Trainers and Course Offerings query.

To Use a PivotChart

1

• **Click Queries on the Objects bar, right-click the Trainers and Course Offerings query, and then click Open on the shortcut menu.**

• **Click the View button arrow, and then click PivotChart View. Click View on the menu bar.**

The PivotChart and View menu appear (Figure 6-70). The drop areas currently do not appear.

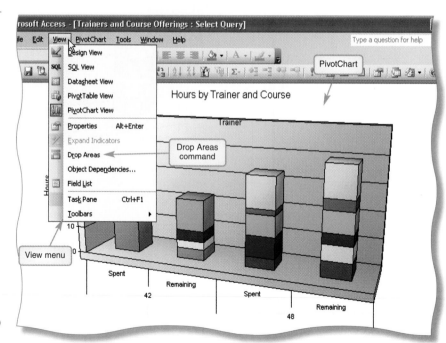

FIGURE 6-70

2

• **Click Drop Areas on the View menu, and then click the Trainer Number arrow.**

The list of available trainers appears (Figure 6-71).

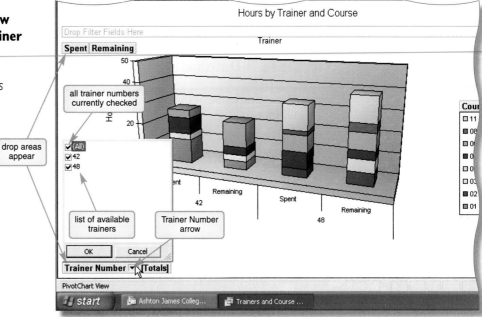

FIGURE 6-71

3

• **Click the check box for trainer number 42 to remove the check mark, and then click the OK button.**

Trainer number 42 no longer appears on the PivotChart (Figure 6-72).

4

• **Click the Close Window button for the window containing the PivotChart.**

• **Click the No button when asked if you want to save your changes.**

The PivotChart is closed. The changes are not saved. The next time you open the PivotChart, the changes you just made will not be reflected.

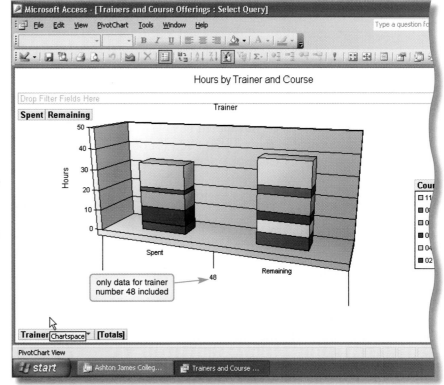

FIGURE 6-72

Closing the Database and Quitting Access

The following steps close the database and quit Access.

To Close a Database and Quit Access

1 **Click the Close Window button for the Ashton James College : Database window.**

2 **Click the Close button for the Microsoft Office Access window.**

Access and the database close.

Project Summary

In Project 6, you learned how to create and use macros. Using Switchboard Manager, you created the switchboard, the switchboard pages, and the switchboard items. You also used the Switchboard Manager to assign actions to the buttons on the switchboard pages. You saw how to use the completed switchboard. You created a PivotTable and a PivotChart associated with a query. In the process, you saw how to customize various aspects of both the PivotTable and PivotChart as well as how to use them.

 If you have a SAM user profile, you may have access to hands-on instruction, practice, and assessment of the skills covered in this project. Log in to your SAM account and go to your assignments page to see what your instructor has assigned.

What You Should Know

Having completed this project, you should be able to perform the tasks below. The tasks are listed in the same order they were presented in this project. For a list of the buttons, menus, toolbars, and commands introduced in this project, see the Quick Reference Summary at the back of this book and refer to the Page Number column.

1. Open a Database   (AC 316)
2. Create a Macro   (AC 317)
3. Add Actions to a Macro   (AC 319)
4. Run a Macro   (AC 322)
5. Modify a Macro   (AC 322)
6. Copy and Paste a Macro   (AC 326)
7. Modify the Copied Macro   (AC 327)
8. Create Additional Macros   (AC 329)
9. Create a Switchboard   (AC 330)
10. Create Switchboard Pages   (AC 332)
11. Modify the Main Switchboard Page   (AC 333)
12. Modify the Other Switchboard Pages   (AC 335)
13. Open a Switchboard   (AC 337)
14. Close the Switchboard and Database   (AC 338)
15. Create the New Tables   (AC 341)
16. Import the Data   (AC 342)
17. Relate Several Tables   (AC 342)
18. Create the Query   (AC 344)
19. Create a PivotTable   (AC 347)
20. Change Properties in a PivotTable   (AC 349)
21. Close the Query and Save the PivotTable Changes   (AC 350)
22. Use a PivotTable   (AC 350)
23. Create a PivotChart and Add a Legend   (AC 355)
24. Change the Chart Type   (AC 356)
25. Change PivotChart Organization   (AC 358)
26. Assign Axis Titles   (AC 359)
27. Remove Drop Areas   (AC 360)
28. Add a Chart Title   (AC 360)
29. Close the Query and Save the PivotChart Changes   (AC 362)
30. Use a PivotChart   (AC 362)
31. Close a Database and Quit Access   (AC 364)

Learn It Online

Instructions: To complete the Learn It Online exercises, start your browser, click the Address bar, and then enter the Web address scsite.com/ac2003/learn. When the Access 2003 Learn It Online page is displayed, follow the instructions in the exercises below. Each exercise has instructions for printing your results, either for your own records or for submission to your instructor.

1 Project Reinforcement TF, MC, and SA

Below Access Project 6, click the Project Reinforcement link. Print the quiz by clicking Print on the File menu for each page. Answer each question.

2 Flash Cards

Below Access Project 6, click the Flash Cards link and read the instructions. Type 20 (or a number specified by your instructor) in the Number of playing cards text box, type your name in the Enter your Name text box, and then click the Flip Card button. When the flash card is displayed, read the question and then click the ANSWER box arrow to select an answer. Flip through Flash Cards. If your score is 15 (75%) correct or greater, click Print on the File menu to print your results. If your score is less than 15 (75%) correct, then redo this exercise by clicking the Replay button.

3 Practice Test

Below Access Project 6, click the Practice Test link. Answer each question, enter your first and last name at the bottom of the page, and then click the Grade Test button. When the graded practice test is displayed on your screen, click Print on the File menu to print a hard copy. Continue to take practice tests until you score 80% or better.

4 Who Wants To Be a Computer Genius?

Below Access Project 6, click the Computer Genius link. Read the instructions, enter your first and last name at the bottom of the page, and then click the PLAY button. When your score is displayed, click the PRINT RESULTS link to print a hard copy.

5 Wheel of Terms

Below Access Project 6, click the Wheel of Terms link. Read the instructions, and then enter your first and last name and your school name. Click the PLAY button. When your score is displayed, right-click the score and then click Print on the shortcut menu to print a hard copy.

6 Crossword Puzzle Challenge

Below Access Project 6, click the Crossword Puzzle Challenge link. Read the instructions, and then enter your first and last name. Click the SUBMIT button. Work the crossword puzzle. When you are finished, click the Submit button. When the crossword puzzle is redisplayed, click the Print Puzzle button to print a hard copy.

7 Tips and Tricks

Below Access Project 6, click the Tips and Tricks link. Click a topic that pertains to Project 6. Right-click the information and then click Print on the shortcut menu. Construct a brief example of what the information relates to in Access to confirm you understand how to use the tip or trick.

8 Newsgroups

Below Access Project 6, click the Newsgroups link. Click a topic that pertains to Project 6. Print three comments.

9 Expanding Your Horizons

Below Access Project 6, click the Expanding Your Horizons link. Click a topic that pertains to Project 6. Print the information. Construct a brief example of what the information relates to in Access to confirm you understand the contents of the article.

10 Search Sleuth

Below Access Project 6, click the Search Sleuth link. To search for a term that pertains to this project, select a term below the Project 6 title and then use the Google search engine at google.com (or any major search engine) to display and print two Web pages that present information on the term.

11 Access Online Training

Below Access Project 6, click the Access Online Training link. When your browser displays the Microsoft Office Online Web page, click the Access link. Click one of the Access courses that covers one or more of the objectives listed at the beginning of the project on page AC 314. Print the first page of the course before stepping through it.

12 Office Marketplace

Below Access Project 6, click the Office Marketplace link. When your browser displays the Microsoft Office Online Web page, click the Office Marketplace link. Click a topic that relates to Access. Print the first page.

1 Creating a Macro and a PivotTable for Begon Pest Control

Instructions: For this assignment, you will use three files: Begon Pest Control.mdb, Category.txt, and Work Orders.txt. If you are using the Microsoft Office Access 2003 Complete or the Microsoft Office Access 2003 Comprehensive text, open the Begon Pest Control database that you used in Project 5 or see your instructor for information about accessing the files required for this book. The Category.txt and Work Orders.txt files are text files that are on the Data Disk.

You will create two new tables for the Begon Pest Control database. The Work Orders table contains information on the type of work the customer needs done. The structure for the Work Orders table is shown in Figure 6-73. Some customers require more than one type of service. For each record to be unique, the primary key for the Work Orders table must be the combination of the Customer Number and the Category Number. A one-to-many relationship exists between the Customer table and the Work Orders table. The Category table contains information on the service category. The structure for the Category table is shown in Figure 6-74. A one-to-many relationship exists between the Category table and the Work Orders table. Perform the following tasks:

1. Start Access and open the Begon Pest Control database.
2. Create a macro to open the Technician/Customer Report you created in Project 4. Save the macro as Print Technician/Customer Report. Run the macro to print the report.
3. Create the Work Orders table using the structure shown in Figure 6-73. The primary key is the combination of Customer Number and Category Number. Use Work Orders as the name of the table.

Structure of Work Orders Table				
FIELD NAME	**DATA TYPE**	**FIELD SIZE**	**PRIMARY KEY?**	**DESCRIPTION**
Customer Number	Text	4	Yes	Customer Number (Portion of Primary Key)
Category Number	Text	2	Yes	Category Number (Portion of Primary Key)
Total Hours (est)	Number			Estimate of Total Hours Required

FIGURE 6-73

4. Create the Category table using the structure shown in Figure 6-74. Use Category as the name of the table.

Structure of Category Table				
FIELD NAME	**DATA TYPE**	**FIELD SIZE**	**PRIMARY KEY?**	**DESCRIPTION**
Category Number	Text	2	Yes	Category Number (Primary Key)
Category Description	Text	50		Description of Category

FIGURE 6-74

Apply Your Knowledge

5. Import the Work Orders text file into the Work Orders table and then import the Category text file into the Category table. For each table, be sure to check the First Row Contains Column Headings box. The data is in delimited format with each field separated by tabs.

6. Open the Relationships window and establish a one-to-many relationship between the Category table and the Work Orders table and between the Customer table and the Work Orders table. Print the Relationships window by making sure the Relationships window is open, clicking File on the menu bar, and then clicking Print Relationships. When Access displays the Print Preview window, click the Print button on the Print Preview toolbar. Do not save the report.

7. Create a query for the Work Orders table. Include all fields in the query and save the query as Customers and Categories.

8. Open the Customers and Categories query and switch to PivotTable view. Create the PivotTable shown in Figure 6-75. Save the changes to the layout of the query. Print the PivotTable.

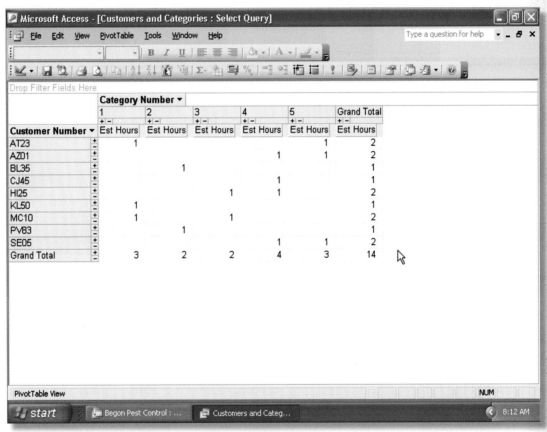

FIGURE 6-75

9. Hide the details for category number 4 and print the PivotTable again. Do not save the changes to the layout of the query.

1 Creating Macros, a Switchboard, a PivotTable, and a PivotChart for the Birds2U Database

Problem: The management of Birds2U would like an easy way to access the various tables, forms, and reports, by simply clicking a button or two. This would make the database much easier to maintain and update. Management also needs to track items that are being reordered from suppliers. Management must know when an item was ordered and how many were ordered. Birds2U may place an order with a supplier one day and then find it needs to order more of the same item before the original order is filled.

Instructions: If you are using the Microsoft Office Access 2003 Complete or the Microsoft Office Access 2003 Comprehensive text, open the Birds2U database that you used in Project 5 or see your instructor for information about accessing the files required in this book. Perform the following tasks:

1. Create macros that will perform the following tasks: (a) Open the Item Update Form, (b) Open the Supplier Master Form, (c) Open the Item Table, (d) Open the Supplier Table, (e) Preview the Inventory Report, (f) Preview the On Hand Value Report, (g) Preview the Supplier/Item Report, (h) Print the Inventory Report, (i) Print the On Hand Value Report, and (j) Print the Supplier/Item Report.
2. Create a switchboard for the Birds2U database. Use the same design for your switchboard pages as the one illustrated in this project. For example, the View Form switchboard page should have three choices: Item Update Form, Supplier Master Form, and Return to Main Switchboard. Include all the forms, tables, and reports for which you created macros in Step 1.
3. Run the switchboard and correct any errors.
4. Create a table in which to store the item reorder information using the structure shown in Figure 6-76. Use Reorder as the name of the table. Add the data shown in Figure 6-76 to the Reorder table. Print the table.

Structure of Reorder Table				
FIELD NAME	DATA TYPE	FIELD SIZE	PRIMARY KEY?	DESCRIPTION
Item Code	Text	4	Yes	Item Code (Portion of Primary Key)
Date Ordered	Date/Time (Change Format property to Short Date)		Yes	Date Item Ordered (Portion of Primary Key)
Number Ordered	Number			Number of Items Ordered

Reorder table		
ITEM CODE	DATE ORDERED	NUMBER ORDERED
BB01	7/15/2005	3
BB01	7/27/2005	1
BO22	8/1/2005	2
BO22	8/9/2005	2
BS10	8/25/2005	2
LM05	8/1/2005	4
LM05	8/15/2005	2
PM05	8/18/2005	2

FIGURE 6-76

5. Add the Reorder table to the Relationships window and establish a one-to-many relationship between the Item table and the Reorder table. Print the Relationships window by making sure the Relationships window is open, clicking File on the menu bar, and then clicking Print Relationships. When Access displays the Print Preview window, click the Print button on the Print Preview toolbar. Do not save the report.

In the Lab

6. Create a query that joins the Reorder table, Item table, and Supplier table. Include the item code from the Reorder table, the supplier code and number on hand from the Item table, and the number ordered from the Reorder table in the design grid. Run the query and save the query as Supplier and Number of Items.

7. Open the Supplier and Number of Items query and switch to PivotTable view. Create the PivotTable shown in Figure 6-77. Print the PivotTable.

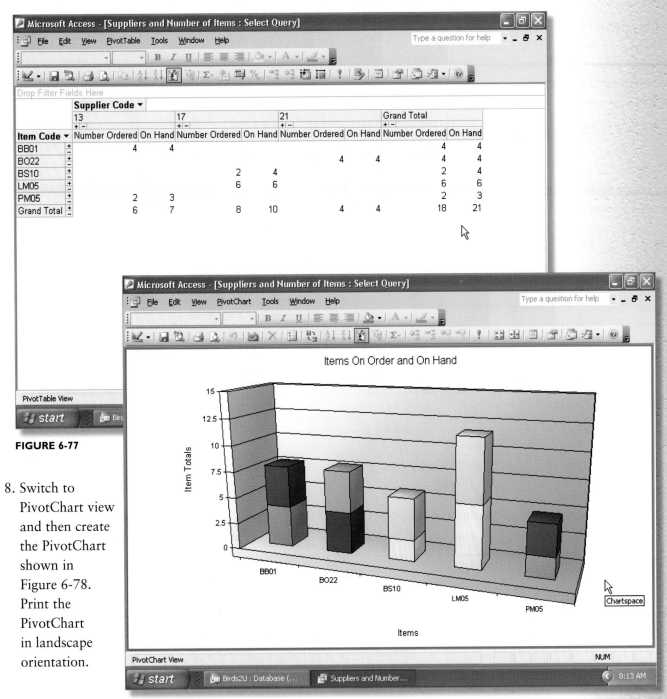

FIGURE 6-77

8. Switch to PivotChart view and then create the PivotChart shown in Figure 6-78. Print the PivotChart in landscape orientation.

FIGURE 6-78

In the Lab

2 Creating Macros, a Switchboard, a PivotTable, and a PivotChart for the Babbage Bookkeeping Database

Problem: Babbage Bookkeeping would like an easy way to access the various tables, forms, and reports by simply clicking a button or two. This would make the database much easier to maintain and update. The company also needs to keep track of when bookkeeping services were performed so it can bill clients properly.

Instructions: For this assignment, you will use two files: Babbage Bookkeeping.mdb and Accounts.xls. If you are using the Microsoft Office Access 2003 Complete or the Microsoft Office Access 2003 Comprehensive text, use the Babbage Bookkeeping database that you used in Project 5 or see your instructor for information about accessing the files required for this book. Accounts.xls is an Excel workbook that is on the Data Disk. Perform the following tasks:

1. Create macros that will perform the following tasks: (a) Open the Client Update Form, (b) Open the Bookkeeper Master Form, (c) Open the Client Table, (d) Open the Bookkeeper Table, (e) Preview the Balance Due Report, (f) Preview the Client Income Report, (g) Preview the Bookkeeper/Client Report, (h) Print the Balance Due Report, (i) Print the Client Income Report, and (j) Print the Bookkeeper/Client Report.

2. Create a switchboard for the Babbage Bookkeeping database. Use the same design for your switchboard pages as the one illustrated in this project. For example, the View Form switchboard page should have three choices: Open Client Update Form, Open Bookkeeper Master Form, and Return to Main Switchboard. Include all the forms, tables, and reports for which you created macros in Step 1.

3. Run the switchboard and correct any errors.

4. Create a table in which to store the account information using the structure shown in Figure 6-79. Use Accounts as the name of the table. Import the Accounts workbook to the Accounts table. Print the table.

Structure of Accounts Table				
FIELD NAME	DATA TYPE	FIELD SIZE	PRIMARY KEY?	DESCRIPTION
Client Number	Text	3	Yes	Client Number (Portion of Primary Key)
Service Date	Date/Time (Change the Format property to Short Date)		Yes	Date that Bookkeeping was Performed (Portion of Primary Key)
Hours Worked	Number			Number of Hours Worked

FIGURE 6-79

5. Add the Accounts table to the Relationships window and establish a one-to-many relationship between the Client table and the Accounts table. Print the Relationships window by making sure the Relationships window is open, clicking File on the menu bar, and then clicking Print Relationships. When Access displays the Print Preview window, click the Print button on the Print Preview toolbar. Do not save the report.

6. Create a query that joins the Accounts, Bookkeeper, and Client tables. Include the client number, service date, and hours worked fields from the Accounts table in the design grid. Calculate the current due amount (hours worked * hourly rate). Run the query and save the query as Total Current Due by Client.

7. Open the Total Current Due by Client query and switch to PivotTable view. Create the PivotTable shown in Figure 6-80. Print the PivotTable.

8. Filter the PivotTable to show only current due amounts for service dates between 8/22/2005 and 8/26/2005. Print the PivotTable and then redisplay all current due amounts.

9. Switch to PivotChart view and then create the PivotChart shown in Figure 6-81. Print the PivotChart in landscape orientation.

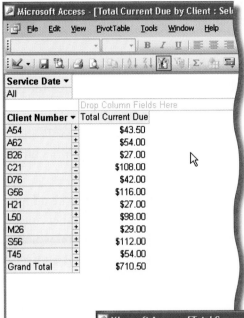

FIGURE 6-80

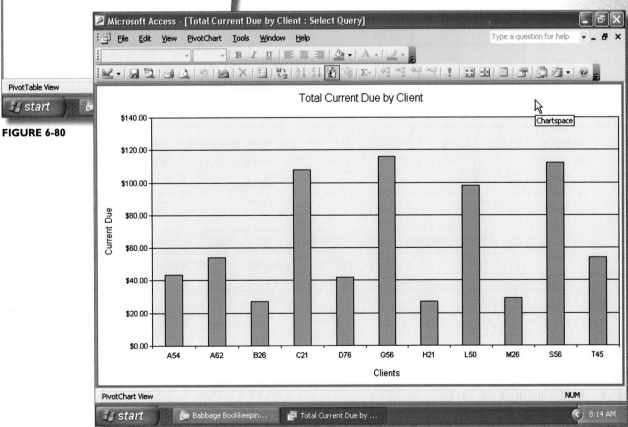

FIGURE 6-81

3 Creating Macros, a Switchboard, and a PivotTable for the City Guide Database

Problem: The chamber of commerce wants an easy way to access various tables, forms, and reports by simply clicking a button or two. The chamber also needs to track active accounts for the current year and wants the ability to change easily the way data is summarized and presented.

Instructions: If you are using the Microsoft Office Access 2003 Complete or the Microsoft Office Access 2003 Comprehensive text, open the City Guide database that you used in Project 5 or see your instructor for information about accessing the files required for this book.

Part 1 Instructions: Create macros to open the Advertiser Update Form and the Ad Rep Master Form. Create macros to preview and to print all the reports in the City Guide database. Create macros to open the tables in the database. Create a switchboard that uses these macros.

Part 2 Instructions: Advertisers contract with the chamber to advertise for one month. The same ad may run for several months or be replaced monthly with an ad of a different size or design. The chamber must track the active accounts for the current year and must be able to query the database for information on which advertisers currently have ads they want to appear in the newcomer's guide. To track this information requires two tables: an Active Accounts table and a Category table. Create these two tables using the structures shown in Figure 6-82. Import the Active Accounts text file into the Active Accounts table and the Ad Categories text file into the Category table. These text files are on your Data Disk. Then, update the relationships for the City Guide database. Print the tables and the Relationships window.

Structure of Active Accounts Table

FIELD NAME	DATA TYPE	FIELD SIZE	PRIMARY KEY?	DESCRIPTION
Advertiser Number	Text	4	Yes	Advertiser Number (Portion of Primary Key)
Ad Month	Text	3	Yes	Month that Ad is to Run (Portion of Primary Key)
Category Code	Text	1		Ad Category

Structure of Category Table

FIELD NAME	DATA TYPE	FIELD SIZE	PRIMARY KEY?	DESCRIPTION
Category Code	Text	1	Yes	Category Code (Primary Key)
Category Description	Text	50		Description of Ad Category

FIGURE 6-82

Part 3 Instructions: The chamber would like to actively track amount paid and balance amounts by advertiser and ad rep. Create a query for the Advertiser table that includes the advertiser number, ad rep number, advertiser type, amount paid, and balance, and then create the PivotTable shown in Figure 6-83. The chamber wants the ability to filter the data by advertiser type.

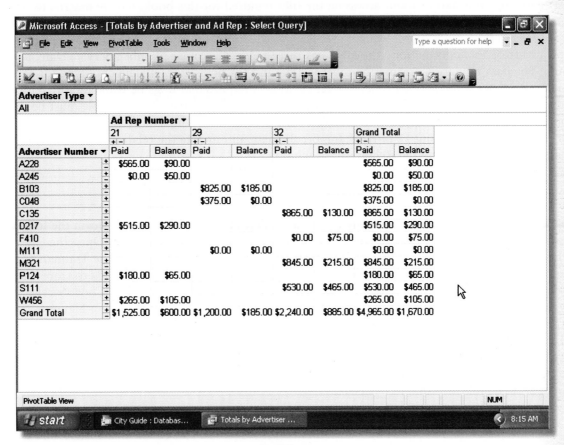

FIGURE 6-83

Cases and Places

The difficulty of these case studies varies:
■ are the least difficult and ■■ are more difficult. The last exercise is a group exercise.

1 ■ Use the College Dog Walkers database that you used in Project 5 for this assignment or see your instructor for information about accessing the files required for this book. Create macros to open the Customer Update Form, the Walker Master Form, the Customer table, and the Walker table. The business needs to keep track of dog-walking services provided to customers. Create a table called Service in which to store this information. The table has three fields: Customer Number, Service Date, and Service Time. The data type for Customer Number is Text and the field size is 4. The data type for Service Date and Service Time is Date/Time. Several customers require that dogs be walked more than once a day. Therefore, for each record to be unique, the primary key for the Service table must be the combination of customer number, service date, and service time. The data for the Service table is in the Services workbook on your Data Disk. Import the data and update the relationships for the database. Print the Service table and the Relationships window.

2 ■ Use the InPerson Fitness Company database and create macros that will perform the following tasks: (a) Open the Client Update Form, (b) Open the Trainer Master Form, (c) Open the Client table, (d) Open the Trainer table, (e) Preview the Trainer/Client Report, and (f) Print the Trainer/Client Report. Create and run a switchboard that uses these macros. The company needs to store information on when personal training services are provided to clients. Create a table called Client Service in which to store this data. The table has the same structure as the Accounts table shown in Figure 6-79 on page AC 370. Change the field size for the Client Number field to four (4). The data for the Client Service table is in the Client Services text file on your Data Disk. Import the data and update the relationships for the database. Print the Client Service table and the Relationships window. Edit the relationship between the Client table and the Client Service table. When a client is deleted, the related records in the Client Service table also should be deleted.

Cases and Places

3 ■■ Use the Regional Books database that you used in Project 5 for this assignment or see your instructor for information about accessing the files required in this book. Create macros to open all forms and tables in the database. Create macros to preview and to print all reports in the database. Create and run a switchboard that uses these macros. The owner of the bookstore has several customers who have purchased books on the layaway plan. He wants to add data on these customers and the books they are buying to the database. Because a customer can purchase more than one book, the primary key for the Book Order table is the combination of Customer Number and Book Code fields. The structures for the Book Order and Customer tables are shown in Figure 6-84. The data for these tables is in the Books workbook on your Data Disk. Update the Regional Books database to include these tables and establish the necessary relationships.

Structure of Book Order Table

FIELD NAME	DATA TYPE	FIELD SIZE	PRIMARY KEY?	DESCRIPTION
Book Code	Text	4	Yes	Book Code (Portion of Primary Key)
Customer Number	Text	3	Yes	Customer Ordering Book (Portion of Primary Key)
Order Date	Date/Time			Date Ordered

Structure of Customer Table

FIELD NAME	DATA TYPE	FIELD SIZE	PRIMARY KEY?	DESCRIPTION
Customer Number	Text	3	Yes	Customer Number (Primary Key)
Last Name	Text	15		Customer Last Name
First Name	Text	15		Customer First Name
Address	Text	15		Address
Phone Number	Text	8		Customer Phone Number (999-9999 version)

FIGURE 6-84

Cases and Places

4 ■■ Use the Campus Housing database that you used in Project 5 for this assignment or see your instructor for information about accessing the files required in this book. Create macros to open all forms and tables in the database. Create macros to preview and to print all reports in the database. Create and run a switchboard that uses these macros. The Housing office would like to store information on potential renters, that is, individuals interested in renting off-campus housing. Because these potential renters can show an interest in more than one rental unit, the primary key for the Property table is the combination of Renter Number and Rental Code. The structure for the Renter table is the same as the Customer table shown in Figure 6-84 on the previous page. Replace Customer with Renter. The Property table contains only the Renter Number and Rental Code fields. Be sure the data types and field size match those in the Renter and Rentals tables, respectively. The data for these tables is in the Property and Renter text files on your Data Disk. Update the Campus Housing database to include these tables and establish the necessary relationships.

5 ■■ **Working Together** As a team, research the differences between a crosstab query and a PivotTable. Modify one of the crosstab queries created previously. What type of modifications are possible to a crosstab query? How difficult is it to make the changes? Discuss when a crosstab is appropriate and when a PivotTable is appropriate and write a short paper that explains these differences. Create a PivotTable for one of the databases described in Cases and Places. The team must have a specific purpose in mind for the PivotTable. Also create a PivotChart for the same database. Write a paragraph that explains how the PivotTable and the PivotChart will help database users.

MICROSOFT
Office Access 2003

Data Access Pages

CASE PERSPECTIVE

Dr. Guernay and his colleagues at Ashton James College are pleased with all the database work that has been done for them thus far. The administration appreciates the ease with which the database can be modified to include additional fields and tables. The administration also likes the ease with which they can query the database. The default values, validation rules, validation text, and the relationships are useful in ensuring the database contains only valid data. They also find the reports, forms, and switchboard to be useful. Because they have found the forms particularly useful, they would like to use a Web page that would be similar to a form in order to view and/or update client data over the Internet. The administration would like to develop a sample of such a Web page, called a data access page, which they then would review. If they determine that it satisfies their needs, they have other requests for data to be accessible over the Web. The first request is to make a list of trainers available over the web. When viewing this data, they would like the option of displaying all the clients for one or more of the trainers appearing on the data access page. In addition, they have found both the PivotTable and the PivotChart to be very useful and would like to be able to view such a PivotTable and PivotChart over the Web. The administration would like to place both a PivotTable and a PivotChart on data access pages. Your task is to help the administration in accomplishing these goals.

As you read through this project, you will learn how to use the Page Wizard as well as the Design window to create data access pages.

Objectives

You will have mastered the material in this Web Feature when you can:

- Create a data access page using the wizard
- Create a grouped data access page in Design view
- Create a PivotTable in a data access page
- Save a PivotChart to a data access page

Introduction

Microsoft Access supports data access pages. A **data access page** is an HTML document that can be bound directly to data in the database. The fact that it is an HTML document implies that it can be run in the Internet Explorer browser. The fact that it is bound directly to the database means that it can access data in the database directly.

Data Access Pages

Figure 1 on the next page shows a sample data access page run in the Internet Explorer browser. Notice that it is similar to a form. Although running in the browser, the data access page is displaying data in the Ashton James College database. Furthermore, the page can be used to update this data. You can use it to change the contents of existing records, to delete records, and to add new records.

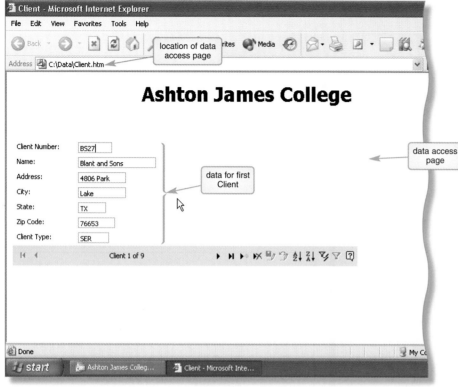

FIGURE 1

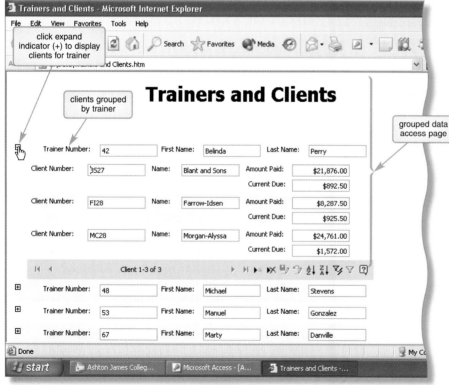

FIGURE 2

In this project, you will learn how to create the data access page shown in Figure 1. This data access page is located in a folder called Data on disk C. The database it is accessing also is located in this folder. In order to use this page on the Internet, both the page and the database would need to be located on some server that would be available to the Internet. The address entered in the browser would be changed to reflect the true location of the page.

You also will learn how to create the data access pages shown in Figures 2, 3, and 4. Figure 2 shows a grouped data access page. The data is grouped by trainer number. Clicking the expand indicator (+) in front of a trainer displays all the clients associated with that trainer. When the clients associated with a trainer appear, the plus sign changes to a minus sign (-). Clicking the minus sign will hide the clients associated with the trainer.

The data access page in Figure 3 contains a PivotTable. The Trainer Number field is in the filter area and can be used to restrict the data reflected in the PivotTable to only clients associated with certain trainers. The Client Number field is in the row area. The Course Number field is in the column area. The Hours Spent and Hours Remaining fields are in the detail area with their captions changed to Spent and Remaining, respectively. Sums of both the Hours Spent and Hours Remaining also are included in the PivotTable.

The data access page in Figure 4 contains a PivotChart. The PivotChart is a 3D Stacked Column chart. The bar heights represent total hours. The x-axis (horizontal axis) shows the trainer numbers subdivided into hours spent and hours remaining.

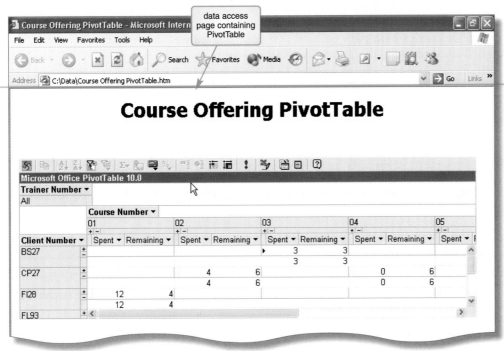

FIGURE 3

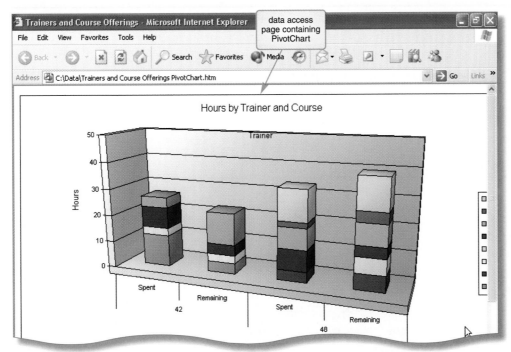

FIGURE 4

Opening the Database

If you are stepping through this project on a computer and want your screen to match the figures in this book, then you should change your computer's resolution to 800 x 600. For more information on how to change the resolution on your computer, see Appendix D. Before carrying out the steps in this project, first you must open the database. The steps on the next page, which start Access and open the database, assume that the database is located in a folder called Data on disk C. (See the note in Project 4 on page AC 197.) If your database is located anywhere else, you will need to make the appropriate adjustments in the steps.

To Open a Database

1 Click the Start button on the Windows taskbar, point to All Programs on the Start menu, point to Microsoft Office on the All Programs submenu, and then click Microsoft Office Access 2003 on the Microsoft Office submenu.

2 If the Access window is not maximized, double-click its title bar to maximize it.

3 If the Language bar appears, right-click it and then click Close the Language bar on the shortcut menu.

4 Click Open on the Database toolbar, and then click Local Disk (C:) in the Look in box. Double-click the Data folder, and then make sure the database called Ashton James College is selected.

5 Click the Open button.

6 If the Security Warning dialog box appears, click the Open button.

The database opens and the Ashton James College : Database window appears.

Creating a Data Access Page

To create a data access page, use the Page Wizard as shown in the following steps.

To Create a Data Access Page Using the Page Wizard

1

• **With the Client table selected, click the New Object button arrow on the Database toolbar.**

• **Click Page and then click Page Wizard.**

• **Click the OK button.**

The Page Wizard dialog box displays the fields in the Client table in the list of available fields. The Client Number field currently is selected (Figure 5).

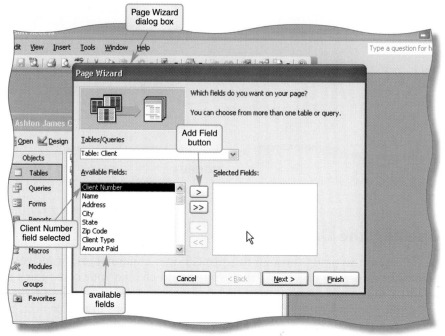

FIGURE 5

2

• **Click the Add Field button to add the Client Number field to the list of selected fields.**

• **Click the Add Field button six more times to add the Name, Address, City, State, Zip Code, and Client Type fields.**

The Client Number, Name, Address, City, State, Zip Code, and Client Type fields are selected (Figure 6).

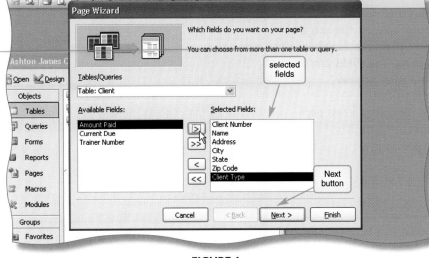

FIGURE 6

3

• **Click the Next button.**

The Page Wizard dialog box appears asking if you want to add any grouping levels (Figure 7).

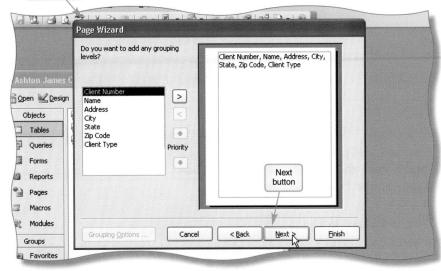

FIGURE 7

4

• **Because you do not need any grouping levels, click the Next button.**

• **Click the Next button a second time, because you do not need to make any changes on the following screen, which enables you to specify a special sort order.**

The Page Wizard dialog box appears asking what title you want for your page (Figure 8).

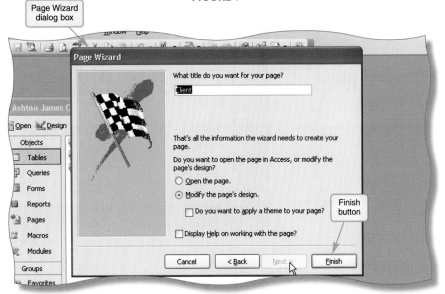

FIGURE 8

5

• **Because Client is acceptable as the page title, click the Finish button. The Field List pane may appear.**

The Client data access page appears (Figure 9).

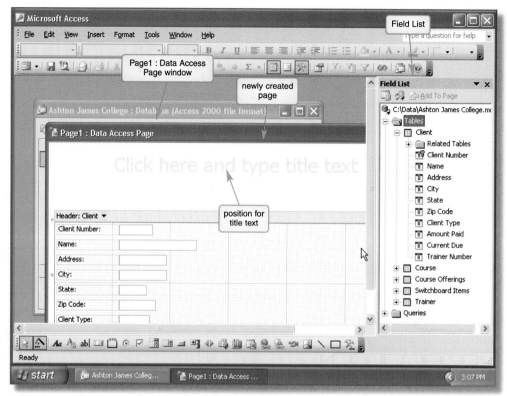

FIGURE 9

6

• **If a Field List pane appears, click the Close button for the Field List pane.**

• **Click anywhere in the portion of the screen labeled "Click here and type title text," and then type** Ashton James College **as the title text.**

The data access page appears (Figure 10). The title is changed to Ashton James College.

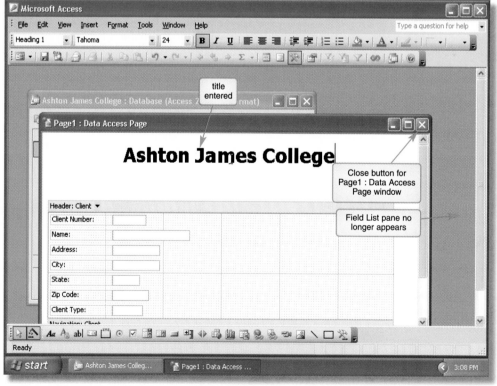

FIGURE 10

7

- **Click the Close button for the Page1 : Data Access Page window to close the window, and then click the Yes button in the Microsoft Office Access dialog box to indicate you want to save your changes.**

- **When the Save As Data Access Page dialog box appears, be sure the Data folder (or whatever folder contains your database) is selected and that the file name is Client.**

The Save As Data Access Page dialog box appears (Figure 11).

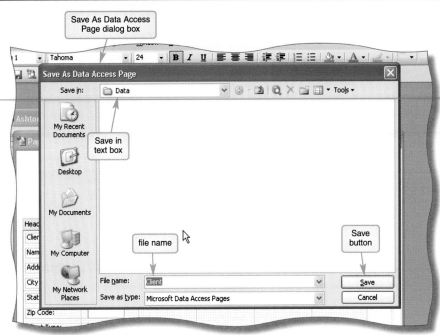

FIGURE 11

8

- **Click the Save button.**

- **If you see a message similar to the one in Figure 12, click the OK button, because the file location you specified is acceptable. [This message indicates that you will need to specify a UNC (Universal Naming Convention) address, rather than the file location you have specified if you want the page to be accessible over a network.]**

The data access page is created.

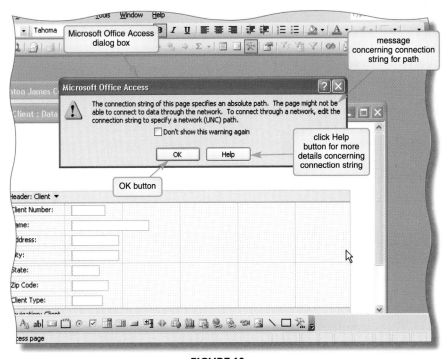

FIGURE 12

Previewing the Data Access Page

If you are connected to the Internet, you can view the data access page in the browser. To do this, you use the Web Page Preview command. When not connected to the Internet, you may not be able to view the data access page using the Web Page Preview command. You still can view the data access page, however, by using the Open command. The steps on the next page illustrate how to preview the data access page that was just created.

To Preview the Data Access Page

1

- **With the Database window appearing, click the Pages object.**
- **Right-click Client.**

The shortcut menu for the Client data access page appears (Figure 13).

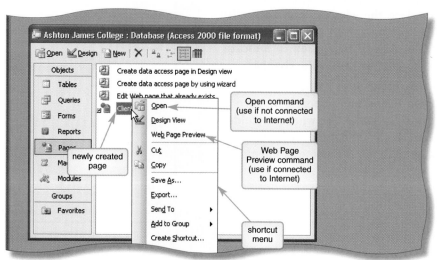

FIGURE 13

2

- **Click Web Page Preview on the shortcut menu. (If not connected to the Internet, click Open on the shortcut menu.) Ensure the window is maximized.**

The page appears within Internet Explorer (Figure 14). If you used the Open command, your screen will look slightly different.

3

- **Close Internet Explorer.**

The page no longer appears.

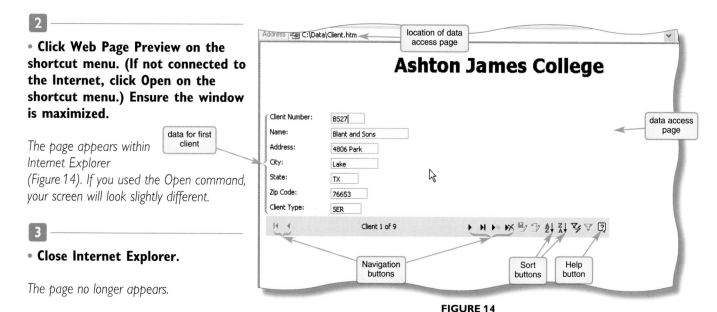

FIGURE 14

Using the Data Access Page

To use the data access page, start Internet Explorer, type the location of the data access page (for example: c:\data\client.htm, if you created the page in the Data folder on disk C), and then press the ENTER key. The page then will appear and look similar to the one in Figure 14.

You can use the navigation buttons, the Sort buttons, and the Filter buttons just as you do when viewing a datasheet or a form in Access. You can get help on the way you use the page by clicking the Help button (Figure 14). A book icon indicates subtopics are available. Double-clicking the icon displays the subtopics. A question mark icon indicates that information on the topic will appear when you click the question mark. In Figure 15, for example, the subtopics for both Getting

Started and Getting Help appear. The question mark in front of "Get Help using a data access page" has been clicked so the information on that topic appears. In addition, the window has been maximized, which makes it easier to read the help information.

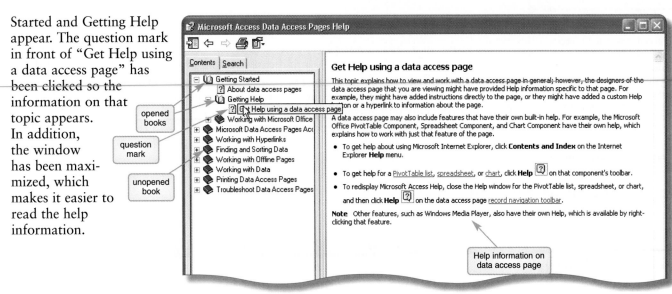

FIGURE 15

Grouped Data Access Pages

You can group records on a data access page that have some common characteristic. For example, you could group clients by trainer number, as in the data access page shown in Figure 2 on page AC 378. Thus, the clients of trainer 42 form one group, the clients of trainer 48 form a second, and the clients of trainer 53 form a third. In the data access page, you can show or hide any of these groups.

To create such a data access page, you can use a wizard. When you do, the wizard will give you an opportunity to specify grouping levels. You also can group in a data access page you are creating in Design view. The following steps show how to create a data access page in Design view.

To Create a Data Access Page in Design View

1 Click Pages on the Objects bar and then click the New button.

2 Be sure Design View is selected in the New Data Access Page dialog box, and then click the OK button.

3 When a message appears indicating that you will not be able to open this data access page in Design view in Access 2000 or Access 2002, click the OK button.

4 If a field list does not appear, click the Field List button on the Page Design toolbar to display a field list.

5 Maximize the window containing the data access page by clicking its title bar.

The data access page appears in a maximized window (Figure 16). A field list appears.

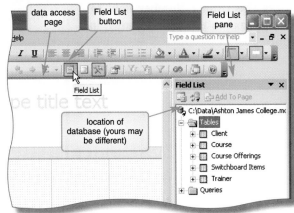

FIGURE 16

Adding the Fields and Grouping

To group in a data access page, you include the fields by dragging them from a field list to the desired position. You indicate grouping by using the Group by Table button on the Page Design toolbar. For example, to indicate grouping by the Trainer table, you first will select the Trainer Number field, and then click the Group by Table button. This will add a section for Trainer above a section for Client. Trainer fields will be in the Trainer section and Client fields will be in the Client section. The following steps illustrate how to add the fields and specify grouping.

To Add the Fields and Grouping

1

• **Click the plus sign in front of Client in the field list.**

• **When the Client fields appear, click the plus sign in front of Related tables, and then click the plus sign in front of the Trainer table listed in the Related Tables section.**

The fields in the Trainer table appear (Figure 17).

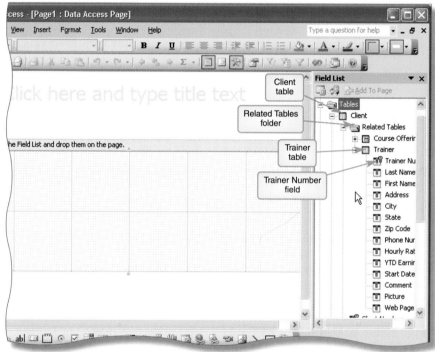

FIGURE 17

2

• **Drag the Trainer Number field to the approximate position shown in Figure 18.**

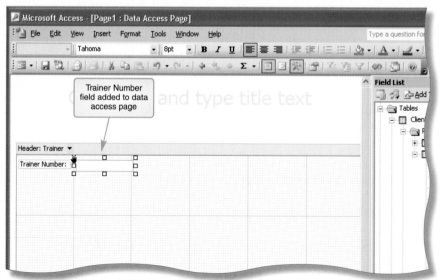

FIGURE 18

3

• **Drag the First Name and Last Name fields to the approximate positions shown in Figure 19.**

• **Drag the labels for the First Name and Last Name fields to the positions shown in the figure.**

• **Click the minus sign (-) in front of the Trainer table so the fields no longer appear, and then drag the Client Number field to the position shown in the figure.**

• **When the Layout Wizard dialog box appears, click the OK button and then click the Trainer Number field to select it.**

The First Name, Last Name, and Client Number fields are added. The Trainer Number field is selected.

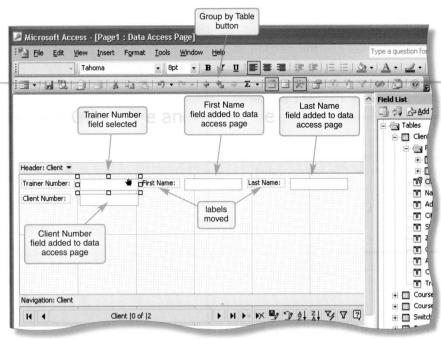

FIGURE 19

4

• **Click the Group by Table button.**

The data is grouped by trainer (Figure 20). A header for the Trainer table is added above the header for the Client table.

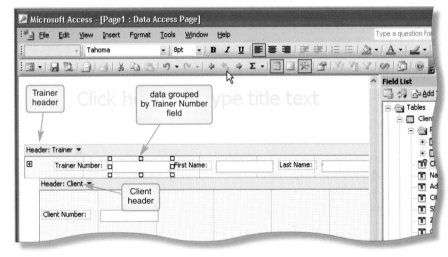

FIGURE 20

5

• **Drag the Client Number field to the approximate position shown in Figure 21.**

• **Drag the Name, Amount Paid, and Current Due fields from the field list to the approximate positions shown in the figure.**

• **Drag the labels to the positions shown in the figure.**

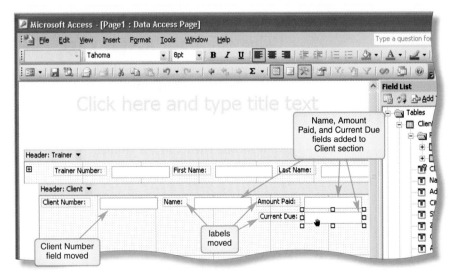

FIGURE 21

6

• **Click anywhere in the portion of the screen labeled "Click here and type title text," and then type** Trainers and Clients **as the title.**

• **Click in any open area of the Client section to select the section, and then drag the lower sizing handle to the approximate position shown in Figure 22.**

The title is added and the Client section is resized.

7

• **Close the window containing the data access page by clicking its Close Window button.**

• **Click the Yes button when asked if you want to save your changes, type** Trainers and Clients **as the file name, and then click the Save button. If you see a message like the one in Figure 12 on page AC 383, click the OK button, because the file location you specified is acceptable. [This message indicates that you will need to specify a UNC (Universal Naming Convention) address, rather than the file location you have specified if you want the page to be accessible over a network.]**

The grouped data access page is created.

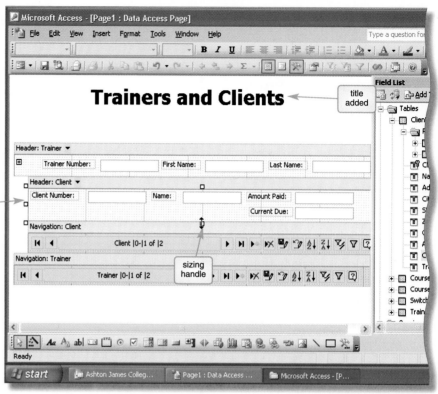

FIGURE 22

Using the Data Access Page

If you are connected to the Internet, you can preview what the page will look like in the browser by using the Web Page Preview command. You also can simply open the data access page using the Open command. In either case, you work with the page in the same manner. The following steps show how to preview the data access page that was just created and then click the plus sign in front of trainer 30 to view all the clients of the trainer.

To Use the Data Access Page

1

• **With the Database window appearing, be sure the Pages object is selected, right-click Trainers and Clients, and then click Web Page Preview on the shortcut menu.**

The data access page appears (Figure 23). Clients currently do not appear.

2

• **Click the plus sign in front of trainer number 42.**

The clients of trainer 42 appear underneath trainer 42 as shown in Figure 2 on page AC 378.

3

• **Close the browser window containing the data access page by clicking its Close button.**

The page no longer appears.

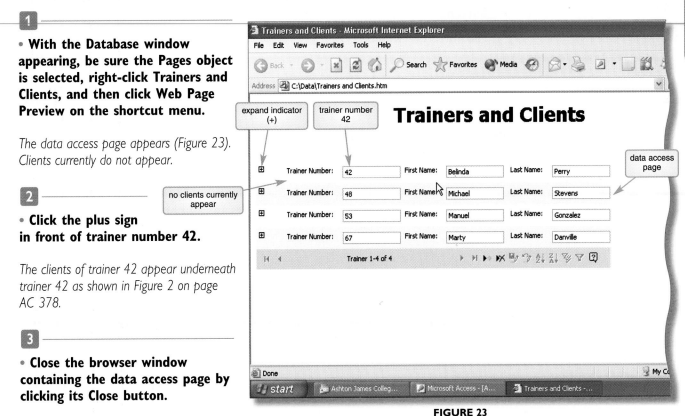

FIGURE 23

PivotTables in Data Access Pages

There are two ways to create a PivotTable in a data access page. You can create a PivotTable view of a table or query and then save the PivotTable as a data access page. Alternatively, you can create a data access page in Design view, place a PivotTable on the data access page, and then place the desired fields in appropriate areas of the PivotTable as you did when you created a PivotTable in Project 6. For the second approach, you first must create a data access page in Design view as illustrated in the following steps.

To Create a Data Access Page in Design View

1 If necessary, click Pages on the Objects bar and then click the New button.

2 Be sure Design View is selected in the New Data Access Page dialog box, and then click the OK button.

3 When a message appears indicating that you will not be able to open this data access page in Design view in Access 2000 or Access 2002, click the OK button.

4 If a field list appears, click the Field List button on the Page Design toolbar to remove the field list.

More About

Publishing to the Internet: Saving Other Objects

You also can publish other objects such as reports and datasheets to the Internet. To publish a datasheet or report to the Internet, save the object as a Web page in HTML format. To do so, select the name of the object in the Database window, click File on the menu bar, and then click Export. In the Save As Type box, click HTML documents.

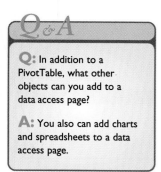

5 If the toolbox does not appear, click the Toolbox button on the Page Design toolbar. Be sure the toolbox is docked at the bottom of the screen. If it is not, drag its title bar to the bottom of the screen and release the left mouse button.

6 Maximize the window.

The data access page appears in Design view.

Creating a PivotTable in a Data Access Page

To create a PivotTable in a data access page, use the Office PivotTable tool in the toolbox and then click the position at which you would like to place the PivotTable. Select the table or query that will form the basis of the PivotTable, display a field list, and then drag the fields for the PivotTable to the appropriate areas.

The following steps show how to create the PivotTable in the data access page.

To Create a PivotTable in a Data Access Page

1

• **Click the Office PivotTable tool in the toolbox, and then point to the approximate position shown in Figure 24.**

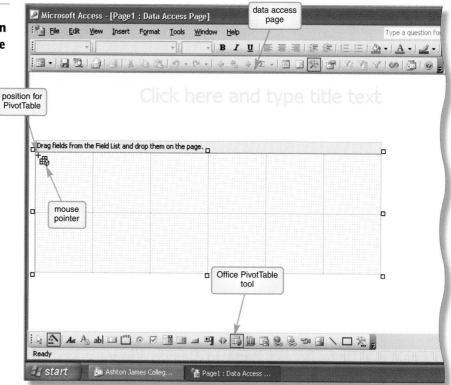

FIGURE 24

2

• Click the position shown in Figure 24 to place the PivotTable. A field list may reappear.

• If a field list reappears, close it by clicking its Close button.

• Right-click the PivotTable and then click Commands and Options on the shortcut menu.

• If necessary, click the "Data member, table, view, or cube name" option button, click the arrow, and then select the Trainers and Course Offerings query.

• Click the Close button in the Commands and Options dialog box.

• Resize the PivotTable to the approximate size shown in Figure 25 by dragging its lower-right sizing handle.

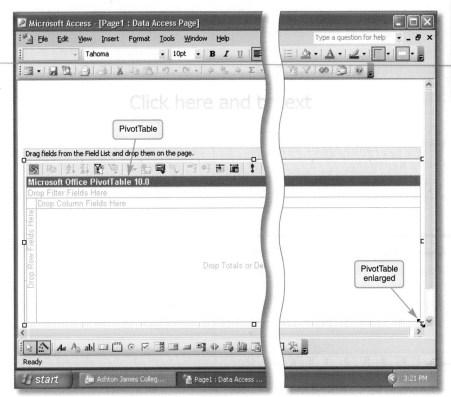

FIGURE 25

3

• Right-click the PivotTable, and then click Field List on the shortcut menu to display the PivotTable Field List pane.

• If the field list does not appear in the position shown in Figure 26, move it to the indicated position by dragging its title bar.

The PivotTable Field List pane appears. It contains only the Trainers and Course Offerings query, the query you identified for the PivotTable.

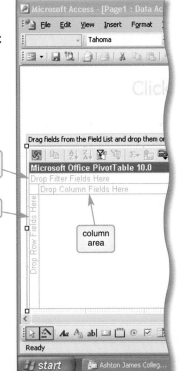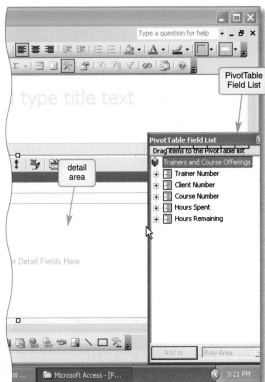

FIGURE 26

4

• **Drag the Client Number field to the row area.**

• **Drag the Course Number field to the column area.**

• **Drag the Trainer Number field to the filter area.**

• **Drag the Hours Spent and Hours Remaining fields to the detail area.**

• **The Hours Remaining field should be to the right of the Hours Spent field in the detail area. If it is not, drag the Hours Remaining field to the right of the Hours Spent field.**

The Client Number field is added to the row area (Figure 27). The Course Number field is added to the column area. The Trainer Number field is added to the filter area. The Hours Spent and Hours Remaining fields are added to the detail area.

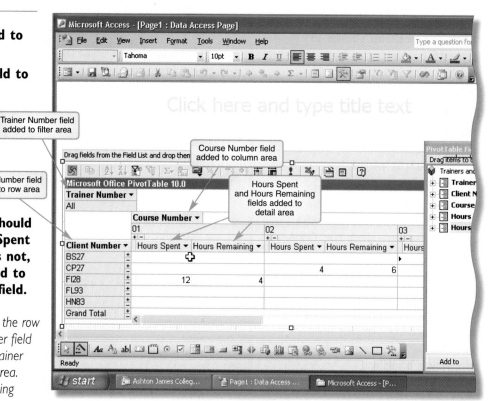

FIGURE 27

5

• **Close the PivotTable Field List pane by clicking its Close button.**

• **Right-click the Hours Spent field, click Commands and Options on the shortcut menu, click the Captions tab, erase the current caption, and type** Spent **as the new caption.**

• **Using the same technique, change the caption for Hours Remaining to** Remaining.

• **Click anywhere in the portion of the screen labeled "Click here and type title text," and then type** Course Offering PivotTable **as the title.**

The caption for the Hours Spent field is changed to Spent (Figure 28). The caption for the Hours Remaining field is changed to Remaining. The title is changed to Course Offering PivotTable.

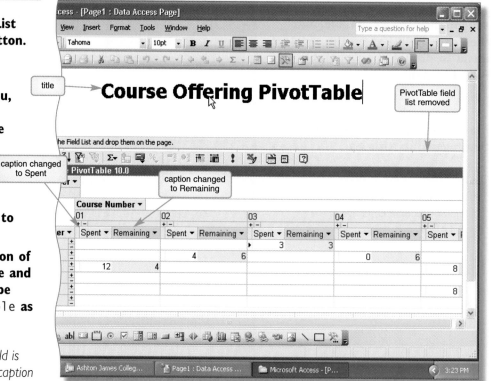

FIGURE 28

6

- **Click the Spent field, and then click the AutoCalc button on the PivotTable toolbar.**

The AutoCalc menu appears (Figure 29).

7

- **Click Sum on the AutoCalc menu.**

- **Click the Remaining field, click the AutoCalc button on the PivotTable toolbar, and then click Sum.**

- **Close the window containing the data access page by clicking its Close Window button.**

- **Click the Yes button when asked if you want to save your changes, type** Course Offering PivotTable **as the field name, and then click the Save button.**

- **If you see a message like the one in Figure 12 on page AC 383, click the OK button, because the file location you specified is acceptable.**

The data access page containing the PivotTable is created.

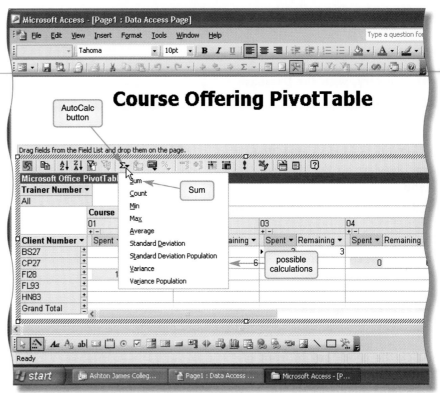

FIGURE 29

Using the PivotTable

You use the PivotTable in the data access page in a similar manner to the way you use PivotTable view for a table or query. You can click appropriate plus or minus signs to hide or show relevant data. You can restrict the data that will be reflected in the PivotTable by clicking an appropriate down arrow and then checking or unchecking items in the list that appears. You also can drag the fields to different locations in the PivotTable to change its organization. The steps on the next page illustrate how to open the data access page, and then restrict the data reflected in the table so clients of trainer 42 are not included.

More About

Microsoft Certification

The Microsoft Office Specialist Certification program provides an opportunity for you to obtain a valuable industry credential — proof that you have the Access 2003 skills required by employers. For more information, see Appendix E, or visit the Access 2003 Certification Web page (scsite.com/ac2003/cert).

To Use the PivotTable

1

• **If necessary, with the Database window appearing, click the Pages object.**

• **Right-click Course Offering PivotTable, and then click Web Page Preview on the shortcut menu.**

• **Click the Trainer Number arrow.**

The data access page appears (Figure 30). The list of trainers also appears.

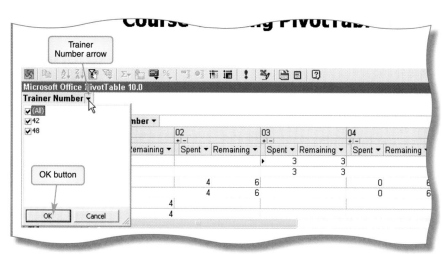

FIGURE 30

2

• **Click the check box in front of trainer 42 to remove the check mark, and then click the OK button.**

The data for clients of trainer 42 no longer is represented in the PivotTable (Figure 31).

3

• **Close the browser window containing the data access page by clicking its Close Window button.**

The page no longer appears.

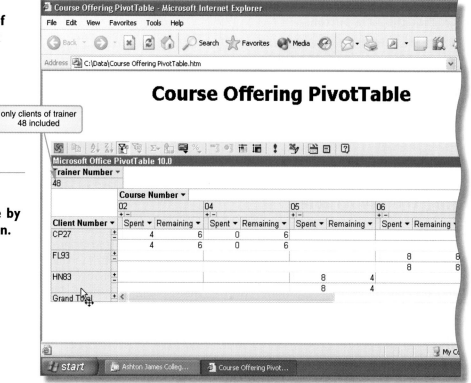

FIGURE 31

Saving a PivotChart to a Data Access Page

You can create a PivotChart on a data access page by first creating the PivotChart as the PivotChart view of a table or query and then saving the PivotChart as a data access page. The following steps show how to save the PivotChart view of the Trainers and Course Offerings query created in Project 6 as a data access page.

To Save a PivotChart to a Data Access Page

1

• **Click Queries on the Objects bar, right-click the Trainers and Course Offerings query, and then click Open on the shortcut menu.**

• **Click the View button arrow, and then click PivotChart View on the View menu.**

• **With the PivotChart appearing, click File on the menu bar, and then click Save As on the View menu.**

• **Change the name from Trainers and Course Offerings to** Trainers and Course Offerings PivotChart**, click the arrow in the As text box, and then select Data Access Page.**

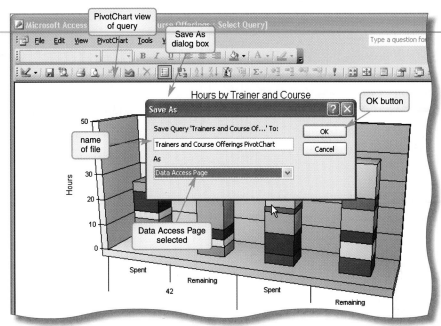

FIGURE 32

The PivotChart and the Save As dialog box appear (Figure 32).

2

• **Click the OK button in the Save As dialog box, be sure the file name is Trainers and Course Offerings PivotChart, and then click the OK button in the New Data Access Page dialog box.**

The data access page containing the PivotChart is created.

3

• **Click the Close Window button twice, once to close the data access page and once to close the PivotChart view of the query.**

• **If asked if you want to save the changes to the layout of the Trainers and Course Offerings query, click the No button.**

The window is closed. Changes to the query layout are not saved.

Using the Data Access Page

You use the PivotChart in the data access page in a similar manner to the way you use the PivotChart view of a table or query. You can display the drop areas and then use them to restrict the data that will be reflected in the PivotChart. You also can display the PivotChart toolbar and use it to change the chart type, to change the chart organization, to show or hide a legend, and so on. The steps on the next page show how to open the data access page when you are connected to the Internet, display a field list, display the drop areas, place the Client Number field in the filter fields area, and then use the Client Number control to restrict the clients whose data is reflected in the PivotChart.

More About

Quick Reference

For a table that lists how to complete the tasks covered in this book using the mouse, menu, shortcut menu, and keyboard, see the Quick Reference Summary at the back of this book, or visit the Access 2003 Quick Reference Web page (scsite.com/ac2003/qr).

To Use the Data Access Page

1

- **With the Database window appearing, click the Pages object.**

- **Right-click Trainers and Course Offerings PivotChart, and then click Web Page Preview on the shortcut menu.**

- **Right-click any open area of the PivotChart.**

The PivotChart appears (Figure 33). The shortcut menu for the PivotChart appears.

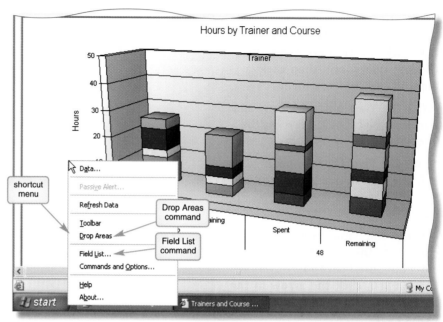

FIGURE 33

2

- **Click Field List on the shortcut menu to display a field list.**

- **Right-click any open area of the PivotChart, and then click Drop Areas on the shortcut menu.**

- **Drag the Client Number field to the filter fields.**

- **Click the Client Number arrow, and then remove the check marks from Client FI28 and Client FL93.**

- **Click the OK button.**

The PivotChart appears (Figure 34). Only course offerings for clients BS27, CP27, and HN83 are reflected in the chart.

3

- **Close the browser window containing the data access page by clicking its Close Window button.**

The page no longer appears.

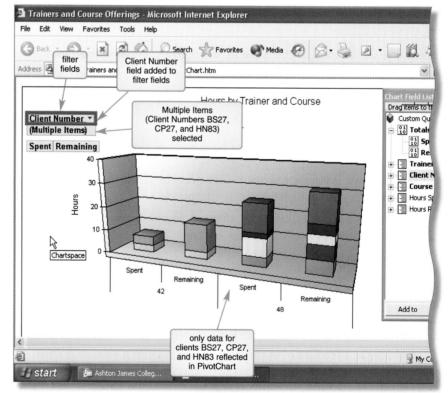

FIGURE 34

Closing the Database and Quitting Access

The following steps close the database and quit Access.

To Close a Database and Quit Access

1 Click the Close Window button for the Ashton James College : Database window.

2 Click the Close button for the Microsoft Access 2003 window.

Web Feature Summary

In this Web Feature, you learned how to create a data access page for the Client table in the Ashton James College database. To do so, you used the Page Wizard. You then saw how to preview the data access page from within Access. You learned how to create and use a grouped data access page that grouped clients by trainer. You also saw how to create a data access page in Design view, and then created a PivotTable in the data access page. The feature also illustrated how to save a PivotChart that was created earlier as a data access page. You also saw how to use each of the data access pages that were created.

 If you have a SAM user profile, you may have access to hands-on instruction, practice, and assessment of the skills covered in this project. Log in to your SAM account and go to your assignments page to see what your instructor has assigned.

What You Should Know

Having completed this Web Feature, you should be able to perform the tasks listed below. The tasks are listed in the same order they were presented in this feature. For a list of the buttons, menus, toolbars, and commands introduced in this Web Feature, see the Quick Reference Summary at the back of this book and refer to the Page Number column.

1. Open a Database   (AC 380)
2. Create a Data Access Page Using the Page Wizard (AC 380)
3. Preview the Data Access Page   (AC 384)
4. Create a Data Access Page in Design View (AC 385)
5. Add the Fields and Grouping   (AC 386)
6. Use the Data Access Page   (AC 389)
7. Create a Data Access Page in Design View (AC 389)
8. Create a PivotTable in a Data Access Page (AC 390)
9. Use the PivotTable   (AC 394)
10. Save a PivotChart to a Data Access Page (AC 395)
11. Use the Data Access Page   (AC 396)
12. Close a Database and Quit Access   (AC 397)

In the Lab

1 Creating Data Access Pages for Begon Pest Control

Problem: Begon Pest Control would like to create Web pages that would allow them to view and/or update customer data over the Internet. The company also would like to make a list of technicians available over the Web. When viewing this data, the company would like the option of displaying all the customers for one or more of the technicians appearing on the data access page.

Instructions: Start Access. Open the Begon Pest Control database that you used in Project 6 or see the inside back cover of this book for instructions for downloading the Data Disk or see your instructor for information about accessing the files required for this book. Perform the following tasks:

1. Use the Page Wizard to create the data access page for the Customer table shown in Figure 35.

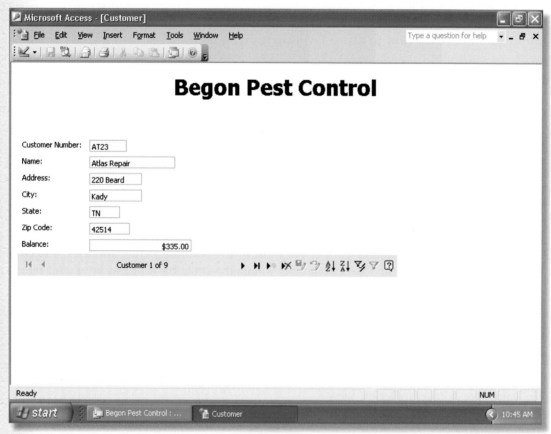

FIGURE 35

2. Print the data access page for customer BL35. To print the page, open the page, click File on the menu bar, and then click Print.
3. Create the grouped data access page shown in Figure 36. The page groups customers by technicians.

In the Lab

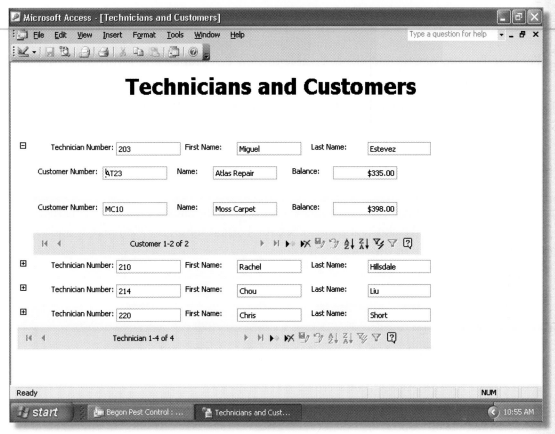

FIGURE 36

4. Open the data access page and then click the First Name field. Click the Sort Ascending button to sort the records in order by first name.
5. Print the data access page.
6. Sort the records in order by technician number and then click the plus sign in front of technician 210. Print the data access page.

In the Lab

2 Creating Data Access Pages for Babbage Bookkeeping

Problem: Babbage Bookkeeping would like to be able to view PivotTables and PivotCharts over the Web.

Instructions: Start Access. Open the Babbage Bookkeeping database that you used in Project 6 or see the inside back cover of this book for instructions for downloading the Data Disk or see your instructor for information about accessing the files required for this book. Perform the following tasks:

1. Open the Total Current Due by Client query that was created previously in Design view.
2. Add the Bookkeeper Number field from the Client table to the query and save the query.
3. Create the data access page shown in Figure 37. The PivotTable uses the modified Total Current Due by Client query. To display current due amounts as currency, right-click the Current Due field, click Commands and Options on the shortcut menu, click the Format tab in the Commands and Options dialog box, and then select Currency in the Number text box.

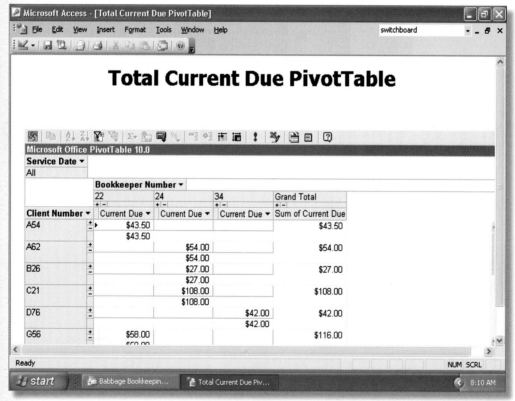

FIGURE 37

4. Save the data access page as Total Current Due PivotTable.
5. Open the data access page and filter the PivotTable to show only current due amounts for service dates between 8/22/2005 and 8/26/2005. Print the PivotTable.
6. Remove the filter to redisplay all service dates. Hide the details for each client number. Print the PivotTable.
7. Open the modified Total Current Due by Client query and then display the query in PivotChart View.
8. Save the PivotChart as a data access page with the name, Total Current Due by Client PivotChart.
9. Print the PivotChart in landscape orientation.

Advanced Report and Form Techniques

PROJECT

7

CASE PERSPECTIVE

The administration at Ashton James College wants a master list of trainers. For each trainer, the report is to include full details for all the clients assigned to the trainer. In addition, for each of these clients for whom courses currently are scheduled, the report should list the specific courses being offered to the client, including the total hours that the course will take as well as the hours already spent on the course. The administration also wants to be able to produce mailing labels for their clients. These labels must align correctly with the particular labels they have purchased and must be sorted by Zip code.

The administration has two additional requests related to improvements in the Client Update Form. First, they would like buttons on the form to assist users in moving to the next record, moving to the previous record, adding a record, deleting a record, and closing the form. Second, they also want users of the form to have a simple way of searching for a client given the client's name. To do so, the administration would like a combo box of customer names to appear on the form. By clicking the combo box arrow, users can display a list of all the client names. To select a client, they will simply click the client's name. The data for that client then will appear in the form. Your task is to help the administration accomplish these goals.

As you read through this project, you will learn how to use the Design window to create a report from scratch. You also will learn how to use the Label Wizard to create mailing labels and how to add command buttons and a combo box to a form.

Advanced Report and Form Techniques

Objectives

You will have mastered the material in this project when you can:

- Create a report in Design view
- Create queries for reports
- Add fields to a report
- Add a subreport to a report
- Modify a subreport
- Add a date
- Add a page number
- Create and print mailing labels
- Add command buttons to forms
- Modify VBA code associated with a command button
- Add a combo box to a form
- Modify properties of a combo box

Introduction

This project creates the report shown in Figure 7-1a. The report is organized by trainer. For each trainer, the report lists the number, first name, and last name. Following the trainer number and name, the report lists data for each client served by that trainer. The client data includes the number, name, address, city, state, Zip code, client type, amount paid, and current due. It also includes any courses currently being offered to the client. For each course, it lists the number, description, total hours the course requires, and hours already spent.

The project also creates mailing labels for the customers. These labels, which are shown in Figure 7-1b, are designed to fit perfectly the type of labels that Ashton James College has purchased.

The addition of a combo box to the Client Update Form created earlier (Figure 7-1c) will allow users to search for clients by name. Command buttons assist the user in performing record and form operations. Appropriate Access wizards are used to create command buttons and combo boxes. The **wizards** create the button or the combo box to the necessary specifications and place it on the form. The wizards also create an event procedure for the button or the combo box. An **event procedure** is a series of steps that Access will carry out when an event, such as the clicking of a command button, occurs. For example, when a user clicks the Delete Record button, the steps in the event procedure created for the Delete Record button will execute. This procedure actually will cause the record to be deleted. Event procedures are written in a language called **Visual Basic for Applications**, or **VBA**. This language is a standard throughout Microsoft applications. In this project, you will make changes as directed in existing VBA procedures. In the next project, you will learn to create your own procedures.

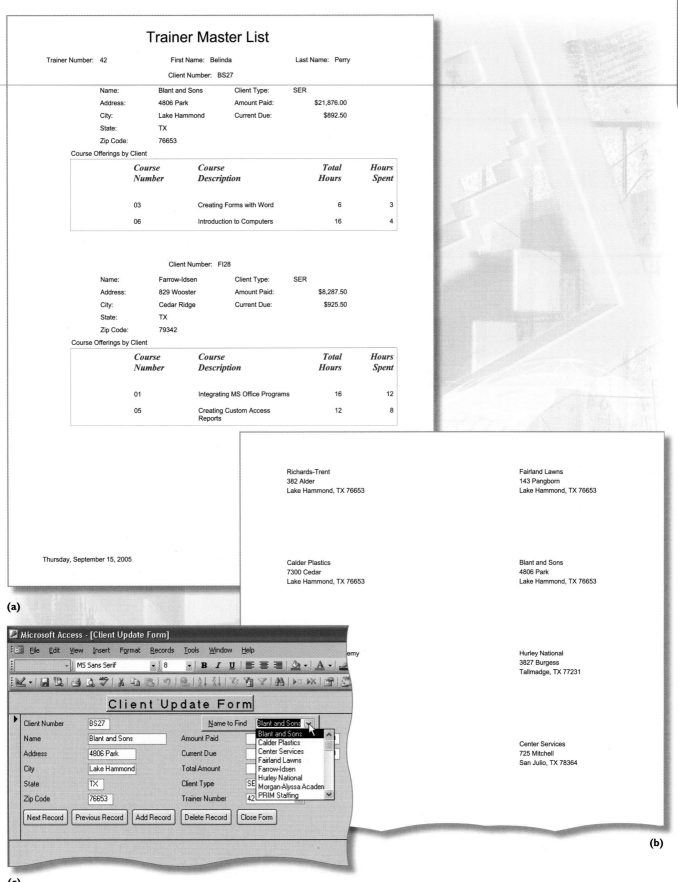

Trainer Master List

Trainer Number: 42   First Name: Belinda   Last Name: Perry

Client Number: BS27

Name:	Blant and Sons	Client Type:	SER
Address:	4806 Park	Amount Paid:	$21,876.00
City:	Lake Hammond	Current Due:	$892.50
State:	TX		
Zip Code:	76653		

Course Offerings by Client

Course Number	Course Description	Total Hours	Hours Spent
03	Creating Forms with Word	6	3
06	Introduction to Computers	16	4

Client Number: FI28

Name:	Farrow-Idsen	Client Type:	SER
Address:	829 Wooster	Amount Paid:	$8,287.50
City:	Cedar Ridge	Current Due:	$925.50
State:	TX		
Zip Code:	79342		

Course Offerings by Client

Course Number	Course Description	Total Hours	Hours Spent
01	Integrating MS Office Programs	16	12
05	Creating Custom Access Reports	12	8

Thursday, September 15, 2005

(a)

Richards-Trent
382 Alder
Lake Hammond, TX 76653

Fairland Lawns
143 Pangborn
Lake Hammond, TX 76653

Calder Plastics
7300 Cedar
Lake Hammond, TX 76653

Blant and Sons
4806 Park
Lake Hammond, TX 76653

...emy

Hurley National
3827 Burgess
Tallmadge, TX 77231

Center Services
725 Mitchell
San Julio, TX 78364

(b)

Microsoft Access - [Client Update Form]

File Edit View Insert Format Records Tools Window Help

MS Sans Serif   8   **B** *I* U

Client Update Form

Client Number	BS27	Name to Find	Blant and Sons
Name	Blant and Sons	Amount Paid	
Address	4806 Park	Current Due	
City	Lake Hammond	Total Amount	
State	TX	Client Type	SE
Zip Code	76653	Trainer Number	42

Blant and Sons
Calder Plastics
Center Services
Fairland Lawns
Farrow-Idsen
Hurley National
Morgan-Alyssa Academy
PRIM Staffing

[Next Record] [Previous Record] [Add Record] [Delete Record] [Close Form]

(c)

FIGURE 7-1

In many cases, the user does not even need to be aware that these event procedures exist. Access creates and uses them automatically. Occasionally, however, a user may wish to make changes to an event procedure. Without making changes, for example, clicking the Add Record button blanks out the fields on the form so a user can enter a new record but does not produce an insertion point in the Client Number field. The fact that there is no insertion point would require the user to take special action, such as clicking the Client Number field, before entering data. A change to the event procedure for the Add Record button corrects this problem.

More About

The Access Help System

Need Help? It is no further away than the Type a question for help box on the menu bar in the upper-right corner of the window. Click the box that contains the text, Type a question for help (Figure 7-2 on page AC 406), type `help`, and then press the ENTER key. Access responds with a list of topics you can click to learn about obtaining help on any Access-related topic. To find out what is new in Access 2003, type `what is new in Access` in the Type a question for help box.

Project Seven — Advanced Report and Form Techniques

The steps in this project show how to create the report shown in Figure 7-1a on the previous page. The report requires two queries that will be used in the report. The report shown in Figure 7-1a contains a **subreport**, which is a report that is contained within another report. The subreport in the report in Figure 7-1a is the portion that lists the open course offerings. The steps in this project create the report shown in the figure from scratch; that is, the steps use Design view rather than the Report Wizard. The subreport is added as part of the process. After creating the report, the steps illustrate how to create mailing labels for the trainers as shown in Figure 7-1b on the previous page.

The steps add the necessary buttons to the Client Update Form. Then, the steps add the combo box that allows users to find a client given the client's name. Finally, steps are presented to complete this process by making the necessary modifications to ensure the buttons and combo box function as intended.

Opening the Database

If you are stepping through this project on a computer and you want your screen to match the figures in this book, then you should change your computer's resolution to 800 × 600. For more information on how to change the resolution on your computer, see Appendix D. Before carrying out the steps in this project, first you must open the database. The following steps, which start Access and open the database, assume that the database is located in a folder called Data on drive C. If your database is located anywhere else, you will need to make the appropriate adjustments in the steps.

To Open a Database

1. **Click the Start button on the Windows taskbar, point to All Programs on the Start menu, point to Microsoft Office on the All Programs submenu, and then click Microsoft Office Access 2003 on the Microsoft Office submenu.**
2. **If the Access window is not maximized, double-click its title bar to maximize it.**
3. **If the Language bar appears, right-click it and then click Close the Language bar on the shortcut menu.**
4. **Click Open on the Database toolbar, and then click Local Disk (C:) in the Look in box. Double-click the Data folder, and then make sure the database called Ashton James College is selected.**
5. **Click the Open button.**

6 If the Security Warning dialog box appears, click the Open button.

The database opens and the Ashton James College : Database window appears.

Creating Reports in Design View

You do not have to use the wizard when you create a report. You can simply create the report in Design view. In the previous reports you created, you used the wizard to create an initial report, and then used Design view to modify the design the wizard created. If you do not use the wizard before moving to Design view, the design will be empty. It is then up to you to place all the fields in the desired locations. It is also up to you to specify any sorting or grouping that is required.

Whether you use the wizard or simply use Design view, you must decide the table or query on which the report is to be based. If the report is to be based on a query, you first must create the query, unless, of course, it already exists.

Creating Queries for Reports

The report you will create requires two queries. The first query relates trainers and clients and the second query relates courses and course offerings. The following steps show how to create the necessary queries.

To Create Queries for the Report

1 If necessary, in the Database window, click Tables on the Objects bar, and then click Trainer. Click the New Object button arrow on the Database window toolbar, and then click Query. Be sure Design View is selected, and then click the OK button. Maximize the window.

2 Right-click any open area in the upper pane, click Show Table on the shortcut menu, click the Client table, click the Add button, and then click the Close button in the Show Table dialog box. Resize the upper and lower panes of the window as well as the field lists so all fields appear.

3 Double-click the Trainer Number, First Name, and Last Name fields from the Trainer table. Double-click the Client Number, Name, Address, City, State, Zip Code, Client Type, Amount Paid, and Current Due fields from the Client table.

4 Close the query by clicking its Close Window button, and then click the Yes button to save the query. Type Trainers and Clients as the name of the query, and then click the OK button.

5 Click Course and then click the New Object button arrow on the Database window toolbar. Click Query. Be sure Design View is selected, and then click the OK button.

6 Right-click any open area in the upper pane, click Show Table on the shortcut menu, click the Course Offerings table, click the Add button, and then click the Close button in the Show Table dialog box. Resize the upper and lower panes of the window as well as the field lists so all fields appear. Double-click the Client Number and Course Number fields from the Course Offerings table. Double-click the Course Description field from the Course table, and then double-click the Total Hours and Hours Spent fields from the Course Offerings table.

More About

Adding Objects

You can add various types of objects to reports in two ways. You can use the Object command on the Insert menu, select the desired type of object (for example, a bitmap image), and then select the specific object you wish to insert (for example, a specific bitmap image on your disk). You also can click the Unbound Object Frame tool on the toolbox and then click the position on the report where you wish to place the object. As with the Object command on the Insert menu, you select the desired type of object and then the specific object you wish to insert.

More About

The Format Painter

If you have added a control to a form or report and want to ensure that it has the same format characteristics as an existing control, you can use the Format Painter. Click the control with the desired characteristics, click the Format Painter button on the toolbar, and then click the control you wish to format.

More About

Subreports

A main report can contain more than one subreport. If the main report is based on a table or query, each subreport must contain information related to the information in the main report. If the main report is not based on a table or query, it simply serves as a container for the subreports, which then have no restrictions on the information they must contain.

7 Close the query by clicking its Close Window button, and then click the Yes button to save the query. Type Course Offerings and Courses **as the name of the query, and then click the OK button.**

The queries are saved.

Creating an Initial Report

Creating the report shown in Figure 7-1a on page AC 403 from scratch involves creating the initial report in Report Design view, adding the subreport, modifying the subreport separately from the main report, and then making the final modifications to the main report.

When you want to create a report from scratch, you begin with the same general procedure as when you want to use the Report Wizard to create the report. The difference is that you will select Design View rather than Report Wizard. The following steps demonstrate how to create the initial version of the Trainer Master List and specify sorting and grouping for the report.

To Create an Initial Report

1

• **If necessary, in the Database window, click Queries on the Objects bar, and then click Trainers and Clients.**

• **Click the New Object button arrow, and then click Report.**

• **Be sure Design View is selected, and then click the OK button.**

• **If necessary, maximize the window and dock the toolbox at the bottom of the screen.**

• **Be sure the field list appears. If it does not, click the Field List button on the Report Design toolbar.**

• **Drag the bottom boundary of the field list down so all fields appear, and then move the field list to the lower-right corner of the screen by dragging its title bar.**

• **Right-click any open area of the Detail section of the report.**

The field list is moved and the shortcut menu appears (Figure 7-2).

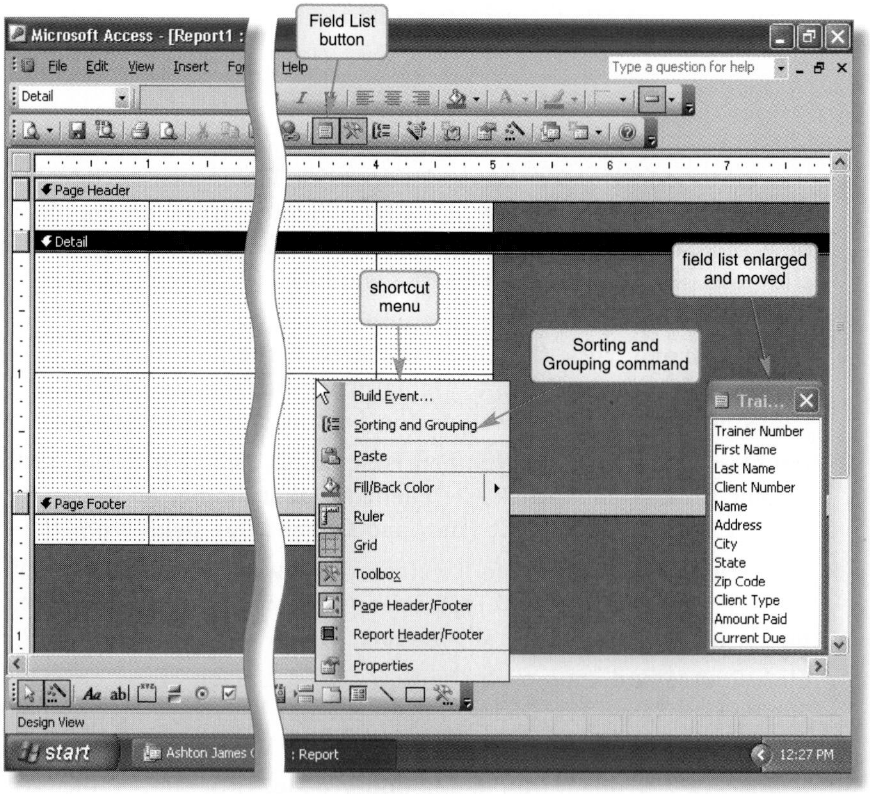

FIGURE 7-2

2

• **Click Sorting and Grouping on the shortcut menu, and then click the down arrow in the Field/Expression box.**

• **Click Trainer Number, click the Group Header property box, click the Group Header property box arrow, and then click Yes.**

• **Click the Keep Together property, click the Keep Together property box arrow, and then click Whole Group in the list of available values for the Keep Together property.**

The Trainer Number field is selected (Figure 7-3). The Group Header property is changed from No to Yes. The value for the Keep Together property is changed to Whole Group.

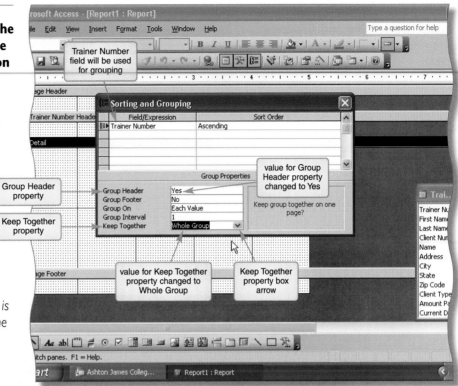

FIGURE 7-3

3

• **Click the Field/Expression box on the second row (the row under Trainer Number), click the down arrow that displays, and then click Client Number in the list of fields that appears.**

The fields are selected for sorting and grouping (Figure 7-4).

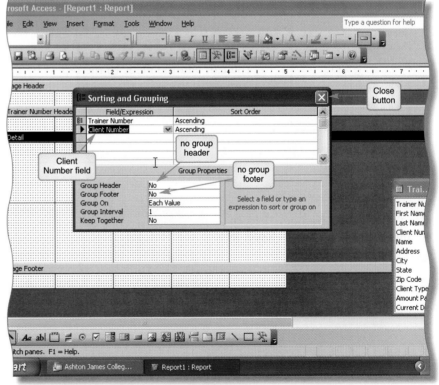

FIGURE 7-4

4

• **Close the Sorting and Grouping dialog box by clicking its Close button.**

The Sorting and Grouping dialog box no longer appears (Figure 7-5). The Trainer Number header now appears in the design.

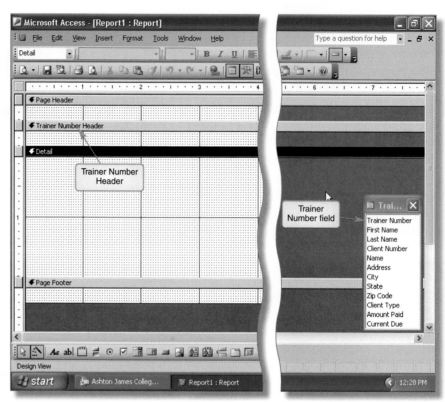

FIGURE 7-5

Adding Fields to the Report

You can add the fields to the report by dragging them from the field list to the appropriate position on the report. The following steps illustrate how to add the fields to the report.

To Add Fields to the Report

1

• **Drag the Trainer Number field to the approximate position shown in Figure 7-6.**

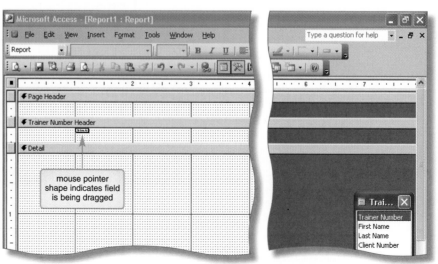

FIGURE 7-6

2

• **Release the left mouse button to place the field.**

• **Use the same techniques to place the First Name and Last Name fields in the approximate positions shown in Figure 7-7.**

• **Adjust the positions of the labels to those shown in the figure. If any field is not in the correct position, drag it to its correct location. To move the control or the attached label separately, drag the large handle in the upper-left corner of the control or label.**

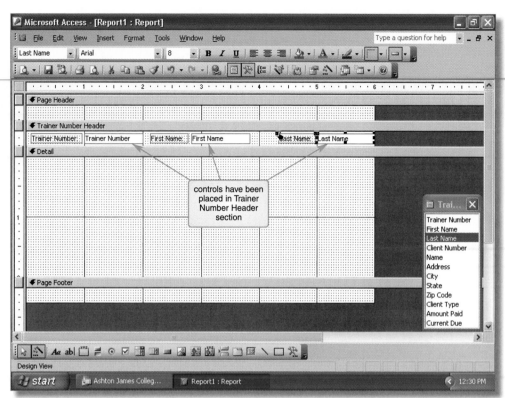

FIGURE 7-7

3

• **Place the remaining fields in the positions shown in Figure 7-8.**

The fields are placed.

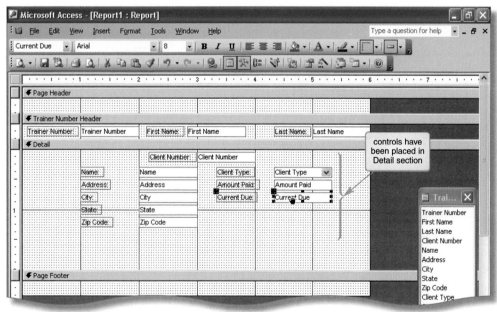

FIGURE 7-8

Saving the Report

Before proceeding with the next steps in the modification of the report, it is a good idea to save your work. The steps on the next page show how to save the current report.

To Save the Report

1

• **Click the Save button on the Report Design toolbar, and then type** Trainer Master List **as the report name.**

The Save As dialog box appears (Figure 7-9).

2

• **Click the OK button.**

The report is saved. The name is Trainer Master List.

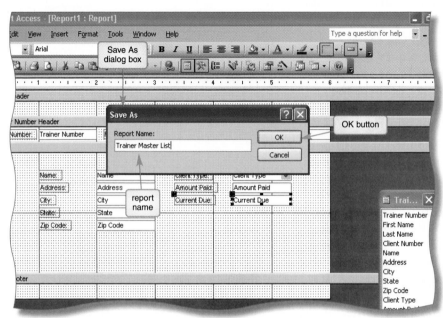

FIGURE 7-9

Adding a Subreport

To add a subreport to a report, you use the Subform/Subreport tool in the toolbox. Provided the Control Wizards button is selected, a wizard will guide you through the process of adding the subreport as in the following steps.

To Add a Subreport

1

• **Close the field list by clicking its Close button.**

• **Be sure the Control Wizards tool is selected, click the Subform/Subreport tool, and then move the pointer, which has changed to a plus sign with a subreport, to the approximate position shown in Figure 7-10.**

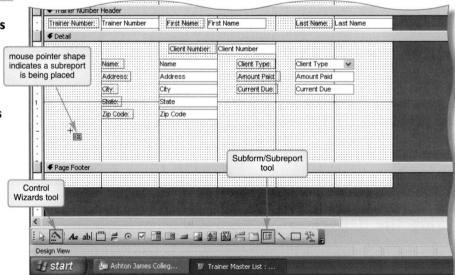

FIGURE 7-10

2

• **Click the position shown in Figure 7-10. Be sure the Use existing Tables and Queries option button is selected.**

The SubReport Wizard dialog box appears (Figure 7-11).

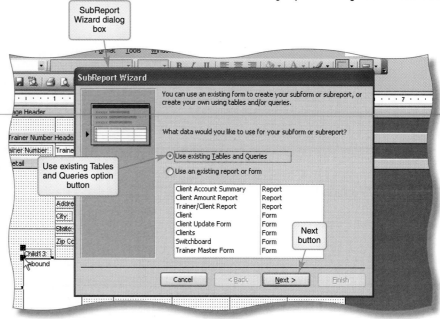

FIGURE 7-11

3

• **Click the Next button. Click the Tables/Queries box arrow.**

The list of available tables and queries appears (Figure 7-12).

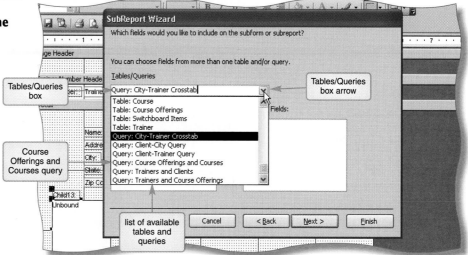

FIGURE 7-12

4

• **Click Query: Course Offerings and Courses, and then click the Add All Fields button.**

All fields in the query are selected (Figure 7-13).

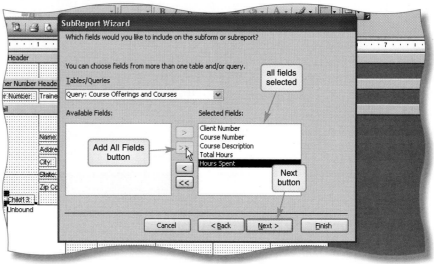

FIGURE 7-13

5

• **Click the Next button and then ensure the "Choose from a list" option button is selected.**

The SubReport Wizard dialog box appears (Figure 7-14). You use this dialog box to indicate the fields that link the main report (referred to as "form" in the sentence) to the subreport (referred to as "subform"). If the fields have the same name, as they often will, you can simply select Choose from a list and then accept the selection Access already has made.

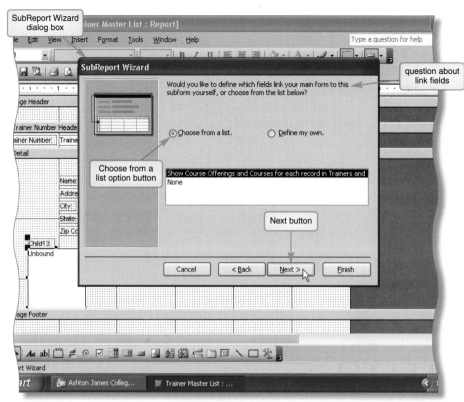

FIGURE 7-14

6

• **Click the Next button and then type** Course Offerings by Client **as the name of the subreport.**

The title is entered (Figure 7-15).

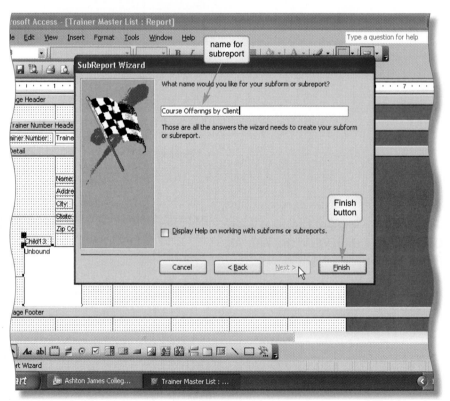

FIGURE 7-15

7

* **Click the Finish button.**
* **If necessary, maximize the window.**
* **If the field list appears, click its Close button.**
* **Drag the subreport to the approximate position shown in Figure 7-16.**

8

* **Close the report design by clicking its Close Window button. Click the Yes button to save the changes.**

The report is saved. The Database window appears.

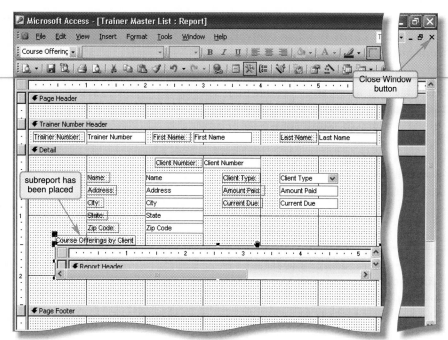

FIGURE 7-16

Modifying the Subreport

The subreport appears as a separate report in the Database window. It can be modified just like any other report. The following steps show how to modify the subreport.

To Modify the Subreport

1

* **Be sure the Reports object is selected, right-click Course Offerings by Client, and then click Design View on the shortcut menu that appears.**
* **If necessary, maximize the window.**
* **Drag the lower boundary of the Report Header section to the approximate position shown in Figure 7-17.**

The design for the subreport appears. The font and style of your headings may be different.

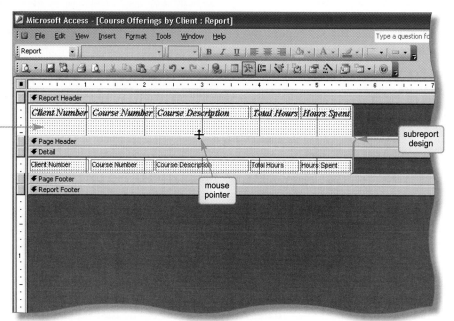

FIGURE 7-17

2

• **Delete the Client Number controls from both the Report Header and Detail sections.**

• **Change the labels in the Report Header section to match those shown in Figure 7-18. (To extend a heading over two lines, press SHIFT+ENTER.)**

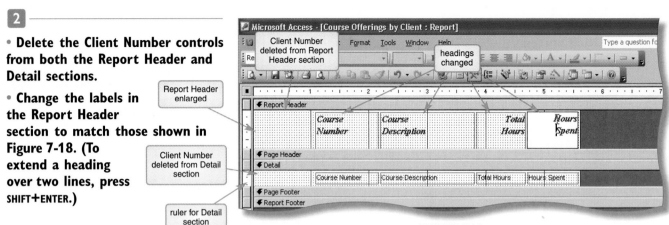

FIGURE 7-18

3

• **Right-click the ruler in the position under the section selector for the detail section to select all the controls in the Detail section and to display the shortcut menu.**

• **Click Properties on the shortcut menu.**

• **Click the Can Grow property, click the arrow that appears, and then click Yes.**

The property sheet appears and the value for the Can Grow property is changed to Yes (Figure 7-19).

4

• **Click the Close button in the Multiple selection property sheet, and then close the subreport by clicking its Close Window button.**

• **Click the Yes button to save the changes.**

The value for the Can Grow property has been changed to Yes. Course description will be spread over several lines.

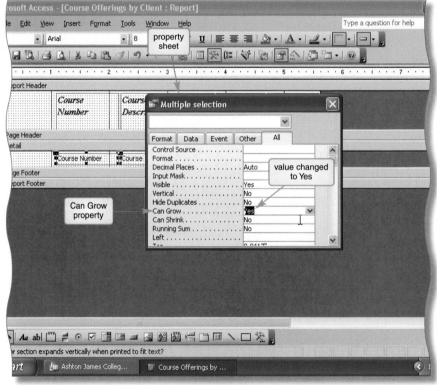

FIGURE 7-19

The subreport has been modified and the changes have been saved.

Adding a Date

To add a date to a report, use the Date and Time command on the Insert menu. When you do, you will be given a choice of date and time formats. After adding the date, you can drag it to the desired position. The following steps demonstrate how to add the date.

To Add a Date

1

• **Be sure the Reports object is selected, right-click Trainer Master List, and then click Design View on the shortcut menu.**

• **If necessary, maximize the window.**

• **Click Insert on the menu bar and then click Date and Time on the Insert menu.**

• **Be sure that Include Date is checked and that Include Time is not checked. Be sure the date format selected is the first of the three options.**

The Date and Time dialog box appears (Figure 7-20).

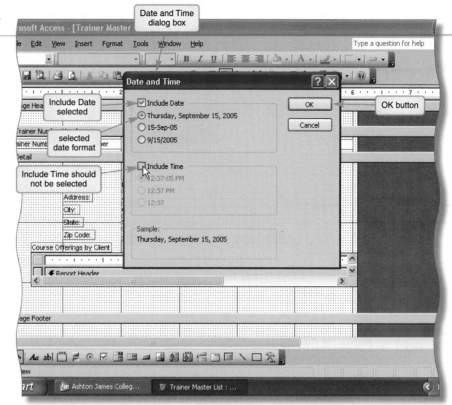

FIGURE 7-20

2

• **Click the OK button to add the date. Click the newly added Date control and point to the boundary but away from any of the handles. The pointer shape changes to a hand as in Figure 7-21.**

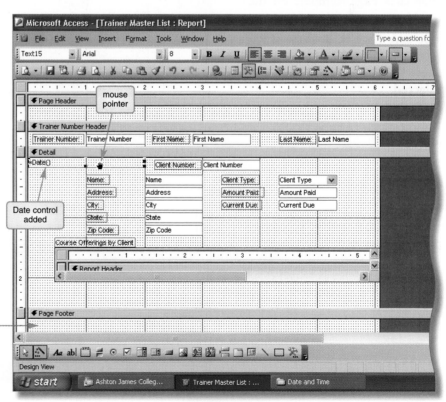

FIGURE 7-21

3

• **Drag the Date control to the position shown in Figure 7-22.**

The date is added to the report.

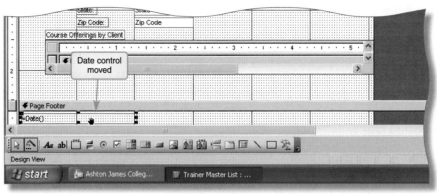

FIGURE 7-22

Adding a Page Number

To add a page number to a report, use the Page Numbers command on the Insert menu. When you do, you will be given a choice of page number formats and positions. The following steps illustrate how to add a page number.

To Add a Page Number

1

• **Click Insert on the menu bar and then click Page Numbers on the Insert menu.**

• **Be sure Page N, Bottom of Page [Footer], Right Alignment, and Show Number on First Page are selected.**

The Page Numbers dialog box appears (Figure 7-23).

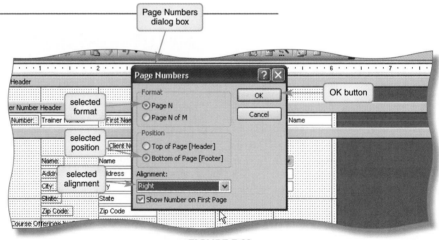

FIGURE 7-23

• **Click the OK button to add a page number.**

The Page Number has been added to the Page Footer (Figure 7-24).

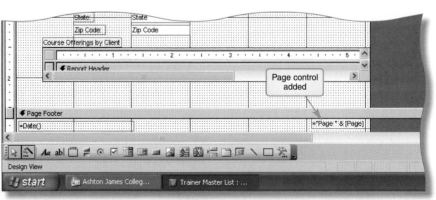

FIGURE 7-24

Adding a Title

A report title is added as a label. Assuming that the title is to appear on each page, it should be added to the page header. (If it only is to appear once at the beginning of the report, it instead would be added to the report header.) The following steps show how to add a title to the page header.

To Add a Title

1

• **Drag the lower boundary of the page header to the approximate position shown in Figure 7-25.**

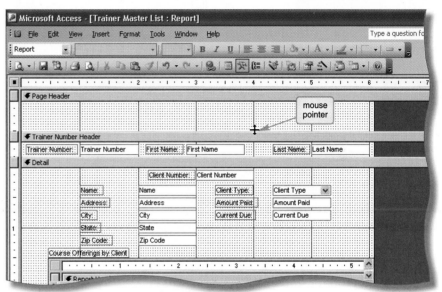

FIGURE 7-25

2

• **Click the Label tool and then move the mouse pointer, which has changed to a plus sign with a label, to the position shown in Figure 7-26.**

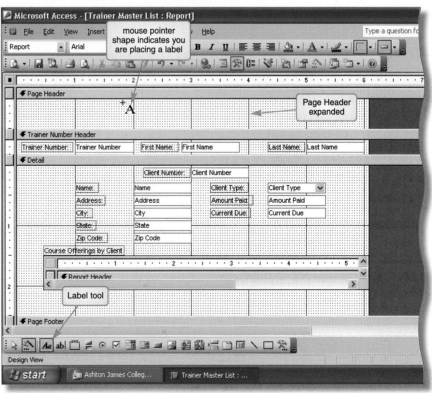

FIGURE 7-26

3

• **Click the mouse pointer in the position in Figure 7-26 on the previous page, and then type** Trainer Master List **as the contents of the label.**

• **Click outside the label to deselect it.**

• **Click the label to select it once again.**

• **Drag the handle in the lower-right corner to expand the label to the size shown in Figure 7-27.**

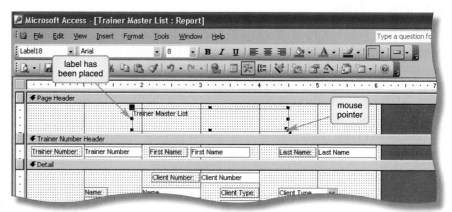

FIGURE 7-27

4

• **Right-click the label containing the title, and then click Properties on the shortcut menu.**

• **Click the down scroll arrow so the Font Size property appears.**

• **Click the Font Size property and then click the Font Size box arrow.**

The list of available font sizes appears (Figure 7-28).

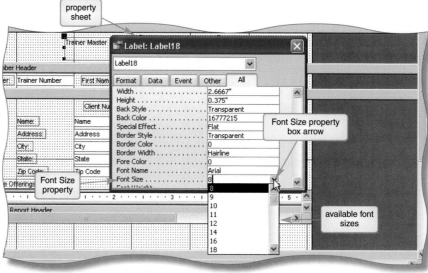

FIGURE 7-28

5

• **Click 18 as the new font size.**

• **Close the property sheet by clicking its Close button.**

• **Drag the right sizing handle of the title so the control better fits the new font size.**

The size of the title is changed (Figure 7-29).

6

• **Close the window containing the report design by clicking its Close Window button.**

• **Click the Yes button to save the changes.**

The report design now is complete.

FIGURE 7-29

Printing a Report

To print a report, right-click the report in the Database window, and then click Print on the shortcut menu. The following steps illustrate how to print the Trainer Master List.

To Print a Report

1 **If necessary, in the Database window, click the Reports object. Right-click Trainer Master List.**

2 **Click Print on the shortcut menu.**

The report prints. It looks similar to the one in Figure 7-1a on page AC 403.

Mailing Labels

In order to print mailing labels, you create a special type of report. When this report prints, the data will appear on the mailing labels aligned correctly and in the order you specify.

Creating Labels

You create labels just as you create reports. There is a wizard, the Label Wizard, that assists you in the process. Using the wizard, you can specify the type and dimensions of the label, the font used for the label, and the content of the label. The following steps illustrate how to create the labels.

To Create Labels

1

• **If necessary, in the Database window, click Tables on the Objects bar, and then click Client. Click the New Object button arrow on the Database window toolbar and then click Report.**

The New Report dialog box appears (Figure 7-30).

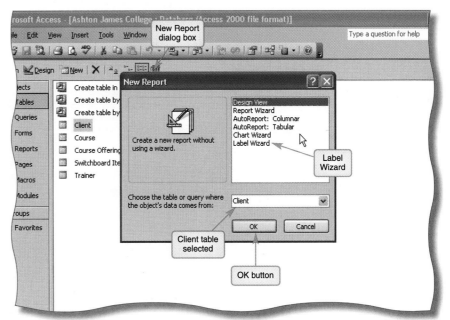

FIGURE 7-30

Microsoft Office
Access 2003

2

• **Click Label Wizard and then click the OK button.**

• **Ensure that English is selected as the Unit of Measure and that Avery is selected in the "Filter by manufacturer" box.**

• **Click C2163 in the Product number list.**

The Label Wizard dialog box appears (Figure 7-31). English and Avery are both selected. Product C2163 is selected.

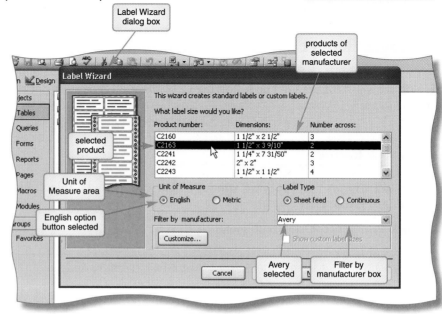

FIGURE 7-31

3

• **Click the Next button.**

The Label Wizard dialog box appears (Figure 7-32). You can use this dialog box to change the font, font size, font weight, and color. You also can specify italics or underlining.

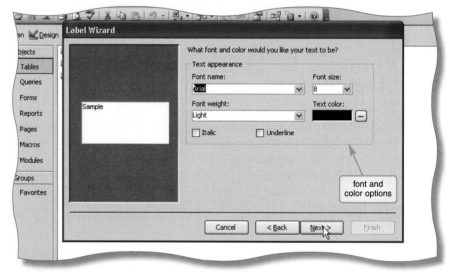

FIGURE 7-32

4

• **Click the Next button to accept the default settings.**

• **Click the Name field and then click the Add Field button.**

The Label Wizard dialog box appears asking for the contents of the mailing labels (Figure 7-33). The Name field has been added to the first row of the label.

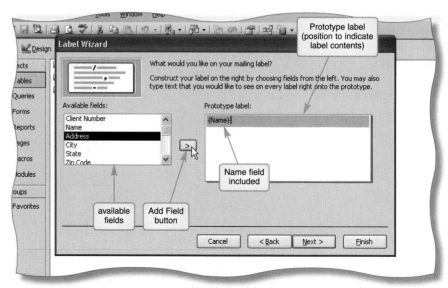

FIGURE 7-33

5

- **Click the second line in the label, and then add the Address field.**
- **Click the third line of the label.**
- **Add the City field, type , (a comma), press the SPACEBAR, add the State field, press the SPACEBAR, and then add the Zip Code field.**

The contents of the label are complete (Figure 7-34).

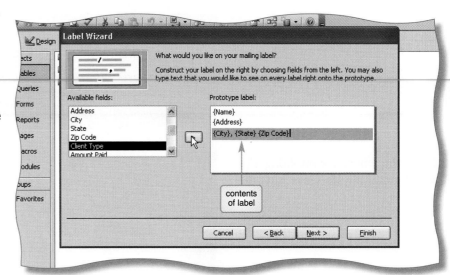

FIGURE 7-34

6

- **Click the Next button.**
- **Select the Zip Code field as the field to sort by, and then click the Add Field button.**

The Zip Code field is selected as the field to sort by (Figure 7-35).

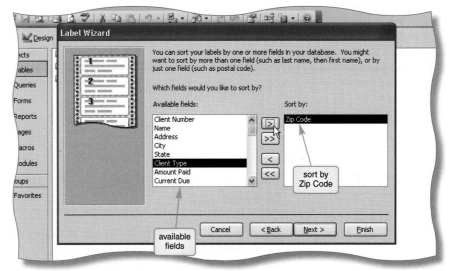

FIGURE 7-35

7

- **Click the Next button.**
- **Ensure the name for the report (that is, the labels) is Labels Client.**

The Label Wizard dialog box appears, requesting a name for the report (Figure 7-36).

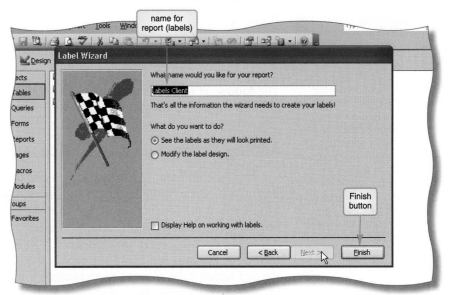

FIGURE 7-36

8

• **Click the Finish button.**

The labels appear (Figure 7-37). They match the ones in Figure 7-1b on page AC 403.

9

• **Close the window containing the labels by clicking its Close button.**

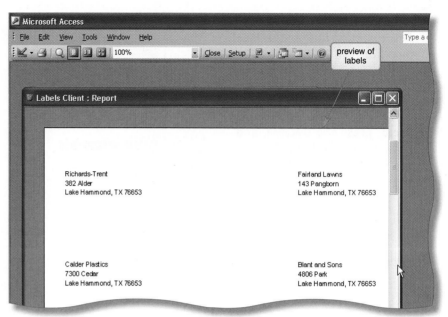

FIGURE 7-37

Printing the Labels

To print the labels, right-click the label report in the Database window, and then click Print on the shortcut menu. The following steps show how to print the labels just created.

To Print Labels

1 **If necessary, in the Database window, click the Reports object. Right-click Labels Client.**

2 **Click Print on the shortcut menu. If a warning message appears, click the OK button.**

The labels print.

Enhancing a Form

The following steps enhance the Client Update Form by adding command buttons and a combo box. In addition, they will place a rectangle around the combo box.

Adding Command Buttons to a Form

To add command buttons, you will use the Control Wizards tool and Command Button tool in the toolbox. Using the series of Command Button Wizard dialog boxes, you must provide the action that should be taken when the button is clicked. Several categories of actions are available.

In the Record Navigation category, you will select the Go To Next Record action for one of the buttons. From the same category, you will select the Go To Previous Record action for another. Other buttons will use the Add New Record and the Delete Record actions from the Record Operations category. The Close Form button will use the Close Form action from the Form Operations category.

The following steps illustrate how to add command buttons to move to the next record, move to the previous record, add a record, delete a record, and close the form.

To Add Command Buttons to a Form

1

• **Click Forms on the Objects bar, and then right-click Client Update Form.**

The shortcut menu appears (Figure 7-38).

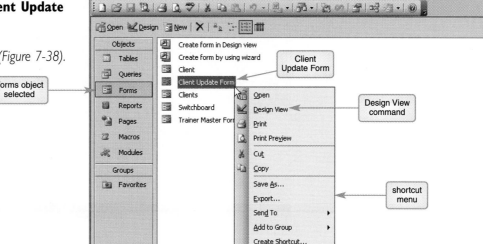

FIGURE 7-38

2

• **Click Design View on the shortcut menu, and ensure the toolbox appears and is docked at the bottom of the screen. (If it does not appear, click the Toolbox button on the toolbar. If it is not docked at the bottom of the screen, drag it to the bottom of the screen to dock it there.)**

• **If a field list appears, remove it by clicking its Close button.**

• **Make sure the Control Wizards tool is selected and the window is maximized.**

The design of the form appears in a maximized window (Figure 7-39).

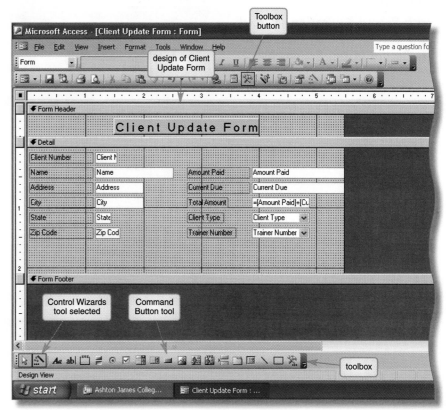

FIGURE 7-39

3

• **Click the Command Button tool and move the mouse pointer, whose shape has changed to a plus sign with a picture of a button, to the position shown in Figure 7-40.**

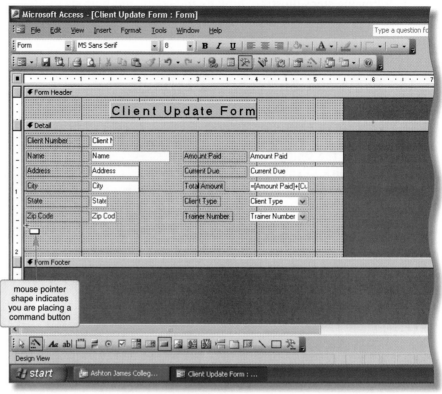

FIGURE 7-40

4

• **Click the position shown in Figure 7-40.**

• **With Record Navigation selected in the Categories box, click Go To Next Record in the Actions box.**

The Command Button Wizard dialog box appears (Figure 7-41). Go To Next Record is selected as the action.

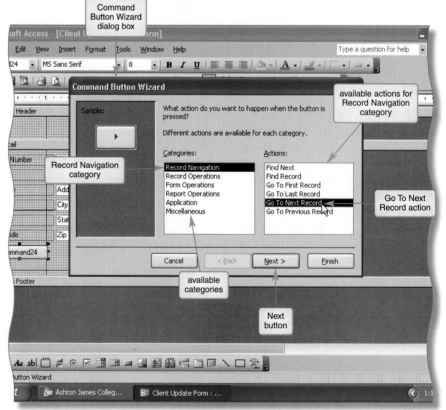

FIGURE 7-41

5

- **Click the Next button.**

The next Command Button Wizard dialog box appears, asking what to display on the button (Figure 7-42). The button can contain either text or a picture.

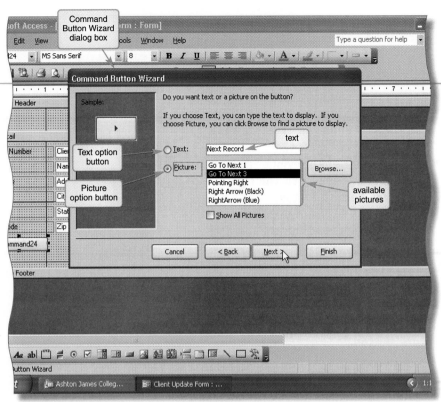

FIGURE 7-42

6

- **Click the Text option button.**
- **Next Record is the desired text and does not need to be changed, so click the Next button.**
- **Type** Next Record **as the name of the button.**

The name of the button appears in the text box (Figure 7-43).

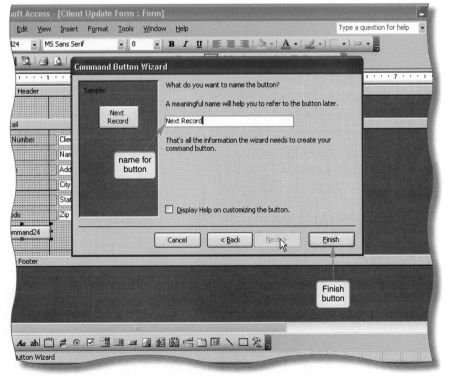

FIGURE 7-43

7

• **Click the Finish button.**

The button appears on the form.

8

• **Use the techniques in Steps 3 through 7 on pages AC 424 through AC 426 to place the Previous Record button directly to the right of the Next Record button.**

• **Click Go To Previous Record in the Actions box, and then type** Previous Record **as the name of the button.**

• **Use the techniques in Steps 3 through 7 to place a button directly to the right of the Previous Record button.**

• **Click Record Operations in the Categories box. Add New Record is the desired action.**

The Command Button Wizard dialog box appears with the selections (Figure 7-44).

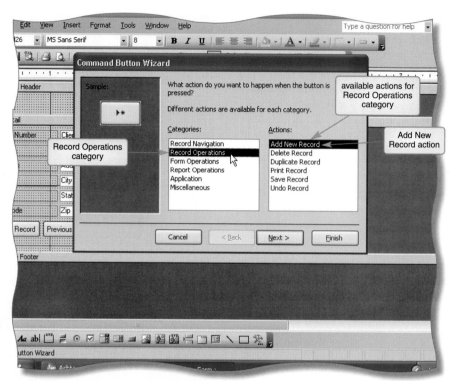

FIGURE 7-44

9

• **Click the Next button and then click Text to indicate that the button is to contain text. Add Record is the desired text.**

• **Click the Next button, type** Add Record **as the name of the button, and then click the Finish button. Use the techniques in Steps 3 through 7 to place the Delete Record and Close Form buttons in the positions shown in Figure 7-45. For the Delete Record button, the category is Record Operations and the action is Delete Record.**

• **For the Close Form button, the category is Form Operations and the action is Close Form.**

• **(If your buttons are not aligned properly, you can drag them to the correct positions.)**

The buttons now have been placed on the form.

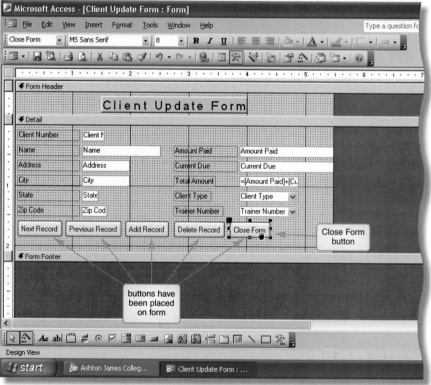

FIGURE 7-45

Combo Boxes

A **combo box**, such as the one shown in Figure 7-1c on page AC 403, combines the properties of a **text box**, a box into which you can type an entry, and a **list box**, a box you can use to display a list. You could type the client's name directly into the box. Alternatively, you can click the Name to Find box arrow, and Access displays a list of client names. To select a name from the list, simply click the name.

Adding a Combo Box to a Form

To create a combo box, use the Combo Box tool in the toolbox. The Combo Box Wizard then will guide you through the steps of adding the combo box. The following steps show how to place a combo box for names on the form.

To Add a Combo Box to a Form

1

• **Make sure the Control Wizards tool is selected, click the Combo Box tool and then move the mouse pointer, whose shape has changed to a small plus sign with a combo box, to the position shown in Figure 7-46.**

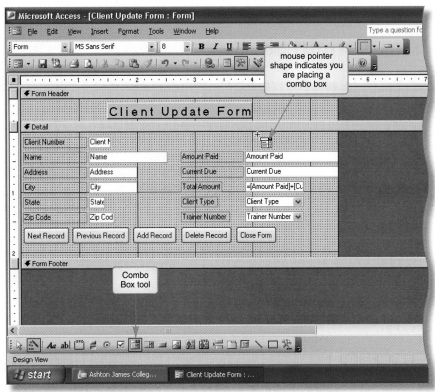

FIGURE 7-46

2

• **Click the position shown in Figure 7-46 on the previous page to place a combo box. Click the "Find a record on my form based on the value I selected in my combo box" option button.**

The Combo Box Wizard dialog box appears, instructing you to indicate how the combo box is to obtain values for the list (Figure 7-47).

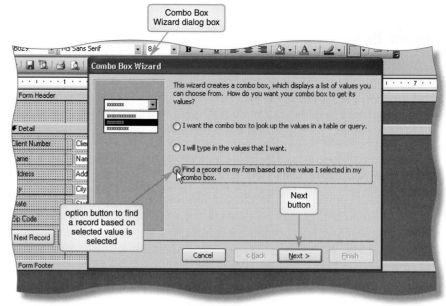

FIGURE 7-47

3

• **Click the Next button, click the Name field, and then click the Add Field button to add Name as a field in the combo box.**

The Name field is selected (Figure 7-48).

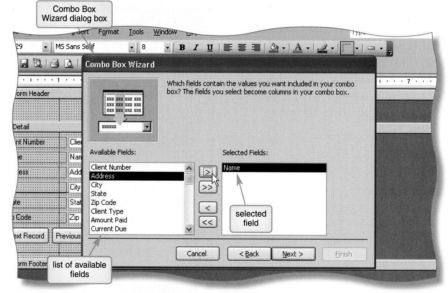

FIGURE 7-48

4

• **Click the Next button.**
• **Point to the right boundary of the column heading.**

The Combo Box Wizard dialog box appears (Figure 7-49) giving you an opportunity to resize the columns in the combo box. The pointer changes to a double-pointing arrow.

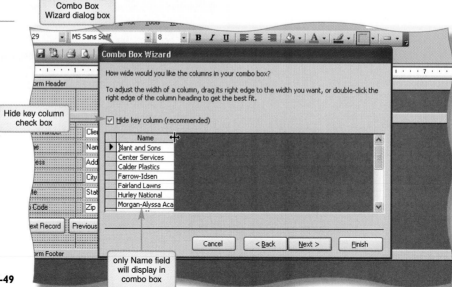

FIGURE 7-49

5

• **Double-click the right boundary of the column heading to resize the column to best fit the data, click the Next button, and then type** &Name to Find **as the label for the combo box.**

The label is entered (Figure 7-50). The ampersand (&) in front of the letter N indicates that users can select the combo box by pressing ALT+N.

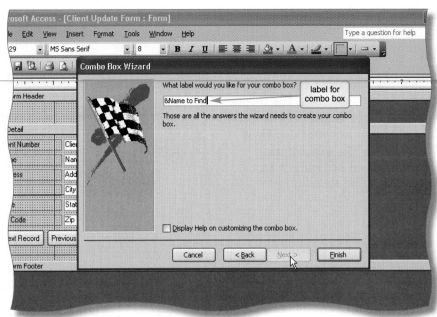

FIGURE 7-50

6

• **Click the Finish button. Position the control and label in the position shown in Figure 7-51.**

The combo box is added. The N in Name is underlined indicating that you can press ALT+N *to select the combo box.*

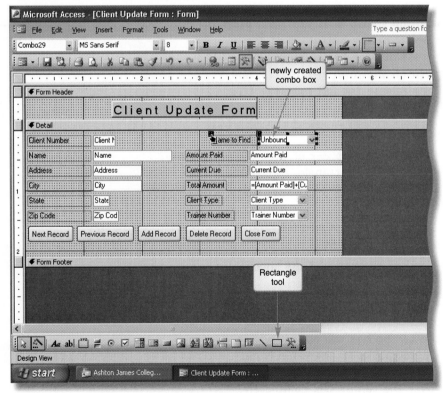

FIGURE 7-51

Placing a Rectangle

In order to emphasize the special nature of the combo box, you will place a rectangle around it. To do so, use the Rectangle tool in the toolbox as the steps on the next page illustrate.

To Place a Rectangle

1

• Click the Rectangle tool in the toolbox and then move the mouse pointer, whose shape has changed to a plus sign accompanied by a rectangle, to the approximate position shown in Figure 7-52.

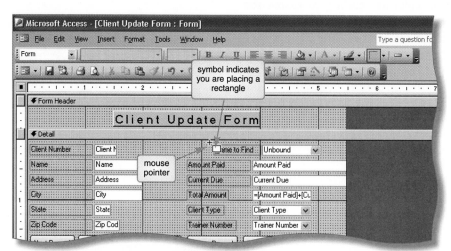

FIGURE 7-52

2

• With the mouse pointer in the position shown in Figure 7-52, press the left mouse button, drag the mouse pointer to the approximate position shown in Figure 7-53, and then release the left mouse button.

3

• Point to the border of the newly created rectangle, right-click, and then click Properties on the shortcut menu.

• Be sure to point to the rectangle, not the combo box.

• Change the value of the Special Effect property to Raised.

• Make sure the value of the Back Style property is Transparent, so the combo box will appear within the rectangle. (If the value is not Transparent, the rectangle would cover the combo box completely and the combo box would not be visible.)

• Close the Rectangle property sheet by clicking its Close button.

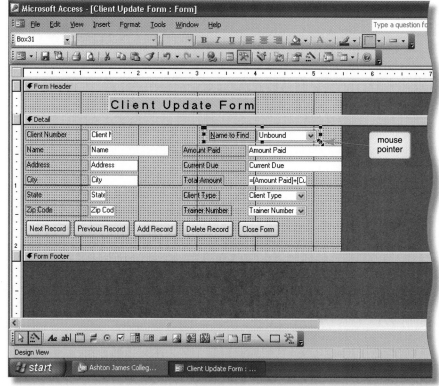

FIGURE 7-53

Closing and Saving a Form

To close a form, close the window using the window's Close button. Then indicate whether you want to save your changes. The following step shows how to close and save the form.

To Close and Save a Form

1 Click the Client Update Form : Form window's Close Window button to close the window, and then click the Yes button to save the design of the form.

Opening a Form

To open a form in the Database window, use the Open command on the shortcut menu. The form will appear and can be used to examine and update data. The following step shows how to open the Client Update Form.

To Open a Form

1

- **With Forms selected on the Objects bar, right-click the Client Update Form to display the shortcut menu.**
- **Click Open on the shortcut menu.**

The form appears with the added buttons and combo box (Figure 7-54).

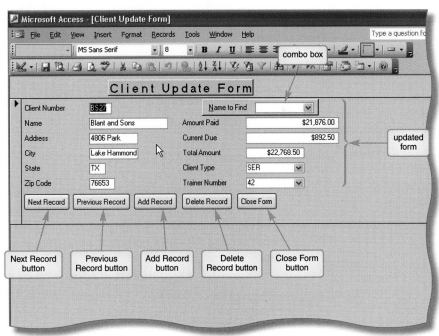

FIGURE 7-54

Using the Buttons

To move around on the form, you can use the buttons to perform the actions you specify. To move to the next record, click the Next Record button. Click the Previous Record button to move to the previous record. Clicking the Delete Record button will delete the record currently on the screen. You will get a message requesting you to verify the deletion before the record actually is deleted. Clicking the Close Form button will remove the form from the screen.

Clicking the Add Record button will clear the contents of the form so you can add a new record. The following step shows how to use the Add Record button.

To Use the Add Record Button

1

• **Click the Add Record button.**

The contents of the form are cleared in preparation for adding a new record (Figure 7-55).

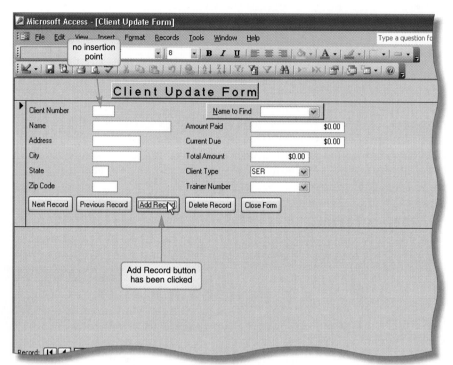

FIGURE 7-55

On the form in Figure 7-55, the contents are cleared, but an insertion point does not appear. Therefore, to begin entering a record, you would have to click the Client Number field before you can start typing. To ensure that an insertion point appears in the Client Number field text box when you click the Add Record button, you must change the focus.

A control is said to have the **focus** when it becomes active; that is, when it becomes able to receive user input through mouse or keyboard actions. At any point in time, only one item on the form has the focus. The Add Record button needs to update the focus to the Client Number field.

Using the Combo Box

Using the combo box, you can search for a client in two ways. First, you can click the combo box arrow to display a list of client names, and then select the name from the list by clicking it. Alternatively, you can begin typing the name. As you type, Access will display automatically the name that begins with the letters you have typed. Once the correct name is displayed, select the name by pressing the TAB key. Regardless of the method you use, the data for the selected client appears on the form once the selection is made.

The following steps first show how to locate the client whose name is Hurley National, and then use the Next Record button to move to the next client.

To Use the Combo Box

1

• **Click the Name to Find box arrow.**

*The list of names appears (Figure 7-56).
The list is not in alphabetical order.*

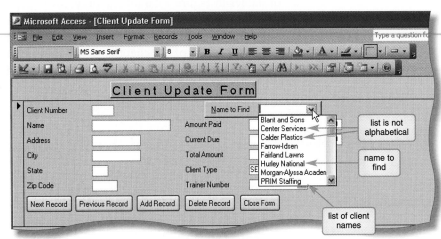

FIGURE 7-56

2

• **Click Hurley National.**

*The data for the client whose name is
Hurley National appears on the form
(Figure 7-57).*

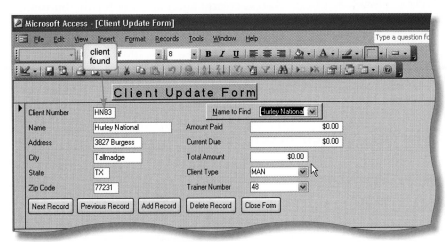

FIGURE 7-57

3

Click the Next Record button.

*The data for the client whose name is
Morgan-Alyssa Academy appears on the
form (Figure 7-58). The combo box still
contains Hurley National.*

FIGURE 7-58

Issues with the Combo Box

Consider the following issues with the combo box. First, if you examine the list of names in Figure 7-56 on the previous page, you will see that they are not in alphabetical order (Center Services comes before Calder Plastics). Second, when you move to a record without using the combo box, the name in the combo box does not change to reflect the name of the client currently on the screen. Third, one way to change the focus from one field to another is to press the TAB key. As you repeatedly press the TAB key, the focus should move through all the fields on the form. It should not move to the combo box, however, because that does not represent a field to be updated.

Modifying the Add Record Button

To display an insertion point automatically when you click the Add Record button, you need to change the focus. To do so, you will use Visual Basic for Applications (VBA). You first must change the name of the control for the Client Number field to a name that does not contain spaces, because spaces are not permitted in names in VBA. You will replace the space with an underscore (_) giving the name, Client_Number. Next, you must add a statement to the VBA code that Access creates automatically for the button click event. The added statement, Client_Number.SetFocus, will move the focus to the control for the Client Number field as soon as the button is clicked.

The following steps illustrate how to change the name of the Client Number control to Client_Number and then add an additional statement to the VBA code that will set the focus to Client_Number.

To Modify the Add Record Button

1

• **Click the View button on the toolbar to return to Design view.**

• **Right-click the control for the Client Number field (the white space, not the label), and then click Properties on the shortcut menu.**

• **Ensure the Name property is selected.**

• **Use the DELETE or BACKSPACE key to erase the current value, and then type Client_Number as the new name.**

The name is changed (Figure 7-59).

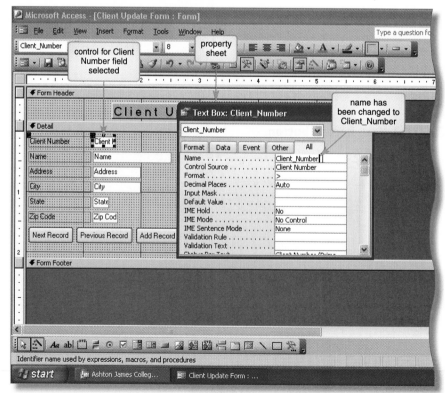

FIGURE 7-59

2

• **Click the Close button to close the Text Box: Client Number property sheet.**

• **Right-click the Add Record button.**

The shortcut menu appears (Figure 7-60).

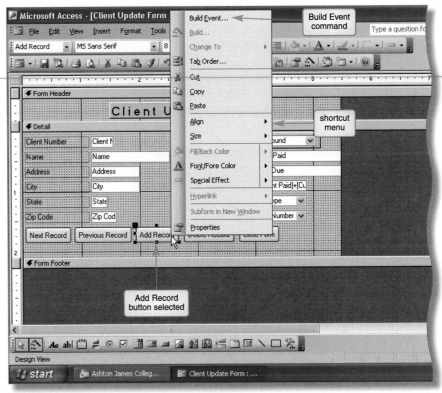

FIGURE 7-60

3

• **Click Build Event on the shortcut menu.**

• **Make sure the window is maximized.**

The VBA code for the Add Record button appears (Figure 7-61). The important line in this code is DoCmd, which stands for Do Command. Following DoCmd, is the command, formally called a method, that will be executed; in this case GoToRecord. Following GoToRecord are the arguments, which are items that provide information that will be used by the method. The only argument necessary in this case is acNewRec. This is a code that indicates that Access is to move to the new record at the end of the table; that is, the position where the new record will be added. This command will not set the focus to any particular field automatically, however, so an insertion point still will not be produced.

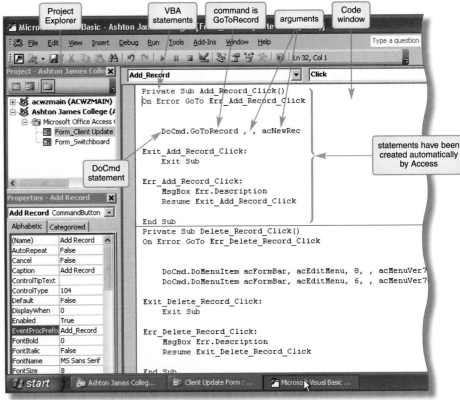

FIGURE 7-61

4

• **Press the down arrow key four times, press the TAB key, and then type** `Client_Number.SetFocus` **as the additional statement.**

• **Press the ENTER key.**

The statement is entered (Figure 7-62). While typing, a box may appear indicating selections for the statement. You may ignore this list. This statement will set the focus in the control named Client_Number as soon as the previous statement (GoToRecord) is executed.

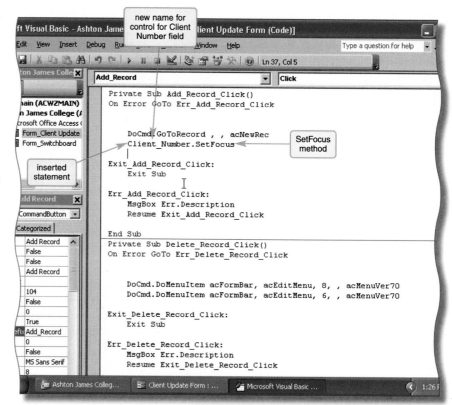

FIGURE 7-62

5

• **Close the Microsoft Visual Basic - Ashton James College - [Form_Client Update Form (Code)] window.**

• **Click the View button arrow on the toolbar, click Form View, and then click the Add Record button.**

An insertion point appears in the Client Number field (Figure 7-63).

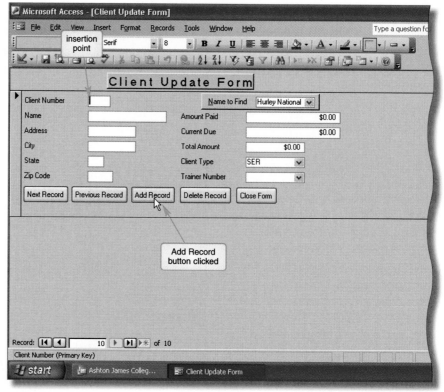

FIGURE 7-63

The large window on the right in Figure 7-61 on page AC 435 is called the Code window. This is the area where you create and modify Visual Basic code. The window on the left is called the Project Explorer, which allows you to navigate among various objects contained in the database on which you are working. The steps in this project do not rely on the Project Explorer and the window may or may not appear on your screen.

Modifying the Combo Box

The following steps modify the query that Access has created for the combo box so the data is sorted by name. The steps then modify the code associated with the On Current event property of the entire form. The modification to the On Current event property will ensure that the combo box is kept current with the rest of the form; that is, it contains the name of the client whose number currently appears in the Client Number field. The final step changes the Tab Stop property for the combo box from Yes to No.

To Modify the Combo Box

1

• **Click the View button on the toolbar to return to Design view.**

• **Right-click the Name to Find combo box (the white space, not the label), and then click Properties on the shortcut menu.**

• **Note the number of your combo box, which may be different from the one shown in Figure 7-64, because it will be important later.**

• **Click the Row Source property.**

The Combo Box: Combo29 property sheet appears. The combo box number is 29 (Combo29). (Yours may be different.) The Row Source property is selected. Depending on where you clicked the Row Source property, the value may or may not be highlighted.

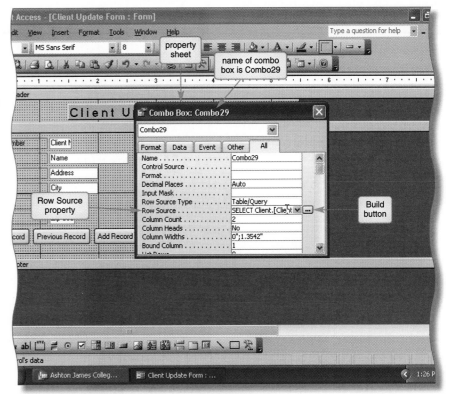

FIGURE 7-64

2

• **Click the Build button.**

The SQL Statement : Query Builder window appears (Figure 7-65). This screen allows you to make changes just as you did when you created queries.

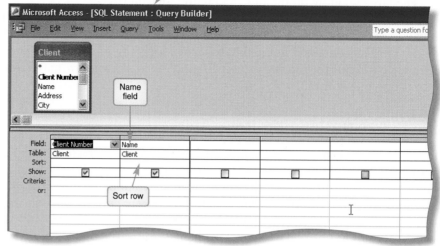

SQL Statement :
Query Builder
window

Name
field

Sort row

FIGURE 7-65

3

• **Click the Sort row in the Name field, click the box arrow that appears, and then click Ascending.**

The sort order is changed to Ascending (Figure 7-66).

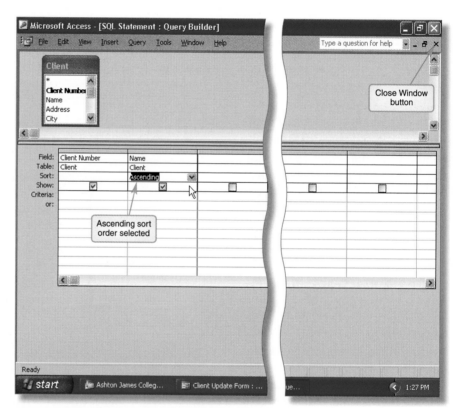

Close Window
button

Ascending sort
order selected

FIGURE 7-66

4

• **Close the SQL Statement : Query Builder window by clicking its Close Window button.**

The Microsoft Office Access dialog box appears (Figure 7-67).

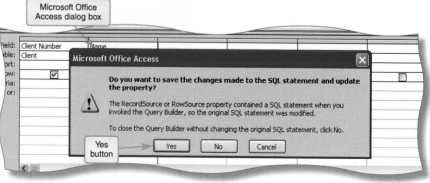

Microsoft Office
Access dialog box

Microsoft Office Access

Do you want to save the changes made to the SQL statement and update the property?

The RecordSource or RowSource property contained a SQL statement when you invoked the Query Builder, so the original SQL statement was modified.

To close the Query Builder without changing the original SQL statement, click No.

Yes
button

[Yes]   [No]   [Cancel]

FIGURE 7-67

5

- **Click the Yes button to change the property, and then close the Combo Box: Combo29 property sheet.**

- **Right-click the form selector (the box in the upper-left corner of the form).**

The shortcut menu for the form appears (Figure 7-68).

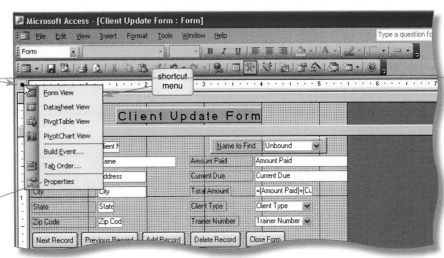

FIGURE 7-68

6

- **Click Properties on the shortcut menu.**

- **Click the down scroll arrow on the Form property sheet until the On Current property appears, and then click the On Current property.**

The Form property sheet appears (Figure 7-69).

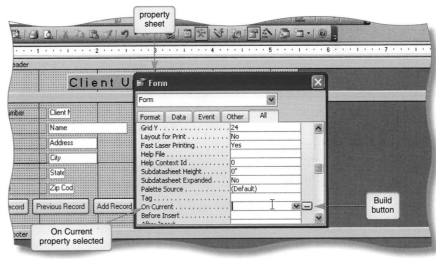

FIGURE 7-69

7

- **Click the Build button and then click Code Builder.**

The Choose Builder dialog box appears (Figure 7-70). Code Builder is selected.

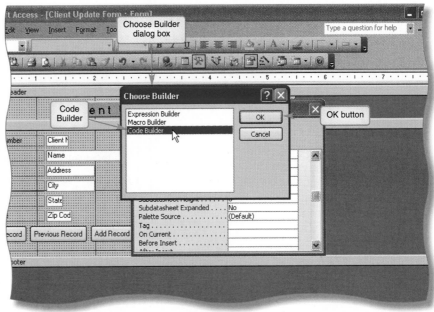

FIGURE 7-70

8

• **Click the OK button.**

Access displays the code generated for the form (Figure 7-71).

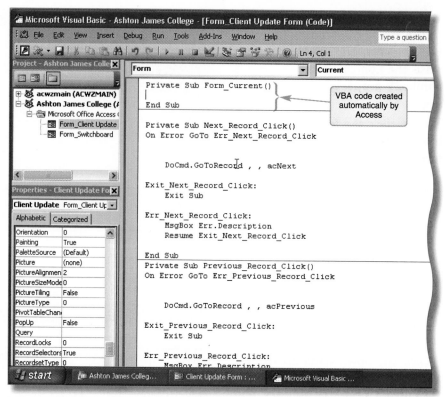

FIGURE 7-71

9

• **Press the TAB key and then type** Combo29 = Client_Number ' Update the combo box **in the position shown in Figure 7-72.**

This statement assumes your combo box is Combo29. If yours has a different number, use your number in the statement instead of 29. This statement will update the contents of the combo box using the client number currently in the Client_Number control. The portion of the statement following the apostrophe is a comment, describing the purpose of the statement.

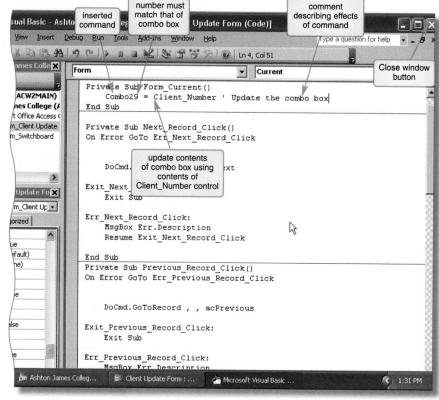

FIGURE 7-72

Click the Close button for the Microsoft Visual Basic - Ashton James College - [Form_Client Update Form (Code)] window, and then close the Form property sheet.

Right-click the Name to Find combo box and then click Properties on the shortcut menu.

Click the down scroll arrow until the Tab Stop property appears, click the Tab Stop property, and then click the Tab Stop property box arrow.

The property sheet for the combo box appears (Figure 7-73).

11

Click No, and then close the Combo Box: Combo29 property sheet.

The modifications to the combo box are complete.

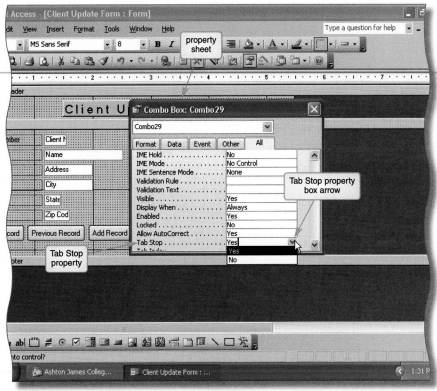

FIGURE 7-73

Using the Modified Combo Box

The problems with the combo box now are corrected. The steps on the next page show how to first search for the client whose name is Hurley National, and then move to the next record in the table to verify that the combo box also will be updated.

To Use the Modified Combo Box

1

• **Click the View button on the toolbar to display the Client Update Form in Form view, and then click the Name to Find box arrow.**

A list of names appears (Figure 7-74). The list is in alphabetical order. (Center Services now comes after Calder Plastics, as it should.)

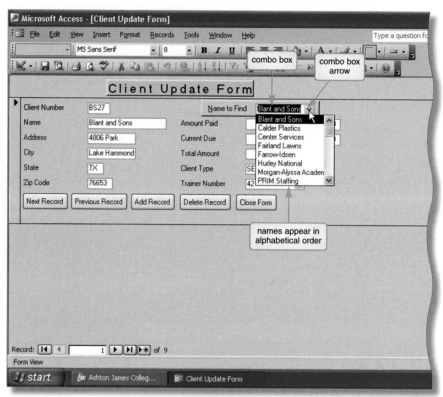

FIGURE 7-74

2

• **Click Hurley National.**

Client HN83 (Hurley National) appears on the form (Figure 7-75).

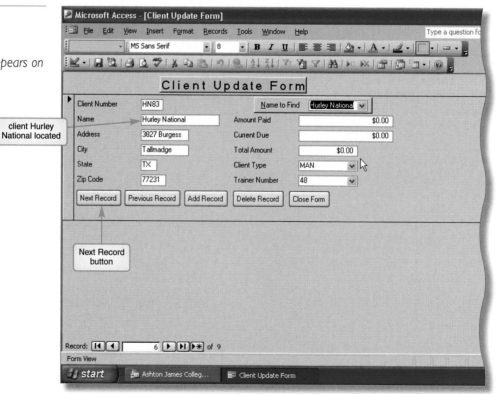

FIGURE 7-75

3

• **Click the Next Record button.**

Client Morgan-Alyssa Academy appears on the form (Figure 7-76). The client's name also appears in the combo box.

4

• **Close the form by clicking its Close Window button, and then click the Yes button to save the changes.**

The changes are saved.

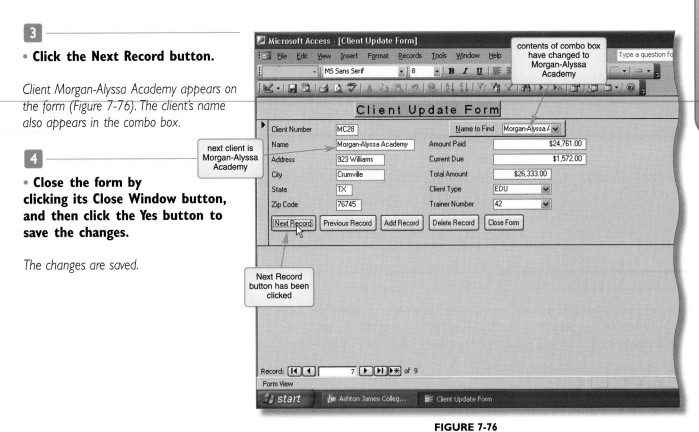

FIGURE 7-76

Closing the Database and Quitting Access

The following steps close the database and quit Access.

To Close a Database and Quit Access

1 Click the Close Window button for the Ashton James College : Database window.

2 Click the Close button for the Microsoft Access window.

More About

Microsoft Certification

The Microsoft Office Specialist Certification program provides an opportunity for you to obtain a valuable industry credential — proof that you have the Access 2003 skills required by employers. For more information, see Appendix E, or visit the Access 2003 Certification Web page (scsite.com/ac2003/cert).

Project Summary

In Project 7, you created the queries to be used by a report. You then learned how to create the report from scratch, using Design view rather than the Report Wizard. In the report, you saw how to use grouping and how to include a subreport. You next learned how to create mailing labels for the Client table. You then learned how to add command buttons to a form and how to create a combo box that can be used for searching. Finally, you learned how to modify a command button and a combo box using Visual Basic for Applications.

If you have a SAM user profile, you may have access to hands-on instruction, practice, and assessment of the skills covered in this project. Log in to your SAM account and go to your assignments page to see what your instructor has assigned.

What You Should Know

Having completed this project, you should be able to perform the tasks below. The tasks are listed in the same order they were presented in this project. For a list of the buttons, menus, toolbars, and commands introduced in this project, see the Quick Reference Summary at the back of this book and refer to the Page Number column.

1. Open a Database   (AC 404)
2. Create Queries for the Report   (AC 405)
3. Create an Initial Report   (AC 406)
4. Add Fields to the Report   (AC 408)
5. Save the Report   (AC 410)
6. Add a Subreport   (AC 410)
7. Modify the Subreport   (AC 413)
8. Add a Date   (AC 415)
9. Add a Page Number   (AC 416)
10. Add a Title   (AC 417)
11. Print a Report   (AC 419)
12. Create Labels   (AC 419)
13. Print Labels   (AC 422)
14. Add Command Buttons to a Form   (AC 423)
15. Add a Combo Box to a Form   (AC 427)
16. Place a Rectangle   (AC 430)
17. Close and Save a Form   (AC 431)
18. Open a Form   (AC 431)
19. Use the Add Record Button   (AC 432)
20. Use the Combo Box   (AC 433)
21. Modify the Add Record Button   (AC 434)
22. Modify the Combo Box   (AC 437)
23. Use the Modified Combo Box   (AC 442)
24. Close a Database and Quit Access   (AC 443)

Learn It Online

Instructions: To complete the Learn It Online exercises, start your browser, click the Address bar, and then enter the Web address scsite.com/ac2003/learn. When the Access 2003 Learn It Online page is displayed, follow the instructions in the exercises below. Each exercise has instructions for printing your results, either for your own records or for submission to your instructor.

1 Project Reinforcement TF, MC, and SA

Below Access Project 7, click the Project Reinforcement link. Print the quiz by clicking Print on the File menu for each page. Answer each question.

2 Flash Cards

Below Access Project 7, click the Flash Cards link and read the instructions. Type 20 (or a number specified by your instructor) in the Number of playing cards text box, type your name in the Enter your Name text box, and then click the Flip Card button. When the flash card is displayed, read the question and then click the ANSWER box arrow to select an answer. Flip through Flash Cards. If your score is 15 (75%) correct or greater, click Print on the File menu to print your results. If your score is less than 15 (75%) correct, then redo this exercise by clicking the Replay button.

3 Practice Test

Below Access Project 7, click the Practice Test link. Answer each question, enter your first and last name at the bottom of the page, and then click the Grade Test button. When the graded practice test is displayed on your screen, click Print on the File menu to print a hard copy. Continue to take practice tests until you score 80% or better.

4 Who Wants To Be a Computer Genius?

Below Access Project 7, click the Computer Genius link. Read the instructions, enter your first and last name at the bottom of the page, and then click the PLAY button. When your score is displayed, click the PRINT RESULTS link to print a hard copy.

5 Wheel of Terms

Below Access Project 7, click the Wheel of Terms link. Read the instructions, and then enter your first and last name and your school name. Click the PLAY button. When your score is displayed, right-click the score and then click Print on the shortcut menu to print a hard copy.

6 Crossword Puzzle Challenge

Below Access Project 7, click the Crossword Puzzle Challenge link. Read the instructions, and then enter your first and last name. Click the SUBMIT button. Work the crossword puzzle. When you are finished, click the Submit button. When the crossword puzzle is redisplayed, click the Print Puzzle button to print a hard copy.

7 Tips and Tricks

Below Access Project 7, click the Tips and Tricks link. Click a topic that pertains to Project 7. Right-click the information and then click Print on the shortcut menu. Construct a brief example of what the information relates to in Access to confirm you understand how to use the tip or trick.

8 Newsgroups

Below Access Project 7, click the Newsgroups link. Click a topic that pertains to Project 7. Print three comments.

9 Expanding Your Horizons

Below Access Project 7, click the Expanding Your Horizons link. Click a topic that pertains to Project 7. Print the information. Construct a brief example of what the information relates to in Access to confirm you understand the contents of the article.

10 Search Sleuth

Below Access Project 7, click the Search Sleuth link. To search for a term that pertains to this project, select a term below the Project 7 title and then use the Google search engine at google.com (or any major search engine) to display and print two Web pages that present information on the term.

11 Access Online Training

Below Access Project 7, click the Access Online Training link. When your browser displays the Microsoft Office Online Web page, click the Access link. Click one of the Access courses that covers one or more of the objectives listed at the beginning of the project on page AC 402. Print the first page of the course before stepping through it.

12 Office Marketplace

Below Access Project 7, click the Office Marketplace link. When your browser displays the Microsoft Office Online Web page, click the Office Marketplace link. Click a topic that relates to Access. Print the first page.

Apply Your Knowledge

1 Applying Advanced Report and Form Techniques to the Begon Pest Control Database

Instructions: Start Access. If you are using the Microsoft Office Access 2003 Comprehensive text, open the Begon Pest Control database that you used in Project 6. Otherwise, see your instructor for information on accessing the files required for this book. Perform the following tasks:

1. Create a query that joins the Technician and Customer tables. Include the Technician Number, First Name, and Last Name fields from the Technician table. Include all fields except the technician number from the Customer table. Save the query as Technicians and Customers.

2. Create a query that joins the Work Orders and Category tables. Include the Customer Number, Category Number, Category Description, and Total Hours (est) fields. Save the query as Work Orders and Categories.

3. Create the report shown in Figure 7-77. The report uses the two queries that you created in Steps 1 and 2. Be sure to include the current date and page numbers on the report. Use the name Technician Master List for the report. The report is in the same style as that demonstrated in the project. Print the report.

4. Create mailing labels for the Customer table. Use Avery labels C2163 and format the label with name on the first line, address on the second line, and city, state, and Zip code on the third line. There is a comma and a space after city and a space between state and Zip code. Sort the labels by Zip code. Print the mailing labels.

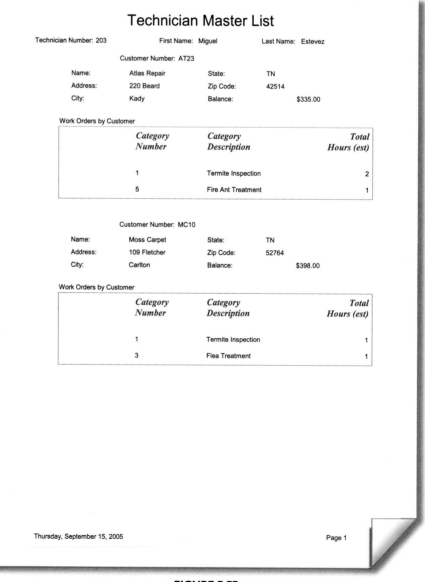

FIGURE 7-77

Apply Your Knowledge

5. Modify the Customer Update Form to create the form shown in Figure 7-78. The form includes command buttons and a combo box to search for customers by name. Be sure to sort the names in ascending order, place a rectangle around the combo box, and update the combo box. The user should not be able to tab to the combo box. When the Add Record button is clicked, the insertion point should be in the Customer Number field.

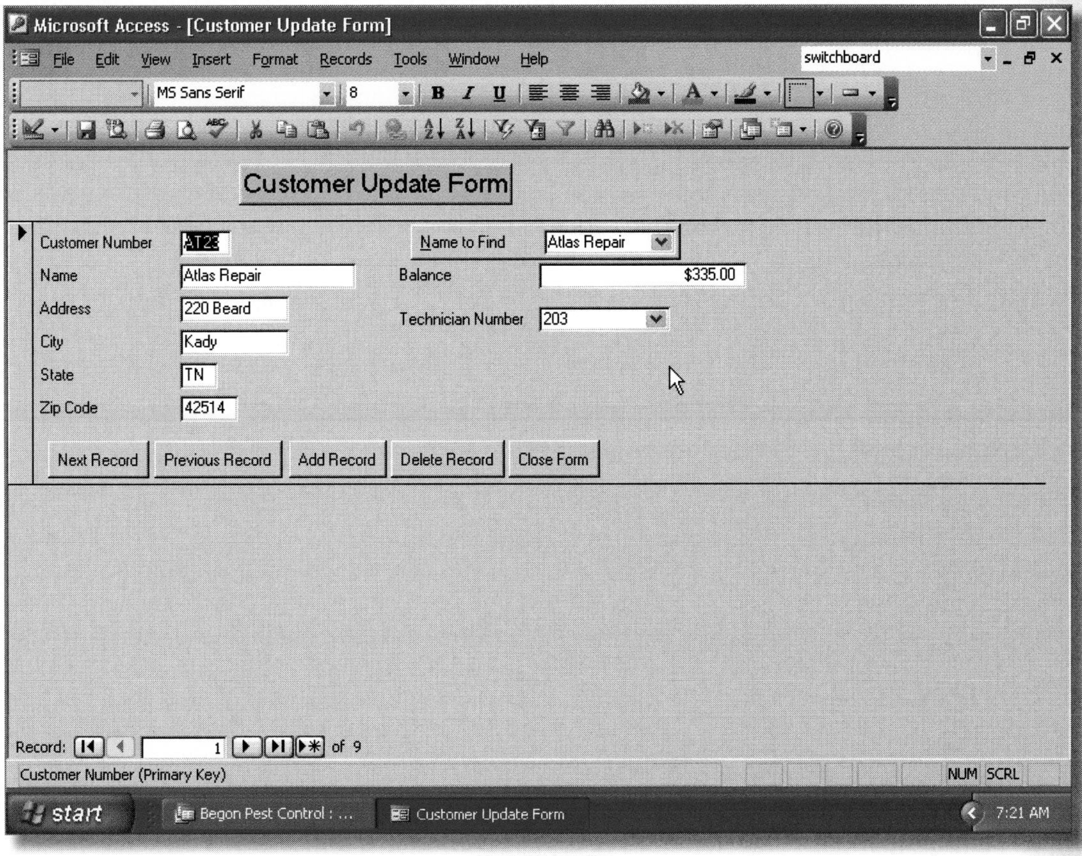

FIGURE 7-78

6. Save and print the form. To print the form, open the form, click File on the menu bar, click Print, and then click Selected Record(s) as the print range. Click the OK button.

In the Lab

1 Applying Advanced Report and Form Techniques to the Birds2U Database

Problem: The management of Birds2U needs a report that displays supplier information as well as information about items and the order status of items. Because employees frequently correspond with suppliers by mail, the company also would like mailing labels. Finally, management would like some improvements to the Item Update Form. This includes placing buttons on the form to make it easier to perform tasks such as adding a record and closing the form as well as an easier way to search for an item given its description.

Instructions: If you are using the Microsoft Office Access 2003 Comprehensive text, open the Birds2U database that you used in Project 6. Otherwise, see your instructor for information on accessing the files required for this book. Perform the following tasks:

1. Create the report shown in Figure 7-79. The report uses the Suppliers and Items query that was previously created as the basis for the main report and the Reorder table as the basis for the subreport. Be sure to include the current date and page numbers on the report. Use the name Supplier Master Report for the report. The report is the same style as that demonstrated in the project. Print the report.

2. Create mailing labels for the Supplier table. Use Avery labels C2163 and format the label with name on the first line, address on the second line, and city, state, and Zip code on the third line. There is a comma and a space after city and a space between state and Zip code. Sort the labels by Zip code. Print the mailing labels.

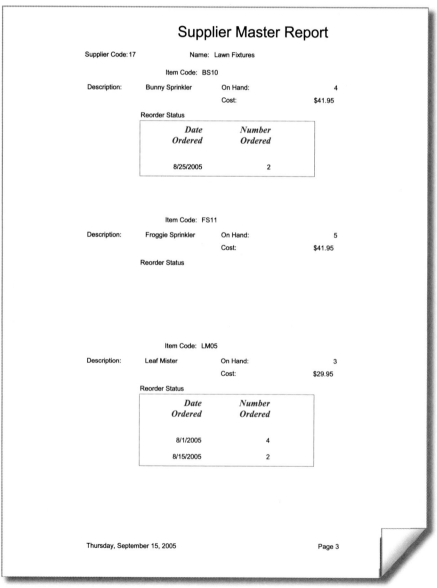

FIGURE 7-79

In the Lab

3. Modify the Item Update Form to create the form shown in Figure 7-80. The form includes command buttons and a combo box to search for items by description. Be sure to sort the descriptions in ascending order, place a rectangle around the combo box, and update the combo box. The user should not be able to tab to the combo box. When the Add Record button is clicked, the insertion point should be in the Item Code field.

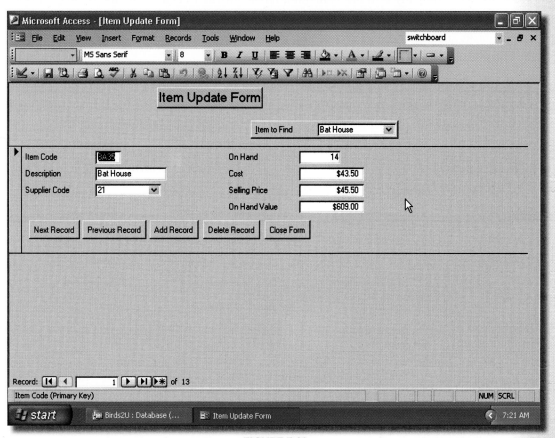

FIGURE 7-80

4. Save and print the form. To print the form, open the form, click File on the menu bar, click Print, and then click Selected Record(s) as the print range. Click the OK button.

In the Lab

2 Applying Advanced Report and Form Techniques to the Babbage Bookkeeping Database

Problem: Babbage Bookkeeping needs a report that displays bookkeeper information as well as information about client accounts. The company also needs mailing labels for their clients. Finally, Babbage Bookkeeping would like some improvements to the Client Update Form. This includes placing buttons on the form to make it easier to perform tasks such as adding a record and closing the form as well as an easier way to search for a client given the client's name.

Instructions: If you are using the Microsoft Office Access 2003 Comprehensive text, open the Babbage Bookkeeping database that you used in Project 6. Otherwise, see your instructor for information on accessing the files required for this book.

Perform the following tasks:

1. Create the report shown in Figure 7-81. The report uses a query as the basis for the main report and the Accounts table as the basis for the subreport. Be sure to include the current date and page numbers on the report. Use the name Bookkeeper Master List for the report. The report is in a similar style as that demonstrated in the project. Note that the page number format is different. Print the report.

2. Create mailing labels for the Client table. Use Avery labels C2163 and format the label with name on the first line, address on the second line, and city, state, and Zip code on the third line. Because the database does not include a state field, type the two-letter abbreviation for your state on the third line in the appropriate location. There is a comma and a space after city and a space between state and Zip code. Sort the labels by Zip code. Print the mailing labels.

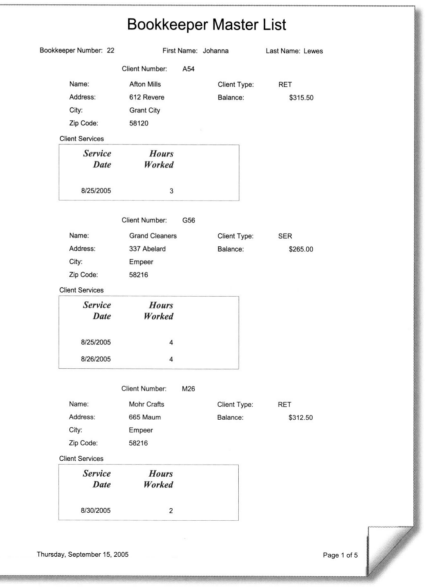

FIGURE 7-81

3. Modify the Client Update Form to create the form shown in Figure 7-82. The form includes command buttons and a combo box to search for clients by name. The command buttons display pictures rather than text. The current date appears in the form header. Be sure to sort the names in ascending order, place a rectangle around the combo box, and update the combo box. The user should not be able to tab to the combo box. When the Add Record button is clicked, the insertion point should be in the Client Number field.

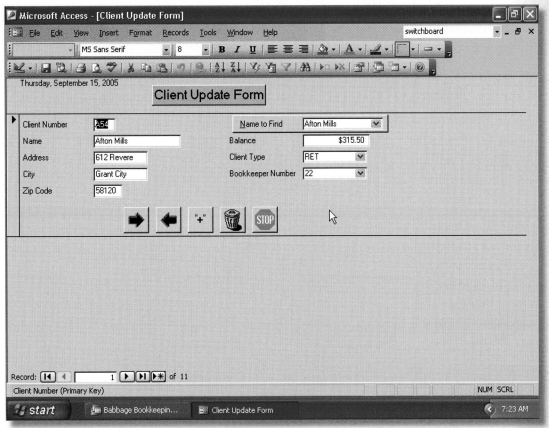

FIGURE 7-82

4. Save and print the form. To print the form, open the form, click File on the menu bar, click Print, and then click Selected Record(s) as the print range. Click the OK button.

In the Lab

3 Applying Advanced Report and Form Techniques to the City Guide Database

Problem: The chamber of commerce needs a report that displays ad rep information as well as information about advertisers. The company also needs mailing labels for their ad reps. Finally, the chamber would like some improvements to the Advertiser Update Form. This includes placing buttons on the form to make it easier to perform tasks such as adding a record and closing the form as well as an easier way to search for an advertiser given the advertiser's name.

Instructions: If you are using the Microsoft Office Access 2003 Comprehensive text, open the City Guide database that you used in Project 6. Otherwise, see your instructor for information on accessing the files required for this book.

Instructions Part 1: Create the report shown in Figure 7-83. The report is similar in style to that demonstrated in the project.

Instructions Part 2: Create mailing labels for the Ad Rep table. Because the database does not include a state field, type the two-letter abbreviation for your state on the third line in the appropriate location.

Instructions Part 3: Modify the Advertiser Update Form to create a form similar to that shown in Figure 7-82 on the previous page. You can use either text or a picture on a command button.

Ad Rep Master Report

Advertiser Number: P124

Name:	Palace Theatre		
Address:	22 Main	Advertiser Type:	SER
Zip Code:	19364	Balance:	$65.00
Telephone Number:	555-8024	Amount Paid:	$180.00

Advertisements

Ad Month	Category Code	Category Description
Aug	1	Quarter Page Ad
Sep	2	Half Page Ad
Jul	2	Half Page Ad

Advertiser Number: W456

Name:	Western Wear		
Address:	345 Oaktree	Advertiser Type:	RET
Zip Code:	19363	Balance:	$105.00
Telephone Number:	555-7913	Amount Paid:	$265.00

Advertisements

Ad Month	Category Code	Category Description
Jul	1	Quarter Page Ad
Aug	2	Half Page Ad
Sep	5	Double Page Ad

Thursday, September 15, 2005   Page 2

FIGURE 7-83

Cases and Places

The difficulty of these case studies varies:
▪ are the least difficult and ▪▪ are more difficult. The last exercise is a group exercise.

1 ▪ Use the College Dog Walkers database that you used in Project 6 for this assignment or see your instructor for information on accessing the files required for this book. Create the report shown in Figure 7-84. Note that the labels for walker first name, walker last name, customer first name, and customer last name have been changed. Modify the Customer Update Form to create a form similar to that shown in Figure 7-78 on page AC 447. You can use either text or a picture on a command button.

Walker Master List

Walker Number: 03   First Name: Johan   Last Name: Cramden

Customer Number: BI34

First Name:	Frank	Last Name:	Bishop
Address:	23 Norwood	Telephone Number:	555-1234
Per Walk Amount:	$12.00	Balance:	$30.00

Dog Walking Services

Service Date	Service Time
9/4/2005	1:30:00 PM
9/5/2005	9:00:00 PM

Customer Number: HA36

First Name:	Bill	Last Name:	Hammer
Address:	314 Easton	Telephone Number:	555-5634
Per Walk Amount:	$12.00	Balance:	$48.00

Dog Walking Services

Service Date	Service Time
9/5/2005	10:00:00 AM

Customer Number: JO45

First Name:	Sylvia	Last Name:	Jones
Address:	44 Norwood	Telephone Number:	555-6754
Per Walk Amount:	$8.00	Balance:	$16.00

Dog Walking Services

Service Date	Service Time
9/5/2005	12:00:00 PM

Thursday, September 15, 2005   Page 1

FIGURE 7-84

Cases and Places

2 ■   Use the InPerson Fitness Company database that you used in Project 6 for this assignment or see your instructor for information on accessing the files required for this book. Create a report for the database that displays information about the trainers as well as information on the trainer's clients. The report should be similar to that shown in Figure 7-81 on page AC 450. Be sure to change the labels for trainer, first name, trainer last name, client first name, and client last name. Modify the Client Update Form to create a form similar to that shown in Figure 7-82 on page AC 451. You can use either text or a picture on a command button.

3 ■■   Use the Regional Books database that you used in Project 6 for this assignment or see your instructor for information on accessing the files required for this book. Create the report shown in Figure 7-85. Modify the Book Update Form to create a form similar to that shown in Figure 7-80 on page AC 449. The form should include a combo box to search for books by title. You can use either text or a picture on a command button.

Publisher Master List

Publisher Code: SI   Publisher Name: SI Publishing

Book Code: 1489

Title:	Hill Country Blues	
Author:	Estelle	Dearling
Paperback	☐	Units On Hand: 1
Book Type:	New	Price: $16.95

Book Orders

Customer Number	First Name	Last Name	Phone Number
005	Terry	Roberts	555-6543
010	Shelly	Stein	555-4567

Book Code: 1534

Title:	Reunion Ranch	
Author:	Dennis	Eaton
Paperback	☑	Units On Hand: 2
Book Type:	New	Price: $5.99

Book Orders

Customer Number	First Name	Last Name	Phone Number
002	Mark	Peterson	555-9876
008	John	Shippers	555-1234

FIGURE 7-85

Cases and Places

4 ■■ Use the Campus Housing database that you used in Project 6 for this assignment or see your instructor for information on accessing the files required for this book. Create the report shown in Figure 7-86. Modify the Rental Update Form to include command buttons to move to the next record, move to the previous record, add a new record, delete a record, print a record, and close the form.

Owner Master List

Owner Code: 50   First Name: Craig   Last Name: Anders

Rental Code: 113

Bedrooms:	2	Parking ✔
Bathrooms:	1	Pets ☐
Lease Term:	9	Rent: $675.00
Distance:	1.00	

Potential Renters

Renter Number	First Name	Last Name	Address	Phone Number
007	Neal	Vandahl	34 Mapleton	555-4321

Rental Code: 117

Bedrooms:	2	Parking ☐
Bathrooms:	2	Pets ☐
Lease Term:	9	Rent: $875.00
Distance:	1.50	

Potential Renters

Renter Number	First Name	Last Name	Address	Phone Number
008	John	Shoppers	567 Cherry	555-1234

Thursday, September 15, 2005   Page 1

FIGURE 7-86

Microsoft Office
Access 2003

Cases and Places

5 ■■ **Working Together** As a team, choose one of the cases and places databases. Then copy and rename the database. Add a report header section to the report created in this project and then create a company letterhead to include in the report header. For example, if you chose the InPerson Fitness Company database, you could create a letterhead that included the company name and the picture of a weightlifter. Add an appropriate picture to the update form. For example, if you chose the Regional Books database, you could add a picture or clip art of a book to the page header for the form. To add a picture or clip art to a report or form, use the Image tool on the toolbox. (See More About Adding Objects on page AC 405.) You can use the clip art that comes with Microsoft Office, download clip art from the Web, or design your own pictures. Experiment with different font styles for the command buttons on the forms.

Using Visual Basic
for Applications (VBA)
and Creating Multi-Page Forms

PROJECT

CASE PERSPECTIVE

The administration at Ashton James College is considering running a promotion. In this promotion, users receive a discount on the amount currently due to Ashton James College for the training they have received. The discount is determined by a promotion factor that is dependent on the client type. Clients whose type is EDU have a promotion factor of 0.95, which represents a five percent discount. Clients whose type is SER have a promotion factor of 0.97 and clients whose type is MAN have a promotion factor of 0.98. The promotion amount is the result of multiplying the current due amount by the appropriate promotion factor.

To assist in determining the effects of this promotion, the administration would like the Client Update Form modified so it includes both the promotion amount and the promotion factor. In addition, users must be able to hide this information whenever necessary. The administration also would like a query that calculates the promotional amounts. There must be a button on the form that users can click to display the results of this query.

Ashton James College also needs a form that lists the number and name of trainers. The form is to contain a subform listing information about the course offerings for clients of the trainer. It also should contain two charts that illustrate the total hours spent by the trainer on each course offering and a Web browser to display the college's home page. Your task is to help the administration accomplish these goals.

As you read through this project, you will learn how to use Visual Basic for Applications (VBA) to customize database applications. You also will learn how to create multi-page forms.

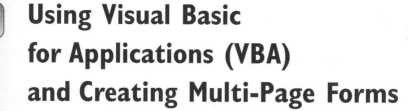
MICROSOFT
Office Access 2003

Using Visual Basic for Applications (VBA) and Creating Multi-Page Forms

PROJECT

8

Objectives

You will have mastered the material in this project when you can:

- Use VBA
- Create functions in a standard module
- Test functions
- Use the functions in a query
- Associate code with an event
- Create Sub procedures
- Correct errors using debugger

- Create code to update controls
- Create a function to run a command
- Create a form using Design view
- Add a tab control
- Add a subform control to a form
- Add a chart to a form
- Add an ActiveX control to a form

More About

The Access Help System

Need Help? It is no further away than the Type a question for help box on the menu bar in the upper-right corner of the window. Click the box that contains the text, Type a question for help (Figure 8-1), type help, and then press the ENTER key. Access responds with a list of topics you can click to learn about obtaining help on any Access-related topic. To find out what is new in Access 2003, type what is new in Access in the Type a question for help box.

Introduction

The form shown in Figure 8-1a has some additions to the previous version of the form. Both the promotion amount and the promotion factor appear on this form. Two additional buttons also appear. The Hide Promotion button will hide the promotion amount, the promotion factor, and the Run Promotion Query button when clicked. In addition, the caption on the button will change to Show Promotion. When the Show Promotion button is clicked, the promotion amount, promotion factor, and the Run Promotion Query button once again will appear. Clicking the Run Promotion Query button will display the promotion query (Figure 8-1b). In order to make these enhancements to the form, you will need to learn to create Visual Basic code.

You also will learn how to create the form shown in Figure 8-2a on page AC 460. The form in Figure 8-2a lists the Trainer Number, First Name, and Last Name fields from the Trainer table. The form is a **multi-page form** because it contains more than one page of information. The form contains a tab control that allows you access to three different pages. Clicking the Datasheet tab displays a page containing a subform. The subform lists the Client Number, Name, Course Number, Total Hours, and Hours Spent for every course offering scheduled for any client assigned to the trainer. Clicking the Charts tab displays a page containing two charts (Figure 8-2b on page AC 460). In both charts, the bars represent the various courses. The height of the bars in the left chart represents the total of the hours scheduled for the course. The height of the bars in the right chart represents the total of the hours already spent. Finally, clicking the Web tab displays a page containing a Web browser. The home page for Ashton James College appears in the browser (Figure 8-2c on page AC 461).

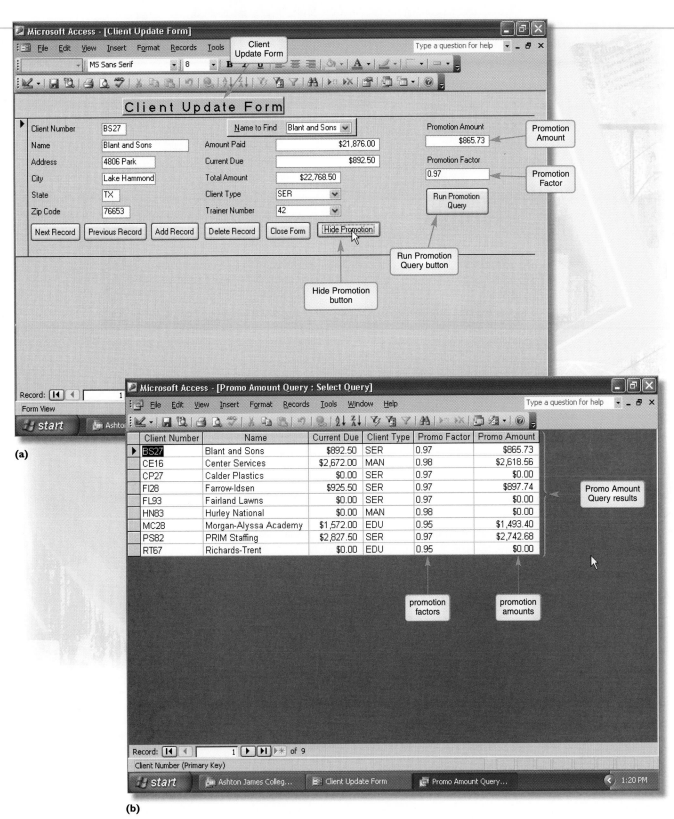

(a)

(b)

FIGURE 8-1

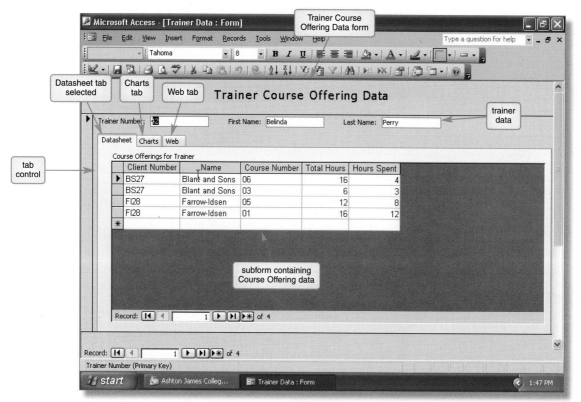

FIGURE 8-2a

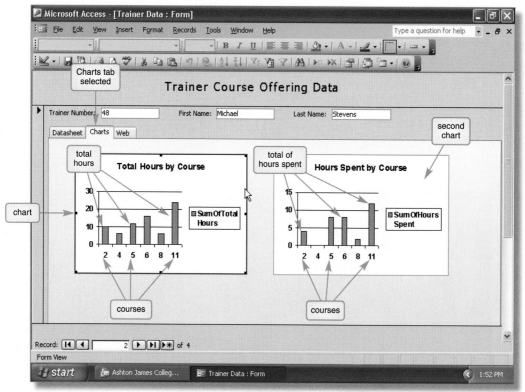

FIGURE 8-2b

FIGURE 8-2c

Project Eight — Using Visual Basic for Applications (VBA) and Creating Multi-Page Forms

The steps in this project show how to add the controls and buttons to support the promotional requirements needed by Ashton James College. The project also illustrates how to create appropriate Visual Basic for Applications (VBA) code to give the form the necessary functionality. The steps create queries that will be used by the multi-page form. Then, the steps create the multi-page form from scratch using Design view. Finally, the steps illustrate how to add a tab control, a subform, two charts, and a Web Browser control to the form.

> **Note:** This project assumes that your database is located in a folder called Data on disk C. If your database is on a floppy disk (drive A), copy your database to disk C or to a network disk. If you do not have access to disk C or a network disk, do not attempt to do the activities in this project. You will not have enough room on your disk.

Opening the Database

If you are stepping through this project on a computer and you want your screen to match the figures in this book, then you should change your computer's resolution to 800 x 600. For more information on how to change the resolution on your computer, see Appendix D. Before carrying out the steps in this project, first you must open the database. The steps on the next page, which start Access and open the database, assume that the database is located in a folder called Data on disk C. If your database is located anywhere else, you will need to make the appropriate adjustments in the steps.

To Open a Database

1 Click the Start button on the Windows taskbar, point to All Programs on the Start menu, point to Microsoft Office on the All Programs submenu, and then click Microsoft Office Access 2003 on the Microsoft Office submenu.

2 If the Access window is not maximized, double-click its title bar to maximize it.

3 If the Language bar appears, right-click it and then click Close the Language bar on the shortcut menu.

4 Click Open on the Database toolbar, and then click Local Disk (C:) in the Look in box. Double-click the Data folder, and then make sure the database called Ashton James College is selected.

5 Click the Open button.

6 If the Security Warning dialog box appears, click the Open button.

The database opens and the Ashton James College : Database window appears.

Visual Basic for Applications (VBA)

Visual Basic for Applications (VBA) is a programming language that can be used with Microsoft Access. As with other programming languages, programs in VBA consist of **code**; that is, a collection of **statements**, also called **commands**, which are instructions that will cause actions to take place when the program executes.

An Access database is composed of objects that have properties and are in turn composed of other objects. Tables, for example, have properties and are in turn composed of fields, which also have properties. (The field properties are shown in the lower pane in the Table Design window.) Forms and reports have properties and contain controls that also have properties. You are familiar with these objects through your manipulation of property sheets.

The key properties when working with VBA deal with **events**, which are actions recognized by these objects. Such properties are called event properties. For example, one of the events associated with a button on a form is clicking the button. The corresponding event property is On Click. If you associate VBA code with the On Click event property, that code will execute whenever the user clicks the button. This approach is referred to as **event-driven programming**. Table 8-1 shows some events associated with actions a user can take and Table 8-2 shows some events associated with data updates.

Table 8-1   Events Associated with User Actions

EVENT	WHEN OCCURS
Activate	Form or report receives focus (that is, is activated)
Click	User presses and releases left mouse button
DblClick	User presses and releases left mouse button twice rapidly
Deactivate	Form or report loses focus (that is, is deactivated)
Enter	Just before a control receives focus
Exit	Just before a control loses focus
GotFocus	Control receives focus
LostFocus	Control loses focus
MouseDown	User presses either mouse button
MouseMove	User moves the mouse
MouseOver	User moves the mouse over the control
MouseUp	User releases mouse button

Table 8-2	Events Associated with Data Updates
EVENT	**WHEN OCCURS**
AfterDelConfirm	User responds Yes when asked to confirm deletion
AfterInsert	New record added to database
AfterUpdate (control)	Value in control changed
AfterUpdate (form)	Record changed in database
BeforeDeleteConfirm	Record deleted, but user has not yet responded when asked to confirm deletion
BeforeInsert	Contents of record entered, but record not yet added to database
BeforeUpdate	Contents of record changed on screen, but update not yet reflected in database
Delete	Record removed from database

Names in VBA

Names in Visual Basic can be up to 255 characters long. Names must begin with a letter and can include letters, numbers, and underscores (_). Unlike names in Access, they cannot contain spaces. Two principal ways exist for handling the restriction on spaces when the name you wish to use contains more than one word. The first is to avoid the space, but place an initial cap on each word. For example, if you wanted the name Show Promotion, you would instead use ShowPromotion. The second is to use an underscore instead of the space. For example, if you wanted the name Current Due, you would instead use Current_Due. In this project, you will use the second method for any name that represents a field in the database and the first method for all others.

Some generally accepted conventions for naming specific items on forms also exist. Names of command buttons begin with cmd, names of text boxes begin with txt, and names of labels begin with lbl. For example, you will use cmdPromo as the name of the command button for showing or hiding promotion data. You will use txtPromoAmount as the name of the text box that contains the promotion amount and lblPromoAmount as the name of its attached label.

Statements in VBA

Statements in VBA use **variables**, which are named locations in computer memory. You can place a value in a variable, change the value in a variable, and use the value in a variety of ways, such as computations and comparisons.

The **assignment statement** is used to assign a value to a variable and also to change the value in a variable. For example, the statement on line 1 in Table 8-3 assigns the value 0.95 to a variable called PromoFactor. The statement on line 2 multiplies (*) this value by the value in Current_Due and assigns the result to the variable called PromoAmount.

More About

Names in VBA

The generally accepted conventions for naming specific items on forms used in this project are based on the Leszynski/Redding naming conventions for VBA. For more information on the Leszynski/Redding naming conventions, visit the Access 2003 More About Web page (scsite.com/ac2003/more) and click Names in VBA.

More About

Events

An event can be caused by a user action or by a VBA statement, or it can be triggered by the system. Using properties associated with events, you can tell Access to run a macro, call a Visual Basic function, or run an event procedure in response to an event.

Table 8-3	Assignment Statement
LINE	**STATEMENT**
1	`PromoFactor = 0.95`
2	`PromoAmount = PromoFactor * Current_Due`

Table 8-4   Simple If Statement

LINE	STATEMENT
1	If Client_Type = "EDU" Then
2	PromoFactor = 0.95
3	End If

Table 8-5   If Statement with Else

LINE	STATEMENT
1	If Client_Type = "EDU" Then
2	PromoFactor = 0.95
3	Else
4	PromoFactor = 1
5	End If

Table 8-6   If Statement with ElseIf

LINE	STATEMENT
1	If Client_Type = "EDU" Then
2	PromoFactor = 0.95
3	ElseIf Client_Type = "SER" Then
4	PromoFactor = 0.97
5	ElseIf Client_Type = "MAN" Then
6	PromoFactor = 0.98
7	Else
8	PromoFactor = 1
9	End If

Table 8-7   Example of Comments in VBA Code

LINE	STATEMENT
1	' Determine PromoFactor based on Client Type
2	If Client_Type = "EDU" Then
3	PromoFactor = 0.95 ' Promo factor for Educational clients
4	End If

The If statement performs a test and then takes action. The action to be taken depends on the results of the test. The simplest form of the If statement is illustrated in Table 8-4. In this statement, if the client type is equal to EDU, PromoFactor will be set to 0.95. If the client type is not equal to EDU, no action will be taken. (Because EDU is a text value, it must be enclosed in quotation marks.)

An If statement also can contain the word Else as illustrated in Table 8-5. In this statement, if the client type is equal to EDU, PromoFactor will be set to 0.95. If the client type is not equal to EDU, PromoFactor will be set to 1.

An If statement also can contain ElseIf to perform multiple tests as illustrated in Table 8-6. In this statement, if the client type is equal to EDU, PromoFactor will be set to 0.95. If the client type is equal to SER, PromoFactor will be set to 0.97. If the client type is MAN, PromoFactor will be set to 0.98. If the client type is not equal to any of these values, PromoFactor will be set to 1.

In the above examples, some lines are indented four spaces. This is not necessary, but is done to make the statement more readable.

Comments in VBA

You can include **comments** in VBA code to describe the purpose of the code. To indicate that the text you are entering is a comment and not a VBA statement, place an apostrophe before the comment. The comment can be on a line by itself as on line 1 of Table 8-7. The comment also can appear on the same line with code as on line 3 of the table. Comments are a valuable tool to help make the code more readable.

Procedures in VBA

In VBA, a group of statements that accomplishes some specific task is called a **procedure**. Two different types of procedures exist. A **function procedure**, which usually is simply called a **function**, typically calculates and returns a value. You can use the function in an expression anywhere that you can use expressions (for example, in queries, in controls on forms and reports, and in Visual Basic code). The value calculated by the function then will be used in the expression.

Table 8-8 shows a sample function. It begins with the word Function followed by the name of the function and ends with End Function. The name of the function in the table is PromoFactor. Within the function, PromoFactor is treated as if it were a variable. The purpose of the function is to calculate a value for PromoFactor. The If statement in this function will set PromoFactor to 0.95 if the client type is EDU and to 1 otherwise.

Table 8-8   PromoFactor Function

LINE	STATEMENT
1	`Function PromoFactor(Client_Type)`
2	`    ' Determine PromoFactor based on Client Type`
3	`    If Client_Type = "EDU" Then`
4	`        PromoFactor = 0.95 ' Promo factor for Educational clients`
5	`    Else`
6	`        PromoFactor = 1 ' Promo factor for others`
7	`    End If`
8	
9	`End Function`

The variable in parentheses (Client_Type) is called a **parameter** and allows you to furnish data to the function to be used in calculating the function value. To use the function, you type the name of the function and then in parentheses, specify the value for this parameter. The item that furnishes this value is called an **argument**. For example, if you specified PromoFactor ("EDU"), "EDU" would be the argument. During the execution of the PromoFactor function, Client_Type would be EDU and thus PromoFactor would be set to 0.95.

It is common to use a database field as the argument when using a function as in PromoFactor ([Client Type]). In this case, if the current value in the Client Type field were EDU, the function would calculate a value of 0.95. If instead, the current value in the field is MAN, the function would calculate a value of 1.

The other type of procedure is a Sub procedure. Unlike functions, **Sub procedures**, also called **subroutines**, do not return a value and cannot be used in expressions. Table 8-9 includes a sample Sub procedure that you will learn how to create and use later in this project. It makes the controls containing the promotional amount and promotional factor, as well as the button to run the promotion query, visible. By placing the statements to accomplish this in a procedure, you can use them from a variety of places within the VBA code. All you need to do is include the name of the procedure wherever you want the commands executed.

Table 8-9   ShowPromotion Sub Procedure

LINE	STATEMENT
1	`Public Sub ShowPromotion()`
2	`    txtPromoAmount.Visible = True`
3	`    txtPromoFactor.Visible = True`
4	`    cmdPromoQuery.Visible = True`
5	`End Sub`

Modules in VBA

In VBA, you group procedures in a structure called a **module**. There are two types of modules. A **standard module** contains procedures that are available from anywhere in a database. A **class module** contains procedures for a particular form or report. When you create a procedure for an object on a form or report, Access automatically places the procedure in the class module for that form or report. If you create additional procedures, you can place them in either a standard module or a class module. If the only way the procedure will be used is in connection with a form or report, you should place the procedure on the form's or report's class module. If it will be used more widely than that, placing it in a standard module is the appropriate action. For example, if a function is used both by a control on a report and in a query, it should be in a standard module.

Compilation

In order for Access to execute your programs, they must be translated from Visual Basic into a language that Access can understand and run. This process is called **compilation**. Translating a program formally is called **compiling** a program and the software that performs the translation is called a **compiler**. When a procedure is run that has not been translated previously, the compiler first will attempt to compile (translate) the procedure. Assuming it is successful, the compiled version then is run. If, however, the compiler finds an error, that is, some aspect of the procedure that does not follow the rules of Visual Basic, it will not complete the translation. Instead, it will report the error. You first must correct the error and then try to run the procedure again. If you have an error, compare the statement very carefully with a similar statement from one of the examples in the book to determine the problem and then correct the problem.

Instead of waiting for these errors to be reported when the procedure is run, you can have Access immediately compile a procedure as soon as you have created it by selecting Debug on the menu bar in Visual Basic and then selecting Compile on the Debug menu. The compiler then will attempt to compile the procedure. If it is successful, Access will use the compiled version the next time the procedure is to be run without requiring the compilation step to take place. If there are errors, they are reported immediately and can be corrected while you still are working on the procedure.

More About

VBA and Microsoft Office

The VBA programming language also can be used with Excel, Word, PowerPoint, Publisher, and Outlook application systems. For more information on VBA and Microsoft Office visit the Access 2003 More About Web page (scsite.com/ac2003/more) and click VBA and Microsoft Office.

Using Visual Basic for Applications (VBA)

In the next sections, you will learn how to use Visual Basic for Applications (VBA) to accomplish several tasks. In particular, you will learn how to do the following:

1. Create functions in a standard module to calculate the promotion factor and the promotion amount.
2. Test the functions you just created to ensure they work correctly.
3. Use the functions you just created in a query.
4. Add buttons and controls associated with the promotion amounts to the Client Update Form.
5. Associate code with the cmdPromo_Click Event, that is, the event of clicking the Show Promotion button. If the button currently reads Show Promotion, the promotion data does not appear. Clicking the button will cause the promotion data to appear and also change the caption of the Show Promotion button to Hide Promotion. Clicking the button a second time will hide the promotion data and also change the caption back to Show Promotion. Associated with this change, you also will need to create the ShowPromotion and HidePromotion procedures.
6. Create the code necessary to update the controls that show promotion data. The data will be updated whenever the user moves to a different client on the form, the user updates the client type, or the user updates the current due amount.
7. Create code that will be executed when the form first is loaded to hide the promotion data.

More About

When to Use VBA

You can accomplish many of the same tasks in Access using either macros or VBA. Your database, however, will be easier to maintain if you use VBA. Because macros are separate objects from the objects that use them, a database containing many macros that respond to events on form and report objects can be difficult to maintain. Visual Basic event procedures are built into the object's definition. If you move a form or report from one database to another, the event procedures built into the form or report object move with it.

8. Create a function to run a query and associate this function with the Run Promotion Query button.

9. Examine the complete programs.

Creating Functions in a Standard Module

The functions that calculate the promotional factor and promotional amount should be available to be used throughout the database. In this project, for example, you will use these functions in a query and also from within a form. In order to have functions widely available, they are placed in a standard module. The function to calculate the promotional factor is called PromoFactor and is shown in Table 8-10.

LINE	STATEMENT
	Table 8-10 PromoFactor Function
1	`Function PromoFactor(Client_Type)`
2	`    ' Determine PromoFactor based on Client Type`
3	`    If Client_Type = "EDU" Then`
4	`        PromoFactor = 0.95 ' Promo factor for Educational clients`
5	`    ElseIf Client_Type = "SER" Then`
6	`        PromoFactor = 0.97 ' Promo factor for Service clients`
7	`    ElseIf Client_Type = "MAN" Then`
8	`        PromoFactor = 0.98 ' Promo factor for Manufacturing clients`
9	`    Else`
10	`        PromoFactor = 1 ' Promo factor for others (should not be any)`
11	`    End If`
12	
13	`End Function`

The following is an explanation of the lines in the PromoFactor function:

Line 1. The Function statement indicates that the code between the word Function and the End Function statement (line 13) forms a function. This function is called PromoFactor and has an argument of Client_Type. The statement within this function will assign an appropriate value to PromoFactor.

Line 2. This line is a comment because it begins with an apostrophe. It indicates the purpose of the function.

Line 3. This line begins an If statement. This particular If statement checks to see if the Client_Type is EDU.

Line 4. This line will be executed if the Client_Type is EDU. It will set PromoFactor to 0.95. The portion following the apostrophe is a comment describing the fact that this is the appropriate value for clients whose type is EDU.

Line 5. This line checks to see if the Client_Type is SER.

Line 6. This line will be executed if the Client_Type is SER. It will set PromoFactor to 0.97, the appropriate value for clients whose type is SER.

Line 7. This line checks to see if the Client_Type is MAN.

Line 8. This line will be executed if the Client_Type is MAN. It will set PromoFactor to 0.98, the appropriate value for clients whose type is MAN.

Line 9. There is no test on this line. This final Else indicates the action to be taken if all the previous tests failed; that is, if the client type is something other than EDU, SER, or MAN.

Line 10. This line will be executed if all the other tests failed. It will set the PromoFactor to 1. As the comment indicates, no clients should fall into this category. This is put here just in case a client happened to get into the database with an invalid client type.

Line 11. This line indicates the end of the If statement.

Line 12. This line is intentionally left blank for readability.

Line 13. This line marks the end of the function.

The function to calculate the promotional amount is called PromoAmount and is shown in Table 8-11.

LINE	STATEMENT
	Table 8-11 PromoAmount Function
1	`Function PromoAmount(Client_Type, Current_Due)`
2	`    ' Determine PromoAmount based on Client Type and Current Due`
3	`    PromoAmount = PromoFactor(Client_Type) * Current_Due`
4	
5	`End Function`

The following is an explanation of the lines in the PromoAmount function:

Line 1. The Function statement indicates that the code between the word Function and the End Function statement (line 5) forms a function. This function is called PromoAmount and has two arguments, Client_Type and Current_Due. The statement within this function will assign an appropriate value to PromoAmount.

Line 2. This line is a comment because it begins with an apostrophe. It indicates the purpose of the function.

Line 3. This line will calculate the appropriate value for PromoAmount. It uses the PromoFactor function to find the appropriate factor for a client with the given type. It multiplies this factor by the current due amount, and then sets PromoAmount equal to the result.

Line 4. This line is intentionally left blank for readability.

Line 5. This line marks the end of the function.

The following steps illustrate how to create these functions in a standard module that will be saved with the name Promo Modules.

To Create Functions in a Standard Module

1

• **Click Modules on the Objects bar in the Database window.**

The Modules object is selected (Figure 8-3).

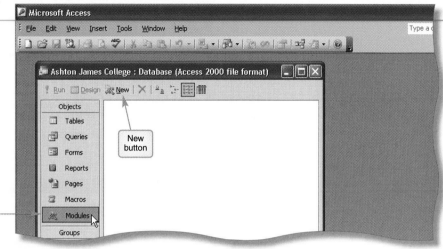

FIGURE 8-3

2

• **Click the New button on the Database window toolbar and be sure the window is maximized.**

The Ashton James College – [Module1 (Code)] window appears (Figure 8-4). Yours may look slightly different. The Project Explorer and Properties window also appear. They may not appear on your screen.

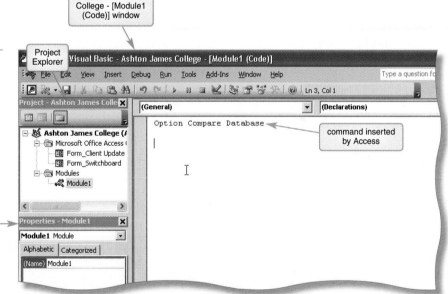

FIGURE 8-4

3

• **Type** Function PromoFactor (Client_Type) **and then press the ENTER key.**

Visual Basic creates a function and adds the End Function statement (Figure 8-5). The insertion point is positioned between the Function statement and the End Function statement.

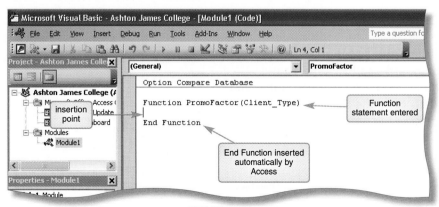

FIGURE 8-5

4

• **Type the statements shown in lines 2 through 12 of Table 8-10 on page AC 467.**

The function is entered (Figure 8-6).

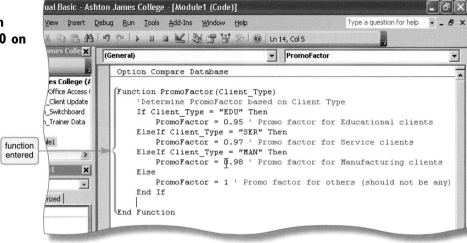

FIGURE 8-6

5

• **Use the DOWN ARROW key to move the insertion point below the End Function statement.**

• **Type** `Function PromoAmount(Client_Type, Current_Due)` **and then press the ENTER key.**

Visual Basic creates a function and adds the End Function statement (Figure 8-7). The insertion point is positioned between the Function statement and the End Function statement.

FIGURE 8-7

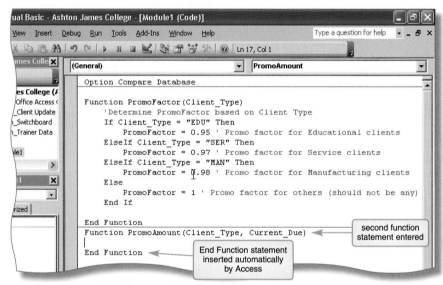

6

• **Type the statements shown in lines 2 through 4 of Table 8-11 on page AC 468.**

The function is entered (Figure 8-8).

7

• **Click the Save button on the Standard toolbar, type** `Promo Modules` **as the module name, and then click the OK button.**

The module is saved as Promo Modules. The functions within it are available for use throughout the database.

FIGURE 8-8

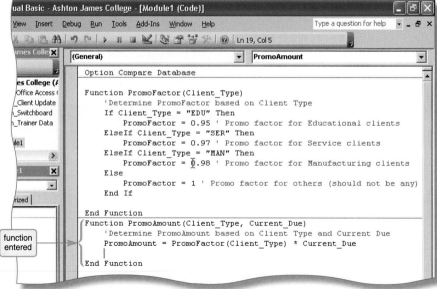

Testing the Functions

Visual Basic provides an easy way to test functions and procedures. You can use the Immediate window. When you do so, you can type a question mark, followed by the procedure name along with values for any arguments. To test if the PromoFactor function calculates the right value for clients of type EDU, for example, you would type ?PromoFactor("EDU") in the Immediate window, press the ENTER key, and then see if the correct value is displayed. To test if the PromoAmount function calculates the right amount for a client whose type is EDU and whose current due amount is $10,000, you would type ?PromoAmount("EDU",10000) in the Immediate window, press the ENTER key, and see if the correct value is displayed. The following steps demonstrate how to perform these tests.

To Test Functions in the Immediate Window

1

• **Click View on the menu bar, and then click Immediate Window on the View menu.**

• **Type** ?PromoFactor("EDU") **in the Immediate window, and then press the ENTER key.**

Visual Basic displays 0.95, which is the correct factor for a client type of EDU (Figure 8-9).

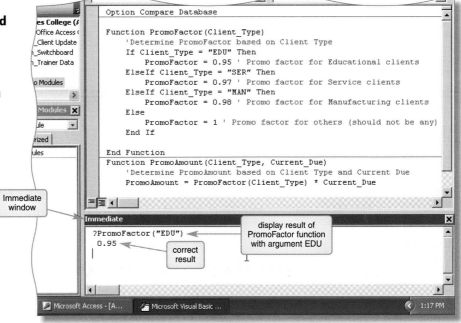

FIGURE 8-9

2

• **Type** ?PromoAmount("EDU",10000) **in the Immediate window, and then press the ENTER key.**

Visual Basic displays 9500 ($9,500), which is the correct amount for a client type of EDU and a current due amount of 10000 ($10,000) (Figure 8-10).

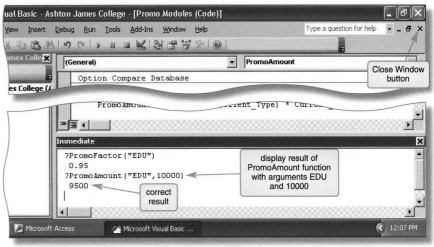

FIGURE 8-10

3

• **Click the Close button for the Microsoft Visual Basic – Ashton James College – [Promo Modules (Code)] window to close the window.**

The Database window appears (Figure 8-11).

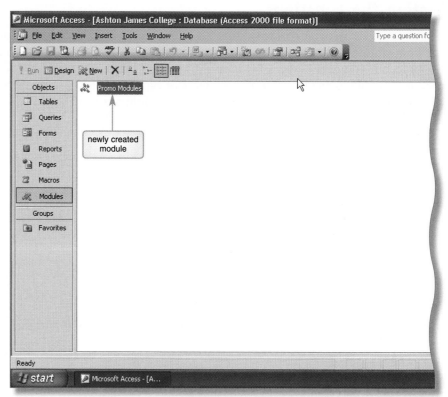

newly created module

FIGURE 8-11

Testing

Testing is only one piece of a larger process known as debugging. Debugging is the process of locating and fixing errors in a program. Compile time errors usually are caused by mistakes in grammar and punctuation (syntax errors) or by mistakes in constructing the code. Run-time errors occur when the code is executed. An example of a run-time error is attempting to divide by zero. Logic errors occur when the program does not perform as intended and produces incorrect results. Testing will help you uncover both run-time and logic errors.

To complete the tests, you would use similar steps to see if the correct values are calculated for clients of other types. You also would test with an invalid value, for example, NON.

Using the Functions in a Query

With the functions stored in a standard module, they are available to be used anywhere in the database. To use a function, type the name of the function and then place the appropriate argument or arguments in parentheses. If the arguments happen to be field names, enclose the field names in square brackets. To calculate the appropriate factor for a client, for example, the expression would be PromoFactor([Client Type]). The appropriate expression for the promotion amount would be PromoAmount([Client Type],[Current Due]). In addition, this expression is to be formatted as currency with two decimal places. In some cases, Access does not recognize such an expression as returning a numeric value that can be reformatted. To address this problem, you can multiply the function by 1.00 in the expression. Thus, the expression would be PromoAmount([Client Type],[Current Due]) * 1.00. The following steps show how to use the functions in a query and also reformat the promotional amount as currency.

To Use Functions in a Query

1

- **In the Database window, click Tables on the Objects bar, and then click Client, if necessary.**

- **Click the New Object button arrow on the Database toolbar, and then click Query.**

- **Be sure Design View is selected, and then click the OK button.**

- **Be sure the Query1 : Select Query window is maximized.**

- **Resize the upper and lower panes and the Client field list so all the fields in the Client table appear.**

- **One-by-one double-click the Client Number, Name, Current Due, and Client Type fields.**

- **Right-click the column following Client Type, and then click Zoom on the shortcut menu.**

- **Type** Promo Factor:PromoFactor([Client Type]) **as the expression.**

The expression for the Promo Factor is entered (Figure 8-12).

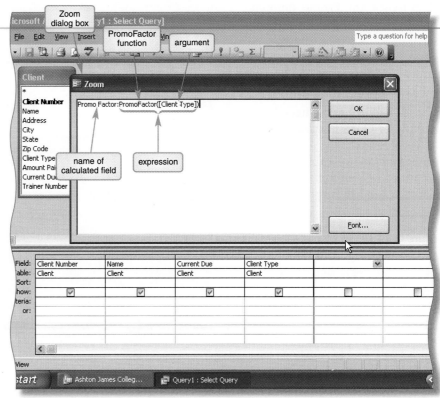

FIGURE 8-12

2

- **Click the OK button.**

- **Right-click the column following Promo Factor, and then click Zoom on the shortcut menu.**

- **Type** Promo Amount:PromoAmount([Client Type],[Current Due])*1.00 **as the expression.**

The expression for the Promo Amount is entered (Figure 8-13).

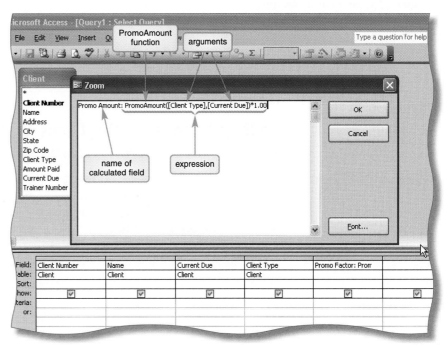

FIGURE 8-13

3

• **Click the OK button.**

• **Right-click the Promo Amount column, click Properties on the shortcut menu, click the Format property on the General tab, click the Format property box arrow, and then click Currency.**

• **Close the property sheet by clicking its Close button.**

The format of the Promo Amount column is changed.

4

• **Run the query, resize each column to best fit the data by double-clicking the right border of the column heading.**

The results appear (Figure 8-14). The promotional factors and promotional amounts are calculated correctly. The columns have been resized to best fit the data.

5

• **Close the window containing the query by clicking its Close Window button, click the Yes button to save the query, type** Promo Amount Query **as the name, and then click the OK button.**

The query is created.

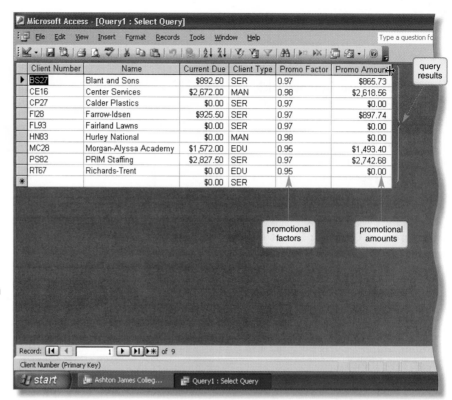

FIGURE 8-14

Adding Buttons to the Client Update Form without the Control Wizards

You add the buttons for showing promotion data and running the promotion query in a similar fashion to the way you added the buttons (Next Record, Previous Record, and so on) in Project 7. In this project, however, you will not use the wizard. Thus, prior to adding the buttons you must make sure the Control Wizards tool is not selected. The following steps first make sure the Control Wizards tool is not selected, add the necessary command buttons, and then change the names and captions.

To Add Command Buttons without the Control Wizards

1

• **Click Forms on the Objects bar, right-click the Client Update Form, click Design View on the shortcut menu, and then maximize the window if it already is not maximized.**

• **If the field list appears, click its Close button.**

• **Be sure the toolbox appears and is docked at the bottom of the screen.**

The Client Update Form appears (Figure 8-15). The Control Wizards tool is selected.

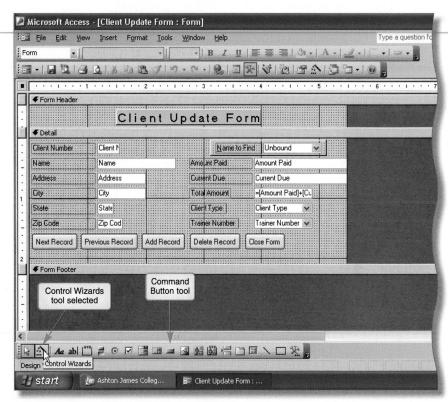

FIGURE 8-15

2

• **If the Control Wizards tool currently is selected, click the tool so it is no longer selected.**

• **Click the Command Button tool and then move the pointer to the approximate position shown in Figure 8-16.**

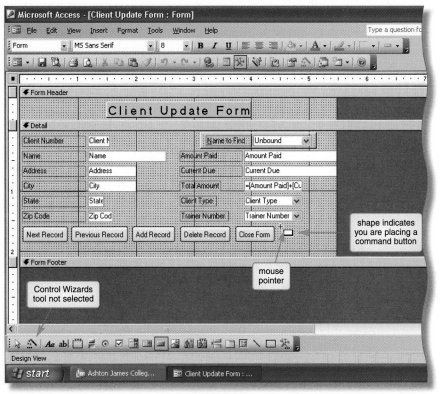

FIGURE 8-16

3

• **Click the position shown in Figure 8-16 on the previous page, right-click the button that is placed on the form, and then click Properties on the shortcut menu.**

The property sheet for the new button appears (Figure 8-17). Your command button name may be different.

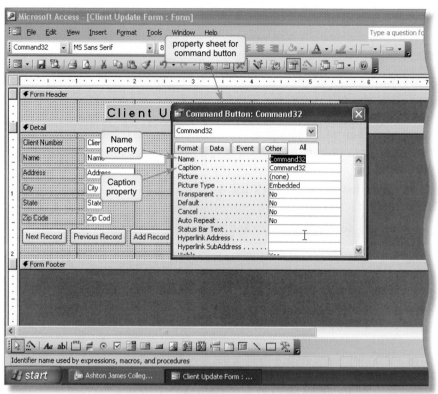

FIGURE 8-17

4

• **Change the value for the Name property to cmdPromo and then change the value for the Caption property to Show Promotion.**

The name and caption are changed (Figure 8-18).

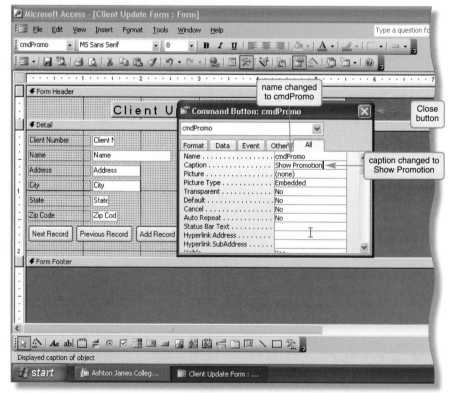

FIGURE 8-18

5

• **Click the Close button for the property sheet, click the Command Button tool in the toolbox and then move the pointer to the approximate location shown in Figure 8-19.**

6

• **Click the position shown in Figure 8-19, right-click the button that is placed on the form, and then click Properties on the shortcut menu.**

• **Change the Name property to cmdPromoQuery and then change the Caption property to Run Promotion Query.**

• **Click the Close button for the property sheet.**

• **Drag the lower sizing handle for the button so the entire caption (Run Promotion Query) appears.**

The button is added. The entire caption appears (Figure 8-20 on the next page).

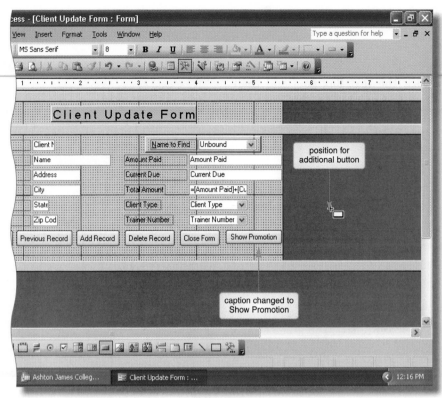

FIGURE 8-19

Adding Controls to the Client Update Form

You add the Promotion Amount and Promotion Factor controls to the Client Update Form as text boxes, just as you have done on other forms. The steps on the next page illustrate how to add the necessary controls. Once added, the steps move the attached label so it is above the control rather than to the left. The steps also change the names of the controls and attached labels, as well as the captions of the labels.

To Add Controls to a Form

1

• **Click the Text Box tool and then move the pointer to the approximate position shown in Figure 8-20.**

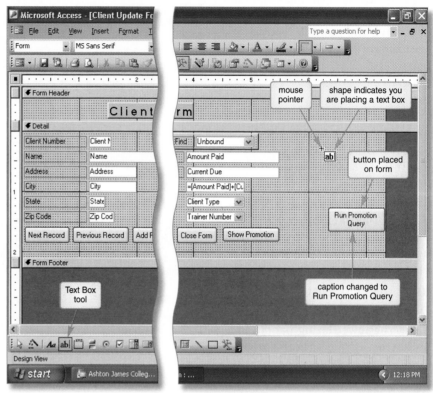

FIGURE 8-20

2

• **Click the position shown in Figure 8-20, point to the Move handle for the label, and then drag the label to the position shown in Figure 8-21.**

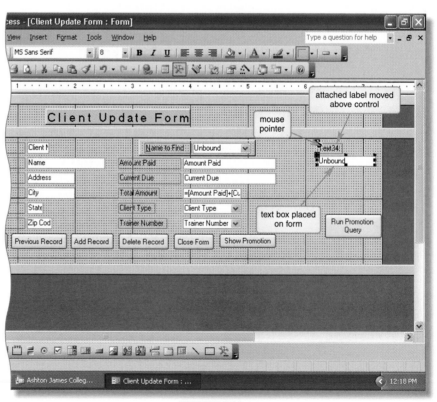

FIGURE 8-21

3

• **Right-click the control (the white space, not the label), click Properties on the shortcut menu, change the name to txtPromoAmount, change the format to Currency, and change the number of decimal places to 2.**

The property sheet for the control appears (Figure 8-22). The name is changed to txtPromoAmount, the format is changed to Currency, and the number of decimal places is changed to 2.

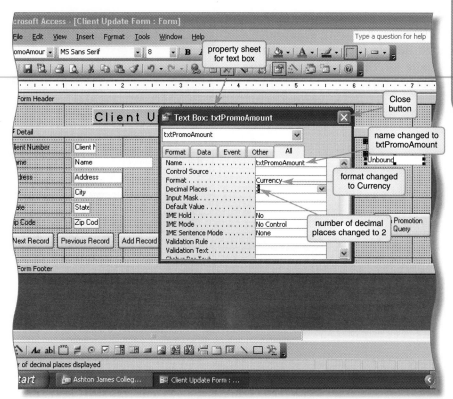

FIGURE 8-22

4

• **Close the property sheet for the control, right-click the label, and then click Properties on the shortcut menu.**

• **Change the name to lblPromoAmount and the caption to Promotion Amount.**

The property sheet for the control appears (Figure 8-23). The name is changed to lblPromoAmount and the caption is changed to Promotion Amount.

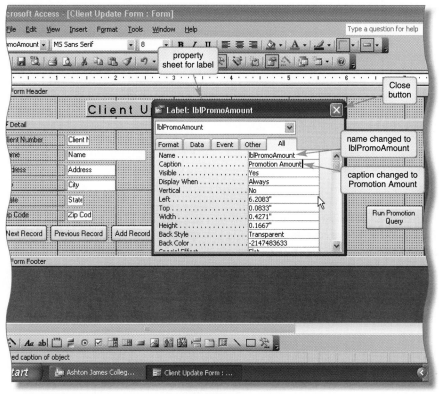

FIGURE 8-23

5

• **Close the property sheet, and then double-click the right sizing handle for the label so the entire label appears.**

The label is changed (Figure 8-24).

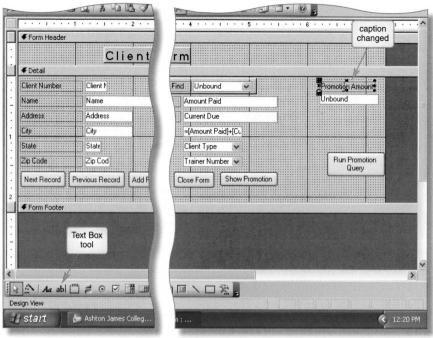

FIGURE 8-24

6

• **Click the Text Box tool in the toolbox and then move the pointer to the approximate position shown in Figure 8-25.**

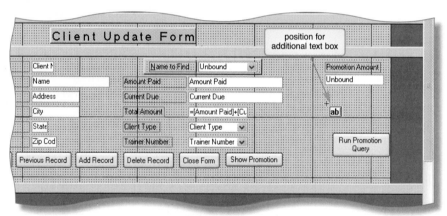

FIGURE 8-25

7

• **Click the position shown in Figure 8-25, move the label so it is above the control, right-click the control, click Properties on the shortcut menu, change the name to txtPromoFactor, and the number of decimal places to 2.**

The label is moved above the control (Figure 8-26). The property sheet appears. The name and number of decimal places are changed.

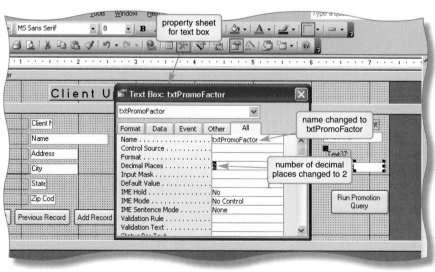

FIGURE 8-26

8

• **Close the property sheet by clicking its Close button.**

• **Right-click the label, click Properties on the shortcut menu, change the name to lblPromoFactor, and the caption to Promotion Factor.**

• **Close the property sheet and then resize the label so the entire label appears.**

The label is changed (Figure 8-27).

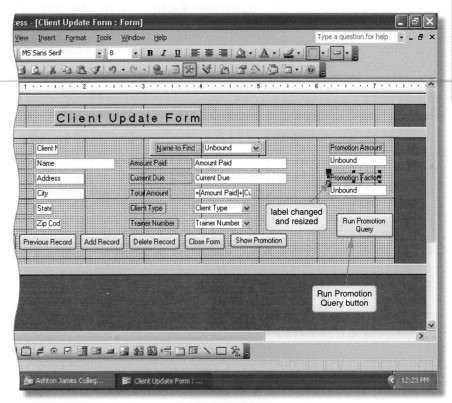

FIGURE 8-27

9

• **Click the Run Promotion Query button.**

• **Move the Run Promotion Query button so it lines up under the newly added controls (Figure 8-28).**

The promotion controls and button now are on the form.

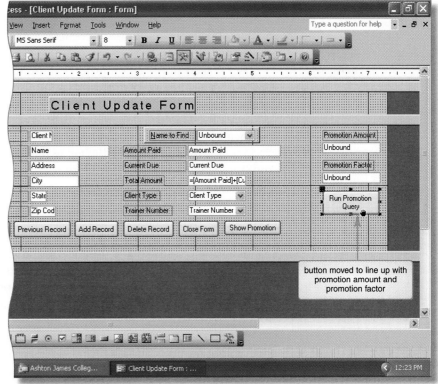

FIGURE 8-28

Associating Code with the cmdPromo_Click Event

In order to show or hide the promotion data by clicking the cmdPromo button, you need to create a Sub procedure that will be executed when the user clicks the button. Access automatically assigns the name cmdPromo_Click to this procedure. The procedure is shown in Table 8-12.

LINE	STATEMENT
Table 8-12	**cmdPromo_Click Sub Procedure**
1	`Private Sub cmdPromo_Click()`
2	`    ' Update button caption and take appropriate action`
3	`    If cmdPromo.Caption = "Show Promotion" Then`
4	`        cmdPromo.Caption = "Hide Promotion"`
5	`        ShowPromotion ' Display promotion info`
6	`    Else`
7	`        cmdPromo.Caption = "Show Promotion"`
8	`        HidePromotion ' Hide promotion info`
9	`    End If`
10	
11	`End Sub`

More About

Saving

If you want to have multiple versions of the Client Update Form, click Save As on the File menu and then save the form as Client Update Form v1 in Design view. Continue with the steps in the next section. Use the Save As command to save a new version of the form after each change to the form design. For example, after you associate the cmdPromo_Click Event with the cmdPromo button, use the Save As command to save the form as Client Update Form v2. This allows you to return to an earlier version if you find mistakes that are too cumbersome to correct in the present version.

The following is an explanation of the lines in the cmdPromo_Click Sub procedure:

Line 1. The Sub statement indicates that the code between the word Sub and the End Sub statement (line 11) forms a Sub procedure. This procedure is called cmdPromo_Click and has no arguments.

Line 2. This line is a comment because it begins with an apostrophe. It indicates the action that the procedure will accomplish.

Line 3. This If statement checks to see if the current value in the Caption property of the control named cmdPromo is equal to Show Promotion. If so, the statements on lines 4 and 5 will be executed.

Line 4. This statement will change the value of the Caption property for the cmdPromo control to Hide Promotion.

Line 5. This statement runs a procedure called ShowPromotion. The ShowPromotion procedure, which has yet to be created, will display the promotion amount, the promotion factor, and the button that can be clicked to run the Promotion Amount query.

Line 6. The Else statement indicates that the following statements (lines 7 and 8) are to be executed in the event the condition is false; that is, the caption for the cmdPromo button is *not* equal to Show Promotion.

Line 7. This statement will change the value of the Caption property for the cmdPromo control to Show Promotion.

Line 8. This statement runs a procedure called HidePromotion. The HidePromotion procedure, which has yet to be created, will hide the promotion amount, the promotion factor, and the button that can be clicked to run the Promotion Amount query.

Line 9. This line indicates the end of the If statement.

Line 10. This line is intentionally left blank for readability.

Line 11. This line marks the end of the Sub procedure.

The following steps illustrate how to create the necessary code and associate it with the On Click property.

To Associate Code with an Event

1

• **Right-click the cmdPromo button (the button whose caption is Show Promotion), click Properties on the shortcut menu, scroll down so the On Click property appears, and then click the On Click property.**

The property sheet for the cmdPromo button appears (Figure 8-29). The On Click property is selected.

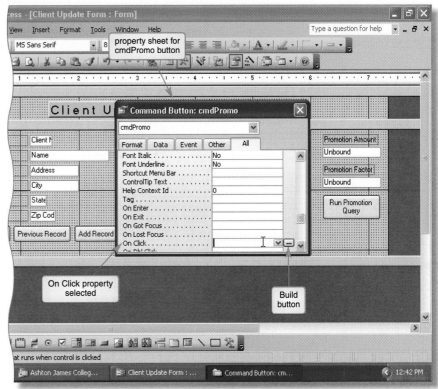

FIGURE 8-29

2

• **Click the Build button, click Code Builder in the Choose Builder dialog box, and then click the OK button.**

The code for cmdPromo_Click, that is, clicking the cmdPromo button, appears (Figure 8-30). The Immediate window, which may be blank on your screen, appears beneath the Code window.

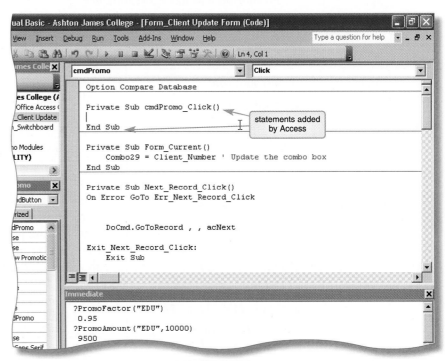

FIGURE 8-30

3

- **Close the Immediate window by clicking its Close button** so more of the Visual Basic code is visible.
- **Type the statements on lines 2 through 10 shown in Table 8-12 on page AC 482.**

The code for the cmdPromo_Click event is entered (Figure 8-31). The Immediate window no longer appears. A Properties window may appear below the Project Explorer window. You will not use either the Project Explorer or the Properties windows.

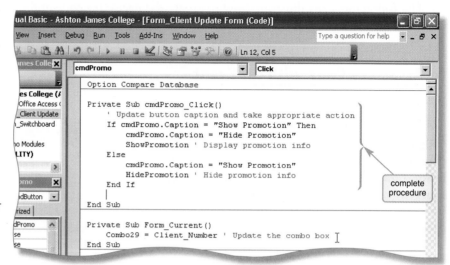

FIGURE 8-31

Creating the ShowPromotion and HidePromotion Sub Procedures

An item on a form will appear, that is, be visible, if its Visible property is set to True. Thus, a procedure to make the promotion amount, the promotion factor, and the button to run the promotion query visible would contain the statements shown in Table 8-13.

The following is an explanation of the lines in the Show Promotion Sub procedure:

Line 1. The Sub statement indicates that the code between the word Sub and the End Sub statement (line 5) forms a Sub procedure. This procedure is called Show Promotion and has no arguments.

Line 2. This line sets the Visible property for the control named txtPromoAmount to True so the control will appear.

Line 3. This line sets the Visible property for the control named txtPromoFactor to True so the control will appear.

Line 4. This line sets the Visible property for the command button named cmdPromoQuery to True so the button will appear.

Line 5. This line marks the end of the Sub procedure.

If an item's Visible property is set to False, it will not appear. Thus, a procedure to hide the promotion amount, the promotion factor, and the button to run the promotion query would contain the statements shown in Table 8-14.

The following is an explanation of the lines in the HidePromotion Sub procedure:

Line 1. The Sub statement indicates that the code between the word Sub and the End Sub statement (line 5) forms a Sub procedure. This procedure is called HidePromotion and has no arguments.

Table 8-13   ShowPromotion Procedure

LINE	STATEMENT
1	`Public Sub ShowPromotion()`
2	`    txtPromoAmount.Visible = True`
3	`    txtPromoFactor.Visible = True`
4	`    cmdPromoQuery.Visible = True`
5	`End Sub`

Table 8-14   HidePromotion Procedure

LINE	STATEMENT
1	`Public Sub HidePromotion()`
2	`    txtPromoAmount.Visible = False`
3	`    txtPromoFactor.Visible = False`
4	`    cmdPromoQuery.Visible = False`
5	`End Sub`

Line 2. This line sets the Visible property for the control named txtPromoAmount to False so the control will not appear.

Line 3. This line sets the Visible property for the control named txtPromoFactor to False so the control will not appear.

Line 4. This line sets the Visible property for the command button named cmdPromoQuery to False so the button will not appear.

Line 5. This line marks the end of the Sub procedure.

The following steps show how to create these procedures as part of the VBA code for the form.

To Create Sub Procedures

1

• **Click the Insert Module button arrow on the Standard toolbar.**

The list of available objects to be inserted appears (Figure 8-32).

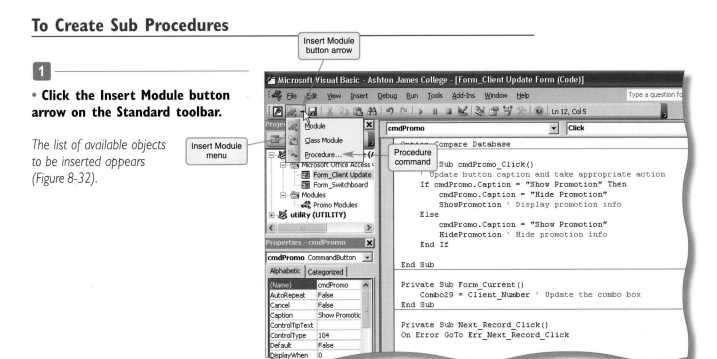

FIGURE 8-32

2

• **Click Procedure.**

• **Type** ShowPromotion **as the name of the procedure in the Add Procedure dialog box.**

The Add Procedure dialog box appears (Figure 8-33). The type (Sub) and scope (Public) already selected are acceptable.

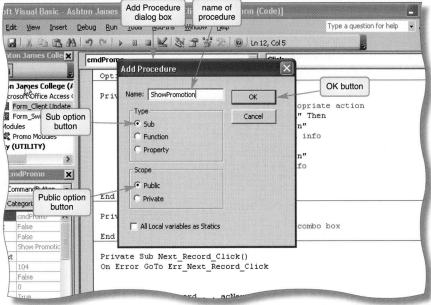

FIGURE 8-33

3

• **Click the OK button and then type the statements on lines 2 through 4 for the ShowPromotion procedure shown in Table 8-13 on page AC 484.**

The code for the ShowPromotion procedure is entered (Figure 8-34).

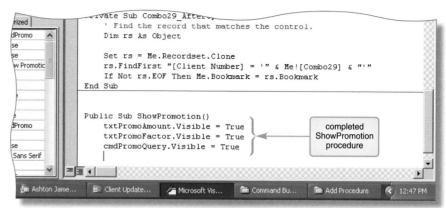

FIGURE 8-34

4

• **Use the techniques in Steps 1 through 3 to create the HidePromotion procedure from Table 8-14 on page AC 484.**

The code for the HidePromotion procedure is entered (Figure 8-35).

5

• **Click the Close button for the Microsoft Visual Basic – Ashton James College – [Form_Client Update Form (Code)] window and then click the Close button for the cmdPromo property sheet.**

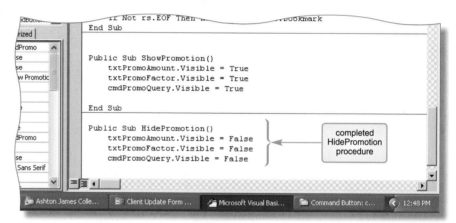

FIGURE 8-35

The ShowPromotion and HidePromotion procedures now have been created and are available for use.

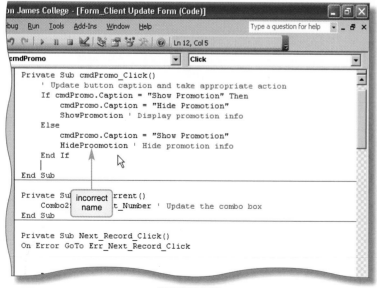

FIGURE 8-36

Correcting Mistakes

As discussed earlier, you can have Access immediately compile a procedure as soon as you have created it by clicking Debug on the menu bar in Visual Basic and then clicking Compile on the Debug menu. Any errors are reported immediately. You then can examine your code carefully and make any necessary corrections.

It is not essential that you use this command. If you do not, you may get errors when you attempt to use your form. For example, Figure 8-36 contains an error. The word HidePromotion contains an extra o (HideProomotion). Consequently, this does not match the name of the HidePromotion procedure that it is attempting to use.

This code is associated with the clicking of the button named cmdPromo (the button containing the words, Show Promotion). When you use the form and click this button, Access will detect the error as it attempts to execute this code. Access will display the error in the manner shown in Figure 8-37. It shows the code containing the error and the specific line containing the error is highlighted. A description of the error appears in the dialog box. You can click the Help button to get help on the meaning of the message that appears.

To correct the error, you first must click the OK button in the Microsoft Visual Basic dialog box. You then will see a screen like the one in Figure 8-38. You actually are running the debugger, with the command containing the error highlighted. In addition, the procedure that was being executed also is highlighted. If you are familiar with program debuggers, you will find that this debugger contains the typical features you expect in a debugger including the ability to step through code, set break points, and so on. You do not need to use these features to determine this type of error, however. You already know which command is incorrect; you just need to determine what is wrong. You should compare the statement very carefully with a similar statement from one of the examples in the book.

To exit the debugger, click the Reset button on the Standard toolbar (Figure 8-38). You then can make the necessary corrections. To test the corrected code, return to the form and repeat whatever action you were in the process of executing. In this example, you would once again click the button labeled Show Promotion.

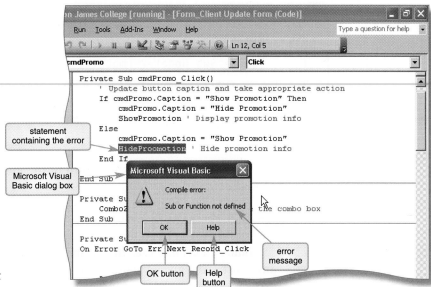

FIGURE 8-37

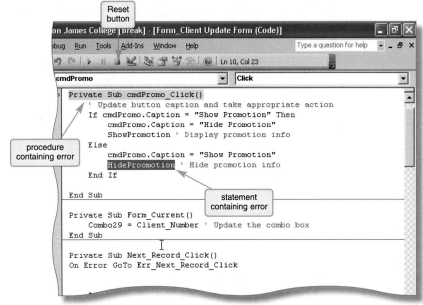

FIGURE 8-38

Creating Code to Update the Controls

To update the promotion amount and the promotion factor, set the Value property for the txtPromoAmount to the result calculated by the PromoAmount function and set the txtPromoFactor to the value calculated by the PromoFactor function. The complete procedure is shown in Table 8-15 on the next page.

Table 8-15   UpdatePromoData Procedure

LINE	STATEMENT
1	Public Sub UpdatePromoData()
2	txtPromoAmount.Value = PromoAmount([Client Type], [Current Due])
3	txtPromoFactor.Value = PromoFactor([Client Type])
4	End Sub

The following is an explanation of the lines in the UpdatePromoData Sub procedure:

Line 1. The Sub statement indicates that the code between the word Sub and the End Sub statement (line 4) forms a Sub procedure. This procedure is called UpdatePromoData and has no arguments.

Line 2. This line uses the PromoAmount function to calculate the appropriate amount for the given client type and current due amount. It then changes the Value property of the txtPromoAmount control to the result of this calculation.

Line 3. This line uses the PromoFactor function to calculate the appropriate factor for the given client type. It then changes the Value property of the txtPromoFactor control to the result of this calculation.

Line 4. This line marks the end of the Sub procedure.

Once this procedure is created, it can be called (used) from other procedures. In particular, it could be used in the Form_Current procedure, which guarantees the promotional data will be updated whenever you move from one client to another. It also could be used from other procedures. For example, using it in a Current_Due_AfterUpdate procedure would guarantee that the values would be updated immediately after a user changed the current due amount. Using it in an AfterUpdate procedure for the Client Type combo box would guarantee that the values would be updated immediately after a user changes the Client Type.

The following steps include a statement to call the UpdatePromoData procedure in the Form_Current procedure and then create the UpdatePromoData procedure. The steps also include statements to call the UpdatePromoData procedure from within both the Combo32_AfterUpdate and Current_Due_After update procedures.

To Create Code to Update Controls

1

• **Right-click the form selector (the small box in the upper-left corner of the form), click Properties, and then click the On Current property.**

The property sheet for the form appears (Figure 8-39). The On Current property is selected. The current value, Event Procedure, indicates that an event procedure already has been created for this property. The procedure to which this refers is the one you created when you updated the On Current property to ensure the combo box always contained the correct name.

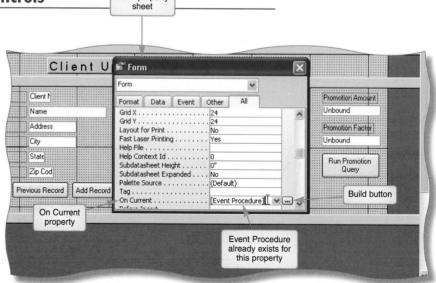

FIGURE 8-39

2

- Click the Build button.
- Click in front of the letter E in End Sub.

The code for the Form_Current procedure appears (Figure 8-40). It contains the statement added earlier to update the combo box.

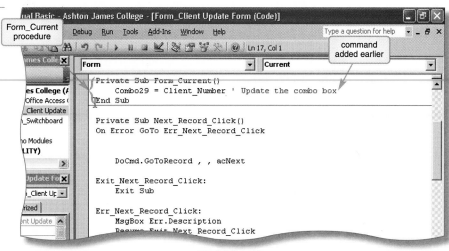

FIGURE 8-40

3

- Add the additional statement shown in Figure 8-41.

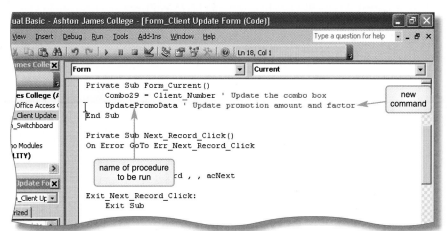

FIGURE 8-41

4

- Click the Insert Module button arrow on the Standard toolbar, click Procedure, be sure the Sub and Public option buttons are selected in the Add Procedure dialog box, type UpdatePromoData as the name of the procedure, and then click the OK button.

- Type the statements on lines 2 and 3 for the UpdatePromoData procedure shown in Table 8-15.

The code for the UpdatePromoData is entered (Figure 8-42).

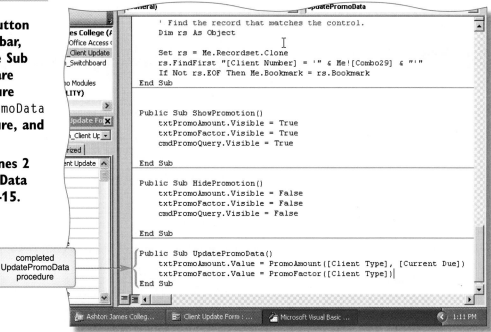

FIGURE 8-42

5

• Click the Close button for the Microsoft Visual Basic – Ashton James College – [Form_Client Update Form (Code)] window to close the window.

• Close the Form property sheet.

• Right-click the combo box for Client Type, click Properties on the shortcut menu, click the After Update property, click the Build button, click Code Builder in the Choose Builder dialog box, and then click the OK button.

• Add the statement shown in Figure 8-43 to the Combo18_AfterUpdate procedure. (Your number may be different.)

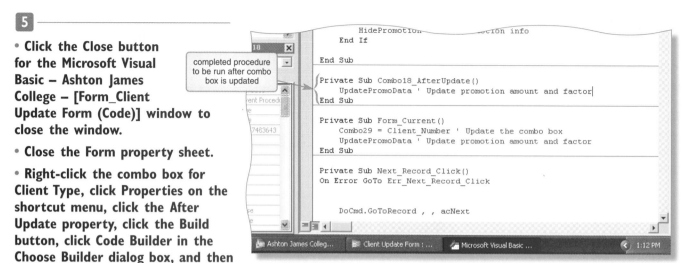

FIGURE 8-43

The procedure for updating promotion data after the value in the combo box is entered.

6

• Click the Close button for the Microsoft Visual Basic – Ashton James College – [Form_Client Update Form (Code)] window to close the window.

• Click the Close button for the Combo Box: Combo 18 property sheet.

• Right-click the control for the Current Due field (the white space, not the label), click Properties on the shortcut menu, click the After Update property, click the Build button, click Code Builder in the Choose Builder dialog box, and then click the OK button.

• Add the statement shown in Figure 8-44 to the Current_Due_AfterUpdate procedure.

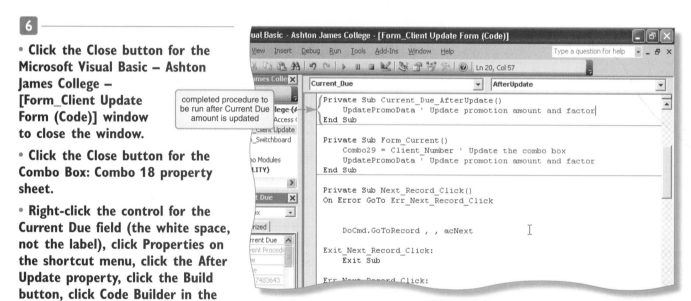

FIGURE 8-44

The procedure for updating promotion data after the value in the Current Due field is complete.

7

• Click the Close button for the Microsoft Visual Basic – Ashton James College – [Form_Client Update (Code)] window to close the window and then close the Text Box: Current Due property sheet.

The Visual Basic window closes and the form design again appears.

Creating a Form Load Event Procedure

There are occasions where there is some special action to be taken when a form first loads into memory. Such an action would be included in a Form Load event procedure, that is, a procedure executed when the Form Load event occurs. For this form, the promotion amount, the promotion factor, and the button to run the Promotion Amount query should all be hidden when the form first appears. To accomplish this, create a Form Load Event procedure containing the single statement, HidePromotion. The following steps illustrate how to create such a procedure.

To Create a Form Load Event Procedure

1

• **Right-click the form selector, click Properties on the shortcut menu, scroll down so the On Load property appears, and then click the On Load property.**

The property sheet for the form appears (Figure 8-45). The On Load property is selected.

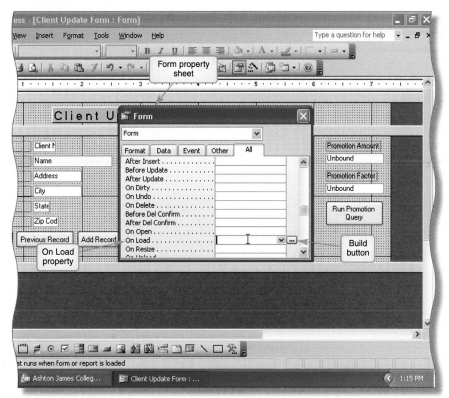

FIGURE 8-45

2

• **Click the Build button, click Code Builder in the Choose Builder dialog box, and then click the OK button.**

• **Add the statement shown in Figure 8-46 to the Form_Load procedure.**

The Form_Load procedure is created.

3

• **Click the Close button for the Microsoft Visual Basic – Ashton James College – [Form_Client Update Form (Code)] window to close the window, and then close the Form property sheet.**

The Visual Basic window closes and the form design again appears.

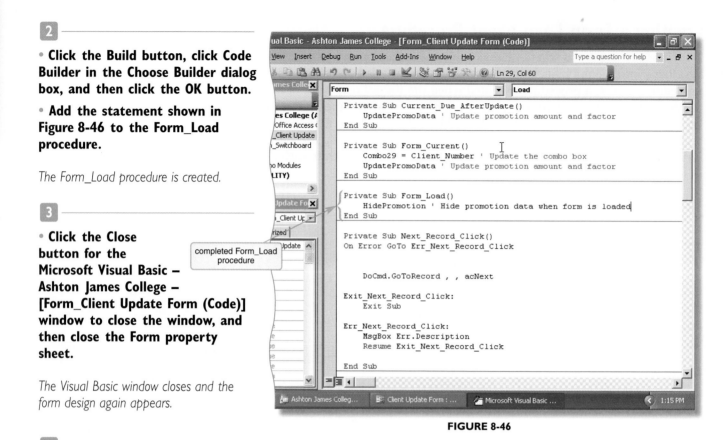

FIGURE 8-46

4

• **Click the Close Window button for the window containing the form design.**

• **When asked if you want to save your changes, click the Yes button.**

The form design no longer appears. The changes are saved.

Table 8-16 Common Methods for DoCmd	
METHOD	**PURPOSE**
ApplyFilter	Sets a filter
Close	Closes open object (form, report, table, query)
FindRecord	Locates a record
GoToRecord	Moves to a specific record
Maximize	Maximizes a window
OpenForm	Opens a form
OpenQuery	Opens a query
OpenReport	Opens a report
Printout	Prints object
RunCommand	Runs a command
ShowAllRecords	Removes filter

Creating a Function to Run a Query

You learned earlier to carry out actions using macros. You can carry out the same actions within VBA code by using DoCmd. (You encountered this function in Project 7 in the Access-generated code for the Add Record button.)

To use DoCmd, type DoCmd followed by a period and then the action. Any arguments are listed after the action separated by commas. Formally, DoCmd is an **object** and the action to be carried out is a **method**. Some of the most common methods you can use with the DoCmd object are shown in Table 8-16. To determine the appropriate arguments for any of these methods, use Help and search for the method. To determine the arguments for the OpenQuery method, for example, use Help and search for OpenQuery.

The RunPromoAmountQuery function is shown in Table 8-17. The key statement is the DoCmd statement on line 4, which uses the OpenQuery method to run a query. The remaining statements are included for **error handling**.

If an error occurs, for example, someone deletes the query so there is no query to run when you click the button, your program will abruptly terminate. Instead of terminating, it would be better for the program to handle the error by displaying a message indicating the problem that has occurred, having the user click an OK button, and then continuing. The additional statements handle any errors that may occur in this fashion.

Table 8-17   RunPromoAmountQuery Function

LINE	STATEMENT
1	`Function RunPromoAmountQuery()`
2	`On Error GoTo RunPromoAmountQuery_Err`
3	
4	`    DoCmd.OpenQuery "Promo Amount Query", acNormal, acReadOnly`
5	
6	`RunPromoAmountQuery_Exit:`
7	`    Exit Function`
8	
9	`RunPromoAmountQuery_Err:`
10	`    MsgBox Error$`
11	`    Resume RunPromoAmountQuery_Exit`
12	
13	`End Function`

The following is an explanation of the lines in the RunPromoAmountQuery function:

Line 1. The Function statement indicates that the code between the word Function and the End Function statement (line 13) forms a function. This function is called RunPromoAmountQuery. It has no arguments.

Line 2. This line indicates that if an error occurs while the function is running, Access is to move immediately to line 9, the line labeled RunPromoAmountQuery_Err.

Line 3. This line is intentionally left blank for readability.

Line 4. This line runs the OpenQuery method of the DoCmd object. The arguments are the name of the query (Promo Amount Query), the view in which the results are to appear (acNormal, which means Datasheet view), and the data mode (acReadOnly). ReadOnly indicates that the users cannot change data when running this query; they can simply view the results.

Line 5. This line is intentionally left blank for readability.

Line 6. This is a label. It is used by the statement in line 11.

Line 7. This line terminates the function; that is, when this line is executed, the function is complete.

Line 8. This line is intentionally left blank for readability.

Line 9. This is the label that is referenced in the On Error statement in line 2. If an error occurs while this procedure is running, Access will move immediately to this line.

Line 10. This line uses the MsgBox statement to display the contents of Error$, a special variable that automatically contains a description of the error that occurred, and then force the user to click the OK button to continue.

Line 11. This line resumes the running of the procedure at the line with the specified label. In this case, the line with this label is line 6 so the next action to be taken is the action specified on line 7, which is to terminate the function. Thus, as soon as the user has reviewed the error message and clicked the OK button, the function terminates and the user would be returned to the form.

Line 12. This line is intentionally left blank for readability.

Line 13. This line marks the end of the function.

The following steps illustrate how to create this function and then use it to run the query whenever the Run Promotion Query button is clicked.

To Create a Function to Run a Query

1

• **Click Modules on the Objects bar in the Database window, right-click Promo Modules, and then click Design View on the shortcut menu.**

• **Be sure the window is maximized.**

• **Click below the End Function for the second function (PromoAmount), type** Function RunPromoAmountQuery(), **and then press the ENTER key.**

Visual Basic creates a function and adds the End Function statement (Figure 8-47). The insertion point is positioned between the Function statement and the End Function statement.

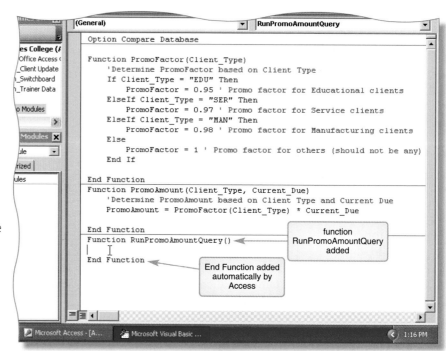

FIGURE 8-47

2

• **Type the statements on lines 2 through 12 shown in Table 8-17 on the previous page.**

The statements for the RunPromoAmountQuery are entered (Figure 8-48).

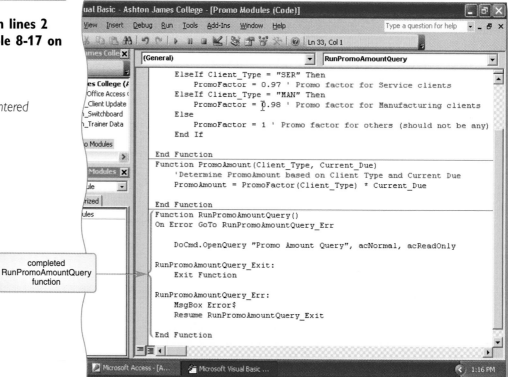

FIGURE 8-48

3

• **Click the Close button for the Microsoft Visual Basic – Ashton James College – [Promo Modules (Code)] window to close the window.**

The Visual Basic window is closed and the Database window appears.

4

• **Click Forms on the Objects bar in the Database window, right-click the Client Update Form, click Design View on the shortcut menu, and then maximize the window if it already is not maximized.**

• **Right-click the button whose caption is Run Promotion Query, click Properties on the shortcut menu, click the On Click property in the Command Button: cmdPromoQuery property sheet, and then type =RunPromoAmountQuery() as the value for the On Click property.**

The value for the On Click property is entered (Figure 8-49). Only the final portion currently appears.

5

• **Close the property sheet by clicking its Close button, and then click the Close Window button for the window containing the form design.**

• **When asked if you want to save your changes, click the Yes button.**

The form design no longer appears. The changes are saved.

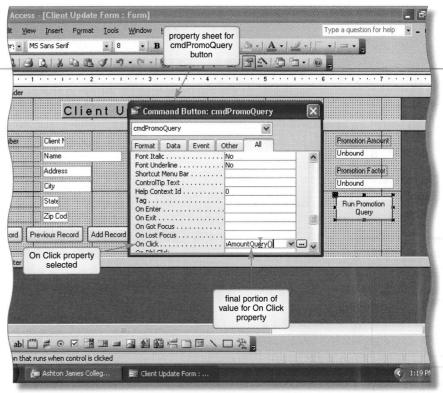

FIGURE 8-49

Using the Form

The form now can be used like any other form. The steps on the next page show how to open the form and use the newly added buttons and controls.

To Use the Form

1

• **With the Database window appearing and the Forms object selected, right-click the Client Update Form, and then click Open on the shortcut menu.**

The form appears (Figure 8-50). The promotion data and Run Promotion Query buttons do not appear.

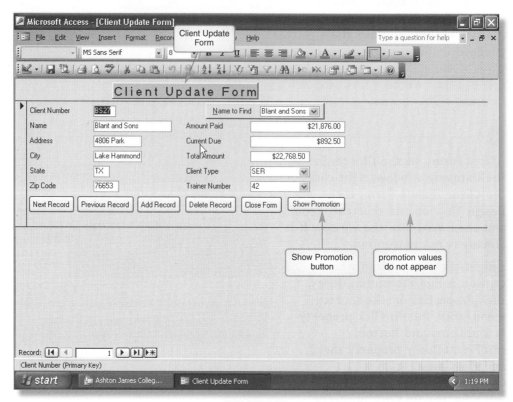

FIGURE 8-50

2

• **Click the Show Promotion button.**

The promotion data and Run Promotion Query buttons appear (Figure 8-51). The caption that had read Show Promotion now reads Hide Promotion. The Promotion Amount and Promotion Factor values have been calculated appropriately.

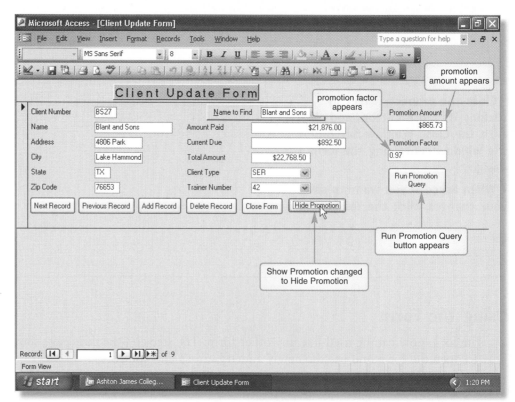

FIGURE 8-51

3

• **Click the Run Promotion Query button.**

The query results appear (Figure 8-52).

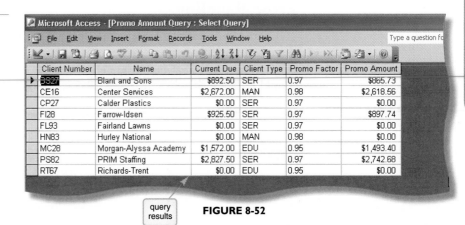

query results

FIGURE 8-52

4

• **Close the window containing the query by clicking its Close Window button.**

• **Use the Client Type combo box to change the client type for Blant and Sons to EDU.**

The query no longer appears (Figure 8-53). Blant and Sons appears on the form with the client type changed to EDU. The Promotion Amount and Promotion Factor values have been updated appropriately.

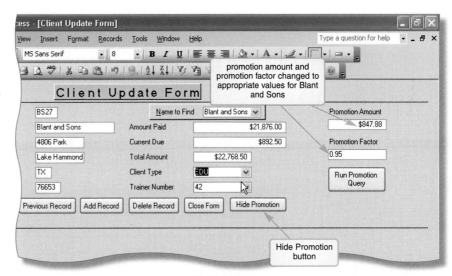

promotion amount and promotion factor changed to appropriate values for Blant and Sons

Hide Promotion button

FIGURE 8-53

5

• **Click the Hide Promotion button.**

The promotion data and Run Promotion Query buttons no longer appear (Figure 8-54).

6

• **Close the form by clicking the Close Form button.**

The form no longer appears.

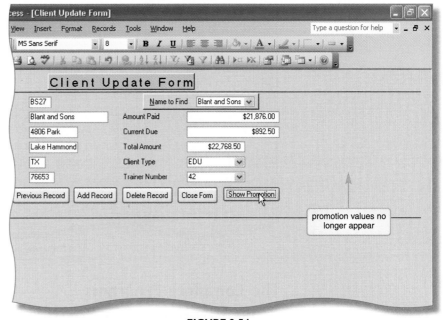

promotion values no longer appear

FIGURE 8-54

Error Handling

The error handling statements in the RunPromoAmountQuery function will display an appropriate message in case there is an error. If, for example, the query referenced in the DoCmd statement does not exist for some reason, the message would indicate this fact. In Figure 8-55, the name of the query, Promo Amnt Query, is incorrect.

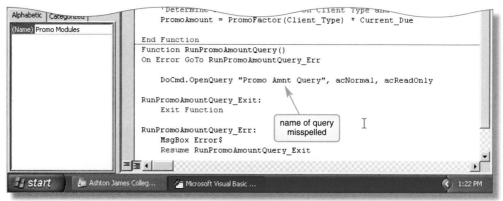

FIGURE 8-55

If a user of the form clicked the Run Promotion Query button with this error, Access would display the message shown in Figure 8-56.

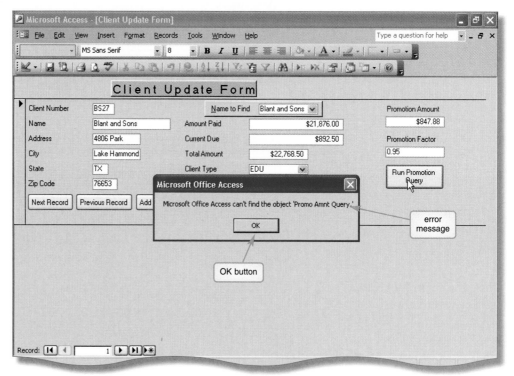

FIGURE 8-56

The Complete Programs

The complete programs are shown in Table 8-18, which shows the standard module, and Table 8-19 on pages AC 500 through AC 503, which shows the form's class module, that is, the code associated with the form.

Table 8-18	Contents of Promo Modules Standard Module
LINE	**STATEMENT**
1	Option Compare Database
2	
3	Function PromoFactor(Client_Type)
4	' Determine PromoFactor based on Client Type
5	If Client_Type = "EDU" Then
6	PromoFactor = 0.95 ' Promo factor for Educational clients
7	ElseIf Client_Type = "SER" Then
8	PromoFactor = 0.97 ' Promo factor for Service clients
9	ElseIf Client_Type = "MAN" Then
10	PromoFactor = 0.98 ' Promo factor for Manufacturing clients
11	Else
12	PromoFactor = 1 ' Promo factor for others (should not be any)
13	End If
14	
15	End Function
16	
17	Function PromoAmount(Client_Type, Current_Due)
18	' Determine PromoAmount based on Client Type and Current Due
19	PromoAmount = PromoFactor(Client_Type) * Current_Due
20	
21	End Function
22	
23	Function RunPromoAmountQuery()
24	On Error GoTo RunPromoAmountQuery_Err
25	
26	DoCmd.OpenQuery "Promo Amount Query", acNormal, acReadOnly
27	
28	RunPromoAmountQuery_Exit:
29	Exit Function
30	
31	RunPromoAmountQuery_Err:
32	MsgBox Error$
33	Resume RunPromoAmountQuery_Exit
34	
35	End Function

The following is an explanation of the lines in the table:

Line 1. This line is inserted automatically. It indicates the method to be used to compare and sort text data. The Database option, which is the one Access includes automatically, means that normal alphabetical order will be used.

Lines 3-15. This is the PromoFactor function. It was discussed on page AC 467.
Lines 17-21. This is the PromoAmount function. It was discussed on page AC 468.
Lines 23-35. This is the RunPromoAmountQuery function. It was discussed on page AC 493.

Table 8-19 Code Associated with Client Update Form

LINE	STATEMENT
1	`Option Compare Database`
2	
3	`Private Sub cmdPromo_Click()`
4	`    ' Update button caption and take appropriate action`
5	`    If cmdPromo.Caption = "Show Promotion" Then`
6	`        cmdPromo.Caption = "Hide Promotion"`
7	`        ShowPromotion ' Display promotion info`
8	`    Else`
9	`        cmdPromo.Caption = "Show Promotion"`
10	`        HidePromotion ' Hide promotion info`
11	`    End If`
12	
13	`End Sub`
14	
15	`Private Sub Combo18_AfterUpdate()`
16	`    UpdatePromoData ' Update promotion amount and factor`
17	`End Sub`
18	
19	`Private Sub Current_Due_AfterUpdate()`
20	`    UpdatePromoData ' Update promotion amount and factor`
21	`End Sub`
22	
23	`Private Sub Form_Current()`
24	`    Combo29 = Client_Number ' Update the combo box`
25	`    UpdatePromoData ' Update promotion amount and factor`
26	`End Sub`
27	
28	`Private Sub Form_Load()`
29	`    HidePromotion ' Hide promotion data when form is loaded`
30	`End Sub`
31	
32	`Private Sub Next_Record_Click()`
33	`On Error GoTo Err_Next_Record_Click`
34	
35	

Table 8-19 Code Associated with Client Update Form

LINE	STATEMENT
36	DoCmd.GoToRecord , , acNext
37	
38	Exit_Next_Record_Click:
39	Exit Sub
40	
41	Err_Next_Record_Click:
42	MsgBox Err.Description
43	Resume Exit_Next_Record_Click
44	
45	End Sub
46	Private Sub Previous_Record_Click()
47	On Error GoTo Err_Previous_Record_Click
48	
49	
50	DoCmd.GoToRecord , , acPrevious
51	
52	Exit_Previous_Record_Click:
53	Exit Sub
54	
55	Err_Previous_Record_Click:
56	MsgBox Err.Description
57	Resume Exit_Previous_Record_Click
58	
59	End Sub
60	Private Sub Add_Record_Click()
61	On Error GoTo Err_Add_Record_Click
62	
63	
64	DoCmd.GoToRecord , , acNewRec
65	Client_Number.SetFocus
66	
67	Exit_Add_Record_Click:
68	Exit Sub
69	
70	Err_Add_Record_Click:
71	MsgBox Err.Description
72	Resume Exit_Add_Record_Click
73	
74	End Sub

(continued)

Table 8-19   Code Associated with Client Update Form (continued)

LINE	STATEMENT
75	`Private Sub Delete_Record_Click()`
76	`On Error GoTo Err_Delete_Record_Click`
77	
78	
79	`    DoCmd.DoMenuItem acFormBar, acEditMenu, 8, , acMenuVer70`
80	`    DoCmd.DoMenuItem acFormBar, acEditMenu, 6, , acMenuVer70`
81	
82	`Exit_Delete_Record_Click:`
83	`    Exit Sub`
84	
85	`Err_Delete_Record_Click:`
86	`    MsgBox Err.Description`
87	`    Resume Exit_Delete_Record_Click`
88	
89	`End Sub`
90	`Private Sub Close_Form_Click()`
91	`On Error GoTo Err_Close_Form_Click`
92	
93	
94	`    DoCmd.Close`
95	
96	`Exit_Close_Form_Click:`
97	`    Exit Sub`
98	
99	`Err_Close_Form_Click:`
100	`    MsgBox Err.Description`
101	`    Resume Exit_Close_Form_Click`
102	
103	`End Sub`
104	`Private Sub Combo31_AfterUpdate()`
105	`    ' Find the record that matches the control.`
106	`    Dim rs As Object`
107	
108	`    Set rs = Me.Recordset.Clone`
109	`    rs.FindFirst "[Client Number] = '" & Me![Combo31] & "'"`
110	`    If Not rs.EOF Then Me.Bookmark = rs.Bookmark`
111	`End Sub`
112	
113	`Public Sub ShowPromotion()`

LINE	STATEMENT
	Table 8-19 Code Associated with Client Update Form
114	`        txtPromoAmount.Visible = True`
115	`        txtPromoFactor.Visible = True`
116	`        cmdPromoQuery.Visible = True`
117	`End Sub`
118	
119	`Public Sub HidePromotion()`
120	`        txtPromoAmount.Visible = False`
121	`        txtPromoFactor.Visible = False`
122	`        cmdPromoQuery.Visible = False`
123	`End Sub`
124	
125	`Public Sub UpdatePromoData()`
126	`        txtPromoAmount.Value = PromoAmount([Client Type], [Current Due])`
127	`        txtPromoFactor.Value = PromoFactor([Client Type])`
128	`End Sub`

The following is an explanation of the lines in the table:

Line 1. This line is inserted automatically. It indicates the method to be used to compare and sort text data. The Database option, which is the one Access includes automatically, means that normal alphabetical order will be used.

Lines 3-13. This is the cmdPromo_Click procedure. It was discussed on page AC 482.

Lines 15-17. This is the procedure to update promotion data after the data in the Client Type combo box is changed. It was discussed on page AC 490.

Lines 19-21. This is the procedure to update promotion data after the data in the Current Due control is changed. It was discussed on page AC 490.

Lines 23-26. This is the procedure that will be executed whenever a different record appears (for example, after the Next Record button is clicked). The statement on line 24, which updates the combo box with the correct client's name, was discussed on page AC 440 in Project 7. The statement on line 25, which runs the UpdatePromoData procedure to update the promotion amount and promotion factor, was discussed on page AC 489.

Lines 28-30. This is the procedure that will be executed when the form is loaded. The statement on line 29 runs the procedure to hide the promotion amount, the promotion factor, and the button to run the Promotion Amount query. It was discussed on page AC 492.

Lines 32-45. This is the procedure that will be executed when the Next Record button is clicked. It was added automatically by Access and was not changed.

Lines 46-59. This is the procedure that will be executed when the Previous Record button is clicked. It was added automatically by Access and was not changed.

Lines 60-74. This is the procedure that will be executed when the Add Record button is clicked. It was added automatically by Access. The statement on line 65 updates the focus to display an insertion point in the control for the Client Number field. It was discussed on page AC 436.

Lines 75-89. This is the procedure that will be executed when the Delete Record button is clicked. It was added automatically by Access and was not changed.

Lines 90-103. This is the procedure that will be executed when the Close Form button is clicked. It was added automatically by Access and was not changed.

Lines 104-111. This is the procedure that will be executed when the combo box for finding a client is updated. It was added automatically by Access and was not changed.

Lines 113-117. This is the ShowPromotion procedure. It was discussed on page AC 484.

Lines 119-123. This is the HidePromotion procedure. It was discussed on page AC 484.

Lines 125-128. This is the UpdatePromoData procedure. It was discussed on page AC 488.

More About

Subforms

A main form does not need to be based on a table or query. If the main form is not based on a table or query, it still can contain one or more subforms. The main form simply serves as a container for the subforms, which then have no restrictions on the information they must contain.

Creating a Form Using Design View

You have learned how to use the Form Wizard to create a variety of forms. You also can create a form without the wizard by simply using Design view. You will be presented with a blank form on which you can place all the necessary controls. On the form you create in this project, you will need to place a subform, two charts, and a Web browser.

Creating a Query for the Subform

The subform is based on data in a query, so you first must create the query. The following steps illustrate how to create the query for the subform.

To Create a Query

1 If necessary in the Database window, click Tables on the Objects bar, and then click Client. Click the New Object button arrow on the Database toolbar. Click Query. Be sure Design View is selected, and then click the OK button. Maximize the Query1 : Select Query window if it is not already maximized. Resize the upper and lower panes and the Client field list so all the fields in the Client table appear.

2 Right-click any open area in the upper pane, click Show Table on the shortcut menu, click the Course Offerings table, click the Add button, and then click the Close button. Resize the upper and lower panes and the Client field list so all the fields in the Client table appear. Double-click the Trainer Number field from the Client table.

3 Double-click the Client Number and Name fields from the Client table. Double-click the Course Number, Total Hours, and Hours Spent fields from the Course Offerings table.

4 Select Ascending as the sort order for both the Trainer Number and Client Number fields.

5 Close the query by clicking its Close Window button. Click the Yes button to save the query. Type Clients and Course Offerings as the name of the query, and then click the OK button.

The query is created.

Creating a Form

When you want to create a form from scratch, you begin with the same general procedure as when you want to use the Form Wizard. The difference is that you will select Design View instead of Form Wizard. The following steps demonstrate how to create the form.

To Create a Form

1

• **If necessary in the Database window, click Tables on the Objects bar, and then click Trainer.**

• **Click the New Object button arrow on the Database toolbar.**

• **Click Form.**

• **Be sure Design View is selected, and then click the OK button.**

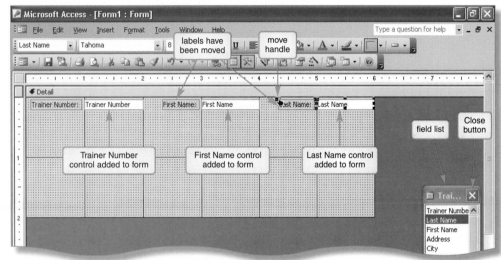

FIGURE 8-57

2

• **Be sure the field list appears and the window is maximized. (If it does not, click the Field List button on the Form Design toolbar.)**

• **Drag the Trainer Number, First Name, and Last Name fields to the approximate positions shown in Figure 8-57.**

• **Move the attached labels for the First Name and Last Name fields to the positions shown in the figure by dragging their move handles.**

3

• **Close the field list by clicking its Close button.**

The field list no longer appears. The fields have been placed on the form.

Using Tab Controls to Create a Multi-Page Form

You can create a **multi-page form**, a form that includes more than a single page, by inserting a page break at the desired location. An alternative that produces a nice-looking and easy-to-use multi-page form is to insert a tab control. Once you have done so, users can change from one page to another by clicking the desired tab.

The steps on the next page illustrate how to insert a tab control with three tabs — Datasheet, Charts, and Web. Users will be able to click the Datasheet tab in the completed form to view work order data in Datasheet view. Clicking the Charts tab will display two charts representing work order data. Clicking the Web tab will display a Web browser showing the Ashton James College home page.

Other Ways

1. Click Forms on Objects bar, click New button, click Design View
2. Click Forms on Objects bar, double-click Create form in Design view
3. On Insert menu click Form, click Design View
4. In Voice Command mode, say "Forms, New"

To Use Tab Controls to Create a Multi-Page Form

1

• **Click the Tab Control tool and move the mouse pointer to the approximate location shown in Figure 8-58.**

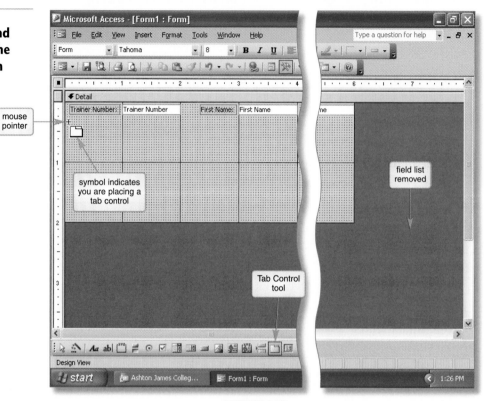

FIGURE 8-58

2

• **Click the position shown in Figure 8-58.**

A tab control appears on the form (Figure 8-59). There currently are two tabs on the control. (Yours may have different numbers.)

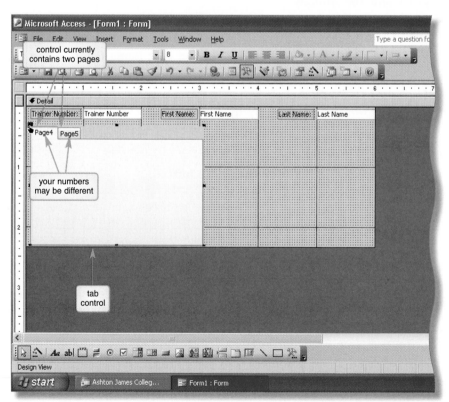

FIGURE 8-59

3

• **Right-click the tab control, and then click Insert Page on the shortcut menu.**

• **Click the leftmost tab, right-click the tab control, and then click Properties on the shortcut menu.**

• **Change the name to Datasheet.**

The property sheet appears (Figure 8-60). The leftmost tab is selected. The name is changed to Datasheet.

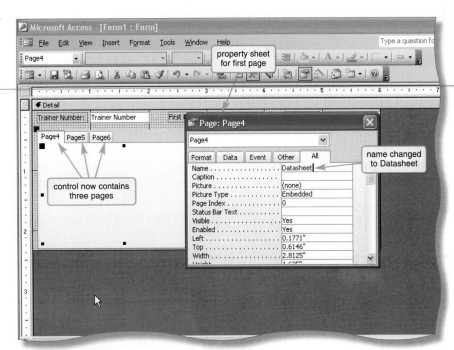

FIGURE 8-60

4

• **Close the property sheet by clicking its Close button.**

• **Right-click the middle tab, select Properties on the shortcut menu, change the name to Charts, and then close the property sheet.**

• **Right-click the rightmost tab, select Properties on the shortcut menu, change the name to Web, and then close the property sheet.**

• **Click the leftmost tab.**

• **Resize the tab control to the approximate size shown in Figure 8-61 by dragging the appropriate sizing handles.**

The tab names are changed and the tab control is resized. The leftmost tab is selected.

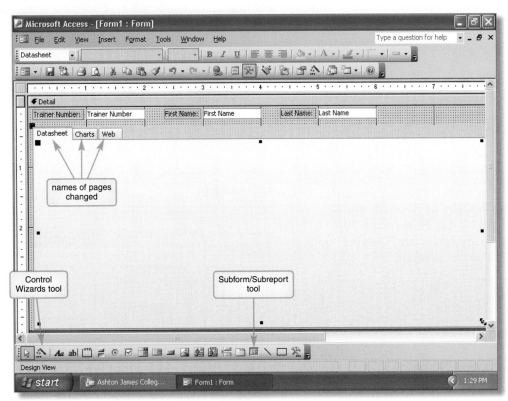

FIGURE 8-61

Placing a Subform

To place a subform on a form, you use the Subform/Subreport tool in the toolbox. Provided the Control Wizards tool is selected, a wizard will guide you through the process of adding the subform as demonstrated in the following steps.

To Place a Subform

1

• **Be sure the Control Wizards tool is selected, click the Subform/Subreport tool in the toolbox, and then move the mouse pointer to the approximate position shown in Figure 8-62.**

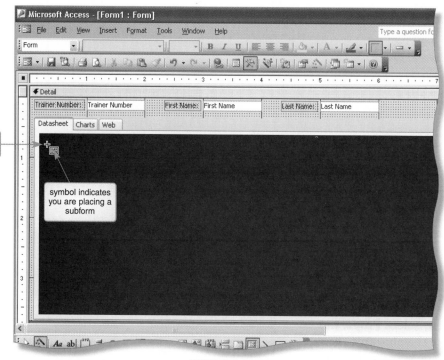

FIGURE 8-62

2

• **Click the position shown in Figure 8-62. Be sure the "Use existing Tables and Queries" option button is selected.**

The SubForm Wizard dialog box appears (Figure 8-63).

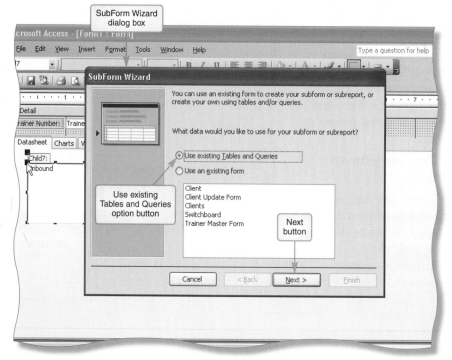

FIGURE 8-63

3

- **Click the Next button.**
- **Click the Tables/Queries box arrow and then click the Clients and Course Offerings query.**
- **Click the Add All fields button.**

The Clients and Course Offerings query is selected (Figure 8-64). All fields are selected.

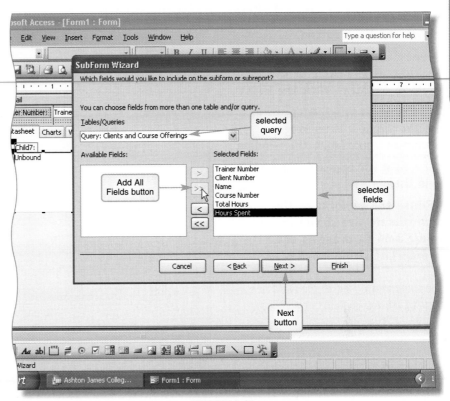

FIGURE 8-64

4

- **Click the Next button.**
- **Be sure the "Choose from a list" option button is selected.**

The SubForm Wizard dialog box appears, asking how you wish to link the main form and subform (Figure 8-65).

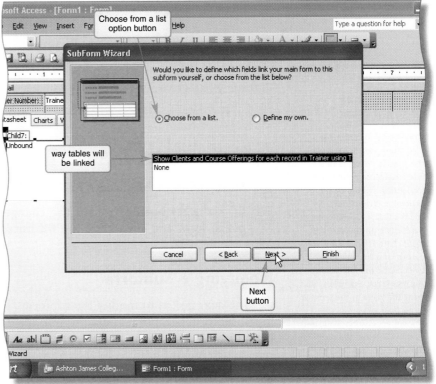

FIGURE 8-65

5

- **Click the Next button.**
- **Type** Course Offerings for Trainer **as the name of the subform and then click the Finish button.**
- **If the window is no longer maximized, maximize the window.**
- **If a field list appears, close the field list.**
- **Resize the subform to the approximate size shown in Figure 8-66 by dragging the appropriate sizing handles.**

The subform is added to the Datasheet page of the tab control.

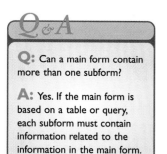

Q: Can a main form contain more than one subform?

A: Yes. If the main form is based on a table or query, each subform must contain information related to the information in the main form.

More About

Conditional Formatting

Conditional formatting is formatting that depends on the specific contents of a control. To use conditional formatting, right-click the control in Design view, and then click Conditional Formatting on the shortcut menu. Enter the desired conditions, and then click the buttons for the formatting you want. For example, if you want the value in the control to be bold whenever the amount is between $0.00 and $1,000.00, enter the condition that indicates that the field value is between 0 and 1000. Next, click the Bold button. Complete the process by clicking the OK button. Values between $0.00 and $1,000 will be bold. Other values will not.

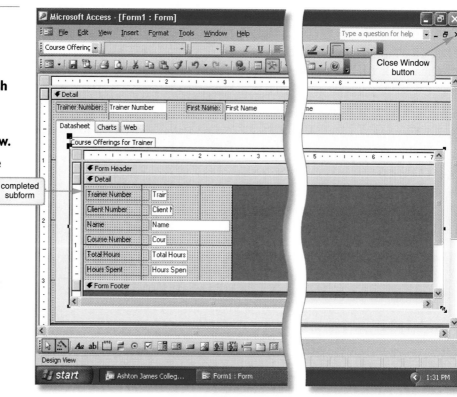

FIGURE 8-66

Closing and Saving the Form

To close a form, close the window using the Close Window button. Then indicate whether you want to save your changes. The following steps show how to close and save the form.

To Close and Save a Form

1. **Close the form by clicking its Close Window button.**

2. **Click the Yes button to save the changes. Type** Trainer Data **as the name of the form and then click the OK button.**

Modifying a Subform

The next task is to modify the subform. The Trainer Number field needed to be in the subform because it is used to link the data in the subform to the data in the main form. It is not supposed to appear in the form, however. In addition, the remaining columns need to be resized to appropriate sizes. The following steps illustrate how to first remove the Trainer Number field and then convert to Datasheet view to resize the remaining columns.

To Modify a Subform

- **In the Database window, click Forms on the Objects bar, right-click the Course Offerings for Trainer form, and then click Design View on the shortcut menu.**
- **Click the Trainer Number control, and then press the DELETE key to delete the control.**
- **Click the View button.**

The subform appears in Datasheet view (Figure 8-67). The Trainer Number field has been removed.

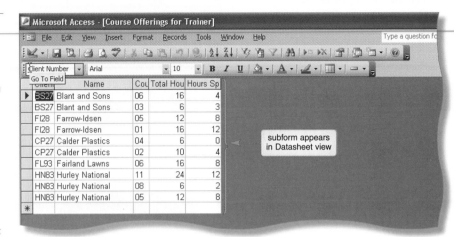

subform appears in Datasheet view

FIGURE 8-67

- **Resize each column to best fit the data by double-clicking the right boundary of the column's field selector.**
- **Close the subform by clicking its Close Window button.**
- **Click the Yes button to save the changes.**

The subform has been changed.

Inserting Charts

To insert a chart, use the Chart command on the Insert menu. The Chart Wizard then will ask you to indicate the fields to be included on the chart and the type of chart you wish to insert. The following steps illustrate how to insert a chart.

To Insert Charts

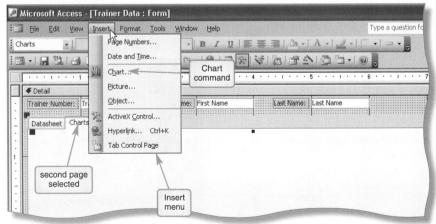

- **In the Ashton James College: Database window, be sure Forms is selected on the Objects bar, right-click Trainer Data and then click Design View on the shortcut menu.**
- **Be sure the window is maximized, and then close the field list if it appears.**
- **Click the Charts tab and then click Insert on the menu bar.**

The Insert menu appears (Figure 8-68). The Charts tab is selected.

Chart command

second page selected

Insert menu

FIGURE 8-68

Microsoft Office
Access 2003

2

• **Click Chart and then move the pointer to the approximate position shown in Figure 8-69.**

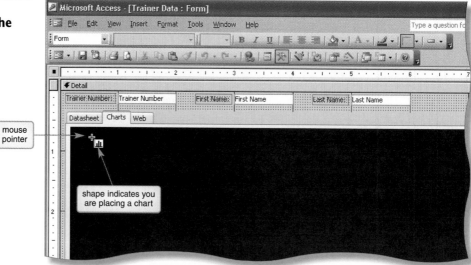

FIGURE 8-69

3

• **Click the position shown in Figure 8-69.**

• **Click the Queries option button in the Chart Wizard dialog box, click the Clients and Course Offerings query, and then click the Next button.**

• **Select the Course Number and Total Hours fields by clicking them and then clicking the Add Field button.**

The Chart Wizard dialog box appears (Figure 8-70). The fields for the chart have been selected.

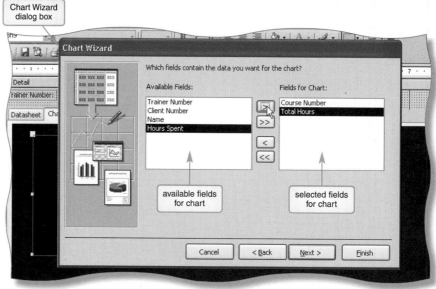

FIGURE 8-70

4

• **Click the Next button.**

• **Be sure the chart in the upper-left corner is selected.**

The Chart Wizard dialog box displays various types of charts (Figure 8-71). Use this box to select the type of chart you want to produce. A description of the selected chart type appears in the dialog box.

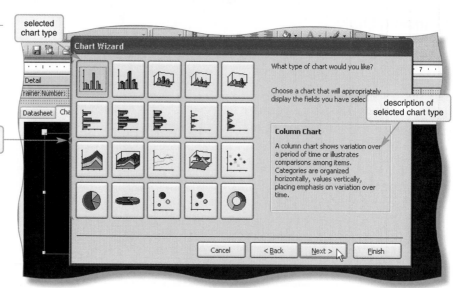

FIGURE 8-71

5

• **Click the Next button.**

The Chart Wizard dialog box displays the layout of the chart (Figure 8-72). The correct items have been placed on the chart in the correct positions. (If not, you could drag the items to the correct positions.)

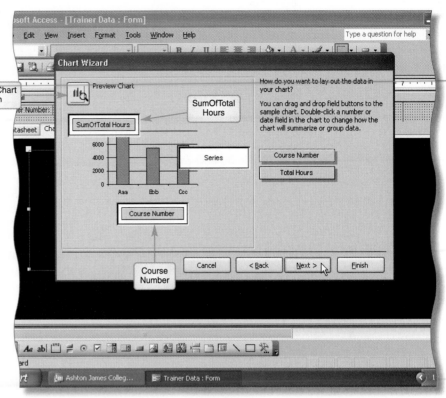

FIGURE 8-72

6

• **Click the Next button.**

The Chart Wizard dialog box appears, indicating the fields that will be used to link the document and the chart (Figure 8-73). Linking the document and the chart ensures that the chart will reflect accurately the data for the correct trainer, that is, the trainer who currently appears in the form.

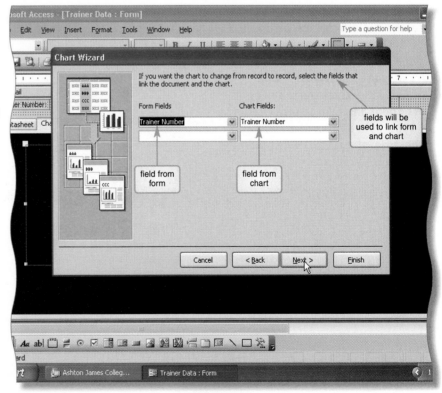

FIGURE 8-73

7

• **Click the Next button, type** Total Hours by Course **as the title, and then click the Finish button.**

The chart appears (Figure 8-74). The title is changed. The data in it is fictitious. The data simply represents the general way the chart will look. Yours may be different.

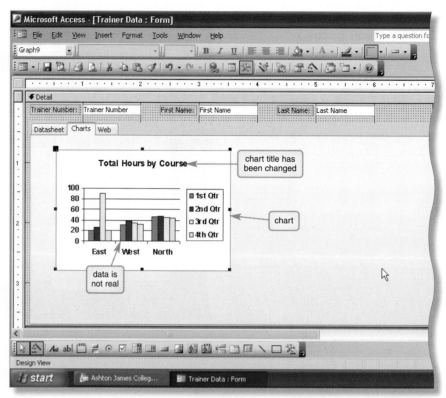

FIGURE 8-74

8

• **Use the techniques shown in Steps 1 through 7 on pages AC 511 through AC 514 to add a second chart at the position shown in Figure 8-75. In this chart, select Hours Spent instead of Total Hours and type** Hours Spent by Course **as the title of the chart instead of Total Hours by Course.**

The chart is inserted.

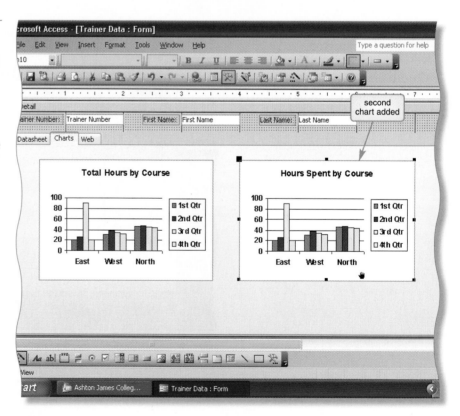

FIGURE 8-75

Other Ways

1. In Voice Command mode, say "Insert, Chart"

Adding an ActiveX Control

When you created forms, you worked with several of the special built-in Microsoft Access controls. These included: text box, label, command button, combo box, rectangle, and so on. Many additional controls, called **ActiveX controls**, also are available. These controls are similar to the others except that they are not part of Access and typically have been developed to work with a variety of applications. There are a wide variety of ActiveX controls available, both from Microsoft and from other sources. In general, to find how to use a particular control, consult the documentation provided with the control.

Many ActiveX controls are installed automatically along with Office. One of the most popular of these is the Calendar control, which enables you to display a calendar on a form. The following steps use another popular control, the Microsoft Web Browser control, to display a Web page on a form. To use the Microsoft Web Browser control, you first add it to the form by selecting it from a list of available ActiveX controls. This places the control on the form. You also will indicate during the loading of the form the Web page that should be displayed.

To indicate the Web page, include a statement similar to the following in the Form_Load procedure: me!WebBrowser1.navigate followed by the URL for the Web page to be displayed. For example, you will use the statement me!WebBrowser1.navigate "http://www.scsite.com/ac2003/ajc.html" in the procedure that will be executed when the form is loaded. In this statement, the me keyword followed by the exclamation point simply indicates that what follows is part of the current object, that is, the form that is being loaded. The name following the exclamation point is the name of the control. The navigate method of the control is used to open the indicated Web page.

The steps on the next page illustrate how to add the Web Browser control to the form and make the necessary change to the Form_Load procedure.

More About

ActiveX Controls

ActiveX controls are objects with embedded code usually written in the Visual Basic or the C++ programming language. ActiveX controls can be used by many different applications in the Windows environment. The slider boxes and counters used on Web pages are other examples of ActiveX controls. ActiveX controls are similar in concept and implementation to Java applets. For more information about ActiveX controls, visit the Access 2003 More About Web page (scsite.com/ac2003/more) and click ActiveX Controls.

More About

The Me Keyword

The Me keyword always refers to the current object. If used within a form, Me is the simplest way to reference the form.

To Add an ActiveX Control

1

• **Click the third tab, the one labeled Web on the tab control.**

• **Click Insert on the menu bar, and then click ActiveX Control on the Insert menu to display the Insert ActiveX Control dialog box.**

• **Select Microsoft Web Browser in the Select an ActiveX Control list and then click the OK button.**

• **Be sure the Web browser just added is selected.**

The Microsoft Web Browser is added to the Web page on the tab control (Figure 8-76).

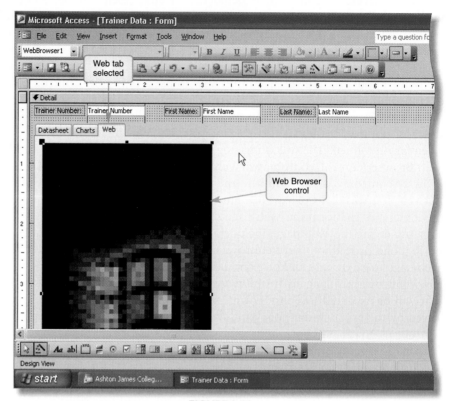

FIGURE 8-76

2

• **Drag the right sizing handle and then drag the lower sizing handle to change the size of the Web Browser control to the one shown in Figure 8-77.**

• **Right-click the control and then click Properties on the shortcut menu to display the property sheet. (In the figure, this already has been done.)**

The property sheet for the Web Browser control appears. The name of the control is WebBrowser1 (yours may be different).

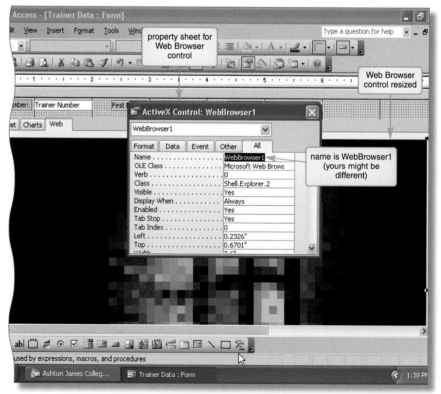

FIGURE 8-77

• **Note the number of your Web Browser control, which may be different from the one shown in Figure 8-77.**

• **Click the Close button for the property sheet.**

• **Right-click the form selector, click Properties on the shortcut menu, scroll down so the On Load property appears, and then click the On Load property.**

• **Click the Build button, click Code Builder in the Choose Builder dialog box, and then click the OK button.**

• **Type** me!WebBrowser1.navigate "http://www.scsite.com/ac2003/ ajc.html" **as the statement in the Form_Load procedure.**

The Form_Load procedure is created (Figure 8-78). If the name of your Web Browser control is not WebBrowser1, substitute the name of your control for WebBrowser1 in the statement. If you do not have access to the Internet, you can replace the http address with the version furnished with your Data Disk (for example, "a:\ajc.html" or "c:\data\ajc.html").

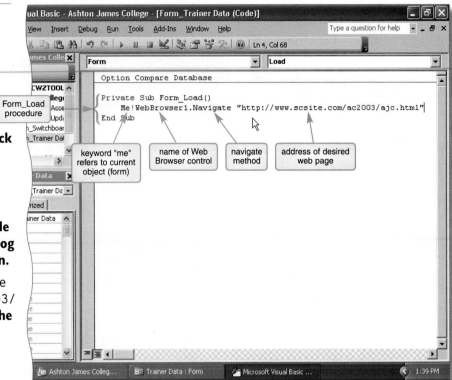

FIGURE 8-78

• **Click the Close button for the Microsoft Visual Basic – Ashton James College – [Form_Trainer Data (Code)] window to close the window.**

• **Click the Close button for the property sheet.**

The Visual Basic window and the property sheet are closed and the form design again appears.

Adding a Title

The form in Figure 8-2a on page AC 460 contains a title. To add a title to a form created in Design view, first use Form Header/Footer on the View menu to add a form header. Next, expand the form header to allow room for the title. You then can use the Label tool in the toolbox to place the label in the form header and type the title in the label. The steps on the next page show how to add a title to the form.

Other Ways

1. In Voice Command mode, say "Insert, ActiveX Control"

More About

The Quick Reference

For a table that lists how to complete the tasks covered in this book using the mouse, menu, shortcut menu, and keyboard, see the Quick Reference Summary at the back of this book, or visit the Access 2003 Quick Reference Web page (scsite.com/ac2003/qr).

To Add a Title

1

• **Click View on the menu bar, and then click Form Header/Footer on the View menu.**

• **Drag the lower boundary of the form header so the header is approximately the size shown in Figure 8-79.**

The form header is expanded. The subform design appears. (Yours may show a name instead of the subform design.)

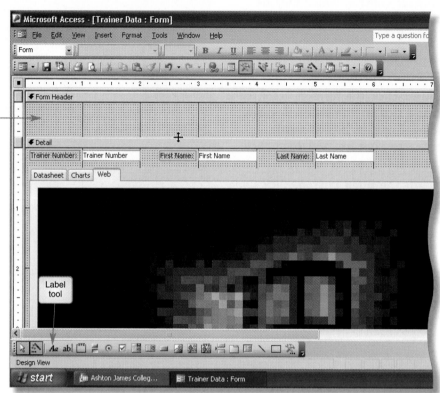

FIGURE 8-79

2

• **Click the Label tool in the toolbox, click the approximate upper-left corner of the label for the title shown in Figure 8-80, drag the pointer so the label is the approximate size of the one shown in the figure, and then type** `Trainer Course Offering Data` **as the title.**

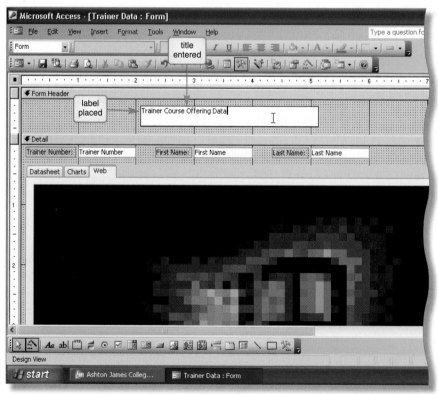

FIGURE 8-80

3

- **Click outside the label to deselect it, right-click the label, and then click Properties on the shortcut menu.**
- **Change the value of the Font Size property to 14 and the value of the Text Align property to Distribute.**
- **Close the property sheet.**

The changes to the title are complete (Figure 8-81).

4

- **Close the form by clicking its Close Window button.**
- **When asked if you want to save your changes, click the Yes button.**

The form is closed and the changes are saved.

FIGURE 8-81

Using the Form

You use this form, just like the other forms you have created and used. To move from one tabbed page to another, simply click the desired tab. The corresponding page then will appear.

The steps on the next page show how to use the form.

More About

Microsoft Certification

Microsoft Office Certification provides an opportunity for you to obtain a valuable industry credential — proof that you have the Access skills required by employers. For more information, see Appendix E, or visit the Access 2003 Certification Web page (scsite.com/ac2003/cert).

To Use the Form

1

• **Right-click the Trainer Data form in the Database window, and then click Open on the shortcut menu.**

The completed form appears (Figure 8-82).

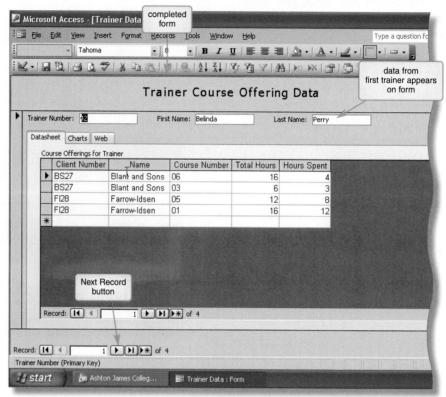

FIGURE 8-82

2

• **Click the Next Record button for trainers (the one in the set of navigation buttons at the bottom of the screen) to move to the second trainer.**

• **Click the Next Record button for Course Offerings (the one in the navigation buttons under the subform) three times.**

The second trainer appears on the form (Figure 8-83). The fourth work order for this trainer is highlighted.

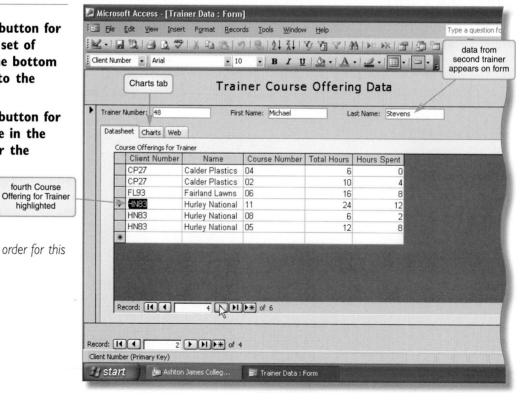

FIGURE 8-83

3

• **Click the Charts tab.**

The charts for the second trainer's work order data appear (Figure 8-84). Across the bottom of the charts are the courses (2, 4, 5, 6, 8, and 11 for this trainer). The height of the bars represents the total hours. For course 2, for example, the bar has a height of 10 in the first chart, indicating the trainer has a total of 10 hours that ultimately will be spent for offerings of course 2. The height of the corresponding bar in the second chart is 4, indicating that the trainer already has spent 4 hours for offerings of this course.

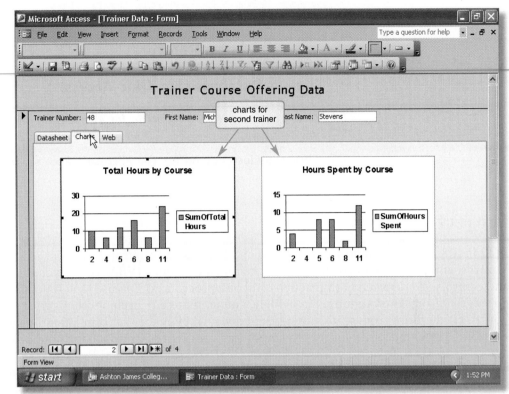

FIGURE 8-84

4

• **Click the Web tab.**

The Web page for Ashton James College appears (Figure 8-85). If you are not connected to the Internet, you may see a message indicating the Web page is unavailable.

5

• **Close the form by clicking its Close Window button.**

The form no longer appears.

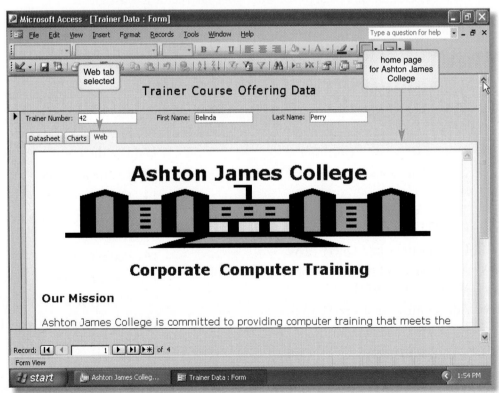

FIGURE 8-85

Closing the Database and Quitting Access

The following steps close the database and quit Access.

To Close a Database and Quit Access

1 **Click the Close Window button for the Ashton James College : Database window.**

2 **Click the Close button for the Microsoft Access window.**

Project Summary

In Project 8, you learned how to add command buttons and controls to a form without using the Control Wizards, and then how to create Visual Basic for Applications (VBA) code to add functionality to the buttons and controls. You created both functions and Sub procedures. You used the functions both in the form and in a query. You grouped procedures in a module, and used these to accomplish a variety of tasks. You also learned how to create forms from scratch using Design view. You made the form a multi-page form by adding a tab control. On the three pages of the tab control, you added a subform, charts, and a Web Browser control.

 If you have a SAM user profile, you may have access to hands-on instruction, practice, and assessment of the skills covered in this project. Log in to your SAM account and go to your assignments page to see what your instructor has assigned.

What You Should Know

Having completed this project, you should be able to perform the tasks below. The tasks are listed in the same order they were presented in this project. For a list of the buttons, menus, toolbars, and commands introduced in this project, see the Quick Reference Summary at the back of this book and refer to the Page Number column.

1. Open a Database   (AC 462)
2. Create Functions in a Standard Module (AC 469)
3. Test Functions in the Immediate Window (AC 471)
4. Use Functions in a Query   (AC 473)
5. Add Command Buttons without the Control Wizards   (AC 475)
6. Add Controls to a Form   (AC 478)
7. Associate Code with an Event   (AC 483)
8. Create Sub Procedures   (AC 485)
9. Create Code to Update Controls   (AC 488)
10. Create a Form Load Event Procedure   (AC 491)
11. Create a Function to Run a Query   (AC 494)
12. Use the Form   (AC 496)
13. Create a Query   (AC 504)
14. Create a Form   (AC 505)
15. Use Tab Controls to Create a Multi-Page Form (AC 506)
16. Place a Subform   (AC 508)
17. Close and Save a Form   (AC 510)
18. Modify a Subform   (AC 511)
19. Insert Charts   (AC 511)
20. Add an ActiveX Control   (AC 516)
21. Add a Title   (AC 518)
22. Use the Form   (AC 520)
23. Close a Database and Quit Access   (AC 522)

Learn It Online

Instructions: To complete the Learn It Online exercises, start your browser, click the Address bar, and then enter the Web address scsite.com/ac2003/learn. When the Access 2003 Learn It Online page is displayed, follow the instructions in the exercises below. Each exercise has instructions for printing your results, either for your own records or for submission to your instructor.

1 Project Reinforcement TF, MC, and SA

Below Access Project 8, click the Project Reinforcement link. Print the quiz by clicking Print on the File menu for each page. Answer each question.

2 Flash Cards

Below Access Project 8, click the Flash Cards link and read the instructions. Type 20 (or a number specified by your instructor) in the Number of playing cards text box, type your name in the Enter your Name text box, and then click the Flip Card button. When the flash card is displayed, read the question and then click the ANSWER box arrow to select an answer. Flip through Flash Cards. If your score is 15 (75%) correct or greater, click Print on the File menu to print your results. If your score is less than 15 (75%) correct, then redo this exercise by clicking the Replay button.

3 Practice Test

Below Access Project 8, click the Practice Test link. Answer each question, enter your first and last name at the bottom of the page, and then click the Grade Test button. When the graded practice test is displayed on your screen, click Print on the File menu to print a hard copy. Continue to take practice tests until you score 80% or better.

4 Who Wants To Be a Computer Genius?

Below Access Project 8, click the Computer Genius link. Read the instructions, enter your first and last name at the bottom of the page, and then click the PLAY button. When your score is displayed, click the PRINT RESULTS link to print a hard copy.

5 Wheel of Terms

Below Access Project 8, click the Wheel of Terms link. Read the instructions, and then enter your first and last name and your school name. Click the PLAY button. When your score is displayed, right-click the score and then click Print on the shortcut menu to print a hard copy.

6 Crossword Puzzle Challenge

Below Access Project 8, click the Crossword Puzzle Challenge link. Read the instructions, and then enter your first and last name. Click the SUBMIT button. Work the crossword puzzle. When you are finished, click the Submit button. When the crossword puzzle is redisplayed, click the Print Puzzle button to print a hard copy.

7 Tips and Tricks

Below Access Project 8, click the Tips and Tricks link. Click a topic that pertains to Project 8. Right-click the information and then click Print on the shortcut menu. Construct a brief example of what the information relates to in Access to confirm you understand how to use the tip or trick.

8 Newsgroups

Below Access Project 8, click the Newsgroups link. Click a topic that pertains to Project 8. Print three comments.

9 Expanding Your Horizons

Below Access Project 8, click the Expanding Your Horizons link. Click a topic that pertains to Project 8. Print the information. Construct a brief example of what the information relates to in Access to confirm you understand the contents of the article.

10 Search Sleuth

Below Access Project 8, click the Search Sleuth link. To search for a term that pertains to this project, select a term below the Project 8 title and then use the Google search engine at google.com (or any major search engine) to display and print two Web pages that present information on the term.

11 Access Online Training

Below Access Project 8, click the Access Online Training link. When your browser displays the Microsoft Office Online Web page, click the Access link. Click one of the Access courses that covers one or more of the objectives listed at the beginning of the project on page AC 458. Print the first page of the course before stepping through it.

12 Office Marketplace

Below Access Project 8, click the Office Marketplace link. When your browser displays the Microsoft Office Online Web page, click the Office Marketplace link. Click a topic that relates to Access. Print the first page.

Apply Your Knowledge

1 Applying Advanced Form Techniques to the Begon Pest Control Database

Instructions: Start Access. If you are using the Microsoft Office Access 2003 Comprehensive text, open the Begon Pest Control database that you used in Project 7. Otherwise, see your instructor for information about accessing the files required for this book. Perform the following tasks:

1. Open the Work Orders and Categories query that you created in Project 7 in Design view. Modify the query to sort the results in ascending order first by Customer Number and then by Category Number. Save the changes to the query.
2. Add a command button to the Customer Update Form that will run the Work Orders and Categories query. Place the button to the right of the Name to Find combo box. The button should display Run Work Orders Query as the caption. The function that you create for the button should be part of a standard module called Query Module and should include error handling. Save the changes to the form.
3. Open the form and click the Run Work Orders Query button and print the query results.
4. Create a query that joins the Customer and Work Orders table. Include the Technician Number, Customer Number, Name, Category Number, and Total Hours (est) fields in the query results. Sort the query in ascending order by Technician Number, Customer Number, and Category Number. Save the query as Customers and Work Orders.
5. Create the Technician Workorder Data form shown in Figure 8-86. The subform that appears in the Datasheet tab uses the Customers and Work Orders query. Use the Ashton James College home page for the Web tab.

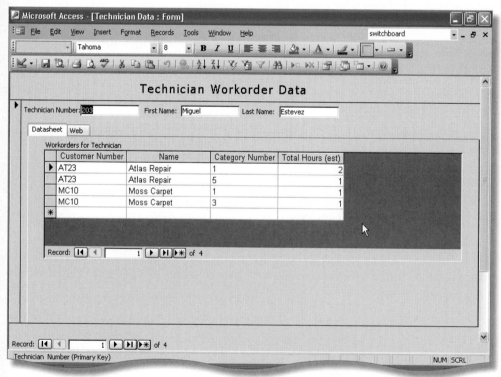

FIGURE 8-86

6. Save and print the form shown in Figure 8-86. To print the form, open the form, click File on the menu bar, click Print, and then click Selected Record(s) as the Print Range. Click the OK button.

In the Lab

1 Applying Advanced Form Techniques to the Birds2U Database

Problem: The management of Birds2U has some additional requests. Because the company gives a five percent discount to all nature centers, it wants a button added to the form that will display the discounted selling price. Management also wants an additional form, one that lists the supplier code and name as well as any items that are on order with the supplier. The form should include a chart that graphically illustrates the total number ordered for each item.

Instructions: Start Access. If you are using the Microsoft Office Access 2003 Comprehensive text, open the Birds2U database that you used in Project 7. Otherwise, see your instructor for information about accessing the files required for this book. Perform the following tasks:

1. Modify the Item Update Form that you created in Project 7. To modify this form, you will need to do the following:
   a. Create a function in a standard module to calculate the discounted amount.
   b. Create a control to display the discounted amount and create the code necessary to update the control. The data will be updated whenever the user moves to a different item on the form or the user updates the selling price. Display the discounted amount to the right of the selling price.
   c. Add a button to show the discount price. If the button currently reads Show Discount Price, the discount amount does not appear and clicking the button will cause the discount amount to appear and the caption for the button to change to Hide Discount Price. Clicking the button a second time will hide the discount amount and also change the caption back to Show Discount Price. Position this button next to the Close Form button on the form.
   d. Create code that will be executed when the form first is loaded to hide the discount amount.
2. Save and print the form. To print the form, open the form, click File on the menu bar, click Print and then click Selected Record(s) as the print range. Click the OK button.
3. Use the Next Record button to move to the record for item code, BB01. Click the Show Discount Price button and print the form.
4. Change the selling price for the record to $87.00 and print the form again.
5. Create a query that joins the Item, Reorder, and Supplier tables. Display the Supplier Code, Name, Item Code, Description, Date Ordered, and Number Ordered fields. Save the query as Reorder Items by Supplier.
6. Create the Open Reorders by Supplier form shown in Figure 8-87. The subform uses the Reorder Items by Supplier query. The Item Code, Description, Date Ordered, and Number Ordered fields appear in Datasheet view when the Datasheet tab is pressed. The chart uses the Reorder Items by Supplier query and displays the item code on the x-axis and the sum of the number ordered on the y-axis. Save the form.
7. Open the Open Reorders by Supplier form and move to the record for Lawn Fixtures. Click the Datasheet tab and print the form.
8. Click the Chart tab and print the form.

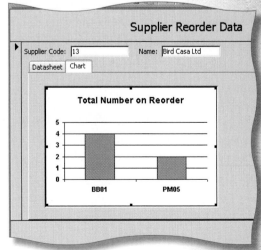

FIGURE 8-87

2 Applying Advanced Form Techniques to the Babbage Bookkeeping Database

Problem: Babbage Bookkeeping has some additional requests. Occasionally, the company offers incentives to clients by applying a credit to client balances. The company wants to be able to display the credit amount on the form. The credit factor is determined by the client type. Finally, the company would like a form that lists the bookkeeper number and name as well as a listing of when bookkeeping services were done. The user should be able to access the company's Web page from the form.

Instructions: If you are using the Microsoft Office Access 2003 Comprehensive text, open the Babbage Bookkeeping database that you used in Project 7. Otherwise, see your instructor for information about accessing the files required for this book. Perform the following tasks:

1. Modify the Client Update Form that you created in Project 7. The form's final appearance should be similar to the Client Update Form shown in Figure 8-1a on page AC 459. To modify this form, you will need to do the following:
   a. Create two functions in a standard module to calculate the credit factor and the amount to credit to the client's balance. Clients with a client type of MAN receive a one percent credit; clients with a client type of RET receive a two percent credit; and clients with a client type of SER receive a three percent credit.
   b. Create controls to display the credit factor and the credit amount and then create the code necessary to update the controls. The data will be updated whenever the client type changes, the user moves to a different client on the form, or the user updates the balance.
   c. Add a button to show the credit data. If the button currently reads Show Credit, the credit factor and credit amount do not appear and clicking the button will cause the credit data to appear and the caption for the button to change to Hide Credit. Clicking the button a second time will hide the credit data and also change the caption back to Show Credit.
   d. Create code that will be executed when the form first is loaded to hide the credit data.
2. Save and print the form. To print the form, open the form, click File on the menu bar, click Print and then click Selected Record(s) as the print range. Click the OK button.
3. Find the record for Mohr Crafts. Click the Show Credit button and print the form.
4. Change the client type for Mohr Crafts to SER and print the form again.
5. Create a query that joins the Client and Accounts tables. Include the Bookkeeper Number, Client Number, Name, Service Date, and Hours Worked fields in the results. Sort the query in ascending order by Bookkeeper Number, Client Number, and Service Date. Save the query as Client Accounts by Bookkeeper.
6. Create the form shown in Figure 8-88. The subform and the chart use the Client Accounts by Bookkeeper query. The chart displays client numbers on the x-axis and the sum of hours worked on the y-axis. Use the Ashton James College Web page for the Web Browser control.
7. Save and print the form shown in Figure 8-88. To print the form, open the form, click File on the menu bar, click Print, and then click Selected Record(s) as the Print Range. Click the OK button.

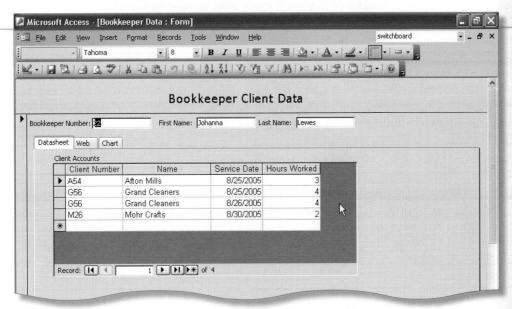

FIGURE 8-88

3 Applying Advanced Form Techniques to the City Guide Database

Problem: The chamber of commerce has some additional requests. First, they want some improvements made to the Advertiser Update Form. The chamber wants to reward its current advertisers for their support. Advertisers will receive a discount on the balance currently owed for advertising. The discount is determined by a promotion factor that is dependent on the advertiser type. Advertisers whose type is DIN or SER have a promotion factor of 0.96 which represents a four percent discount. Advertisers whose type is RET have a promotion factor of 0.98. The promotion amount is the result of multiplying the balance by the appropriate promotion factor. Finally, the company needs a form that will show advertiser accounts by ad rep and display the chamber's home page.

Instructions: If you are using the Microsoft Office Access 2003 Comprehensive text, open the City Guide database that you used in Project 7. Otherwise, see your instructor for information about accessing the files required for this book.

Instructions Part 1:   Modify the Advertiser Update Form to meet the chamber's requirements. The form should be similar in appearance to that shown in Figure 8-1a on page AC 459. Be sure to create code that updates the controls when the advertiser type changes and when the balance changes.

Instructions Part 2:   Create the form shown in Figure 8-89.

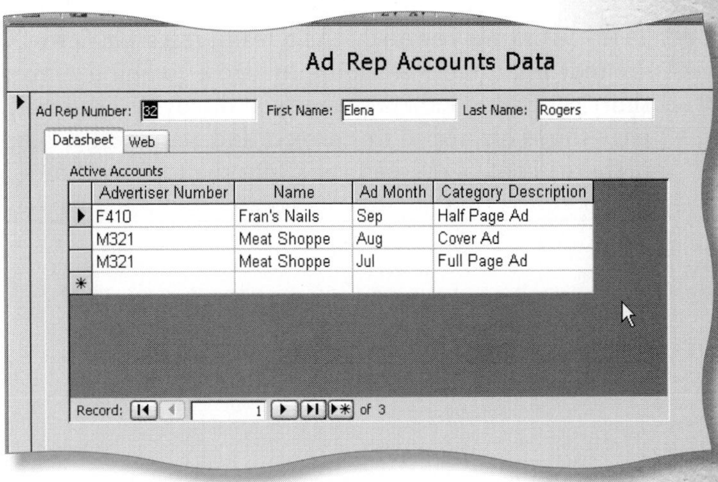

FIGURE 8-89

Cases and Places

The difficulty of these case studies varies:
■ are the least difficult and ■■ are more difficult. The last exercise is a group exercise.

1 ■ Use the College Dog Walkers database that you used in Project 7 for this assignment or see your instructor for information about accessing the files required for this book. Add a command button to the Customer Update Form that when clicked will open the Walker Master List report created in Project 7. Be sure to include error handling.

2 ■ Use the InPerson Fitness Company database that you used in Project 7 for this assignment or see your instructor for information about accessing the files required for this book. Create a form for the InPerson Fitness database that is similar to the form shown in Figure 8-88 on the previous page. Use the Ashton James College Web page for the Web tab or select your own Web page reference.

3 ■■ Use the Regional Books database that you used in Project 7 for this assignment or see your instructor for information about accessing the files required for this book. The bookstore has decided to join with other merchants in offering senior citizens a 10 percent discount. Modify the Book Update Form to create a form that is similar to the Item Update Form described in In the Lab 1.

4 ■■ Use the Campus Housing database that you used in Project 7 for this assignment or see your instructor for information about accessing the files required for this book. To encourage students to seek off-campus housing, the university has convinced property owners to discount the rental amounts for a limited time. Craig Anders will offer a five percent discount. Della Hanley will offer a three percent discount and Alan Kindall will offer a six percent discount. Modify the Rental Update Form to reflect these discounted rents. The form should be similar to that shown in Figure 8-1a on page AC 459. Create a multi-page form that displays potential renters by owner as well as the university's Web page.

5 ■■ **Working Together** As a team, research ActiveX controls. What are ActiveX controls and why are they important? What are the most common ActiveX controls and how are they used? Write a short paper that explains what you discovered through your research. Then, choose one of the multi-page forms created in this project and add another page to the form. Select an ActiveX control and place the control on the form. Print the form and turn in the form and the paper to your instructor.

Administering a Database System

CASE PERSPECTIVE

The administration of Ashton James College (AJC) has decided that they need a database administrator. Several activities have been determined that the individual in charge of administering the database must perform. The activities include analyzing tables for possible duplication, analyzing performance to see where improvements could be made, and producing complete system documentation. The administrator can enable automatic error checking and determine the types of errors for which Access automatically should check. The administrator can assist users by specifying smart tags, which are buttons that appear in fields in tables or controls on forms and that assist users in accomplishing various tasks. The administrator also can assist in importing from, or linking to, lists on SharePoint Services sites. The administrator can specify necessary custom input masks to assist users in entering data in the correct format. The administrator can assist users by ensuring that the switchboard appears automatically whenever they open the database. The administrator should consider the use of both passwords and encoding to protect the database from unauthorized use. To support remote access to the database, administration could include the creation, use, and synchronization of replicas. AJC also wants the database administrator to investigate other ways of protecting their data, including splitting the database, creating an MDE version of the database, and specifying different permissions concerning the use of the database to different users. Your task is to assist the database administrator in these various duties.

As you read through this project, you will learn how to carry out the important duties of a database administrator.

Office Access 2003

Administering a Database System

Objectives

You will have mastered the material in this project when you can:

- Convert a database to an earlier version of Access
- Use the Table Analyzer, Performance Analyzer, and Documenter
- Enable and use automatic error checking
- Create a custom input mask
- Create and use smart tags
- Import and link SharePoint Services lists and use online collaboration

- Set startup options
- Set and remove passwords
- Encode a database
- Set the macro security level
- Use replication and synchronize the Design Master and the replica
- Split a database
- Create an MDE File
- Specify user-level security

Introduction

Administering a database system encompasses a variety of activities (Figure 9-1). Administration can include conversion of a database to an earlier version. Database system administration usually includes such activities as analyzing tables for potential problems, analyzing performance to see if changes are warranted to make the system perform more efficiently, and documenting the various objects in the database. It can include the use of automatic error checking as well as such steps as the creation of custom input masks to assist in the data entry process. The inclusion of smart tags in tables, queries, forms, and reports is part of the administration of a database system as is the sharing of database data via SharePoint Services. Securing the database through the use of passwords and encoding also is part of the administration of a database system as is the setting of startup options. Supporting remote users through replication (making copies of the database for remote use) also falls in the category of administering a database as does the setting of the appropriate macro security level. Another important area of

database administration is the protection of the database. This protection includes splitting the database into a front-end and a back-end database as well as the creation of an MDE file, a file in which all VBA source code is compiled and then removed from the database. Protection also includes assigning specific permissions to users concerning the types of activities they can perform on the various objects in the database. Figure 9-1 summarizes some of the various types of activities involved in administering a database.

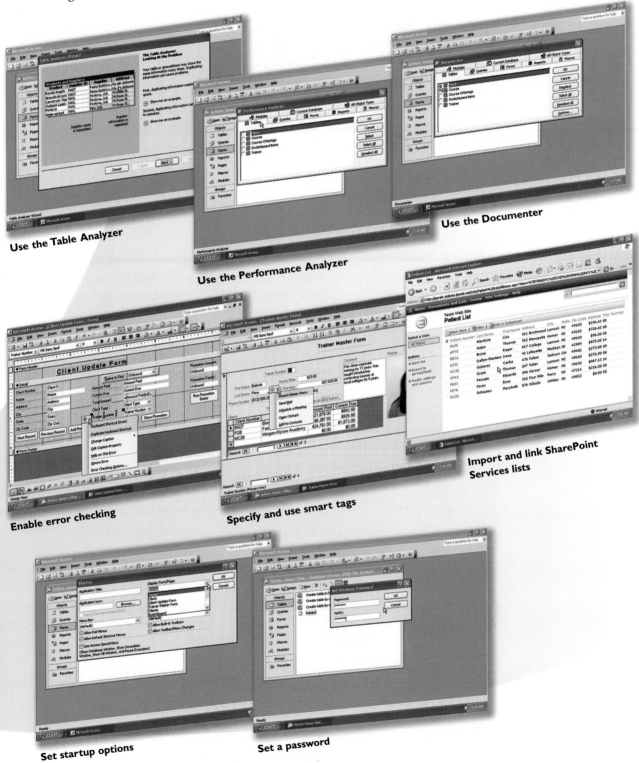

Use the Table Analyzer

Use the Performance Analyzer

Use the Documenter

Enable error checking

Specify and use smart tags

Import and link SharePoint Services lists

Set startup options

Set a password

FIGURE 9-1

More About

The Access Help System

Need Help? It is no further than the Type a question for help box on the menu bar in the upper-right corner of the window. Click the box that contains the text, Type a question for help (Figure 9-4 on page AC 534), type help, and then press the ENTER key. Access responds with a list of topics you can click to learn about obtaining help on any Access-related topic. To find out what is new in Access 2003, type what is new in Access in the Type a question for help box.

Project Nine — Administering a Database System

The steps in this project begin by creating an Access 97 version of the database for a particular user. Next, the use of three Access tools — the Table Analyzer, the Performance Analyzer, and the Documenter are illustrated. The steps show how to enable automatic error checking and determine the types of error checking available. The steps also illustrate creating a custom input mask and specifying smart tags on a table and a form. The use of SharePoint Services lists, including how to import a list to a table in a database and how to link a list are discussed. The steps set a startup option so the switchboard automatically appears when the database is opened. Other commands secure the database by setting a password and encoding the database. The concepts behind macro security level are explained. Steps are presented to create a replica for remote users of the database and to use the replica to update the database. Finally, the steps show additional ways of securing a database. This includes splitting a database into front-end and back-end databases and creating an MDE file, which is a file where VBA code is compiled, editable source code is removed from the database, and the database is compacted. Other methods of securing a database include specifying user-level security in which various groups and users are assigned specific permissions concerning the objects in the database.

Opening the Database

If you are stepping through this project on a computer and you want your screen to match the figures in this book, then you should change your computer's resolution to 800 × 600. For more information on how to change the resolution on your computer, see Appendix D. Before carrying out the steps in this project, first you must open the database. The following steps, which demonstrate how to start Access and open the database, assume that the database is located in a folder called Data on disk C. If your database is located anywhere else, you will need to make the appropriate adjustments in the steps.

To Open a Database

1. **Click the Start button on the Windows taskbar, point to All Programs on the Start menu, point to Microsoft Office on the All Programs submenu, and then click Microsoft Office Access 2003 on the Microsoft Office submenu.**

2. **If the Access window is not maximized, double-click its title bar to maximize it.**

3. **If the Language bar appears, right-click it and then click Close the Language bar on the shortcut menu.**

4. **Click Open on the Database toolbar, and then click Local Disk (C:) in the Look in box. Double-click the Data folder, and then make sure the Ashton James College database is selected.**

5. **Click the Open button.**

6. **If the Security Warning dialog box appears, click the Open button.**

The database opens and the Ashton James College : Database window appears.

Microsoft Access Tools

Microsoft Access has a variety of tools that are useful in administering databases. These include tools to convert a database to an earlier version of Access, to analyze table structures, to analyze performance, and to create detailed documentation.

Q & A

Q: Can I convert an Access 97 database to an Access 2000 or Access 2002 - 2003 version?

A: Yes. To convert an Access 97 database, use the same Convert Database command and select the appropriate Access version for your needs.

Converting a Database to an Earlier Version

If you have stored your database in the default Access 2000 format, any user of Access 2000 can access the database. Occasionally, you might encounter someone who needs to use your database, but who uses Access 97. Such a user cannot access the data directly. You need to convert the database to the earlier version in order for the user to access it. Once you have done so, the user can use the converted version. To convert the database, use the Convert Database command as in the following steps.

To Convert a Database to an Earlier Version

1

• **Click Tools on the menu bar, point to Database Utilities on the Tools menu, and then point to Convert Database on the Database Utilities submenu.**

The Convert Database submenu appears (Figure 9-2).

2

• **Click To Access 97 File Format.**

• **Type** Ashton James College 97 **as the name of the file, and then click the Save button in the Convert Database Into dialog box.**

• **If a warning message appears, click the OK button.**

The Access 97 version of the database is created and available for use.

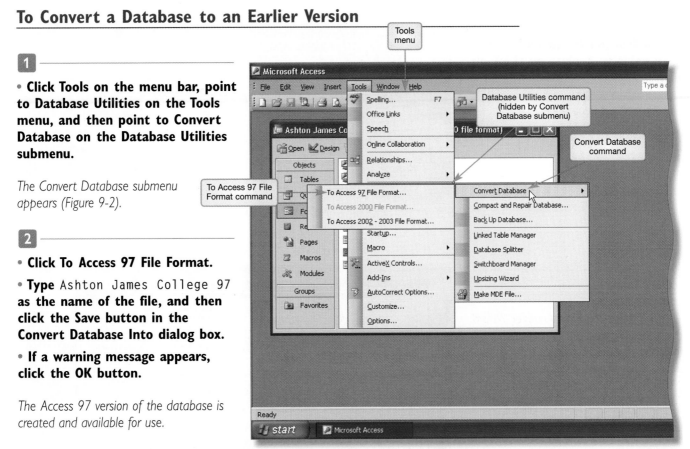

FIGURE 9-2

Other Ways

1. In Voice Command mode, say "Tools, Database Utilities, Convert Database, To Access 97 File Format"

It is important to realize that any changes made in the converted version, will not be reflected in the original. Assuming the original version still is going to be used, the converted version should be used for retrieval purposes only. Otherwise, if you make changes they will appear in one version and not the other, making your data inconsistent.

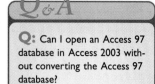

Q: Can I open an Access 97 database in Access 2003 without converting the Access 97 database?

A: Yes. To open an earlier version of an Access database in Access 2003, click Open on the Database toolbar, click the previous version Access database in the Open dialog box, click the Open button, and then in the Convert/Open Database dialog box, click Open Database.

Using the Table Analyzer

Access contains an Analyze tool that performs three separate functions. This tool can analyze tables while looking for potential redundancy (duplicated data). The Analyze tool also can analyze performance and check to see if there is any way to make queries, reports, or forms more efficient. Then, the tool will make suggestions for possible changes. The final function of the analyzer is to produce detailed documentation of the various tables, queries, forms, reports, and other objects in the database.

The Table Analyzer examines tables for **redundancy**, which is duplicated data. If redundancy is found, the Table Analyzer will suggest ways to split the table in order to eliminate the redundancy. The following steps illustrate how to use the Table Analyzer.

To Use the Table Analyzer

1

• **Click Tools on the menu bar, and then point to Analyze on the Tools menu.**

The Analyze submenu appears (Figure 9-3).

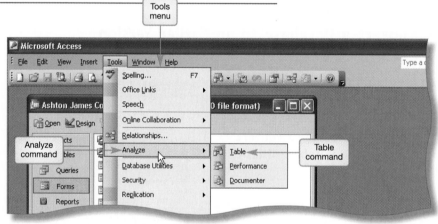

FIGURE 9-3

2

• **Click Table.**

Access displays the Table Analyzer Wizard dialog box (Figure 9-4). The message indicates that tables may store duplicate information, which can cause problems. If a dialog box appears asking to install the Table Analyzer Wizard, check with your instructor before proceeding.

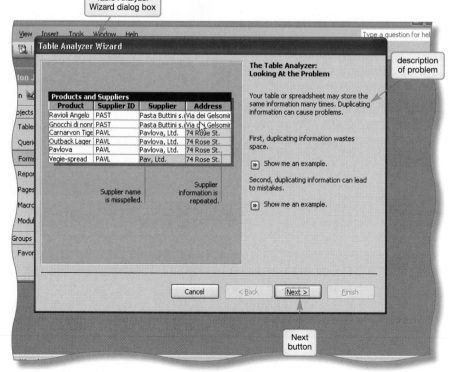

FIGURE 9-4

3

• **Click the Next button.**

The Table Analyzer Wizard displays a message indicating that the wizard will suggest ways to split the original table to remove duplicate information (Figure 9-5).

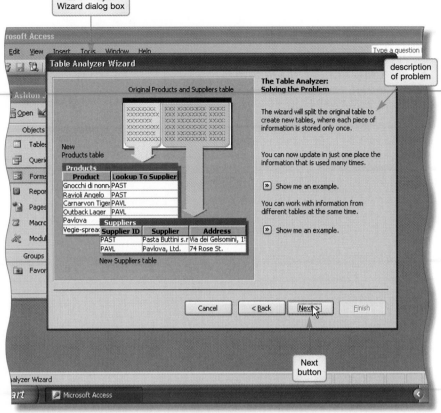

FIGURE 9-5

4

• **Click the Next button.**

• **Make sure the Client table is selected.**

The Client table is selected (Figure 9-6).

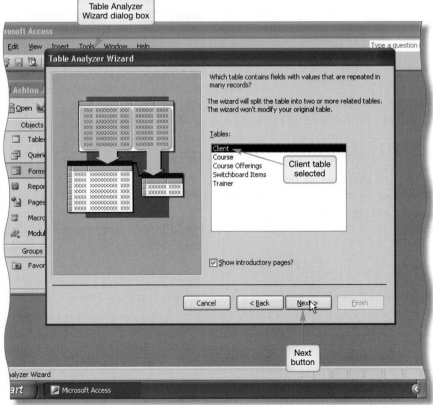

FIGURE 9-6

5

• **Click the Next button.**

• **Be sure the "Yes, let the wizard decide" option button is selected.**

The Table Analyzer Wizard dialog box appears (Figure 9-7). The wizard will decide what fields go in what tables.

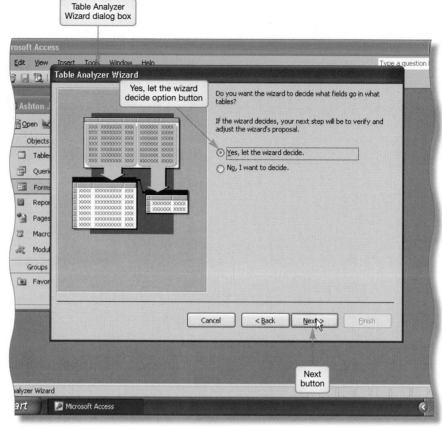

FIGURE 9-7

6

• **Click the Next button.**

The Table Analyzer Wizard dialog box appears (Figure 9-8). It indicates duplicate information (for example, City, State, Zip Code). Your screen may be different.

7

• **Because the type of duplication identified by the analyzer does not pose a problem, click the Cancel button.**

The structure is not changed.

Other Ways

1. Click Analyze button arrow on Database toolbar, click Analyze Table
2. In Voice Command mode, say "Analyze, Analyze Table"

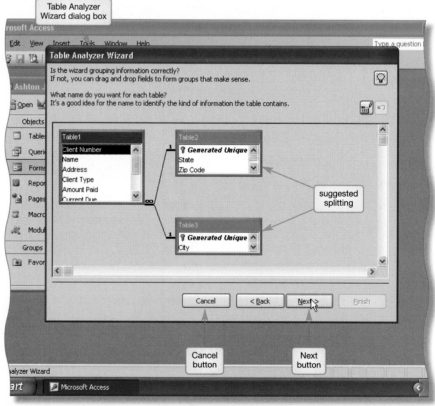

FIGURE 9-8

Using the Performance Analyzer

The Performance Analyzer will examine the tables, queries, reports, forms, and other objects in your system, looking for changes that would improve the efficiency of your database. This could include changes to the way data is stored as well as changes to the indexes created for the system. Once it has finished, it will make recommendations concerning possible changes. The following steps demonstrate how to use the Performance Analyzer.

To Use the Performance Analyzer

1

- **Click Tools on the menu bar, point to Analyze on the Tools menu, and then click Performance on the Analyze submenu.**

- **If necessary, click the Tables tab.**

The Performance Analyzer appears (Figure 9-9). The Tables tab is selected so all the tables appear.

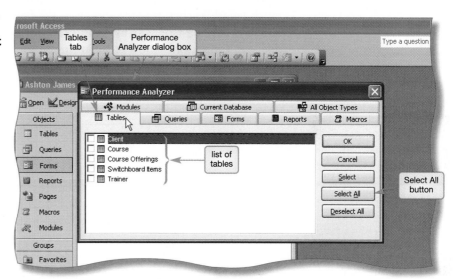

FIGURE 9-9

2

- **Click the Select All button to select all tables.**

- **Click the OK button.**

The Performance Analyzer displays the results of its analysis (Figure 9-10). The Performance Analyzer indicates that you might consider changing the data type of the Course Number field from Text to Long Integer, which is an efficient number format for both computations and data storage.

3

- **Click the Close button.**

The Performance Analyzer no longer appears.

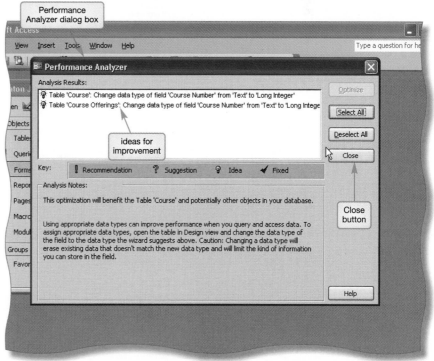

FIGURE 9-10

At this point, you can decide whether to follow the advice given by the Performance Analyzer. You also may decide to make a change to improve performance even though the change was not indicated by the Performance Analyzer. If you have a query that is processing a large amount of data and the query is sorted on a particular field, you probably will want an index built on that field. If one does not exist, you should create it.

Using the Documenter

The Documenter allows you to produce detailed documentation of the various tables, queries, forms, reports, and other objects in your database. Figure 9-11 shows a portion of the documentation of the Client table. The complete documentation is much lengthier than the one shown in the figure. In the actual documentation, all fields would display as much information as the Client Number field. In this documentation, only those items of interest are shown for the other fields.

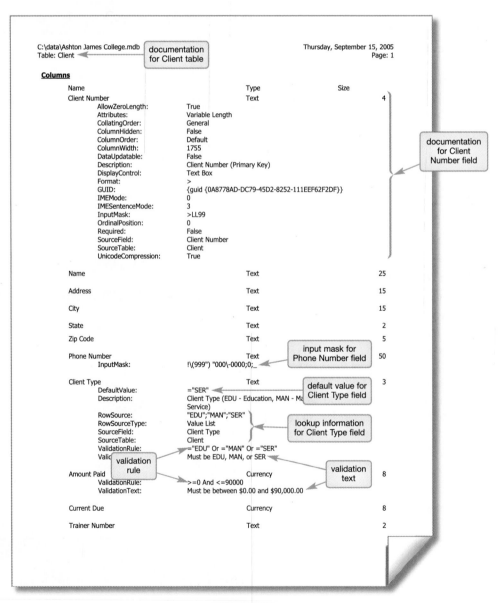

FIGURE 9-11

Notice that the documentation of the Phone Number field includes the input mask. Notice also the documentation of the Client Type field contains the default value, the description, and the row source associated with the Lookup information for the field. The documentation for both the Client Type and Amount Paid fields contains validation rules and validation text.

The following steps show how to use the Documenter to produce documentation for the Client table.

To Use the Documenter

1

• **Click Tools on the menu bar, point to Analyze on the Tools menu, and then click Documenter on the Analyze submenu.**

• **Click the Tables tab and then click the Client check box.**

The Documenter appears (Figure 9-12).

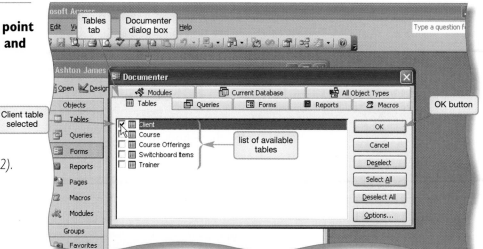

FIGURE 9-12

2

• **Click the OK button.**

Access displays the Object Definition window (Figure 9-13). You can print the documentation by clicking the Print button. You also can save the documentation by using the Export command on the File menu.

3

• **Click the Print button on the Print Preview toolbar to print the documentation.**

• **Close the window by clicking its Close button.**

The documentation no longer appears.

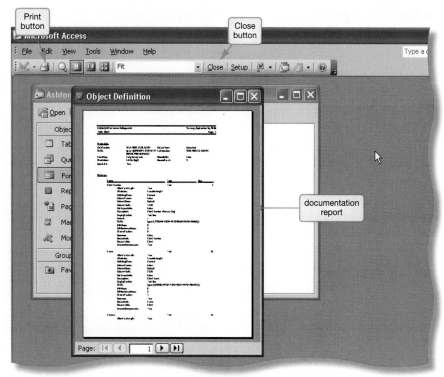

FIGURE 9-13

Table 9-1 Types of Errors	
DATA TYPE	DESCRIPTION
Unassociated label and control	A label and control are selected that are not associated with each other.
New unassociated labels	A newly added label is not associated with any other control.
Keyboard shortcut errors	A shortcut key is invalid. This can happen because an unassociated label has a shortcut key, there are duplicate shortcut keys assigned, or a blank space is assigned as a shortcut key.
Invalid control properties	A control property is invalid. For example, the property can contain invalid characters.
Common report errors	The report has invalid sorting or grouping specifications or the report is wider than the page size.

Automatic Error Checking

Access can automatically check for several types of errors in forms and reports. When it detects an error, it warns you about the existence of the error. Access also provides you with options for correcting it. The types of errors that Access can detect are shown in Table 9-1.

Enabling Error Checking

In order for automatic error checking to take place, it must be enabled. The following steps show how to enable error checking.

To Enable Error Checking

• **Click Tools on the menu bar.**

The Tools menu appears (Figure 9-14).

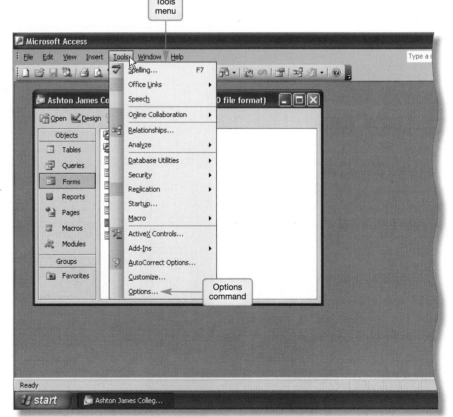

FIGURE 9-14

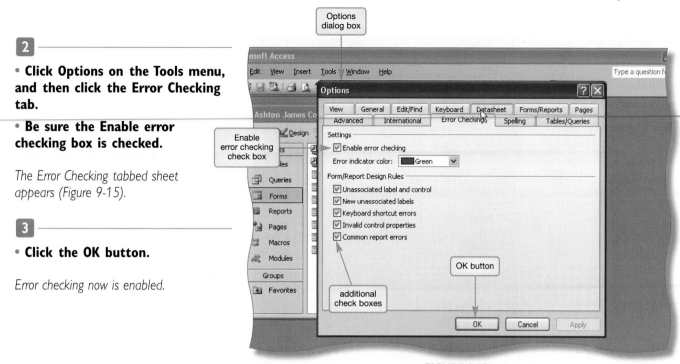

2

• **Click Options on the Tools menu, and then click the Error Checking tab.**

• **Be sure the Enable error checking box is checked.**

The Error Checking tabbed sheet appears (Figure 9-15).

3

• **Click the OK button.**

Error checking now is enabled.

FIGURE 9-15

In Figure 9-15, all the other check boxes are checked, indicating all the various types of automatic error checking that are possible will take place. If there was a particular type of error checking that you did not wish to take place, you would remove its check mark before clicking the OK button.

Error Indication

If an error occurs, a small triangle called an **error indicator**, appears in the appropriate field or control. In Figure 9-16, the label for Trainer Number is changed to include an ampersand (&) before the letter N. This will make the letter N a keyboard shortcut for this control, which is a problem because the letter N is already a shortcut for Name to Find.

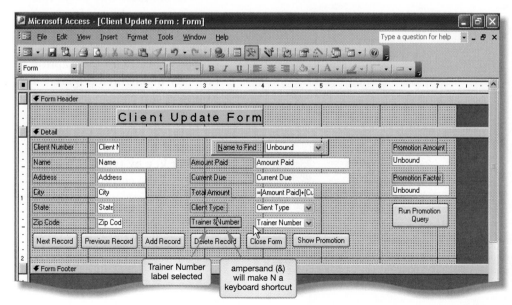

FIGURE 9-16

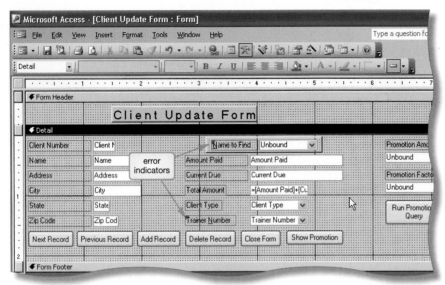

FIGURE 9-17

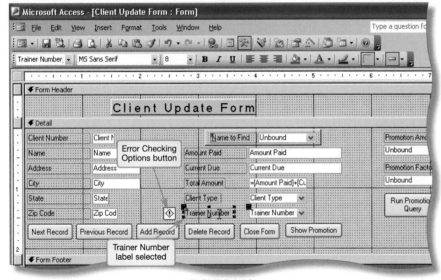

FIGURE 9-18

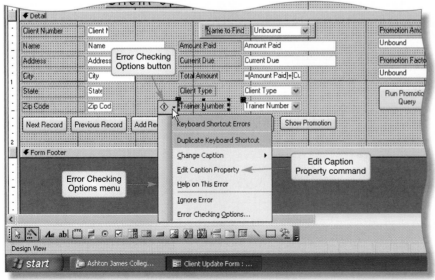

FIGURE 9-19

Once the change is complete, an error indicator appears in both controls in which the letter N is the keyboard shortcut as shown in Figure 9-17.

Selecting a control containing an error indicator will display an Error Checking Options button. In Figure 9-18, the Error Checking Options button appears next to the Trainer Number label, which currently is selected.

Clicking the Error Checking Options button produces the Error Checking Options menu as shown in Figure 9-19. The first line in the menu is simply a statement of the type of error that occurred, and the second is a description of the specific error. The Change Caption command gives a submenu of the captions that can be changed. The Edit Caption Property command allows you to change the caption directly and is the simplest way to correct this error. The Help on This Error command gives help on the specific error that occurred. You can choose to ignore the error by using the Ignore Error command. The final command, Error Checking Options, allows you to change the same error checking options you saw when you first enabled error checking.

The simplest way to fix this error is to edit the caption property. Clicking the Edit Caption Property command produces a property sheet with the Caption property highlighted (Figure 9-20). You then can change the Caption property to make another letter the shortcut key. For example, you could make the letter T the shortcut key by typing &Trainer Number as the entry.

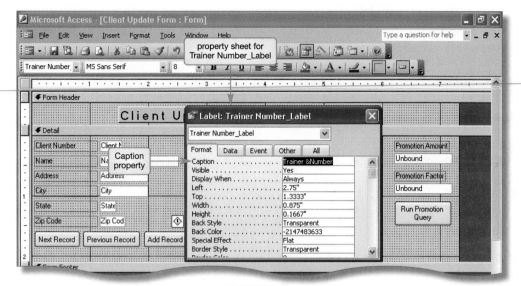

FIGURE 9-20

Custom Input Masks

A way to prevent users from entering data that does not have a certain format is to use an input mask. You may have already used the Input Mask Wizard to create an input mask. Using the wizard, you can select the input mask that meets your needs from a list. This often is the best way to create the input mask.

If the input mask you need to create is not similar to any in the list, you can create a custom input mask by entering the appropriate characters as the value for the Input Mask property. In doing so, you use the symbols from Table 9-2.

For example, to indicate that client numbers must consist of two letters followed by two numbers, you would enter LL99. The Ls in the first two positions indicate that the first two positions must be letters. Using L instead of a question mark indicates that the users must enter these letters; that is, they are not optional. With the question mark, they could leave these posi-

Table 9-2	Input Mask Symbols	
SYMBOL	**TYPE OF DATA ACCEPTED**	**DATA ENTRY OPTIONAL**
0	Digits (0 through 9) without plus (+) or minus (-) sign. Positions left blank appear as zeros.	No
9	Digits (0 through 9) without plus (+) or minus (-) sign. Positions left blank appear as spaces.	Yes
#	Digits (0 through 9) with plus (+) or minus (-) sign. Positions left blank appear as spaces.	Yes
L	Letters (A through Z).	No
?	Letters (A through Z).	Yes
A	Letters (A through Z) or digits (0 through 9).	No
a	Letters (A through Z) or digits (0 through 9).	Yes
&	Any character or a space.	No
C	Any character or a space.	Yes
<	Converts any letter entered to lowercase.	Does not apply
>	Converts any letter entered to uppercase.	Does not apply
!	Characters typed in the input mask fill it from left to right.	Does not apply
\	Character following the slash is treated as a literal in the input mask.	Does not apply

tions blank. The 9s in the last two positions indicate that the users must enter digits (0 through 9). Using 9 instead of 0 indicates that they could leave these positions blank; that is, they are optional. Finally, to ensure that any letters entered are converted to uppercase, you would use the > symbol at the beginning of the input mask. The complete mask would be >LL99.

The following steps show how to create a custom input mask for the Client Number field.

To Create a Custom Input Mask

1

• **If necessary, click the Tables object to be sure the tables appear.**

• **Right-click Client and then click Design View on the shortcut menu.**

• **Maximize the window containing the design by double-clicking its title bar.**

• **With the Client Number field selected, click the Input Mask property, and then type** >LL99 **as the value.**

The input mask for the Client Number field is entered (Figure 9-21).

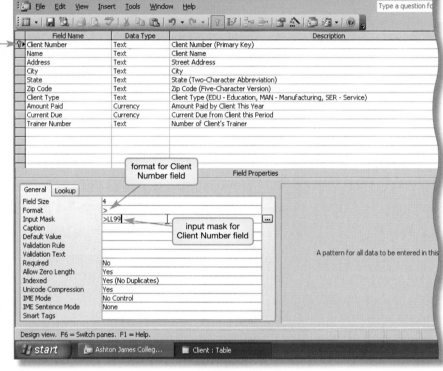

FIGURE 9-21

2

• **Close the window containing the design by clicking its Close Window button.**

• **When prompted to save the changes, click the Yes button.**

The changes are saved.

From this point on, anyone entering a client number will be restricted to letters in the first two positions and numeric digits in the last two. Further, any letters entered in the first two positions will be converted to uppercase.

In Figure 9-21, the Client Number field has both a custom input mask and a format. Technically, you do not need both. When the same field has both an input mask and a format, the format takes precedence. Because the format specified for the Client Number field is the same as the input mask (uppercase), it will not affect the data.

Smart Tags

In Access, a **smart tag** is a button that appears in a table, query, form, or report that assists users in accomplishing various tasks including connecting to the Web. Smart tags are available in other Office applications as well. You can assign smart tags to fields in tables and queries. You also can assign smart tags to controls in forms and reports.

Showing Smart Tags

In addition to assigning smart tags, you need to take special action to be sure that the smart tags appear. There actually are two options you have to address. One option concerns smart tags appearing in forms and reports. The other concerns smart tags appearing in tables and queries.

To Show Smart Tags in Forms and Reports

1. Click Tools on the menu bar.
2. Click Options on the Tools menu.
3. Click the Forms/Reports tab.
4. Be sure the Show Smart Tags on Forms check box is checked.
5. Click the OK button.

To Show Smart Tags in Tables and Queries

1. Click Tools on the menu bar.
2. Click Options on the Tools menu.
3. Click the Datasheet tab.
4. Be sure the Show Smart Tags on Datasheets check box is checked.
5. Click the OK button.

Hiding Smart Tags

Just as you need to take special action to be sure that smart tags appear, you also need to take special action to hide the smart tags, that is, to be sure that the smart tags do not appear. Again there are two options you have to address. One concerns forms and reports. The other concerns tables and queries.

To Hide Smart Tags in Forms and Reports

1. Click Tools on the menu bar.
2. Click Options on the Tools menu.
3. Click the Forms/Reports tab.
4. Be sure the Show Smart Tags on Forms check box is not checked.
5. Click the OK button.

More About

Smart Tags

Smart tags improve productivity and save time because you can perform actions in Access that you usually would use other programs, such as Outlook and Word to perform. For more information about smart tags, visit the Access 2003 More About Web page (scsite.com/ac2003/more) and click Smart Tags.

To Hide Smart Tags in Tables and Queries

1. Click Tools on the menu bar.
2. Click Options on the Tools menu.
3. Click the Datasheet tab.
4. Be sure the Show Smart Tags on Datasheets check box is not checked.
5. Click the OK button.

Adding a Smart Tag to a Field in a Table

You use the Smart Tag property for a field to add a smart tag to the field. The following steps illustrate how to add a smart tag to the Last Name field in the Trainer table.

To Add a Smart Tag to a Field in a Table

1

• **With the Tables object selected, right-click the Trainer table.**

• **Click Design View on the shortcut menu and make sure the window is maximized.**

• **Click the row selector for the Last Name field.**

• **Click the Smart Tags text box.**

An insertion point appears in the Smart Tags text box (Figure 9-22). The Build button appears.

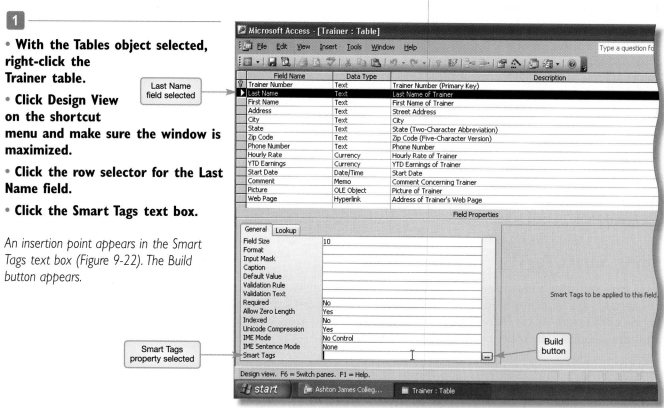

FIGURE 9-22

2

- Click the Build button.
- Click the check box for the Person Name smart tag.

The list of available smart tags appears (Figure 9-23). Your list may be different. The Person Name smart tag is selected. The possible actions for the selected smart tag appear in the Actions box.

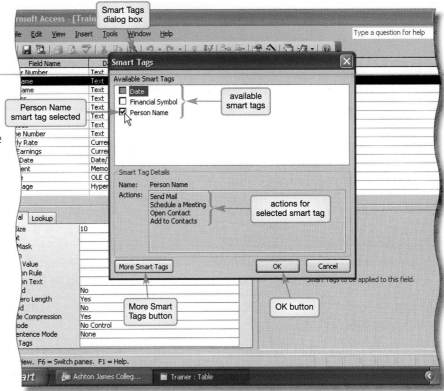

FIGURE 9-23

3

- Click the OK button.

An appropriate entry for the selected smart tag appears in the Smart Tags text box (Figure 9-24).

4

- Close the window containing the table by clicking its Close Window button.
- Save your changes by clicking the Yes button.

The smart tag has been added.

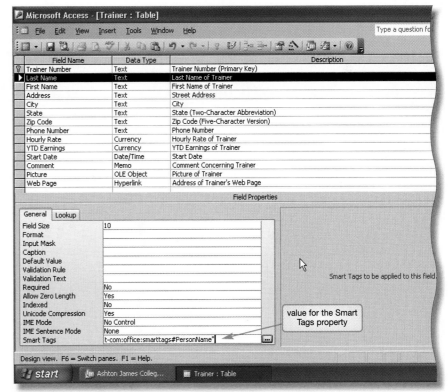

FIGURE 9-24

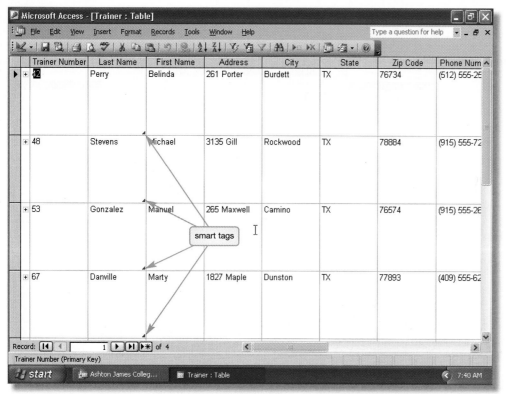

FIGURE 9-25

Using the Smart Tag in the Table

After you have created a smart tag for a field in a table, it will appear in the field whenever you view the table. In Figure 9-25, for example, the small triangles indicate smart tags.

When you click a field containing a smart tag, the Smart Tag Actions button will appear. In Figure 9-26, the Smart Tag Actions button for the last name Perry appears next to the field.

Clicking the Smart Tag Actions button produces a menu of possible actions (Figure 9-27). You can click an action on this menu to take the corresponding action.

FIGURE 9-26

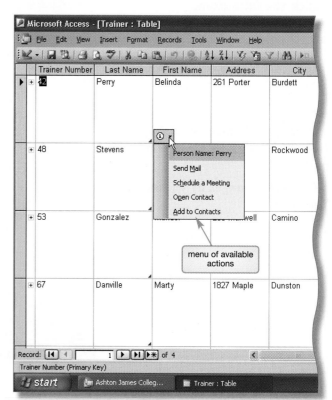

FIGURE 9-27

Adding a Smart Tag to a Control in a Form or Report

You also can add smart tags to controls in forms and reports. The following steps demonstrate how to add a smart tag to a control in a form.

To Add a Smart Tag to a Control in a Form

- **Click Forms on the Objects bar.**
- **Right-click the form called Trainer Master Form.**
- **Click Design View on the shortcut menu and maximize the window, if necessary.**
- **If a field list appears, close the field list by clicking its Close button.**
- **Right-click the Last Name control.**
- **Click Properties on the shortcut menu.**
- **Be sure the All tab is selected. Scroll down until the Smart Tags property appears, and then click the Smart Tags property.**

An insertion point appears in the Smart Tags text box (Figure 9-28). The Build button appears.

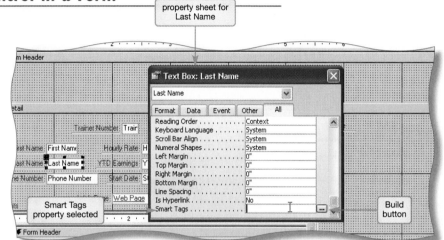

FIGURE 9-28

- **Click the Build button.**
- **Click the check box for the Person Name smart tag.**

The list of available smart tags appears (Figure 9-29). Your list may be different. The Person Name smart tag is selected. The possible actions for the selected smart tag appear in the Actions box.

3

- **Click the OK button.**

The smart tag is added to the control.

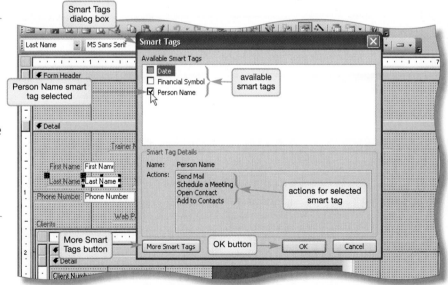

FIGURE 9-29

4

- **Close the property sheet.**
- **Close the Design window containing the Trainer Master Form by clicking its Close Window button.**
- **Click the Yes button to save the change.**

The change is saved.

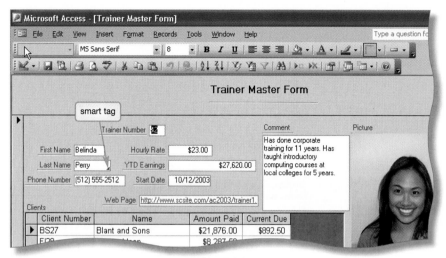

FIGURE 9-30

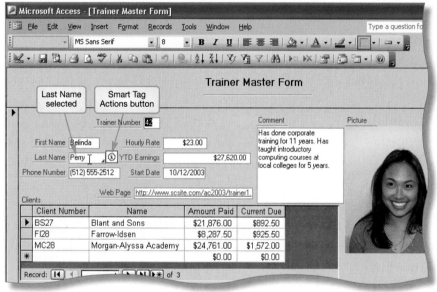

FIGURE 9-31

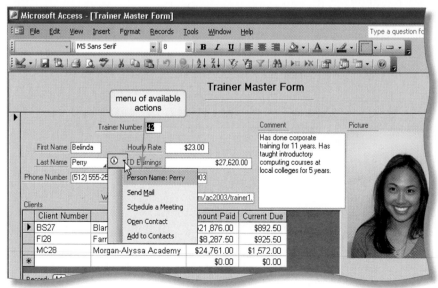

FIGURE 9-32

Using the Smart Tag in the Form

Once you have created a smart tag for a control in a form, it will appear whenever you view the form as shown in Figure 9-30.

When you click a field containing a smart tag, the Smart Tag Actions button will appear. In Figure 9-31, the Smart Tag Actions button for the Last Name control appears next to the control.

Clicking the Smart Tag Actions button produces a menu of possible actions (Figure 9-32). You can click an action on this menu to take the corresponding action.

Additional Smart Tags

To use other smart tags created by Microsoft or by other companies, click the More Smart Tags button, and then search the Web for the desired smart tag.

SharePoint Services

Similarly to other applications, Access allows you to share data with others using SharePoint Services. You can import, export, and link data to a SharePoint Services site. The data will reside on the site in the form of a SharePoint Services list.

SharePoint Services Lists

A SharePoint Services list is similar to a table in a database. The list is a grid with column headings, which are similar to field names, and data in the columns that match the column headings. Figure 9-33 shows a list with information about patients in a clinic. The first column heading is Patient Number, and the items in the column are patient numbers. The second column heading is Last Name, and the items in the column are last names. Above the list are buttons you can use to add a new item, filter the items that appear, and also to edit the data in Datasheet view, which is very similar to Datasheet view in Access.

If you click a particular item, such as the patient number of the first patient, and then click the arrow that appears, you will see a menu of available actions (Figure 9-34). You can edit or delete the item by clicking the appropriate command on the menu.

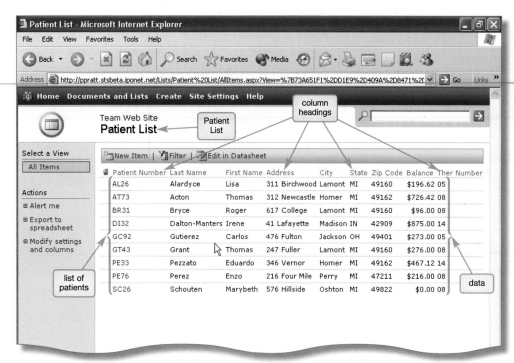

FIGURE 9-33

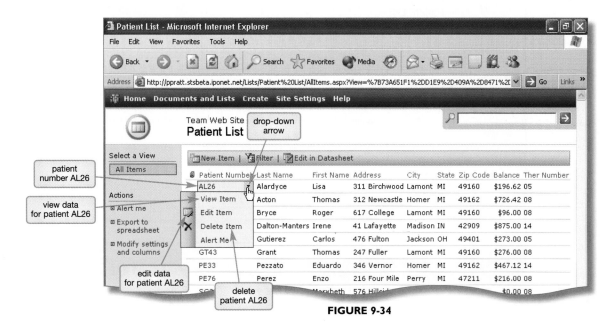

FIGURE 9-34

If you click View Item, you will see the data for just this one patient (Figure 9-35). You then could edit or delete the item by clicking the appropriate button. You also could add a new item by clicking the New Item button. You can return to the list by clicking the Go Back to List button.

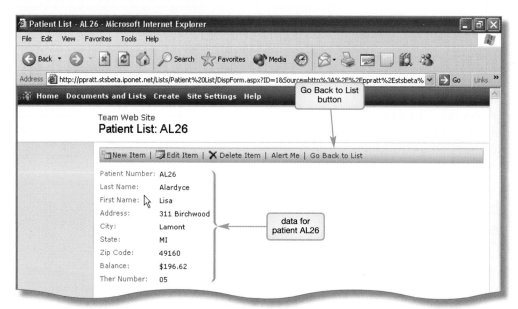

FIGURE 9-35

To move from the list to Datasheet view, point to the Edit in Datasheet button as in Figure 9-36, and then click the button.

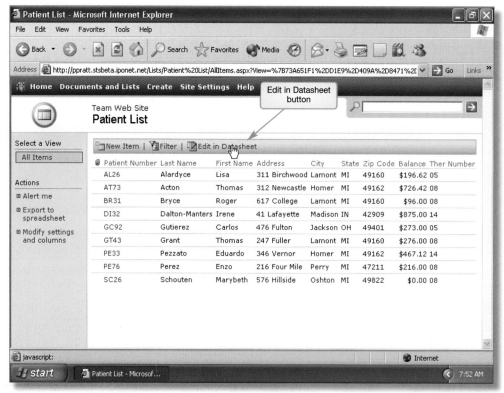

FIGURE 9-36

In Datasheet View, you can edit data as you would in Access. You also can click the drop-down arrow for any column name to produce a menu similar to the one in Figure 9-37. You can use this menu to change the sort order or to filter the items that appear.

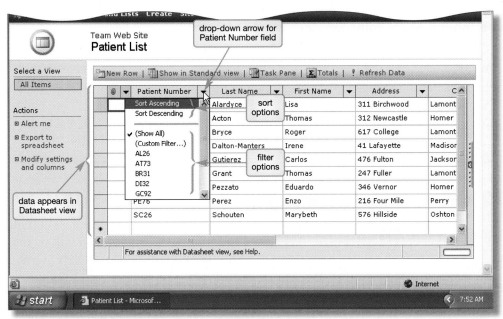

FIGURE 9-37

You can include totals for any numeric items on the list. To do so, click the Totals button. The total will be displayed at the bottom of the column as in Figure 9-38. In the figure, the right scroll arrow has been clicked four times so the Balance column appears on the screen.

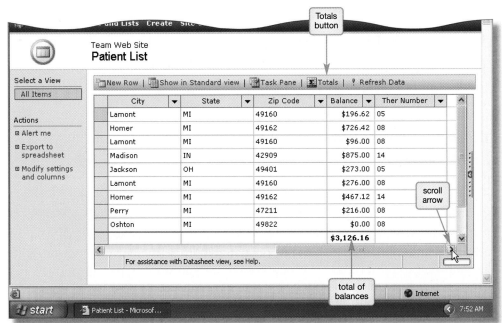

FIGURE 9-38

Importing a SharePoint Services List

From Access, you can import a SharePoint Services list to a table in a database just as you can import data from other sources. In the process, you will need to identify the SharePoint site where the list is located.

To Import a SharePoint Services List

1. Click File on the menu bar.
2. Point to Get External Data and then click Import.
3. Click the Files of type arrow, scroll down until Windows SharePoint Team Services appears, and then click Windows SharePoint Team Services.

4. Follow the directions in the Import SharePoint Team Services Wizard. You will need to identify the site that contains the data; your user name and password; the list you want to retrieve; and the views of the list you want (typically you will choose All Items, which will be the only option). Once you have done so, you will click the Finish button.
5. After the import is complete, click the OK button.

The imported table is shown in Figure 9-39. The name of the table is Patient List: All Items. Access also has added automatically the ID and Attachments fields.

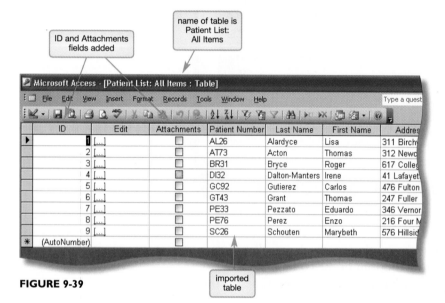

FIGURE 9-39

Linking SharePoint Services Lists

Just as you can import a SharePoint Services list to a table in a database, you also can link one. In the process, you identify the SharePoint site where the list is located.

To Link a SharePoint Services List

1. Click File on the menu bar.
2. Point to Get External Data and then click Link Tables.
3. Click the Files of type arrow, scroll down until Windows SharePoint Team Services appears, and then click Windows SharePoint Team Services.
4. Follow the directions in the Link to SharePoint Team Services Wizard. You will need to identify the site that contains the data; your user name and password; the list you want to retrieve; and the views of the list you want (typically you will choose All Items, which will be the only option). Once you have done so, you will click the Finish button.
5. After the link is complete, click the OK button.

The linked table appears in the Database window preceded by the symbol that indicates it is linked (Figure 9-40).

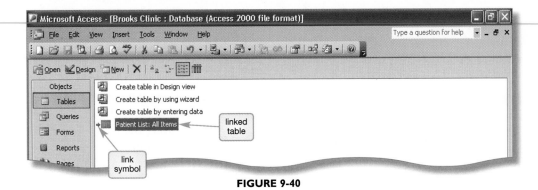

FIGURE 9-40

Figure 9-41 shows the table in Datasheet view.

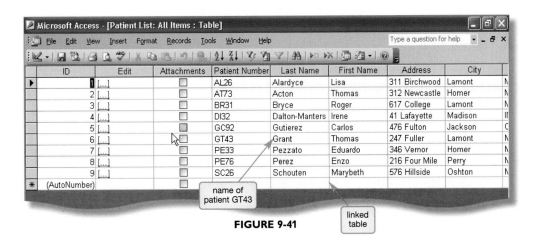

FIGURE 9-41

Using a Linked Table

Because this is a linked table, any change is reflected automatically in the corresponding SharePoint Services list. In Figure 9-42, for example, the name of patient GT43 is changed from Grant to Grantson.

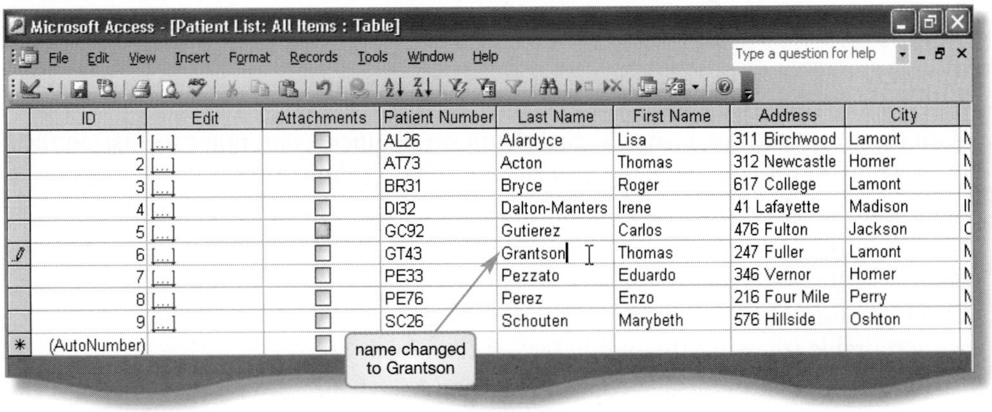

FIGURE 9-42

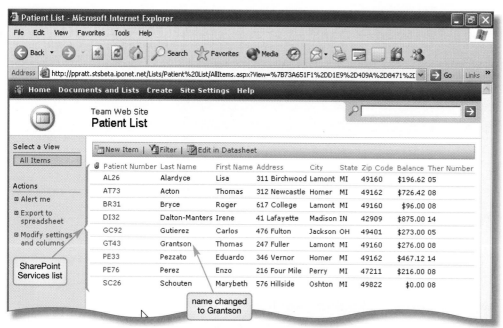

The corresponding SharePoint Services list is shown in Figure 9-43. The change to the name of patient GT43 is reflected in the list. If you already had the SharePoint Services list open when you made the change to the linked table, the change would not immediately be reflected on your screen.

FIGURE 9-43

More About

SharePoint Services

Windows SharePoint Services allow you to share information, collaborate on documents and collect team knowledge over an intranet or the Internet. For more information about SharePoint Services, visit the Access 2003 More About Web page (scsite.com/ac2003/more) and click SharePoint Services.

Creating a SharePoint Services List

You can create a SharePoint Services list directly on a SharePoint Services site. You also can create one by exporting an Access table or an Excel worksheet. The process for creating one from an Access table is similar to exporting a table to any other format. The only difference is that you select SharePoint Services in the Files of Type box, and then identify the site to which you wish to export the data.

The process in Excel is slightly different in that you first must convert the worksheet to a list. You then publish the list to the SharePoint Services site. The following steps illustrate how to create a SharePoint Services list from an Excel worksheet and then how to publish the list to the SharePoint Services site.

To Create a SharePoint Services List from an Excel Worksheet

1. With the worksheet appearing in Excel, click Data on the menu bar, point to List on the Data menu, and then click Create List on the List submenu.
2. Make sure the Create List dialog box contains the correct information concerning the location of your list and that the My list has headers check box is checked, and then click the OK button.

To Publish an Excel List to a SharePoint Services Site

1. With the list appearing in Excel, click Data on the menu bar, point to List on the Data menu, and then click Publish List on the List submenu.
2. Indicate the address of the SharePoint Services site, be sure the Link to the new SharePoint List check box is checked, enter a name for your list (a description is optional), and then click the Next button.
3. Check the list of columns and corresponding data types. Assuming they are acceptable (they usually will be), click the Finish button.
4. When a dialog box indicates your list was published successfully, click the OK button.

Your list now is on the SharePoint Services site and is available for use.

Online Collaboration

The Microsoft Office applications include a collaborative feature that allows you and your colleagues to share and make changes to a database online. You either can schedule in advance using Microsoft Outlook or start an online meeting from within an Access database. If your colleagues are available and decide to accept your invitation, the online meeting begins. The initiator (host) of an online meeting and all participants must have Microsoft NetMeeting installed on their computers, but only the initiator needs to have the database management system installed.

To Start an Online Meeting

1. Click Tools on the menu bar.
2. Point to Online Collaboration and then click Meet Now.
3. Follow the directions in the NetMeeting dialog box. You will need to enter information about yourself so other participants can find you and see you in the meeting. You also will need to enter the name of the server. After the correct information is entered, click the OK button.

Using Online Collaboration

The initiator (host) controls the online meeting. The host can allow collaboration by the meeting participants and can turn off collaboration at anytime. When collaboration is turned on, participants can take turns making changes to the Access database. When collaboration is turned off, only the host can make changes but the other participants are able to view the database and any changes the host makes to the database.

To Turn On Online Collaboration

1. On the Online Meeting toolbar, click Allow others to edit.

The first time another participant wants to take control of the database, the individual double-clicks anywhere in the Access data file. Subsequently, the individual only needs to click anywhere in the Access data file to regain control.

Database Options

You can use the Startup command to set **startup options**, that is, actions that will be taken automatically when the database first is opened. The steps on the next page demonstrate how to use the Startup command to ensure that the switchboard appears automatically when the Ashton James College database is opened.

To Set Startup Options

1

• **Click Tools on the menu bar.**

The Tools menu appears (Figure 9-44).

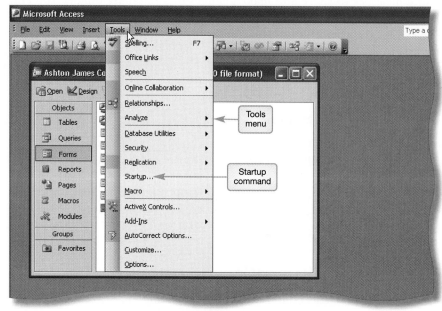

FIGURE 9-44

2

• **Click Startup and then click the Display Form/Page box arrow.**

The Startup dialog box appears (Figure 9-45). The list of available forms and pages appears.

3

• **Click Switchboard and then click the OK button.**

The switchboard now will appear whenever the database is opened.

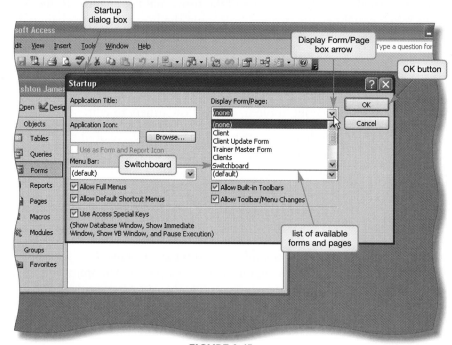

FIGURE 9-45

Setting Passwords

In order to set a password, the database must be open in exclusive mode. The following steps open the Harton-Janes Clinic database in exclusive mode in preparation for setting a password.

To Open a Database in Exclusive Mode

1 Close the Ashton James College : Database window.

2 Click the Open button on the Database toolbar.

3 If necessary, click Local Disk (C:) in the Look in box, and then double-click the Data folder (assuming your database is stored in a folder called Data).

4 Make sure the Harton-Janes Clinic database is selected, and then click the Open button arrow (not the button itself).

5 Click Open Exclusive in the list that appears.

6 If the Security Warning dialog box appears, click the Open button.

The database opens in exclusive mode and the Harton-Janes Clinic : Database window appears.

With the database open in exclusive mode, the following steps illustrate how to set a password.

To Set a Password

1

• **Click Tools on the menu bar, and then point to Security on the Tools menu.**

The Security submenu appears (Figure 9-46).

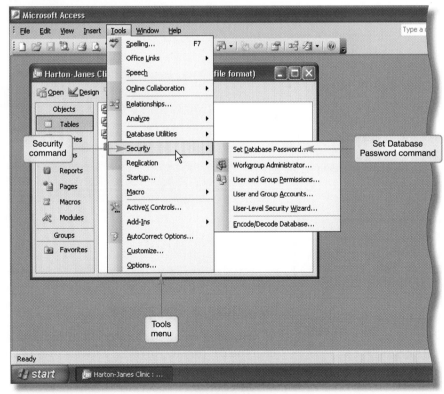

FIGURE 9-46

2

• **Click Set Database Password.**

• **Type your password in the Password text box in the Set Database Password dialog box. Asterisks, not the actual characters, appear as you type your password.**

• **Press the TAB key and then type your password again in the Verify text box.**

• **Be sure to remember the password that you type.**

• **You will use it again in the next sections.**

The password is entered in both the Password text box and the Verify text box (Figure 9-47).

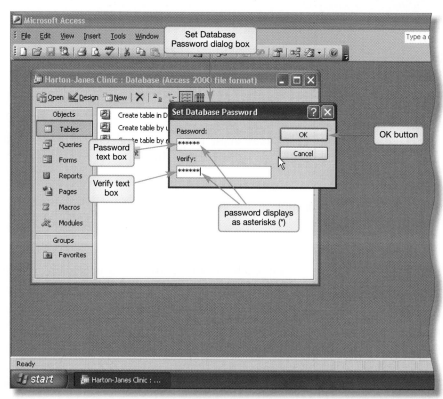

FIGURE 9-47

3

• **Click the OK button.**

The password is entered. From this point on, whenever a user opens the database, the user will be required to enter the password in the Password Required dialog box (Figure 9-48).

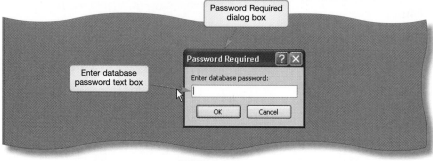

FIGURE 9-48

More About

Encoding

The encoding process requires Access to make an additional copy of the database, which is called the encoded version. Once the process is complete, the original will be deleted. During the process, however, there must be sufficient disk space available for both versions of the database. If not, the process will fail.

Encoding a Database

Encoding refers to the storing of the data in the database in an encoded (encrypted) format. Anytime a user stores or modifies data in the database, the database management system (DBMS) will encode the data before actually updating the database. Before a legitimate user retrieves the data via the DBMS, the data will be decoded. The whole encoding process is transparent to a legitimate user; that is, he or she is not even aware it is happening. If an unauthorized user attempts to bypass all the controls of the DBMS and get to the database through a utility program or a word processor, however, he or she will be able to see only the encoded, and unreadable, version of the data.

In order to encode/decode a database, the database must be closed. The following steps demonstrate how to encode a database using the Encode/Decode Database command.

To Encode a Database

1

• **Close the window containing the database by clicking its Close button.**

• **Click Tools on the menu bar, and then click Security on the Tools menu.**

The Security submenu appears (Figure 9-49).

2

• **Click Encode/Decode Database.**

• **Select the Harton-Janes Clinic database, and then click the OK button.**

• **Enter your password and then click the OK button in the Password Required dialog box.**

• **Type** Harton-Janes Clinic Enc **as the file name in the File name box, and then click the Save button.**

The database is encoded. The encoded version is called Harton-Janes Clinic Enc.

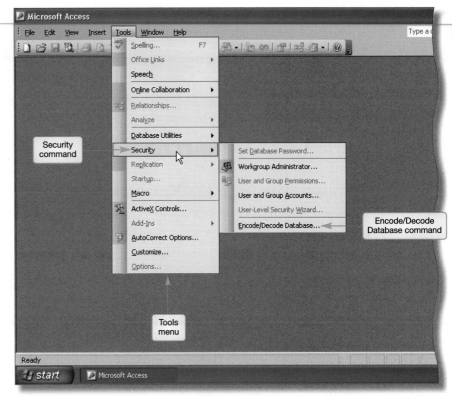

FIGURE 9-49

Removing a Password

If you no longer feel a password is necessary, you can remove it by using the Unset Database Password command as the steps on the next page illustrate.

Other Ways

1. In Voice Command mode, say "Tools, Security, Encode Decode Database"

To Remove a Password

• **Open the Harton-Janes Clinic database in exclusive mode** (see the steps on page AC 559).

• **You will need to enter your password when requested.**

• **Click Tools on the menu bar, and then point to Security on the Tools menu.**

The Security submenu appears (Figure 9-50).

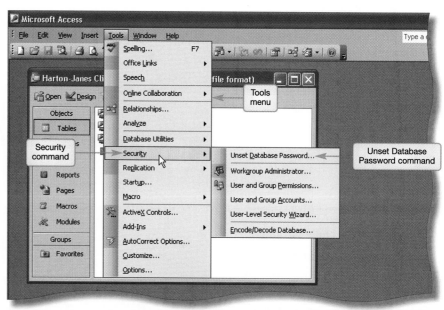

FIGURE 9-50

2

• **Click Unset Database Password.**

• **Type the password in the Unset Database Password dialog box.**

The Unset Database Password dialog box appears (Figure 9-51).

3

• **Click the OK button.**

The password is removed.

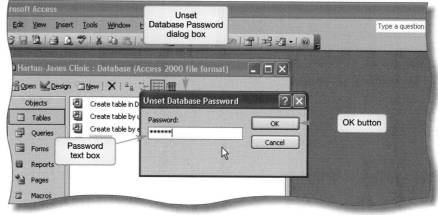

FIGURE 9-51

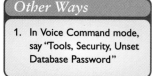

Other Ways

1. In Voice Command mode, say "Tools, Security, Unset Database Password"

Users will no longer need to enter a password when they open the database.

Macro Security

A macro virus is a computer virus that can affect a macro. Protection against this type of virus is called macro security. Three levels of macro security exist. The levels are described in Table 9-3.

To specify which level of security you want Access to use (the default is medium), you need to set the macro security level.

Table 9-3 Macro Security Levels	
LEVEL	**DESCRIPTION**
High	Only run macros that are digitally signed and confirmed to be from a trusted source.
Medium	Warning displayed prior to running a macro from a source not on list of trusted sources.
Low	All macros can be run.

To Set the Macro Security Level

1. Click Tools on the menu bar.
2. Point to Macro on the Tools menu.
3. Click Security.
4. If necessary, click the Security Level tab.
5. Click the desired security level.

Replication

Replication is the process of making multiple copies, called **replicas**, of a database. The original database is called the **Design Master**. The replicas then can be used at different locations. To make sure the Design Master reflects the changes made in the various replicas, the Design Master and the replicas will be **synchronized** periodically. This ensures that all databases reflect all the changes that have been made.

Creating a Replica

To create a replica, be sure the database to be replicated is open, and then use the Create Replica command on the Tools menu. The following steps demonstrate how to open the Harton-Janes Clinic database and then create a replica.

To Create a Replica

1

• **Click Tools on the menu bar, point to Replication, and then point to Create Replica.**

The Tools menu appears (Figure 9-52). The Replication submenu also appears.

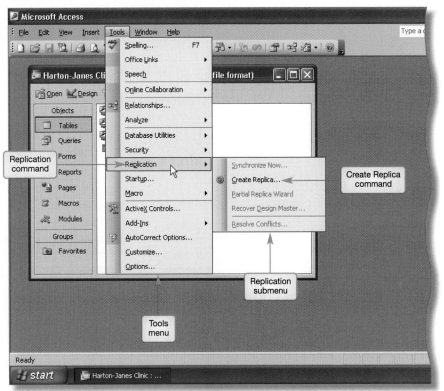

FIGURE 9-52

Microsoft Office
Access 2003

2

• **Click Create Replica.**

The Microsoft Office Access dialog box appears (Figure 9-53). The message indicates that the database must be closed before creating a replica. If you click the Yes button, the database will be closed and converted to a Design Master.

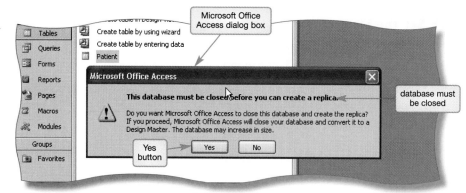

FIGURE 9-53

3

• **Click the Yes button.**

• **When asked if you want Microsoft Access to make a backup of your database, click the Yes button.**

• **Be sure the Save in box contains the location where you want to place the replica.**

• **Be sure the default name, Replica of Harton-Janes Clinic appears in the File name text box as the name of the replica.**

The Location of New Replica dialog box appears (Figure 9-54).

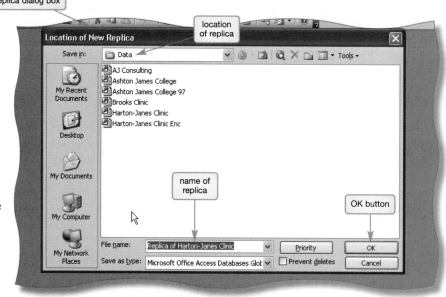

FIGURE 9-54

4

• **Click the OK button.**

The Microsoft Office Access dialog box appears (Figure 9-55). It indicates that the database has been converted to a Design Master and that the replica has been created.

5

• **Click the OK button.**

The replica is created and available for use.

6

• **Close the Database window for the Harton-Janes Clinic : Design Master by clicking its Close button.**

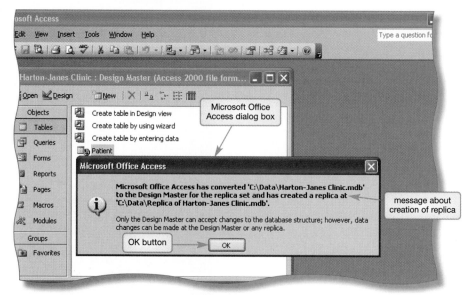

FIGURE 9-55

Using a Replica

You can use a replica similar to any other database, except that you cannot change the structure of any of the objects in your database. The following steps show how to open the replica, add a record, and change one of the names.

To Use the Replica

1

• **Click Open on the Database toolbar, and then click Local Disk (C:) in the Look in box.**

• **Double-click the Data folder, make sure the database called Replica of Harton-Janes Clinic is selected, and then click the Open button.**

• **With the Tables object selected, right-click Patient.**

The shortcut menu appears (Figure 9-56). The symbol in front of Patient indicates that it is a replica.

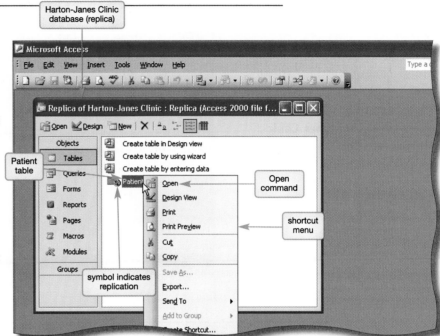

FIGURE 9-56

2

• **Click Open on the shortcut menu, and then click the New Record button.**

• **Type the final record shown in Figure 9-57.**

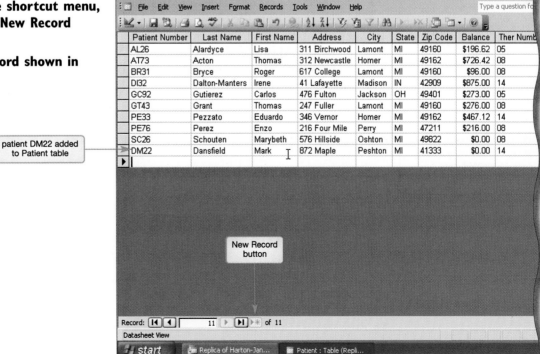

FIGURE 9-57

3

• **Click the last name of patient number SC26, erase the current name, and then type** Timson **as the new name.**

The changes are made (Figure 9-58).

4

• **Click the Close button for the window containing the Patient table.**

• **Click the Close button for the Replica of Harton-Janes Clinic : Database window.**

The table no longer appears and the database closes.

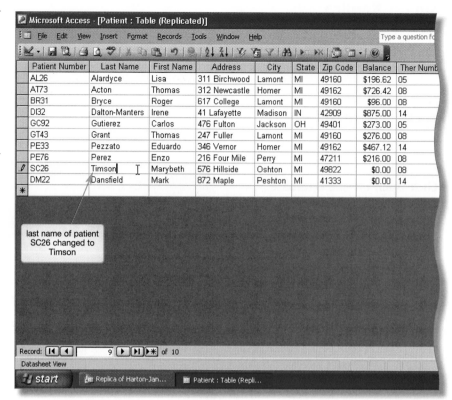

last name of patient SC26 changed to Timson

FIGURE 9-58

More About

Replication

When many users are using their own replicas, potential problems in synchronizing the data exist. A user adding a work order for a customer in one replica, while another user is deleting the same customer from a different replica would pose problems during synchronization. For more information concerning replication, visit the Access 2003 More About Web page (scsite.com/ac2003/more) and click Replication.

Synchronizing the Design Master and the Replica

Now that the replica has been updated, the data in the Design Master and the data in the replica no longer match. In order for them to match, the updates to the replica also must be made to the Design Master. Microsoft Access will make these updates automatically, using a process called **synchronization**. In order to synchronize the Design Master and the replica, the Design Master must be open in exclusive mode. The following steps illustrate how to open the Harton-Janes Clinic database in exclusive mode and then synchronize the Design Master and the replica.

To Synchronize the Design Master and the Replica

1

• **Click the Open button on the Database toolbar.**

• **If necessary, click Local Disk (C:) in the Look in box, and then double-click the Data folder (assuming your database is stored in a folder called Data).**

• **Make sure the Harton-Janes Clinic database is selected.**

• **Click the Open button arrow (not the button itself).**

• **Click Open Exclusive in the list that appears.**

• **Click Tools on the menu bar, and then point to Replication.**

The Design Master is open (Figure 9-59). The Tools menu and the Replication submenu appear.

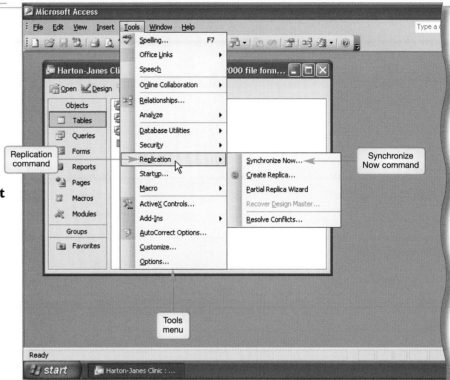

FIGURE 9-59

2

• **Click Synchronize Now.**

• **If necessary, click the Directly with Replica option button in the Synchronize Database 'Harton-Janes Clinic' dialog box, and then click the OK button.**

• **When a message appears indicating that Microsoft Access must close the database in order to perform the synchronization, click the Yes button.**

The databases are synchronized. Access displays the message shown in Figure 9-60 when the process is complete.

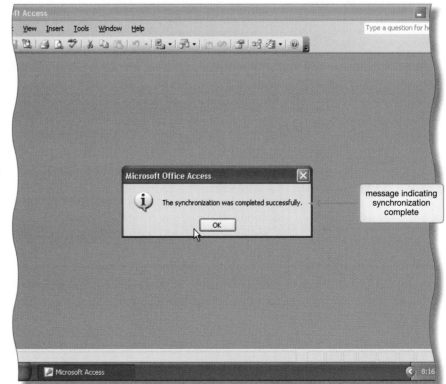

FIGURE 9-60

3

- Click the **OK** button in the Microsoft Office Access dialog box.
- Click the **Close** button for the Harton-Janes Clinic : Design Master Database window.

The database closes.

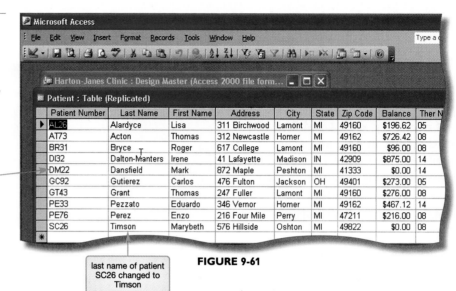

patient DM22 added to Patient table

last name of patient SC26 changed to Timson

FIGURE 9-61

The data in the replicated database (the Design Master) now incorporates the changes made earlier to the replica, as shown in Figure 9-61.

Protecting a Database through Splitting

In many cases, users would like to develop their own custom forms, reports, queries, or other objects. If each user develops such custom objects, the database can become cluttered and confusing. Many reports, for example, could be developed by a different user for a different purpose. Further, unless some special action is taken, there is nothing to protect one user's object (for example, a report or form) from modification by another user.

A better approach is to **split** the database into two databases, one called the **back-end database** that contains only the table data, and another database called the **front-end database** that contains the other objects. While there only would be a single copy of the back-end database, each user could have his or her own copy of the front-end database. A user would create the desired custom objects in his or her own front-end database, thereby not interfering with any other user. Also, if additional security is desired, front-end databases can be secured using the advanced security techniques described later in this project.

If a database has Visual Basic for Applications (VBA) code associated with it, you can protect this code by saving your database as an **MDE file**. In an MDE version, all VBA code is compiled, and then the source code (that is, the original code) is removed from the database. This makes the database smaller and also prevents any modifications to the VBA code.

It is very important that you save your original database in case you ever need to make changes to the VBA code. Because the VBA code is removed from the MDE file, you cannot use it to make such changes.

Converting to 2002 – 2003 Format

You can split a database in Access 2000 format. To create an MDE file, however, the database must be stored in 2002 - 2003 format. To prepare for the next activities in this section, you will create a version of the Ashton James College database in

Access 2002-2003 format called Ashton James College Converted. To do so, use the Convert Database command on the Database Utilities submenu as illustrated in the following steps.

To Convert to 2002 – 2003 Format

1 Open the Ashton James College database. If the Security Warning dialog box appears, click the Open button.

2 Click the Close button for the Main Switchboard window.

3 Click Tools on the menu bar, point to Database Utilities on the Tools menu, point to Convert Database on the Database Utilities submenu, and then click To Access 2002 – 2003 File Format.

4 Be sure the Save in text box contains the location where you wish to store the converted file, type Ashton James College Converted as the file name, and then click the Save button.

5 Click the OK button in the Microsoft Office Access dialog box.

6 Click the Close button for the Ashton James College : Database window.

The database is converted. The name of the resulting database is Ashton James College Converted.

Splitting the Database

To split a database, make sure the database to be split is open, and then select the Database Splitter command on the Database Utilities submenu. You then will identify a name and location for the back-end database that will be created by the splitter. The following steps show how to split the Ashton James College Converted database.

To Split the Database

1

• **Open the Ashton James College Converted database that you created in the previous steps. If the Security Warning dialog box appears, click the Open button.**

• **When the Main Switchboard window appears, close it by clicking its Close button.**

• **With the Database window appearing, click Tools on the menu bar, and then point to Database Utilities on the Tools menu.**

The Database Utilities submenu appears (Figure 9-62).

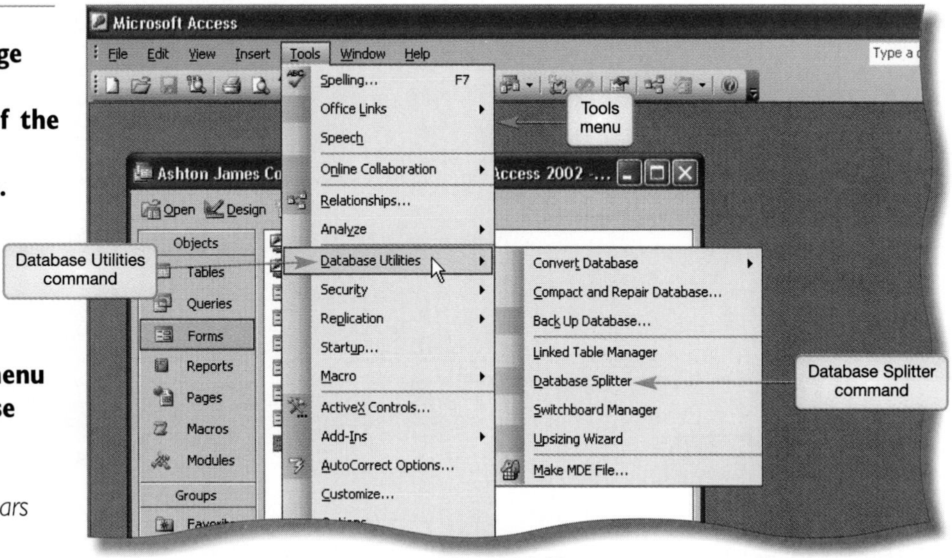

FIGURE 9-62

2

• **Click Database Splitter on the Database Utilities submenu.**

The Database Splitter dialog box appears (Figure 9-63). The message indicates the effect of splitting a database and some reasons for doing so.

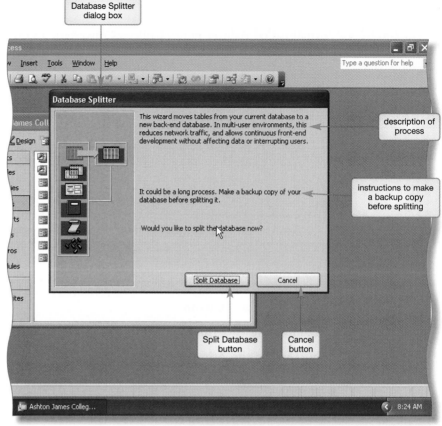

FIGURE 9-63

3

• **Click the Split Database button. Be sure the file name in the Create Back-end Database dialog box that appears is Ashton James College Converted_be.mdb, and then click the Split button.**

The Database Splitter dialog box appears (Figure 9-64).

4

• **Click the OK button.**

The database is split.

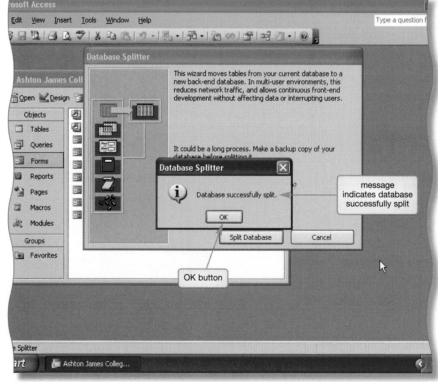

FIGURE 9-64

Other Ways

1. In Voice Command mode, say "Tools, Database Utilities, Database Splitter"

The Front-End and Back-End Databases

The database now has been split into separate front-end and back-end databases. The front-end database is the one that you will use. This database contains all the queries, reports, forms, and so on, from the original database. The front-end database only contains links to the tables, however, instead of the tables themselves (Figure 9-65). The back-end database contains the actual tables, but does not contain any other objects.

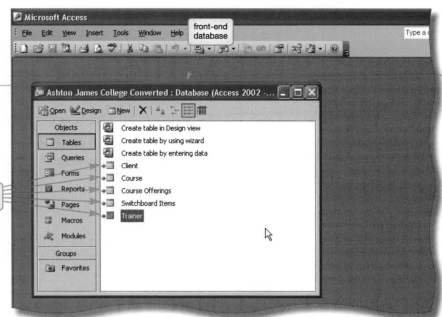

FIGURE 9-65

Creating an MDE File

To create an MDE file, the database needs to be stored in 2002 - 2003 format. Provided that it is, you create the MDE file by using the Make MDE File command on the Database Utilities submenu of the Tools menu. The following steps show how to create an MDE file for the Ashton James College Converted database.

To Create an MDE File

1

• **Click the Close button for the Ashton James College Converted : Database window.**

• **Click Tools on the menu bar, and then point to Database Utilities on the Tools menu.**

The Database Utilities submenu appears (Figure 9-66).

2

• **Click Make MDE File.**

• **Double-click Ashton James College Converted in the Database to Save as MDE dialog box.**

• **When the Save MDE As dialog box appears, be sure the Save as type box contains MDE File (*.mde).**

• **Click the Save button.**

The MDE file is created.

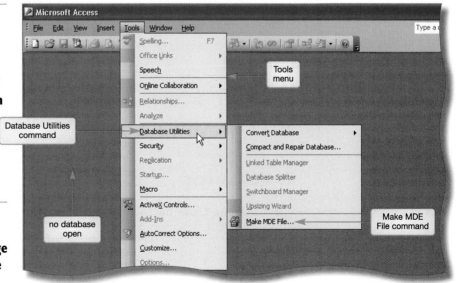

FIGURE 9-66

More About

MDE Files

If the database is replicated, you first must remove replication before creating an MDE file. When you do create an MDE file, users still are able to update data and run reports but they are not able to view, create, or modify forms or reports in Design view. Users also cannot import or export forms or reports.

Using the MDE File

You use an MDE file just as you use the databases with which you now are familiar with two exceptions. First, you must select MDE files in the Files of type box when opening the file. Second, you will not be able to modify any source code because the source code has been removed. If you clicked Modules, for example, and then right-clicked Promo Modules, you would find that the Design View command on the shortcut menu is dimmed, as are most other commands (Figure 9-67).

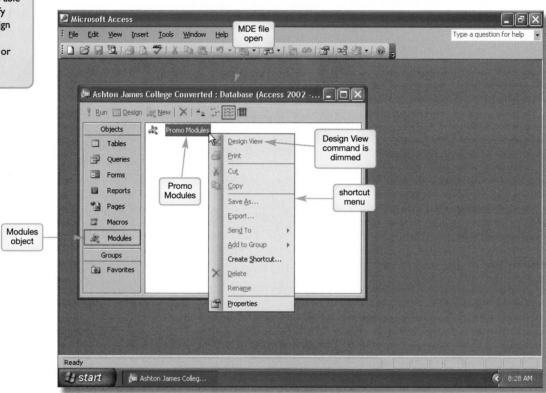

FIGURE 9-67

Quitting Access

The following step quits Access.

To Quit Access

1 **Click the Close button for the Microsoft Access window.**

Access closes.

Advanced Security

In Access, it is possible to specify **user-level security**, that is, an approach to security in which different users have different permissions concerning the objects they can access in the database. One user, for example, may be able to add records to a certain table, but not to change or delete existing records. Another may be able to perform any updates to the table, but not change the table's design. A third may be able to change the design, but not update the data. The same types of permissions apply to all objects in the database: tables, queries, forms, reports, and other objects.

Permissions can be assigned either to individual users or to entire groups of users. One common practice is to create groups, called **workgroups**, assign appropriate permissions to the group, and then assign each user to an appropriate workgroup based on the permissions the user requires. Information about workgroups, users, and permissions is stored in a special file, called a **workgroup information file**.

When using user-level security, each user is identified by a personal ID and password. Before accessing the database, the user must furnish the ID and password. If either is invalid, the user will not be able to access any data in the database. If both are valid, the user can perform any actions for which he or she has permission.

User-Level Security Wizard

You used the Security submenu on the Tools menu earlier to set a database password and to encode a database. Other options on this menu allow an individual to administer workgroups, set permissions, and manage user and group accounts (Figure 9-68). The User-Level Security Wizard command on the Security submenu allows you to use a wizard to perform many of these tasks in a guided fashion.

When you use the Security Wizard, you first must decide which workgroup information file you wish to use. You can

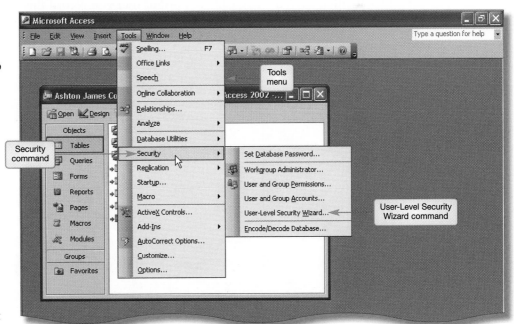

FIGURE 9-68

create a new file or modify your current file, provided that you have permission to do so. In order to create a new workgroup information file, make sure the Create a new workgroup information file option button is selected before you click the Next button (Figure 9-69 on the next page).

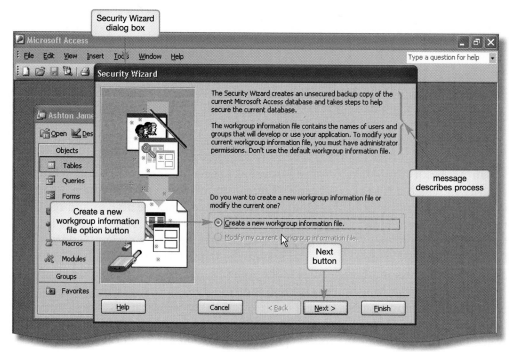

FIGURE 9-69

In the next step, you identify the name and location of the file containing workgroup information (Figure 9-70). You also need to enter a **workgroup ID** (**WID**). As the information in the Security Wizard dialog box indicates, the WID is a unique alphanumeric string that is 4 – 20 characters in length. You can accept the one that the wizard is suggesting or, if you prefer, change it to some other value. In either case, it is critically important that you record this ID somewhere so you have it for future reference. If there is any problem with the workgroup file, you will need this information to make the necessary corrections.

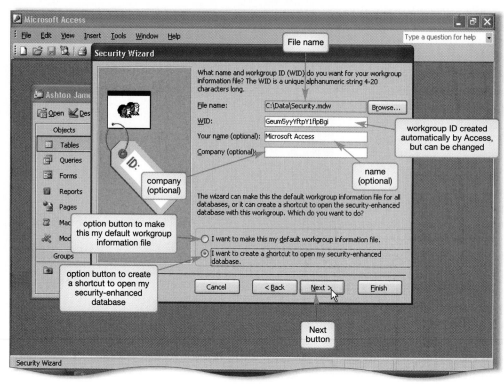

FIGURE 9-70

In this dialog box, you also indicate whether this workgroup file is to become your **default workgroup information file**, the file that will be used whenever you start Access. As an alternative, you can create a shortcut to open the database you are securing. When you use this shortcut, the database will be opened using the workgroup you have just created. If the information in the workgroup is specific to this database, creating a shortcut is typically the approach you will want to take.

The next step in using the wizard is to decide whether all objects in the database are to be secured (Figure 9-71). By default, all objects are secured. Usually this is appropriate. If you have some object, that you do not want secured, click the appropriate tab so the object appears, and then click the check box in front of the object to remove the check mark.

Access has several built-in groups that automatically are assigned appropriate collections of permissions (Figure 9-72). You can select any of these groups that you feel would be appropriate for your security needs by placing a check mark in the check box in front of the group. The wizard creates a group ID for any group you select automatically. You can, if desired, change the group ID. The available groups and corresponding permissions are shown in Table 9-4.

FIGURE 9-71

Table 9-4 Groups and Associated Permissions	
GROUP	**PERMISSIONS**
Backup Operators	Open database exclusively to perform backup and compacting operations, but cannot view any objects.
Full Data Users	Edit data, but cannot alter any object's design.
Full Permissions	Full permissions for all objects, but cannot assign permissions to anyone else.
New Data Users	Read and insert data, but cannot update or delete data. Cannot alter any object's design.
Project Designers	Edit data and object. Cannot alter tables or relationships.
Read-Only Users	Read data. Cannot alter data or any object's design.
Update Data Users	Read and update data, but cannot insert or delete data. Cannot alter any object's design.

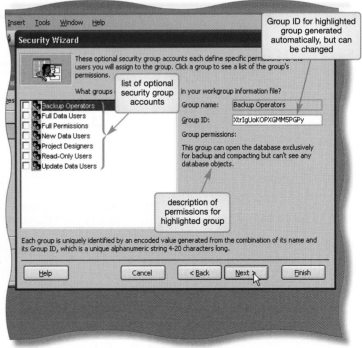

FIGURE 9-72

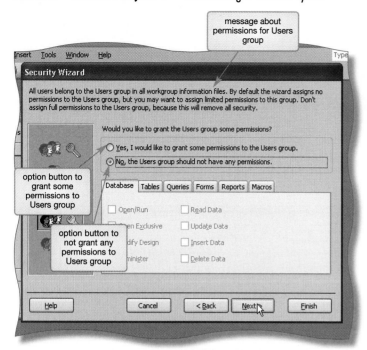

FIGURE 9-73

The next step in using the wizard is to decide whether or not to assign permissions to the Users group (Figure 9-73). There is a default Users group in every workgroup information file. All users automatically belong to this group, whether or not they belong to any other group. Thus, every user would receive automatically any permissions assigned to the Users group. Typically, you do not want to grant any permissions to this group. Rather, you grant permissions to the other groups you specify. You also may grant permissions directly to certain specific users.

The next step is to add new users (Figure 9-74). To add a user, select Add New User, and then type the user name and password. You either can accept the Personal ID (PID) that the wizard has assigned or assign one of your own. Once you have made these changes, click the Add This User to the List button to add the user. In the figure, users Pratt, Last, Shelly, and Cashman have been added. The Administrator user was created automatically.

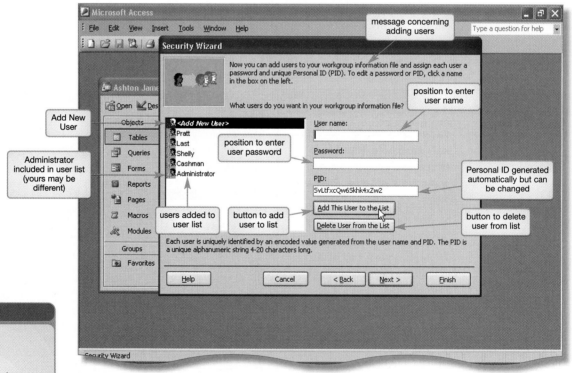

FIGURE 9-74

The next step is to assign users to groups (Figure 9-75). You can do so in one of two ways. You first can select a user and then select the groups to which the user is to be assigned. Alternatively, you first can select a group and then select all the users to be assigned to the group. To carry out either of these operations, first select the option button that corresponds to the approach you want to take. Then, make the appropriate selections.

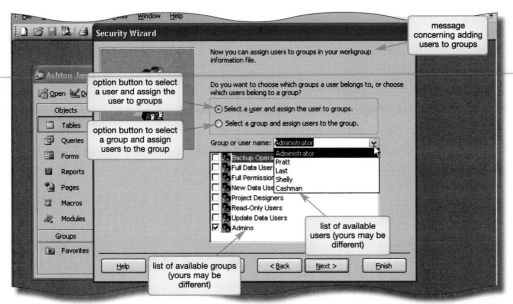

FIGURE 9-75

To complete the process, you need to indicate the location and name for the backup copy of the unsecured database (Figure 9-76). After you have done so and clicked the Finish button, the wizard will create the backup database and encode the secured database. The wizard also will update the workgroup information file to reflect the users, groups, and permissions you have assigned. Finally, it will generate and display a report giving detailed information about the users and groups in the workgroup information file. You should print and save this report in case there is ever a problem with the workgroup information file. You will need the information in this file to correct the problem. Once the process is complete, you will need to restart Access in order for the security you specified to take effect.

Working with a Secured Database

When you open a secured database, you will be asked for a name and password. If you are not able to enter a valid name and password combination, you will be unable to open the database. A valid combination identifies you as a legitimate user of the database. You then can take the actions corresponding to the permissions you have been assigned. If you try to take an action for which you have not been granted permission, Access will display an error message and will not allow you to take the action.

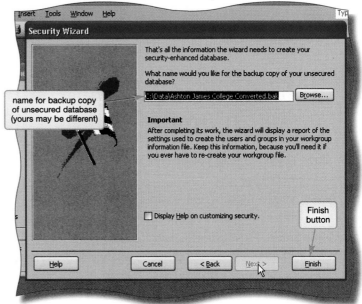

FIGURE 9-76

Project Summary

Project 9 introduced you to the issues involved in administering a database system. You saw how to create an Access 97 version of the database. You learned how to use the Table Analyzer, the Performance Analyzer, and the Documenter. You learned how to enable automatic error checking as well as the types of error checking available. You created a custom input mask. You specified and saw how to use smart tags on a table and a form. You saw SharePoint Services lists and learned how to import and link these lists to tables in a database. You set a startup option so the switchboard automatically appears when the database is opened. You saw how to secure the database by setting a password and encoding the database. You saw the effect of the macro security level and how to change it. You created a replica for remote users of the database and updated the database via the replica. You split a database into front-end and back-end databases and you created an MDE file, which is a file where VBA code is compiled, editable source code is removed from the database, and the database is compacted. You also learned how to specify user-level security.

 If you have a SAM user profile, you may have access to hands-on instruction, practice, and assessment of the skills covered in this project. Log in to your SAM account and go to your assignments page to see what your instructor has assigned.

What You Should Know

Having completed this project, you should be able to perform the tasks below. The tasks are listed in the same order they were presented in this project. For a list of the buttons, menus, toolbars, and commands introduced in this project, see the Quick Reference Summary at the back of this book and refer to the Page Number column.

1. Open a Database   (AC 532)
2. Convert a Database to an Earlier Version (AC 533)
3. Use the Table Analyzer   (AC 534)
4. Use the Performance Analyzer   (AC 537)
5. Use the Documenter   (AC 539)
6. Enable Error Checking   (AC 540)
7. Create a Custom Input Mask   (AC 544)
8. Show Smart Tags in Forms and Reports (AC 545)
9. Show Smart Tags in Tables and Queries (AC 545)
10. Hide Smart Tags in Forms and Reports (AC 545)
11. Hide Smart Tags in Tables and Queries (AC 546)
12. Add a Smart Tag to a Field in a Table   (AC 546)
13. Add a Smart Tag to a Control in a Form (AC 549)
14. Import a SharePoint Services List   (AC 554)
15. Link a SharePoint Services List   (AC 554)

16. Create a SharePoint Services List from an Excel Worksheet   (AC 556)
17. Publish an Excel List to a SharePoint Services Site (AC 556)
18. Start an Online Meeting   (AC 557)
19. Turn On Online Collaboration   (AC 557)
20. Set Startup Options   (AC 558)
21. Open a Database in Exclusive Mode   (AC 559)
22. Set a Password   (AC 559)
23. Encode a Database   (AC 561)
24. Remove a Password   (AC 562)
25. Set the Macro Security Level   (AC 563)
26. Create a Replica   (AC 563)
27. Use the Replica   (AC 565)
28. Synchronize the Design Master and the Replica (AC 567)
29. Convert to 2002 - 2003 Format   (AC 569)
30. Split the Database   (AC 569)
31. Create an MDE File   (AC 571)
32. Quit Access   (AC 572)

Learn It Online

Instructions: To complete the Learn It Online exercises, start your browser, click the Address bar, and then enter the Web address scsite.com/ac2003/learn. When the Access 2003 Learn It Online page is displayed, follow the instructions in the exercises below. Each exercise has instructions for printing your results, either for your own records or for submission to your instructor.

1 Project Reinforcement TF, MC, and SA

Below Access Project 9, click the Project Reinforcement link. Print the quiz by clicking Print on the File menu for each page. Answer each question.

2 Flash Cards

Below Access Project 9, click the Flash Cards link and read the instructions. Type 20 (or a number specified by your instructor) in the Number of playing cards text box, type your name in the Enter your Name text box, and then click the Flip Card button. When the flash card is displayed, read the question and then click the ANSWER box arrow to select an answer. Flip through Flash Cards. If your score is 15 (75%) correct or greater, click Print on the File menu to print your results. If your score is less than 15 (75%) correct, then redo this exercise by clicking the Replay button.

3 Practice Test

Below Access Project 9, click the Practice Test link. Answer each question, enter your first and last name at the bottom of the page, and then click the Grade Test button. When the graded practice test is displayed on your screen, click Print on the File menu to print a hard copy. Continue to take practice tests until you score 80% or better.

4 Who Wants To Be a Computer Genius?

Below Access Project 9, click the Computer Genius link. Read the instructions, enter your first and last name at the bottom of the page, and then click the PLAY button. When your score is displayed, click the PRINT RESULTS link to print a hard copy.

5 Wheel of Terms

Below Access Project 9, click the Wheel of Terms link. Read the instructions, and then enter your first and last name and your school name. Click the PLAY button. When your score is displayed, right-click the score and then click Print on the shortcut menu to print a hard copy.

6 Crossword Puzzle Challenge

Below Access Project 9, click the Crossword Puzzle Challenge link. Read the instructions, and then enter your first and last name. Click the SUBMIT button. Work the crossword puzzle. When you are finished, click the Submit button. When the crossword puzzle is redisplayed, click the Print Puzzle button to print a hard copy.

7 Tips and Tricks

Below Access Project 9, click the Tips and Tricks link. Click a topic that pertains to Project 9. Right-click the information and then click Print on the shortcut menu. Construct a brief example of what the information relates to in Access to confirm you understand how to use the tip or trick.

8 Newsgroups

Below Access Project 9, click the Newsgroups link. Click a topic that pertains to Project 9. Print three comments.

9 Expanding Your Horizons

Below Access Project 9, click the Expanding Your Horizons link. Click a topic that pertains to Project 9. Print the information. Construct a brief example of what the information relates to in Access to confirm you understand the contents of the article.

10 Search Sleuth

Below Access Project 9, click the Search Sleuth link. To search for a term that pertains to this project, select a term below the Project 9 title and then use the Google search engine at google.com (or any major search engine) to display and print two Web pages that present information on the term.

11 Access Online Training

Below Access Project 9, click the Access Online Training link. When your browser displays the Microsoft Office Online Web page, click the Access link. Click one of the Access courses that covers one or more of the objectives listed at the beginning of the project on page AC 550. Print the first page of the course before stepping through it.

12 Office Marketplace

Below Access Project 9, click the Office Marketplace link. When your browser displays the Microsoft Office Online Web page, click the Office Marketplace link. Click a topic that relates to Access. Print the first page.

Apply Your Knowledge

1 Administering the Begon Pest Control Database

Instructions: Start Access. If you are using the Microsoft Office Access 2003 Comprehensive text, open the Begon Pest Control database that you used in Project 8. Otherwise, see the inside back cover for instructions for downloading the Data Disk or see your instructor for information about accessing the files required for this book. Perform the following tasks:

1. Use the Table Analyzer to analyze the Customer table. On your own paper, list the results of the analysis.
2. Use the Performance Analyzer to analyze all the tables and queries in the Begon Pest Control database. On your own paper, list the results of the analysis.
3. Use the Documenter to produce documentation for the Category table. Print the documentation.
4. Create a custom input mask for the Customer Number field in the Customer table. The first two characters of the customer number must be uppercase letters and the last two characters must be digits. No position may be blank. On your own paper, list the input mask you created.
5. Create a smart tag for the Last Name field in the Technician table. On your own paper, list the smart tag you created.
6. Open the Customer Update Form and create a smart tag for the Name field. On your own paper, list the steps to add the smart tag.
7. Create an encoded version of the Begon Pest Control database. Use Begon Pest Control Enc as the file name.

In the Lab

1 Administering the Birds2U Database

Problem: Birds2U has asked you to administer the Birds2U database system. The management has determined a number of activities that you must perform. These include analyzing performance, setting startup options, creating input masks and smart tags, converting the database to an earlier version, and splitting the database.

Instructions: If you are using the Microsoft Office Access 2003 Comprehensive text, open the Birds2U database that you used in Project 8. Otherwise, see the inside back cover for instructions for downloading the Data Disk or see your instructor for information about accessing the files required for this book. Perform the following tasks:

1. Use the Performance Analyzer to analyze all the tables and queries in the Birds2U database. On your own paper, list the results of the analysis.
2. Use the Documenter to print the documentation for the Reorder table.
3. Supplier Code is a field in both the Item and Supplier tables. Create an input mask for the Supplier Code field in both tables. On your own paper, list the input mask that you created.
4. Modify the startup option so the switchboard opens automatically when the Birds2U database opens.
5. Open the Supplier Master Report and create a smart tag for the Name field. On your own paper, list the steps to add the smart tag.
6. Convert the database to an Access 97 version for a user who does not have the latest version of Microsoft Office Access.
7. Split the database into two databases.
8. Open the front-end database and open the switchboard form in Design view.
9. Add a label to the upper-left corner of the form and type your name in the label. To add a label, use the Label tool in the toolbox.
10. Change the font color to white and the font size to 12.
11. Print the form. To print the form, open the form, click File on the menu bar, click Print, and then click Selected Record(s) as the Print Range. Click the OK button.

2 Administering the Babbage Bookkeeping Database

Problem: Babbage Bookkeeping has asked you to administer the Babbage Bookkeeping database system. The management has determined a number of activities that you must perform. These include analyzing performance, setting startup options, creating input masks, and replicating and synchronizing the database.

Instructions: If you are using the Microsoft Office Access 2003 Comprehensive text, open the Babbage Bookkeeping database that you used in Project 8. Otherwise, see the inside back cover for instructions for downloading the Data Disk or see your instructor for information about accessing the files required for this book. Perform the following tasks:

1. Use the Performance Analyzer to analyze all the tables and queries in the Babbage Bookkeeping database. On your own paper, list the results of the analysis.
2. Use the Documenter to print the documentation for the Accounts table.
3. Bookkeeper Number is a field in both the Client and Bookkeeper tables. Create an input mask for the Bookkeeper Number field in both tables. On your own paper, list the input mask that you created.
4. Modify the startup option so the switchboard opens automatically when the Babbage Bookkeeping database opens.
5. Create a replica of the database.
6. Open the replica, change the name for client A54 to Afton Clothing Mills, and then add the following record to the Accounts table:

T45	8/31/2005	4

7. Synchronize the replica with the Design Master.
8. Open the Design Master and print the Client table and the Accounts table.

In the Lab

3 Administering the City Guide Database

Problem: The chamber of commerce is considering having you administer their database system. To test your qualifications, the chamber has asked you to perform a number of administrative tasks.

Instructions: If you are using the Microsoft Office Access 2003 Comprehensive text, open the City Guide database that you used in Project 8. Otherwise, see the inside back cover for instructions for downloading the Data Disk or see your instructor for information about accessing the files required for this book. Perform the following tasks:

Instructions Part 1: The chamber is concerned that some database operations are not as efficient as they should be. Analyze the database and report your findings to the chamber.

Instructions Part 2: The chamber would like an easy way to select an advertiser name and send them an e-mail. The chamber wants to be able to do this from within the Advertiser table and the Advertiser Update Form. The chamber also wants the switchboard to display when the database is opened and wants to prevent unauthorized users from getting to the database through a utility program or a word processor.

Instructions Part 3: Errors are occurring because individuals are entering incorrect values, for example, text instead of numbers, in the Advertiser table for the Advertiser Number, Zip Code, and Ad Rep Number.

Cases and Places

The difficulty of these case studies varies:
■ are the least difficult and ■■ are more difficult. The last exercise is a group exercise.

1 ■ Use the College Dog Walkers database that you used in Project 8 for this assignment or see your instructor for information about accessing the files required for this book. Perform the following database administration tasks and answer the questions about the database.

a. Run the Table Analyzer on all tables and describe the results of the analysis.

b. Run the Performance Analyzer on all tables and queries and describe the results of the analysis.

c. Set a password for the College Dog Walkers database. Why did you choose that particular password? What will happen if you try to open the College Dog Walkers database and cannot remember your password?

d. Create an Access 97 version and an Access 2002 – 2003 version of the College Dog Walkers database. Why would you need to convert a database to an earlier version?

e. Encode the database. What is the purpose of encoding?

f. Split the database. What happens when you split the database?

g. Create an MDE file. What happens to VBA code when you create an MDE file?

2 ■ Replicate the InPerson Fitness Company database. Use the replica and add yourself as a client. Use MN05 as the client number and assign yourself to trainer 207. Your balance and amount paid amounts are both 0. Add a record to the Client Service table for yourself. Synchronize the Design Master and the replica. Use the Design Master to print the updated tables.

3 ■■ Use the Regional Books database to experiment with macro level security. Start with a low level of security. Open the database and run at least two macros. Record what happens. Repeat this procedure for each level of security.

4 ■■ If you have your instructor's permission, use the User-Level Security Wizard to create user-level security for the Campus Housing database.

5 ■■ **Working Together** If you have your instructor's permission and the ability to use a Web server, experiment with both SharePoint Services and online collaboration. Select one of the cases and places databases to use for collaboration. As a team, prepare a report that details your experiences.

SQL Feature: Using SQL

CASE PERSPECTIVE

Dr. Gernaey and his colleagues at Ashton James College are pleased with the database of trainers and clients. The administration appreciates the functionality and flexibility provided by the various forms and reports. They like being able to access these forms and reports through the switchboard. They also understand the way Access tools can be used to support the work of a database administrator. The newer features of Access, such as smart tags and the use of SharePoint Services have enabled AJC to collaborate with other colleges providing corporate training. Recent problems on campus with e-mail security have made AJC aware of how important it is to have security procedures in place for the AJC database. The administration particularly appreciates the ability to query the database using the Access query facility. They have one final request, however, and it concerns queries. The administration realizes that there is a database language for queries that seems to be universal. The language, which is called SQL and is supported by virtually every DBMS, is an extremely powerful tool for querying a database. The administration wants to learn to use this language. In the process, they would like to create a wide variety of SQL queries.

Your task is to assist the administration of AJC in learning more about SQL and how to use it to answer questions.

As you read through this project, you will learn how to query a database using the SQL query language.

Objectives

You will have mastered the material in this project when you can:

- Change the font or font size
- Include fields and criteria in SQL queries
- Use computed fields and built-in functions in SQL queries
- Sort the results in SQL queries
- Use multiple functions in the same command
- Group the results in SQL queries
- Join tables in SQL queries
- Compare with Access-generated SQL

Introduction

The language called **SQL (Structured Query Language)** is a very important language for querying and updating databases. It is the closest thing to a universal database language, because the vast majority of database management systems, including Access, use it in some fashion. Although some users will be able to do all their queries through the query features of Access instead of SQL, those in charge of administering and maintaining the database system certainly should be familiar with this important language.

Similarly to creating queries in Design view, SQL furnishes users a way of querying relational databases. In SQL, however, the user must type commands to obtain the desired results, instead of making entries in the design grid as shown in Figure 1a on the next page. Queries then are run just as they are in Design view to produce the results. The results for the query in Figure 1a are shown in Figure 1b on the next page.

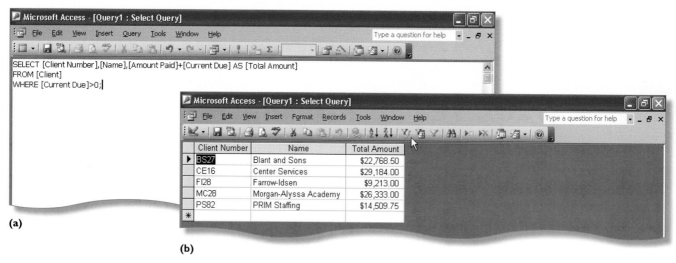

FIGURE 1

SQL was developed under the name SEQUEL at the IBM San Jose research facilities as the data manipulation language for IBM's prototype relational model DBMS, System R, in the mid-1970s. In 1980, it was renamed SQL to avoid confusion with an unrelated hardware product called SEQUEL. It is used as the data manipulation language for IBM's current production offerings in the relational DBMS arena — SQL/DS and DB2. Most relational DBMSs, including Microsoft Access, use a version of SQL as a data manipulation language.

Some people pronounce SQL by pronouncing the three letters, that is, ess-que-ell. It is very common, however to pronounce it as the name under which it was developed originally, that is, sequel. This text assumes you are pronouncing it as the word, sequel. That is why you will see the word, a, used before SQL. If it were pronounced ess-que-ell, you would use the word, an, before SQL. For example, this text will refer to "a SQL query" rather than "an SQL query."

Opening the Database

If you are stepping through this project on a computer and you want your screen to match the figures in this book, then you should change your computer's resolution to 800 x 600. For more information on how to change the resolution on your computer, see Appendix D. Before carrying out the steps in this project, first you must open the database. The following steps, which start Access and open the database, assume that the database is located in a folder called Data on disk C. If your database is located anywhere else, you will need to make the appropriate adjustments in the steps.

To Open a Database

1 Click the Start button on the Windows taskbar, point to All Programs on the Start menu, point to Microsoft Office on the All Programs submenu, and then click Microsoft Office Access 2003 on the Microsoft Office submenu.

2 If the Access window is not maximized, double-click its title bar to maximize it.

3 If the Language bar appears, right-click it and then click Close the Language bar on the shortcut menu.

4 Click Open on the Database toolbar, and then click Local Disk (C:) in the Look in box. Double-click the Data folder, and then make sure the Ashton James College database is selected.

5 Click the Open button.

6 If the Security Warning dialog box appears, click the Open button.

7 When the Switchboard appears, close the Switchboard by clicking its Close button.

The database opens and the Ashton James College : Database window appears. The Switchboard does not appear.

Changing the Font or Font Size

You can change the font and/or the font size for queries using the Options command on the Tools menu and then the Tables/Queries tab. There usually is not a compelling reason to change the font, unless there is a strong preference for some other font. It often is worthwhile to change the font size, however. With the default size of 8, the queries can be hard to read. Increasing the font size to 10 can make a big difference. The following steps show how to change the font size for SQL queries to 10.

To Change the Font Size

1

• **Click Tools on the menu bar, and then click Options on the Tools menu.**

• **Click the Tables/Queries tab.**

• **Click the Size box arrow, and then click 10 in the list that appears.**

The value in the Size box is changed to 10 (Figure 2).

2

• **Click the OK button.**

The font size for queries is changed.

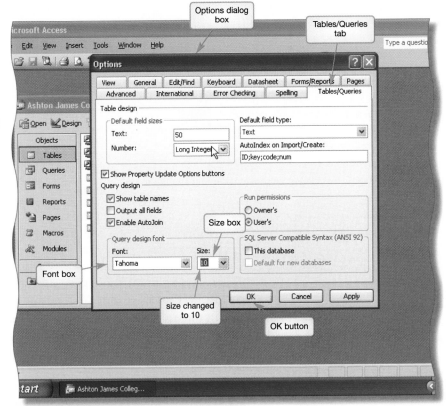

FIGURE 2

Creating a New SQL Query

You begin the creation of a new **SQL query**, which is a query expressed using the SQL language, just as you begin the creation of any other query in Access. The only difference is that you will use SQL view instead of Design view. The following steps illustrate how to create a new SQL query.

To Create a New SQL Query

 1

- **If necessary, click the Queries object and then click the New button on the Database window toolbar.**
- **Be sure Design View is selected and then click the OK button.**
- **When the Show Table dialog box appears, click its Close button.**
- **Be sure the Query1 : Select Query window is maximized.**
- **Click the View button arrow.**

The list of available views appears (Figure 3).

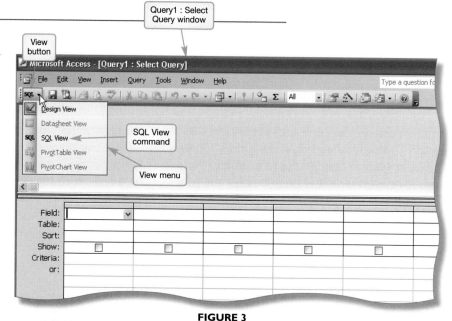

FIGURE 3

2

- **Click SQL View.**

The Query1 : Select Query window appears in SQL view (Figure 4).

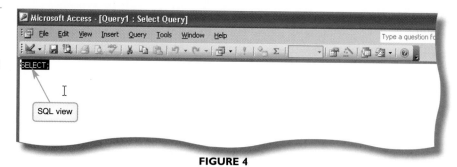

FIGURE 4

Other Ways

1. On View menu click SQL View
2. In Voice Command mode, say "View, SQL View"

Q&A

Q: Can I change the font size for datasheets?

A: Yes. To change the font size for datasheets, click Tools on the menu bar, click Options, click the Datasheet tab, and then make the appropriate changes.

The basic form of SQL expressions is quite simple: SELECT-FROM-WHERE. After the SELECT, you list those fields you want to appear. The fields will appear in the results in the order in which they are listed in the expression. After the FROM, you list the table or tables involved in the query. Finally, after the WHERE, you list any criteria that apply to the data you want to retrieve. The command ends with a semicolon (;).

SQL has no special format rules. In this text, you place the word FROM on a new line, then place the word WHERE, when it is used, on the next line. This makes the commands easier to read. Words that are part of the SQL language are entered in uppercase and others are entered in a combination of uppercase and lowercase. Because it is a common convention, and necessary in some versions of SQL, place a semicolon (;) at the end of each command.

Unlike some other versions of SQL, Microsoft Access allows spaces within field names and table names. There is a restriction, however, to the way such names are used in SQL queries. When a name containing a space appears in SQL, it must be enclosed in square brackets. For example, Client Number must appear as [Client Number] because the name includes a space. On the other hand, City does not need to be enclosed in square brackets because its name does not include a space. In order to be consistent, all names in this text will be enclosed in square brackets. Thus, the City field would appear as [City] even though the brackets technically are not required.

Including Only Certain Fields

To include only certain fields, list them after the word SELECT. If you want to list all rows in the table, you do not need to include the word WHERE. The following steps list the number, name, amount paid, and current due amount of all clients.

To Include Only Certain Fields

1

• **Type** SELECT [Client Number],[Name],[Amount Paid],[Current Due] **as the first line of the command, and then press the ENTER key.**

• **Type** FROM [Client]; **as the second line.**

The command is entered (Figure 5).

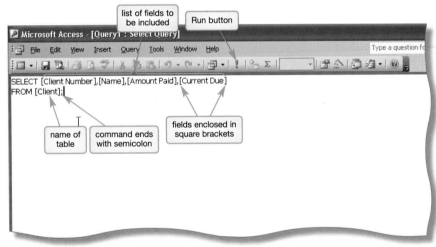

FIGURE 5

2

• **Click the Run button.**

• **If instructed to do so, print the results by clicking the Print button on the Query Datasheet toolbar.**

The results appear (Figure 6). Only the fields specified are included.

Client Number	Name	Amount Paid	Current Due
BS27	Blant and Sons	$21,876.00	$892.50
CE16	Center Services	$26,512.00	$2,672.00
CP27	Calder Plastics	$8,725.00	$0.00
FI28	Farrow-Idsen	$8,287.50	$925.50
FL93	Fairland Lawns	$21,625.00	$0.00
HN83	Hurley National	$0.00	$0.00
MC28	Morgan-Alyssa Academy	$24,761.00	$1,572.00
PS82	PRIM Staffing	$11,682.25	$2,827.50
RT67	Richards-Trent	$0.00	$0.00
*		$0.00	$0.00

FIGURE 6

Preparing to Enter a New SQL Query

To enter a new SQL query, you could close the window, click the No button when asked if you want to save your changes, and then begin the process from scratch. A quicker alternative is to use the View menu and then select SQL View. You then will be returned to SQL view with the current command appearing. At that point, you could erase the current command and then enter a new one. (If the next command is similar to the previous one, it may be simpler to modify the current command instead of erasing it and starting over.) The following steps show how to prepare to enter a new SQL query.

To Prepare to Enter a New SQL Query

1

• **Click the View button arrow.**

The list of available views appears (Figure 7).

2

• **Click SQL View.**

The command once again appears in SQL view.

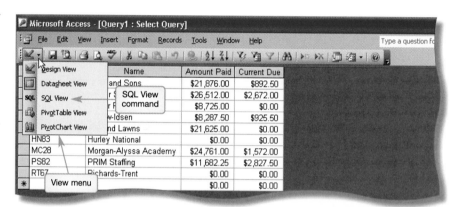

FIGURE 7

Including All Fields

To include all fields, you could use the same approach as in the previous steps, that is, list each field in the Client table after the word SELECT. There is a shortcut, however. Instead of listing all the field names after SELECT, you can use the asterisk (*) symbol. This indicates that you want all fields listed in the order in which you described them to the system during data definition. The following steps illustrate how to list all fields and all records in the Client table.

To Include All Fields

1

• **Delete the current command, type** SELECT * **as the first line of the command, and then press the ENTER key.**

• **Type** FROM [Client]; **as the second line.**

The command is entered (Figure 8).

asterisk (*) indicates all fields are to be included

Run button

```
SELECT *
FROM [Client];
```

FIGURE 8

2

- **Click the Run button.**

- **If instructed to do so, print the results by clicking the Print button.**

The results appear (Figure 9). All fields in the Client table are included.

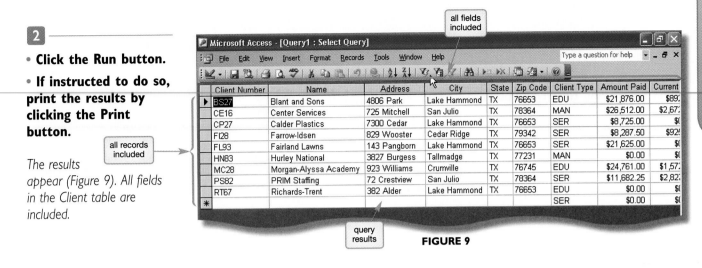

all fields included

all records included

query results

FIGURE 9

Using a Criterion Involving a Numeric Field

To restrict the records to be displayed, include the word WHERE followed by a criterion as part of the command. If the field involved is a numeric field, you simply type the value. To list the client number and name of all clients whose current due amount is 0, for example, you would type the condition [Current Due]=0 as shown in the following steps.

To Use a Criterion Involving a Numeric Field

1

- **Click the View button arrow, click SQL View, and then delete the current command.**

2

- **Type** SELECT [Client Number],[Name] **as the first line of the command, and then press the ENTER key.**

- **Type** FROM [Client] **as the second line, and then press the ENTER key.**

- **Type** WHERE [Current Due]=0; **as the third line.**

The command is entered (Figure 10).

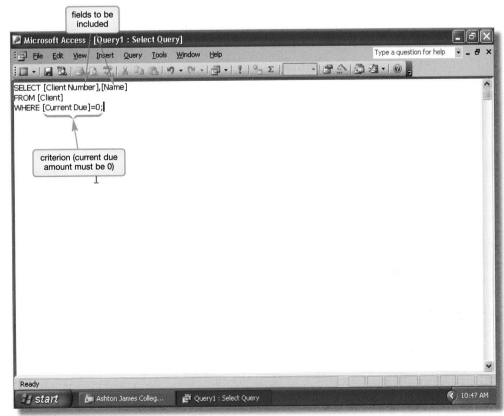

fields to be included

criterion (current due amount must be 0)

FIGURE 10

3

• **Click the Run button.**

• **If instructed to do so, print the results by clicking the Print button.**

The results appear (Figure 11). Only those clients for which the current due amount is $0.00 are included.

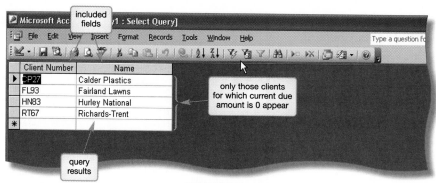

FIGURE 11

Table 1 Comparison Operators	
COMPARISON OPERATOR	**MEANING**
=	Equal to
<	Less than
>	Greater than
<=	Less than or equal to
>=	Greater than or equal to
<> or !=	Not equal to

The criterion following the word WHERE in the preceding query is called a simple criterion. A **simple criterion** has the form: field name, comparison operator, then either another field name or a value. The possible comparison operators are shown in Table 1. Note that there are two different versions for "not equal to" (<> and !=). You must use the one that is right for your particular implementation of SQL. If you use the wrong one, your system will let you know instantly. Simply use the other.

Using a Criterion Involving a Text Field

If the criterion involves a text field, the value must be enclosed in single quotation marks. The following example lists all clients located in Lake Hammond, that is, all clients for whom the value in the City field is Lake Hammond.

To Use a Criterion Involving a Text Field

1

• **Click the View button arrow, click SQL View, and then delete the current command.**

2

• **Type** SELECT [Client Number],[Name] **as the first line of the command, and then press the ENTER key.**

• **Type** FROM [Client] **as the second line, and then press the ENTER key.**

• **Type** WHERE [City]='Lake Hammond'; **as the third line.**

The command is entered (Figure 12).

FIGURE 12

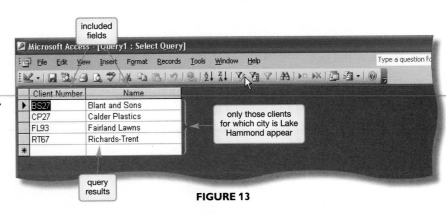

FIGURE 13

3

- **Click the Run button.**

- **If instructed to do so, print the results by clicking the Print button.**

The results appear (Figure 13). Only those clients located in Lake Hammond are included.

Using Compound Criteria

The criteria you have seen so far are called simple criteria. The next examples require compound criteria. **Compound criteria** are formed by connecting two or more simple criteria using AND, OR, and NOT. When simple criteria are connected by the word AND, all the simple criteria must be true in order for the compound criterion to be true. When simple criteria are connected by the word OR, the compound criterion will be true whenever any of the simple criteria are true. Preceding a criterion by NOT reverses the truth or falsity of the original criterion. That is, if the original criterion is true, the new criterion will be false; if the original criterion is false, the new one will be true.

The following steps illustrate how to use compound criteria to display the names of those clients located in Lake Hammond and for whom the current due amount is 0.

To Use a Compound Criterion

1

- **Click the View button arrow, click SQL View, and then delete the current command.**

2

- **Type** SELECT [Client Number],[Name] **as the first line of the command, and then press the ENTER key.**

- **Type** FROM [Client] **as the second line, and then press the ENTER key.**

- **Type** WHERE [City]='Lake Hammond' **as the third line, and then press the ENTER key.**

- **Type** AND [Current Due]=0; **as the fourth line.**

The command is entered (Figure 14).

FIGURE 14

3

• **Click the Run button.**

• **If instructed to do so, print the results by clicking the Print button.**

The results appear (Figure 15). Only those clients located in Lake Hammond and with a current due amount of $0.00 are included.

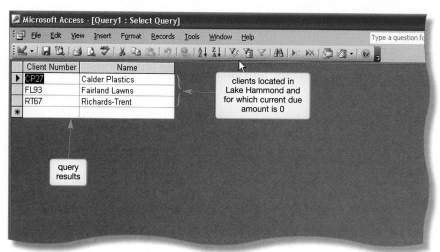

FIGURE 15

You use the same method to form compound criteria involving OR. Simply use the word OR instead of the word AND. In that case, the results would contain those records that satisfied either criterion.

Using the Word Not in a Criterion

To use the word NOT in a criterion, precede the criterion with the word NOT. The following steps illustrate how to list the numbers and names of the clients not located in Lake Hammond.

To Use NOT in a Criterion

1

• **Click the View button arrow, click SQL View, and then delete the current command.**

2

• **Type** SELECT [Client Number],[Name] **as the first line of the command, and then press the ENTER key.**

• **Type** FROM [Client] **as the second line, and then press the ENTER key.**

• **Type** WHERE NOT [City]='Lake Hammond'; **as the third line.**

The command is entered (Figure 16).

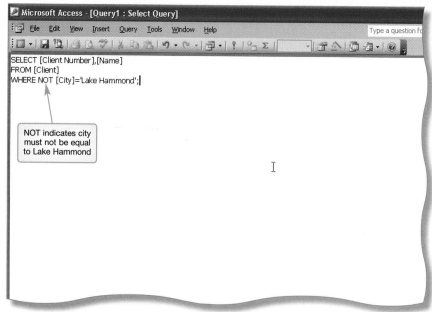

FIGURE 16

3

- **Click the Run button.**
- **If instructed to do so, print the results by clicking the Print button.**

The results appear (Figure 17). Only those clients not located in Lake Hammond are included.

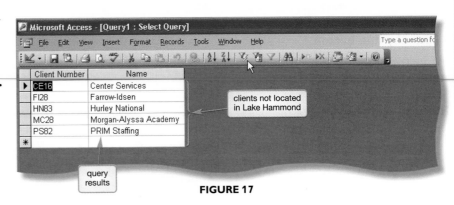

FIGURE 17

Using Computed Fields

Just as with queries created in Design view, you can include fields in queries that are not in the database, but that can be computed from fields that are. Such a field is called a **computed** or **calculated field**. Such computations can involve addition (+), subtraction (-), multiplication (*), or division (/). The query in the following steps includes the total amount, which is equal to the amount paid amount plus the current due amount.

To name the computed field, follow the computation with the word AS and then the name you wish to assign the field. The following steps show how to assign the name Total Amount to the computed field. The steps also list the Client Number and Name for all clients for which the current due amount is greater than 0.

Q & A

Q: Can I assign a different name to an existing field?

A: Yes. To do so, use the word AS and follow it with the name you wish to assign the field. For example, the command, SELECT [Name] AS [Client Name] FROM [Client];, displays the Client Name column heading in the query result.

To Use a Computed Field

1

- **Click the View button arrow, click SQL View, and then delete the current command.**

2

- **Type** SELECT [Client Number],[Name],[Amount Paid]+[Current Due] AS [Total Amount] **as the first line of the command, and then press the ENTER key.**
- **Type** FROM [Client] **as the second line, and then press the ENTER key.**
- **Type** WHERE [Current Due]>0; **as the third line.**

The command is entered (Figure 18).

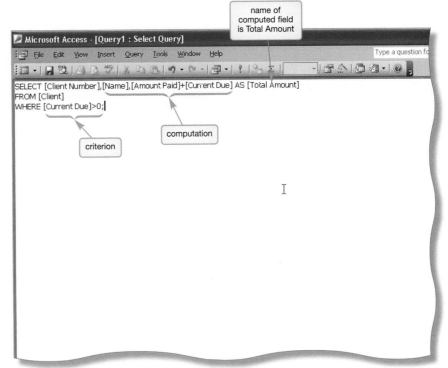

FIGURE 18

3

- **Click the Run button.**
- **If instructed to do so, print the results by clicking the Print button.**

The results appear (Figure 19). The total amount is calculated appropriately. Only those clients with a current due amount greater than 0 are included.

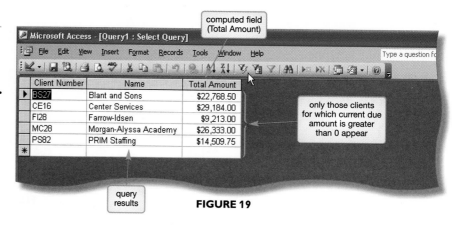

computed field (Total Amount)

only those clients for which current due amount is greater than 0 appear

query results

FIGURE 19

More About

Sorting in SQL

In SQL, you can sort in descending order by following the sort key with DESC in the ORDER BY clause. If you have two sort keys, you could choose to sort one in descending order and the other in ascending order. For example, ORDER BY [Trainer Number], [Current Due] DESC; would sort on ascending Trainer Number and descending Current Due.

Sorting

The field on which data is to be sorted is called a **sort key**, or simply a **key**. If the data is to be sorted on two fields, the more important key is called the **major sort key** (also referred to as the **primary sort key**) and the less important key is called the **minor sort key** (also referred to as the **secondary sort key**). To sort the output, you include the words ORDER BY, followed by the sort key. If there are two sort keys, the major sort key is listed first.

The following steps list the client number, name, amount paid amount, current due amount, and trainer number for all clients. The data is to be sorted by trainer number. Within the clients having the same trainer number, the data is to be sorted further by amount paid amount. This means that the Trainer Number field is the major (primary) sort key and the Amount Paid field is the minor (secondary) sort key.

To Sort the Results

1

- **Click the View button arrow, click SQL View, and then delete the current command.**

2

- **Type** SELECT [Client Number],[Name],[Amount Paid],[Current Due],[Trainer Number] **as the first line of the command, and then press the ENTER key.**

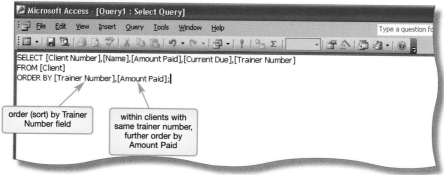

order (sort) by Trainer Number field

within clients with same trainer number, further order by Amount Paid

FIGURE 20

- **Type** FROM [Client] **as the second line, and then press the ENTER key.**
- **Type** ORDER BY [Trainer Number],[Amount Paid]; **as the third line.**

The command is entered (Figure 20). By default, the records will be sorted in ascending order.

3

- **Click the Run button.**

- **If instructed to do so, print the results by clicking the Print button.**

The results appear (Figure 21). The clients are sorted by trainer number. Within the clients of a particular trainer, the results further are sorted by amount paid.

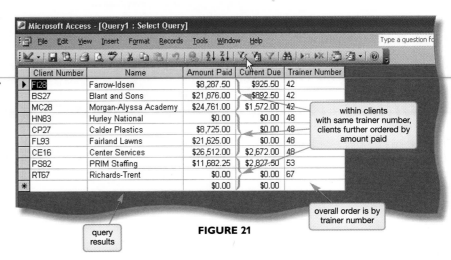

FIGURE 21

Using Built-In Functions

SQL has **built-in** functions (also called **aggregate** functions) to calculate the number of entries, the sum or average of all the entries in a given column, and the largest or smallest of the entries in a given column. In SQL, these functions are called COUNT, SUM, AVG, MAX, and MIN, respectively.

The following steps demonstrate how to count the number of clients assigned to trainer number 42. To do so, use the COUNT function with an asterisk (*).

To Use a Built-In Function

1

- **Click the View button arrow, click SQL View, and then delete the current command.**

2

- **Type** SELECT COUNT(*) **as the first line of the command, and then press the ENTER key.**

- **Type** FROM [Client] **as the second line, and then press the ENTER key.**

- **Type** WHERE [Trainer Number]='42'; **as the third line.**

The command is entered (Figure 22).

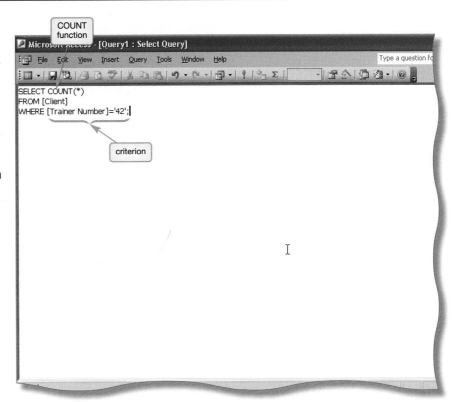

FIGURE 22

3

• **Click the Run button.**

• **If instructed to do so, print the results by clicking the Print button.**

The results appear (Figure 23). There are three clients for trainer number 42. The heading Expr1000 is a default heading assigned by Access.

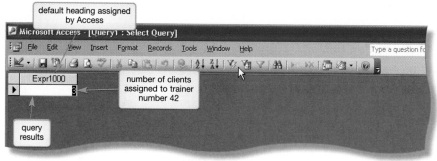

FIGURE 23

Using Multiple Functions in the Same Command

The only differences between COUNT and SUM, other than the obvious fact that they are computing different statistics, are that first, in the case of SUM, you must specify the field for which you want a total, instead of an asterisk (*) and second, the field must be numeric. You could not calculate a sum of names or addresses, for example. The following steps show how to use both the COUNT and SUM functions to count the number of clients and calculate the SUM (total) of their Amount Paid amounts.

To Use Multiple Functions in the Same Command

1

• **Click the View button arrow, click SQL View, and then delete the current command.**

2

• **Type** SELECT COUNT(*),SUM([Amount Paid]) **as the first line of the command, and then press the ENTER key.**

• **Type** FROM [Client]; **as the second line.**

The command is entered (Figure 24).

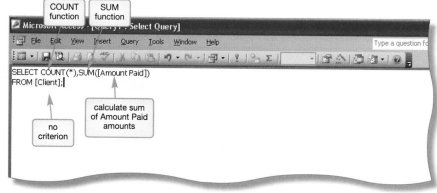

FIGURE 24

3

• **Click the Run button.**

• **If instructed to do so, print the results by clicking the Print button.**

The results appear (Figure 25). The number of clients (9) and the total of the amounts paid ($123,468.75) both appear.

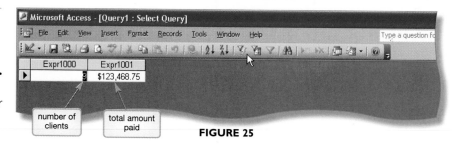

FIGURE 25

The use of AVG, MAX, and MIN is similar to SUM. The only difference is that a different statistic is calculated.

Grouping

Grouping means creating groups of records that share some common characteristic. In grouping work orders by client number, for example, the work orders of client BS27 would form one group, the work orders of client EU28 would be a second, the work orders of client FL93 would form a third, and so on.

The following steps calculate the totals of the Amount Paid fields, called Total Paid, and the Current Due fields, called Total Due, for the clients of each trainer. To calculate the totals, the command will include the SUM([Amount Paid]) and SUM([Current Due]). To get totals for the clients of each trainer the command also will include the words GROUP BY followed by the field used for grouping, in this case, Trainer Number.

Including GROUP BY Trainer Number will cause the clients for each trainer to be grouped together; that is, all clients with the same trainer number will form a group. Any statistics, such as totals, appearing after the word SELECT will be calculated for each of these groups. It is important to note that using GROUP BY does not imply that the information will be sorted. To produce the results in a particular order, you also should use ORDER BY as illustrated in the following steps. The steps also rename the total amount paid as Total Paid and the total current due as Total Due by including appropriate AS clauses.

To Use Grouping

1

• **Click the View button arrow, click SQL View, and then delete the current command.**

2

• **Type** SELECT [Trainer Number],SUM([Amount Paid]) AS [Total Paid],SUM([Current Due]) AS [Total Due] **as the first line of the command, and then press the ENTER key.**

• **Type** FROM [Client] **as the second line, and then press the ENTER key.**

• **Type** GROUP BY [Trainer Number] **as the third line, and then press the ENTER key.**

• **Type** ORDER BY [Trainer Number]; **as the fourth line.**

The command is entered (Figure 26).

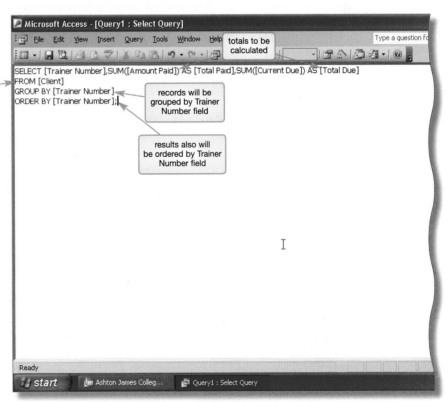

FIGURE 26

3

- **Click the Run button.**

- **If instructed to do so, print the results by clicking the Print button.**

The results appear (Figure 27). The first row represents the group of clients of trainer 42. For these clients, the total paid is $54,924.50 and the total due is $3,390.00.

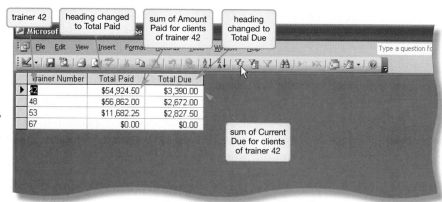

trainer 42 | heading changed to Total Paid | sum of Amount Paid for clients of trainer 42 | heading changed to Total Due

sum of Current Due for clients of trainer 42

FIGURE 27

When rows are grouped, one line of output is produced for each group. The only things that may appear are statistics calculated for the group or fields whose values are the same for all rows in a group. For example, it would make sense to display the trainer number, because all the clients in the group have the same trainer number. It would not make sense to display the client number, because the client number will vary from one row in a group to another. (SQL could not determine which client number to display for the group.)

Restricting the Groups that Appear

In some cases you only want to display certain groups. For example, you may want to display only those trainers for whom the sum of the Current Due amounts are greater than $3,000. This restriction does not apply to individual rows, but instead to groups. Because WHERE applies only to rows, it is not appropriate to accomplish the kind of restriction you have here. Fortunately, there is a word that is to groups what WHERE is to rows. The word is HAVING and its use is shown in the following steps.

To Restrict the Groups that Appear

1

- **Click the View button arrow and then click SQL View.**

2

- **Click the beginning of the fourth line (ORDER BY [Trainer Number];), and then press the ENTER key.**

- **Click the beginning of the new blank line, and then type** HAVING SUM([Current Due])>3000 **as the new fourth line.**

The command is entered (Figure 28).

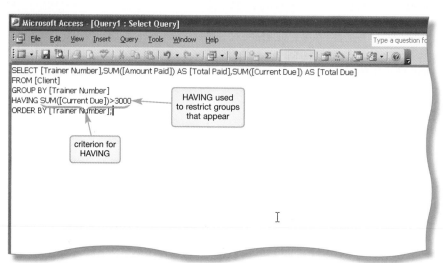

SELECT [Trainer Number],SUM([Amount Paid]) AS [Total Paid],SUM([Current Due]) AS [Total Due]
FROM [Client]
GROUP BY [Trainer Number]
HAVING SUM([Current Due])>3000
ORDER BY [Trainer Number];

HAVING used to restrict groups that appear

criterion for HAVING

FIGURE 28

3

- **Click the Run button.**
- **If instructed to do so, print the results by clicking the Print button.**

The results appear (Figure 29). Only those groups for which the sum of the Current Due is greater than $3,000.00 appear. In this case, there is only one such group, the group for trainer 42.

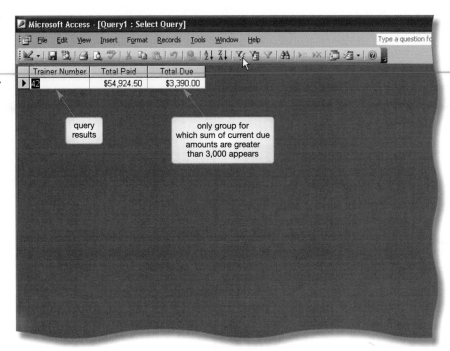

FIGURE 29

Joining Tables

Many queries require data from more than one table. Just as with creating queries in Design view, it is necessary to be able to **join** tables, that is, to find rows in two tables that have identical values in matching fields. In SQL, this is accomplished through appropriate criteria following the word WHERE.

If you wish to list the client number, name, trainer number, first name of the trainer, and last name of the trainer for all clients, you need data from both the Client and Trainer tables. The Trainer Number field is in both tables, the Client Number field is only in the Client table, and the First Name and Last Name fields are only in the Trainer table. You need to access both tables in your SQL query, as follows:

1. After the word SELECT, you indicate all fields you wish to appear.
2. After the word FROM, you list all tables involved in the query.
3. After the word WHERE, you give the criterion that will restrict the data to be retrieved to only those rows from the two tables that match, that is, to the rows that have common values in matching fields.

There is a problem, however. The matching fields are both called Trainer Number. There is a field in the Client table called Trainer Number, as well as a field in the Trainer table called Trainer Number. In this case, if you only enter Trainer Number, it will not be clear which table you mean. It is necessary to **qualify** Trainer Number, that is, to specify to which field in which table you are referring. You do this by preceding the name of the field with the name of the table, followed by a period. The Trainer Number field in the Client table, for example is [Client].[Trainer Number].

The steps on the next page demonstrate how to list the client number, name, trainer number, first name of the trainer, and last name of the trainer for all clients.

More About

Joins in SQL

Different types of joins can be implemented in SQL. For example, in joining clients and course offerings in such a way that a client will display even if it has no open course offerings, you would need to perform a type of join called an outer join. For more information, visit the Access 2003 More About Web page (scsite.com/ac2003/more) and click Joins in SQL.

To Join Tables

1

• **Click the View button arrow, click SQL View, and then delete the current command.**

2

• **Type** SELECT [Client Number],[Name],[Client]. [Trainer Number],[First Name],[Last Name] **as the first line of the command, and then press the ENTER key.**

• **Type** FROM [Client],[Trainer] **as the second line, and then press the ENTER key.**

• **Type** WHERE [Client].[Trainer Number]=[Trainer].[Trainer Number]; **as the third line.**

The command is entered (Figure 30).

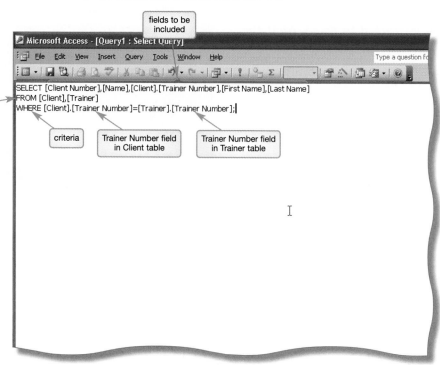

FIGURE 30

3

• **Click the Run button.**

• **If instructed to do so, print the results by clicking the Print button.**

The results appear (Figure 31). The results include the appropriate data from both the Client table and the Trainer table.

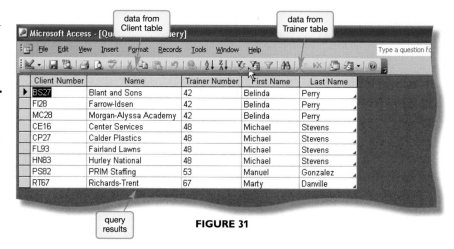

FIGURE 31

More About

The Quick Reference

For a table that lists how to complete the tasks covered in this book using the mouse, menu, shortcut menu, and keyboard, see the Quick Reference Summary at the back of this book, or visit the Access 2003 Quick Reference Web page (scsite.com/ac2003/qr).

Note that whenever there is potential ambiguity, you must qualify the fields involved. It is permissible to qualify other fields as well, even if there is no confusion. For example, instead of [Name], you could have typed [Client].[Name] to indicate the Name field in the Client table. Some people prefer to qualify all fields and this is not a bad approach. In this text, you only will qualify fields when it is necessary to do so.

You can restrict the records to be included in a join by creating a compound criterion. The criterion will include the criterion necessary to join the tables along with a criterion to restrict the records. The criteria will be connected with AND.

The following steps show how to list the client number, name, trainer number, first name of the trainer, and last name of the trainer for all clients for which the current due amount is greater than 0.

To Restrict the Records in a Join

1

• **Click the View button arrow, and then click SQL View.**

2

• **If necessary, click immediately after the semicolon on the third line.**

• **Press the BACKSPACE key to delete the semicolon, and then press the ENTER key.**

• **Type** AND [Current Due] > 0; **as the fourth line.**

The command is entered (Figure 32).

3

• **Click the Run button.**

• **If instructed to do so, print the results by clicking the Print button.**

The results appear (Figure 33). Only those clients for which the current due is greater than $0.00 appear.

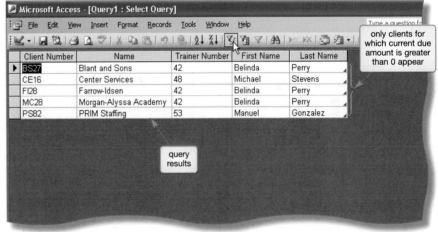

FIGURE 32

FIGURE 33

In some cases, you will need data from more than two tables. The steps on the next page, for example, illustrate how to include the client number and name from the Client table. The query also includes the course number, total hours, and hours spent from the Course Offerings table as well as the course description, which only is found in the Course table. Thus, the query must include the Course Offerings, Course, and Client tables.

The Course and Course Offerings table are related by the Course Number column that they have in common. The specific condition to relate these tables is [Course].[Course Number]=[Course Offerings].[Course Number]. Likewise, the Client and Course Offerings table are related by the Client Number column that they have in common. The condition to relate these two tables is [Client].[Client Number]=[Course Offerings].[Client Number]. These conditions must be related with AND as shown in the steps on the next page.

More About

Microsoft Certification

Microsoft Office Certification provides an opportunity for you to obtain a valuable industry credential — proof that you have the Access skills required by employers. For more information, see Appendix E, or visit the Access 2003 Certification Web page (scsite.com/ac2003/cert).

To Join Multiple Tables

1

• **Click the View button arrow, click SQL View, and then delete the current command.**

2

• **Type** SELECT [Course Offerings].[Client Number], [Name],[Course Offerings].[Course Number],[Course Description], **as the first line of the command, and then press the ENTER key.**

• **Type** [Total Hours],[Hours Spent] **as the second line of the command, and then press the ENTER key.**

• **Type** FROM [Course Offerings],[Course],[Client] **as the third line, and then press the ENTER key.**

• **Type** WHERE [Course].[Course Number]=[Course Offerings].[Course Number] **as the fourth line, and then press the ENTER key.**

• **Type** AND [Client].[Client Number]=[Course Offerings].[Client Number]; **as the fifth line.**

The command is entered (Figure 34).

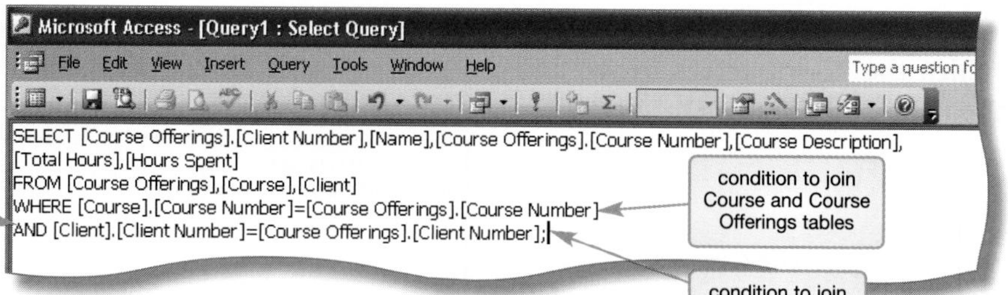

conditions connected by AND

condition to join Course and Course Offerings tables

condition to join Client and Course Offerings tables

FIGURE 34

3

• **Click the Run button. Resize each column to best fit the data by double-clicking the right edge of its field selector.**

• **If instructed to do so, print the results by clicking the Print button.**

The results appear (Figure 35).

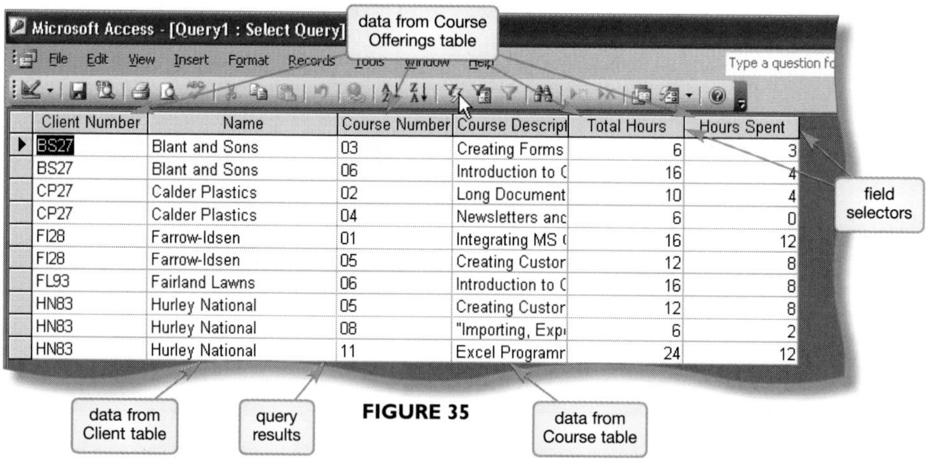

data from Course Offerings table

Client Number	Name	Course Number	Course Descript	Total Hours	Hours Spent
BS27	Blant and Sons	03	Creating Forms	6	3
BS27	Blant and Sons	06	Introduction to (	16	4
CP27	Calder Plastics	02	Long Document	10	4
CP27	Calder Plastics	04	Newsletters and	6	0
FI28	Farrow-Idsen	01	Integrating MS (	16	12
FI28	Farrow-Idsen	05	Creating Custor	12	8
FL93	Fairland Lawns	06	Introduction to (	16	8
HN83	Hurley National	05	Creating Custor	12	8
HN83	Hurley National	08	"Importing, Expr	6	2
HN83	Hurley National	11	Excel Programr	24	12

field selectors

data from Client table

query results

FIGURE 35

data from Course table

More About

Access-Generated SQL

After creating an SQL command, you can move to Design view. Access automatically fills in the design grid appropriately to match your SQL command. Then, you can return to SQL view and again see the command. If you make any changes in the design grid before returning to SQL view, however, Access will reformat your command as an Access-Generated SQL command.

To create a SQL query that joins data from more than two tables, it is best to take it one step at a time, as follows:

1. List all the columns to be included after the word SELECT. If the name of any column appears in more than one table, precede the column name with the table name (that is, qualify it).
2. List all the tables involved in the query after the word FROM.
3. Taking the tables involved one pair at a time, put the condition that relates the tables after the word WHERE. Join these conditions with AND. If there are any other conditions, include them after the word WHERE and connect them to the others with the word AND.

Closing the Query and Restoring the Font Size

The following steps show how to close the query and restore the font size to its default setting.

To Close a Query and Restore the Font Size

1 Click the Close Window button for the Microsoft Access - [Query1 : Select Query] window.

2 Click Tools on the menu bar, and then click Options on the Tools Menu. Click the Tables/Queries tab.

3 Click the Size box arrow, and then click 8 in the list that appears. Click the OK button.

The font size is changed to 8.

Comparison with Access-Generated SQL

When you create a query in Design view, Access automatically creates a corresponding SQL query that is similar to the queries you have created. The Access query shown in Figure 36, for example, includes the Client Number and Name. The City field has a criterion (Lake Hammond), but the City field will not appear in the results. The View menu appears in the figure.

The corresponding SQL query is shown in Figure 37. The query is very similar to the queries you have entered, but there are three slight differences. First, the fields are qualified (Client.[Client Number] and Client.Name), even though they do not need to be. (Only one table is involved in the query, so no qualification is necessary.) Second, the Name field is not enclosed in square brackets. The field legitimately is not enclosed in square brackets because there are no spaces or other special characters in the field name. Finally, there are extra parentheses in the criteria.

Both the style used by Access and the style you have been using are legitimate. The choice of style is a personal preference.

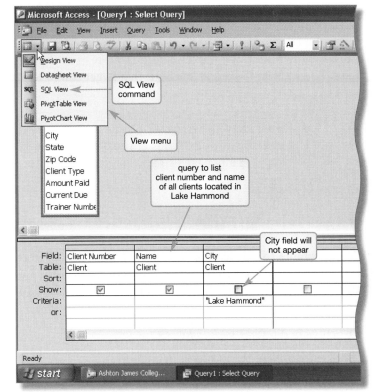

FIGURE 36

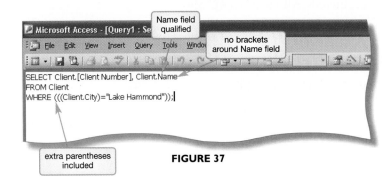

FIGURE 37

Closing the Database and Quitting Access

The following steps close the database and quit Access.

To Close a Database and Quit Access

1 **Click the Close Window button for the Ashton James College : Database window.**

2 **Click the Close button for the Microsoft Access window.**

Access and the database close.

SQL Feature Summary

In this SQL Feature, you learned how to create SQL queries. You saw how to include fields in a query. You learned to use criteria involving both numeric and text fields as well as how to use compound criteria. You used computed fields, and saw how to rename the computation. You sorted the results of a query. You used the built-in functions. You grouped records in a query and also restricted the groups that appeared in the results. You saw how to join two tables, and how to restrict the records in a join. You learned how to join multiple tables. Finally, you looked at the SQL that is generated automatically by Access.

 If you have a SAM user profile, you may have access to hands-on instruction, practice, and assessment of the skills covered in this project. Log in to your SAM account and go to your assignments page to see what your instructor has assigned.

What You Should Know

Having completed this feature, you should be able to perform the tasks below. The tasks are listed in the same order they were presented in this feature. For a list of the buttons, menus, toolbars, and commands introduced in this feature, see the Quick Reference Summary at the back of this book and refer to the Page Number column.

1. Open a Database   (AC 586)
2. Change the Font Size   (AC 587)
3. Create a New SQL Query   (AC 588)
4. Include Only Certain Fields   (AC 589)
5. Prepare to Enter a New SQL Query   (AC 590)
6. Include All Fields   (AC 590)
7. Use a Criterion Involving a Numeric Field (AC 591)
8. Use a Criterion Involving a Text Field   (AC 592)
9. Use a Compound Criterion   (AC 593)
10. Use NOT in a Criterion   (AC 594)
11. Use a Computed Field   (AC 595)
12. Sort the Results   (AC 596)
13. Use a Built-In Function   (AC 597)
14. Use Multiple Functions in the Same Command (AC 598)
15. Use Grouping   (AC 599)
16. Restrict the Groups that Appear   (AC 600)
17. Join Tables   (AC 602)
18. Restrict the Records in a Join   (AC 603)
19. Join Multiple Tables   (AC 604)
20. Close a Query and Restore the Font Size (AC 605)
21. Close a Database and Quit Access   (AC 606)

In the Lab

1 Querying the Begon Pest Control Database Using SQL

Problem: The management of Begon Pest Control would like to learn more about SQL and has determined a number of questions it wants SQL to answer. You must obtain the answers to the questions posed by management.

Instructions: Start Access. If you are using the Microsoft Office Access 2003 Comprehensive text, open the Begon Pest Control database that you used in Project 9. Otherwise, see the inside back cover for instructions for downloading the Data Disk or see your instructor for information about accessing the files required for this book. Perform the following tasks:

1. Open Microsoft Office Word, create a new document, and then type your name at the top. With both Access and Word open on the desktop, create the queries in SQL in Steps 2 through 8 below. For each query, run the query, print the query results, and copy the SQL command to the Word document. To copy the SQL command, highlight the command, click Copy on the Query Design toolbar, switch to Word, and then click Paste on the Standard toolbar.
2. Find all records in the Customer table where the balance is less than $300.00. Display the customer number, name, and technician number.
3. Find all records in the Customer table where the balance is greater than $350.00 and the city is Carlton. Display all fields in the result.
4. Find all records in the Customer table where the Zip code is not 42514.
5. Display the customer number, name, technician number, first name, and last name for all customers. Sort the results in ascending order by technician number and customer number.
6. Display the customer number, name, category description, and estimated total hours for all customers that have work orders.
7. Restrict the records retrieved in Step 6 above to only those work orders where the estimated total hours are greater than 1.
8. Display and print the average balance grouped by technician number. Be sure to name the average balance as Average Balance.
9. Print the Word document that includes the SQL commands used in Steps 2 through 8.

In the Lab

2 Querying the Birds2U Database Using SQL

Problem: The management of Birds2U would like to learn more about SQL and has determined a number of questions it wants SQL to answer. You must obtain the answers to the questions posed by management.

Instructions: Start Access. If you are using the Microsoft Office Access 2003 Comprehensive text, open the Birds2U database that you used in Project 9. Otherwise, see the inside back cover for instructions for downloading the Data Disk or see your instructor for information about accessing the files required for this book. Perform the following tasks:

1. Open Microsoft Office Word, create a new document, and then type your name at the top. With both Access and Word open on the desktop, create the queries in SQL in Steps 2 through 8 below. For each query, run the query, print the query results, and copy the SQL command to the Word document. To copy the SQL command, highlight the command, click Copy on the Query Design toolbar, switch to Word, and then click Paste on the Standard toolbar.

2. Find all records in the Item table where the difference between the cost of the item and the selling price of the item is greater than $4.00. Display the item code, description, cost, and selling price.

3. Display the item code, description, number ordered, cost, and total cost (cost * number ordered) for all items. Be sure to name the computed field, Total Cost.

4. Display the item code, description, date ordered, number ordered, and supplier name for all items.

5. Restrict the records retrieved in Step 4 above to those items where the number ordered is greater than 2.

6. Find the total number of reordered items for each item. Display the item code and total number ordered. Sort the results by item code.

7. Find the average cost by supplier.

8. Find the average cost by supplier for those items that have an average cost less than $30.00.

9. Print the Word document that includes the SQL commands used in Steps 2 through 8.

Appendix A

Microsoft Office Access Help System

Using the Access Help System

This appendix shows you how to use the Access Help system. At anytime while you are using Access, you can interact with its Help system and display information on any Access topic. It is a complete reference manual at your fingertips.

As shown in Figure A-1, five methods for accessing the Access Help system are available:

1. Microsoft Access Help button on the Database toolbar
2. Microsoft Access Help command on the Help menu
3. Function key F1 on the keyboard
4. Type a question for help box on the menu bar
5. Office Assistant

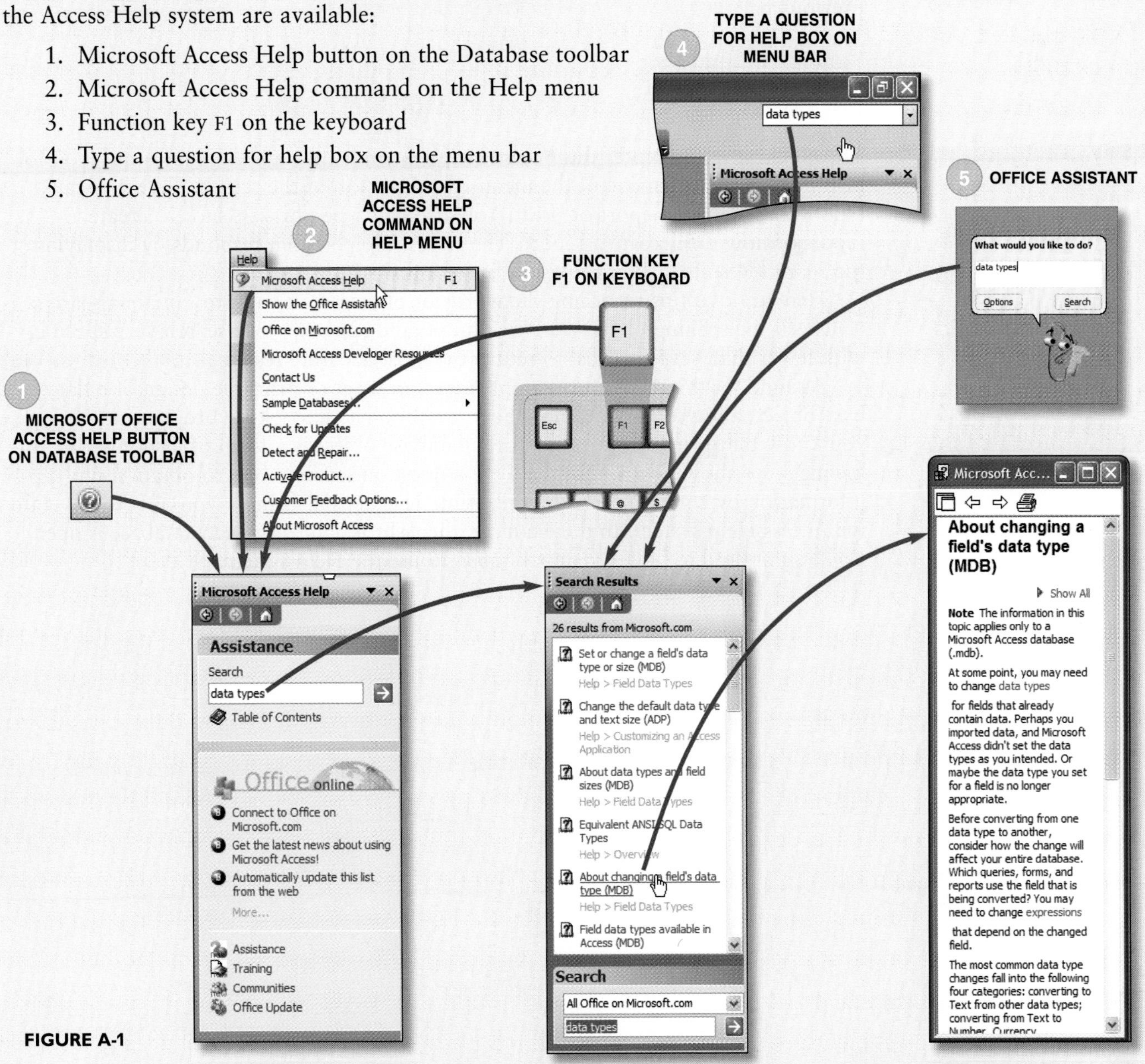

FIGURE A-1

(a) Microsoft Access Help Task Pane

(b) Search Results Task Pane

(c) Microsoft Access Help Window

All five methods result in the Access Help system displaying a task pane on the right side of the Access window. The first three methods cause the **Microsoft Office Access Help task pane** to appear (Figure A-1a on the previous page). This task pane includes a Search text box in which you can enter a word or phrase on which you want help. Once you enter the word or phrase, the Access Help system displays the Search Results task pane (Figure A-1b on the previous page). With the Search Results task pane displayed, you can select specific Help topics.

As shown in Figure A-1, methods 4 and 5 bypass the Microsoft Access Help task pane and immediately display the **Search Results task pane** (Figure A-1b) with a list of links that pertain to the selected topic. Thus, the result of any of the five methods for accessing the Access Help system is the Search Results task pane. Once the Access Help system displays this task pane, you can choose links that relate to the word or phrase on which you searched. In Figure A-1, for example, data types was the searched topic, and the link chosen, About changing a field's data type (MDB), resulted in the Access Help system displaying the Microsoft Office Access Help window with information about changing a field's data type (Figure A-1c on the previous page).

Navigating the Access Help System

The quickest way to enter the Access Help system is through the Type a question for help box on the right side of the menu bar at the top of the screen. Here you can type words, such as report or print. You also can type phrases, such as create a report or how do I create a report. The Access Help system responds by displaying the Search Results task pane with a list of links.

Here are two tips regarding the words or phrases you enter to initiate a search: (1) check the spelling of the word or phrase; and (2) keep your search very specific, with fewer than seven words, to return the most accurate results.

Assume for the following example that you want to print the design of a database object, and you do not know how to do it. The likely keyword is print, because you know that printing the design of a database object is a form of printing. The following steps show how to use the Type a question for help box to obtain useful information by entering the keyword print. The steps also show you how to navigate the Access Help system. In the example, the Ashton James College database is open. You do not need to have a database open to use the Help system.

To Obtain Help Using the Type a Question for Help Box

1

• **Click the Type a question for help box on the right side of the menu bar, type** print **and then press the ENTER key.**

The Access Help system displays the Search Results task pane on the right side of the window. The Search Results task pane includes 30 resulting links (Figure A-2). If you do not find what you are looking for, you can modify or refine the search in the Search area at the bottom of the Search Results task pane. The results returned in your Search Results task pane may be different.

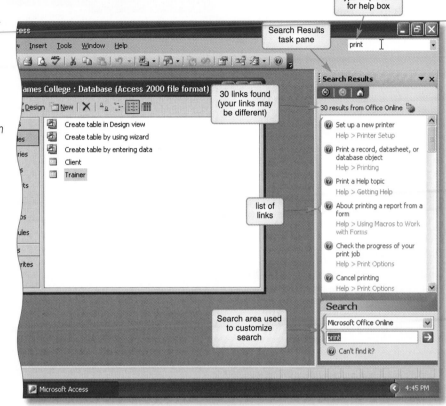

FIGURE A-2

2

• **Scroll down to the bottom of the list of links in the Search Results task pane and then click the Print the design of a database or a database object (MDB) link.**

• **When the Access Help system displays the Microsoft Office Access Help window, click its Auto Tile button in the upper-right corner of the window.**

The Access Help system displays the Microsoft Office Access Help window with the desired information about printing the design of a database or a database object (Figure A-3). With the Microsoft Office Access Help window and Microsoft Office Access window tiled, you can read the information in one window and complete the task in the other window.

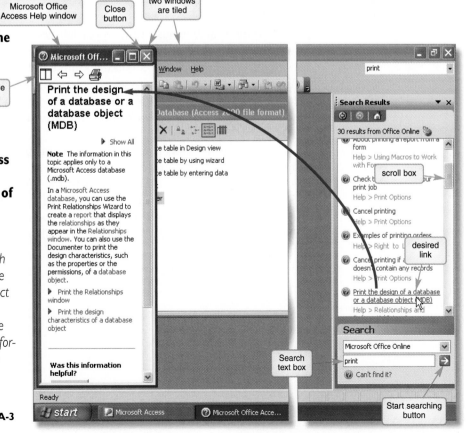

FIGURE A-3

3

• **Double-click the Microsoft Office Access Help window title bar.**

The Microsoft Office Access Help window is maximized so it fills the entire screen (Figure A-4). If you are connected to the Internet, you can give Microsoft your opinion as to whether the information was helpful by clicking the Yes or No button at the bottom of the page.

4

• **Click the Restore Down button on the right side of the Microsoft Office Access Help window title bar to return to the tiled state shown in Figure A-3.**

• **Click the Close button on the Microsoft Office Access Help window title bar.**

The Microsoft Office Access Help window closes and the database is active.

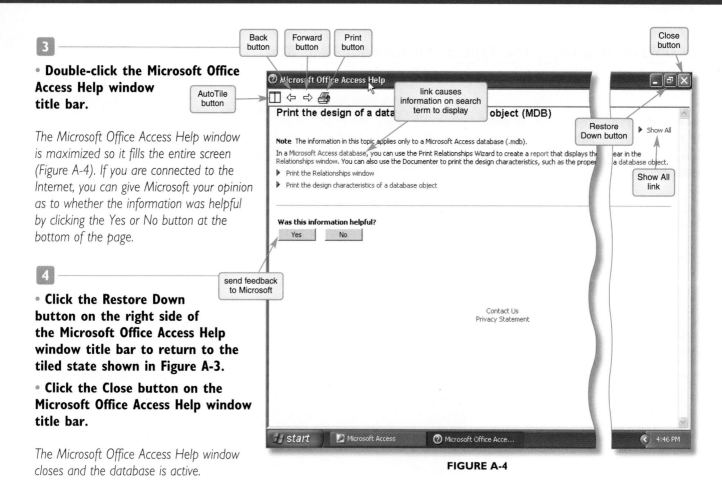

FIGURE A-4

Use the four buttons in the upper-left corner of the Microsoft Office Access Help window (Figure A-4) to tile or untile, navigate through the Help system, or print the contents of the window. As you click links in the Search Results task pane, the Access Help system displays new pages of information. The Access Help system remembers the links you visited and allows you to redisplay the pages visited during a session by clicking the Back and Forward buttons (Figures A-3 on the previous page and A-4).

If none of the links presents the information you want, you can refine the search by entering another word or phrase in the Search text box in the Search Results task pane (Figure A-3). If you have access to the Web, then the scope is global for the initial search. **Global** means all the categories listed in the Search box of the Search area in Figure A-5 are searched. For example, you can restrict the scope to **Offline Help**, which results in a search of related links only on your hard disk.

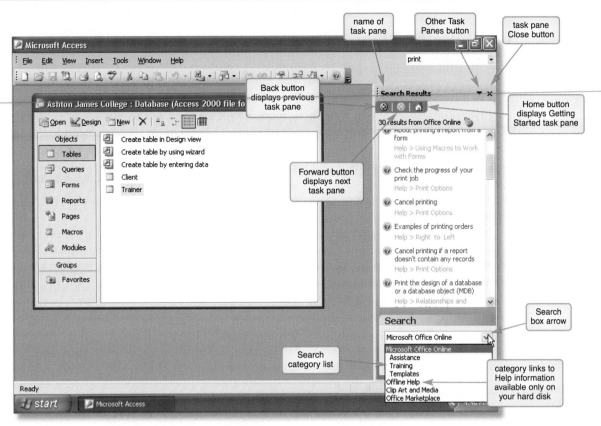

FIGURE A-5

Figure A-5 shows several additional features of the Search Results task pane with which you should be familiar. The buttons immediately below the name of the task pane allow you to navigate between task panes. The Other Task Panes button and the Close button on the Search Results task pane title bar let you change task panes and close the active task pane.

As you enter questions and terms in the Type a question for help box, the Access Help system adds them to its list. Thus, if you click the Type a question for help box arrow, a list of previously used words and phrases are displayed (Figure A-6).

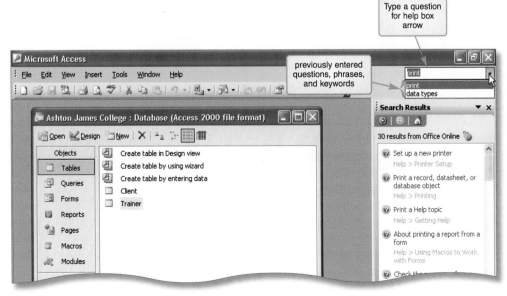

FIGURE A-6

The Office Assistant

The **Office Assistant** is an icon (middle of Figure A-7) that Access displays in the Access window while you work. For the Office Assistant to appear, it must be activated by invoking the Show the Office Assistant command on the Help menu. This Help tool has multiple functions. First, it will respond in the same way as the Type a question for help box with a list of topics that relate to the entry you make in the text box at the bottom of the Office Assistant balloon. The entry can be in the form of a word or phrase as if you were talking to a person. For example, if you want to learn more about creating a report, in the balloon text box, you can type any of the following words or phrases: report, create a report, how do I create a report, or anything similar.

In the example in Figure A-7, the phrase, create a report, is entered into the Office Assistant balloon. The Office Assistant responds by displaying the Search Results task pane with a list of links from which you can choose. Once you click a link in the Search Results task pane, the Access Help system displays the information in the Microsoft Office Access Help window (Figure A-7).

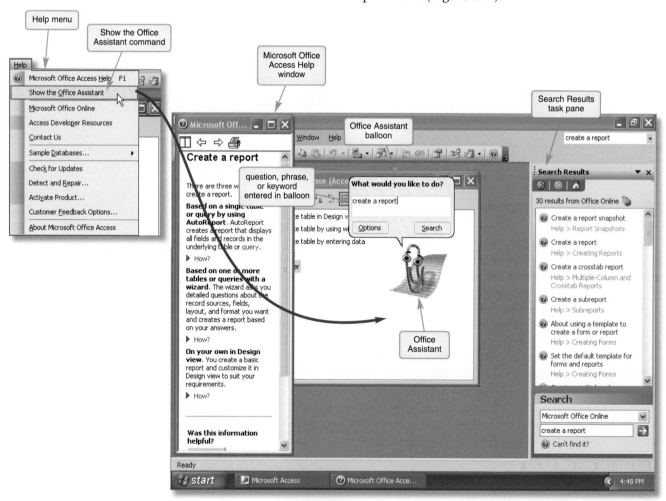

FIGURE A-7

Second, the Office Assistant monitors your work and accumulates tips during a session on how you might increase your productivity and efficiency. The accumulation of tips must be enabled. You enable the accumulation of tips by right-clicking the Office Assistant, clicking Options on the shortcut menu, and then selecting the types of tips you want accumulated. You can view the tips at anytime. The accumulated tips appear when you activate the Office Assistant balloon. Also, if at anytime you see a lightbulb above the Office Assistant, click it to display the most recent tip. If the Office Assistant is hidden, then the lightbulb shows on the Microsoft Office Access Help button on the Database toolbar.

You hide the Office Assistant by invoking the Hide the Office Assistant command on the Help menu or by right-clicking the Office Assistant and then clicking Hide on the shortcut menu. The Hide the Office Assistant command shows on the Help menu only when the Office Assistant is active in the Access window. If the Office Assistant begins showing up on your screen without you instructing it to show, then right-click the Office Assistant, click Options on the shortcut menu, click the Use the Office Assistant check box to remove the check mark, and then click the OK button.

Third, if the Office Assistant is active in the Access window, then Access displays all program and system messages in the Office Assistant balloon.

You may or may not want the Office Assistant to appear on the screen at all times. As indicated earlier, you can hide it and then show it later through the Help menu. For more information about the Office Assistant, type office assistant in the Type a question for help box and then click the links in the Search Results task pane.

Help Buttons in Dialog Boxes and Subsystem Windows

As you invoke commands that display dialog boxes or other windows, such as the Print Preview window, you will see buttons and links that offer helpful information. Figures A-8a and A-8b (on the next page) shows the types of Help buttons and links you will see as you work with Access.

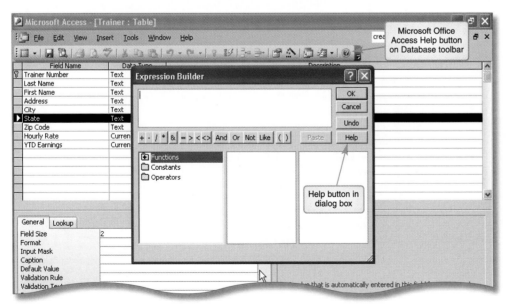

FIGURE A-8a

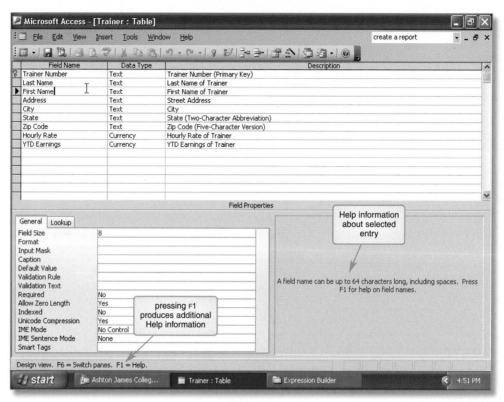

FIGURE A-8b

Other Help Commands on the Help Menu

Thus far, this appendix has discussed the first two commands on the Help menu:
(1) the Microsoft Office Access Help command (Figure A-1 on page APP 1) and
(2) the Show the Office Assistant command (Figure A-7 on page APP 6). Several
additional commands are available on the Help menu as shown in Figure A-9.
Table A-1 summarizes these commands.

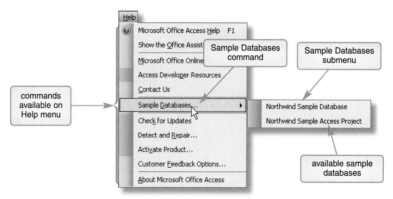

FIGURE A-9

Table A-1 Summary of Other Help Commands on the Help Menu

COMMAND ON HELP MENU	FUNCTION
Microsoft Office Online	Activates your browser, which displays the Microsoft Office Online Home page. The Microsoft Office Online Home page contains links that can improve your Office productivity.
Access Developer Resources	Activates your browser, which displays information and links specific to developing applications using Microsoft Office Access.
Contact Us	Activates your browser, which displays Microsoft contact information and a list of useful links.
Sample Databases	Produces the Sample Databases submenu with a list of available sample databases that you can use to explore various features of Microsoft Access.
Check for Updates	Activates your browser, which displays a list of updates to Office 2003. These updates can be downloaded and installed to improve the efficiency of Office or to fix an error in one or more of the Office applications.
Detect and Repair	Detects and repairs errors in the Access program.
Activate Product	Activates Access if it has not already been activated.
Customer Feedback Options	Gives or denies Microsoft permission to collect anonymous information about your hardware.
About Microsoft Office Access	Displays the About Microsoft Access dialog box. The dialog box lists the owner of the software and the product identification. You need to know the product identification if you call Microsoft for assistance. The three buttons below the OK button are the System Info button, the Tech Support button, and the Disabled Items button. The System Info button displays system information, including hardware resources, components, software environment, and applications. The Tech Support button displays technical assistance information. The Disabled Items button displays a list of disabled items that prevents Access from functioning properly.

Use Help

1 Using the Type a Question for Help Box

Instructions: Perform the following tasks using the Access Help system.

1. Use the Type a question for help box on the menu bar to get help on lookup fields.
2. Click About creating a field that looks up or list values in tables (MDB) in the list of links in the Search Results task pane. Tile the windows. Double-click the Microsoft Access Help window title bar to maximize it. Click the Show All button. Read and print the information. At the top of the printout, write down the number of links the Access Help system found.
3. One at a time, click two additional links in the Search Results task pane and print the information. Hand in the printouts to your instructor. Use the Back and Forward buttons to return to the original page.
4. Use the Type a question for help box to search for information on calculated fields. Click the About calculations in a query (MDB) link in the Search Results task pane. When the Microsoft Access Help window is displayed, maximize the window. Read and print the information. One at a time, click the links on the page and print the information for any new page that displays. Close the Microsoft Access Help window.
5. For each of the following words and phrases, click one link in the Search Results task pane, click the Show All link, and then print the page: table; record; field; database design; primary key; foreign key; and referential integrity.

2 Expanding on the Access Help System Basics

Instructions: Use the Access Help system to understand the topics better and answer the questions listed below. Answer the questions on your own paper, or hand in the printed Help information to your instructor.

1. Show the Office Assistant. Right-click the Office Assistant and then click Animate! on the shortcut menu. Repeat invoking the Animate command to see various animations. Right-click the Office Assistant, click Options on the shortcut menu, click the Reset my tips button, and then click the OK button. Click the lightbulb above the Office Assistant. If you see the lightbulb, it indicates that the Office Assistant has a tip to share with you.
2. Use the Office Assistant to find help on filtering records. Print the help information for three links in the Search Results task pane. Close the Microsoft Access Help window. Hand in the printouts to your instructor. Hide the Office Assistant.
3. Press the F1 key. Search for information on Help. Click the first two links in the Search Results task pane. Read and print the information for both.
4. One at a time, invoke the first three commands in Table A-1 on the previous page. Print each page. Click two links on one of the pages and print the information. Hand in the printouts to your instructor.
5. Click About Microsoft Access on the Help menu. Click the Tech Support button and print the resulting page. Click the System Info button. Below the Components category, print the CD-ROM and Display information. Hand in the printouts to your instructor.

Speech and Handwriting Recognition

Introduction

This appendix discusses the Office capability that allows users to create and modify databases using its alternative input technologies available through **text services**. Office provides a variety of text services, which enable you to speak commands and enter text in an application. The most common text service is the keyboard. Other text services include speech recognition and handwriting recognition.

The Language Bar

The **Language bar** allows you to use text services in the Office applications. You can utilize the Language bar in one of three states: (1) in a restored state as a floating toolbar in the Access window (Figure B-1a or Figure B-1b if Text Labels are enabled); (2) in a minimized state docked next to the notification area on the Windows taskbar (Figure B-1c); or (3) hidden (temporarily closed and out of the way). If the Language bar is hidden, you can activate it by right-clicking the Windows taskbar, pointing to Toolbars on the shortcut menu (Figure B-1d), and clicking Language bar on the Toolbars submenu. If you want to close the Language bar, right-click the Language bar and then click Close the Language bar on the shortcut menu (Figure B-1e).

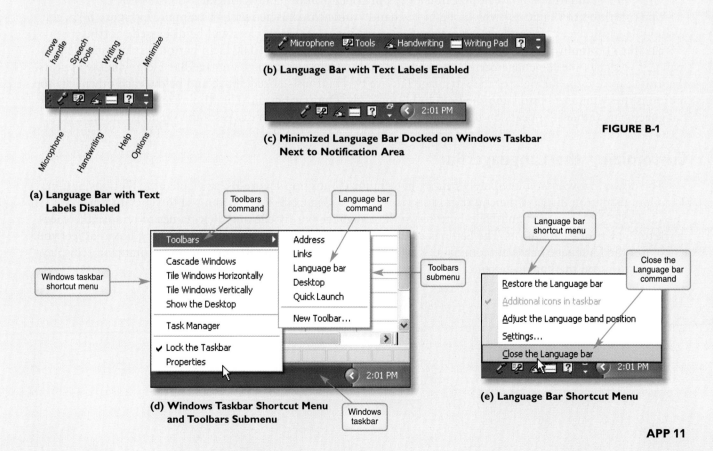

(a) Language Bar with Text Labels Disabled

(b) Language Bar with Text Labels Enabled

(c) Minimized Language Bar Docked on Windows Taskbar Next to Notification Area

(d) Windows Taskbar Shortcut Menu and Toolbars Submenu

(e) Language Bar Shortcut Menu

FIGURE B-1

When Windows was installed on your computer, the installer specified a default language. For example, most users in the United States select English (United States) as the default language. You can add more than 90 additional languages and varying dialects such as Basque, English (Zimbabwe), French (France), French (Canada), German (Germany), German (Austria), and Swahili. With multiple languages available, you can switch from one language to another while working in Access. If you change the language or dialect, then text services may change the functions of the keys on the keyboard, adjust speech recognition, and alter handwriting recognition. If a second language is activated, then a Language icon appears immediately to the right of the move handle on the Language bar. This appendix assumes that English (United States) is the only language installed. Thus, the Language icon does not appear in the examples in Figure B-1 on the previous page.

Buttons on the Language Bar

The Language bar shown in Figure B-2a contains seven buttons. The number of buttons on your Language bar may be different. These buttons are used to select the language, customize the Language bar, control the microphone, control handwriting, and obtain help.

The first button on the left is the Microphone button, which enables and disables the microphone. When the microphone is enabled, text services adds two buttons and a balloon to the Language bar (Figure B-2b). These additional buttons and the balloon will be discussed shortly.

The second button from the left is the Speech Tools button. The Speech Tools button displays a menu of commands (Figure B-2c) that allow you to hide or show the balloon on the Language bar; train the Speech Recognition service so that it can interpret your voice better; add and delete words from its dictionary, such as names and other words not understood easily; and change the user profile so more than one person can use the microphone on the same computer.

The third button from the left on the Language bar is the Handwriting button. The Handwriting button displays the Handwriting menu (Figure B-2d), which lets you choose the Writing Pad (Figure B-2e), Write Anywhere (Figure B-2f), or the on-screen keyboard (Figure B-2g). The On-Screen Symbol Keyboard command on the Handwriting menu displays an on-screen keyboard that allows you to enter special symbols that are not available on a standard keyboard. You can choose only one form of handwriting at a time.

The fourth button indicates which one of the handwriting forms is active. For example, in Figure B-2a, the Writing Pad is active. The handwriting recognition capabilities of text services will be discussed shortly.

The fifth button from the left on the Language bar is the Help button. The Help button displays the Help menu. If you click the Language Bar Help command on the Help menu, the Language Bar Help window appears (Figure B-2h). On the far right of the Language bar are two buttons stacked above and below each other. The top button is the Minimize button and the bottom button is the Options button. The Minimize button minimizes the Language bar so that it appears on the Windows taskbar. The next section discusses the Options button.

Customizing the Language Bar

The down arrow icon immediately below the Minimize button in Figure B-2a is called the Options button. The Options button displays a menu of text services options (Figure B-2i). You can use this menu to hide the Speech Tools, Handwriting, and Help buttons on the Language bar by clicking their names to remove the check mark to the left of each button. The Settings command on the Options menu displays a dialog box that lets you customize the Language bar. This command will be discussed shortly. The Restore Defaults command redisplays hidden buttons on the Language bar.

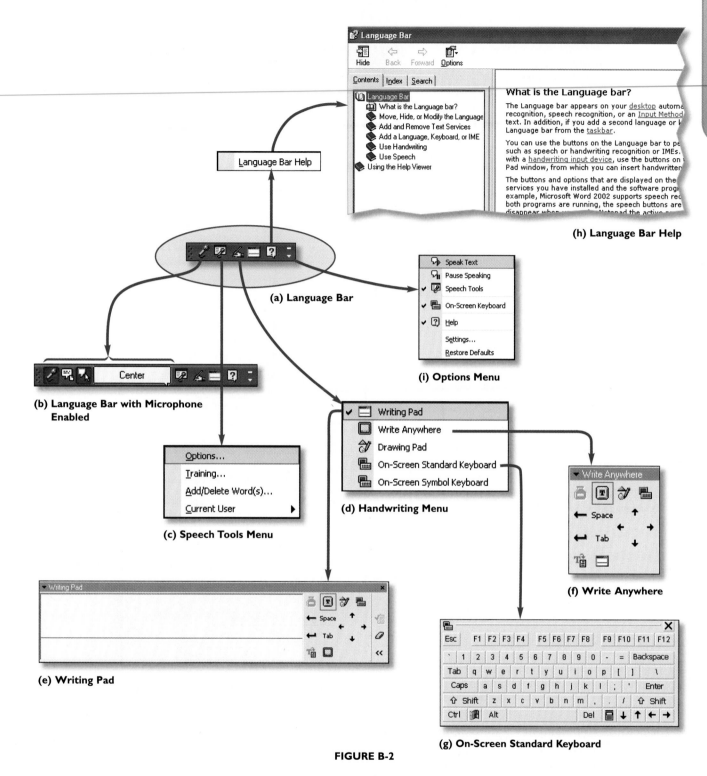

(h) Language Bar Help

(a) Language Bar

(b) Language Bar with Microphone Enabled

(i) Options Menu

(c) Speech Tools Menu

(d) Handwriting Menu

(f) Write Anywhere

(e) Writing Pad

(g) On-Screen Standard Keyboard

FIGURE B-2

If you right-click the Language bar, a shortcut menu appears (Figure B-3a on the next page). This shortcut menu lets you further customize the Language bar. The Minimize command on the shortcut menu docks the Language bar on the Windows taskbar. The Transparency command in Figure B-3a toggles the Language bar between being solid and transparent. You can see through a transparent Language bar (Figure B-3b on the next page). The Text Labels command toggles on text labels on the Language bar (Figure B-3c on the next page) and off (Figure B-3b).

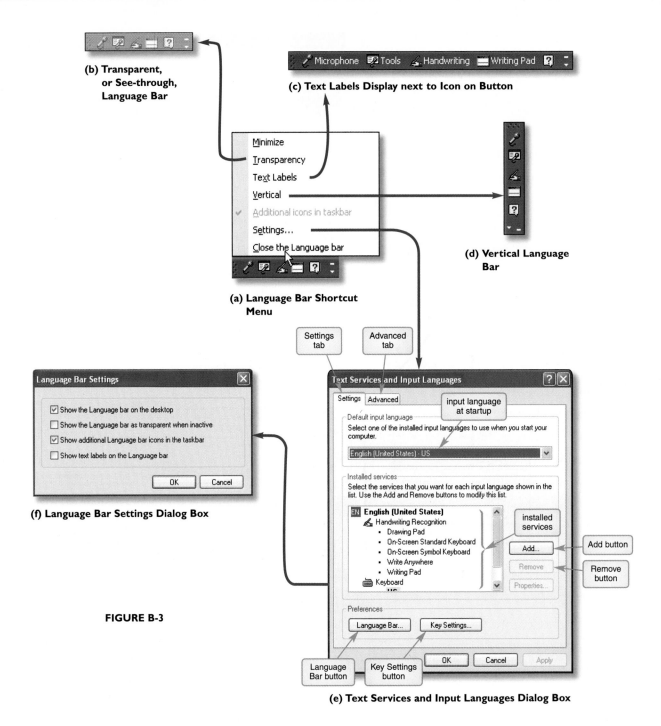

(b) Transparent, or See-through, Language Bar

(c) Text Labels Display next to Icon on Button

(a) Language Bar Shortcut Menu

(d) Vertical Language Bar

(f) Language Bar Settings Dialog Box

FIGURE B-3

(e) Text Services and Input Languages Dialog Box

The Settings command in Figure B-3a displays the Text Services and Input Languages dialog box (Figure B-3e). The Text Services and Input Languages dialog box allows you to add additional languages, add and remove text services, modify keys on the keyboard, modify the Language bar, and extend support of advanced text services to all programs, including Notepad and other programs that normally do not support text services (through the Advanced tab). If you want to remove any one of the services in the Installed services list, select the service, and then click the Remove button. If you want to add a service, click the Add button. The Key Settings button allows you to modify the keyboard. If you click the Language Bar button in the Text Services and Input Languages dialog box, the Language Bar Settings dialog box appears (Figure B-3f). This dialog box contains Language bar options, some of which are the same as the commands on the Language bar shortcut menu shown in Figure B-3a.

The Close the Language bar command on the shortcut menu shown in Figure B-3a closes or hides the Language bar. If you close the Language bar and want to redisplay it, see Figure B-1d on page APP 11.

Speech Recognition

The **Speech Recognition service** available with Office enables your computer to recognize human speech through a microphone. The microphone has two modes: dictation and voice command (Figure B-4). You switch between the two modes by clicking the Dictation button and the Voice Command button on the Language bar. These buttons appear only when you turn on Speech Recognition by clicking the Microphone button on the Language bar (Figure B-5a on the next page). If you are using the Microphone button for the very first time in Access, it will require that you check your microphone settings and step through voice training before activating the Speech Recognition service.

The Dictation button places the microphone in Dictation mode. In **Dictation mode**, whatever you speak is entered as text in the active cell. The Voice Command button places the microphone in Voice Command mode. In **Voice Command mode**, whatever you speak is interpreted as a command. If you want to turn off the microphone, click the Microphone button on the Language bar or in Voice Command mode say, "Mic off" (pronounced mike off). It is important to remember that minimizing the Language bar does not turn off the microphone.

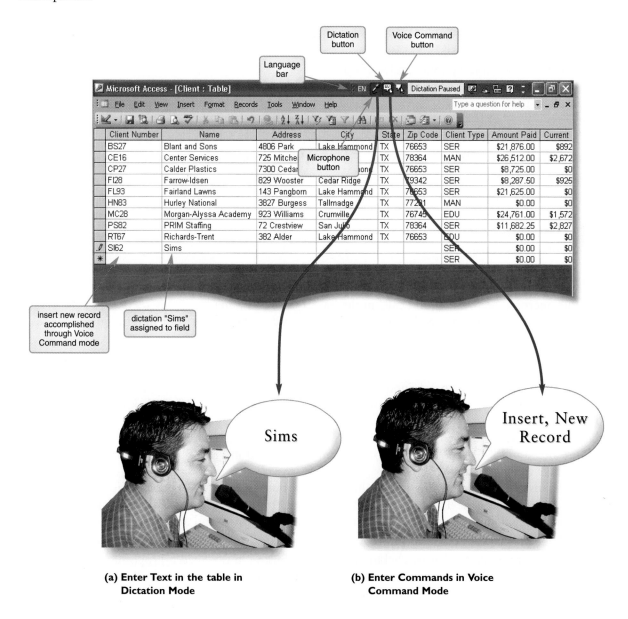

(a) Enter Text in the table in
Dictation Mode

(b) Enter Commands in Voice
Command Mode

FIGURE B-4

The Language bar speech message balloon shown in Figure B-5b displays messages that may offer help or hints. In Voice Command mode, the name of the last recognized command you said appears. If you use the mouse or keyboard instead of the microphone, a message will appear in the Language bar speech message balloon indicating the word you could say. In Dictation mode, the message, Dictating, usually appears. The Speech Recognition service, however, will display messages to inform you that you are talking too soft, too loud, too fast, or to ask you to repeat what you said by displaying, What was that?

Getting Started with Speech Recognition

For the microphone to function properly, you should follow these steps:

1. Make sure your computer meets the minimum requirements.
2. Start Access. Activate Speech Recognition by clicking Tools on the menu bar, pointing to Speech, and then clicking Speech Recognition on the Speech submenu.
3. Set up and position your microphone, preferably a close-talk headset with gain adjustment support.
4. Train Speech Recognition.

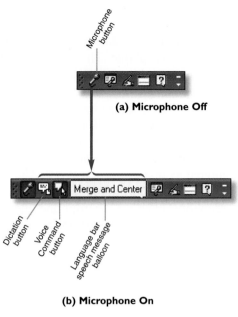

(a) Microphone Off

(b) Microphone On

FIGURE B-5

The following sections describe these steps in more detail.

SPEECH RECOGNITION SYSTEM REQUIREMENTS For Speech Recognition to work on your computer, it needs the following:

1. Microsoft Windows 98 or later or Microsoft Windows NT 4.0 or later
2. At least 128 MB RAM
3. 400 MHz or faster processor
4. Microphone and sound card

SETUP AND POSITION YOUR MICROPHONE Set up your microphone as follows:

1. Connect your microphone to the sound card in the back of the computer.
2. Position the microphone approximately one inch out from and to the side of your mouth. Position it so you are not breathing into it.
3. On the Language bar, click the Speech Tools button, and then click Options on the Speech Tools menu (Figure B-6a).
4. When text services displays the Speech input settings dialog box (Figure B-6b), click the Advanced Speech button. When text services displays the Speech Properties dialog box (Figure B-6c), click the Speech Recognition tab.
5. Click the Configure Microphone button. Follow the Microphone Wizard directions as shown in Figures B-6d, B-6e, and B-6f. The Next button will remain dimmed in Figure B-6e until the volume meter consistently stays in the green area.
6. If someone else installed Speech Recognition, click the New button in the Speech Properties dialog box and enter your name. Click the Train Profile button and step through the Voice Training dialog boxes. The Voice Training dialog boxes will require that you enter your gender and age group. It then will step you through voice training.

You can adjust the microphone further by clicking the Settings button in the Speech Properties dialog box (Figure B-6c). The Settings button displays the Recognition Profile Settings dialog box that allows you to adjust the pronunciation sensitivity and accuracy versus recognition response time.

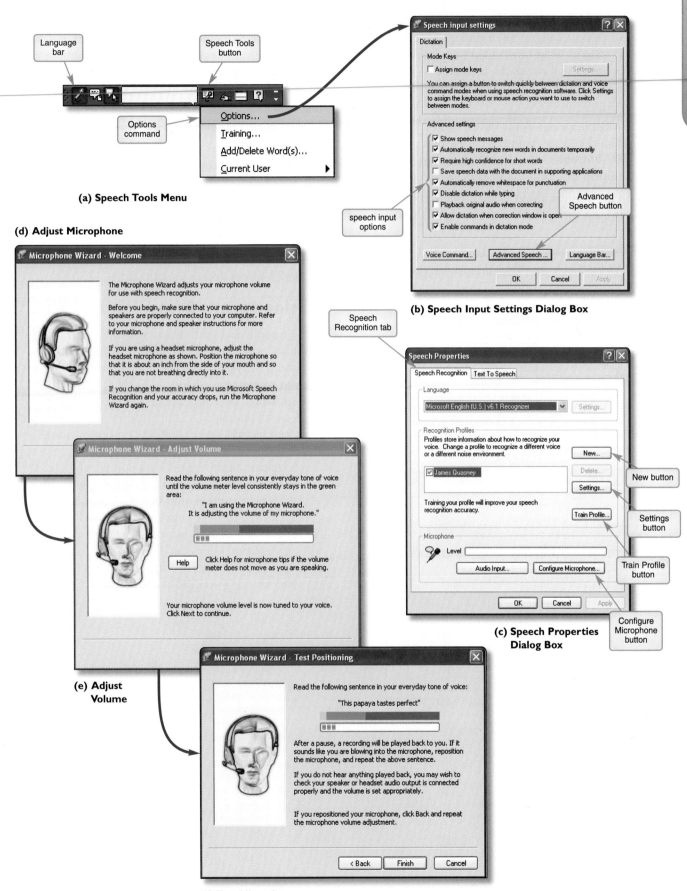

(a) Speech Tools Menu

(d) Adjust Microphone

(e) Adjust Volume

(f) Test Microphone

(b) Speech Input Settings Dialog Box

(c) Speech Properties Dialog Box

FIGURE B-6

TRAIN THE SPEECH RECOGNITION SERVICE   The Speech Recognition service will understand most commands and some dictation without any training at all. It will recognize much more of what you speak, however, if you take the time to train it. After one training session, it will recognize 85 to 90 percent of your words. As you do more training, accuracy will rise to 95 percent. If you feel that too many mistakes are being made, then continue to train the service. The more training you do, the more accurately it will work for you. Follow these steps to train the Speech Recognition service:

1. Click the Speech Tools button on the Language bar and then click Training (Figure B-7a).
2. When the Voice Training dialog box appears (Figure B-7b), click one of the sessions and then click the Next button.
3. Complete the training session, which should take less than 15 minutes.

If you are serious about using a microphone to speak to your computer, you need to take the time to go through at least three of the eight training sessions listed in Figure B-7b.

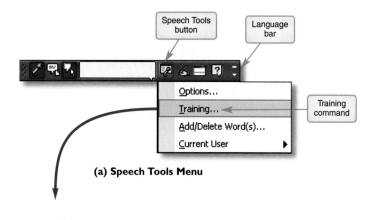

(a) Speech Tools Menu

Using Speech Recognition

Speech recognition lets you enter text into a table similarly to speaking into a tape recorder. Instead of typing, you can dictate text that you want to assign to fields, and you can issue voice commands. In Voice Command mode, you can speak menu names, commands on menus, toolbar button names, and dialog box option buttons, check boxes, list boxes, and button names. Speech recognition, however, is not a completely hands-free form of input. Speech recognition works best if you use a combination of your voice, the keyboard, and the mouse. You soon will discover that Dictation mode is far less accurate than Voice Command mode. Table B-1 lists some tips that will improve the Speech Recognition service's accuracy considerably.

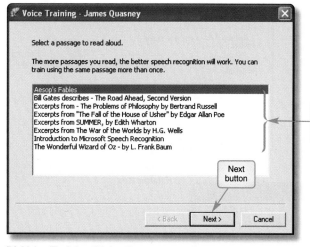

(b) Voice Training Dialog Box

FIGURE B-7

NUMBER	TIP
Table B-1	**Tips to Improve Speech Recognition**
1	The microphone hears everything. Though the Speech Recognition service filters out background noise, it is recommended that you work in a quiet environment.
2	Try not to move the microphone around once it is adjusted.
3	Speak in a steady tone and speak clearly.
4	In Dictation mode, do not pause between words. A phrase is easier to interpret than a word. Sounding out syllables in a word will make it more difficult for the Speech Recognition service to interpret what you are saying.
5	If you speak too loudly or too softly, it makes it difficult for the Speech Recognition service to interpret what you said. Check the Language bar speech message balloon for an indication that you may be speaking too loudly or too softly.
6	If you experience problems after training, adjust the recognition options that control accuracy and rejection by clicking the Settings button shown in Figure B-6c on page APP 17.
7	When you are finished using the microphone, turn it off by clicking the Microphone button on the Language bar or in Voice Command mode, say "Mic off." Leaving the microphone on is the same as leaning on the keyboard.
8	If the Speech Recognition service is having difficulty with unusual words, then add the words to its dictionary by using the Add/Delete Word(s) command on the Speech Tools menu (Figure B-8a). The last names of individuals and the names of companies are good examples of the types of words you should add to the dictionary.
9	Training will improve accuracy; practice will improve confidence.

The last command on the Speech Tools menu is the Current User command (Figure B-8a). The Current User command is useful for multiple users who share a computer. It allows them to configure their own individual profiles, and then switch between users as they use the computer.

For additional information on the Speech Recognition service, enter speech recognition in the Type a question for help box on the menu bar.

Handwriting Recognition

Using the Office **Handwriting Recognition service**, you can enter text and numbers into Access by writing instead of typing. You can write using a special handwriting device that connects to your computer or you can write on the screen using your mouse. Four basic methods of handwriting are available by clicking the Handwriting button on the Language bar: Writing Pad; Write Anywhere; Drawing Pad; and On-Screen Keyboard. Although the on-screen keyboard does not involve handwriting recognition, it is part of the Handwriting menu and, therefore, will be discussed in this section.

If your Language bar does not include the Handwriting button, then for installation instructions, enter install handwriting recognition in the Type a question for help box on the menu bar.

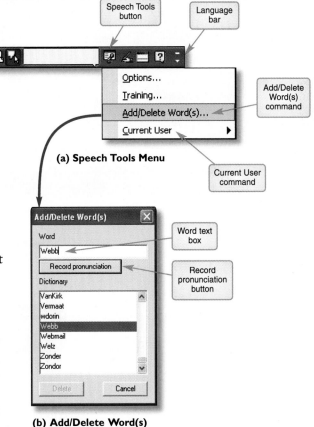

(a) **Speech Tools Menu**

(b) **Add/Delete Word(s) Dialog Box**

FIGURE B-8

Writing Pad

To display the Writing Pad, click the Handwriting button on the Language bar and then click Writing Pad (Figure B-9). The **Writing Pad** resembles a notepad with one or more lines on which you can use freehand to print or write in cursive. With the Text button enabled, you can form letters on the line by moving the mouse while holding down the mouse button. To the right of the notepad is a rectangular toolbar. Use the buttons on this toolbar to adjust the Writing Pad, select cells, and activate other handwriting applications.

Consider the example in Figure B-9. With the insertion point in the City field, the word, Lee, is written in cursive on the **Pen line** in the Writing Pad. As soon as the word is complete, the Handwriting Recognition service automatically assigns the word to the City field.

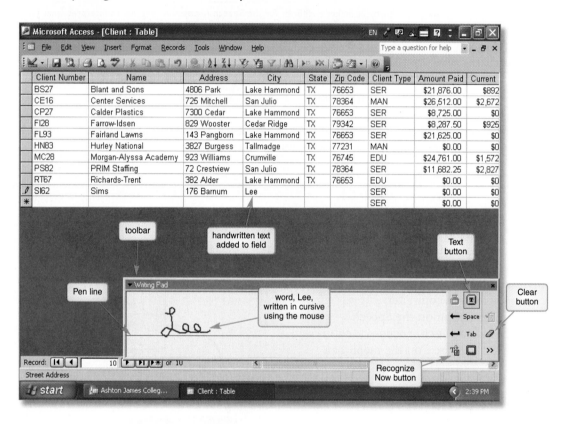

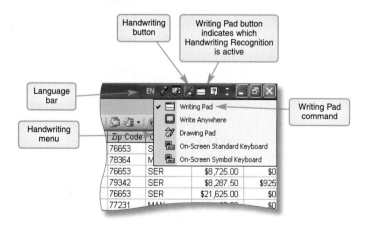

FIGURE B-9

You can customize the Writing Pad by clicking the Options button on the left side of the title bar and then clicking the Options command (Figure B-10a). Invoking the Options command causes the Handwriting Options dialog box to display. The Handwriting Options dialog box contains two sheets: Common and Writing Pad. The Common sheet lets you change the pen color and pen width, adjust recognition, and customize the toolbar area of the Writing Pad. The Writing Pad sheet allows you to change the background color and the number of lines that are displayed in the Writing Pad. Both sheets contain a Restore Default button to restore the settings to what they were when the software was installed initially.

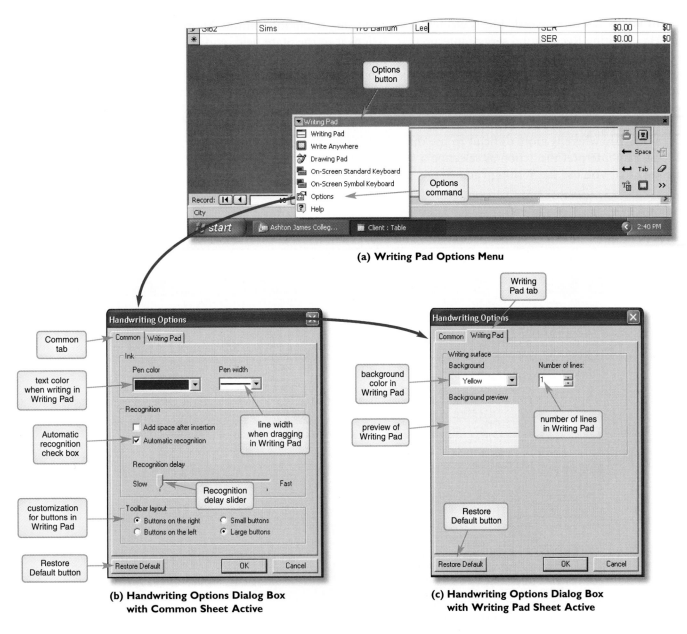

(a) Writing Pad Options Menu

(b) Handwriting Options Dialog Box
with Common Sheet Active

(c) Handwriting Options Dialog Box
with Writing Pad Sheet Active

FIGURE B-10

When you first start using the Writing Pad, you may want to remove the check mark from the Automatic recognition check box in the Common sheet in the Handwriting Options dialog box (Figure B-10b). With the check mark removed, the Handwriting Recognition service will not interpret what you write in the Writing Pad until you click the Recognize Now button on the toolbar (Figure B-9 on page APP 20). This allows you to pause and adjust your writing.

The best way to learn how to use the Writing Pad is to practice with it. Also, for more information, enter handwriting recognition in the Type a question for help box on the menu bar.

Write Anywhere

Rather than use Writing Pad, you can write anywhere on the screen by invoking the Write Anywhere command on the Handwriting menu (Figure B-11) that appears when you click the Handwriting button on the Language bar. In this case, the entire window is your writing pad.

In Figure B-11, the word, TX, is written in cursive using the mouse button. Shortly after the word is written, the Handwriting Recognition service interprets it, assigns it to the State field, and erases what was written.

It is recommended that when you first start using the Writing Anywhere service that you remove the check mark from the Automatic recognition check box in the Common sheet in the Handwriting Options dialog box (Figure B-10b on the previous page). With the check mark removed, the Handwriting Recognition service will not interpret what you write on the screen until you click the Recognize Now button on the toolbar (Figure B-11).

Write Anywhere is more difficult to use than the Writing Pad, because when you click the mouse button, Access may interpret the action as selecting a field rather than starting to write. For this reason, it is recommended that you use the Writing Pad.

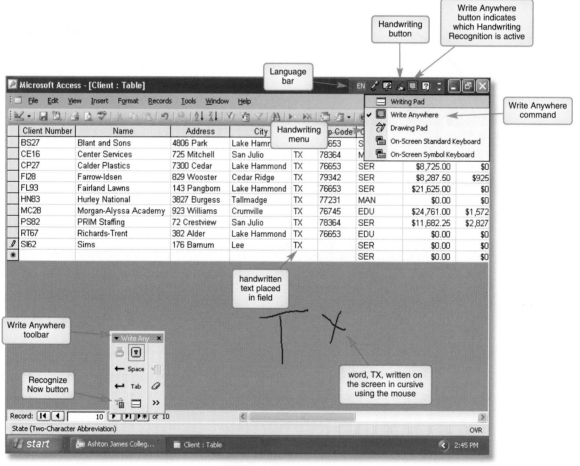

FIGURE B-11

On-Screen Keyboard

The On-Screen Standard Keyboard command on the Handwriting menu (Figure B-12) displays an on-screen keyboard. The **on-screen keyboard** lets you enter data into a field by using your mouse to click the keys. The on-screen keyboard is similar to the type found on handheld computers.

The On-Screen Symbol Keyboard command on the Handwriting menu (Figure B-12) displays a special on-screen keyboard that allows you to enter symbols that are not on your keyboard, as well as Unicode characters. **Unicode characters** use a coding scheme capable of representing all the world's current languages.

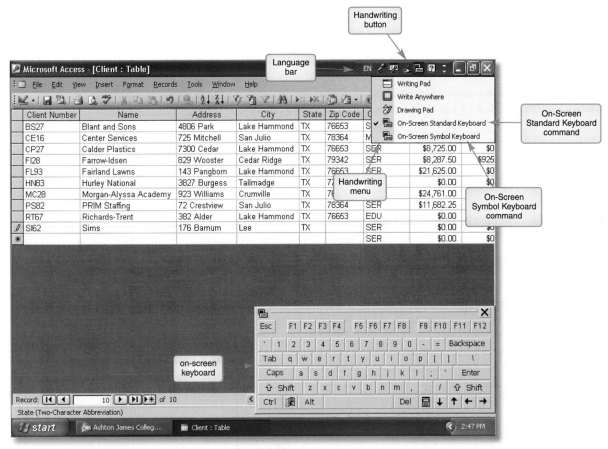

FIGURE B-12

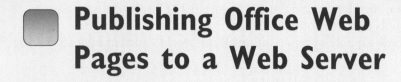

Appendix C

Publishing Office Web Pages to a Web Server

With the Office applications, you use the Save as Web Page command on the File menu to save the Web page to a Web server using one of two techniques: Web folders or File Transfer Protocol. A **Web folder** is an Office shortcut to a Web server. **File Transfer Protocol** (**FTP**) is an Internet standard that allows computers to exchange files with other computers on the Internet.

You should contact your network system administrator or technical support staff at your ISP to determine if their Web server supports Web folders, FTP, or both, and to obtain necessary permissions to access the Web server. If you decide to publish Web pages using a Web folder, you must have the Office Server Extensions (OSE) installed on your computer.

Using Web Folders to Publish Office Web Pages

When publishing to a Web folder, someone first must create the Web folder before you can save to it. If you are granted permission to create a Web folder, you must obtain the URL of the Web server, a user name, and possibly a password that allows you to access the Web server. You also must decide on a name for the Web folder. Table C-1 explains how to create a Web folder.

Office adds the name of the Web folder to the list of current Web folders. You can save to this folder, open files in the folder, rename the folder, or perform any operations you would to a folder on your hard disk. You can use your Office program or Windows Explorer to access this folder. Table C-2 explains how to save to a Web folder.

Using FTP to Publish Office Web Pages

When publishing a Web page using FTP, you first must add the FTP location to your computer before you can save to it. An FTP location, also called an **FTP site**, is a collection of files that reside on an FTP server. In this case, the FTP server is the Web server.

To add an FTP location, you must obtain the name of the FTP site, which usually is the address (URL) of the FTP server, and a user name and a password that allows you to access the FTP server. You save and open the Web pages on the FTP server using the name of the FTP site. Table C-3 explains how to add an FTP site.

Office adds the name of the FTP site to the FTP locations list in the Save As and Open dialog boxes. You can open and save files using this list. Table C-4 explains how to save to an FTP location.

Table C-1 Creating a Web Folder

1. Click File on the menu bar and then click Save As (or Open).
2. When the Save As dialog box (or Open dialog box) appears, click My Network Places on the My Places bar, and then click the Create New Folder button on the toolbar.
3. When the Add Network Place Wizard dialog box appears, click the Next button. If necessary, click Choose another network location. Click the Next button. Click the View some examples link, type the Internet or network address, and then click the Next button. Click Log on anonymously to deselect the check box, type your user name in the User name text box, and then click the Next button. Enter the name you want to call this network place and then click the Next button. Click the Finish button.

Table C-2 Saving to a Web Folder

1. Click File on the menu bar and then click Save As.
2. When the Save As dialog box appears, type the Web page file name in the File name text box. Do not press the ENTER key.
3. Click My Network Places on the My Places bar.
4. Double-click the Web folder name in the Save in list.
5. If the Enter Network Password dialog box appears, type the user name and password in the respective text boxes and then click the OK button.
6. Click the Save button in the Save As dialog box.

Table C-3 Adding an FTP Location

1. Click File on the menu bar and then click Save As (or Open).
2. In the Save As dialog box, click the Save in box arrow and then click Add/Modify FTP Locations in the Save in list; or in the Open dialog box, click the Look in box arrow and then click Add/Modify FTP Locations in the Look in list.
3. When the Add/Modify FTP Locations dialog box appears, type the name of the FTP site in the Name of FTP site text box. If the site allows anonymous logon, click Anonymous in the Log on as area; if you have a user name for the site, click User in the Log on as area and then enter the user name. Enter the password in the Password text box. Click the OK button.
4. Close the Save As or the Open dialog box.

Table C-4 Saving to an FTP Location

1. Click File on the menu bar and then click Save As.
2. When the Save As dialog box appears, type the Web page file name in the File name text box. Do not press the ENTER key.
3. Click the Save in box arrow and then click FTP Locations.
4. Double-click the name of the FTP site to which you wish to save.
5. When the FTP Log On dialog box appears, enter your user name and password and then click the OK button.
6. Click the Save button in the Save As dialog box.

Appendix D

Changing Screen Resolution and Resetting the Access Toolbars and Menus

This appendix explains how to change your screen resolution in Windows to the resolution used in this book. It also describes how to reset the Access toolbars and menus to their installation settings.

Changing Screen Resolution

The **screen resolution** indicates the number of pixels (dots) that your system uses to display the letters, numbers, graphics, and background you see on your screen. The screen resolution usually is stated as the product of two numbers, such as 800 × 600. An 800 × 600 screen resolution results in a display of 800 distinct pixels on each of 600 lines, or about 480,000 pixels. The figures in this book were created using a screen resolution of 800 × 600.

The screen resolutions most commonly used today are 800 × 600 and 1024 × 768, although some Office specialists operate their computers at a much higher screen resolution, such as 2048 × 1536. The following steps show how to change the screen resolution from 1024 × 768 to 800 × 600.

To Change the Screen Resolution

1

- **If necessary, minimize all applications so that the Windows desktop appears.**
- **Right-click the Windows desktop.**

Windows displays the Windows desktop shortcut menu (Figure D-1).

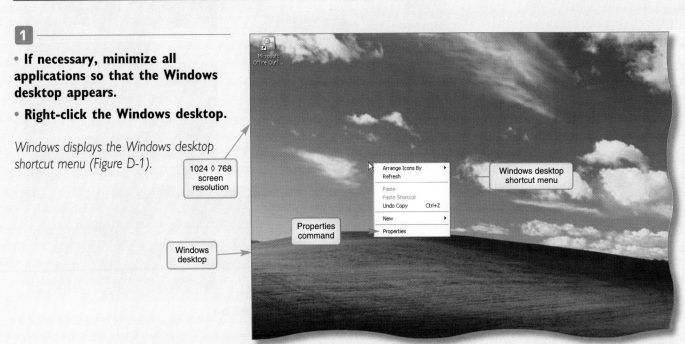

1024 ◊ 768 screen resolution

Properties command

Windows desktop

Windows desktop shortcut menu

FIGURE D-1

2

• **Click Properties on the shortcut menu.**

• **When Windows displays the Display Properties dialog box, click the Settings tab.**

Windows displays the Settings sheet in the Display Properties dialog box (Figure D-2). The Settings sheet shows a preview of the Windows desktop using the current screen resolution (1024 × 768). The Settings sheet also shows the screen resolution and the color quality settings.

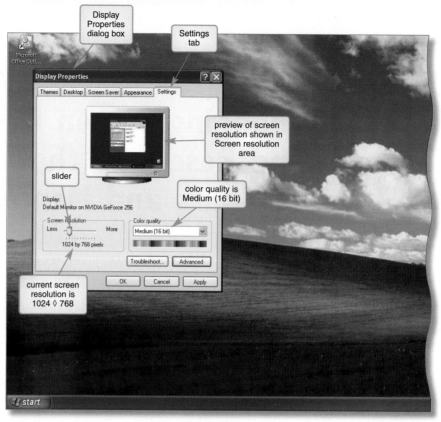

FIGURE D-2

3

• **Drag the slider in the Screen resolution area to the left so that the screen resolution changes to 800 × 600.**

The screen resolution in the Screen resolution area changes to 800 × 600 (Figure D-3). The Settings sheet shows a preview of the Windows desktop using the new screen resolution (800 × 600).

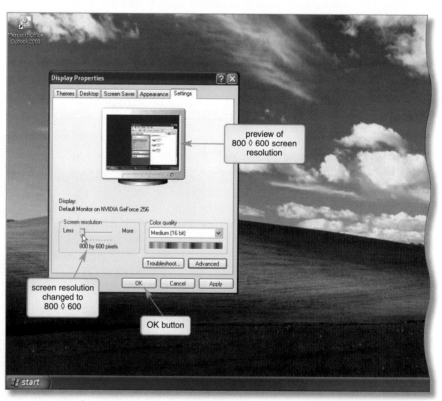

FIGURE D-3

4

• **Click the OK button.**

• **If Windows displays the Monitor Settings dialog box, click the Yes button.**

Windows changes the screen resolution from 1024 × 768 to 800 × 600 (Figure D-4).

800 ◊ 600 screen resolution

FIGURE D-4

As shown in the previous steps, as you decrease the screen resolution, Windows displays less information on your screen, but the information increases in size. The reverse also is true: as you increase the screen resolution, Windows displays more information on your screen, but the information decreases in size.

Resetting the Access Toolbars and Menus

In Microsoft Access, you can personalize toolbars and menus. You can change the toolbar or toolbars that appear by using the Toolbars command on the View menu, and then selecting the toolbars you want to appear. You also can change the buttons that appear on a particular toolbar by using the Toolbar Options button (see Figure D-5 on the next page). In addition, Access personalizes the commands on the menus based on their usage. Each time you start Access, the toolbars and menus have the same settings as the last time you used the application. This appendix shows you how to reset usage data, that is, how to clear menu and toolbar settings. Resetting usage data does not affect the location of the toolbars, nor does it change any buttons you might have added using the Customize dialog box. To reverse these changes, you need to reset the toolbar. The steps on the next page show how to reset the usage data and also the Database toolbar.

To Reset Menu and Toolbar Usage Data

1

• **Start Access following the steps outlined at the beginning of Project 1.**

• **Click View on the menu bar, and then point to Toolbars.**

The View menu and Toolbars submenu appear (Figure D-5).

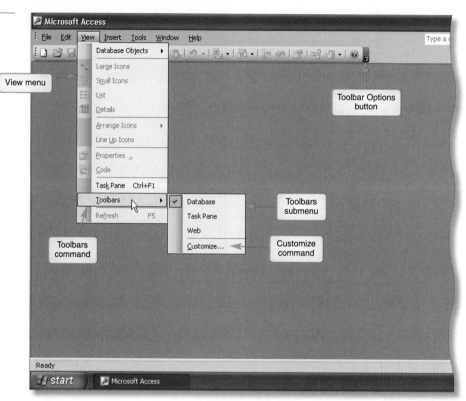

FIGURE D-5

2

• **Click Customize on the Toolbars submenu.**

• **When Access displays the Customize dialog box, if necessary, click the Options tab.**

Access displays the Customize dialog box (Figure D-6). The Customize dialog box contains three sheets used for customizing the Access toolbars and menus.

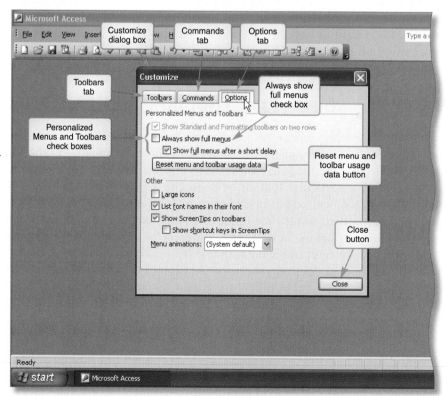

FIGURE D-6

3

• **Click the Reset menu and toolbar usage data button.**

The Microsoft Office Access dialog box displays a message indicating the actions that will be taken and asks if you are sure you want to proceed (Figure D-7).

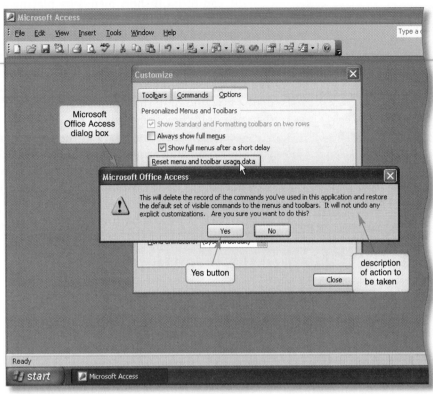

FIGURE D-7

4

• **Click the Yes button in the Microsoft Office Access dialog box.**

• **Click the Toolbars tab in the Customize dialog box and then click Database (the word Database and not the check box in front of it) in the Toolbars list.**

The Customize dialog box displays the Toolbars sheet with Database highlighted in the Toolbars list (Figure D-8).

5

• **Click the Reset button.**

• **When the Microsoft Office Access dialog box appears, asking if you are sure you want to reset the changes made to the Database toolbar, click the OK button.**

• **Repeat the process for any other toolbar you want to reset.**

6

• **Click the Close button in the Customize dialog box.**

Access resets the Database toolbar to its installation settings.

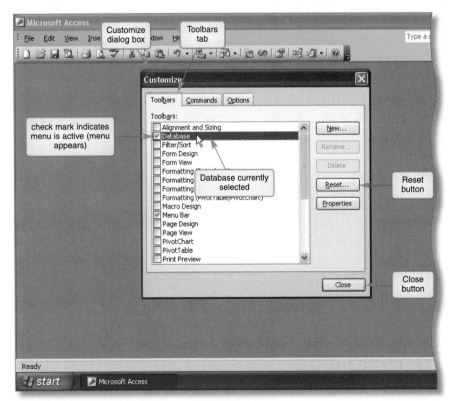

FIGURE D-8

Other Ways

1. Click Toolbar Options button on Database toolbar, point to Add or Remove Buttons, click Customize, click Options tab, click Reset menu and toolbar usage data button to reset usage data, click Yes button, click Close button
2. Click Toolbar Options button on Database toolbar, point to Add or Remove Buttons, click Customize, click Toolbars tab, click toolbar name, click Reset button to reset toolbar to installation settings, click OK button, click Close button
3. Right-click toolbar, click Customize, click Options tab, click Reset menu and toolbar usage data button to reset usage data, click Yes button, click Close button
4. Right-click toolbar, click Customize on shortcut menu, click Toolbars tab, click toolbar name, click Reset button to reset toolbar to installation settings, click OK button, click Close button
5. In Voice Command mode, say "View, Toolbars, [desired toolbar name], Reset, OK, Close"

You can turn off short menus by placing a check mark in the Always show full menus check box in the Customize dialog box (see Figure D-6 on page APP 28).

One other task you can complete through the Customize dialog box in Figure D-6 is to add buttons to toolbars and commands to menus. To add buttons, click the Commands tab in the Customize dialog box and drag the commands to a toolbar. To add commands to a menu, click the Commands tab in the Customize dialog box and drag the commands to the menu name. When the menu appears, you then can drag the commands to the desired menu location.

Access considers the menu at the top of the Access window to be a toolbar. If you add commands to menus as described in the previous paragraph and want to reset them to their installation settings, do the following: (1) Click Toolbars on the View menu; (2) click Customize; (3) click the Toolbars tab; (4) scroll down in the Toolbars list and click Menu Bar; (5) click the Reset button; (6) click the OK button; and (7) click the Close button.

Appendix E

Microsoft Office Specialist Certification

What Is Microsoft Office Specialist Certification?

Microsoft Office Specialist certification provides a framework for measuring your proficiency with the Microsoft Office 2003 applications, such as Microsoft Office Word 2003, Microsoft Office Excel 2003, Microsoft Office Access 2003, Microsoft Office PowerPoint 2003, and Microsoft Office Outlook 2003. The levels of certification are described in Table E-1.

Table E-1 Levels of Microsoft Office Specialist Certification			
LEVEL	**DESCRIPTION**	**REQUIREMENTS**	**CREDENTIAL AWARDED**

Microsoft Office Specialist	Indicates that you have an understanding of the basic features in a specific Microsoft Office 2003 application	Pass any ONE of the following:
		  Microsoft Office Word 2003
		  Microsoft Office Excel 2003
		  Microsoft Office Access 2003
		  Microsoft Office PowerPoint 2003
		  Microsoft Office Outlook 2003
			Candidates will be awarded one certificate for each of the Specialist-level exams they have passed:
			  Microsoft Office Word 2003
			  Microsoft Office Excel 2003
			  Microsoft Office Access 2003
			  Microsoft Office PowerPoint 2003
			  Microsoft Office Outlook 2003

Microsoft Office Expert	Indicates that you have an understanding of the advanced features in a specific Microsoft Office 2003 application	Pass any ONE of the following:
		  Microsoft Office Word 2003 Expert
		  Microsoft Office Excel 2003 Expert
			Candidates will be awarded one certificate for each of the Expert-level exams they have passed:
			  Microsoft Office Word 2003 Expert
			  Microsoft Office Excel 2003 Expert

Microsoft Office Master	Indicates that you have a comprehensive under-standing of the features of four of the five primary Microsoft Office 2003 applications	Pass the following:
		  Microsoft Office Word 2003 Expert
		  Microsoft Office Excel 2003 Expert
		  Microsoft Office PowerPoint 2003
		And pass ONE of the following:
		  Microsoft Office Access 2003 or
		  Microsoft Office Outlook 2003
			Candidates will be awarded the Microsoft Office Master certificate for fulfilling the requirements.

Why Should You Be Certified?

Being Microsoft Office certified provides a valuable industry credential — proof that you have the Office 2003 applications skills required by employers. By passing one or more Microsoft Office Specialist certification exams, you demonstrate your proficiency in a given Office 2003 application to employers. With more than 400 million people in 175 nations and 70 languages using Office applications, Microsoft is targeting Office 2003 certification to a wide variety of companies. These companies include temporary employment agencies that want to prove the expertise of their workers, large corporations looking for a way to measure the skill set of employees, and training companies and educational institutions seeking Microsoft Office 2003 teachers with appropriate credentials.

The Microsoft Office Specialist Certification Exams

You pay $50 to $100 each time you take an exam, whether you pass or fail. The fee varies among testing centers. The **Microsoft Office Expert** exams, which you can take up to 60 minutes to complete, consist of between 40 and 60 tasks that you perform on a personal computer in a simulated environment. The tasks require you to use the application just as you would in doing your job. The **Microsoft Office Specialist** exams contain fewer tasks, and you will have slightly less time to complete them. The tasks you will perform differ on the two types of exams. After passing designated Expert and Specialist exams, candidates are awarded the **Microsoft Office Master** certificate (see the requirements in Table E-1 on the previous page).

How to Prepare for the Microsoft Office Specialist Certification Exams

The Shelly Cashman Series offers several Microsoft-approved textbooks that cover the required objectives of the Microsoft Office Specialist certification exams. For a listing of the textbooks, visit the Shelly Cashman Series Microsoft Office Specialist Center at scsite.com/winoff2003/cert. Click the link Shelly Cashman Series Microsoft Office 2003-Approved Microsoft Office Textbooks (Figure E-1). After using any of the books listed in an instructor-led course, you should be prepared to take the indicated Microsoft Office Specialist certification exam.

How to Find an Authorized Testing Center

To locate a testing center, call 1-800-933-4493 in North America, or visit the Shelly Cashman Series Microsoft Office Specialist Center at scsite.com/winoff2003/cert. Click the link Locate an Authorized Testing Center Near You (Figure E-1). At this Web site, you can look for testing centers around the world.

Shelly Cashman Series Microsoft Office Specialist Center

The Shelly Cashman Series Microsoft Office Specialist Center (Figure E-1) lists more than 15 Web sites you can visit to obtain additional information about certification. The Web page (scsite.com/winoff2003/cert) includes links to general information about certification, choosing an application for certification, preparing for the certification exam, and taking and passing the certification exam.

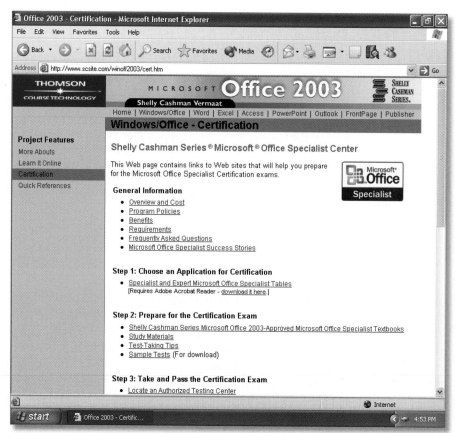

FIGURE E-1

Microsoft Office Specialist Certification Maps for Microsoft Office Access 2003

This book has been approved by Microsoft as courseware for Microsoft Office Specialist certification. Table E-2 lists the skill sets and activities you should be familiar with if you plan to take the specialist-level examination for Microsoft Office Access 2003. There is no expert-level examination for Microsoft Office Access 2003.

Table E-6   Specialist-Level Skill Sets, Activities, and Locations in Book for Microsoft Office Access 2003

SKILL SET	SKILL BEING MEASURED	SKILL DEMONSTRATED IN BOOK	SKILL EXERCISE IN BOOK
I. Structuring Databases	A. Create Access databases	AC 10	AC 56-64 (In The Lab 1-3, Cases and Places 1-5)
	B. Create and modify tables	AC 15, AC 159, AC 127-130	AC 63 (Cases and Places 3), AC 171 (Cases and Places 3), AC 167-172 (All Exercises)
	C. Define and modify field types	AC 130, AC 147	AC 169 (In The Lab 2 Step 5f, In The Lab 3 Part 1), AC 172 (Cases and Places 5)
	D. Modify field properties	AC 127-128, AC 140-144, AC 160, AC 263, AC 265	AC 167-172 (All Exercises), AC 304 (Apply Your Knowledge, Steps 1, 3), AC 312 (Cases and Places 3)
	E. Create and modify one-to-many relationships	AC 151, AC 342	AC 171-172 (Cases and Places 1-4), AC 374 (Cases and Places 2)
	F. Enforce referential integrity	AC 152, AC 342	AC 167 (Apply Your Knowledge Step 17), AC 169 (In The Lab 1 Step 13), AC 170 (In The Lab 2 Step 11), AC 170 (In The Lab 3 Part 3), AC 171-172 (Cases and Places 1-4), AC 374-376 (All Cases and Places)
	G. Create and modify queries	AC 34, AC 37, AC 104, AC 154	AC 55 (Apply Your Knowledge Steps 3-6), AC 60 (In The Lab 2 Step 2), AC 62 (In The Lab Part 3), AC 63-64 (Cases and Places 3-4), AC 109 (Apply Your Knowledge Step 8), AC 111 (In The Lab 2 Step 12), AC 112 (Cases and Places 5), AC 172 (Cases and Places 4), AC 171 (Cases and Places 3), AC 172 (Cases and Places 5), AC 376 (Cases and Places 5)
	H. Create forms	AC 38, AC 228, AC 274	AC 57 (In The Lab 1 Step 8), AC 61 (In the Lab 3 Part 1), AC 64 (Cases and Places 4), AC 249-256 (All Exercises), AC 304-312 (All Exercises)
	I. Add and modify form controls and properties	AC 227, AC 232, AC 235, AC 237, AC 241, AC 286, AC 288	AC 249-256 (All Exercises)
	J. Create reports	AC 43, AC 198, AC 217	AC 55-64 (All Exercises)
	K. Add and modify report control properties	AC 209	AC 249-256 (All Exercises)
	L. Create a data access page	AC 380	AC 398 (In The Lab 1)
II. Entering Data	A. Enter, edit and delete records	AC 23, AC 28, AC 116, AC 119, AC 125	AC 54-64 (All Exercises), AC 167-172 (All Exercises)
	B. Find and move among records	AC 27	AC 55 (Apply Your Knowledge Step 1), AC 57 (In The Lab 1 Step 9), AC 60 (In The Lab 2 Step 3), AC 62 (In The Lab 3 Part 2)
	C. Import data to Access	AC 176-180	AC 191 (In The Lab 1)
III. Organizing Data	A. Create and modify calculated fields and aggregate functions	AC 96-97, AC 99-103	AC 110 (In The Lab 1 Step 11), AC 111 (In The Lab 3 Part 3), AC 112 (Cases and Places 3), AC 110 (In The Lab 1 Steps 12, 13), AC 111 (In The Lab 2 Step 11, In The Lab 3 Part 3), AC 112 (Cases and Places 1-4)
	B. Modify form layout	AC 211, AC 216	AC 254 (In The Lab 3), AC 256 (Cases and Places 5)
	C. Modify report layout and page setup	AC 30-31, AC 212, AC 222	AC 170 (In The Lab 3 Parts 2-3), AC 254 (In The Lab 3), AC 256 (Cases and Places 5)

Table E-6 Specialist-Level Skill Sets, Activities, and Locations in Book for Microsoft Office Access 2003

SKILL SET	SKILL BEING MEASURED	SKILL DEMONSTRATED IN BOOK	SKILL EXERCISE IN BOOK
	D. Format datasheets	AC 131-135	AC 171 (Cases and Places 2)
	E. Sort records	AC 86-89, AC 155, AC 205, AC 240	AC 167 (Apply Your Knowledge Step 15), AC 171-172 (Cases and Places 2, 4), AC 256 (Cases and Places 5)
	F. Filter records	AC 121, AC 123	AC 167 (Apply Your Knowledge Step 13), AC 169 (In The Lab 2 Step 9)
IV. Managing Databases	A. Identify object dependencies	AC 299	AC 312 (Cases and Places 5)
	B. View objects and object data in other views	AC 23, AC 29-31, AC 42, AC 202, AC 208, AC 347, AC 354, AC 384	AC 54-64 (All Exercises), AC 170 (In The Lab 3), AC 366 (Apply Your Knowledge), AC 368-373 (In The Lab 1-3), AC 376 (Cases and Places 5)
	C. Print database objects and data	AC 29-31, AC 47, AC 72, AC 242	AC 54-64 (All Exercises, AC 109-112 (All Exercises), AC 249-256 (All Exercises), AC 304-312 (All Exercises)
	D. Export data from Access	AC 181, AC 183, AC 184, AC 185-187	AC 192 (In The Lab 2)
	E. Back up a database	AC 162-163	AC 167 (Apply Your Knowledge Step 18), AC 170 (In The Lab 2 Step 12), AC 171 (Cases and Places 1-2)
	F. Compact and repair databases	AC 163-164	AC 169 (In The Lab 1 Step 14), AC 170 (In The Lab 2 Step 12), AC 171 (Cases and Places 1-2)

Appendix F

 Database Design

Introduction

This appendix illustrates a method for designing a database to satisfy a set of requirements. In the process, you must identify the tables in the database, the columns in the tables, the primary keys of the tables, and the relationships between the tables.

The appendix begins by examining some important concepts concerning relational databases and then presents the design methodology. To illustrate the process, the requirements for the Ashton James College database are given. Then, the design methodology is used to create the database design. The appendix concludes by examining normalization, a process that you can use to identify and fix potential problems in database designs.

Relational Databases

A **relational database** is a collection of tables similar to the tables for Ashton James College that appear in Figure F-1 on the next page. The Client table contains information about the clients to which Ashton James College provides training services. The college assigns each client to a specific trainer. The Trainer table contains information about the trainers to whom these clients are assigned.

The Course table lists the specific courses that the trainers at Ashton James College offer to their clients. Each course has a number and a description. The table also includes the total hours for which the course usually is offered and the increments, that is, the standard time blocks in which the course usually is offered. The first row, for example, indicates that course 01 is Integrating MS Office Programs. The course typically is offered in 4-hour increments for a total of 16 hours.

The Course Offerings table contains a client number, a course number, the total number of hours for which the course is scheduled, and the number of hours already spent in the course. The second record shows that client number BS27 currently has scheduled course 06 (Introduction to Computers). The course is scheduled for 16 hours, of which 4 hours already have been spent in class.

The formal term for a table is relation. A **relation** is essentially a two-dimensional table. If you study the tables shown in Figure F-1, however, you might see that there are certain restrictions you can place on relations. Each column in a table should have a unique name, and entries in each column should match this column name. For example, in the Zip Code column, all entries should in fact *be* Zip codes. In addition, each row should be unique. After all, if two rows in a table contain identical data, the second row does not provide any information that you do not already have. In addition, for maximum flexibility, the order in which columns and rows appear in a table should be immaterial. Finally, a table's design is less complex

Client

CLIENT NUMBER	NAME	ADDRESS	CITY	STATE	ZIP CODE	AMOUNT PAID	CURRENT DUE	TRAINER NUMBER
BS27	Blant and Sons	4806 Park	Lake Hammond	TX	76653	$21,876.00	$892.50	42
CE16	Center Services	725 Mitchell	San Julio	TX	78364	$26,512.00	$2,672.00	48
CP27	Calder Plastics	7300 Cedar	Lake Hammond	TX	76653	$8,725.00	$0.00	48
EU28	Elba's Furniture	1445 Hubert	Tallmadge	TX	77231	$4,256.00	$1,202.00	53
FI28	Farrow-Idsen	829 Wooster	Cedar Ridge	TX	79342	$8,287.50	$925.50	42
FL93	Fairland Lawn	143 Pangborn	Lake Hammond	TX	76653	$21,625.00	$0.00	48
HN83	Hurley National	3827 Burgess	Tallmadge	TX	77231	$0.00	$0.00	48
MC28	Morgan-Alyssa	923 Williams	Crumville	TX	76745	$24,761.00	$1,572.00	42
PS82	PRIM Staffing	72 Crestview	San Julio	TX	78364	$11,682.25	$2,827.50	53
TE26	Telton-Edwards	5672 Anderson	Dunston	TX	77893	$8,521.50	$0.00	48

Trainer

TRAINER NUMBER	LAST NAME	FIRST NAME	ADDRESS	CITY	STATE	ZIP CODE	HOURLY RATE	YTD EARNINGS
42	Perry	Belinda	261 Porter	Burdett	TX	76734	$23.00	$27,620.00
48	Stevens	Michael	3135 Gill	Rockwood	TX	78884	$21.00	$23,567.50
53	Gonzalez	Manuel	265 Maxwell	Camino	TX	76574	$24.00	$29,885.00
67	Danville	Marty	1827 Maple	Dunston	TX	77893	$20.00	$0.00

Course

COURSE NUMBER	COURSE DESCRIPTION	HOURS	INCREMENTS
01	Integrating MS Office Programs	16	4
02	Long Documents with Word	8	4
03	Creating Forms with Word	6	6
04	Newsletters and Graphics with Word	6	6
05	Creating Custom Access Reports	12	4
06	Introduction to Computers	16	4
07	Preventing Pain and Injury at Your Computer	4	2
08	Importing, Exporting, and Linking Data	6	3
09	Presentation Authoring Using PowerPoint	16	4
10	Access Database Projects (ADP)	12	4
11	Excel Programming	24	4

Course Offerings

CLIENT NUMBER	COURSE NUMBER	TOTAL HOURS	HOURS SPENT
BS27	03	6	3
BS27	06	16	4
CP27	02	10	4
CP27	04	6	0
FI28	01	16	12
FI28	05	12	8
FL93	06	16	8
HN83	05	12	8
HN83	08	6	2
HN83	11	24	12

FIGURE F-1

if you restrict each position in the table to a single entry; that is, you do not permit multiple entries (often called **repeating groups**) in the table. These restrictions lead to the following definition:

A relation is a two-dimensional table in which:

1. The entries in the table are single-valued; that is, each location in the table contains a single entry.
2. Each column has a distinct name (technically called the attribute name).
3. All values in a column are values of the same attribute (that is, all entries must match the column name).
4. The order of columns is immaterial. You can view the columns in any order you want.
5. Each row is distinct; that is, no two rows are identical.
6. The order of rows is immaterial. You can view the rows in any order you want.

A relational database is a collection of relations. Rows in a table (relation) often are called **records** or **tuples**. Columns in a table (relation) often are called **fields** or **attributes**.

To show the structure of a relational database, there is a commonly accepted shorthand representation: you write the name of the table and then within parentheses list all of the columns in the table. Each table should appear on its own line. Using this method, you would represent the Ashton James College database as follows:

Client (Client Number, Name, Address, City, State, Zip Code, Amount Paid, Current Due, Trainer Number)

Trainer (Trainer Number, Last Name, First Name, Address, City, State, Zip Code, Hourly Rate, YTD Earnings)

Course (Course Number, Course Description, Hours, Increments)

Course Offerings (Client Number, Course Number, Total Hours, Hours Spent)

The Ashton James College database does contain some duplicate column names. For example, the Trainer Number column appears in *both* the Trainer table *and* the Client table. Suppose a situation exists wherein the two columns might be confused. If you write Trainer Number, how would the computer or another individual know which Trainer Number column in which table you intended to use? When duplicate column names exist in a database, you need to indicate the column to which you are referring. One common approach to this problem is to write both the table name and the column name, separated by a period. Thus, you would write the Trainer Number column in the Client table as Client.Trainer Number and the Trainer Number column in the Trainer table as Trainer.Trainer Number. Technically, when you combine a column name with a table name, you say that you **qualify** the column names. It is *always* acceptable to qualify column names, even if there is no possibility of confusion. If confusion may arise, however, it is *essential* to qualify column names.

Functional Dependence

In the Ashton James College database (Figure F-1), a given client number in the database will correspond to a single client because client numbers are unique. Thus, you could look up a client number and find a single name that corresponds to it (often written as Client Number → Name). No ambiguity exists. Formally, if you know a value for an attribute guarantees that you also know a single value for a second attribute, the second attribute is said to be **functionally dependent** on the first. Thus, Name is functionally dependent on Client Number because if you know a value for Client Number, you automatically know a single value for Name.

If you were given a city and asked to find a single client's name, however, you could not do it. Given Lake Hammond as the city, for example, you would find three client names (Blant and Sons, Calder Plastics, and Fairland Lawn). Formally, you would say the Client Name is *not* functionally dependent on City.

In the Trainer table, Last Name is functionally dependent on Trainer Number. If you are given a value for Trainer Number, for example 42, you will find a *single* last name, Perry, associated with it.

In the Client table, Name is not functionally dependent on Trainer Number. Given the Trainer Number 42, for example, you would not be able to find a single client name, because 42 appears on more than one row in the table.

In the Course Offerings table, Hours Spent is not functionally dependent on Client Number. Client Number does not give enough information. For example, there is a row on which Client Number is BS27 and Hours Spent is 3 and another row on which Client Number is also BS27, but Hours Spent is 4. Hours Spent also is not functionally dependent on Course Number, because Course Number does not give enough information. For example, there is a row on which Course Number is 06 and Hours Spent is 4 and another row on which Course Number also is 06, but Hours Spent is 8.

Hours Spent actually is functionally dependent on the combination (formally called the **concatenation**) of Client Number and Course Number. Given a client number *and* a course number, you can determine a single value for Hours Spent.

Primary Key

The **primary key** of a table (relation) is the column or minimum collection of columns that uniquely identifies a given row in that table. In the Trainer table, the trainer's number uniquely identifies a given row. For example, Trainer Number 42 occurs in only one row of the table. Thus, Trainer Number is the primary key.

The primary key provides an important way of distinguishing one row in a table from another. Primary keys typically are represented by underlining the column or collection of columns that comprise the primary key for each table in the database. Thus, the complete representation for the Ashton James College database is as follows:

Client (<u>Client Number</u>, Name, Address, City, State, Zip Code, Amount Paid, Current Due, Trainer Number)

Trainer (<u>Trainer Number</u>, Last Name, First Name, Address, City, State, Zip Code, Hourly Rate, YTD Earnings)

Course (<u>Course Number</u>, Course Description, Hours, Increments)

Course Offerings (<u>Client Number</u>, <u>Course Number</u>, Total Hours, Hours Spent)

The primary key of the Course Offerings table consists of two columns, Client Number and Course Number. Total Hours and Hours Spent neither are dependent on just Client Number nor are they dependent on just Course Number. Rather they are dependent on the combination of Client Number and Course Number. Thus, neither Client Number nor Course Number alone can be the primary key.

Occasionally (but not often) there might be more than one possibility for the primary key. For example, if the Ashton James College database included the trainer's Social Security number in the Trainer table, either the trainer number or the Social Security number could serve as the primary key. In this case, both columns are referred to as candidate keys. Similarly to a primary key, a **candidate key** is a column or collection of columns on which all columns in the table are functionally dependent — the definition for primary key really defines candidate key as well. From all the candidate keys, one is chosen to be the primary key.

Database Design

This section presents a specific database design methodology, given a set of requirements that the database must support. The section then presents a sample of such requirements and illustrates the design method by designing a database to satisfy these requirements.

Design Method

The following steps illustrate how to design a database for a set of requirements.

1. Read through the requirements and identify the entities (objects) involved. Assign names to the entities. If, for example, the design involves departments and employees, you could assign the names Department and Employee. If the design involves customers, orders, and parts, you could assign the names Customer, Order, and Part.

2. Identify a unique identifier for each entity. For example, if one of the entities is parts, you would determine what it takes to uniquely identify each individual part. In other words, what enables the organization to distinguish one part from another? For a part entity, it may be Part Number. For a customer entity, it may be Customer Number. If there is no such unique identifier, it is probably a good idea to add one. Perhaps the previous system was a manual one in which customers were not assigned numbers, in which case this would be a good time to add customer numbers to the system.

3. Identify the attributes for all the entities. These attributes will become the columns in the tables. It is possible that more than one entity has the same attribute. At Ashton James College, for example, clients and trainers both have addresses, cities, states, and Zip codes. To clarify this, you can follow the name of the attribute with the corresponding entity in parentheses. Thus, Address (Client) would be the address of a client, whereas Address (Trainer) would be the address of a trainer.

4. Identify the functional dependencies that exist among the attributes.

5. Use the functional dependencies to identify the tables. You do this by placing each attribute with the attribute or minimum combination of attributes on which it is functionally dependent. The attribute or attributes on which all other attributes in the relation are dependent will be the primary key of a relation. The remaining attributes will be the other columns in the relation. Once you have determined all the columns in the relation, you can assign an appropriate name to the relation.

6. Identify any relationships between tables by looking for matching columns.

The following sections illustrate the design process by designing the database for Ashton James College. The next section gives the requirements that this database must support, and the last section creates a database design based on those requirements.

Requirements for the Ashton James College Database

The Ashton James College database must support the following requirements:

1. For a client, store the client number, name, address, city, state, Zip code, amount paid, and the amount that is currently due.

2. For a trainer, store the trainer number, last name, first name, address, city, state, Zip code, hourly rate, and YTD earnings.

3. For a course, store the course number, course description, hours, and increments. In addition, for each offering of the course, store the number of the client for whom the course is offered, the total hours required for the course, and the number of hours already spent.

4. Each client has a single trainer to which the client is assigned. Each trainer may be assigned many clients.

5. A client may be offered many courses and a course may be offered to many clients.

Database Design Example

The following represents the application of the design methodology for the Ashton James College requirements.

1. There are three entities: clients, trainers, and courses. The names assigned to them are Client, Trainer, and Course, respectively.

2. The unique identifier for clients is the client number. The unique identifier for trainers is the trainer number. The unique identifier for courses is the course number. The names assigned to these identifiers are Client Number, Trainer Number, and Course Number, respectively.

3. The attributes are:
   Client Number
   Name
   Address (Client)
   City (Client)
   State (Client)
   Zip Code (Client)
   Amount Paid
   Current Due
   Trainer Number
   Last Name
   First Name
   Address (Trainer)
   City (Trainer)
   State (Trainer)
   Zip Code (Trainer)
   Hourly Rate
   YTD Earnings
   Course Number
   Course Description
   Hours
   Increments
   Total Hours
   Hours Spent

Parentheses after an attribute indicate the entity to which the attribute corresponds. For example, Address (Client) represents the address of a client whereas Address (Trainer) represents the address of a trainer.

4. The functional dependencies among the attributes are:
   Client Number → Name, Address (Client), City (Client), State (Client), Zip Code (Client), Amount Paid, Current Due, Trainer Number
   Trainer Number → Last Name, First Name, Address (Trainer), City (Trainer), State (Trainer), Zip Code (Trainer), Hourly Rate, YTD Earnings
   Course Number → Course Description, Hours, Increments
   Client Number, Course Number → Total Hours, Hours Spent

The client's name, address, city, state, Zip code, amount paid, and current due are dependent only on Client Number. Because a client has a single trainer, the trainer number is dependent on Client Number as well. The trainer's last name, first name, address, city, state, Zip code, hourly rate, and YTD earnings are dependent only on Trainer Number. A course description, the number of hours for the course, and the increments in which the course is offered are dependent only on Course Number. The total hours for a particular course offering as well as the hours already spent are dependent on the combination of Client Number and Course Number.

5. The tables are:

  Client (<u>Client Number</u>, Name, Address, City, State, Zip Code, Amount Paid, Current Due, Trainer Number)

  Trainer (<u>Trainer Number</u>, Last Name, First Name, Address, City, State, Zip Code, Hourly Rate, YTD Earnings)

  Course (<u>Course Number</u>, Course Description, Hours, Increments)

  Course Offerings (<u>Client Number</u>, <u>Course Number</u>, Total Hours, Hours Spent)

The primary keys are underlined.

6. The following are the relationships between the tables:

 a. The Client and Trainer tables are related using the Trainer Number fields.

 b. The Client and Course Offerings tables are related using the Client Number fields.

 c. The Course and Course Offerings tables are related using the Course Number fields.

Normalization

After you create your database design, you should analyze it to make sure the design is free of potential problems. To do so, you use a process called normalization. The **normalization** process enables you to identify the existence of potential problems. This process also supplies methods for correcting these problems.

The normalization process involves converting tables into various types of **normal forms**. A table in a particular normal form possesses a certain desirable set of properties. Several normal forms exist, the most common being first normal form (1NF), second normal form (2NF), third normal form (3NF), and fourth normal form (4NF). The forms create a progression in which a table that is in 1NF is better than a table that is not in 1NF; a table that is in 2NF is better than one that is in 1NF; and so on. The goal of normalization is to take a table or collection of tables and produce a new collection of tables that represents the same information but is free of problems.

First Normal Form

A relation (table) that contains a **repeating group** (or multiple entries for a single row) is called an **unnormalized relation**. Removal of repeating groups is the starting point in the goal for tables that are as free of problems as possible. A table (relation) is in **first normal form** (1NF) if it does not contain repeating groups.

As an example, you might have created the following Course Offerings table, in which there is a repeating group consisting of Course Number, Total Hours, and Hours Spent. In the example, there is one row per client with Course Number, Total Hours, and Hours Spent repeated as many times as necessary.

Course Offerings (<u>Client Number</u>, (Course Number, Total Hours, Hours Spent))

The table is Course Offerings and the primary key is Client Number. The inner parentheses indicate that there is a repeating group. The repeating group contains three attributes or columns, Course Number, Total Hours, and Hours Spent. This means that for a single client, there can be multiple combinations of course number, total hours, and hours spent as illustrated in Figure F-2.

Course Offerings			
CLIENT NUMBER	COURSE NUMBER	TOTAL HOURS	HOURS SPENT
BS27	03	6	3
	06	16	4
CP27	02	10	4
	04	6	0
FI28	01	16	12
	05	12	8
FL93	06	16	8
HN83	05	12	8
	08	6	2
	11	24	12

FIGURE F-2

To convert the table to 1NF, remove the repeating group to give the following:

Course Offerings (<u>Client Number</u>, <u>Course Number</u>, Total Hours, Hours Spent)

The corresponding example of the new table is shown in Figure F-3.

Course Offerings			
CLIENT NUMBER	COURSE NUMBER	TOTAL HOURS	HOURS SPENT
BS27	03	6	3
BS27	06	16	4
CP27	02	10	4
CP27	04	6	0
FI28	01	16	12
FI28	05	12	8
FL93	06	16	8
HN83	05	12	8
HN83	08	6	2
HN83	11	24	12

FIGURE F-3

Note that the second row of the unnormalized table (Figure F-2) indicates that client CP27 currently is being offered both course 02 and course 04. In the normalized table, this information is represented by *two* rows, the third and the fourth (Figure F-3). The primary key for the unnormalized Course Offerings table was the Client Number only. The primary key for the normalized table now is the combination of Client Number and Course Number.

In general, when converting a non-1NF table to 1NF, the primary key typically will include the original primary key concatenated with the key of the repeating group; that is, the column that distinguishes one occurrence of the repeating group from another within a given row in the table. In this case, Course Number is the key to the repeating group and thus becomes part of the primary key of the 1NF table.

Second Normal Form

Even though the following table is in 1NF, problems exist that will cause you to want to restructure the table. You might have created the following Course Offerings table:

Course Offerings (<u>Client Number</u>, Name, <u>Course Number</u>, Course Description, Total Hours, Hours Spent)

with the functional dependencies:

Client Number → Name

Course Number → Course Description

Client Number, Course Number → Total Hours, Hours Spent

This notation indicates that Client Number alone determines Name, Course Number alone determines Course Description, but it requires *both* a Client Number *and* a Course Number to determine either Total Hours or Hours Spent. Consider the sample of this table shown in Figure F-4.

Course Offerings

CLIENT NUMBER	NAME	COURSE NUMBER	COURSE DESCRIPTION	TOTAL HOURS	HOURS SPENT
BS27	Blant and Sons	03	Creating Forms with Word	6	3
BS27	Blant and Sons	06	Introduction to Computers	16	4
CP27	Calder Plastics	02	Long Documents with Word	10	4
CP27	Calder Plastics	04	Newsletters and Graphics with Word	6	0
FI28	Farrow-Idsen	01	Integrating MS Office Programs	16	12
FI28	Farrow-Idsen	05	Creating Custom Access Reports	12	8
FL93	Fairland Lawn	06	Introduction to Computers	16	8
HN83	Hurley National	05	Creating Custom Access Reports	12	8
HN83	Hurley National	08	Importing, Exporting, and Linking Data	6	2
HN83	Hurley National	11	Excel Programming	24	12

FIGURE F-4

The description of a specific client, BS27 for example, occurs multiple times in the table. This redundancy causes several problems. It is certainly wasteful of space, but that is not nearly as serious as some of the other problems. These other problems are called **update anomalies** and they fall into four categories:

1. **Update.** A change to the name of client BS27 requires not one change to the table, but several — you must change each row in which BS27 appears. This certainly makes the update process much more cumbersome; it is more complicated logically and takes longer to update.

2. **Inconsistent data.** There is nothing about the design that would prohibit client BS27 from having two or more different names in the database.

3. **Additions.** There is a real problem when you try to add a new course and its description to the database. Because the primary key for the table consists of both Client Number and Course Number, you need values for both of these to add a new row. If you have a client to add but there are as yet no courses scheduled for it, what do you use for a course number? The only solution would be to make up a dummy course number and then replace it with a real course number once the client requests a course. Certainly this is not an acceptable solution.

4. **Deletions.** In Figure F-4 on the previous page, if you delete client HN83 from the database, you also *lose* all the information about course 11. For example, you would no longer know that the description of course 11 is Excel Programming.

These problems occur because there is a column, Name, that is dependent on only a portion of the primary key, Client Number, and *not* on the complete primary key. The problem with Course Description, is that it is dependent on only the Course Number. This leads to the definition of second normal form. Second normal form represents an improvement over first normal form because it eliminates update anomalies in these situations. In order to understand second normal form, you need to understand the term nonkey column.

A column is a **nonkey column** (also called a **nonkey attribute**) if it is not a part of the primary key. A table (relation) is in **second normal form** (2NF) if it is in first normal form and no nonkey column is dependent on only a portion of the primary key.

Note that if the primary key of a table contains only a single column, the table is automatically in second normal form. In that case, there would not be any column dependent on only a portion of the primary key.

To correct the problems, convert the table to a collection of tables in second normal form. The following is a method for performing this conversion.

First, take each subset of the set of columns that make up the primary key, and begin a new table with this subset as its primary key. For the Course Offerings table, this would give:

(<u>Client Number</u>,

(<u>Course Number</u>,

(<u>Client Number</u>, <u>Course Number</u>,

Next, place each of the other columns with the appropriate primary key; that is, place each one with the minimal collection of columns on which it depends. For the Course Offerings table, this would yield:

(<u>Client Number</u>, Name)

(<u>Course Number</u>, Course Description)

(<u>Client Number</u>, <u>Course Number</u>, Total Hours, Hours Spent)

Each of these new tables now can be given a name that is descriptive of the meaning of the table, such as Client, Course, and Course Offerings. Figure F-5 shows samples of the tables involved.

Client

CLIENT NUMBER	NAME
BS27	Blant and Sons
CP27	Calder Plastics
FI28	Farrow-Idsen
FL93	Fairland Lawn
HN83	Hurley National

Course

COURSE NUMBER	COURSE DESCRIPTION
01	Integrating MS Office Programs
02	Long Documents with Word
03	Creating Forms with Word
04	Newsletters and Graphics with Word
05	Creating Custom Access Reports
06	Introduction to Computers
08	Importing, Exporting, and Linking Data
11	Excel Programming

Course Offerings

CLIENT NUMBER	COURSE NUMBER	TOTAL HOURS	HOURS SPENT
BS27	03	6	3
BS27	06	16	4
CP27	02	10	4
CP27	04	6	0
FI28	01	16	12
FI28	05	12	8
FL93	06	16	8
HN83	05	12	8
HN83	08	6	2
HN83	11	24	12

FIGURE F-5

The new design eliminates the update anomalies. A client name occurs only once for each client, so you do not have the redundancy that you did in the earlier design. Changing the name of a client is now a simple process involving a single change. Because the name of a client occurs in a single place, it is not possible to have multiple names for the same client in the database at the same time.

To add a new client, you create a new row in the Client table and thus there is no need to have a course offering already scheduled for that client. Also, deleting client HN83 does not cause course 11 to be deleted from the Course table, and thus you still have its description (Excel Programming) in the database. Finally, you have not lost any information in the process. The data in the original design can be reconstructed from the data in the new design.

Third Normal Form

Problems still can exist with tables that are in 2NF as illustrated in the following Client table:

Client (<u>Client Number</u>, Name, Address, City, State, Zip Code, Amount Paid, Current Due, Trainer Number, Last Name, First Name)

The functional dependencies in this table are:

Client Number → Name, Address, City, State, Zip Code, Amount Paid, Current Due, Trainer Number

Trainer Number → Last Name, First Name

Client Number determines all the other columns. In addition, Trainer Number determines Last Name and First Name.

Because the primary key of the table is a single column, the table is automatically in second normal form. As the sample of the table shown in Figure F-6 demonstrates, however, this table has problems similar to those encountered earlier, even though it is in 2NF. In this case, it is the name of a trainer that can occur many times in the table (see trainer 42, Belinda Perry, for example).

Client

CLIENT NUMBER	NAME	...	AMOUNT PAID	CURRENT DUE	TRAINER NUMBER	LAST NAME	FIRST NAME
BS27	Blant and Sons	...	$21,876.00	$892.50	42	Perry	Belinda
CE16	Center Services	...	$26,512.00	$2,672.00	48	Stevens	Michael
CP27	Calder Plastics	...	$8,725.00	$0.00	48	Stevens	Michael
EU28	Elba's Furniture	...	$4,256.00	$1,202.00	53	Gonzalez	Manuel
FI28	Farrow-Idsen	...	$8,287.50	$925.50	42	Perry	Belinda
FL93	Fairland Lawn	...	$21,625.00	$0.00	48	Stevens	Michael
HN83	Hurley National	...	$0.00	$0.00	48	Stevens	Michael
MC28	Morgan-Alyssa	...	$24,761.00	$1,572.00	42	Perry	Belinda
PS82	PRIM Staffing	...	$11,682.25	$2,827.50	53	Gonzalez	Manuel
TE26	Telton-Edwards	...	$8,521.50	$0.00	48	Stevens	Michael

FIGURE F-6

This redundancy results in the same set of problems described previously with the Course Offerings table. In addition to the problem of wasted space, you have similar update anomalies, as follows:

1. **Updates.** A change to the name of a trainer requires not one change to the table, but several. Again the update process becomes very cumbersome.

2. **Inconsistent data.** There is nothing about the design that would prohibit a trainer from having two different names in the database. On the first row, for example, the name for trainer 42 might read Belinda Perry; whereas on the fifth row (another row on which the trainer number is 42), the name might be Belinda Stevens.

3. **Additions.** In order to add trainer 87, whose name is Penny Ortiz, to the database, she must have at least one client. If she has not yet been assigned any clients, either you cannot record the fact that her name is Penny Ortiz or you have to create a fictitious client for her to represent. Again, this is not a desirable solution to the problem.

4. **Deletions.** If you were to delete all the clients of trainer 42 from the database, then you also would lose all information concerning trainer 42.

These update anomalies are due to the fact that Trainer Number determines Last Name and First Name, but Trainer Number is not the primary key. As a result, the same Trainer Number and consequently the same Last Name and First Name can appear on many different rows.

You have seen that 2NF is an improvement over 1NF, but in order to eliminate 2NF problems, you need an even better strategy for creating tables in the database. Third normal form provides that strategy. Before looking at third normal form, however, you need to become familiar with the special name that is given to any column that determines another column (like Trainer Number in the Client table).

Any column (or collection of columns) that determines another column is called a **determinant**. Certainly the primary key in a table is a determinant. In fact, by definition, any candidate key is a determinant. (Remember that a candidate key is a column or collection of columns that could function as the primary key.) In this case, Trainer Number is a determinant, but it certainly is not a candidate key, and that is the problem.

A table is in **third normal form** (3NF) if it is in second normal form and if the only determinants it contains are candidate keys.

This definition is not the original definition of third normal form. This more recent definition, which is preferable to the original, also is referred to as **Boyce-Codd normal form** (**BCNF**). In this text, it simply is referred to as third normal form, however.

You now have identified the problem with the Client table: it is not in 3NF. What you need is a scheme to correct the deficiency in the Client table and in all tables having similar deficiencies. Such a method follows.

First, for each determinant that is not a candidate key, remove from the table the columns that depend on this determinant, but do not remove the determinant. Next, create a new table containing all the columns from the original table that depend on this determinant. Finally, make the determinant the primary key of this new table.

In the Client table, for example, Last Name and First Name are removed because they depend on the determinant Trainer Number, which is not a candidate key. A new table is formed, consisting of Trainer Number as the primary key, Last Name and First Name. Specifically:

Client (<u>Client Number</u>, Name, Address, City, State, Zip Code, Amount Paid,
Current Due, Trainer Number, Last Name, First Name)

is replaced by:

Client (<u>Client Number</u>, Name, Address, City, State, Zip Code, Amount Paid,
Current Due, Trainer Number)

and

Trainer (<u>Trainer Number</u>, Last Name, First Name)

Figure F-7 shows samples of the tables involved.

Client

CLIENT NUMBER	NAME	...	AMOUNT PAID	AMOUNT DUE	TRAINER NUMBER
BS27	Blant and Sons	...	$21,876.00	$892.50	42
CE16	Center Services	...	$26,512.00	$2,672.00	48
CP27	Calder Plastics	...	$8,725.00	$0.00	48
EU28	Elba's Furniture	...	$4,256.00	$1,202.00	53
FI28	Farrow-Idsen	...	$8,287.50	$925.50	42
FL93	Fairland Lawn	...	$21,625.00	$0.00	48
HN83	Hurley National	...	$0.00	$0.00	48
MC28	Morgan-Alyssa	...	$24,761.00	$1,572.00	42
PS82	PRIM Staffing	...	$11,682.25	$2,827.50	53
TE26	Telton-Edwards	...	$8,521.50	$0.00	48

Trainer

TRAINER NUMBER	LAST NAME	FIRST NAME
42	Perry	Belinda
48	Stevens	Michael
53	Gonzalez	Manuel

FIGURE F-7

This design corrects the previously identified problems. A trainer's name appears only once, thus avoiding redundancy and making the process of changing a trainer's name a very simple one. It is not possible with this design for the same trainer to have two different names in the database. To add a new trainer to the database, you add a row in the Trainer table so it is not necessary to have a pre-existing client for the trainer. Finally, deleting all the clients of a given trainer will not remove the trainer's record from the Trainer table, so you retain the trainer's name; all the data in the original table can be reconstructed from the data in the new collection of tables. All previously mentioned problems have indeed been solved.

In the Lab

1 Designing a Database

Instructions: Answer the following questions on your own paper.

1. List three relational table characteristics that are violated in the table shown in Figure F-8.

Item

DATE	ITEM NUMBER	NUMBER ORDERED	DATE	PRICE
11/01/05	BA35	10	11/12/05	$43.50
11/01/05	BB05	1	11/09/05	$82.10
	BE19	1	Friday	$39.80
11/03/05	BU24	4	11/13/05	$36.10
11/03/05	HF01	2	11/12/05	$11.35
11/04/05	BA35	2	11/12/05	$43.50
	GF12	4	$14.80	$14.80
11/04/05	BB05	1	11/15/05	$82.10
11/03/05	HF01	2	11/12/05	$11.35
11/04/05	SF03	2	11/13/05	$ 8.05

FIGURE F-8

2. The following table is a student's first attempt to create a database design:
   Student (<u>Student Number</u>, Student Name, Number Credits, Advisor Number, Advisor Name, (Course Number, Description, Grade))
   a. Identify the functional dependencies.
   b. Convert this table to an equivalent collection of tables in 3NF.
3. The following table concerns invoice information. For a given invoice (identified by the invoice number), there will be a single customer. The customer's number, name, and address appear on the invoice as well as the invoice date. Also, there may be several different parts appearing on the invoice. For every part that appears, the part number, description, price, and number shipped will be displayed. Convert this table into an equivalent collection of tables in 3NF.
   Invoice (<u>Invoice Number</u>, Customer Number, Last Name, First Name, Street, City, State, Zip Code, Invoice Date, (Part Number, Part Description, Price, Number Shipped))
4. Consider the following collection of requirements for Alisa Vending Services:
   - For each driver, the company keeps track of driver's name, unique Social Security number, and a telephone number.
   - For each truck, the company keeps track of a unique truck ID number, truck color, and truck max weight.
   - One driver can be assigned to more than one truck.
   - Each truck can be assigned to only one driver.
   - Based on these requirements, create a set of 3NF relations.

Index

Quick Reference Summary

In Microsoft Office Access 2003, you can accomplish a task in a number of ways. The following table provides a quick reference to each task presented in this textbook. The first column identifies the task. The second column indicates the page number on which the task is discussed in the book. The subsequent four columns list the different ways the task in column one can be carried out. You can invoke the commands listed in the MOUSE, MENU BAR, and SHORTCUT MENU columns using Voice commands.

Microsoft Office Access 2003 Quick Reference Summary

TASK	PAGE NUMBER	MOUSE	MENU BAR	SHORTCUT MENU	KEYBOARD SHORTCUT
Add Chart	AC 511		Insert | Chart		
Add Combo Box	AC 235, AC 237	Combo Box tool			
Add Command Button	AC 423	Command Button tool			
Add Date	AC 415		Insert | Date and Time		
Add Drop Areas	AC 360		View | Drop Areas		
Add Field	AC 129	Insert Rows button	Insert | Rows	Insert Rows	INSERT
Add Fields Using Field List	AC 408	Drag field			
Add Group of Records	AC 139	Query Type button arrow | Append Query	Query | Append Query	Query Type | Append Query	
Add Label	AC 241	Label tool			
Add Page Number	AC 416		Insert | Page Number		
Add Record	AC 23, AC 116	New Record button	Insert | New Record		
Add Rectangle	AC 430	Rectangle tool			
Add Smart Tag	AC 546	Smart Tag property | Build button			
Add Subform	AC 508	Subform/Subreport tool			
Add Subreport	AC 410	Subform/Subreport tool			
Add Switchboard Item	AC 334, AC 336	New button			
Add Switchboard Page	AC 332	New button			
Add Table to Query	AC 92	Show Table button	Query | Show Table	Show Table	
Add Text Box	AC 232	Text Box tool			
Advanced Filter/Sort	AC 124		Records | Filter | Advanced Filter Sort		

TASK	PAGE NUMBER	MOUSE	MENU BAR	SHORTCUT MENU	KEYBOARD SHORTCUT
Align Controls	AC 212		Format | Align	Align	
Apply Filter	AC 121, AC 123	Filter By Selection or Filter By Form button	Records | Filter		
Calculate Statistics	AC 100	Totals button	View | Totals	Totals	
Change Chart Type	AC 356	Chart Type button	PivotChart | Chart Type	Chart Type	
Change Font for Tables and Queries	AC 587		Tools | Options | Tables/Queries | Font box or Size box		
Change Group of Records	AC 136	Query Type button arrow | Update Query	Query | Update Query	Query Type | Update Query	
Change Margins	AC 222	Setup	File | Page Setup | Margins tab	Page Setup	
Change PivotChart Organization	AC 358	By Row/By Column button	PivotChart | By Row/By Column		
Change Property	AC 215, AC 243	Properties button	View | Properties	Properties	F4
Change Tab Order	AC 295		View | Tab Order	Tab Order	
Clear Query	AC 75		Edit | Clear Grid		
Close Database	AC 26	Close Window button	File | Close		
Close Form	AC 39	Close Window button	File | Close		
Close Query	AC 73	Close Window button	File | Close		
Close Table	AC 21	Close Window button	File | Close		
Collapse Subdatasheet	AC 153	Expand indicator (-)			
Compact a Database	AC 163		Tools | Database Utilities | Compact and Repair		
Convert Database to Another Version	AC 533		Tools | Database Utilities | Convert Database		
Create Calculated Field	AC 96			Zoom	SHIFT+F2
Create Data Access Page	AC 380	New Object button arrow | Page	Insert | Page		
Create Database	AC 10	New button	File | New		CTRL+N
Create Form	AC 38, AC 228	New Object button arrow | AutoForm	Insert | AutoForm		
Create Form Using Design View	AC 505	Double-click Create Form in Design View	Insert | Form | Design View		
Create Index	AC 161	Indexes button	View | Indexes		
Create Input Mask	AC 263	Input Mask property box			
Create Labels	AC 419	New Object button arrow | Report | Label Wizard	Insert | Report | Label Wizard		
Create Lookup Wizard Field	AC 147	Text arrow | Lookup Wizard			
Create Macro	AC 317	New Object button arrow | Macro	Insert | Macro		
Create MDE File	AC 571		Tools | Database Utilities | Make MDE File		
Create PivotChart	AC 347	View button arrow | PivotChart View	View | PivotChart View	PivotChart View	
Create PivotTable	AC 355	View button arrow | PivotTable View	View | PivotTable View	PivotTable View	

Microsoft Office Access 2003 Quick Reference Summary

TASK	PAGE NUMBER	MOUSE	MENU BAR	SHORTCUT MENU	KEYBOARD SHORTCUT
Create PivotTable in Data Access Page	AC 390	Office PivotTable tool	Insert | Office PivotTable		
Create Query	AC 68	New Object button arrow | Query	Insert | Query		
Create Replica	AC 563		Tools | Replication | Create Replica		
Create Report	AC 43	New Object button arrow | Report	Insert | Report		
Create Report Using Design View	AC 406	Double-click Create Report in Design View	Insert | Report | Design View		
Create Snapshot	AC 184		File | Export, select SNP as file type	Export, select SNP as file type	
Create SQL Query	AC 588	View button arrow | SQL View	View | SQL View	SQL View	
Create Standard Module	AC 469	Module Object | New button	Insert | Module		
Create Sub Procedure	AC 485	Insert Module button arrow | Procedure	Insert | Procedure		
Create Switchboard	AC 330		Tools | Database Utilities | Switchboard Manager		
Create Table	AC 17	Tables object | Create table in Design View or Create table by using wizard	Insert | Table		
Crosstab Query	AC 104	New Object button arrow | Query	Insert | Query		
Default Value	AC 142	Default Value property box			
Delete Field	AC 130	Delete Rows button	Edit | Delete	Delete Rows	DELETE
Delete Group of Records	AC 138	Query Type button arrow | Delete Query	Query | Delete Query	Query Type | Delete Query	
Delete Record	AC 125	Delete Record button	Edit | Delete Record	Delete Record	DELETE
Enable Error Checking	AC 540		Tools | Options | Error Checking		
Encode Database	AC 561		Tools | Security | Encode/Decode Database		
Exclude Duplicates	AC 87	Properties button	View | Properties | Unique Values Only	Properties | Unique Values Only	
Exclude Field from Query Results	AC 78	Show check box			
Expand Subdatasheet	AC 153	Expand indicator (+)			
Export Data Using Drag and Drop	AC 183	Drag object to desired application			
Export Data Using Export Command	AC 183		File | Export	Export	
Field Size	AC 19, AC 127	Field Size property box			
Field Type	AC 20	Data Type box arrow | appropriate type			Appropriate letter
Filter Records	AC 121, AC 123	Filter By Selection or Filter By Form button	Records | Filter		
Font in Datasheet	AC 133		Format | Font	Font	
Format	AC 144	Format property box			

Microsoft Office Access 2003 Quick Reference Summary *(continued)*

TASK	PAGE NUMBER	MOUSE	MENU BAR	SHORTCUT MENU	KEYBOARD SHORTCUT
Format a Calculated Field	AC 98	Properties button	View | Properties	Properties	
Format Datasheet	AC 134		Format | Datasheet	Datasheet	
Group Data Access Page	AC 386	Group by Table button			
Group in Query	AC 103	Totals button	View | Totals		
Hide Smart Tags in Forms and Reports	AC 545		Tools | Options | Forms/Reports, be sure Show Smart Tags is not checked		
Hide Smart Tags in Tables and Queries	AC 546		Tools | Options | Datasheet, be sure Show Smart Tags is not checked		
Import	AC 177		File | Get External Data | Import	Import	
Import SharePoint Services List	AC 554		File | Get External Data | Import | Files of type arrow | Windows SharePoint Services		
Include All Fields in Query	AC 78	Double-click asterisk in field list			
Include Field in Query	AC 71	Double-click field in field list			
Join Properties	AC 94		View | Join Properties	Join Properties	
Key Field	AC 19	Primary Key button	Edit | Primary Key	Primary Key	
Link	AC 180		File | Get External Data | Link Tables	Link Tables	
Link SharePoint Services List	AC 554		File | Get External Data | Link Tables | Files of type arrow | Windows SharePoint Services		
Modify Switchboard Page	AC 333, AC 335	Edit button			
Move Control	AC 230	Drag control			
Move to Design View	AC 291	View button	View | Design View	Design View	
Move to First Record	AC 27	First Record button			CTRL+UP ARROW
Move to Last Record	AC 27	Last Record button			CTRL+DOWN ARROW
Move to Next Record	AC 27	Next Record button			DOWN ARROW
Move to Previous Record	AC 27	Previous Record button			UP ARROW
Open Database	AC 26	Open button	File | Open		CTRL+O
Open Form	AC 116	Forms object | Open button		Open	Use ARROW keys to move highlight to name, then press ENTER key
Open Table	AC 26	Tables object | Open button		Open	Use ARROW keys to move highlight to name, then press ENTER key
Preview Table	AC 30	Print Preview button	File | Print Preview	Print Preview	
Print Relationships	AC 151		File | Print Relationships		
Print Report	AC 47	Print button	File | Print	Print	CTRL+P
Print Results of Query	AC 72	Print button	File | Print	Print	CTRL+P

Microsoft Office Access 2003 Quick Reference Summary

TASK	PAGE NUMBER	MOUSE	MENU BAR	SHORTCUT MENU	KEYBOARD SHORTCUT
Print Table	AC 30	Print button	File | Print	Print	CTRL+P
Quit Access	AC 50	Close button	File | Exit		ALT+F4
Relationships (Referential Integrity)	AC 150	Relationships button	Tools | Relationships		
Remove Control	AC 222	Cut button	Edit | Cut	Cut	DELETE
Remove Filter	AC 122	Remove Filter button	Records | Remove Filter/Sort		
Remove Password	AC 562		Tools | Security | Unset Database Password		
Resize Column	AC 131, AC 268	Drag right boundary of field selector	Format | Column Width	Column Width	
Resize Control	AC 282	Drag sizing handle			
Resize Row	AC 268	Drag lower boundary of row selector	Format | Row Height	Row Height	
Resize Section	AC 224	Drag section boundary			
Restructure Table	AC 126	Tables object | Design button		Design View	
Return to Select Query Window	AC 72	View button arrow	View | Design View		
Run Query	AC 71	Run button	Query | Run		
Save Form	AC 39	Save button	File | Save		CTRL+S
Save PivotChart as Data Access Page	AC 395		File | Save As		
Save Query	AC 80	Save button	File | Save		CTRL+S
Save Table	AC 21	Save button	File | Save		CTRL+S
Search for Record	AC 117	Find button	Edit | Find		CTRL+F
Select Fields for Report	AC 44	Add Field button or Add All Fields button			
Set Macro Security Level	AC 563		Tools | Macro | Security		
Set Password	AC 559		Tools | Security | Set Database Password		
Set Startup Options	AC 558		Tools | Startup		
Show Legend	AC 355	Show Legend button	PivotChart | Show Legend		
Show Smart Tags in Forms and Reports	AC 545		Tools | Options | Forms/Reports, be sure Show Smart Tags is checked		
Show Smart Tags in Tables and Queries	AC 545		Tools | Options | Datasheet, be sure Show Smart Tags is checked		
Simple Query Wizard	AC 34	New Object button arrow | Query	Insert | Query		
Sort and Group in Report	AC 205	Sorting and Grouping button	View | Sorting and Grouping	Sorting and Grouping	
Sort Data in Query	AC 86	Sort row | Sort row arrow | type of sort			
Sort Records	AC 155	Sort Ascending or Sort Descending button	Records | Sort | Sort Ascending or Sort Descending	Sort Ascending or Sort Descending	

Microsoft Office Access 2003 Quick Reference Summary *(continued)*

TASK	PAGE NUMBER	MOUSE	MENU BAR	SHORTCUT MENU	KEYBOARD SHORTCUT
Specify User-Level Security	AC 573		Tools | Security | User-Level Security Wizard		
Split a Database	AC 567		Tools | Database Utilities | Database Splitter		
Start Online Meeting	AC 557		Tools | Online Collaboration | Meet Now		
Switch Between Form and Datasheet Views	AC 41, AC 120	View button arrow	View | Datasheet View		
Synchronize Design Master and Replica	AC 567		Tools | Replication | Synchronize Now		
Top-Values Query	AC 89	Top Values button	View | Properties	Properties	
Update Hyperlink Field	AC 271	Insert Hyperlink	Insert | Hyperlink	Hyperlink | Edit Hyperlink	CTRL+K
Update OLE Field	AC 269		Insert | Object	Insert Object	
Use AND Criterion	AC 84				Place criteria on same line
Use Documenter	AC 539	Analyze button arrow | Documenter	Tools | Analyze | Documenter		
Use OR Criterion	AC 85				Place criteria on separate lines
Use Performance Analyzer	AC 537	Analyze button arrow | Analyze Performance	Tools | Analyze | Performance		
Use Table Analyzer	AC 534	Analyze button arrow | Analyze Table	Tools | Analyze | Table		
Validation Rule	AC 141	Validation Rule property box			
Validation Text	AC 141	Validation Text property box			
View Object Dependencies	AC 299		View | Object Dependencies		